# WOMEN:
## A FEMINIST PERSPECTIVE
### SECOND EDITION

Edited by
## JO FREEMAN

 Mayfield Publishing Company

Library of Congress Catalog Card Number: 78-64593

International Standard Book Number: 0-87484-422-3

Manufactured in the United States of America

Mayfield Publishing Company, 285 Hamilton Avenue, Palo Alto, California 94301

This book was set in Baskerville and Korinna by the Lienett Company and was printed and bound by the George Banta Company. Sponsoring editor was Alden C. Paine, copy editor was Cheryl Smith, and Carole Norton supervised editing. Production supervisor was Michelle Hogan, the book was designed by Nancy Sears, and art for the cover and part title pages is by Nan Golub.

# Contents

# PART 5
# INSTITUTIONS OF SOCIAL CONTROL

# PART 6
# FEMINISM

# The Contributors

**JO FREEMAN** is the author of *The Politics of Women's Liberation* (1975), winner of a 1975 American Political Science Association prize as the Best Scholarly Work on Women and Politics. She has been an organizer and participant in the women's liberation movement since its inception A founder and editor of the first national new feminist newsletter, *Voice of the Women's Liberation Movement,* she is currently a member of the National Organization for Women, The National Women's Political Caucus, The Women's Caucus for Political Science, and the Women's Martial Arts Union. She has published articles on feminism, social movements, law, public policy, sex-role socialization, organizational theory, education, and party politics in *Nation, Ms., Valparaiso Law Review, Trans-action, School Review, Liberal Education, American Journal of Sociology, Intellect, Political Science Quarterly, Acta Sociologica, Prospects,* and numerous anthologies.

**KAREN L. ADAMS** is a part-time lecturer in the Anthropology Department at Wayne State University and a doctoral candidate in Linguistics at the University of Michigan. She has participated in the Women's Studies Program at the University of Michigan in various capacities, including that of teaching assistant. Her major area of interest is the relationship between language and society.

**ELIZABETH M. ALMQUIST** is Associate Professor of Sociology at North Texas State University. She is author of *Sex Roles, Tradition and Change* (1977) coauthor (with Janet Chafetz, Barbara Chance, and Judy Corder-Bolz) of *Men, Women and Society,* a nonsexist introductory sociology text. She and Shirley S. Angrist published *Careers and Con-*

*tingencies: How College Women Juggle with Gender* (1975), which traces the development of women's career aspirations during their four years of college. They are currently investigating the career implementations and feminist activities of the same women during the ten years following college and graduation.

**PAULINE B. BART** is Associate Professor of Sociology in Psychiatry at the Abraham Lincoln Medical School of the University of Illinois, Chicago. She teaches behavioral science to medical students and conducts interdisciplinary seminars on sex roles and health issues to students in sociology and the health professions. Dr. Bart taught the first course on women at the University of California, Berkeley, is one of the founders of Sociologists for Women in Society, and was first chairperson for the Sex Roles section of the American Sociological Association. She is currently principal investigator of an NIMH-funded grant, "Avoiding Rape: A Study of Victims and Avoiders," and has interviewed 93 women about their experiences. Her published works include "Portnoy's Mother's Complaint," "A Funny Thing Happened On the Way to the Orifice: Women in Gynecology Textbooks," coauthored by Diana Scully (*American Journal of Sociology,* January 1973), and *The Student Sociologist's Handbook* (with Linda Frankel).

**ROSALYN FRAAD BAXANDALL** teaches Women's History in the American Studies program at State University of New York, College at Old Westbury. She is editor of *America's Working Women,* and has contributed articles on day care to many publications. Long active in day care, she is now also involved with the PTA. She is a member of CARASA, Coalition for Abortion Rights and Against Sterilization Abuse. She is currently preparing a book about changes in capitalism and sexuality in the 1920's.

**INGE BELL** is a Professor of Sociology at Pitzer College, Claremont, California, where she specializes in innovative teaching with special emphasis on placing students in the social science fields and encouraging them to work toward societal change. Her published works include "The Non-Voter" (*Berkeley Journal of Sociology,* 1955), "Status Discrepancy and the Radical Rejection of Nonviolence" (*Sociological Inquiry,* 1967), *CORE and the Strategy of Nonviolence* (1967), "The Double Standard" (*Transaction,* November 1970), and *A Student Involvement Manual* (1971; 42 research projects for students). She has been studying Eastern philosophy for four years and is currently seeking publication for "Buddhist Sociology."

**JESSIE BERNARD** is a Research Scholar at Pennsylvania State University. She has received the Kurt Lewin Award from the Society for the Psychological Study of Social Problems, the first Emeriti Award presented by Pennsylvania State University, and the Outstanding Achievement Award of the American Association of University Women, among many others. The Jessie Bernard Award was established in 1976 by the American Sociological Association. Dr. Bernard chaired the opening of International Women's Year at the United Nations and presented the opening address. A small sampling of her published works includes *Academic Women* (1964), *The Sex Game: Communication between the Sexes* (1968), *Sociology: Nurses and Their Patients in a Modern Society* (1970), and *Self-Portrait of a Family* (1978). She is a Visiting Research Scholar at the National Institute of Education, HEW; and Scholar-In-Residence, United States Commission on Civil Rights.

**NADEAN BISHOP** is Coordinator of Women's Studies and Associate Professor of English Literature at Eastern Michigan University, Ypsilanti. She has chaired sections at the Modern Language Association and MMLA on Women's Studies, Bibliography, Children's Literature, Women in Literature, and Matthew Arnold, and has read numerous papers at conferences on Women's Studies pedagogy and administration. Under grants from the Ford and Carnegie Foundations, she became Associate Director of the Institute for Administrative Advancement for its six-week session in Madison, 1975. She has contributed poetry and articles to such journals as *Human Behavior, The Wordsworth Circle,* and *The Radical Teacher,* and has a chapter on Women in Literature in *The Contemporary American Woman.*

**FRANCINE D. BLAU** is Assistant Professor of Economics and Labor and Industrial Relations at the University of Illinois at Urbana-Champaign, where her teaching includes courses on women in the labor market. She has been a discussant at such meetings as the Conference on the National Longitudinal Surveys (Washington, D.C., 1977), The Southwestern Assembly on Women and the American Economy (Dallas, 1977), and the Conference on Occupational Career Analysis (Greensboro, 1976). Her published works include "Economists' Approaches to Sex Segregation in the Labor Market. An Appraisal," with

Carol Jusenius (*Signs,* Spring 1976), "Sex Segregation of Workers by Enterprise in Clerical Occupations" (in *Labor Market Segmentation,* 1975), "Women's Place in the Labor Market" (*American Economic Review,* May 1972), *Equal Pay in the Office* (1977), and she is working with Lawrence Kahn on "Race and Sex Differences in the Probability of Quits and Layoffs" and "Wage Consequences of Job Turnover," both under grants from the Employment and Training Administration.

**MERRY BOLT** is a Research Associate in the Section of Gastroenterology, Billings Hospital, University of Chicago, and is involved in nutrition-related research. During 1969–1971 she was active in Zero Population Growth and Illinois Citizens for the Medical Control of Abortion.

**MARY EASTWOOD** is an attorney in the Office of Legal Counsel U. S. Department of Justice, and has served as technical legal assistant to the Citizens' Advisory Council on the Status of Women. She is the author of several published articles on legal theory and women's rights, and was a founding member of the National Organization for Women (NOW), Federally Employed Women (FEW), and Human Rights for Women (HRW). She is a member of the Board of Directors of HRW, and is Vice President of the FEW Legal and Education Fund and 2nd Vice President of the National Woman's Party.

**ROSLYN L. FELDBERG** is an Assistant Professor of Sociology at Boston University, where she has been active in developing and teaching the Women's Studies Program. As a member of the Women's Research Center of Boston, she has been conducting a study of single-parent families, and has written several articles about family life and divorced motherhood. She is currently collaborating with Evelyn Glenn on a study of women clerical workers and a course about women and work.

**EVELYN NAKANO GLENN** is an Assistant Professor of Sociology at Boston University. Her main interest is the area of women and work, and she is currently collaborating with Roslyn Feldberg under a National Institute of Mental Health grant. They are studying clerical work, exploring such facets as work consciousness and links between work and family life. Glenn is also doing research on the Japanese–American domestic worker, examining the relationships between work, aging, and ethnicity.

KATHLEEN GOUGH was a Research Associate in Anthropology at the University of British Columbia, Vancouver, when she wrote for this collection. She is the co-editor (with David M. Schneider) of *Matrilineal Kinship* (1974), and (with Hari P. Sharma) of *Imperialism and Revolution n South Asia* (1973). She has contributed numerous articles on family roles and kinship in India to scholarly journals and anthologies.

HELEN MAYER HACKER is a Professor of Sociology at Adelphi University, Garden City, N.Y. She is the author of a number of widely reprinted articles concerning gender roles, including, in addition to the one contained in the present volume, "Why Can't a Woman  .?" (*The Humanist*, January–February 1971) and "Women as a Minority Group Twenty Years Later" (*International Journal of Group Tensions*, March 1974), an update of "The New Burdens of Masculinity" (*Marriage and Family Living*, August 1957). She contributed chapters entitled "Class and Race Differences in Gender Roles" and "Gender Roles from a Cross-Cultural Perspective" to *Gender and Sex in Society* (Lucile Doberman, ed., 1975). Her module "The Social Roles of Women and Men· A Sociological Approach" (1975) appears in *Women's Studies: The Social Realities* (Barbara Bellow Watson, ed., 1976). She is currently compiling a monograph on "Changes in Women's Attitudes toward Work," as well as a study of same-sex and cross-sex friendship.

NANCY M. HENLEY is an Associate Professor of Psychology at the University of Lowell, Massachusetts. She has worked with the Association for Women in Psychology and with *State of Mind* (formerly *Radical Therapist/Rough Times*), a journal of alternatives in and to psychology. Her research in recent years has focused on women and communication, both verbal and nonverbal. Dr. Henley's published works include "Politics of Touch" (*Berkeley Journal of Sociology*, 1973), *Body Politics: Power, Sex, and Nonverbal Communication* (1977), and co-edited with Barrie Thorne, *Language and Sex: Difference and Dominance* (1975).

DIANNE F. HERMAN is a Ph.D. candidate at Penn State, and is currently working on her dissertation, "Violence in the Modern American Family: A Political Analysis." She has taught at Lycoming College and Bloomsburg State College, both in Pennsylvania, but is now writing full time.

**JUDITH HOLE** is a Producer for CBS News, currently producing seg-- ments of *Magazine,* a once-a-month broadcast primarily for women. She has long been active in the women's movement at CBS, and helped conceive and develop some innovative career programs. She is co- author, with Ellen Levine, of *Rebirth of Feminism* (1971).

**VIOLA KLEIN** was a Reader (equivalent to Associate Professor) of Sociol- ogy at Reading University, Berkshire, Eng., until her sudden death in 1973. She is the author of *The Feminine Character: History of an Ideology* (1946 and 1973), *Women's Two Roles* (with Alva Myrdal, 1956), *Britain's Married Women Workers* (1965), *Women Workers* (1965), and a large number of articles and monographs on related subjects.

**WENDY LARSEN,** an attorney, was clerking for a Justice of the Illinois Supreme Court and served on the Women's Rights Committee of the American Civil Liberties Union when she co-authored her article for this collection. She is a former Editor-in-Chief of the *DePaul Law Review.* She received her B.D. degree from the University of Chicago and her J.D. from DePaul University, Chicago.

**ELLEN LEVINE** has returned to school and is studying law at New York University School of Law. Her previous endeavors include *Rebirth of Feminism,* with Judith Hole (1971); co-editing of the journal *Notes from the Third Year;* co-editing with Anne Loedt and others of *Radical Feminism* (1973); *All She Needs . . . ,* a book of feminist cartoons; and directing the Broadcast/Film Division of Consumers Union.

**JUDITH LORBER** is an Associate Professor of Sociology at Brooklyn College, The City University of New York. She has done research on surgical patients and community mental health centers, and is currently engaged in a study of the work lives of female and male physicians. Her publications include articles on patients in a general hospital, women and medical sociology, illness as deviance, equality of the sexes and care of children, and ghetto community mental health center workers. She has held office in the American Sociological Association, the Society for the Study of Social Problems, the Eastern Sociological Society, and Sociologists for Women in Society. She has been a consul- tant to the first American Medical Women's Association Leadership Workshop, a participant in the 1977 Conference on Leadership and Authority for Women in the Health Professions, and a consultant to the U. S. Commission on the Civil Rights Sex Discrimination in Medical Advertising Project.

**NAOMI B. LYNN** is an Associate Professor of Political Science at Kansas State University. She is president of the Kansas Chapter of the American Society for Public Administration, former national president of the Women's Caucus for Political Science, and a member of the Executive Council of the Midwest Political Science Association. She is co-author of *The Fulbright Premise: Senator J. William Fulbright's Views on Presidential Power,* and a contributor to numerous journals including *American Journal of Political Science, The Journal of Military and Political Sociology,* and *Public Personnel Management.* Her published articles include "Societal Punishment and Aspects of Female Political Participation" (in *A Portrait of Marginality,* 1977) and "Women and Political Socialization: The Impact of Motherhood" (in *Women in Politics,* 1974).

**MARY NELSON** received her Ph.D. in Social Psychology in 1975 from the University of California. She has worked as an investigator for the Agricultural Labor Relations Board in the Imperial Valley, California, and developed a simulation game, based on the history of the Salinas Valley since the 1930's, for teaching negotiation skills to farm workers. From February 1976 to September 1977 she travelled in Latin America, supporting herself by working as a maid on a cattle ranch in Paraguay, baker's assistant in Peru, seamstress on an island in northern Brazil, waitress in a hotel in Bolivia, and English teacher in Salvador, Brazil.

**LETITIA ANNE PEPLAU** is an Assistant Professor of Social Psychology at the University of California, Los Angeles. She has recently co-edited, with C. Hammen, a special volume of the *Journal of Social Issues* on "Sexual Behavior: Social Psychological Perspectives." Her research focuses on close relationships, and has included studies of heterosexual, lesbian, and gay male relationships.

**LINDA PHELPS** is a Research Assistant at the Institute for Community Studies in Kansas City, Missouri. She was a founder of the Kansas City Women's Liberation Union, and has published several articles in Women's Movement Publications, including "What Is the Difference: Women's Rights and Women's Liberation."

**BARBARA BOVEE POLK** is a curriculum specialist in the Community College System of the University of Hawaii, Honolulu. She holds a Ph.D. in Social Psychology from the University of Michigan, and has taught Sex Roles and methods courses in sociology and social psychology. Several of her articles have appeared in professional journals and published anthologies.

**BARBARA KATZ ROTHMAN** is a Ph.D. candidate in Sociology at New York University and is currently completing her dissertation, "Women, Health and Reproduction: Defining and Negotiating Reality." She has taught medical sociology, sex roles, and other courses at Brooklyn College and other area colleges, as well as a continuing education program for nurses at Downstate Medical Center. Her published works include "Childbirth as Negotiated Reality" (*Symbolic Interaction,* 1978) and "The Way We Live Now: In Which a Sensible Woman Persuades Her Doctor, Her Family and Her Friends to Help Her Give Birth at Home" (*Ms. Magazine,* December 1976). She has lectured on women's health issues at colleges and health institutions, as well as on television and radio.

**KAY LEHMAN SCHLOZMAN** is Assistant Professor of Political Science at Boston College, where she teachers courses in American Politics. She has published numerous articles in scholarly journals and is currently collaborating on a book about the political and social consequences of contemporary unemployment in the United States.

**LAURA SHAPIRO** is a freelance writer whose work has appeared in *Mother Jones, Rolling Stone, Ms.,* and *Boston Magazine.* From 1969 to 1977 she wrote regularly for *The Real Paper* and *The Boston Globe.*

**PAULINE TERRELONGE STONE** is an Assistant Professor of Political Science and Afroamerican and African Studies at the University of Michigan at Ann Arbor. She has taught courses on "Women in Political Theory" and "Black Women in America," and is a member of the Committee on the Status of Women of the American Political Science Association and Editor of the Newsletter of the National Conference of Black Political Scientists. She is the author of articles in a number of scholarly journals on the subject of black politicians in American society, and has done research on women in the Caribbean.

NORMA WARE is a doctoral candidate in Anthropology and Linguistics at the University of Michigan, and has completed her dissertation on the impact of cultural double-binding on communication among professional women. She has been active in various capacities in the Women's Studies Program at the University for several years.

LENORE J. WEITZMAN is a National Fellow at the Hoover Institution at Stanford University. Her major work has focused on the legal regulation of intimate relationships through laws governing marriage and divorce, and she is currently studying the relationship between law and social behavior. Her book *The Marriage Contract* will be published by Prentice-Hall this year, and she is writing a monograph with Herma Hill Kay and Ruth B. Dixon at the Center for the Study of Law and Society at the University of California at Berkeley, dealing with the social and legal effects of California's no-fault divorce law.

BARBARA M. WERTHEIMER is an Associate Professor at the New York State School of Industrial and Labor Relations, Cornell University, and Director of the Institute for Education and Research on Women and Work. She is a long-time labor educator and the author of many books and articles in this field and on the subject of women's role in the work force, past and present. Her most recent book is *We Were There: The Story of Working Women in America* (1977).

MARTHA STURM WHITE is a Research Psychologist at the University of California, San Francisco, where she teaches and has recently completed a study of a new role in the nursing profession, the nurse practitioner. Her pioneering book on adult development, *The Next Step,* was published in 1964 while she was on the staff of the Radcliffe Institute; since then she has been active in developing guidance workshops for women, and in conducting further research in adult development, particularly that of educated and professional women. A forthcoming article will present a new scale measuring androgynous competency. She has taught at Boston University, Cornell University, and San Francisco State University.

ANNE WILSON is a doctoral candidate in Sociology at Johns Hopkins University, having completed an M.S. in Family and Community Development at the University of Maryland.

# Preface

The first edition of this book was put together as a labor of love and published primarily as an act of faith. It had its genesis in 1968, at the first national conference of what was to become the younger branch of the women's liberation movement. Many of us at that conference had just begun reading everything we could find on women, and in that traditional era we were appalled at the scarcity of perceptive writings and only occasionally delighted by a gem that sparkled with new ideas. There were no books or anthologies presenting a feminist perspective on women's status, and those books about women that were not written from a wholly traditional view generally discounted feminism as out-moded, extreme, or both.

Ironically for a group that has since produced so much writing, most of us then felt unable to express our rising consciousness in words. Why not, we thought, do the next best thing? Why not bring together those few existing pieces that were worthwhile and save other women the task of seeking them out? That was a job I took on. Unfortunately, at the same time, I started working for my Ph.D. in political science. It took two years longer to publish the anthology than it did to get the degree.

During the years I worked on the book it grew and changed with the movement. Of the earliest selections, only those by Hacker and Klein were retained in the first edition (and in the second). The rest represented the new research of that time, the new thinking, and the new interpretations of old research inspired by the women's liberation movement.

The first edition articles came from a variety of sources. I placed ads in most of the burgeoning feminist media, and some organizations, notably the Women's History Research Library of Berkeley and KNOW of Pittsburgh, included special notices with their regular mailings. The response was overwhelming. Hundreds of articles and proposals poured in, and well over a year was spent reading and editing them.

From the beginning the standards were high. This book was to contain pieces that were comprehensive, lucidly written, and well grounded in scholarly research. Needless to say, the submissions I received in response to ads were not uniform in style and approach; nor did they cover all the topics needed. Hence I also collected movement pamphlets and other publications on women, attended feminist meetings, and audited panel discussions on women at professional meetings to find potential authors.

During this period both scholarly and popular writing on women was increasing exponentially, with feminist insights sparking analysis of the contradictions in women's lives in every conceivable sphere. Simultaneously, it was becoming harder and harder to interest a publisher in the book. Some who had expressed tentative interest when I first began sending out the prospectus decided as the book took shape that "this women's thing" was a fad and what market there was, was already glutted. Then one of my authors discussed the book with the traveling editor of a small house on the West Coast. That editor was Alden Paine. He wrote to me, I sent the manuscript, and after I agreed to decrease its length by one-third, National Press Books (soon to become Mayfield Publishing Company) sent me a contract.

As the book went to press, almost everything about it (except the quality of the articles) was an unknown. Owing to its size and recent name change, the publisher was unknown. I was an unknown. All but a few of the authors were unknowns. The potential readership was unknown. All publishing involves some risk, but this was extraordinary.

Since this is the *second* edition, I needn't point out that love and faith carried the day. Women's studies courses grew and spread, and both teachers and students found the volume an appropriate introductory text. The reason the courses spread, even in an atmosphere of skepticism and a period of declining college enrollments, is that feminism is not a fad, but a national consciousness that is fundamentally changing the fabric of all our lives.

Despite the considerable political and personal pleasure I felt at the book's success (and at the chagrin of publishers who had turned it down), I must admit I was not overjoyed when Mayfield told me to start preparing a second edition; I hadn't yet recovered from the seven years spent on the first one. Once convinced it had to be done, however, I had to make some hard decisions about what to delete and what to add. Some decisions made themselves: not all authors were available to update their contributions; a few articles no longer had the same impact as they had earlier; feedback from users of the text identified some that were not widely assigned in class. And, insofar as possible, I wanted to replace reprints with original articles and to survey the current issues.

This time the "advertising" for submissions was restricted to a one-time announcement in each of the newsletters of Sociologists for Women in Society and the Women's Caucus for Political Science. These alone elicited more than fifty papers and proposals. In addition, having learned with the first edition that advertising can yield limited results despite heavy responses, I had in the intervening years collected papers on women from sociology, psychology and political science conventions. Surprisingly, when I finally sat down to mine that collection, I found only one paper that "fit" the book. I also asked feminist faculty for names of young scholars doing new research that might be written up for undergraduate readers, and kept my eyes open for other writers who might contribute to the volume. This "grapevine" netted more final pieces than any other approach—and with far less reading of proposals and writing of rejection letters. (With this edition, I have probably now written as many rejection letters as I have received, and have yet to decide which is the more unpleasant experience.)

Despite my apprehensions, the creation of the second edition proved much easier than the first. Not only does success beget success, but I could now draw upon a network of feminist scholars who were engaged in the kind of substantive research I was looking for, and who moreover were committed to reaching a wide audience. Thus in many ways the compilation of the second edition reflected the maturation of the scholarly side of the women's movement.

Collection was only the beginning. As manuscripts came in, they had to be appraised, edited, and often revised. Every selection had to be clear, internally consistent, and accurate. Data contradictions between articles had to be resolved, and owing to space restrictions, overlaps had to be avoided. Footnotes had to be checked, quotes verified, statistics updated, a few new tables added and a few eliminated. For the tables and statistics I was thankful for the contribution of Barbara Farah of Michigan's Center for Political Studies, and for the cooperation of numerous government employees, in particular Elizabeth

Waldman, Beverly Johnson, Howard Hayghe, Anne Young, and Carl Rosenfeld, each of whom I called on many times. I now know more about how to interpret (and misinterpret) the mountains of numerical data the government collects than I ever thought I wanted to know.

Throughout this process, most of the authors came through magnificently. They juggled class schedules to get copy in on time; they understood when sections of their articles were eliminated to avoid overlapping with others; they revised and updated as necessary and responded to numerous requests and inquiries. The Mayfield editorial and production staff—named on the copyright page—performed similarly, occasionally under adverse conditions.

The book that emerged from all this effort contains not only an enormous amount of painstaking research and original thinking but some information that cannot easily be found anywhere else. The reader will find this a useful reference book as well as a general text. What can't be found in the articles can probably be found in sources cited in the notes. But while accuracy, thoroughness, and the use of the most recent data are stressed throughout, the true strength of the book rests not in its facts but in its ideas, and in the comprehensive orientation provided by a feminist perspective.

# Introduction

The feminist perspective can best be understood in contrast to the traditional view, for each arises from a dramatically different set of premises. The traditionalist view looks at the many ways in which women differ from men and concludes that these differences reflect some basic intrinsic difference that far transcends reproductive capacities. The traditionalist notes that historically women have always had less power, less influence, and fewer resources than men, and assumes this must accord with some natural order. The feminist perspective looks at the many similarities between the sexes and concludes that women and men have equal potential for individual development. Differences in the realization of that potential, therefore, must result from externally imposed restraints, from the influence of social institutions and values. The feminist view holds that so long as society prescribes sex roles and social penalties for those who deviate from them, no meaningful choice exists for members of either sex. Such roles and restraints are incisively examined and challenged in this book, in the belief that only by first understanding their origins and manifestations can we gain the wisdom to dismantle them and create a more just society.

The organization of the book allows readers to begin by looking at their own lives, then moves out in widening circles to bring in the social and historical context of woman's present-day status. It concludes with a section on feminism as the historical and contemporary challenge to that status. Nonetheless, owing to the scope of many of the pieces and the very nature of their topics, the global and the personal are often combined.

In Part 1, Wilson, Bolt, and Larsen show how the most intimate of functions, reproduction, has been one of the most highly controlled aspects of human life, and how our historically pro-natalist attitude has been used to justify women's confinement to home and family duties. Bishop argues that this confinement has been institutionalized in part through restrictions on abortions, which would allow women to choose when they wish to be mothers; and Rothman points out how both the reproductive and mothering functions have been co-opted by the medical establishment to its own ends. Phelps tells us that women have been alienated from their own sexuality by the so-called sexual liberation of the sixties; yet, says Herman, because we live in a "rape culture," women are held responsible for the sex act even when it takes place against their will.

The family has been the primary social institution to inform women's lives, and the patriarchal family has been perhaps the single most pervasive and effective means of confining and controlling their achievements. In Part 2, Gough puts the family in an historical and anthropological context; Peplau shows how power is wielded in the mating game called dating; Bernard cuts through the sentimentality of the mother role to reveal the flesh-and-blood creature who is the mother; and Baxandall explores the continuing need for adequate day-care facilities to aid U. S. employed mothers, pointing out how the absence of such facilities operates as a disincentive to women seeking employment outside the home.

It is via socialization and education that women are steered away from participating in the major social and economic institutions of our society. In Part 3, Weitzman contributes a major tour de force of the socialization literature with her own interpretation of how and why women emerge from this process in the way they do. Bell and Bart examine the consequences for older women of accepting the social norms of the female life cycle, and Freeman analyzes how women who have escaped or surmounted many of the early barriers can still be subtly (and not so subtly) discriminated against in graduate school.

In Part 4, the economic consequences of society's channeling are clearly delineated by Blau, who points out that there are two distinct labor markets—one male and one female—and the latter is economically depressed. Woman's share in the total income earned in this country, by and large, is not proportionate to her productive contribution. Women's share in unemployment, however, is considerable. The last decade has seen a rise in the women's labor force participation rate, and also a rise in the overall unemployment rate. Some have asserted that the unemployment rate has been artificially inflated by women who claim they want jobs when they don't really need to work. Because women are assumed to be "secondary workers" the hardships they endure with unemployment are assumed to be less arduous than those of male "breadwinners." Schlozman demolishes these myths by showing why women's increased participation rate in no way explains the current high overall unemployment rate, and why the hardships women experience when they are unemployed are not different from men's. Glenn and Feldberg focus on clerical work to show how increased employment of women in this occupation has led to decreased benefits. It is clear that income is more directly related to the sex of the employee than to the requirements of the job. Wertheimer delves into labor history to document women's valiant, but often unwelcome, contribution to the labor movement; White examines how even the most scientific of professions erects barriers to women's effectiveness; and Lorber looks at some of the noneconomic reasons why women are excluded from male domains in the work world.

More overt institutions of social control are analyzed in Part 5. Eastwood discusses the role of law both in suppressing women and in rectifying discrimination, documenting the significant legal gains made by the women's liberation movement. Lynn does the same in the sphere of politics. Almquist documents the synergistic effect of racism and sexism for black women. Nelson turns to history to analyze the original witch hunts, which she attributes to medieval society's fear of a new economic independence among women, and Shapiro looks at some contemporary forms of violence used to suppress women's independence. More subtle spheres of control are charted by two complementary pieces, one by Henley and Freeman on nonverbal communication and the other by Adams and Ware on language; both reveal the pervasiveness of sexism in interpersonal dealings, as well as the ways in which everyday conversation constantly reinforces prescribed sex-role behaviors in our society. And once again Hacker sums it up, as she did before most of us even heard of feminism, by pointing out that in every way except numerically, women are a minority group.

The last section, Part 6, is devoted to feminism past and present, a subject well worth a book in itself. Although Klein's historical treatment is primarily concerned with events in England, the patterns of development of oppression and dawning feminist awareness there were similar to those in the United States, and hers is still the best succinct analysis to date. Hole and Levine detail accomplishments of the first feminist wave in the United States; Freeman does the same for the current wave. Stone advocates the relevance of feminism for black women and identifies barriers to its active acceptance, and Polk provides heuristic models that enable us to analyze the intellectual bases of various contemporary feminist arguments and activities.

The articles in this book are not merely a critique of society; implicitly, they take to task the scholarly disciplines whose research and concepts they draw upon. These disciplines, like the institutions and agencies of society at large, are dominated by those on the inside. They still reflect, to a great degree, the traditionalist point of view, and with it a desire to explain, justify, and maintain the status quo of human and institutional relationships. The result is too often a consistency of approach that is almost stifling. It may be politically convenient to view the world through the most comfortable lenses, but the resulting distortion is scientifically unacceptable  Only when one changes position, views the world from another stance, and relaxes one's claim to a monopoly on truth can new knowledge be gained.

The papers in this book show how feminist thought can contribute to this process by providing a new perspective from which to reexamine basic concepts in many spheres of learning. They not only point out the sexist prejudices of old research but show how new human opportunities can be created by changing outworn institutions and values. A feminist perspective is practical as well as theoretical; it illuminates possibilities for the future as well as criticizes the limitations of the present.

Yet these new ideas can have real meaning only within the context of a political movement organized to put them into practice. They will not be adopted merely because they appear in print. For proof of this fact, we need only look at what happened during and after the last feminist movement. We are, after all, not the first scholars to challenge traditional attitudes toward women. Within the limits of the scholarly tools then available to them, our feminist forebears did this once before. One has only to visit the library of the National Women's Party in Washington or the Schlesinger Library in Cambridge, Mass. or the library of the Fawcett Society in London to realize the magnitude of their work. And one has only to think about how this work was relegated to dusty shelves and ignored after the last wave of feminism ended to feel a certain amount of despair: clearly new ideas are not espoused by society on the basis of merit alone.

Thus we are in the position of calling "new" what is in fact very old. The feminist ideas of today are "new" only in the sense that most people now alive have not been exposed to them until recently, and in the sense that the more advanced methodology of the scholarly disciplines can "renew" their significance. But if we are not to repeat history—if we are not to see our own volumes ultimately join those others on the dusty shelves—we cannot complacently assume that they will be readily embraced. Instead we must recognize the political context in which such ideas thrive, and we must work to maintain that context until they are thoroughly incorporated into the everyday frame of mind.

# PART 1 THE BODY AND ITS CONTROL

## Merry Bolt, Anne Wilson, and Wendy Larsen

# Woman's Biology— Mankind's Destiny: The Population Explosion and Women's Changing Roles

*The family is not our world — the world is our family.*
*—Anonymous*

The issues of population growth and women's liberation are both often featured topics in the media, yet the fundamental interdependency between them tends to be overlooked. As long as motherhood continues to be defined as a woman's essential role and outside employment or other major responsibilities seen as simply an addition to that role, real "equal opportunity" is impossible; and as long as women's roles continue to be defined in expectation of universal motherhood, population stabilization will be difficult to achieve.

Woman's biology has been used to explain how traditional sex roles have developed and why they are similar in so many cultures. In this "biological" view, woman's lesser physical strength leads naturally to her lesser power and status, and her vulnerability during pregnancy and lactation sets limits to her achievement. Often an innately different psychology is ascribed to the female, based on the nurturant qualities required by motherhood, or on a maternal instinct or drive. Sometimes these real and supposed differences have been eulogized;[1] simultaneously, and without conscious contradiction, however, they have served to justify and maintain women's inferior status, and to dictate a certain role (motherhood as the primary career) as peculiarly appropriate to women.

Historically, women have had little control over their reproductive function. Motherhood was almost inevitable for any sexually active, fertile woman. Such fecundity only slightly overbalanced the high death rate, however, and was necessary for survival of the species. Biology *was* destiny; the idea of separating procreative functions from other female sex roles was rarely entertained.

As long as a high death rate existed, positive attitudes toward marriage and reproduction were desirable. We should keep in mind when we analyze these attitudes that periodic famine, disease, and war have taken heavy tolls in human populations even in relatively recent recorded history. The Black Death, for example, may have killed more than a quarter of the population of England and Europe within a two-year time span in the fourteenth century.[2] World War II claimed millions of lives only forty years ago; and even today, thousands are dying in Subsaharan Africa owing to a combination of age-old scourges. Nevertheless, death rates in most parts of the world have now dropped dramatically, due primarily to a decline in infant and child mortality,[3] which has a more serious effect on population growth than a drop in deaths among people aged 45–60. Population growth depends not only on fertility rates, but also on survival to reproductive age. Thus, despite the trend to smaller families in certain countries, we still face a problem of excess fertility both in the United States and in the world as a whole.

Much has been said about the nature and extent of the population problem. The world now has four billion people and will probably have two billion more by the turn of the century.[4] In the United States all this talk has caused less concern than one might expect, because it has been followed by talk of our having achieved zero population growth (ZPG) and of our now experiencing a "baby bust" instead of a "baby boom."[5]

Contrary to the impression some have gained from the news media, the United States is a long way from ZPG. Our natural growth rate has indeed slowed down to about 0.6 percent per year (doubling every 116 years).[6] At the same time, however, projections based on present fertility trends seem to indicate that fertility may be about at replacement level, where one child survives to replace each adult. This would result in ZPG when the age structure of the population becomes stable approximately 72 years from now (the average lifespan), if fertility remains at this low level.* While there is some evidence that this slower population growth is due in part to a shift in the ideal family size, [7] the decline has been paralleled by economic recession. Thus it is difficult to tell how much is a real decline and how much is merely delayed fertility that could lead to another baby boom if economic conditions improve.[8]

Still, Americans constitute only 5 percent of the world's population,[9] and many people find it hard to understand why it is important to limit growth in this country at all. The connection between affluent America and the rest of the world is not obvious. Most Americans do not realize how dependent we are on the resources of the world to support our standard of living, and how inequitable distribution of those resources supports our illusion of abundance. Yet even in our own country, hunger and malnutrition exist amidst plenty because substantial numbers of people do not have the money to buy nutritious food. Economic surpluses are not necessarily real surpluses. This situation can be seen more clearly when we look at trade between developed and underdeveloped nations. We tend to feel in this country that we are feeding the world singlehandedly with our shipments of excess wheat. But protein is the actual limiting nutritional factor, and we in the United States import more pounds of protein than we export.[10] Peru, which was once a major producer of protein-rich fish meal, exported most of it to Europe, the United States, and Japan to be used for livestock and poultry feed, while there was widespread protein malnutrition in Peru

---

*Technical distinctions in demographic terms are not the issue here. Adroit choice of appropriate data can support almost any conclusion. Furthermore, demographic projections require estimates that are inherently unreliable. For a fuller discussion of the actual problems and distinctions see the original report by George Grier (see note 5) or the 1972 Population Reference Bureau publication, "Population Statistics: What do they Mean?" (see note 4).

and the rest of Latin America.* Similarly, the energy crisis has exposed our dependence on other countries' selling us their resources (in this case, oil) cheaply.** At the same time that we are trying to maintain our lifestyle at the expense of the future development of the rest of the world, however, we tout the glories of technology and development, encouraging everyone to aspire to owning two cars, an air-conditioned four-bedroom house, a swimming pool, and a color TV.[11]

Ecologists have warned that there is no simple technological solution to our environmental problems.[12] Unfortunately, population experts have tended to ignore these warnings. The solutions they propose to the population problem range from increasing the availability of contraceptives, finding safer, more effective contraceptives, and giving free abortions, to licensing parenthood.[13] Although some of these proposals have merit (it makes no sense, for example, to force people to have babies they don't want at the same time one is encouraging people to forgo having babies they do want), people's lives and particularly women's lives are involved in these decisions. Typically the desires of the people involved are highhandedly dismissed as unimportant, or important only as an obstacle to the public welfare.

Meanwhile, people—including women—continue to want too many children. Although concern about overpopulation has removed some of the societal-duty aspect of parenthood, and expected family size is at an all-time low, people still expect families of a size somewhat above the replacement level of 2.1 children per couple.[14] Also, people continue to have unplanned children.[15] Research seems to indicate that couples are more likely to practice effective contraception when they have reached or exceeded their desired family size, and that desired family size is a fair, if conservative, predictor† of actual fertility.[16] We would argue,

---

*And when the Peruvian anchovy fishing collapsed, the price of chicken and other meat soared in the United States. See C. P. Idyll, "The Anchovy Crisis," *Scientific American*, 228:6 (1973), 22–29.

**According to the Seventh Annual report of the Council on Environmental Quality, 1976, page 102 (available from U.S. Government Printing Office), about 40% of our annual oil consumption is imported.

†An exception to this is the poor, who tend to expect—and find—birth control to be ineffective, and who tend to be somewhat fatalistic about family planning. See Catherine S. Chilman, "Some Psychological Aspects of Fertility, Family Planning, and Population Policy in the United States," in J. T. Fawcett, ed., *Psychological Perspectives on Population* (New York: Basic Books, 1973), especially p. 177; and Lee Rainwater, *And the Poor Get*

then, that as long as marriage and motherhood are regarded and promulgated as a woman's primary role, women will continue to want "too many" children.

The pronatalist attitudes of our society and government have a long history behind them that is not easily erased. The Biblical tradition, one primary source of Western views on sex and women, sees men and women as incomplete without each other; in relation to each other through marriage and parenthood they form the image of divine life. The primary emphasis in this sexual relationship is on producing offspring, especially boys, as it is through posterity that a Jew participates in the Messianic age. After the Exile, every Jewish man had to marry and to produce at least one son and one daughter; sterility made the marriage void.

Christianity, developing under the influence of Greek asceticism and Eastern religions, gradually downgraded sex. The Roman Catholic tradition, as seen especially in Aquinas, saw sex as a hindrance to the spiritual life, therefore sinful and in need of justification. Reproduction—and only reproduction—can provide this justification because it brings souls into the world as candidates for salvation; thus the Catholic position on birth control.

In not banning either birth control or divorce, Protestantism sowed the seeds of a change in the status of women. However, that change was a long time coming; the Reformation envisioned no change in basic attitudes toward women and sex. Luther maintained that men and women had originally been created equal, but that since a woman had been largely responsible for the Fall, women must be subject to their husbands and bear the pain of labor and the responsibility of childrear-

---

*Children* (Chicago: Quadrangle Books, 1960). It is just a myth, however, that the poor, black mothers receiving Aid to Dependent Children are largely responsible for population growth in this country, and that if they would just restrain themselves from having children they can't afford (through compulsory abortion or sterilization, for example), the problem would be solved. In 1975, 81 percent of all births were to white women, compared to 16 percent to blacks. Seventy-four percent of all white births and 68 percent of all black births were first or second children. See "Population Myths," a 1977 publication of Zero Population Growth, Inc., 1346 Connecticut Ave., N.W., Washington, D.C. 20036. Also, most poor families in this country are white (Ehrlich and Ehrlich, p. 322). If black and Spanish-speaking people in this country (rich or poor) had had *no* children at all during the 1960's, our population would be merely 4 percent smaller, compared to the 13 percent attributable to the white majority (Commission on Population Growth and the American Future, pp. 71–72).

ing. With Protestantism's lesser emphasis on celibacy and virginity, marriage did become a more honorable estate, although the only justification for sex was still procreation.

Nineteenth-century science made it possible to question literal interpretations of the Bible. Simultaneously, nineteenth-century industrial development restricted the family to immediate relatives and narrowed the wife's role as men left the farms and home industries for the factories.[17] With advances in sanitation and public health, the death rate began to drop, followed by the birth rate,[18] and feminism developed. Ironically, the "biology is destiny" credo seemed to reach full flower even as people began to control their fertility and the birth rate fell in Great Britain and the United States. Pressures designating motherhood as the natural path to feminine fulfillment seem to have intensified into a sentimental mystique under the auspices of Freud and Queen Victoria just as women caught a glimpse of other options. There was fear of "race suicide" if feminism took hold.

The birth rate declined further during the Great Depression of the 1930's.[19] Although fertility never dropped even to the present level, and although our population continued to grow, people tended to attribute to the statistics a mind of their own, and to fear that the downward trend might be extrapolated out to zero and the end of mankind.

From associating economic depression and contraction with a declining birth rate, it seemed natural conversely to associate prosperity and industrial expansion with a rising birth rate, and to create the "growth is good" ethic that characterized the post-war years. Population growth was seen as beneficial to the economy and therefore desirable.[20] Having children might almost have been considered a civic duty. Lee Rainwater's study of attitudes toward childbearing, presumably reflecting the feelings prevalent during the late 1950's and early 1960's found agreement that it was selfish not to have children, that people should have all the children they can afford.[21] Economists reinforced this belief even to the end of the 1960's, predicting disaster if zero population growth should ever be attained.

The post-industrial decline in family size was somewhat balanced by a trend for more women to marry and to marry at younger ages.[22] It is not unreasonable to assume that this in part reflects stronger societal pressure toward a norm of universal marriage (better dead than unwed)[23] and parenthood as well as a relaxation of obstacles to marriage as individual autonomy increased with industrialization. Of American women born in 1902–5, almost one in ten remained single despite few apparent alternatives to marriage at that time; and of those who did marry, about a third had only one child or no children at all.[24] Reliable estimates are of course difficult to obtain in a time of flux such as this, but as of 1976, projections for American women born in 1946–51 (now aged 25–29) are that only one in twenty will not marry. Of those marrying, only 6.4 percent expect to remain childless, and 11.2 percent expect to have one child.[25]

This sort of phenomenon has circular effects, for as marriage becomes nearly universal, the unmarried do not fit in. They find the world organized by and for couples. A few years later in the life cycle, when all their friends have had children, the childless feel out of place as discussions turn to *Sesame Street* and diaper service. It is not just women talking about domestic matters that leads to a feeling of exclusion, for men are prone to replay the latest Little League game, inning by inning. Those not experiencing similar joys and frustrations are not appreciated, particularly if they should respond by talking about how much they enjoy their own, freer lifestyle.

American industry has carefully fostered society's pronatalist prejudices while cashing in on them, selling the marriage ideal along with its deodorant, mouthwash, and orange-blossom-scented douches; selling the motherhood ideal with toothpaste, floor wax, and ersatz orange juice. "Mothers of the Year" are honored for producing more little consumers. It is interesting to speculate why ads for feminine deodorant sprays are acceptable for television, while contraceptive devices are not. Contraceptives, in fact, are not extensively advertised anywhere, even where there are no laws forbidding such ads.

The American government, too, has traditionally given official sanction to the sex-role norms, reflecting both the dominant social values and the view that a large population is beneficial in maintaining military strength. The present federal income tax structure gives tax advantages to those married, but only if one partner does not work. Families with children are allowed additional deductions to their tax bill. Similarly, social security benefits are often greater for married women who have never worked than for women who have worked all their lives. At the local level, where the basic tax is the property tax, the family with twelve children pays no more for the expenses of schools, recreational facilities, transportation, police, and fire protection than the family with no children, except insofar as larger families may tend to own larger and thus possibly more valuable homes.

There has been talk of changing the official pronatalism, but little has actually been done.* The Population Stabilization Resolution initiated by Congress in 1972 was not passed. The President's Commission on Population and the American Future came out with an excellent report, but President Nixon refused to accept it, and impounded the funds that would have put the Population Education Act into effect. Presidents Ford and Carter have not taken significant action since then. In 1977 the House established a Select Committee on Population; hopefully it will resume the 1972 efforts.

Unofficially, pressure to marry and have children seems reinforced even today by holdovers of the puritan ethic. "Getting married and settling down" is still prescribed as an antidote to irresponsibility. Those who fear themselves to be selfish and egocentric may have large families to prove to themselves and others that they are not selfish and self-centered.[26] The norm that parents should be mature may be taken to mean that those who forego parenthood are immature, or that having children in and of itself makes one mature.

Childlessness has become more socially acceptable, perhaps, and there is at least one national organization[27] lobbying to end discrimination against the single and childless. Yet most mothers probably perceive this new attitude as a devaluation of their life's work, and hope that their daughters do not take such talk too seriously. The evidence seems to be that generally their daughters do share their values. Sorensen reported in 1972 that 92 percent of the teenage girls interviewed in his survey expected ultimately to marry and have children.[28]

Even among some feminists who are challenging the old restrictive role, motherhood may become very important. It can be used to prove both to society and to these women themselves that they are indeed "normal females" with the proper maternal instincts. It keeps them from being called man-hating or unloving or frustrated, castrating females.

In the face of all these pressures to marry and reproduce, perhaps the institutions of marriage and parenthood—and thus, inevitably,

---

*This inaction is, in part, due to the problem of finding measures that will not adversely affect the children of large families who should not be made innocent victims in any attempt to discourage large families.

woman's traditional role—should be reexamined. For if they really are all glamour and romance, the one true path to personal happiness, maturity, and self-actualization, if they bring security, love, and a stable, lifelong source of companionship and emotional gratification, why are they sold so hard? We must begin to recognize that the traditional feminine role not only contributes to overpopulation, but also commonly fails to live up to its promises of fulfillment.

Sunday supplements make it hard to ignore that one in three or four American marriages ends in divorce.[29] Even for lasting marriages, the picture is often unattractive. J. R. Udry states after a review of the data: "The young person contemplating marriage might be advised that the *usual* experience is gradual devitalization, although none will accept this as representing his own future."[30]

Still, it requires strength not to conform and there are indications that those with lower ego strength and poorer social adjustment tend to be among the first to seek the social security of early marriage.[31] Society seldom questions the decision of a woman to "give up everything" and marry, but it often questions the motives of those who want more than marriage. In a study of the adjustment of unmarried women, Baker found that when a single woman took a positive view of her state, her chances of feeling fulfilled were as good as those of married women.[32] Unfortunately, our society does all it can to make it difficult for women past a certain age to take a positive view of being single.

Similarly, parenthood continues to be romanticized, perhaps even more than marriage. One may recognize that one's parents' marriage was less than ideal, but, by logical necessity, children grow up in, and are therefore best acquainted with, families with children. Alternative adult models are scarce, particularly in suburbia. It may be difficult to escape the idea that parenthood is the normal culmination of every adult's life.

Whether all people are ideally suited to parenthood, and will derive their major life satisfactions from it is open to question, however. Family research does not substantiate the myths that children patch up unhappy marriages and generally contribute to marital euphoria.

Practically speaking, moreover, children are expensive. Recent (1975–76) estimates are than an American family with an annual income of $10,500–13,500 will spend about $35,000 per child between birth and age 18. If annual income is $16,500–20,000 the cost per child will be in excess of $50,000.[33] It takes another $8,000–10,000 to put each child through college. Under current economic conditions of recession and inflation, children are not merely a serious responsibility but a severe economic strain for struggling couples.

Worse, the intangible benefits that are supposed to compensate parents for their sacrifices are not always forthcoming. Several studies of marital satisfaction show wives' complaints increasing with the advent of children, reaching a peak when children begin school and then tapering off somewhat, particularly when the husband retires.[34] Although one should be cautious in attributing the wives' rising dissatisfaction directly to the influence of children, nonetheless it does conflict with the idealized pattern wherein children are supposed to revitalize and strengthen the relationship between their parents, and bring new love and happiness into the family. In a more carefully controlled longitudinal study, wives' complaints of lack of attention from their husbands increased following the birth of a first child.[35] Masters and Johnson, studying pregnancy, report that a substantial number of husbands begin affairs during their wives' pregnancies, and often continue them afterwards.[36]

If we seem unduly cynical, let us add that we are not suggesting that there are no happy marriages or that parenthood is always disappointing and lacking in gratification. Happy marriages do exist, and children can be a great source of joy and satisfaction in their appreciation of life.* We only wish to suggest that marriage and parenthood are undesirable as a universal goal and ideal. No one should rush into them, be pushed into them, or drift into them for lack of other alternatives. Parenthood especially is something to be planned, to be undertaken seriously and realistically, with a full understanding of the problems, responsibilities, and restrictions attendant upon bringing another person into the world. Children are more than cute pets; they have identities all their own and may or may not fulfill their parents' expectations.

The obstacles in the way of a career for the well-socialized woman are still great today, and the escape hatch to instant identity through

---

*For a description of some satisfying marriages and families, see John F. Cuber and Peggy G. Harroff, *Sex and the Significant Americans* (Baltimore: Penguin Books, 1965). These "vital" marriages are not suggested as ideal relationships, but simply as possible; the actual sex roles portrayed may appear somewhat dated.

motherhood is always open. As a mother, a woman may receive all the praise and attention she felt lacking before. Unfortunately the discovery that motherhood is not always enough often comes too late for the situation to be easily rectified, for children require a long-term commitment and a large part of the family resources. Returning to a career after dropping out is often difficult. Certain kinds of training become obsolete rapidly, especially in the technical and scientific fields, and refresher courses do not always exist. Educational institutions are not geared to the needs of women who have children to care for, and neither are most jobs. These conditions need to be changed so that women will not be trapped in a cycle of housewifery where producing and rearing children is the only creative option readily available to them.

Once a woman begins having children, social forces seem to conspire to keep her at home. Unless they have no husbands or are otherwise forced to work, mothers are expected to stay home with preschool children, even though maternal employment apparently does the children no harm under normal conditions of adequate care and parental affection.[37] On the contrary, some evidence suggests that women who want to work are "better mothers" if they follow their inclination than if they stay home out of duty.[38] Maternal employment may sometimes positively benefit children by fostering greater independence.[39] But the image of even school-age children returning to an empty house and an empty cookie jar continues to pull at heartstrings as if there were no other choices.

One or two children are not a full-time, lifelong career. The three or four children our mothers had were not, either, but since our mothers were encouraged to ignore this problem, they were confronted with twenty or thirty empty years between the time their children left home and the time their husbands retired. Many of them have entered the labor market, yet such women often feel trapped—too old to start a new career and unable to find challenging work fully utilizing their potential.

We must finally accept careers outside the home as the rule rather than the exception. If marriage and childbearing are placed in this perspective, then women may be able to plan more realistically to achieve satisfaction through their own abilities and efforts rather than solely through the lives of their husbands and children, probably to the relief of both of those groups.

To achieve this end, however, women will have to come to terms both with their own sexuality and with heterosexual relations in general. Without birth control (including abortion), biology is still destiny. Both premarital sex and births out of wedlock are increasingly common among adolescents.[40] About half of unmarried nineteen-year-old females in the United States are estimated to be sexually active.[41] Unfortunately, casual sex is often characterized by casual contraception and inaccurate sexual knowledge.[42] Sexual freedom carries with it as great a potential for the exploitation of women as did the traditional role. Possibly, indeed, a greater potential, for it places on women the entire burden of child support as well as childrearing, if responsible paternity is not insisted upon.

Women seem intent on pleasing men, inside or outside of marriage. Insofar as this is reciprocated by men's genuinely caring about the welfare of their sex partners, this is not necessarily bad. However, women need to recognize their vulnerability, and to be prepared to look after themselves.* Unintentional motherhood resulting from "sexual liberation" curtails a woman's options as severely as do culturally imposed social and psychological definitions of sex roles—and often at an earlier age.

Only when women are truly free, both culturally and biologically, to be producers of ideas, art, inventions, and leadership as well as of babies, will we have come very far toward a real solution to the population crisis in this country.

## NOTES

1   Ashley Montague, *The Natural Superiority of Women* (New York: Macmillan, 1968).

2   William L. Langer, "The Black Death," *Scientific American,* 210:2 (1964), 114–21.

3   The American Assembly, Columbia Univ., *The Population Dilemma,* 2nd ed., ed. by Philip Hauser (Englewood Cliffs, N.J.: Prentice-Hall, 1969), p. 15.

4   Population Reference Bureau, Inc. (PRB), *1977 World Population Data Sheet,* available at Bureau headquarters, 1754 N St. NW, Washington, D.C. 20036; Paul Ehrlich and

---

*Only 28 percent of Sorensen's nonvirgin males "often worried" about making a girl pregnant. Forty-six percent of the males who were sexually active at the time of the study had sometimes "just trusted to luck that the girl wouldn't become pregnant," during the preceding month. See Robert C. Sorensen, *Adolescent Sexuality in Contemporary America,* pp. 305, 453.

Anne Ehrlich, *Population, Resources and Environment,* 2nd ed. (San Francisco: W. H. Freeman, 1972), p. 50.

5  George Grier, "Baby Bust Replaces Baby Boom," report released by Washington Center for Metropolitan Studies, 1717 Massachusetts Ave. NW, Washington, D.C., 1971.

6  PRB, *1977 World Population Data Sheet.*

7  Bureau of the Census, "Birth Expectations of American Wives: June 1973," and "Birth Expectation and Fertility, June 1972." *Current Population Reports,* Series P-20 #254.

8  Philip Hauser, "Population Outlook," testimony before the Special Sub-Committee on Human Resources, U.S. Senate Committee on Labor and Public Welfare, Washington, D.C., Oct. 14, 1971.

9  PRB, *1977 World Population Data Sheet.*

10  Ehrlich and Ehrlich, pp. 112–13.

11  For further discussion of the interrelations between population and other problems, see Donella Meadows, Dennis Meadows, Jørgen Randers, and William Behrens, III, *The Limits to Growth* (New York: Universe Books, 1972); Commission on Population Growth and the American Future, *Population and the American Future,* G.P.O., Stock #5258–2002, Washington, D.C., 1972; Committee on Resources and Man, National Academy of Sciences–National Research Council, *Resources and Man* (San Francisco: W. H. Freeman & Co., 1969); Paul Ehrlich, *The Population Bomb,* 2nd ed. (New York: Ballantine Books, Inc., 1971); Georg Borgstrom, "The Food and People Dilemma," (Belmont, Ca.: Duxbury Press, 1974).

12  Barry Commoner, *The Closing Circle: Nature, Man and Technology* (New York: Knopf, 1971); Garrett Hardin, *Exploring New Ethics for Survival: the Voyage of the Spaceship Beagle* (New York: Viking Press, 1972).

13  Lenni W. Kangas, "Integrated Incentives for Fertility Control," *Science,* 169 (1970), 1278–83; Edgar R. Chasteen, *The Case for Compulsory Birth Control* (Englewood Cliffs, N.J.: Prentice-Hall, 1971); Roger W. McIntire, "Parenthood Training or Mandatory Birth Control: Take Your Choice," *Psychology Today,* 7:5 (1973), 34; Bernard Berelson, "Beyond Family Planning," *Science,* 163 (1969), 533–43.

14  Bureau of the Census, "Birth Expectations: 1973" and ". . . 1972."

15  Commission on Population Growth and the American Future, p. 97.

16  Lee Rainwater, *Family Design: Marital Sexuality, Family Size and Contraception* (Chicago: Aldine, 1965), pp. 228–30; "Birth Expectations: 1972," p. 2.

17  W. A. O'Neil, *Everyone Was Brave: The Rise and Fall of Feminism in America* (Chicago: Quadrangle Books, 1969), p. 4.

18  Commission on Population Growth and the American Future, pp. 16–17.

19  R. E. Miles, "The Population Challenge of the '70's," *Population Bulletin,* 16:1 (1970), 7.

20  Commission on Population Growth and the American Future, p. 41.

21  Rainwater, 1965, pp. 280–81.

22  Bureau of the Census, "Marriage, Divorce, and Remarriage by Year of Birth: June 1971," *Current Population Reports,* Series P-20 #239, 1972, pp. 4–5.

23   Jessie Bernard, *Women and the Public Interest* (Chicago: Aldine-Atherton, 1971), p. 180.

24   N. B. Ryder, "The Emergence of a Modern Fertility Pattern: United States, 1917–66," in *Fertility and Family Planning*, ed. S. J. Behrman, L. Corsa, and R. Freedman (Ann Arbor: University of Michigan Press, 1970), pp. 102–04.

25   Bureau of the Census, Current Population Reports, Series P-20, no. 308, "Fertility of American Women: June 1976," (Washington, D.C.: U.S. Government Printing Office, Table 12).

26   Rainwater, 1965, pp. 194–95.

27   NON (National Organization for Non-Parents), 806 Reistertown Road, Baltimore, Maryland 21208.

28   Robert C. Sorensen, *Adolescent Sexuality in Contemporary America* (New York: World Publishing, 1973), p. 358.

29   Bureau of the Census, Current Population Reports, Series P-20, no. 297, "Number, Timing and Duration of Marriage and Divorce in the United States: June 1975," Table G.

30   J. R. Udry, *The Social Context of Marriage* (Philadelphia: Lippincott, 1966), p. 301.

31   K. W. Bartz and F. I. Nye, "Early Marriage: A Propositional Formulation," *Journal of Marriage and the Family*, 32 (1970), 258; Floyd M. Martinson, "Ego Deficiency As a Factor in Marriage," *American Sociological Review*, 20 (1955), 163.

32   Luther G. Baker, Jr., "The Personality and Social Adjustment of the Never-Married Woman," *Journal of Marriage and the Family*, 30 (1968), 473.

33   Thomas J. Epenshade, "The value and cost of children," *Population Bulletin*, 32:1 (Population Reference Bureau, Inc., 1977, see note 4).

34   Wesley Burr, "Satisfactions with Various Aspects of Marriage Over the Life Cycle: A Random Middle Class Sample," *Journal of Marriage and the Family*, 32 (1970), 54; Boyd Rollins and Harold Feldman, "Marital Satisfaction over the Family Life Cycle," *Journal of Marriage and the Family*, 32 (1970), 20; Karen S. Renne, "Correlates of Dissatisfaction in Marriage," *Journal of Marriage and the Family*, 32 (1970), 54; J. R. Hurley and D. Palonen, "Marital Satisfaction and Child Density Among University Student Parents," *Journal of Marriage and the Family*, 29 (1967), 483.

35   Robert G. Ryder, "Longitudinal Data Relating Marriage Satisfaction and Having a Child," *Journal of Marriage and the Family*, 35 (1973), 604.

36   Ruth Brecher and Edward Brecher, "Sex During and After Pregnancy," in *An Analysis of Human Sexual Response* ed. by Brecher and Brecher (New York: New American Library, 1966), p. 93.

37   L. W. Hoffman and F. I. Nye, *The Employed Mother in America* (Chicago: Rand McNally, 1963).

38   Marion Yarrow, Phyllis Scott, Louise de Leeuw and Christine Heinig, "Child Rearing in Families of Working and Non-Working Mothers," *Sociometry*, 25:2 (1962), 102–40.

39   Faye H. Von Mering, "Professional and Non-Professional Women as Mothers," *The Journal of Social Psychology*, 42 (1955), 21–34.

40  Wendy H. Baldwin, "Adolescent Pregnancy and Childbearing—Growing Concerns for Americans," *Population Bulletin*, 31:2 (Population Reference Bureau, 1976, see note 4).

41  *Ibid.*, p. 16; Sorensen, p. 189; Commission on Population Growth and the American Future, p. 85.

42  *Ibid.*, pp. 17–18; Commission on Population Growth and the American Future, p. 85; pp. 303–27.

# Linda Phelps

# Female Sexual
Alienation

In the last few years, the so-called sexual revolution has turned sour. The end of inhibition and
the release of sexual energies so often thought of
as initiating the revolutionary culture are now
beginning to be seen as just another fraud. After
the countless rapes at music festivals and anti-war
gatherings, after the demands raised at People's
Park (Berkeley, California, 1969) for "Free Land,
Free Dope, Free Women," after the analyses of
(male) rock culture, women are beginning to
realize that nothing new has happened in male-
female sexual relations. What we have is simply a
more sophisticated (and thus more insidious) version of male sexual culture, a kind of sexual

*Another version of this article appeared in *Liberation* (May
1971) and in *The Ladder* (August-September 1971).

"freedom" that has meant more opportunity for men, not a new kind of experience for women. At first it was, perhaps, a new experience for women as traditional, puritanical notions of female sexuality were partly discarded. But underneath the guilt that we had learned were needs for self-protection that were much more real. Somehow the rules of the game were still male.

Many of us who only a few years before had felt sexually "liberated" now suddenly found ourselves more sympathetic with the problems of our mothers and grandmothers—feeling a loss of interest in sex, a hatred of sex, or a disgust with our own sexual fantasies. This turn-about happened very fast in many cases, and I think it happened because we opened ourselves up in consciousness-raising and a lot of bad feelings that we did not quite understand floated to the top. It has been good to get these feelings out and look at them. But can we explain them, can we understand what has happened to our sexuality?

I would like to suggest that we can understand the distortion of female sexuality if we conceptualize it as a special case of alienation.

Alienation is a much-used and little-explained term. Put simply, it refers to the progressive sense of separation between our selves or personalities and everything around us that occurs when we are powerless. As Ernest Becker put it in an important essay on alienation: "People break down when they aren't 'doing'—when the world around them does not reflect the active involvement of their own creative powers. . . . Alienated man [sic] is man separated from involvement with and responsibility for the effective use of his *self-powers.*" The opposite of powerlessness is self-actualization; and the healthy, self-actualizing human being moves through the world as an autonomous source of action, in touch with her/his own experience.

Since self-actualization seems so obviously preferable, it is worth asking precisely how alienation comes about in our lives as individuals. Becker[1] suggests several ways in his tri-dimensional analysis of alienation.

1) *Alienation occurs along the dimension of time.* As children we learn certain patterns of behavior that bring us approval and help us function in the world. But as we grow older, we face situations not covered by the old patterns, situations calling for new kinds of behavior. If our early childhood training has been too rigid, we cannot go beyond the old patterns, and we become increasingly unable to handle our own experiences. Withdrawal is a natural response in these circumstances.

2) *Alienation also occurs within the dimension of the roles we play.* We are called upon to play more than one role in life, and sometimes the behavior expected in one role conflicts with the behavior expected in another. These contradictions set us at odds with parts of our lives. Not only are females confined to a small number of socially acceptable roles, but they are given conflicting messages about these roles. Motherhood, for example, is viewed as a sacred task, but mothers are not taken seriously when they act outside their kitchens and homes. Child-rearing is seen as a woman's job, but a woman must not use her intuition or experience in doing it; (largely male) psychologists, child psychiatrists, and educational researchers will tell her how. Girls are encouraged to become educated, but discouraged from doing anything meaningful with that education.

3) *The third dimension of alienation* is more complex. Put simply, it *is the stage at which* the conflicts just described become too severe, the gaps between thought and experience, mind and body become too great, and *an actual breakdown of self is likely to occur.* It is this kind of breakdown that makes people unable to function and lands them in mental hospitals. Becker calls this extreme form of alienation "schizophrenia" and I would like to adopt his usage, realizing that powerlessness can sometimes drive us literally "out of our minds." R. D. Laing is probably right in his contention that there is no such thing as "schizophrenia" as that term has usually been used in the mental health field,* yet for want of another term I would like to use it here in the specialized sense explained above: an extreme form of alienation in which people lose touch with their own experience of reality.

This tri-dimensional concept of alienation is complex, but I think it can help us understand some parts of our own experience of male-female sexual relationships, especially if we extend it to include a political dimension. Both Laing and Becker describe alienation as growing out of power relationships between people as well as out of the

---

*R. D. Laing and A. Esterson, *Sanity, Madness, and the Family: Families of Schizophrenics* (Baltimore, Md.: Penguin Books, 1970). As Laing sees it, behaviors that have often been called schizophrenic are understandable reactions to social situations in which people are powerless, their experiences and perceptions denied and mystified by others. A woman in Laing's study broke down when she lost "any sense of being the agent of her own thoughts and words" (p. 42). Another young woman who had been in a mental hospital for ten years felt that "she was forbidden to see for herself and think for herself. Any expression of her own was simply ignored, disparaged, ridiculed" (p. 60).

condition of being human. As human beings we come to understand and experience ourselves as we interact with other people. It is in grappling with the outside world, in trying out our powers of thought and emotion, that we become full, self-actualized people. In this self-directed behavior, we test ourselves and gain some understanding of ourselves and our environment. And the more positive and successful experiences we build up, the more secure we are as whole persons. This is the mechanism by which we become liberated; the reverse process is alienation.

As alienated people, we begin to deny our own reality; we lose important parts of ourselves. When alienation becomes extreme, we take refuge in a world of *symbols;* we become accustomed to relating to symbol-objects rather than person-objects and in doing so we lose contact with our own self-powers.

I would argue that as females we become sexually alienated, at points even schizophrenic, because we relate neither to ourselves as self-directed persons nor to our partners as the objects of our desire, but to a false world of symbol and fantasy. This fantasy world that veils our experience is the world of sex as seen through male eyes. It is a world where eroticism is defined in terms of female powerlessness, dependency, and submission. It is a world of sado-masochistic sex.

If this seems doubtful, think of the erotic themes of most of the novels, comic books, movies, jokes, cartoons, and songs ever published. The most frequent sexual theme is the drama of conquest and submission: the male takes the initiative and the female waits, waits in a thousand variations on a single theme—eagerly, coyly, shyly, angrily, and, at the outer edge of pornography and fantasy, against her will. Usually it is more subtle. The female stands in awe of the hero's abilities, his powers; she is willing when he takes the initiative, guides her by the elbow, puts his arm around her waist, maneuvers her into the bedroom. What is it that makes such descriptions arousing? Not a mere catalogue of anatomy, for this may not even be given, but the tension in the social situation as male advances on female, whether she is willing or not.

Such submission is acceptable in our culture if the man is superior, and this leads to the search for the man who is smarter, taller, more self-confident—someone to look up to and thus worthy of giving in to.

In each of our lives, there was a first man for whom we were prepared like lambs for the slaughter. My fantasy of him was a composite of Prince Valiant, Gary Cooper, and my father. Trained in submission, in silence, I awaited him through a series of *adolescent boyfriends who were not masterful enough to fit the dream* . . . because I would not really graduate to the estate of womanhood until I had been taken by a strong man.[2]

Our culture's eroticism mirrors the power dynamics between the sexes, but in a particularly cruel way. With the right man and the right circumstances, the picture of female powerlessness can be highly arousing. In this way, sexism gets built into our very biological impulses.

A rather narrow form of male-dominated heterosexuality has become the norm which shapes our sexual impulses. In a study of sexual behavior,[3] psychologist Abe Maslow confirmed this norm, reporting that women who find their male partners more dominant than they are usually make the best sexual "adjustment." For example, a very sexually active woman in his study failed to reach orgasm with several male partners because she considered them weaker than herself and thus could not "give in to them." Thus, "normal" sexual happiness occurs in our society when the male plays the dominant role.

If we come to view male-dominated heterosexuality as the only healthy form of sex, it is because we are bombarded with that model for our sexual fantasies long before we experience sex itself. Sexual images of conquest and submission pervade our imagination from an early age and determine how we will later look upon and experience sex. Through the television set and the storybook, we live out in imagination society's definition of sex and love. Rapunzel waits in her tower for years in hopes of the young prince who will free her body from its imprisonment. Sleeping Beauty's desires slumber until they are awakened and fulfilled by the kiss of the young prince. The sexual fable in the stories of these fairy-tale princesses is quite clear, and very nearly as powerful today as it was a century ago. There are few women, no matter how intelligent, no matter how dedicated to the pursuit of a goal, who will not finally be conquered—and like it. And if they are not conquered, it is understood that no man desired them anyway.

By experiencing such sexual fantasies at an early age, women become alienated from their own later experiences (Becker's first dimension). Locked early into a set of fantasy images that define female sexual roles as passive, they must deny feelings that do not fit the definition. And so all-pervasive is the male bias of our culture that we seldom notice that the fantasies we take in, the images that describe to us how to act, are male fantasies about females. In a male world, female sexuality is from the beginning unable to get a clear picture of itself.

Moreover, also from the beginning, women experience Becker's second dimension of alienation: the role of woman as a sexual being is subject to contradictory evaluations by society. Young girls become attuned to society's ambivalent view of female sexuality. Women are considered synonomous with sex, yet female sexuality is seen as valid only under certain conditions, such as marriage. Even in more permissive ages like our own, there are still limits. One of these is the point where a female can be labeled promiscuous. Another is the point where she attempts to exercise any power: women who initiate and direct sexual activity with male partners find that they have gone too far and are feared and rejected as "castrators."

In all these ways, female sexuality becomes distorted, swallowed up in a fantasy world of symbol-objects rather than real people. Like the schizophrenic, we are alienated from our own experience and from our own powers of initiation. This form of alienation affects sex directly: it means that women do not often take the initiative in relation to men. As Becker describes it:

> Schizophrenic passivity is a direct reflex of the abrogation of one's powers in the face of the object. . . . If you relate to an object under your own initiatory powers, then it becomes an object which enriches your own nature. If you lack initiatory powers over the object, it takes on a different value, for it then becomes an individual which crowds your own nature. . . . A girl really comes to exist as a feminine sex object for the adolescent only as he learns to exercise active courtship powers in relation to her.[4]

If women become objects of sexual desire for men in the social process of male-initiated relationships, how does the male become an object of sexual desire for the female? In a sense, perhaps he does not. It is not clear, in fact, that the male body *per se* is arousing for women, certainly not in the same way that the female body is for men. Indeed, many women find the male body ugly. They respond narcissistically to the bombardment of images of the female body as sexual stimuli, and think of sex in terms of what is being done to them rather than projecting sexual desire onto the male. The female is taught to be the object of sexual desires rather than to be a self-directed sexual being oriented toward another; she is taught to be adored rather than adoring. As Schulamith Firestone points out in *The Dialectic of Sex,* "Cultural distortion of sexuality also explains how female sexuality gets twisted in narcissism: women make love to themselves vicariously through the man rather than directly making love to him.[5]

Two things would seem to happen to female sexuality. On the one hand, with little acceptable sexual imagery—either male or female—available in this culture for women, many do not allow themselves any sexual desires or fantasies at all. (Masters and Johnson, having found that many women who could not focus on sexual imagery had difficulty having orgasm, have tried to encourage sexual fantasy through the reading of arousing material.) Women who do have fantasies often have the same sado-masochistic ones as men do. In these fantasy episodes, the female does not always play the masochistic role. She may take the part of the male, the female, or an onlooker, but there is almost always a powerless female in the scene.

How do women tolerate a situation in which men control and define the experience of sex? Only, I believe, in the same way the schizophrenic tolerates his/her world—by separation from it. We experience our sexuality in symbolic terms at the expense of active physical involvement. Sex is reinterpreted to us by society in symbolic messages of passivity and conquest. Like the symbolic world of the schizophrenic, women's fantasy life—our desire to be taken, overpowered, mastered—allow us to play the passive role and perhaps even to enjoy it *if we fully accept the world as defined by men.* Caught between the demands of a male-dominated society and the demands of our own self-definition, we survive by fully accepting the masochistic symbol-world given to us by male society at the expense of our own experience. In fact, our physical experience has been denied and distorted for so long that most of us are not even aware of the sacrifice we have made. We are only uneasy that all is not well.

Yet ultimately in the lives of those women for whom fantasy and reality become too far apart, a crisis occurs. The crisis may arise in some cases merely because the male becomes demystified after years of marriage. It is hard to hold onto fantasies of male power when confronted with the reality of a pot-bellied, lethargic husband. In other cases, as more women become involved in the women's movement, the whole fragile structure of fantasy and power may fall along with the myth of male supremacy. Such a crisis most commonly results either in a transfer of fantasy to a new male or in a loss of interest in sex altogether.

Women, then, are alienated from their sexuality along several dimensions. From an early age, we are alienated from ourselves as sexual beings by a male society's ambivalent definition of our sexuality: we are sexy, but we are pure; we are insatiable, but we are frigid; we have beautiful bodies, but we must paint and shave and deodorize them. We are also alienated because we are separated from our own experience by the prevailing male cultural definition of sex—the male fantasy of active man and passive woman. From an early age, our sexual impulses are turned back upon ourselves in the narcissistic counterpart of the male fantasy world. In social relations with men, we are alienated from ourselves as initiating, self-directed persons. Only a few women are able to hold all these contradictory parts together. Far more are now beginning to question whether they should have to try.

Calling into question our traditional female role, however, has meant calling into question more and more layers of our experience. With this questioning has come the discovery that there is very little worth saving in male-female relations as we have known them. Kate Millett showed us in *Sexual Politics* that fascism—the relations of dominance and submission that begin with sex and extend throughout our society—is at the very core of our cultural experience. So it is with little joy and much sadness that we peel back the layers of our consciousness and see our sexual experience for what it really is. And it is also with much sadness that we admit that there is no easy answer. It does no good to say that we have been merely the victims of male power plays. For whatever reasons, the sado-masochistic content is in the heads of women too. As long as female powerlessness is the unspoken reality of much of our cultural imagination, then women will want to be conquered. As long as our cultural vision for the future is the projection of male desires, women will not be able to understand even their own alienation.

To say this is to suggest some ways out of our cultural and sexual alienation. Yet we should never assume, as we often do, that the pervasive sexual distortion will easily be corrected. We have pushed beyond the economic revolution and the cultural revolution to come face to face with the real sexual revolution, and we are not sure just what we have left in the way of hope and affirmation.

Perhaps the most courageous and in the long run the most positive thing we can do is to acknowledge the pain we feel now and the profound damage we have sustained—and in doing so avoid despair. Sometimes it is necessary to touch bottom in order to push up for air.

## NOTES

1   Ernest Becker, "Mills' Social Psychology and the Great Historical Convergence on the Problem of Alienation," in Irving Horowitz, ed., *The New Sociology, Essays in Social Science and Social Theory in Honor of C. Wright Mills* (New York: Oxford University Press, 1964), pp. 108–33.

2   *Motherlode*, vol. 1 no. 1, p. 1.

3   A. H. Maslow, "Self-Esteem (Dominance-feeling) and Sexuality in Women," in Hendrick M. Ruitenbeek, *Psychoanalysis and Female Sexuality* (New Haven, Conn.: College and University Press, 1966), pp. 161–97.

4   Becker, *op. cit.*, p. 125.

5   Shulamith Firestone, *The Dialectic of Sex* (New York: William Morrow, 1970), p. 78.

# Barbara Katz Rothman

# Women, Health, and Medicine

Women are not only people: *woman* is a subject one can study, even specialize in within medicine. Obstetricians and gynecologists are medicine's, and perhaps society's, generally recognized "experts" on the subject of women, especially women's bodies: our health, reproductive functioning, and sexuality.[1] Obstetrics is the branch of medicine concerning the care of women during pregnancy, labor, and the time surrounding childbirth,[2] similar in some ways to midwifery. Gynecology is the "science of the diseases of women, especially those affecting the sex organs."[3] There is no comparable "science" of the study of men, *their* diseases and/or reproductive functions. An attempt by urologists in 1891 to develop an "andrology" specialty came to nothing.[4]

At its simplest, we can think of a medical specialty as arising out of pre-existing needs. People have heart attacks: the medical specialty of cardiology develops. Or the amount of knowledge generated in a field grows so enormously that no one person can hope to master it all: physicians "carve out" their own areas of specialization. Increasing knowledge about cancer thus led to the specialty of oncology, and subspecialities within oncology.

But the development of a medical specialty is not necessarily the creation of a key for an already existing lock. Medical "needs" do not necessarily predate the specialty, even though the specialty is presumably organized to meet those needs. This has been made quite clear in the work of Thomas Szasz on the relatively recent expansion of medicine into such "social problem" areas as alcoholism, gambling and suicide.[5] Medicine doesn't have the "cures" for these problems but by defining them in medical terms, as sickness, the physician gains political control over the societal response: punishment becomes "treatment," desired or not, successful or not. Similarly, medical control over childbirth, lactation, menopause, and other women's health issues was not based on superior ability to deal with these concerns.

The case of Jacoba Felice de Almania, a woman tried for the illegal practice of medicine in 1322, illustrates this point. In her defense Jacoba Felice de Almania had witnesses who testified that she never charged unless she cured, and that her cures were successful where other "legal" (male) practitioners had failed. However, since she had not attended a medical school (medical schools being closed to women) she was not licensed to practice medicine. That she saw women who did not want to go to a male practitioner, that she was successful did not matter. "Efficacy of treatment was not the criteria for determining who was or was not a legitimate medical practitioner, but the educational requirements and membership in the faculty of an organized group were the most important factors."[6] In essence, what professional control over medicine says is, "We may not be able to help you, but we are the only ones qualifed to try."

Vern Bullough, in his analysis of the development of medicine as a profession, writes that during the middle ages, "One obvious group outside of the control of the university physician was the midwife, but during the period under study the university physician generally ignored this whole *area of medicine*. Midwives might or might not be qualified, but this *was not a matter of public concern* (emphasis added)."[7] More accurately, one might state not that physicians ignored this "area of medicine," but that midwifery and its concerns were outside of medicine, just as matters that were undoubtedly of concern *to women* existed outside of the "public" concern. Until pregnancy and childbirth were defined as medical events, midwifery was in no sense a branch, area, or interest of medicine as a profession.

Medical expansion into the area of childbirth began before the development of asepsis, surgical techniques, anesthesia: any of what we now consider the contributions of obstetrics. And yet, even without the technology, by the beginning of the nineteenth century medicine had begun the redefinition of childbirth from a family or religious event to a medical one, needing medical presence for its safe conduct.[8]

Midwives treated childbirth in the larger context of women's lives. Midwives did not and do not deliver babies. They teach women how to give birth. Brack has called the role of the midwife "total"—she helped in the socialization of the mother to her new status, both as teacher and as role model. "The midwife's relation to the woman was both diffuse and affective, while the physician role demanded specificity and affective neutrality."[9] Midwives taught how to birth babies, how to nurse them, how to care for the babies and for the mothers own body. Physicians deliver babies and move on. The physician "isolated the laboring woman and her delivery of the infant from the rest of the childbearing experience, and defined it as a medical and surgical event which required specialized knowledge."[10] As one modern nurse-midwife has said of obstetrics residents: "They want us to stay with the woman in labor and just call them when she's ready to deliver. To them, that's the whole thing."

At the time that physicians were taking over control of childbirth, it is virtually unarguable that the non-interventionist, supportive techniques of the midwives were safer for both the birthing woman and her baby. The physicians' approaches included bleeding to "syncope" (until the woman fainted), tobacco infusion enemas, frequent non-sterile examinations, and other surgical and chemical interventions.[11] In the 1910's and 20's, as American physicians successfully ousted midwives, the midwives' safety records remained better than the physicians'. In Newark a midwifery program in 1914–16 achieved maternal mortality rates as low as 1.7 per thousand, while in Boston, where midwives were banned, the rates were 6.5 per 1000. Similarly, infant mortality rates in Newark were 8.5 per 1000 contrasted with 37.4 in Boston.[12] In Washington, as the percentage of births reported by midwives shrank from 50 percent in 1903 to 15 percent in 1912, infant mortality in the first day, first week, and first month of life all increased. New York's dwindling corps of midwives did significantly better than did New York doctors in preventing both stillbirths and post partum infection.[13]

The physician's separation of the "delivery" of the baby from its larger socio-emotional context has its roots as far back as Rene Descartes' concept of mind-body dualism. To Descartes, the body was a machine whose structure and operation falls within the province of human knowledge, as distinguished from the mind which God alone can know. Though even the Hippocratic principles state that the mind and body should be considered together, "Experience shows that most physicians . . . irrespective of their professional activities and philosophical views on the nature of the mind, behave in practice as if they were still Cartesian dualists. Their conservative attitudes are largely a matter of practical convenience."[14]

The medical models used for convenience are that diseases are the bad-guys which the good-guy medications can take care of; that the body breaks down and needs repair; that repair can be done in the hospital like a car in the shop; and that once "fixed," the person can be returned to the community. The earliest models were largely mechanical; later models worked more with chemistry; and newer more sophisticated medical writing describes computer-like programming; but the basic points remain the same. It was a useful model when dealing with the problems facing medicine at the turn of the century: primarily bacterial and viral disease-causing agents and simple accidents and trauma. It has never worked well for understanding the problems that women face in dealing with doctors, including the experience of childbirth. While midwifery was learned by apprentice, doctors were instructed in the use of forceps, as well as techniques of normal delivery, by "book learning," by discussion, by the use of wooden models, and infrequently by watching another doctor at work. Wertz, in her study of the development of obstetrics, has pointed out that "By regarding the female body as a machine, European doctors found that they could measure the birth canal and predict whether or not the child could pass through."[15] Stories of women delivering while their doctors scrubbed for a Caesarian section were told, probably with much relish, and similar stories continue to be part of the lore of midwifery. Among the stories midwives tell each other are the tales of women who were told that they could never deliver vaginally, and then went on to have normal births of over-sized babies.

In the nineteenth and early twentieth centuries midwives and physicians were in direct competition for patients, and not only for their fees. Newer, more clinically oriented medical training demanded "teaching material," so that even the immigrant and poor women were desired as patients.[16] The displacement of the midwife by the male obstetrician can be better understood in terms of this competition than as an ideological struggle or as "scientific advancement." Physicians, unlike the unorganized, disenfranchised midwives, had access to the power of the state through their professional associations. They were thus able to control licensing legislation, in state after state restricting the midwife's sphere of activity and imposing legal sanctions against her.[17]

The legislative changes were backed up by the attempt to win public disapproval for midwifery and support for obstetrics. Physicians accused midwives of ignorance and incompetence, and attacked midwifery practices as "meddlesome." Rather than upgrading the midwives and teaching the skills physicians thought necessary, the profession of medicine refused to train women either as midwives or as physicians.[18] Physicians argued repeatedly that medicine was the appropriate profession to handle birth because "normal pregnancy and parturition are exceptions and to consider them to be normal physiologic conditions was a fallacy."[19] Childbirth became redefined as a medical rather than a social event, and the roles and care surrounding it were reorganized to suit medical needs.[20]

Once professional dominance was established in the area of childbirth, obstetrics rapidly expanded into the relatively more sophisticated area of gynecology. The great obstetricians of the nineteenth century were invariably gynecologists[21] (and of course all men). Among other effects, this linking of obstetrics and gynecology further reinforced the obstetrical orientation toward pathology.

One of the earliest uses of the developing field of gynecology was the overt social control of women through surgical removal of various of her sexual organs. Surgical removal of the clitoris (clitoridectomy) or, less dramatically, its foreskin (circumcision) and removal of the ovaries (oopherectomy or castration) were used to check women's "mental disorders." The first gynecologist to do a clitoridectomy was an Englishman, in 1858.[22] In England, the procedure was harshly criticized, and not repeated by others after the death of the originator in 1860. In America, however, clitoridectomies were done regularly from the late 1860's through till at least 1904[23] and then sporadically until as recently as the late 1940's.[24] The procedure was used to terminate sexual desire or sexual behavior, something deemed pathological in women. Circumcisions were done on women of all ages to stop masturbation up until at least 1937.[25]

More widespread than clitoridectomies or circumcisions were oopherectomies for psychological "disorders." Interestingly, the female gonads were removed not when women were "too female"—i.e., too passive or dependent, but when women were too masculine—assertive, aggressive, "unruly." Oopherectomies for "psychiatric" reasons were done in America between 1872 and 1946.[26] (By the 1940's prefrontal lobotomies were gaining acceptance as psychosurgery.)

The developing medical control of women was not limited to extreme cures for psychiatric problems. The physical health and stability of even the most well-adjusted, lady-like women was questioned. Simply by virtue of gender, women were (and are) subject to illness labeling.

One explanation for women's vulnerability to illness labeling lies in the functionalist approach to the sociology of health. Talcott Parsons has pointed out that it is a functional requirement of any social system that there be a basic level of health of its members.[27] Any definition of illness that is too lenient would disqualify too many people from fulfilling their functions and would impose severe strains on the social system. System changes, such as war, can make changes in standards of health and illness generally set for members. This works on an individual level as well, standards of health and illness being related to social demands: a mild headache will excuse a student from attending class, but not from taking final exams. A logical extension of this is that the less valued a person or group's contribution to society, the more easily they are labeled ill.

Women are not always seen as functional members of society, as people doing important things. This has historically and cross-culturally been especially true of the women of the upper classes in patriarchal societies, where it is a mark of status for a man to be able to afford to keep a wife who is not performing any useful function. A clear, if horrifying, example of this is the traditional Chinese practice of foot-binding. By crippling girls, men were able to show that they could afford to have wives and daughters who do nothing. It is a particularly disturbing example of conspicuous consumption. But we do not have to turn to faraway places to see women defined as useless. In Ehrenreich and English's historical analysis of the woman patient, *Complaints and Disorders,* they speak of the late nineteenth and early twentieth century "lady of leisure." "She was the social ornament that proved a man's success; her idleness, her delicacy, her childlike ignorance of 'reality' gave a man the 'class' that money alone could not provide."[28]

The practice of creating physical deformity in women can be seen in our history as well. A woman researcher who studied menstrual problems among college women between 1890 and 1920 found that women in the earlier period probably were somewhat incapacitated by menstruation, just as the gynecologists of the day were claiming. However, she did not attribute the menstrual problems to women's "inherent disabilities" or "overgrowth of the intellect" as did the male physicians: she related it to dress styles. Women in the 1890's carried some fifteen pounds of skirts and petticoats, hanging from a tightly corseted waist. As skirts got lighter and waists were allowed to be larger, menstruation ceased to be the problem it had been.[29] In the interest of science, women might try the experiment of buckling themselves into a painfully small belt and hanging a fifteen pound weight from it. One might expect weakness, fatigue, shortness of breath, even fainting: all the physical symptoms of women's "inherent" disability. And consider further the effects of bleeding as a treatment for the problem.

It follows from Parsons' analysis that in addition to actually creating physical disability (the bound feet of the Chinese, the deforming corsetry of our own history), women were more easily *defined* as sick when they were not seen as functional social members. At the same time in our history that the upper class women were "delicate," "sickly," and "frail," the working class women were well enough to perform the physical labor of housework, both their own and the upper classes', as well as to work in the factories and fields. Because ". . . however sick or tired working class women might have been, they certainly did not have the time or money to support a cult of invalidism. Employers gave no time off for pregnancy or recovery from childbirth, much less for menstrual periods, though the wives of these same employers often retired to bed on all these occasions."[30] The working class women were seen as strong and healthy, and for them, pregnancy, menstruation, and menopause were not allowed to be incapacitating.

These two themes: *the treatment of the body as a machine,* and *the lesser functional importance assigned to women,* still account for much of the medical treatment of women.

Contemporary physicians do not usually speak of the normal female reproductive functions as diseases. The exception, to be discussed below, is menopause. The other specifically female reproductive functions—menstruation, pregnancy, childbirth, and lactation—are regularly asserted in medical texts to be normal and healthy phenomena. However, these statements are made within the context of teaching the medical "management," "care," "supervision," and "treatment" of each of these "conditions."

Understood in limited mechanical terms, each of these normal female conditions or happenings is a complication, stress on an otherwise normal system. Medicine has fared no better than any other discipline in arriving at a working model of women that does not take men as the comparative norm.

For example, while menstruation is no longer viewed as a disease, it is seen as a complication in the female system, contrasted to the reputed biologic stability of the supposedly noncycling male.[31] As recently as 1961 the American Journal of Obstetrics and Gynecology was still referring to women's "inherent disabilities" in explanations of menstruation:

> Women are known to suffer at least some inconvenience during certain phases of the reproductive cycle, and often with considerable mental and physical distress. Woman's awareness of her inherent disabilities is thought to create added mental and in turn physical changes in the total body response, and there result problems that concern the physician who must deal with them.[32]

Research on contraception displays the same mechanistic biases. The claim has been made that contraceptive research has concentrated on the female rather than the male because of the sheer number of potentially vulnerable links in the female chain of reproductive events.[33] Reproduction is clearly a more complicated process for the female than the male. While we might claim that it is safer to interfere in a simpler process, medicine has tended to view the number of points in the female reproductive process as distinct entities. Reproduction is dealt with not as a complicated organic process, but as a series of discrete points, like stations on an assembly line, with more for female than for male.

The alternative to taking the female system as a complication of the "basic" or "simpler" male system is of course to take female as the working norm. In this approach, a pregnant woman is compared only to pregnant women, a lactating breast compared only to other lactating breasts. Pregnancy, lactation, etc. are accepted not only as nominally healthy variations, but as truly normal states. To take the example of pregnancy, women *are* pregnant; it's not something they "have" or "catch" or even "contain." Pregnancy involves physical changes: they are not, as medical texts frequently call them, "symptoms" of pregnancy. Pregnancy is not a disease; its changes are no more "symptoms" than the growth spurt or development of pubic hair are "symptomatic" of puberty. There may be diseases or complications of pregnancy, but the pregnancy itself is neither disease nor complication.

In contrast, the working model of pregnancy that medicine has arrived at is that a pregnant woman is a woman with an insulated parasitic capsule growing inside. The pregnancy, while physically located within the woman, is still seen as "external" to her, not a part of her. The capsule within has been seen as virtually omniscient and omnipotent, reaching out and taking what it needs from the mother-host, at her expense if necessary, while protected from all that is bad or harmful.

The pregnancy, in this medical model, is almost entirely a mechanical event in the mother. She differs from the nonpregnant only in the presence of this thing growing inside her. Differences other than the mechanical are accordingly seen as symptoms to be treated, so that the woman can be kept as "normal" as possible through the "stress" of the pregnancy. Pregnancy is not necessarily inherently unhealthy in this model, but it is frequently associated with changes other than the growth of the uterus and its contents, and these changes are seen as unhealthy. For example, hemoglobin (iron) is lower in pregnant women than nonpregnant, making pregnant women appear (by nonpregnant standards) anemic. They are then treated for this anemia with iron supplements. Water retention, or edema, is greater in pregnant women than nonpregnant, and they are treated with limits placed on their salt intake and with diuretics. Pregnant women tend to gain weight over that accounted for by the fetus, placenta, and amniotic fluid. They are treated for this weight gain with strict diets, sometimes even with "diet pills." And knowing that these changes are likely to occur in pregnant women, American doctors have tried to treat all pregnant women with iron supplements, limits on salt and calorie intake, and many with diuretics, in the name of "preventive medicine."

What is particularly important to note is that these "treatments" of entirely normal phenomena are frequently not perceived by the medical profession as interventions or disruptions. Rather, the physician sees himself as assisting nature, restoring the woman to normality. Bogden, in her study of the development of obstetrics, reports that an 1800's non-interventionist physician, as opposed to a "regular" physician, would give a laboring woman a catheter, some castor oil or milk of magnesia, bleed her a pint or so, administer ergot, use poultices to blister her, and "Any of these therapies would be administered in the interests of setting the parturient up for an easier, less painful labor and delivery, while still holding to the belief that the physician was letting nature take its course."[34] Wertz says that currently medicine has redefined "natural childbirth," in response to consumer demand for it, to include any of the following techniques: spinal or epidural anesthesia, inhalation anesthesia in the second stage of labor, forceps, epesiotomy, induced labor.[35] Each of these techniques increases the risk of childbirth for mothers and babies.[36] Under the title "Normal Delivery," an obstetric teaching film purports to show "the use of various drugs and procedures used to facilitate normal delivery." Another "Normal Delivery" film is "a demonstration of a normal, spontaneous delivery, including a paracervical block, epesiotomy. . . ."

The use of estrogens provides an even better example of how medicine views the body as a machine that can be "run" or "managed" without being changed. Estrogens are female hormones; in medicine they are seen as femininity in a jar. In the widely selling *Feminine Forever*, Dr. Robert A. Wilson, pushing "estrogen replacement therapy" for all menopausal women, calls estrogen levels as detected by examination of cells from the vagina, a woman's "femininity index."[38] As estrogen levels naturally drop off after menopause a woman is, according to Dr. Wilson, losing her "femininity." Interestingly, estrogen levels are also quite low while a woman is breast-feeding, something not usually socially linked to a "loss of femininity."

Menopause remains the one normal female process that is still overtly referred to as a "disease" in the medical literature. To some physicians, menopause is a *deficiency disease,* and the use of estrogens is restoring the woman to her "normal" condition. Here we must reconsider the question of women's functional importance in the social system. Middle-aged housewives have been called the last of the "ladies of leisure," having outlived their social usefulness as wife-mothers, and having been allowed no alternatives. While oopherectomies and clitorectomies are no longer being done on upper class women as they were a hundred years ago, to "cure" all kinds of dubious "ills," older women are having hysterectomies (surgical removal of the uterus) at alarming rates.[39] Much more typical of modern medicine, however, is the use of chemical rather than surgical "therapy." Because the social changes and demands for readjustment of middle age roughly coincide with the time of menopause, menopause becomes the "illness" for which women can be treated.

Estrogens have been used in virtually every stage of the female reproductive cycle, and usually with the argument that they return the woman to normal, or are a "natural" treatment. Estrogens are used in puberty, to keep girls from getting "unnaturally" tall; to treat painful menstruation; as contraception, supposedly mimicking pregnancy; as a chemical abortion in the "morning after" pill; to replace supposedly missing hormones and thus to prevent miscarrages; to dry up milk and return women to the "normal" nonlactating state; and in menopause to return women to the "normal" cycling state. For all the claims of normality and "natural" treatment, at this writing approximately half of these uses of estrogens have been shown to cause cancer. The use of estrogens in pregnancy was the first to be proven carcinogenic: daughters of women who had taken estrogens (notably DES, a particular synthetic estrogen) are at risk for the development of a rare cancer of the vagina.[40] The sequential birth control pill was taken off the market as the danger of cancer of the lining of the uterus (endometrial cancer) became known, and similarly estrogens taken in menopause have been shown to increase the risk of endometrial cancer by as much as fourteen times after seven years of use.[42]

The model of the body as a machine, which can be regulated, controlled, and "managed" by medical treatments, is not working. "Femininity" or physical "femaleness" is not something that comes in a jar and can be manipulated.

Nor are women accepting the relegation to secondary functional importance, as wives and mothers of men. In rejecting the viewpoint that we bear men's children for them, we are reclaiming our bodies. When pregnancy is seen not as the presence of a (man's) fetus in a woman, but as a condition of the woman herself, attitudes toward contraception, infertility, abortion, and childbirth all change. When pregnancy is perceived as a condition of the woman then abortion, for example, is primarily a response to that condition.

The women's health movement has grown as an important part of the women's liberation movement. In some of its work, the movement has been geared toward consumerism within medicine, seeking better medical care and a wider range of services for women. While better trained, more knowledgeable, and more *humane* physicians are a high priority, what the self-help and lay midwifery groups are doing goes much deeper than that. I believe that these women are reconstructing the pre-obstetrics and gynecology model of women's health. They are redefining women's health in fundamentally women's terms.

Women's self-help groups and clinics are teaching women how to examine their own bodies, not in the never-ending search for pathology in which physicians are trained, but to learn more about health. Medical technology and physicians are clearly useful in treating illness, but do we really want physicians to be "treating" health? It is entirely possible for a woman to fit herself for a diaphragm, do a pap smear and a breast examination (all with help and instruction if she needs it) and never adopt the "patient" role. It is also possible for a woman to go through a pregnancy and birth her baby with good, knowledgable, *caring* help, but without becoming a "patient" under the "supervision" of a physician.

Redefining normality within the context of the female reproductive system will take time. We have all been imbued with the medical model of women's bodies and health, and it is hard to work past that. Redefining women in women's terms is not a problem unique to health. It is an essential feminist issue.

**REFERENCES**

1  Diana Scully and Pauline Bart, "A Funny Thing Happened on the Way to the Orifice: Women in Gynecology Textbooks," *American Journal of Sociology*, 78 (1971), 1045–1050.

2  *Gould Medical Dictionary*, 3rd Ed. (New York: McGraw-Hill, 1972), p. 1056.

3  *Gould Medical Dictionary*, p. 658.

4  G. J. Barker-Benfield, *The Horrors of the Half-Known Life* (New York: Harper and Row, 1976), p. 88.

5  Thomas Szasz, *The Theology of Medicine* (New York: Harper Colophon, 1977).

6  Vern Bullough, *The Development of Medicine as a Profession* (New York and Switzerland: Karger, 1966), p. 101.

7   Bullough, p. 102.

8   Janet Carlisle Bogdan, "Nineteenth Century Childbirth: Its Context and Meaning," paper presented at the third Berkshire Conference on the History of Women, June 9–11, 1976, p. 2.

9   Datha Clapper Brack, "The Displacement of the Midwife: Male Domination in a Formerly Female Occupation," unpublished, 1976, p. 4.

10  Brack, "The Displacement of the Midwife," p. 5.

11  Bogdan, "Nineteenth Century Childbirth."

12  Frances E. Kobrin, "The American Midwife Controversy: A Crisis in Professionalization," *Bulletin of the History of Medicine* (1966), p. 355.

13  Kobrin, "The American Midwife Controversy," p. 355.

14  Rene Dubos, *Man, Medicine and Environment* (New York: New American Library, 1968), p. 79.

15  Dorothy C. Wertz, "Childbirth as a Controlled Workspace: From Midwifery to Obstetrics," paper presented at the 71st Annual Meeting of the American Sociological Association, 1976, p. 5.

16  Barbara Ehrenreich and Deirdre English, *Witches, Midwives and Nurses* (Old Westbury, N.Y.: Feminist Press, 1973), p. 33.

17  Brack, "The Displacement of the Midwife."

18  Bogdan, "Nineteenth Century Childbirth," p. 8.

19  Kobrin, "The American Midwife Controversy," p. 353.

20  Brack, "The Displacement of the Midwife," p. 1.

21  Barker-Benfield, *The Horrors of the Half-Known Life,* p. 83.

22  *Ibid.,* p. 120.

23  Barker-Benfield, *The Horrors of the Half-Known Life,* p. 120.

24  Ehrenreich and English, *Complaints and Disorders* (Old Westbury, N.Y.: Feminist Press, 1973).

25  Barker-Benfield, *The Horrors of the Half-Known Life,* p. 120.

26  *Ibid.,* p. 121.

27  Talcott Parsons, "Definitions of Health and Illness in Light of American Value Systems," in Jaco, *Patients, Physicans and Illnesses* (New York: Free Press, 1958).

28  Ehrenreich and English, *Complaints and Disorders*, p. 16.

29  Vern Bullough and Martha Voght, "Women, Menstruation and Nineteenth-Century Medicine," paper presented at the 45th annual meeting of the American Association for the History of Medicine, 1972.

30  Ehrenreich and Englisn, *Complaints and Disorders*, p. 47.

31  Estelle Ramey, "Men's Cycles (They Have Them Too, You Know)," *Ms.* (1972), 8–14.

32  Milton Abramson and John R. Torghele, *American Journal of Obstetrics and Gynecology* (1961), p. 223.

33  Sheldon Segal, "Contraceptive Research: A Male Chauvinist Plot?", *Family Planning Perspectives* (July 1972).

34   Janet Carlisle Bogdan, "Nineteenth Century Childbirth: The Politics of Reality," paper presented at the 71st annual meeting of the American Sociological Association, 1976, p. 11.

35   Wertz, "Childbirth as a Controlled Workspace," p. 15.

36   Doris Haire, *The Cultural Warping of Childbirth* (Hillside, N.J.: International Childbirth Education Association, 1972).

37   *Educational Materials for Obstetrics and Gynecology,* American College of Obstetrics and Gynecology, 1974.

38   Robert A. Wilson, *Feminine Forever* (New York: Pocket Books, 1968).

39   John Bunker, "Surgical Manpower," *New England Journal of Medicine* (January 15, 1970).

40   Arthur Herbst, J. Ulfelder and D. C. Poskanzer, "Adenocarcinoma of the Vagina," *New England Journal of Medicine,* (April 22, 1971), pp. 871–81.

41   Barbara Seaman and Gideon Seaman, M.D., *Women and the Crisis in Sex Hormones* (New York: Rawson Associates Publishers, Inc., 1977), p. 78.

42   Harry Ziel and William Finkle, "Estrogen Replacement Therapy," *New England Journal of Medicine* (December 4, 1975).

# Dianne Herman

# The Rape Culture

When Susan Griffin wrote, "I have never been free of the fear of rape," she touched a responsive chord in most women.[1] Every woman knows the fear of being alone at home late at night or the terror that strikes her when she receives an obscene phone call. She knows also of the "mini-rapes"—the pinch in the crowded bus, the wolf whistle from a passing car, the stare of a man looking at her bust during a conversation. Griffin has argued, ". . . rape is a kind of terrorism which severely limits the freedom of women and makes women dependent on men."[2]

Women live their lives according to a rape schedule.

> There is what might be called a universal curfew on women in this country. Whenever a woman walks alone at night, whenever she hitchhikes, she is aware that she is violating

well-established rules of conduct and, as a result, that she faces the possibility of rape. If in one of these situations she *is* raped, the man will almost always escape prosecution and the woman will be made to feel responsible because she was somehow "asking for it."[3]

One solution to this problem is suggested by Golda Meir. When a Cabinet meeting discussed the number of assaults at night on women, one minister suggested that the women stay home after dark. Meir replied, "But it's the men who are attacking the women. If there's to be a curfew, let the men stay home, not the women."[4] Golda Meir's suggestion wouldn't strike us as funny or odd if we did not assume that women must bear the responsibility for men's sexual aggression.

Underlying this view of rape is a traditional concept of male and female sexuality, one which assumes that males are sexually aggressive and females are sexually passive. Those sharing these assumptions conclude that rape is a natural act which arises out of a situation where men, when unrestrained by convention or threat of punishment, will sexually attack women. Thus the only way to stop rape is not to allow the opportunity for it to happen by insisting that women avoid "dangerous" situations or by providing a deterrent through stiff penalties. An example of this mentality is Judge Archie Simonson's 1977 explanation when he released on probation a 15-year-old boy who raped a girl in a high school stairwell. "This community is well-known to be sexually permissive," he said. "Should we punish a 15- or 16-year-old boy who reacts to it normally?"[5]*

Most studies on rape take as a given the aggressive nature of male sexuality. Hans von Hentig wrote in the early fifties that the incidence of rape reflects a demographic imbalance in the society where there are too many males as compared to females in the population. Yet studies sympathetic to his basic premise have found no relationship between a lack of females for male sexual outlet and rape.[6] Along the same lines, proposals have been made to make prostitution legal in the hope that the incidence of rape will decrease. As researchers point out, however, ". . . three cities that had allowed open prostitution actually experienced a decline in rape and other sexual assaults after prostitution was

---

*Simonson's comment provoked a successful recall campaign by his Madison, Wisconsin constituents. He was replaced by a female lawyer who won the judgeship with the support of local feminist groups.

prohibited."[7] Because rape is held to be a natural behavior there have been few attempts to understand the cultural conditions that give rise to this crime.

But animals in their natural habitat do not rape, and many societies have existed where rape is not known.[8] According to Margaret Mead in *Sex and Temperament*, the Arapesh do not "have any conception of the male nature that might make rape understandable to them."[9] Among the Arapesh, men and women are both expected to act toward each other with gentleness and concern. Thus there is no reason to maintain the assumption that rape is a natural act.

Anthropological studies like those of Margaret Mead have demonstrated that sexual attitudes and practices are learned, not instinctual. In this country people are raised to believe that men are sexually active and aggressive while women are sexually passive and submissive. Since it is assumed men can't control their desires, every young woman is taught that she must be the responsible party in any sexual encounter. In such a society men and women are trained to believe that the sexual act involves domination. Normal heterosexual relations are pictured as consisting of an aggressive male forcing himself on a woman who seems to fear sex but unconsciously wants to be overpowered.

So diffuse is the aggressive-passive, dominant-submissive, me-Tarzan, you-Jane nature of the relationship between the sexes that in our culture there is a close association between violence and sexuality. Words that are slang sexual terms, for example, frequently accompany assaultive behavior or gestures. "Fuck-you" is meant as a brutal attack in verbal terms. In the popular culture, "James Bond alternately whips out his revolver and his cock, and though there is no known connection between the skills of a gun-fighter and love-making, pacifism seems suspiciously effeminate."[10] The imagery of sexual relations between males and females in books, songs, advertising and films is frequently that of a sado-masochistic relationship thinly veiled by a romantic facade. Thus it is very difficult in our society to differentiate rape from "normal" heterosexual relations. Indeed our culture can be characterized as a rape culture because the image of heterosexual intercourse is based on a rape model of sexuality.

If healthy heterosexuality were characterized by loving, warm and reciprocal satisfaction then rape could be defined as sex without consent and involving therefore either domination or violence. Instead rape is legally defined as sexual intercourse by a male with a female, *other than his wife,* without the consent of the woman and effected by force, duress, intimidation, or deception as to the nature of the act. The spousal exemption in the law means that a husband cannot be guilty of personally raping his wife, even if he forces intercourse against her will. This loophole implicitly states that *violent, unwanted* sex has little to do with the definition of rape. Instead, rape is *illegal* sex by a man who has no rights over the woman. In other words, in the law's eyes violence in sexual intercourse is permissible, but sexual relations with a woman who is not one's property is not. The statutory rape laws support this contention very well because, in this instance, rape is simply intercourse outside marriage with a minor who is considered too young to render legal consent (as a minor, her property—her body—is still controlled by others).

From their inception, rape laws have been established, not to protect women, but to protect women's property value for men.

> Society's view of rape was purely a matter of economics—of assets and liabilities. When a married woman was raped, her husband was wronged, not her. If she was unmarried, her father suffered since his investment depreciated. It was the monetary value of a woman which determined the gravity of the crime. Because she had no personal rights under the law, her own emotions simply didn't matter.[11]

Because rape meant that precious merchandise was irreparably damaged, the severity of the punishment was dependent on whether the victim was a virgin. In some virgin rapes biblical law ordered that the rapist marry the victim since she was now devalued property.[12] The social status of the victim was also important, as a woman of higher social status was more valuable.

While these laws are no longer present in the same form, attitudes and customs have remained much the same. For example, "shot-gun weddings" are still with us, and rape is far more likely to be prosecuted if the woman is a virgin of the middle or upper class who is attacked by a lower-class male.[13] Rape is least prosecuted if the victim is black. The rape of poor, black women is not an offense against men of power. But as Eldridge Cleaver has explained, the black male who sexually assaults a white woman is seen as a vengeful castrator, deserving of the most severe punishment.[14]

In a society in which a man's worth is measured by his ability to be aggressive, the rapist is demonstrating that he is more masculine than a man who cannot protect, hold on to and control his woman. "In raping another man's woman, a man may aggrandize his own manhood and concurrently reduce that of another man."[15] Rape is an offense that one man commits against another. Thus the husband whose wife has been sexually violated may not only question his own masculinity but may also feel that his wife participated in some way in her own victimization or enjoyed the experience. His self-esteem is thus lowered not only by the rapist but by his wife's presumed complicity.

Husbands who blame their wives may view the rape as marital infidelity. Victims have reported that their husband's inability to "adjust" to the fact that the rape had occurred was the cause of their divorce.[16] The more immediate response of husbands, however, is anger and rage directed at the rapist. One husband said, for example, "It's a matter of territorial imperative. I fantasized ways of getting back at him, like shoving a shot-gun down his throat and pulling the trigger until it quit clicking."[17] Another husband admitted, "I wanted to kill that bastard. I wanted to destroy him for what he'd done to me."[18] The overwhelming need for revenge not only allows men to express their anger at being humiliated, but it also serves to restore their self-esteem in socially prescribed ways by acting in a "manly," aggressive fashion.

One of the most surprising findings of studies on rape is that the rapist is normal in personality, appearance, intelligence, behavior and sexual drive.[19] According to Amir, the only significant psychological difference between the rapist and the normal, well-adjusted male appears to be the greater tendency of the former to express rage and violence. But this finding probably tends to overemphasize the aggressive personality characteristics of rapists, since generally only imprisoned rapists have been studied. Those few rapists who are sentenced to prison tend to be the more obviously violent offenders. In fact, studies by some researchers have found one type of rapist who is fairly meek and mild-mannered.[20] What is clear is that the rapist is not an exotic freak. Rather rape evolves out of a situation in which "normal" males feel a need to prove themselves to be "men" by displaying dominance over females.

In our society men demonstrate their competence as people by being "masculine." Part of this definition of masculinity involves a contempt for anything feminine or for females in general. Reported rapes, in fact, are frequently associated with some form of ridicule and sexual humiliation, such as urinating on the victim, anal intercourse, fellatio, and ejaculation in the victim's face and hair. Insertion into the woman's vagina of broomsticks, bottles and other phallic objects is not an uncommon *coup de grâce*.[21] The overemphasis on values of toughness expresses itself in a disregard for anything associated with fragility. In the rapist's view, his assertion of maleness is automatically tied to a violent repudiation of anything feminine.

Nothing supports more convincingly the premise that rape in our society is the act of a male attempting to assert his masculinity than the studies that have been conducted on homosexual rapes in prisons. Interestingly, researchers have discovered that aggressors in prison rape cases usually have little or no prior history of homosexual behavior.[22] They do not consider themselves homosexuals, and neither do the other inmates. Rather, they equate their actions with those of an aggressive, heterosexual male. They are often called "jockers" or "wolves" by other inmates, terms that characterize them as males. One researcher commented with some astonishment,

> We were struck by the fact that the typical sexual aggressor does not consider himself to be a homosexual, or even to have engaged in homosexual acts. This seems to be based upon his startlingly primitive view of sexual relationships, one that defines as male whichever partner is aggressive and as homosexual whichever partner is passive.[23]

While the other inmates and the aggressors consider their behavior normal under circumstances of heterosexual deprivation, Davis has noted that sexual release is not the primary motivation of the rapist. Rather the motive appears to be the need of some males in prison to exercise control and domination over others.

> A primary goal of the sexual aggressor, it is clear, is the conquest and degradation of his victim. We repeatedly found that aggressors used such language as "Fight or fuck," "We're gonna make a girl out of you."[24]

The attempt to control other men, and in fact to transform them into women (passive, sexual objects), demonstrates to the rapist, himself, and to others of the prison population that he is in fact a "real man." Genet wrote, "a male that fucks another male is a double-male."[25] Being removed from the heterosexual world, the prison rapist needs to affirm his identity as a male by being dominant over less "masculine" men. "A man who has become accustomed to validating his masculinity through regular interaction with members of the opposite sex may suddenly find his ego-image in grave jeopardy once a prison sentence consigns him to an all-male world."[26] Imprisonment knocks out whatever props the rapist may have established to prove his masculinity. Only the demonstration of sexual and physical prowess can stave off feelings of emasculation in the limited environment of the prison.

Many prison rapists display little, if any, concern for the attitudes or feelings of their partners. One study reported that a group of 17 men raped one inmate over the course of four hours.[27] Another prisoner was raped repeatedly even after he was bleeding from his rectum, had become ill and vomited. But the callousness of the rapist's attitude toward his victim is required by the prison culture. For in the narrow view of sexuality subscribed to by most inmates, one is either a "woman" or a "man." If any member of the prison population displays emotion or vulnerability, he is likely to be tagged a "woman" and is therefore open to sexual attack. It is for this reason that many inmates refuse to aid the victim and may actually take part in a gang-bang themselves. In a world where one is either dominant and a rapist or submissive and a victim, the pressures to be the former are so great that many men find themselves forced to be the sexual violators of others.

In addition, many rapists believe that women enjoy sado-masochistic sex. One group of authors has said of the rape offender,

> He sees her struggle and protestation not as a refusal but as part of
> her own sexual excitation. "Women like to get roughed up, they
> enjoy a good fight." This belief is maintained even when the victim
> is literally fighting for her life and the offender has to brutally
> injure her to force her to submit to intercourse.[28]

In one instance where a 63-year-old woman was robbed and raped at gunpoint by a 24-year-old man, her assailant threw her a kiss and said before running away, "I bet I made your day."[29] Some offenders have been incredulous when arrested, complaining that they may have been a little rough, but the women enjoyed their advances. The rapist's attraction to dominance and violence stems from his view of sexuality which he interprets to mean "man ravishes, woman submits."[30]

One of the most overlooked aspects of rape is that it is frequently a group phenomenon. In Amir's study, 43 percent of the cases involved two or more offenders. Out of a total of 646 cases, 370 were single rapes, 105 were pair rapes and 171 were group rapes.[31] The rapist in a group rape is not only expressing his hostility toward women and asserting his masculinity to himself, but he is also proving his manhood to others. Group rapes are usually characterized by a considerable amount of violence, "even though this is one situation in which no brutality, no threat even, would be necessary to subdue the victim."[32] The measure of masculinity is not just the ability to have sexual intercourse with a female, but the ability to exert control over her, and control is equated with dominance. "Through the forcing of the victim to sexual relations the rapist expresses, proves, tests, and gains his image of masculinity, which involves sexual as well as social dominance over women."[33] In addition, acts of sexual humiliation are more common in group rapes.[34] The age group most likely to be offenders in either pair or group rapes are youths in the 10 to 14 age bracket.[35]

In general, rapists tend to be very young. Amir found offenders were most likely to be between 15 and 19 years old.[36] According to the *Uniform Crime Reports*, published by the F.B.I., the age grouping of males between 16 and 24 constitutes the greatest concentration of arrests for forcible rape. Fifty-seven percent of the men charged with this crime in 1976 were under 25.[37] But on reflection this should come as no surprise, for adolescence is the time when most males probably feel the most doubts about their masculinity and the consequent need to affirm it. Brownmiller captures this insight in a personal reflection.

> They are desperately trying to learn the way to be successful men. When I have stood, almost mesmerized, on my Fourteenth Street subway platform and watched a gang of youths methodically assault a gum machine for its pennies—in escalation of a dare—I could only think *That could be my body.*[38]

Perhaps this need of some men to prove their masculinity to themselves and to others explains why rape is so common in war. The U.S. military has generally eulogized the values of masculinity and emphasized aggressiveness: The Marines built their image on their ability to form "men" out of adolescent youths. The stressing of soldiers as "real men" gives those who lead armies a perfect mechanism by which to keep in line those who might otherwise question the validity of a military conquest. Cowardice in the face of the enemy is equated with femininity. At the same time, however, the real dangers of combat cause many men to question their masculinity. Such situations are ripe for rape.

In 1966, an American patrol held a 19-year-old Vietnamese girl captive for several days, taking turns raping her and finally murdering her. The sergeant planned the crime in advance, telling the soldiers during the mission's briefing that the girl would improve their "morale." When one soldier refused to take part in the rape, the sergeant called him "queer" and "chicken," another testified later that he joined in the assault to avoid such insults.[39]

While violence is particularly associated with rape, it is not absent from ordinary heterosexual relations. In Kanin and Kirkpatrick's study of male sexual aggression in dating and courtship relations in the late 1950's, first-semester college women were asked to report forceful sexual attempts they considered offensive. Behavior considered repugnant to the women included forced necking, petting above and below the waist, attempted intercourse and rape. Of the 291 responding women, 56 percent reported themselves offended at least once during the academic year at some level of erotic intimacy.[40] A large proportion of these were serious sexual assaults.

The experiences of being offended were not altogether associated with trivial situations as shown by the fact that 20.9% were offended by forceful attempts to intercourse and 6.2% by "aggressively forceful attempts at sexual intercourse in the course of which menacing threats or coercive infliction of physical pain were employed."[41]

Those women most likely to experience forced petting or intercourse were regular dates, "pinned" or engaged to their attackers.[42] This contradicts one of the most common myths attached to the crime of rape: the notion that the rapist is a stranger to his victim. When the word rape is mentioned, most people conjure up images of a woman alone walking late at night in a bad section of a large city. She is being followed by a tall, dark (black?) male who overtakes her, throws her in an alley and rapes her. Perhaps the only accurate parts of this image are that rape is much more likely to occur in urban areas and at night.[43]

The myth that rape is committed only by a stranger serves to keep many women from reporting an incident or of even defining an unpleasant sexual episode as attempted rape. It also serves to keep the men involved from construing their actions to be those of a rapist.

The male learns the same basic mythology of rape as the woman. He is aware of the notion that rape can only be committed by a stranger. This definition can serve as a justification since it precludes the possibility that he can be called a rapist after an encounter with a woman who knew his name.[44]

Nonetheless, in the majority of reported cases victims know their offenders. In Amir's study of rape in Philadelphia in 1958 and 1960, approximately one-third of all forcible rapes were committed by neighbors, close friends, boyfriends, family friends or relatives. In only 42 percent of the 646 cases was the rapist a complete stranger. Amir has commented,

> Girls who trusted their boyfriends and those whose families had confidence in their friends or relatives were not spared from becoming victims of rape. In 21% of primary relationships men forfeited their trusted position and committed the crime of rape.[45]

The fact that victim and offender are acquainted in such a high percentage of reported cases has sometimes been interpreted to mean that large numbers of rapes are victim-precipitated. Amir classified rape cases as victim-precipitated when

> . . . the victims actually—or so it was interpreted by the offender— agreed to sexual relations but retracted before the actual act or did not resist strongly enough when the suggestion was made by the offenders. The term applies also to cases in which the victim enters vulnerable situations charged with sexuality, especially when she uses what could be taken as an invitation to sexual relations.[46]

Despite such a broad definition, Amir found that only 19 percent of all rapes in his study were victim-precipitated. Some of the factors in these types of rapes were where victims had "bad" reputations, where victims met offenders in a bar, at a picnic or party, or where victims were involved in "primary relationships," excluding relatives.

It is difficult to imagine, however, that offenders could misinterpret the sexual signals they thought they were receiving given the finding that the closer the relationship between the participants in rape, the greater is the use of physical force. In fact in Amir's own study, neighbors and acquaintances were the most likely to engage in brutal rape. Amir was forced to conclude that rape between people who know each other is not the result of a sexual encounter in which a woman "teases" a man.

In general, the analysis of the interpersonal relations between victim and offender lent support to those who reject the myth of the offender who attacks victims unknown to him. But equally rejected is the notion that rape is generally an affair between, or a result of intimate relations between victim and rapist.[47]

Once it is understood that rape occurs quite commonly between people who are acquainted, other findings about this crime start to make sense. Most studies, for example, report that about half of all rapes occur in the victim's or rapist's home.[48] Another 15 percent occur in automobiles.[49] Car rapes are especially likely to involve participants who are intimate.

In addition, the rapist and his victim are generally of the same race and age. Ninety percent of all reported rapes are intra-racial, not inter-racial, occurrences.[50] One reason the myth that black men rape white women dies hard is because these cases frequently receive the most publicity. In a study of rape in Philadelphia, it was discovered that the two major newspapers, when they reported on rape cases, mentioned mainly interracial offenses. Intra-racial rapes were only occasionally mentioned.[51]

The myth also survives that most rapes are spontaneous. However, statistics compiled from reported rapes show that the overwhelming majority are planned. In one study, 71 percent of all reported rapes were prearranged and another 11 percent were partially planned. Only 18 percent were impulsive acts.[52] Planning is most common in cases of group rape, but even where the rapist is acting alone, a majority of the rapes involve some manipulations on the part of the offender to place his victim in a vulnerable situation that he can exploit. It is often assumed that the rapist had no prior intent to commit rape but was overcome by the sexual provocations of his victim. The conventional scenario is one of a man who is sexually aroused by a seductive woman.

But the image of the rape victim as seductive and enticing is also at odds with reality. Rapes have been committed on females as young as six months and as old as 93. Most victims tend to be very young. In Amir's study, 20 percent were between 10 and 14, another 25 percent were between 15 and 19.[53] According to data compiled in 1974 by Women Organized Against Rape, 41 percent of rape victims seen in hospital emergency rooms in Philadelphia were 16 or younger. The category with the highest frequency of victims was the age range between 13 and 16 years old.[54]

Most convicted rapists tend to project the blame on others, particularly the victim. Schultz found that the sex offender is twice as likely to insist on his innocence as the general offender.[55] "In two-thirds of the cases one hears, 'I'm here on a phoney beef,' or 'I might have been a little rough with her but she was asking for it,' or 'I might have done it but I was too drunk to remember'."[56] They also rationalize their act by labeling their victims "bad" women.

The amazing thing is that the offender's view of the situation and of his victim is not that far removed from that of society in general. For just as the rapist blames his victim, so do the police, prosecutors, judges, juries, friends and relatives.

Women have often complained that their veracity is in question when they report charges of rape. The first public agency with which a woman makes contact after she reports a rape is usually the police, and they have often been less than sympathetic to rape complaints. Some officers have actually asked victims questions such as "How many orgasms did you have?," or "Didn't I pick you up last week for prostitution?"[57] A 1971 California police textbook, *Patrol Procedure*, begins its discussion on sexual assaults with the statement, "Forcible rape is one of the most falsely reported crimes."[58]

The police have considerable discretion in determining whether a crime has been committed. In 1976, according to the F.B.I., 19 percent of all forcible rapes reported to the police were unfounded.[59] Unfounding simply means that the police have decided not to advise prosecution.

A study conducted in 1966 of the procedures used by the Philadelphia Police Department in unfounding rape cases discovered that one of the major factors for the unfounding of a case was the moral appraisal of the victim by the police. For example, if the woman had been drinking, police in most instances dismissed her charges.[60] Police were also most likely to unfound cases involving black participants and least likely to do so when victim and offender were both white.[61]

According to many studies, one of the most frequent causes of unfounding rape is a prior relationship between the participants. Forty-three percent of all date rapes in the Philadelphia study were unfounded. The police, according to the researcher, seemed to be more concerned that the victim had "assumed the risk" than they were with the fact that she had not given consent to intercourse.[63]

Another common reason police unfound cases is the apparent lack of force in the rape situation. The extent of injuries seems to be even more important in the decision to unfound than whether the offender has a weapon.[64] There is no requirement that a businessman must forcibly resist when mugged or forfeit protection under the law. But proof of rape, both to the police and in court, is often in the form of resistance, and resistance is substantiated by the extent of injuries suffered by the victim. Yet local police departments frequently advise women not to resist if faced with the possibility of rape.

> In a confusion partially of their own making, local police precincts point out contradictory messages: they "unfound" a rape case because, by the rule of their own male logic, the woman did not show normal resistance; they report on an especially brutal rape case and announce to the press that the multiple stab wounds were the work of an assailant who was enraged because the woman resisted.[65]

In other words the victim is told that if she was raped it was because she did not resist enough. But if she fights back and is raped and otherwise assaulted, police blame her again for bringing about her own injuries because of her resistance.

The number of unfounded rapes is probably underestimated because of police practices. Police may turn away a complaint and not file an incident report at all. Or rape complaints may be categorized as "investigations of persons"—a catchall for incidents requiring an investigation report but for which there is insufficient information for classification into other crime categories. If further investigation confirms police doubts and the case is closed, then the incident is not recorded as an unfounded rape complaint. Because of these police practices, one author estimates that the F.B.I.'s 19 percent unfounding rate is far too low and that the true figure is probably at least 50 percent.[66] Other investigators who have interviewed police personnel have found from their comments that police believe that 80 percent to 90 percent of the rapes reported to them are not really rapes. In addition, the Philadelphia study found that the prosecutor's office was even less likely than the police to believe that the victim had been forced against her will to have intercourse.[67]

Police and prosecuting practices that are demeaning to rape victims have been criticized recently, and there are indications that some changes are being made. A study in 1974, for example, found that about half of the police departments surveyed had, in the last three years, instituted some innovations in their methods of handling rape cases—notably in providing specialized training to officers or in assigning women to investigate.[68] In 1975, however, after a 15-month nationwide investigation, the U.S. Law Enforcement Assistance Administration concluded that the response by police, prosecutors and hospitals toward rape victims is "generally poorly coordinated and inadequate."[69] Studies continue to find that, "the credibility of the rape victim is questioned more than that of any other victims of crime."[70] In 1976 almost half of the prosecutors' offices surveyed in a national study admitted using polygraph examinations in many instances because they suspected the alleged rape victim was lying.[71]

For many women, the experience of having their account of the events scrutinized, mocked, or discounted continues in the courtroom. Women have often said they were made to feel that they, not the defendants, were the persons on trial. According to Burgess and Holmstrom, "Going to court, for the victim, is as much of a crisis as the actual rape itself."[72] They quote one victim shortly after she appeared in district court:

> I felt like crying. I felt abused. I didn't like the questions the
> defense was asking. I felt accused—guilty till proven innocent. I
> thought the defense lawyer made it a big joke.[73]

They relate how one twelve-year-old girl had a psychotic break during the preliminary court process.[74]

The victim, by taking the case to court, incurs extensive costs, both psychological and financial. Expecting to testify just once, she is likely to have to repeat her story at the hearing for probable cause, to the grand jury and in superior court sessions. To convey the discomfort of such a process, feminists have recommended that individuals imagine having to tell an audience all of the details of their last sexual experience.

Financially, the time away from work nearly always stretches beyond expectations. According to Burgess and Holmstrom, the victims they accompanied to court were often forced to sit three and four hours in the court house, only to be told that the case had been continued. After they and their witnesses had taken time off from work and, in some cases, traveled great distances, they were less enthusiastic about the idea of seeing justice done.[75] Wood has said, "Due to the traumatic experience which a victim must go through in order to attempt to secure the attacker's successful prosecution, it is amazing any rape cases come to trial."[76]

Rape is different from ordinary criminal cases in that special rules of evidence may be used in court.[77] The one issue with which the courts are concerned is not whether intercourse took place, but whether there was consent at the moment of coitus.[78] However, in order to convict on the charge of rape, the courts have generally not deemed the word of the complainant against that of the defendant to be sufficient evidence for conviction. Instead many states require corroboration.

A corroboration rule requires that the testimony of the victim be supported by independent "inculpatory" evidence before a jury may consider that the testimony supports a guilty verdict.[79] While the corroboration rule has been criticized, it is still used in many states in rape cases.

> Although most jurisdictions still pay lip service to the common law rule which permits a conviction based upon the uncorroborated testimony of the complainant, corroboration is usually required whenever the testimony is incredible, contradictory, or improbable. Moreover, several states have, by statute, required corroboration in all rape cases; a number of others have required it in special circumstances; and still others do not require it, but prefer it.[80]

Nothing comparable to the restrictions on evidence in rape cases exists elsewhere in criminal law, even when similar circumstances have been present. There is no corroboration required, for example, for physical assault, a crime as likely as rape to take place without the presence of witnesses.[81] In addition, while assault is an offense that is equally subject to intentional falsification, it lacks many of the discouragements that accompany rape accusations. The corroboration rule has meant that, in some states, conviction for rape is practically impossible to obtain. In 1971, for instance, before New York amended its corroboration statute. New York City had 2,415 "founded" rape complaints but only 18 cases that resulted in conviction.[82] As LeGrand has stated, "Juries exist, after all, to decide whose testimony is most credible, and they are instructed to convict only if satisfied of the accused's guilt. There should be no special rules for rape."[83]

Whether a state has a corroboration requirement or not is usually beside the point, however, since juries frequently are likely to introduce extraordinary rules of evidence in rape cases. Kalven and Zeisel conducted an analysis of jurors' reactions to many crimes, including rape, in over 3,500 trials. They found that in rape cases the jury does not consider solely the issue of consent during intercourse but also include as relevant to conviction any suggestions of contributory behavior on the part of the victim.[84] In a sense juries have created an extra-legal defense. If the complainant somehow "assumed the risk" of rape, juries will commonly find the defendant guilty of some lesser crime or acquit him altogether.[85] "A 17-year-old girl was raped during a beer drinking party. The jury *probably acquitted,* according to the judge, because they thought the girl asked for what she got."[86] According to Medea and Thompson, in one case " . . . a woman who responded with 'Fuck-off' when approached lost her case because 'fuck' is a sexually exciting word . . ."[87] If the victim knew the offender previously, especially as an intimate, juries will be reluctant to convict.

> In one case of "savage rape," the victim's jaw was fractured in two places. The jury nevertheless acquitted because it found that there may have been sexual relations on previous occasions, and the parties had been drinking on the night of the incident.[88]

Defense attorneys often attempt to get acquittals for their defendants by tarnishing the image of the victim in the eyes of the jury. A woman " . . . may be asked whether she wears a bra, whether she frequents bars, whether she enjoys sexual intercourse. The purpose, of course, is to create the impression that she consented to—or encouraged—the rapist."[89] In some states the complainant's past sexual conduct can be introduced in the trial but not the defendant's, even if he has been guilty of past sexual offenses.[90] It is argued that if a woman has in the past consented to sexual relations outside of marriage, she is probably more likely to have consented to any resulting sexual relationships. An "unchaste" woman is also presumed to be of low moral character and thus more likely to lie. Needless to say, it is impossible, according to police and prosecutors, for a prostitute to be raped.

As a consequence of these practices, rape is a crime that is very rarely punished. In reported rape cases where police *do* believe the victim, only about half of rape offenders are actually arrested. Even if the police catch up with an accused rapist, however, he is unlikely to be convicted. In 1976, for example, of all adult men arrested, only 67 percent were prosecuted for rape, and of these 49 percent resulted in acquittals or dismissals, while another 9 percent were found guilty of lesser offenses. Even though they constitute a large proportion of offenders, juveniles were even more likely to be treated leniently by the courts, with only 20 percent being officially charged with forcible rape.[91] In some jurisdictions, the conviction rate, based on arrests, is only 3 percent.[92]

Using F.B.I. statistics, LeGrand calculated that

> . . . a man who rapes a woman who reports the rape to police has roughly seven chances out of eight of walking away without any conviction. Assuming only one woman in five reports the rape, his chances increase to 39 out of 40. If these figures take into account the high percentage of those who receive probation or suspended sentences, his chances of escaping incarceration are in the vicinity of 98 to 99 out of 100. Forcible rape has a lower conviction rate than any other crime listed in the *Uniform Crime Reports.*[93]

Most individuals convicted of rape serve a sentence of no longer than four years, except when the victim is white and the offender is black. Of the 455 men executed for rape from 1930 to 1967, 405 were black.[94] Black males, however, are not uniformly punished the most severely. If their victims are black females, they are likely to receive the most lenient sentences. In a study of rape convictions in Baltimore in 1967, "Of the four categories of rapist and victim in a racial mix, blacks received the stiffest sentences for raping white women and the mildest sentences for raping black women."[95]

There is a bias in the criminal justice system against rape complaints that seems to be based on the fear that women frequently accuse innocent men of rape. This position is sometimes stated explicitly as, for example, in this comment in the *University of Pennsylvania Law Review:*

> Women often falsely accuse men of sexual attacks to extort money, to force marriage, to satisfy a childish desire for notoriety, or to attain personal revenge. Their motives include hatred, a sense of shame after consenting to illicit intercourse, especially when pregnancy results, and delusion.[96]

Many states still allow judges to include in the jury charge a version of the "Hale instructions": "Rape is an accusation easily made and hard to be proved, and harder to be defended by the party accused, though never so innocent."[97]

These kinds of attitudes, however, are not limited to the legal profession. The general public believes "a woman with her skirt up can run faster than a man with his pants down," and medical experts argue "rape cannot be perpetrated by *one man* alone on an adult woman of good health and vigor."[98] The famous sexologist, Alfred Kinsey, has stated that the only difference between a rape and a good time depends on whether the girl's parents were awake when she finally got home.[99]

The claim that women easily make false accusations of rape is refuted even by the F.B.I. According to the *Uniform Crime Report,* " ... law enforcement administrators recognize that this offense is probably one of the most under-reported crimes."[100] Medea and Thompson discovered that 70 percent of the women in their sample did not report the crime.[101] A number of studies have estimated that only 20 percent of all forcible rapes are reported to authorities.

The disbelief of judges, juries, police and prosecutors that a rape victim faces is compounded by the distrust she encounters from family and friends when she admits she has been raped. Responses of parents, relatives, friends and spouses are either anger at the victim for being foolish enough to get raped or anger at the rapist for the humiliation and shame that family members will suffer as a result of the attack.

The three responses that Burgess and Holmstrom recorded from parents of child victims of rape were:

1 blaming the assailant—"If we ever find out who did it, there won't be enough left to pick him up if I see him."

2 blaming the child—"We have her on punishment for one month. She can't go out and see any of her friends. Only one friend she can telephone and no friends permitted in the house. This is because of what happened."

3 blaming themselves—"My wife is not well and says she is going to commit suicide. She says she is not good as a mother and wants to kill herself. What should I do?"[102]

Facing disbelief on every side, victims do blame themselves. In fact much of the psychological discomfort suffered by women who have been raped is their belief that they were in part responsible for their own sexual violation. Women frequently ask themselves why they let it happen. "There is a strong desire for the victim to try and think of how she could undo what has happened. She reports going over in her mind how she might have escaped from the assailant, how she might have handled the situation differently."[103] For many women the aftermath of the rape is worse than the physical pain of the actual rape. They are plagued by feelings of guilt, shame, loss of self-esteem and humiliation. Many rapes go unreported because victims have been unjustifiably convinced that they were guilty of precipitating the attack.[104] This is even more probable in cases where the victim knows the offender. Some women have confessed that it was only when they were involved in more healthy relationships that they realized that their initial introduction into sex was rape.

The attitude of victims of rape can be characterized as one more of despair than of resentment or anger. They have been taught, and many have assumed, the responsibility for male sexuality. When they are raped, they feel that they have failed, and that they are at fault. Medea and Thompson have argued that many female rape victims feel like they are sentinels who have fallen asleep while on guard duty.

> The male is the aggressor, the soldier laying siege to the castle; the woman is the guardian of the gate, and defender of the sacred treasure. If the male forces his way in with a battering ram and captures the treasure, he has succeeded in his purpose. There is no cause for guilt or remorse. The woman, on the other hand, has failed in her purpose. She has allowed the treasure to be taken and feels herself to be at fault. She suffers from feelings of guilt, besides the feelings of violation, humiliation and defeat.[105]

In a rape culture, even the victims believe that men are naturally sexual aggressors. Their response to the rape is to blame themselves for not taking proper precautions and not to demand a change in the behavior of men.

As long as sex in our society is construed as a dirty, low and violent act involving domination of a male over a female, rape will remain a common occurrence.

It is the logical outcome of things if men act according to the "masculine mystique" and women act according to the "feminine mystique." But rape does not have to occur. Its presence is an indication of how widely held are traditional views of appropriate male and female behavior and how strongly they are enforced. Our society is a rape culture because it fosters and encourages rape by teaching males and females that it is natural and normal that sexual relations involve aggressive behavior on the part of males. To see an end to rape, people must be able to envision a relationship between the sexes that involves sharing, warmth and equality and to bring about a social system in which those values are fostered.

## NOTES

1　Susan Griffin, "Rape: The All-American Crime," *Ramparts*, 10:3 (September 1971), p. 26.

2　*Ibid.*, p. 35.

3　Andra Medea and Kathleen Thompson, *Against Rape* (New York: Farrar, Straus and Girous, 1974), pp. 4–5.

4　Meir quoted in Letty Cotton Pogrebin, "Do Women Make Men Violent?", *Ms.*, 3:5 (1974), p. 55.

5　"Judge in Wisconsin Calls Rape By Boy 'Normal' Reaction," *New York Times*, May 27, 1977, p. 9.

6　Menachem Amir, "Forcible Rape," *Federal Probation*, 31:1 (1967), p. 51.

7　Paul M. Kinsie, "Sex Crimes and the Prostitution Racket." *Journal of Social Hygiene*, 36 (1950), pp. 250–52.

8　Susan Brownmiller, *Against Our Will: Men, Women and Rape* (New York: Simon and Schuster), 1975, pp. 12–13.

9　Margaret Mead, *Sex and Temperament in Three Primitive Societies* (New York: Dell, 1968), p. 110.

10　Griffin, p. 27.

11　Carol V. Horos, *Rape* (New Canaan, Connecticut: Tobey Publishing Company, Inc., 1974), p. 4.

12　*Ibid.*, p. 5.

13　National Institute of Law Enforcement and Criminal Justice, *Forcible Rape, A National Survey of the Response by Prosecutors, Volume One* (Washington, D.C.: U.S. Government Printing Office, 1977), p. 17, 27.

14　Eldridge Cleaver, *Soul On Ice* (New York: Dell-Delta/Ramparts, 1968).

15　Griffin, p. 33.

16　Kurt Weis and Sandra S. Borges, "Victimology and Rape: The Case of the Legitimate Victim," *Issues in Criminology*, 8:2 (Fall 1973), p. 105.

17　Jerrold K. Footlick, "Rape Alert," *Newsweek*, November 10, 1975, p. 71.

18　Horos, p. 96.

19　Menachem Amir, *Patterns in Forcible Rape* (Chicago: University of Chicago Press, 1971), p. 314. See also Benjamin Karpman, *The Sexual Offender and His Offenses* (New York: Julian Press, Inc., 1954), pp. 38–39.

20　See, for example, Camille E. LeGrand, "Rape and Rape Laws: Sexism in Society and Law," *California Law Review*, 61:3 (1973), p. 922 and Murray L. Cohen, Ralph Garofalo, Richard Boucher and Theoharis Seghorn, "The Psychology of Rapists," *Seminars in Psychiatry*, 3:3 (August 1971), p. 317.

21　Brownmiller, p. 195.

22　George L. Kirkham, "Homosexuality in Prison," in James M. Henslin, ed., *Studies in the Sociology of Sex* (New York: Appleton-Century-Crofts, 1971), p. 340.

23　Alan J. Davis, "Sexual Assaults in the Philadelphia Prison System," in John A. Gagnon and William Simon, eds., *The Sexual Scene* (United States, no city: Aldine Publishing Co., 1970), pp. 122–23.

24  *Ibid.*, p. 123.
25  Jean Genet, *Our Lady of the Flowers,* translated by Bernard Frechtman (New York: Grove Press, 1963), p. 253.
26  Kirkham, p. 327.
27  Davis, p. 110.
28  Cohen *et. al.*, p. 322.
29  Horos, p. 22.
30  Pogrebin, p. 52.
31  Amir, *Patterns in Forcible Rape,* p. 334.
32  Medea and Thompson, p. 34.
33  Amir, *Patterns in Forcible Rape,* p. 309.
34  Brownmiller, p. 196.
35  Amir, *Patterns in Forcible Rape,* p. 343.
36  *Ibid.*, p. 52.
37  Clarence M. Kelley, *Crime in the United States, 1976, Uniform Crime Report* (Washington, D.C.: U.S. Government Printing Office, 1977), pp. 16–17.
38  Brownmiller, p. 194.
39  Lucy Komisar, *Violence and the Masculine Mystique* (Pittsburgh: KNOW, Inc., no date), p. 6.
40  Clifford Kirkpatrick and Eugene Danin, "Male Sex Aggression on a University Campus," *American Sociological Review,* 22:1 (February 1957), p. 53.
41  *Ibid.*
42  Eugene J. Kanin, "Male Aggression in Dating-Courtship Relations," *American Journal of Sociology,* 63:2 (September 1957), p. 200.
43  Amir, *Patterns in Forcible Rape,* p. 339.
44  Weis and Borges, p. 87.
45  Menachem Amir, "The Role of the Victim in Sex Offenses," in H. L. P. Resnick and Marvin E. Wolfgang, eds., *Secual Behaviors: Social, Clinical and Legal Aspects* (Boston: Little, Brown and Company, 1972), p. 151.
46  Amir, "Forcible Rape," p. 57.
47  Amir, *Patterns in Forcible Rape,* p. 346.
48  Medea and Thompson, p. 134.
49  Amir, "Forcible Rape," p. 57.
50  About 5% of rapes are committed in association with another felony such as burglary and robberv. These rapes are the few in which interracial rape occurs and in which victims te:id to be older than their attackers. See, for example, Amir, *Patterns in Forcible Rape,* p. 343.
51  "Police Discretion and the Judgment that a Crime Has Been Committed—Rape in Philadelphia," Comment in *University of Pennsylvania Law Review,* 117:2 (1968), p. 318.
52  Amir, *Patterns in Forcible Rape,* p. 341.
53  *Ibid.*, p. 52.

54   Women Organized Against Rape, *W.O.A.R. Data* (Philadelphia: mimeo, 1975), p. 1.

55   Leroy Schultz, "Interviewing the Sex Offender's Victim," *Journal of Criminal Law, Criminology and Police Science,* 50:5 (January-February 1960), p. 451.

56   R. J. McCaldon, "Rape," *Canadian Journal of Corrections,* 9:1 (January 1967), p. 47.

57   Pamela Lakes Wood, "The Victim in a Forcible Rape Case: A Feminist View," *American Criminal Law Review,* 7:2 (1973), p. 348.

58   Brownmiller, p. 364.

59   *Uniform Crime Report,* 1976, p. 16.

60   "Police Discretion and the Judgment that a Crime Has Been Committed—Rape in Philadelphia," p. 292.

61   *Ibid.,* p. 304.

62   See, for example, Duncan Chappell, *et. al.,* "Forcible Rape: A Comparative Study of Offenses Known to the Police in Boston and Los Angeles," in James M. Henslin, ed., *Studies in the Sociology of Sex* (New York: Appleton-Century-Crofts, 1971), p. 180.

63   *Ibid.,* p. 291.

64   *Ibid.,* p. 299.

65   Brownmiller, p. 402.

66   "Police Discretion and the Judgment that a Crime Has Been Committed—Rape in Philadelphia," p. 279.

67   *Ibid.*

68   National Institute of Law Enforcement and Criminal Justice, p. 46.

69   Footlick, p. 70.

70   Lisa Brodyaga *et. al, Rape and Its Victims: A Report for Citizens, Health Facilities, and Criminal Justice Agencies* (Washington, D.C.: U.S. Government Printing Office, 1975), p. 15. See also E. Galton, "Police Processing of Rape Complaints," *American Journal of Criminal Law,* 4 (Winter 1975–1976), pp. 15–30.

71   National Institute of Law Enforcement and Criminal Justice, pp. 22–23.

72   Ann Wolbert Burgess and Lynda Lytle Holmstrom, *Rape: Victims of Crisis* (Bowie, Maryland: Robert J. Brady, Company, 1974), p. 197.

73   *Ibid.*

74   *Ibid.,* p. 211.

75   *Ibid.,* p. 200.

76   Wood, p. 335.

77   "The Rape Corroboration Requirement: Repeal Not Reform," Notes in *The Yale Law Journal,* 81:7 (1972), p. 1366.

78   "Police Discretion and the Judgment that a Crime Has Been Committed—Rape in Philadelphia," p. 279.

79   "The Corroboration Rule and Crimes Accompanying a Rape," Comment in *University of Pennsylvania Law Review,* 118:3 (1970), p. 461.

80   Wood, p. 336.

81  "The Rape Corroboration Requirement: Repeal Not Reform," p. 1375.

82  Wood, p. 372.

83  LeGrand, p. 939.

84  Wood, p. 372.

85  "The Rape Corroboration Requirement: Repeal Not Reform," p. 1379.

86  Wood, pp. 341–42.

87  Medea and Thompson, p. 121.

88  Wood, pp. 344–45.

89  Footlick, p. 72.

90  LeGrand, p. 935.

91  *Uniform Crime Report, 1976,* pp. 16–17.

92  Brownmiller, p. 175.

93  LeGrand, p. 927.

94  Angela Davis, "Joanne Little: The Dialectics of Rape," *Ms.,* 3, 12 (June 1975), p. 106.

95  "Negroes Accuse Maryland Bench: Double Standard Is Charged in Report on Rape Cases," *New York Times,* September 18, 1967, p. 33.

96  "The Corroboration Rule and Crimes Accompanying a Rape," p. 460.

97  Footlick, p. 72.

98  Julia R. and Herman Schwendinger, "Rape Myths: In Legal, Theoretical, and Everyday Practice," *Crime and Social Justice,* 1 (1974), p. 19.

99  Brownmiller, p. 276.

100  *Uniform Crime Report,* 1976, p. 16.

101  Medea and Thompson, p. 135.

102  Burgess and Holmstrom, pp. 60–62.

103  *Ibid.,* p. 41.

104  Schwendinger, p. 18.

105  Medea and Thompson, pp. 24–25.

# Nadean Bishop

# Abortion:
# The Controversial
# Choice

"Reproductive freedom" has been a major demand of the women's liberation movement for
most of its existence, as well as one of its most
controversial issues. In fact, whether or not "reproductive freedom" was even a women's rights
issue was a subject of major debate at the 1967
national convention of the National Organization
for Women, and the vote to include it in a
Women's Bill of Rights cost NOW its conservative
wing a year later.

Although "reproductive freedom" includes an
entire gamut of issues such as sex education, access to contraception, and an end to forced sterilization of poor and minority women, at its core is
the question of abortion. Controversy over abortion preceded the women's movement by many
centuries, and its resurgence as a contemporary
issue was not initiated by feminists. The American

Civil Liberties Union was the first national organization to support it publicly, in 1965, and ACLU has sponsored the key court cases since then. National organizations to repeal abortions laws have developed independently of the feminist movement, but the issue has nonetheless become thoroughly identified as a feminist issue. Consequently, an argument that was originally expressed in terms of the right to privacy and medical safety is now primarily debated in terms of a woman's right to control her own body.

The result is that the "pro" and "con" sides do not speak to the same issue or from the same concerns. "Pro" does not mean "pro-abortion"; it means "pro-choice." Many who would not choose to terminate a pregnancy of their own argue that every woman should have the right to choose when and under what circumstances she will bear a child. Birth control measures sometimes fail, victims of rape and incest must have some recourse, tests may show deformity of the embryo, the number of children already born may be too large (and unwanted children may become neglected or beaten children). But regardless of the reasons, the choice should be that of the pregnant woman. It is her body, and her right to make that choice. And society should not penalize her for it by forcing her to bear an unwanted child or to take the risk of an illegal abortion, which can usually only be had under medically unsafe conditions. From this perspective "reproductive freedom" cannot be separated from any of the other women's rights issues; every woman must be free to determine her own life, and she cannot do so with the fear of an unplanned interruption for child-rearing.

Those opposed are more concerned with the "right to life" than the "right to choose." They argue that life exists from conception, and that "abortion forfeits the very basic right to life from which all other rights proceed."[1] Because this argument makes an as-yet-unproved assumption about when life begins, it is basically a religious argument, and is highly identified with religious forces. Although the "right to life" has been strongly supported by fundamentalist protestants and orthodox Jews, the Catholic hierarchy (though not necessarily the laity) has been a major backer of efforts to ban or restrict abortion.

Thus it is worth comparing what the major religious faiths have to say, even though "pro-choice" advocates would say that any legislation which imposes a single interpretation of when life begins denies the religious freedom guaranteed by the First Amendment.

The testimony of Jewish Rabbi Balfour Brickner before a House subcommittee in March of 1976 provides a succinct history of the position of Judaism on abortion: Many Orthodox Jewish authorities advise against abortion except "when a woman is impregnated through rape or incest or when it is clear that continuation of pregnancy to birth would constitute a clear danger to the life and/or health of the mother." But the official position differs. "In Judaism, the fetus in the womb is not a person (lav nefesh hu) until it is born. . . . Thus there is no capital liability for foeticide. By this reckoning, abortion cannot be considered murder." This interpretation is made from the scriptural admonition in Exodus 21:22: "If a man strike, and wound a pregnant woman so that her fruit be expelled, but no harm befall her, then shall he be fined as her husband shall assess, and the matter placed before the judges." Talmudic commentators on this passage conclude that the one responsible "is not culpable for murder, since the unborn fetus is not considered a person."[2]

In direct contrast to the Jewish position that life begins at birth is the official pronouncement of the Roman Catholic Church that life begins at the moment of conception. Thus, for the Roman Catholic hierarchy, any aborting of the fetus is condemned as murder. Pope Paul has maintained a hard line on abortion, asserting that the life of the fetus takes precedence over the life of the mother. The fetus is to be carried to term even if the pregnancy resulted from incest or rape and even if the life or mental health of the mother is in jeopardy.

It is startling in the light of theological rigidity and expected conformity that so many Catholics disagree with this official position. A 1976 Knight-Ridder poll shows 76 percent of Catholics polled agreeing with the statement: "If a woman wants to have an abortion, that is a matter for her and her doctor to decide and the government should have nothing to do with it." Protestants polled said yes 82 percent of the time and 98 percent of Jews polled agreed.[3] In 1977 the National Opinion Research Center in Chicago reported that 37 percent of Catholics polled said "Abortion should be permitted if a woman was married and did not want more [children]" and 45 percent approved of abortion if a woman "cannot afford any more children."[4]

Catholic theologians have not always opposed abortion on the grounds of life beginning with conception. St. Jerome, translator of the Vulgate Bible, said in a letter to a female student, Algasis, "Seeds are gradually formed in the uterus, and it [abortion] is not reputed homicide until the scattered elements receive their appearances and members." St. Augustine too said "the law does not provide that the act [abortion] pertains to homicide, for there cannot yet be said to be a live soul in a body that lacks sensation when it is not formed in flesh and so not yet endowed with sense." Pope Gregory XIV in 1591 in the Codicis Juris Fontes returned to the practice of allowing abortions up to 40 days, following the Aristotelian ruling on ensoulment, thus overturning the 1588 prohibition of abortion by Sixtus V.[5]

It was not until 1869 that the Catholic Church under Pope Pius IX forbade all abortions. This dogma has been reaffirmed since, most strongly in the 1974 Declaration on Procured Abortion which states: "The First Right of the Human Person is his life. Never, under any pretext may a woman resort to abortion. Nor can one exempt women from what nature demands of them." This dogma is vehemently opposed by such Catholic women as Dr. Janet Furlong-Cahill, former professor at St. Mary's, Notre Dame: "Such a stand is designed to leave woman at the mercy, not only of her biological makeup, but also at the mercy of a celibate hierarchy, who claim the right to damn her eternally if she uses methods such as artificial birth control, sterilization or abortion to protect herself against unwanted or dangerous pregnancies."[6]

Protestant denominations have a diversity of opinion regarding when life begins and whether abortion should be allowed. The tes timony of Theressa Hoover, Associate General Secretary of the United Methodist Church, before the House subcommittee may be taken as representative of the sentiments of many Protestants regarding abortion. Ms. Hoover stresses the strong Protestant tradition of "advocating individual responsibility in matters concerning family, sexuality, and community."[7] This belief is rooted in the teachings of Jesus, which admonish Christians to take responsibility for their own lives and make responsible personal decisions. The right to privacy and the autonomy of the individual are basic doctrines that are violated by governmental interference in matters of family planning.

Protestants would almost universally choose the life of the mother over the life of the fetus. As Ms. Hoover expresses it:

A woman suffering from heart disease, diabetes, or cancer, could suffer grave, if not fatal risks if she continued a pregnancy to term. And a woman who is the carrier of a genetic disease, such as sickle cell anemia or Taysachs, which may be transmitted to the fetus, should not be compelled to bear that fetus if she does not choose to after medical tests have confirmed that the fetus is affected. We cannot in good conscience force a woman who has been raped to carry the possible resulting pregnancy to term. To do so would be to totally disregard the anguish which women suffer in such circumstances.[8]

Leaders from eighteen religious persuasions, including Protestants, Jews, and Roman Catholics, joined in 1973 to found the Religious Coalition for Abortion Rights to safeguard the option of legal abortion. The current crusade of RCAR is to counteract the anti-choice minority, headed by the National Conference of Catholic Bishops. The stance of the RCAR is not pro-abortion but pro-choice, a position which parallels that taken by the American Civil Liberties Union: "The union itself offers no comment on the wisdom or the moral implications of abortion, believing that such judgments belong solely in the province of individual conscience and religion."[9]

## LEGAL AND LEGISLATIVE STATUS OF ABORTION

On January 22, 1973, the Supreme Court handed down two landmark decisions regarding abortion: *Roe v. Wade* and *Doe v. Bolton*. "Roe" is the anonymous label given a pregnant unmarried woman in a Texas case, and "Doe" is the name given a pregnant married woman, mother of three, in a Georgia referral. In both cases the Court voted seven to two in support of the Right to Privacy of the women involved and the inability of both Texas and Georgia to establish any "compelling state interest" during the first trimester of pregnancy and limited legal control in subsequent trimesters.

The ruling in *Roe v. Wade* surveyed medical, religious, moral, and historical material before concluding that the Fourteenth Amendment's protection of personal liberty "is broad enough to encompass a woman's decision whether or not to terminate her pregnancy."[10] Having decided this, the Supreme Court set different standards according to the trimester since conception. During the first trimester abortion presents very little danger to the mother and thus there must be no state interference in the decision to terminate the unwanted pregnancy: it is a matter between the patient and her doctor. The only restriction is that the abortion must be done by a physician. After the first trimester the state has the right to specify certain standards for the facilities where the abortion occurs, including after-care services in case of complications, which are more frequent during the second and third trimesters. But even then the state must not limit the reasons for which a woman may seek an abortion.

In dealing with the question of the state's interest in the right of the fetus, *Roe v. Wade* declares that the term "person" as used in the Constitution applies only after birth. The Court declined to intervene in the theological debate regarding the point at which life begins, but it ruled that the state has some interest after viability—the stage after which the fetus may have hope for "meaningful life outside the mother's womb." Thus after the 24th to the 28th week the state may regulate or even forbid abortion unless it is required to save the pregnant woman's life or mental health.[11]

A history of earlier abortion legislation may put *Roe v. Wade* into perspective. The restrictive provisions of the ruling for the final trimester echo the wording of all abortion laws in the United States for the hundred years prior to 1967. For the first 200 years of American history, abortion before the first movement of the fetus was not considered a crime of any kind, and during Colonial times, in keeping with the English common law, willful abortion of a quickened fetus was accounted a simple misdemeanor. In 1803 the British revised their criminal code and made abortion a crime, though with lesser penalties before quickening. Exceptions were normally made if the abortion was necessary to save the life of the pregnant woman. In the United States the first abortion legislation did not come until 1821, and it was not until after the Civil War that most states created statutes superseding British common law. Thereafter the restrictive provisions applied. The removal of nearly all legal controls on abortion followed in 1970 in four states: New York, Washington, Alaska, and Hawaii.[12]

Liberalization of these restrictions was proposed in 1959 in the Model Penal Code of the American Law Institute. The ALI code said a licensed physician could terminate a pregnancy (1) if the life or mental health of the mother was threatened; or (2) if the child was likely to be born with "a grave, permanent, and irremediable mental or physical defect" (such as those caused by the drug thalidomide); or (3) if the woman became pregnant as a result of rape or incest. Colorado in 1967 was the first state to adopt this code for therapeutic abortion and twelve other states adopted variations of it in the ensuing years.[13]

Georgia was one of the states adopting the ALI code, and the 1973 *Doe v. Bolton* case addressed its regulations. Georgia required that abortions be performed in hospitals approved by the Joint Commission on Accreditation, even though only 54 of its 159 counties had such hospitals. The court found this requirement invalid on the basis of equal access as well as a lack of compelling state interest. Also struck down were provisions requiring approval at all stages of pregnancy by two state-licensed physicians and a hospital review committee.

Two crucial questions were pointedly not addressed by either *Roe v. Wade* or *Doe v. Bolton:* the rights of the husband in the case of an adult married woman seeking abortion, and the rights of the parents in the case of a minor. In a 1974 case called *Doe v. Doe,* the Massachusetts Supreme Court ruled that "if the State cannot interfere with the abortion decision before the fetus is viable, except in ways reasonably related to maternal health, it seems highly doubtful that it can come to the husband's assistance with authority it does not itself possess."[14] Rights of the parents in the decision concerning an abortion for their underage daughter are complicated by variable state laws about medical care for minors. Most state courts have ruled that no parental consent can be required and that no parent can force a pregnant girl under 18 years of age to have an abortion if she chooses not to.

But Congress soon began nibbling at the freedom given by the Supreme Court. In late 1976 Rep. Henry Hyde (R, Ill.) attached an amendment to the 1977 Labor/HEW Appropriations Act prohibiting the use of Medicaid money to pay for abortions, except when the life of the mother is in danger or in case of incest or rape. A preliminary injunction against implementation of the amendment was granted, but Hyde appealed the case and a Federal district court dissolved its injunction in August 1977.[15]

At present the states set the policies for approving payments for abortion and other medical services under Medicaid, and the federal government reimburses the states, paying half for the wealthy states and more for others.[16] In deciding on the HEW appropriation for 1978, the Senate and House engaged in six months of rancorous debate over the wording of the proviso concerning funding for reimbursing states for Medicaid payments for abortion. The Congressional Clearinghouse on Women's Rights noted, "No single piece of legislation generated as much controversy as the subject of federal funding of abortion in the Medicaid program."[17] On December 7, 1977, the night before funding for the Department of Labor and HEW was due to expire, the Senate and House settled the impasse with this resolution:

That none of the funds provided for in this paragraph shall be used to perform abortions except where the life of the mother would be endangered if the fetus were carried to term; or except for such medical procedures necessary for the victims of rape or incest which has been reported promptly to a law enforcement agency or public health service; or except in those instances where severe and long-lasting physical health damage to the mother would result if the pregnancy were carried to term when so determined by two physicians.

Nor are payments prohibited for drugs or devices to prevent implantation of the fertilized ovum, or the medical procedures necessary for the termination of ectopic pregnancy.[18]

This drastic limitation to the federal support of Medicaid payments for abortions is combined with a ruling by the United States Supreme Court on June 20, 1977, that "neither federal law or the Constitution requires the states to pay Medicaid benefits for nontherapeutic abortions. By 6 to 3 votes the Court found that nothing in Title XIX of the Social Security Act or the Constitution precluded a state from adopting a policy of favoring normal childbirth over abortion and using its public funds to further that policy."[19] Justice Thurgood Marshall spelled out the implications of this decision in the minority report:

As the Court well knows, these regulations inevitably will have the practical effect of preventing nearly all poor women from obtaining safe and legal abortions.

The enactments challenged here brutally coerce poor women to bear children whom society will scorn for every day of their lives. . . . I am appalled at the ethical bankruptcy of those who preach a "right to life" that means under present social policies, a bare existence in utter misery for so many poor women and their children. . . . Nonwhite women now obtain abortions at nearly twice the rate of whites and it appears that almost 40 percent of minority women—more than five times the proportion of whites—are dependent upon medicaid for their health care. . . . The effect will be to relegate millions of people to lives of poverty and despair.[20]

## WHO GETS AN ABORTION?

A total of 744,600 women received abortions in 1974, following the Supreme Court decision legalizing abortion during the first trimester. The number moved to 1.1 million in 1975 according to statistics released in April of 1977 by the *Center for Disease Control: Abortion Surveillance 1975.*[21] From 1969 through 1975, 4.3 million legal abortions were performed in the United States. The present ratio runs one for every four live births.[22]

Throughout the six years statistics have been collected, one-third of all legal abortions have been performed for women under twenty years of age. Another one-third of those receiving abortions were between twenty and twenty-five and the remaining were over 25 years of age. Contrary to the myth that abortions are sought predominantly by the unmarried adolescent girl who "gets in trouble," two-thirds of all legal abortions are performed for women over twenty, and more than one-fourth of all abortion recipients are married.

SUMMARY TABLE    Characteristics of Women Receiving Abortions, United States, 1972–1975

| Characteristics | Percent distribution[1] | | | |
|---|---|---|---|---|
| | 1972 | 1973 | 1974 | 1975 |
| Residence | | | | |
| Abortion in-state | 56.2 | 74.8 | 86.6 | 89.2 |
| Abortion out-of-state | 43.8 | 25.2 | 13.4 | 10.8 |
| Age | | | | |
| ≤ 19 | 32.6 | 32.7 | 32.7 | 33.1 |
| 20–24 | 32.5 | 32.0 | 31.8 | 31.9 |
| ≥ 25 | 34.9 | 35.3 | 35.6 | 35.0 |
| Race | | | | |
| White | 77.0 | 72.5 | 69.7 | 67.8 |
| Black and others | 23.0 | 27.5 | 30.3 | 32.2 |
| Marital status | | | | |
| Married | 29.7 | 27.4 | 27.4 | 26.1 |
| Unmarried | 70.3 | 72.6 | 72.6 | 73.9 |
| Number of living children | | | | |
| 0 | 49.4 | 48.6 | 47.8 | 47.1 |
| 1 | 18.2 | 18.8 | 19.6 | 20.2 |
| 2 | 13.3 | 14.2 | 14.8 | 15.5 |
| 3 | 8.7 | 8.7 | 8.7 | 8.7 |
| 4 | 5.0 | 4.8 | 4.5 | 4.4 |
| ≥ 5 | 5.4 | 4.9 | 4.5 | 4.2 |

SUMMARY TABLE    (cont'd)

| Characteristics | Percent distribution[1] | | | |
|---|---|---|---|---|
| | 1972 | 1973 | 1974 | 1975 |
| Type of procedure | | | | |
| Curettage | 88.6 | 88.4 | 89.7 | 90.9 |
| Suction | 65.2 | 74.9 | 77.5 | 82.6 |
| Sharp | 23.4 | 13.5 | 12.3 | 8.4 |
| Intrauterine installation | 10.4 | 10.4 | 7.8 | 6.2 |
| Hysterotomy/Hysterectomy | 0.6 | 0.7 | 0.6 | 0.4 |
| Other | 0.5 | 0.6 | 1.9 | 2.4 |
| Weeks of gestation | | | | |
| ≤8 | 34.0 | 36.1 | 42.6 | 44.6 |
| 9–10 | 30.7 | 29.4 | 28.7 | 28.4 |
| 11–12 | 17.5 | 17.9 | 15.4 | 14.9 |
| 13–15 | 8.4 | 6.9 | 5.5 | 5.0 |
| 16–20 | 8.2 | 8.0 | 6.5 | 6.1 |
| ≥ 21 | 1.3 | 1.7 | 1.2 | 1.0 |

[1]Excludes unknowns

SOURCE: *Center for Disease Control: Abortion Surveillance 1975* (Atlanta, Ga.: Center for Disease Control, U.S. Department of Health, Education and Welfare, April 1977), p. iv.

More than two-thirds of those receiving abortions are white, but black women are 2.2 times as likely to have abortions as white women. For example, in 1975 there were 277 legal abortions among white women for each 1,000 live births, but 476 legal abortions among black women for each 1,000 live births.[23]

Perhaps the most striking statistic, however, is that approximately 70 percent of the abortions obtained legally would have been obtained illegally before decriminalization, according to Dr. Christopher Tietze, senior fellow of the Population Center and an expert on the statistics and demographics of family planning.[24] The hazards of illegal abortion are chilling to contemplate. Of course we have no way of knowing the number of women who die from the unsanitary practices of back-alley abortionists, but the Center for Disease Control report shows a drop from 320 known abortion-related fatalities in 1961 to 88 in 1972 and 44 in 1975, with eighteen of these latter coming from illegal abortions.[25] Additional evidence comes from the fact that deaths from the two most common complications of illegal abortions—puerperal sepsis and hemorrhage—dropped from 433 in 1960 to 158 in 1973.[26] Other factors, such as more effective contraceptive techniques and more sanitary facilities, may help, but the legalization of abortion is certainly the major cause for this reduction. The Institute of Medicine report of May 1975 concluded its summation of facts such as these with a strong affirmation of decriminalization of abortion: "Legislation and practices that permit women to obtain abortions in proper medical surroundings will lead to fewer deaths and a lower rate of medical complications than restrictive legislation and practices."[27]

The dominant alternative to abortion, bearing the unwanted baby, has proved to be devastating in terms of the consequent mistreatment of the child. Feminist attorney Jean King quotes a longitudinal study done in Göteborg, Sweden, by Norman and Nancy Polanski, tracing 120 cases after therapeutic abortion was refused. Sixty-eight of the pregnant women found other avenues to abortion. Of the 52 babies born, 14 died before age three. Those surviving were matched with a same-sex child born in the same hospital during the same week, and the pairs were traced for 21 years. Twenty-two became juvenile offenders compared with ten in the control group. They became not only community problems and victims, but victimizers. The study shows the same syndrome that we recognize with battered children: those who are mistreated as they grow up become parents who batter their own offspring. This multiplication of inhumanity could be stopped before it begins by providing readily available methods for terminating unwanted pregnancy.[28] A similar study of Czechoslovakian children whose mothers had twice been denied abortions found the unwanted children to have "poorer health and poorer grades in school and to be less accepted by their peers than other children of similar socioeconomic status, intellectual ability, birth order, and family size."[29]

The answer to the question "Who gets an abortion?" is complicated by two other factors: regional availability and financial situation. Abortions are not available everywhere in the United States: 11 states reported no abortions at all during 1975 because doctors and hospitals refused to perform them. Louisiana's state legislature has made participation in an abortion punishable by death, a law clearly unconstitutional under the Supreme Court decision of 1973, but nonetheless an indication of the deterrents that make legal abortions difficult to obtain. Only 18 percent of the public hospitals and 38 percent of private hospitals in the United States reported performing even one abortion during 1975 and the first quarter of 1976.[30]

The money question is a concern for many women who seek abortions. Abortions have always been available to the woman with money and influence, if not in this country then by flying to Sweden. No such possibility exists for the poor. Of the one million legal abortions performed in 1975, 300,000 were paid for by the federal government. Most of these were financed with Medicaid funds, whose use for abortions has since been prohibited. Yet an estimated 400,000 to 900,000 women who wanted abortions in 1975 still couldn't get them.[31] Now, without Medicaid funds for abortions, HEW officials estimate that the government will have to pay between $450 million and $565 million for medical care and public assistance during the first year after birth, in contrast to the $50 million expended in 1975 for abortions. In addition, HEW says, "without Medicaid support for women who choose abortion, there would be an estimated 125 to 250 deaths annually from illegal and self-induced abortions as well as 12,500 to 25,000 complications requiring hospitalization."[32]

## ABORTION RISKS

Spontaneous abortion occurs in one of every fifteen pregnancies and has been called "Nature's method of birth control" because it eliminates fetal and placental abnormalities. Induced abortions, whether required for therapeutic, socio-economic, eugenic, contraceptive, or circumstantial reasons, have been practiced since ancient times. Gynecological instruments such as probes, dilators, and forceps were found in the ruins of Pompeii. During the Renaissance the physician of Queen Elizabeth I wrote of techniques to remove unwanted material from the uterus by the use of suction.[23]

But what are the risks involved with modern abortion techniques? Abortions performed under medical supervision during the first trimester, which in 1975 was 88 percent of all abortions, offer very little risk compared with other medical practices. Eight times as many women die as a result of full-term pregnancies as from having legal abortions during the first trimester. The maternal death rate is 14 deaths per 100,000 for vaginal deliveries and 111 deaths per 100,000 for caesarean sections, compared to 1.7 per 100,000 for first-trimester abortions. Even surgery for removal of tonsils and adenoids is 3 times as risky as legal abortion during the first 12 weeks. The mortality ratio goes down dramatically to 0.5 for these procedures occurring before the ninth week of gestation. As the gestation period increases, so does the risk. The jump is from 4.2 deaths at 11 to 12 weeks to 17 deaths per 100,000 abortions at 16 to 20 weeks. This still is less than a quarter of the ratio for major surgery such as hysterotomy and hysterectomy, which have a combined mortality of 61.3 deaths per 100,000.[34]

Why would a woman wait until the second trimester? Studies have shown such factors as ambivalence and objection on religious grounds are usually involved, combined with procedural delays and difficulties in getting counseling, the pregnancy test, or the money. Abortion is also necessary in the second trimester for mothers exposed to rubella virus infection, X-rays, or the ingestion of drugs known to damage the fetus. A major factor, however, is that testing for almost 60 inherited metabolic disorders such as Tay-Sachs or mongolism cannot occur until the second trimester. A testing technique called amniocentesis, which affords almost 100 percent accuracy, has been developed. It was performed in 6,000 second-trimester pregnancies between 1967 and 1974 and less than 10 percent of the diagnoses showed an affected fetus.[35] Thus 600 sets of parents were saved the grief of a deformed baby, and 5,400 mothers were able to carry their healthy children to a normal birth.

But what about the psychological effects of legal abortion? Since reliable measures of psychological states before abortion are unavailable, its effects are hard to gauge, but evidence over the last several years indicates that abortion does not cause "any detectable increase in the incidence of mental illness."[36] Some women with previous psychiatric illness have shown aggravated conditions following an abortion. But the Joint Program for the Study of Abortion survey showed only an estimated 0.2 to 0.4 cases of post-abortion psychosis per 1,000 legal abortions, less than half the post-partum rate of 1 to 2 per 1,000 deliveries in the United States.[37]

## BEYOND ABORTION

Abortion is the most controversial aspect of reproductive freedom, but it is not the only one. The U.S. Commission on Civil Rights report on The Right to Limit Childbearing expresses it very well:

Even when the legal right to reproductive choice—including the right to abortion—is secured, not all women can exercise that right equally. Thus, for example, the poor woman who might choose to bear a child may find that the lack of financial assistance, counseling, housing assistance, child care, and health and personal services afford her no alternative but to abort. We cannot be sure, therefore, that every consent is informed consent and is not coerced by social [and] economic factors.[38]

The better world we look toward, in which women have a genuine freedom of choice, would thus be a world in which financial inequities would be alleviated. Following President Carter's decision not to support federal funds for abortion, he directed HEW to put money and staff time into abortion alternative programs that may help bring an end to some inequities. Early proposals include "better adolescent family planning clinics, greater incentives to states to encourage more sexual education in the classroom and incentives to encourage schools to allow teen-age mothers to enroll."[39]

Even "Right to Life" campaigners seem willing to support options to abortion such as improved hospital conditions for maternity patients and medical insurance plans that cover all the costs of giving birth. Child-care facilities for the workers as well as for the very poor engage the energies of feminists and right-to-lifers alike. Reforms in adoption policies to counteract the black market atmosphere of the early seventies are under way, but adoption will never be the answer to the problem of more than a million unwanted babies.[40]

Feminists would go beyond these conservative attempts to overcome the inequities and injustices that make abortion attractive. Sex education, including fertility control information, must be legalized and required in all states to help reduce the thousands of pregnancies entered into out of ignorance. Contraceptives should be provided through low-cost clinics in every community, along with pregnancy testing without parental knowledge or a doctor's order.

A world in which abortion is not the only answer would be one in which a woman's freedom of sexual expression would be accepted as a right, and one in which a woman without a man could bear and raise a child without social stigma. Financial support would be available for those unwed mothers who choose to bring up their children instead of giving them up for adoption. Most of all, control over our bodies means we are not forced by social conditioning or economic pressures to violate our own best interest. Punishment for freedom must never become the norm.

Until this ideal state is achieved, however, feminists will continue to work toward retaining the option of abortion as a court of last resort. As Bella Abzug put it for all of us:

> I am opposed to compulsory abortion. I am opposed to compulsory sterilization. I am also opposed to compulsory pregnancy. Under the Supreme Court decision, no woman anywhere in the United States can be forced to have an abortion. Neither can she be forced to have a baby. She is free to decide, under certain limitations specified by the Supreme Court, whether she should give birth to a child. We are all concerned with the right to life. We must also be concerned with preserving the essence of our democratic society which allows all viewpoints to flourish and compete for support.[41]

## NOTES

1  "...To Form a More Perfect Union...": Justice for American Women, Report of the National Commission on the Observance of International Women's Year (Washington, D.C.: Government Printing Office, 1976), p. 280.

2  Rabbi Balfour Brickner, "Judaism and Abortion," testimony before the Subcommittee on Civil and Constitutional Rights of the Committee on the Judiciary, U.S. House of Representatives, March 24, 1976.

3  "Public Opinion Polls Since the Supreme Court Decisions of 1973" (National Abortion Rights Action League, 706 Seventh Street, S.E., Washington, D.C. 20003, 1976).

4  Susan J. Lowe and Cynthia P. Green, "The Right to Choose: Facts on Abortion" (Zero Population Growth, 1346 Connecticut Avenue, N.W., Washington, D.C. 20036, 1977), p. 4.

5  "Theological Facts of History on Abortion" (Catholics for a Free Choice, 201 Massachusetts Avenue, N.E., Washington, D.C. 20002, 1976).

6  Dr. Janet Furlong-Cahill, "Abortion: the Double Standard" (Catholics for a Free Choice, 1974), p. 5.

7  "Testimony before the Subcommittee on Civil and Constitutional Rights of the Committee on the Judiciary in the U.S. House of Representatives, March 24, 1976" (Religious Coalition on Abortion Rights, 100 Massachusetts Avenue, N.E., Washington, D.C. 20002, 1976).

8  Ibid.

9  "Abortion: Why Religious Organizations in the United States Want to Keep It Legal" (RCAR, 1976).

10  Harriet F. Pilpel, Ruth Jane Zuckerman, and Elizabeth Ogg, "Abortion: Public Issue, Private Decision" (Public Affairs Pamphlet No. 527, 381 Park Avenue South, N.Y. 10016, 1975), p. 2.

11  *Ibid.,* pp. 2, 3.

12  *Ibid,* p. 11.

13  *Ibid.*

14  *Ibid.,* p. 6.

15  "A Review of State Laws and Policies," *Family Planning/Population Report* V6:#4, (Alan Guttmacher Institute, August 1977), p. 45.

16  *Ibid.*

17  *The Congressional Clearinghouse on Women's Rights* V.3:#39 (For the week of December 5, 1977), p. 12.

18  *Ibid.*

19  "A Review of State Laws and Policies," p. 45.

20  *Ibid.,* p. 47.

21  U.S. Department of Health, Education and Welfare, Public Health Service, National Center for Disease Control, Bureau of Epidemiology, *Center for Disease Control: Abortion Surveillance 1975,* (Atlanta, Georgia: Center for Disease Control, April 1977), p. 1. Hereafter cited as CDC.

22  Lowe and Green, p. 1.

23  CDC, p. 25.

24  Lowe and Green, p. 1.

25  CDC, p. 5.

26  Christopher Tietze and Marjorie Cooper Murstein, "Induced Abortion: 1975 Factbook," *Report on Population/Family Planning* (Population Council, December 1975), p. 63.

27  "Institute of Medicine: Legalized Abortion and the Public Health—Summary and Conclusions, May 1975" (National Academy of Sciences, Washington, D.C.), quoted in *Congressional Record,* V.121:#85 (June 3, 1975).

28  Jean King, speech to Abortion Teach-in, November 12, 1971, in Ann Arbor, Michigan.

29  "15 Facts You Should Know About Abortion" (Zero Population Growth, 1976), p. 2.

30  E. Sullivan, *et al.,* "Legal Abortion in the United States, 1975–76," *Family Planning in Perspectives,* IX:3 (1977), p. 121.

31  Terri Schultz, "Though Legal, Abortions Are Not Always Available," New York *Times,* January 2, 1977, IV, p. 8.

32  Lowe and Green, p. 2.

33  Theresa von der Vlugt and P. T. Piotrow, "Uterine Aspiration Techniques," *Population Reports,* Series F., #3 (June 1973).

34  "Institute of Medicine."

35  *Ibid.*

36  *Ibid.*

37  *Ibid.*

38  U.S. Commission on Civil Rights, *Constitutional Aspects of the Right to Limit Childbearing,* by Mary F. Berry, April 1975, p. 96.

39  "HEW Studies Program of Abortion Alternatives," New York *Times*, August 18, 1977, 15:1.

40  Joseph Morgenstern, "The New Faces of Adoption," *Newsweek* (September 13, 1971).

41  "NOW Defends a Woman's Right to Choose," (NOW, 425 13th St., NW, Washington, D.C., 1976).

# PART 2 IN AND OUT OF THE FAMILY

# Kathleen Gough

# The Origin
of the Family

The trouble with the origin of the family is that
no one really knows. Since [Friedrich] Engels
wrote *The Origin of the Family, Private Property and
the State* ... in 1884,* a great deal of new evidence has come in. Yet the gaps are still enormous.

Reprinted, with minor editorial changes, from *Journal of Marriage and the Family* (November 1971), pp. 760–71, with permission of the author and the publisher.

*EDITOR'S NOTE: The full original title of this volume is *Der
Ursprung der Familie, des Privateigenthums und des Staats. Im
Anschluss an Lewis H. Morgan's Forschungen* (Hottingen-Zurich,
1884). It is based on Lewis H. Morgan, *Ancient Society; Or,
Researches in the Lines of Human Progress from Savagery, through
Barbarism to Civilization* (New York, 1877). Ms. Gough has
consulted the English translation of the Engels work: *The
Origin of the Family, Private Property and the State in the Light of
the Researches of Lewis H. Morgan*, 4th ed. (New York and
London, 1942); this is the work referred to in her article as
"Morgan and Engels."

It is not known *when* the family originated, although it was probably between two million and 100,000 years ago. It is not known whether it developed once or in separate times and places. It is not known whether some kind of embryonic family came before, with, or after the origin of language. Since language is the accepted criterion of human-ness, this means that we do not even know whether our ancestors acquired the basics of family life before or after they were human. The chances are that language and the family developed together over a long period. But the evidence is sketchy.

Although the origin of the family is speculative, it is better to speculate with than without evidence. The evidence comes from three sources. One is the social and physical lives of non-human primates—especially the New and Old World monkeys and, still more, the great apes, humanity's closest relatives. The second source is the tools and home sites of prehistoric humans and proto-humans. The third is the family lives of hunters and gatherers of wild provender who have been studied in modern times.

Each of these sources is imperfect: monkeys and apes, because they are *not* pre-human ancestors, although they are our cousins; fossil hominids, because they left so little vestige of their social life; hunters and gatherers, because none of them has, in historic times, possessed a technology and society as primitive as those of early humans. All show the results of long endeavor in specialized, marginal environments. But together, these sources give valuable clues.

## DEFINING THE FAMILY

To discuss the origin of something we must first decide what it is. I shall define the family as "a married couple or other group of adult kinfolk who cooperate economically and in the upbringing of children, and all or most of whom share a common dwelling."

This includes all forms of kin-based household. Some are extended families containing three generations of married brothers or sisters. Some are "grand-families" descended from a single pair of grand-parents. Some are matrilineage households, in which brothers and sisters share a house with the sisters' children, and men merely visit their wives in other homes. Some are compound families, in which one man has several wives, or one woman, several husbands. Others are nuclear families composed of a father, mother and children.

Some kind of family exists in all known human societies, although it is not found in every segment or class of all stratified, state societies. Greek and American slaves, for example, were prevented from forming legal families, and their social families were often disrupted by sale, forced labor, or sexual exploitation. Even so, the family was an ideal which all classes and most people attained when they could.

The family implies several other universals. (1) Rules forbid sexual relations and marriage between close relatives. Which relatives are forbidden varies, but all [known] societies forbid mother-son mating, and most, father-daughter and brother-sister. Some societies allow sex relations, but forbid marriage, between certain degrees of kin. (2) The men and women of a family cooperate through a division of labor based on gender. Again, the sexual division of labor varies in rigidity and in the tasks performed. But in no human society to date is it wholly absent. Child-care, household tasks and crafts closely connected with the household, tend to be done by women; war, hunting, and government, by men. (3) Marriage exists as a socially recognized, durable, although not necessarily lifelong relationship between individual men and women. From it springs social fatherhood, some kind of special bond between a man and the child of his wife, whether or not they are his own children physiologically. Even in polyandrous societies, where women have several husbands, or in matrilineal societies, where group membership and property pass through women, each child has one or more designated "fathers" with whom he has a special social, and often religious, relationship. This bond of *social* fatherhood is recognized among people who do not know about the male role in procreation, or where, for various reasons, it is not clear who the physiological father of a particular infant is. Social fatherhood seems to come from the division and interdependence of male and female tasks, especially in relation to children, rather than directly from physiological fatherhood, although in most societies, the social father of a child is usually presumed to be its physiological father as well. Contrary to the beliefs of some feminists, however, I think that in no human society do men, as a whole category, have *only* the role of insemination, and *no* other social or economic role, in relation to women and children. (4) Men in general have higher status and authority over the women of their families, although older women may have influence, even some authority, over junior men. The omnipresence of male authority, too, goes contrary to the belief of some feminists that in "matriarchal" societies, women were either completely equal to, or had paramount authority over, men, either in the home or in society at large.

It is true that in some matrilineal societies, such as the Hopi of Arizona or the Ashanti of Ghana, men exert little authority over their wives. In some, such as the Nayars of South India or the Minangkabau of Sumatra, men may even live separately from their wives and children, that is, in different families. In such societies, however, the fact is that women and children fall under greater or lesser authority from the women's kinsmen—their eldest brothers, mothers' brothers, or even their grown up sons.

In matrilineal societies, where property, rank, office and group membership are inherited through the female line, it is true that women tend to have greater independence than in patrilineal societies. This is especially so in matrilineal tribal societies where the state has not yet developed, and especially in those tribal societies where residence is matrilocal—that is, men come to live in the homes or villages of their wives. Even so, in all matrilineal societies for which adequate descriptions are available, the ultimate headship of household, lineages, and local groups is usually with men.*

There is in fact no true "matriarchal" as distinct from "matrilineal," society in existence or known from literature, and the chances are that there never has been.† This does not mean that women and men never had relations that were dignified and creative for both sexes, appropriate to the knowledge, skills and technology of their times. Nor does it mean that the sexes cannot be equal in the future, or that the sexual division of labor cannot be abolished. I believe that it can and must be. But it is not necessary to believe myths of a feminist Golden Age in order to plan for parity in the future.

---

*See David M. Schneider and Kathleen Gough, eds., *Matrilineal Kinship* (Berkeley, Calif. 1961), for common and variant features of matrilineal systems.

†The Iroquois are often quoted as a "matriarchal" society, but in fact Morgan himself refers to "the absence of equality between the sexes" and notes that women were subordinate to men, ate after men, and that women (not men) were publicly whipped as punishment for adultery. Warleaders, tribal chiefs, and *sachems* (heads of matrilineal lineages) were men. Women did, however, have a large say in the government of the long-house or home of the matrilocal extended family, and women figured as tribal counsellors and religious officials, as well as in arranging marriages. (Lewis H. Morgan: The League of the *Ho-de-ne Sau-nee* or *Iroquois*, Human Relations Area Files, 1954).

## PRIMATE SOCIETIES

Within the primate order, humans are most closely related to the anthropoid apes (the African chimpanzee and gorilla and the Southeast Asian orang-utan and gibbon), and of these, to the chimpanzee and the gorilla. More distantly related are the Old, and then the New World, monkeys, and finally, the lemurs, tarsiers and treeshrews.

All primates share characteristics without which the family could not have developed. The young are born relatively helpless. They suckle for several months or years and need prolonged care afterwards. Childhood is longer, the closer the species is to humans. Most monkeys reach puberty at about four to five and mature socially between about five and ten. Chimpanzees, by contrast, suckle for up to three years. Females reach puberty at seven to ten; males enter mature social and sexual relations as late as thirteen. The long childhood and maternal care produce close relations between children of the same mother, who play together and help tend their juniors until they grow up.

Monkeys and apes, like humans, mate in all months of the year instead of in a rutting season. Unlike humans, however, female apes experience unusually strong sexual desire for a few days shortly before and during ovulation (the oestrus period), and have intensive sexual relations at that time. The males are attracted to the females by their scent or by brightly colored swellings in the sexual region. Oestrus-mating appears to be especially pronounced in primate species more remote from humans. The apes and some monkeys carry on less intensive, month-round sexuality in addition to oestrus-mating, approaching human patterns more closely. In humans, sexual desires and relations are regulated less by hormonal changes and more by mental images, emotions, cultural rules and individual preferences.

Year-round (if not always month-round) sexuality means that males and females socialize more continuously among primates than among most other mammals. All primates form bands or troops composed of both sexes plus children. The numbers and proportions of the sexes vary, and in some species an individual, a mother with her young, or a subsidiary troop of male juveniles may temporarily travel alone. But in general, males and females socialize continually through mutual grooming* and playing as well as through frequent sex relations. Keeping close to the females, primate males play with their children

---

*Combing the hair and removing parasites with hands or teeth.

and tend to protect both females and young from predators. A "division of labor" based on gender is thus already found in primate society between a female role of prolonged child care and a male role of defense. Males may also carry or take care of children briefly, and non-nursing females may fight. But a kind of generalized "fatherliness" appears in the protective role of adult males toward young, even in species where the sexes do not form long-term individual attachments.

## SEXUAL BONDS AMONG PRIMATES

Some non-human primates do have enduring sexual bonds and restrictions, superficially similar to those in some human societies. Among gibbons a single male and female live together with their young. The male drives off other males and the female, other females. When a juvenile reaches puberty it is thought to leave or be expelled by the parent of the same sex, and eventually find a mate elsewhere. Similar *de facto*, rudimentary "incest prohibitions" may have been passed on to humans from their prehuman ancestors and later codified and elaborated through language, moral custom and law. Whether this is so may become clearer when we know more about the mating patterns of the other great apes, especially of our closest relatives, the chimpanzees. Present evidence suggests that male chimpanzees do not mate with their mothers.

Orang-utans live in small, tree-dwelling groups like gibbons, but their forms are less regular. One or two mothers may wander alone with their young, mating at intervals with a male, or a male-female pair, or several juvenile males, may travel together.

Among mountain gorillas of Uganda, South Indian langurs, and hamadryas baboons of Ethiopia, a single, fully mature male mates with several females, especially in their oestrus periods. If younger adult males are present, the females may have occasional relations with them if the leader is tired or not looking.

Among East and South African baboons, rhesus macaques, and South American woolly monkeys, the troop is bigger, numbering up to two hundred. It contains a number of adult males and a much larger number of females. The males are strictly ranked in terms of dominance based on both physical strength and intelligence. The more dominant males copulate intensively with the females during the latter's oestrus periods. Toward the end of oestrus a female may briefly attach herself to a single dominant male. At other times she may have relations with any male of higher or lower rank provided that those of higher rank permit it.

Among some baboons and macaques the young males travel on the outskirts of the group and have little access to females. Some macaques expel from the troop a proportion of the young males, who then form "bachelor troops." Bachelors may later form new troops with young females.

Other primates are more thoroughly promiscuous, or rather indiscriminate, in mating. Chimpanzees, and also South American howler monkeys, live in loosely structured groups, again (as in most monkey and ape societies) with a preponderance of females. The mother-child unit is the only stable group. The sexes copulate almost at random, and most intensively and indiscriminately during oestrus.

A number of well-known anthropologists have argued that various attitudes and customs often found in human societies are instinctual rather than culturally learned, and come from our primate heritage. They include hierarchies of ranking among men, male political power over women, and the greater tendency of men to form friendships with one another, as opposed to women's tendencies to cling to a man.*

I cannot accept these conclusions and think that they stem from the male chauvinism of our own society. A "scientific" argument which states that all such features of female inferiority are instinctive is obviously a powerful weapon in maintaining the traditional family with male dominance. But in fact, these features are *not* universal among non-human primates, including some of the most closely related to humans. Chimpanzees have a low degree of male dominance and male hierarchy and are sexually virtually indiscriminate. Gibbons have a kind of fidelity for both sexes and almost no male dominance or hierarchy. Howler monkeys are sexually indiscriminate and lack male hierarchies or dominance.

The fact is that among non-human primates male dominance and male hierarchies seem to be adaptations to particular environments, some of which did become genetically established through natural selection. Among humans, however, these features are present in variable degrees and are almost certainly learned, not inherited at all.

---

*See, for example, Desmond Morris, *The Naked Ape*, [Dell, 1969]; Robin Fox, *Kinship and Marriage*, [Penguin, 1968]. [Editor's note: see also Lionel Tiger, *Men in Groups*, Random House, 1969.]

Among non-human primates there are fairly general differences between those that live mainly in trees and those that live largely on the ground. The tree dwellers (for example gibbons, orang-utans, South American howler and woolly monkeys) tend to have to defend themselves less against predators than do the ground-dwellers (such as baboons, macaques or gorillas). Where defense is important, males are much larger and stronger than females, exert dominance over females, and are strictly hierarchized and organized in relation to one another. Where defense is less important there is much less sexual dimorphism (difference in size between male and female), less or no male dominance, a less pronounced male hierarchy, and greater sexual indiscriminancy.

Comparatively speaking, humans have a rather small degree of sexual dimorphism, similar to [that found in] chimpanzees. Chimpanzees live much in trees but also partly on the ground, in forest or semi-forest habitats. They build individual nests to sleep in, sometimes on the ground but usually in trees. They flee into trees from danger. Chimpanzees go mainly on all fours, but sometimes on two feet, and can use and make simple tools. Males are dominant, but not very dominant, over females. The rank hierarchy among males is unstable, and males often move between groups, which vary in size from two to fifty individuals. Food is vegetarian, supplemented with worms, grubs, or occasional small animals. A mother and her young form the only stable unit. Sexual relations are largely indiscriminate, but nearby males defend young animals from danger. The chances are that our prehuman ancestors had a similar social life. Morgan and Engels were probably right in concluding that we came from a state of "original promiscuity" before we were fully human.

## HUMAN EVOLUTION

Judging from the fossil record, apes ancestral to humans, gorillas, and chimpanzees roamed widely in Asia, Europe, and Africa some twelve to twenty-eight million years ago. Toward the end of that period (the Miocene) one appears in North India and East Africa, Ramapithecus, who may be ancestral both to later hominids and to modern humans. His species were small like gibbons, walked upright on two feet, had human rather than ape corner-teeth, and therefore probably used hands rather than teeth to tear their food. From that time evolution toward humanness must have proceeded through various phases until the emergence of modern *Homo sapiens,* about 70,000 years ago.

In the Miocene period before Ramapithecus appeared, there were several time-spans in which, over large areas, the climate became drier and sub-tropical forests dwindled or disappeared. A standard reconstruction of events, which I accept, is that groups of apes, probably in Africa, had to come down from the trees and adapt to terrestrial life. Through natural selection, probably over millions of years, they developed specialized feet for walking. Thus freed, the hands came to be used not only (as among apes) for grasping and tearing, but for regular carrying of objects such as weapons (which had hitherto been sporadic) or of infants (which had hitherto clung to their mothers' body hair).

The spread of indigestible grasses on the open savannahs may have encouraged, if it did not compel, the early ground dwellers to become active hunters rather than to simply forage for small, sick, or dead animals that came their way. Collective hunting and tool use involved group cooperation and helped foster the growth of language out of the call-systems of apes. Language meant the use of symbols to refer to events not present. It allowed greatly increased foresight, memory, planning and division of tasks—in short, the capacity for human thought.

With the change to hunting, group territories became much larger. Apes range only a few thousand feet daily; hunters, several miles. But because their infants were helpless, nursing women could hunt only small game close to home. This then produced the sexual division of labor on which the human family has since been founded. Women elaborated upon ape methods of child care, and greatly expanded foraging, which in most areas remained the primary and most stable source of food. Men improved upon ape methods of fighting off other animals, and of group protection in general. They adapted these methods to hunting, using weapons which for millennia remained the same for the chase as for human warfare.

Out of the sexual division of labor came, for the first time, home life as well as group cooperation. Female apes nest with and provide foraged food for their infants. But adult apes do not cooperate in food getting or nest building. They build new nests each night wherever they may happen to be. With the development of a hunting-gathering complex, it became necessary to have a G.H.Q., or home. Men could bring meat to this place for several days' supply. Women and children could meet men there after the day's hunting, and could bring their vegetable produce for general consumption. Men, women, and children could build joint shelters, butcher meat, and treat skins for clothing.

Later, fire came into use for protection against wild animals, for lighting, and eventually for cooking. The hearth then provided the focus and symbol of home. With the development of cookery, some humans—chiefly women, and perhaps some children and old men— came to spend more time preparing nutrition so that all people need spend less time in chewing and tearing their food. Meals—already less frequent because of the change to a carnivorous diet—now became brief, periodic events instead of the long feeding sessions of apes.

The change to humanness brought two bodily changes that affected birth and child care. These were head-size and the width of the pelvis. Walking upright produced a narrower pelvis to hold the guts in position. Yet as language developed, brains and hence heads grew much bigger relative to body size. To compensate, humans are born at an earlier stage of growth than apes. They are helpless longer and require longer and more total care. This in turn caused early women to concentrate more on child care and less on defense than do female apes.

Language made possible not only a division and cooperation in labor but also all forms of tradition, rules, morality and cultural learning. Rules banning sex relations among close kinfolk must have come very early. Precisely how or why they developed is unknown, but they had at least two useful functions. They helped to preserve order in the family as a cooperative unit, by outlawing competition for mates. They also created bonds *between* families, or even between separate bands, and so provided a basis for wider cooperation in the struggle for livelihood and the expansion of knowledge.

It is not clear when all these changes took place. Climatic change with increased drought began regionally up to 28 million years ago. The divergence between pre-human and gorilla-chimpanzee stems had occurred in both Africa and India at least 12 million years ago. The pre-human stem led to the Australopithecenes of East and South Africa, about 1,750,000 years ago. These were pygmy-like, two-footed, upright hominids with larger-than-ape brains, who made tools and probably hunted in savannah regions. It is unlikely that they knew the use of fire.

The first known use of fire is that of the cave-dwelling hominids (Sinan-thropus, a branch of the Pithecanthropines) at Choukoutien near Peking, some half a million years ago during the second ice age. Fire was used regularly in hearths, suggesting cookery, by the time of the Acheulean and Mousterian cultures of Neanderthal man in Europe, Africa, and Asia before, during, and after the third ice age, some 150,000 to 100,000 years ago. These people, too, were often cave dwellers, and buried their dead ceremonially in caves. Cave-dwelling by night as well as by day was probably, in fact, not safe for humans until fire came into use to drive away predators.

Most anthropologists conclude that home life, the family, and lan-guage had developed by the time of Neanderthal man, who was closely similar and may have been ancestral to modern *Homo sapiens*. At least two anthropologists, however, believe that the Australopithecenes al-ready had language nearly two million years ago, while another thinks that language and incest prohibitions did not evolve until the time of *Homo sapiens* some 70,000 to 50,000 years ago.* I am myself inclined to think that family life built around tool use, the use of language, cookery, and a sexual division of labor, must have been established sometime between about 500,000 and 200,000 years ago.

## HUNTERS AND GATHERERS

Most of the hunting and gathering societies studied in the eighteenth to twentieth centuries had technologies similar to those that were wide-spread in the Mesolithic period, which occurred about 15,000 to 10,000 years ago, after the ice ages ended but before cultivation was invented and animals domesticated.

Modern hunters live in marginal forest, mountain, arctic, or desert environments where cultivation is impracticable. Although by no means "primeval," the hunters of recent times do offer clues to the types of family found during that 99 percent of human history before the agricultural revolution. They include the Eskimo, many Canadian and South American Indian groups, the forest BaMbuti (pygmies) and the desert Bushmen of Southern Africa, the Kadir of South India, the

---

*For the former view, see Charles F. Hockett and Robert Ascher, "The Human Revo-lution," in Yehudi A. Cohen, ed., *Man in Adaptation: The Biosocial Background*, Aldine, 1968; for the latter, Frank B. Livingstone, "Genetics, Ecology and the Origin of Incest and Exogamy," *Current Anthropology*, February 1969.

Veddah of Ceylon, and the Andaman Islanders of the Indian Ocean. About 175 hunting and gathering cultures in Oceania, Asia, Africa, and America have been described in fair detail.

In spite of their varied environments, hunters share certain features of social life. They live in bands of about 20 to 200 people, the majority of bands having fewer than 50. Bands are divided into families, which may forage alone in some seasons. Hunters have simple but ingenious technologies. Bows and arrows, spears, needles, skin clothing, and temporary leaf or wood shelters are common. Most hunters do some fishing. The band forages and hunts in a large territory and usually moves camp often.

Social life is egalitarian. There is of course no state, nor organized government. Apart from religious shamans or magicians, the division of labor is based only on sex and age. Resources are owned communally; tools and personal possessions are freely exchanged. Everyone works who can. Band leadership goes to whichever man has the intelligence, courage, and foresight to command the respect of his fellows. Intelligent older women are also looked up to.

The household is the main unit of economic cooperation, with the men, women, and children dividing the labor and pooling their produce. In 97 percent of the 175 societies classified by G. P. Murdock, hunting is confined to men; in the other three percent it is chiefly a male pursuit. Gathering of wild plants, fruits and nuts is women's work. In 60 percent of societies, only women gather, while in another 32 percent gathering is mainly feminine. Fishing is solely or mainly men's work in 93 percent of the hunting societies where it occurs.

For the rest, men monopolize fighting, although interband warfare is rare. Women tend children and shelters and usually do most of the cooking, processing, and storage of food. Women tend also to be foremost in the early household crafts such as basketry, leather work, the making of skin or bark clothing, and in the more advanced hunting societies, pottery. (Considering that women probably *invented* all of these crafts, in addition to cookery, food storage and preservation, agriculture, spinning, weaving, and perhaps even house construction, it is clear that women played quite as important roles as men in early cultural development.) Building dwellings and making tools and ornaments are variously divided between the sexes, while boat-building is largely done by men. Girls help the women, and boys play at hunting or hunt small game until they reach puberty, when both take on the roles of adults. Where the environment makes it desirable, the men of a whole band or of some smaller cluster of households cooperate in hunting or fishing and divide their spoils. Women of nearby families often go gathering together.

Family composition varies among hunters as it does in other kinds of societies. About half or more of known hunting societies have nuclear families (father, mother and children), with polygynous households (a man, two or more wives, and children) as occasional variants. Clearly, nuclear families are the most common among hunters, although hunters have a slightly higher proportion of polygynous families than do non-hunting societies.

About a third of hunting societies contain some "stem-family" households—that is, older parents live together with one married child and grandchildren, while the other married children live in independent dwellings. A still smaller proportion live in large extended families containing several married brothers (or several married sisters), their spouses, and children.* Hunters have fewer extended and stem families than do non-hunting societies. These larger households become common with the rise of agriculture. They are especially found in large, pre-industrial agrarian states such as ancient Greece, Rome, India, the Islamic empires, China, etc.

Hunting societies also have few households composed of a widow or divorcee and her children. This is understandable, for neither men nor women can survive long without the work and produce of the other sex, and marriage is the way to obtain them. That is why so often young men must show proof of hunting prowess, and girls of cooking, before they are allowed to marry.

The family, together with territorial grouping, provides the framework of society among hunters. Indeed, as Morgan and Engels clearly saw, kinship and territory are the foundations of all societies before the rise of the state. Not only hunting and gathering bands, but the larger and more complex tribes and chiefdoms of primitive cul-

---

*For exact figures, see G. P. Murdock, *World Ethnographic Sample,* American Anthropologist, 1957; Allan D. Coult, *Cross Tabulations of Murdock's World Ethnographic Sample,* University of Missouri, 1965; and G. P. Murdock, *Ethnographic Atlas,* University of Pittsburgh, 1967. In the last-named survey, out of 175 hunting societies, 47 percent had nuclear family households, 38 percent had stem families, and 14 percent had extended families.

tivators and herders organize people through descent from common ancestors or through marriage ties between groups. Among hunters, things are simple. There is only the family, and beyond it the band. With the domestication of plants and animals, the economy becomes more productive. More people can live together. Tribes form, containing several thousand people loosely organized into large kin-groups such as clans and lineages, each composed of a number of related families. With still further development of the productive forces the society throws up a central political leadership, together with craft specialization and trade, and so the chiefdom emerges. But this, too, is structured through ranked allegiances and marriage ties between kin groups.

Only with the rise of the state does class, independently of kinship, provide the basis for relations of production, distribution, and power. Even then, kin groups remain large in the agrarian state and kinship persists as the prime organizing principle within each class until the rise of capitalism. The reduction in significance of the family that we see today is the outgrowth of a decline in the importance of "familism" relative to other institutions, that began with the rise of the state but became speeded up with the development of capitalism and machine industry. In most modern socialist societies, the family is even less significant as an organizing principle. It is reasonable to suppose that in the future it will become minimal or may disappear at least as a legally constituted unit for exclusive forms of sexual and economic cooperation and of child-care.

Morgan and Engels (1942) thought that from a state of original promiscuity, early humans at first banned sex relations between the generations of parents and children, but continued to allow them indiscriminately between brothers, sisters and all kinds of cousins within the band. They called this the "consanguineal family." They thought that later, all mating within the family or some larger kin group became forbidden, but that there was a stage (the "punaluan") in which a group of sisters or other close kinswomen from one band were married jointly to a group of brothers or other close kinsmen from another. They thought that only later still, and especially with the domestication of plants and animals, did the "pairing family" develop in which each man was married to one or two women individually.

These writers drew their conclusions not from evidence of actual group marriage among primitive peoples but from the kinship terms found today in certain tribal and chiefly societies. Some of these equate all kin of the same sex in the parents' generation, suggesting brother-sister marriage. Others equate the father's brothers with the father, and the mother's sisters with the mother, suggesting the marriage of a group of brothers with a group of sisters.

Modern evidence does not bear out these conclusions about early society. All known hunters and gatherers live in families, not in communal sexual arrangements. Most hunters even live in nuclear families rather than in large extended kin groups. Mating is individualized, although one man may occasionally have two wives, or (very rarely) a woman may have two husbands. Economic life is built primarily around the division of labor and partnership between individual men and women. The hearths, caves and other remains of Upper Palaeolithic hunters suggest that this was probably an early arrangement. We cannot say that Engels' sequences are completely ruled out for very early hominids—the evidence is simply not available. But it is hard to see what economic arrangements among hunters would give rise to group rather than individual or "pairing" marriage arrangements, and this Engels does not explain.

Soviet anthropologists continued to believe in Morgan and Engels' early "stages" longer than did anthropologists in the West. Today, most Russian anthropologists admit the lack of evidence for "consanguineal" and "punaluan" arrangements, but some still believe that a different kind of group marriage intervened between indiscriminate mating and the pairing family. Semyonov, for example, argues that in the stage of group marriage, mating was forbidden within the hunting band, but that the men of two neighboring bands had multiple, visiting sex relations with women of the opposite band.*

While such an arrangement cannot be ruled out, it seems unlikely because many of the customs which Semyonov regards as "survivals" of such group marriage (for example, visiting husbands, matrilineage dwelling groups, widespread clans, multiple spouses for both sexes, men's and women's communal houses, and prohibitions of sexual intercourse inside the huts of the village) are actually found not so much among hunters as among horticultural tribes, and even quite

---

*Y. I. Semyonov, "Group Marriage, Its Nature and Role in the Evolution of Marriage and Family Relations," *Seventh International Congress of Anthropological and Ethnological Sciences*, vol. 4, Moscow, 1967.

complex agricultural states. Whether or not such a stage of group marriage occurred in the earliest societies, there seems little doubt that pairing marriage (involving family households) came about with the development of elaborate methods of hunting, cooking, and the preparation of clothing and shelters—that is, with a fully fledged division of labor.

Even so, there *are* some senses in which mating among hunters has more of a group character than in archaic agrarian states or in capitalist society. Murdock's sample shows that sex relations before marriage are strictly prohibited in only 26 percent of hunting societies. In the rest, marriage is either arranged so early that pre-marital sex is unlikely, or (more usually) sex relations are permitted more or less freely before marriage.

With marriage, monogamy is the normal *practice* at any given time for most hunters, but it is not the normal *rule*. Only 19 percent in Murdock's survey prohibit plural unions. Where polygyny is found (79 percent) the most common type is for a man to marry two sisters or other closely related women of the same kin group—for example, the daughters of two sisters or of two brothers. When a woman dies it is common for a sister to replace her in the marriage, and when a man dies, for a brother to replace him.

Similarly, many hunting societies hold that the wives of brothers or other close kinsmen are in some senses wives of the group. They can be called on in emergencies [times of illness]. Again, many hunting societies have special times for sexual license between men and women of a local group who are not married to each other, such as the "lights out" games of Eskimos sharing a communal snow-house. In other situations, an Eskimo wife will spend the night with a chance guest of her husband's. All parties expect this as normal hospitality. Finally, adultery, although often punished, tends to be common in hunting societies, and few if any of them forbid divorce or the remarriage of divorcees and widows.

The reason for all this seems to be that marriage and sexual restrictions are practical arrangements among hunters designed mainly to serve economic and survival needs. In these societies, some kind of rather stable pairing best accomplishes the division of labor and cooperation of men and women and the care of children. Beyond the immediate family, either a larger family group or the whole band has other, less intensive but important, kinds of cooperative activities.

Therefore, the husbands and wives of individuals within that group can be summoned to stand in for each other if need arises. In the case of Eskimo wife-lending, the extreme climate and the need for lone wandering in search of game dictate high standards of hospitality. This evidently becomes extended to sexual sharing.

In the case of sororal polygyny or marriage to the dead wife's sister, it is natural that when two women fill the same role—either together or in sequence—they should be sisters, for sisters are more alike than other women. They are likely to care more for each other's children. The replacement of a dead spouse by a sister or a brother also preserves existing intergroup relations. For the rest, where the economic and survival bonds of marriage are not at stake, people can afford to be freely companionate and tolerant. Hence pre-marital sexual freedom, seasonal group license, and a pragmatic approach to adultry.

Marriages among hunters are usually arranged by elders when a young couple are ready for adult responsibilities. But the couple know each other and usually have some choice. If the first marriage does not work, the second mate will almost certainly be self-selected. Both sexual and companionate love between individual men and women are known and are deeply experienced. With comparative freedom of mating, love is often less separated from or opposed to marriage than in archaic states or even in some modern nations.

## THE POSITION OF WOMEN

Even in hunting societies it seems that women are always in some sense the "second sex," with greater or less subordination to men. This varies. Eskimo and Australian aboriginal women are far more subordinate than women among the Kadar, the Andamanese or the Congo Pygmies—all forest people.

I suggest that women have greater power and independence among hunters when they are important food-obtainers than when they are mainly processors of meat or other supplies provided by men. The former situation is likelier to exist in societies where hunting is small-scale and intensive than where it is extensive over a large terrain, and in societies where gathering is important by comparison with hunting.

In general in hunting societies, however, women are less subordinated in certain crucial respects than they are in most, if not all, of the archaic states, or even in some capitalist nations. These respects include men's ability to deny women sexuality or to force it upon them; to command or exploit their labor or to control their produce; to control or rob them of their children; to confine them physically and prevent their movement; to use them as objects in male transactions; to cramp their creativeness; or to withhold from them large areas of the society's knowledge and cultural attainments.

Especially lacking in hunting societies is the kind of male possessiveness and exclusiveness regarding women that leads to such institutions as savage punishments or death for female adultery, the jealous guarding of female chastity and virginity, the denial of divorce to women, or the ban on a woman's remarriage after her husband's death.

For these reasons, I do not think we can speak, as some writers do, of a class division between men and women in hunting societies. True, men are more mobile than women and they lead in public affairs. But class society requires that one class control the means of production, dictate its use by the other classes, and expropriate the surplus. These conditions do not exist among hunters. Land and other resources are held communally, although women may monopolize certain gathering areas, and men, their hunting grounds. There is rank difference, role difference, and some difference respecting degreees of authority, beteen the sexes, but there is reciprocity rather than domination or exploitation.

As Engels saw, the power of men to exploit women systematically springs from the existence of surplus wealth, and more directly, from the state, social stratification, and the control of property by men. With the rise of the state, because of their monopoly over weapons, and because freedom from child-care allows them to enter specialized economic and political roles, some men—especially ruling-class men—acquire power over other men and over women. Almost all men acquire it over women of their own or lower classes, especially within their own kinship groups. These kinds of male power are shadowy among hunters.

To the extent that men *have* power over women in hunting societies, this seems to spring from the male monopoly of heavy weapons, from the particular division of labor between the sexes, or both. Although men seldom use weapons against women, they *possess* them (or possess superior weapons) in addition to their physical strength. This does give men an ultimate control of force. When old people or babies must be killed to ensure band or family survival, it is usually men who kill them.

Infanticide—rather common among hunters, who must limit the mouths to feed—is more often female infanticide than male.

The hunting of men seems more often to require them to organize in groups than does the work of women. Perhaps because of this, about 60 percent of hunting societies have predominantly virilocal residence. That is, men choose which band to live in (often, their fathers'), and women move with their husbands. This gives a man advantages over his wife in terms of familiarity and loyalties, for the wife is often a stranger. Sixteen to 17 percent of hunting societies are, however, uxorilocal, with men moving to the households of their wives, while 15 to 17 percent are bilocal—that is, either sex may move in with the other on marriage.

Probably because of male cooperation in defense and hunting, men are more prominent in band councils and leadership, in medicine and magic, and in public rituals designed to increase game, to ward off sickness, or to initiate boys into manhood. Women do, however, often take part in band councils; they are not excluded from law and government as in many agrarian states. Some women are respected as wise leaders, story tellers, doctors, or magicians, or are feared as witches. Women have their own ceremonies of fertility, birth, and healing, from which men are often excluded.

In some societies, although men control the most sacred objects, women are believed to have discovered them. Among the Congo Pygmies, religion centers about a beneficent spirit, the Animal of the Forest. It is represented by wooden trumpets that are owned and played by men. Their possession and use are hidden from the women and they are played at night when hunting is bad, someone falls ill, or death occurs. During the playing men dance in the public campfire, which is sacred and is associated with the forest. Yet the men believe that women originally owned the trumpet and that it was a woman who stole fire from the chimpanzees or from the forest spirit. When a woman has failed to bear children for several years, a special ceremony is held. Women lead in the songs that usually accompany the trumpets, and an old woman kicks apart the campfire. Temporary female dominance seems to be thought necessary to restore fertility.

In some hunting societies women are exchanged between local groups, which are thus knit together through marriages. Sometimes, men of different bands directly exchange their sisters. More often there is a generalized exchange of women between two or more groups, or a one-way movement of women within a circle of groups. Sometimes the husband's family pays weapons, tools or ornaments to the wife's in return for the wife's services and later, her children.

In such societies, although they may be well treated and their consent sought, women are clearly the moveable partners in an arrangement controlled by men. Male anthropologists have seized on this as evidence of original male dominance and patrilocal residence Fox and others, for example, have argued that until recently, *all* hunting societies formed out-marrying patrilocal bands, linked together polically by the exchange of women. The fact that fewer than two-thirds of hunting societies are patrilocal today, and only 41 percent have band exogamy, is explained in terms of modern conquest, economic change and depopulation.

I cannot accept this formula. It is true that modern hunting societies have been severely changed, de-cultured, and often depopulated, by capitalist imperialism. I can see little evidence, however, that the ones that are patrilocal today have undergone less change than those that are not. It is hard to believe that in spite of enormous environmental diversity and the passage of thousands, perhaps millions, of years, hunting societies all had band exogamy with patrilocal residence until they were disturbed by western imperialism. It is more likely that early band societies, like later agricultural tribes, developed variety in family life and the status of women as they spread over the earth.

There is also some likelihood that the earliest hunters had matrilocal rather than patrilocal families. Among apes and monkeys, it is almost always males who leave the troop or are driven out. Females stay closer to their mothers and their original site; males move about, attaching themselves to females where availability and competition permit. Removal of the wife to the husband's home or band may have been a relatively late development in societies where male cooperation in hunting assumed overwhelming importance.* Conversely, after the development of horticulture (which was probably invented and is

---

*Upper Paleolithic hunters produced female figurines that were obvious emblems of fertility. The cult continued through the Mesolithic and into the Neolithic period. Goddesses and spirits of fertility are found in some patrilineal as well as matrilineal societies, but they tend to be more prominent in the latter. It is thus possible that in many areas even late Stone Age hunters had matrilocal residence and perhaps matrilineal descent, and that in some regions this pattern continued through the age of horticulture and even—as in the case of the Nayars of Kerola and the Minangkabau of Sumatra—into the age of plow agriculture, of writing, and of the small-scale state.

mainly carried out by women), those tribes in which horticulture predominated over stock-raising were most likely to be or to remain matrilocal and to develop matrilineal descent groups with a relatively high status of women. But where extensive hunting of large animals, or later, the herding of large domesticates, predominated, patrilocal residence flourished and women were used to form alliances between male-centered groups. With the invention of metallurgy and of agriculture as distinct from horticulture after 4000 B.C., men came to control agriculture and many crafts, and most of the great agrarian states had patrilocal residence with patriarchal, male-dominated families.

## CONCLUSIONS

The family is a human institution, not found in its totality in any pre-human species. It required language, planning, cooperation, self-control, foresight, and cultural learning, and probably developed along with these.

The family was made desirable by the early human combination of prolonged child-care with the need for hunting with weapons over large terrains. The sexual division of labor on which it was based grew out of a rudimentary pre-human division between male defense and female child care. But among humans this sexual division of functions for the first time became crucial for food production and so laid the basis for future economic specialization and cooperation.

Morgan and Engels were probably right in thinking that the human family was preceded by sexual indiscriminacy. They were also right in seeing an egalitarian group-quality about early economic and marriage arrangements. They were without evidence, however, in believing that the earliest mating and economic patterns were entirely group relations.

Together with extensive tool use and language, the family was no doubt the most significant invention of the human revolution. All three required reflective thought, which above all accounts for the vast superiority in consciousness that separates humans from apes.

The family provided the framework for all pre-state society and the fount of its creativeness. In groping for survival and for knowledge, human beings learned to control their sexual desires and to suppress their individual selfishness, aggression, and competition. The other side of this self-control was an increased capacity for love—not only the love of a mother for her child, which is seen among apes, but of male for female in enduring relationships, and of each sex for ever-widening groups of humans. Civilization would have been impossible without this initial self-control, seen in incest prohibitions and in the generosity and moral orderliness of primitive family life.

From the start, women have been subordinate to men in certain key areas of status, mobility and public leadership. But before the agricultural revolution, and even for several thousands of years thereafter, the inequality was based chiefly on the unalterable fact of prolonged child-care combined with the exigencies of primitive technology. The extent of inequality varied according to the ecology and the resulting sexual division of tasks. But in any case it was largely a matter of survival rather than of man-made cultural impositions. Hence the impressions we receive of dignity, freedom, and mutual respect between men and women in primitive hunting and horticultural societies. This is true whether these societies are patrilocal, bilocal, or matrilocal, although matrilocal societies, with matrilineal inheritance, offer greater freedom to women than do patrilocal and patrilineal societies of the same level of productivity and political development.

A distinct change occurred with the growth of individual and family property in herds, in durable craft objects and trade objects, and in stable, irrigated farm-sites or other forms of heritable wealth. This crystallized in the rise of the state, about 4000 B.C. With the growth of class society and of male dominance in the ruling class of the state, women's subordination increased, and eventually reached its depths in the patriarchal families of the great agrarian states.

Knowledge of how the family arose is interesting to women because it tells us how we differ from pre-humans, what our past has been, and what have been the biological and cultural limitations from which we are emerging. It shows us how generations of male scholars have distorted or over-interpreted the evidence to bolster beliefs in the inferiority of women's mental processes—for which there is no foundation in fact. Knowing about early families is also important to correct a reverse bias among some feminist writers, who hold that in "matriarchal" societies women were completely equal with or were even dominant over men. For this, too, there seems to be no basis in evidence.

The past of the family does not limit its future. Although the family probably emerged with humanity, neither the family itself nor particular family forms are genetically determined. The sexual division of labor—until recently, universal—need not, and in my opinion should not, survive in industrial society. Prolonged child-care ceases to be a basis for female subordination when artificial birth control, spaced births, small families, patent feeding and communal nurseries allow it to be shared by men. Automation and cybernation remove most of the heavy work for which women are less well equipped than men. The exploitation of women that came with the rise of the state and of class society will presumably disappear in post-state, classless society—for which the technological and scientific basis already exists.

The family was essential to the dawn of civilization, allowing a vast qualitative leap forward in cooperation, purposive knowledge, love, and creativeness. But today the confinement of women in homes and small families—like their subordination in work—artificially limits these human capacities [rather than enhancing them]. It may be that the human gift for personal love will make some form of voluntary, long-term mating and of individual devotion between parents and children continue indefinitely, side by side with public responsibility for domestic tasks and for the care and upbringing of children. There is no need to legislate personal relations out of existence. But neither need we fear a social life in which the family is no more.

# Letitia Anne Peplau*

## Power in Dating Relationships

Americans are sentimental about love. In thinking about romance, we emphasize intimacy and caring; we like to view our lover and the relationship as unique. We deemphasize the part that cultural values and social roles play in determining whom we love and how we conduct ourselves with them.[1] In particular we neglect a crucial aspect of love relationships—power. This paper investigates that facet of romance and how traditional sex roles often tip the balance of power in favor of men.

The traditional formula for dating relationships has two basic themes. First, the man is expected to take the initiative. He asks the woman out, plans activities, provides transportation, and pays the bills. Second, our society's concept of "male superiority" dictates that a woman should

---

*This paper is based on a large-scale research project directed by Zick Rubin in collaboration with Charles T. Hill and the author.

"look up" to the significant man in her life, a stance that is facilitated by his usually being taller, older, and more sophisticated.[2] Feminists have severely criticized this viewpoint. In *Sexual Politics*,[3] Kate Millet argues that patriarchal norms are pervasive and insidious. While male domination may be seen most easily in business, education, religion, or politics, it also extends to personal relationships between the sexes. The family helps perpetuate the power imbalance by teaching children to accept the superior status of men.

In Millet's analysis, romantic love does not elevate the status of women. Rather, the ideology of love hides the reality of women's subordination and economic dependence on men. As television commercials readily illustrate, "love" can be used for the emotional manipulation of women. It is "love" that justifies household drudgery, as well as deference to men. Thus, true equality would require basic changes in the intimate relationships of women and men.

Although traditional views of romantic relationships are under attack, proponents of the old pattern remain strong. A striking example is provided by Helen Andelin, author of *Fascinating Womanhood*[4] and an advocate of a benevolent form of male dominance. In her book and in classes on Fascinating Womanhood around the country, Andelin urges women to accept and enjoy traditional sex roles. Male leadership is a key element.

According to Andelin, women should defer to men and take pleasure in being cared for. The man is "the undisputed head of the family." The woman has a "submissive role, a supporting role and sometimes an active role. . . . But, first she must accept him as her leader, support and obey him."[5] The popularity of *Fascinating Womanhood* indicates that many women endorse this traditional view.

Young couples today are confronted with alternative models for power in romantic relationships. Traditional sex roles prescribe that the man should take the lead. But contemporary thinking favors a more equal balance of power. The research reported in this paper explores the attitudes of a diverse group of student couples about power and assesses the balance of power in each couple's relationship. It also examines factors that affected whether or not couples actually achieved equal power in their relationship.[6]

## THE EGALITARIAN IDEAL

The college students in our sample were staunch supporters of an egalitarian balance of power. When we asked, "Who do you think should have more say about your relationship, your partner or you?", 95 percent of women and 87 percent of men indicated that dating partners should have "exactly equal say." While male dominance may once have been the favored pattern of male-female relations, it was overwhelmingly rejected by the students in this study. It is possible that some students gave the answer they considered socially desirable, rather than their own true opinion. In either case, however, responses indicated a striking change in the type of male-female relationship considered appropriate.

Although students advocated equality, they seldom reported having grown up in an egalitarian family. As one student explained,

> When I was growing up, my father was the Supreme Court in our family. He ran the show. My relationship with Betsy is very different, very egalitarian. We try to discuss things and reach consensus. And that's the way I think it should be.

Only 18 percent of students reported that their parents shared equally in power. A 53 percent majority indicated that the father had more say; the remaining 29 percent reported that the mother had more say. Our data indicated that college students were seeking a different type of relationship from the model set by their parents. A key question was whether those student couples would be successful in achieving the equal-power relationship they desired.

## ASSESSING THE BALANCE OF POWER

Although the word "power" suggests a phenomenon that is obvious and easy to study, this is not the case.[7] Power is often elusive, especially in close relationships. Consider a woman who appears to dominate her boyfriend by deciding what to do on dates, determining which friends the couple sees, and even selecting the boyfriend's new clothes. Is it reasonable to infer that she has a good deal of power in the relationship? Not necessarily. Further investigation might reveal that her boyfriend, a busy pre-med student, disdains such "trivial" matters, and cheerfully delegates decision-making in these areas to his girlfriend. Additionally, he may retain veto power on all decisions, but rarely exercise it because his girlfriend scrupulously caters to his preferences. In this instance, greater power may actually reside with the man, who delegates responsibility, rather than with the woman, who merely implements his preferences.[8]

Power—one person's ability to influence the behavior of another—cannot be directly observed, but must be inferred from actual behavior. The context in which an action occurs and the intentions of the participants largely determine the meaning of the act. Especially in close personal relationships, judgments about power may be difficult to make. In order to assess power in our couples, we asked very general questions about the overall balance of power, as well as more specific questions about particular situations and events.

Despite their support for equality, only 49 percent of the women and 42 percent of the men reported equal power. When the relationship was unequal, it was usually the man who had more say About 45 percent of the men and 35 percent of the women reported that the man had more say, compared to 13 percent and 17 percent respectively who said the woman had more say. Clearly, the relationships these students had were often more traditional than the ideals they espoused.

In answer to more specific questions about power, a similar pattern emerged. Students were asked which partner had more say in five important areas of their relationship: recreation, conversation, sexual activity, amount of time spent together, and activities with other people. In each of these areas, fewer than half the students reported equal power.

More specific questions about hypothetical situations supported these data. For instance, the couple wants to go to a movie, but disagrees about which film to see. About one-third of the students reported that they as a couple would do what the man wanted, one-third what the woman wanted, and one-third were uncertain.

A second situation involved whose friends to go out with:

> You and (      ) are trying to decide how you as a couple will spend the weekend. You really want the two of you to go out with some of your friends, but (      ) wants just as strongly for the two of you to go out with some of his/her friends. Obviously you can't go out with both sets of friends at once. Whom do you as a couple decide to go out with?

Answers to this question showed an interesting sex difference. Half the women were sure that the couple would go out with the man's friends; only 13 percent thought they would go out with their own friends. In contrast, half of the men were undecided about what would happen; 25 percent thought they would go out with the man's friends, and the other 25 percent thought they would go out with the woman's friends. Thus women more often predict a traditional pattern in which the man determines whom the couple sees. Men reflect greater uncertainty, and are equally likely to believe that the man or woman would decide.

Our data also suggested that women may exercise major influence over whether the couple has sexual intercourse or not. At the time of our first questionnaire, slightly over 40 couples were not having intercourse with each other. The major reason given for this was that the woman preferred not to. Further, when we compared women who were not having intercourse to those who were, we found that the no-intercourse women were twice as likely to describe themselves as having greater overall power in the relationship and less likely to report male power.

Many students told us that the simplistic alternatives we offered (e.g., do what he wants versus do what she wants) did not adequately describe their own behavior. Some said they would compromise about which movie to see; others indicated they would take turns, seeing one movie this week and another next week. In some instances, students said they would take other factors into account, such as their partner's mood, or which partner had most recently had their own way about something else. No one decision or event provides a clear indication of the balance of power. As expected, however, people's overall assessment of the balance of power was significantly related to their reports of power in specific situations.

In summary, we have found that fewer than half the student couples in our study believed they had achieved an equal-power relationship. This was true both for a measure of general power, and for reports of power in particular areas. On balance, one person is seen as having greater overall influence in over half the couples in our study.

## TIPPING THE BALANCE OF POWER

Why is it that students who want to have an egalitarian relationship are not successful in achieving one? Our analyses indicated several important factors that affected the balance of power in dating relationships: sex-role attitudes, unequal involvement and personal resources, and the woman's career aspirations.

### Sex-role attitudes

While most students endorsed an ideal of equal power, they varied considerably in their more general attitudes about proper behavior for

**Balance of Power for Traditional, Moderate, and Liberal Couples**

| | Woman's report | | | Man's report | | |
| --- | --- | --- | --- | --- | --- | --- |
| | Man more | Equal | Woman more | Man more | Equal | Woman more |
| Traditionals (72 couples) | 43% | 47% | 10% | 59% | 31% | 10% |
| Moderates (73 couples) | 37 | 45 | 18 | 51 | 34 | 15 |
| Liberals (76 couples) | 24 | 51 | 25 | 25 | 62 | 13 |

men and women. Our questionnaire included a ten-item Sex-Role Attitude Scale. Students indicated their agreement or disagreement with such statements as, "If a couple is going somewhere by car, it's better for the man to do most of the driving" and "If both husband and wife work full time, her career should be just as important as his in determining where the family lives." Responses indicated that some students took staunchly traditional positions, others endorsed strongly feminist positions, and many fell somewhere in between. Dating partners generally held similar attitudes; it was unusual to find an ardent traditionalist dating a feminist partner.

While traditional sex-role attitudes were often associated with unequal relationships, there were important exceptions. For example, over one-third of the most traditional couples reported equal power, as Paul and Peggy illustrate. For them, power was not a prominent issue. While Peggy was considered the expert on cooking and social skills, Paul made decisions about what to do on dates. They divided responsibilities in a traditional way, but believed that overall they had equal power. Nor did all nontraditional couples have equal-power relationships; about 25 percent reported that the man had more say.

In summary, sex-role attitudes often have an important impact on the balance of power in dating relationships. Believing that men and women can perform similar tasks, acknowledging that the woman's career is as important as the man's, and other nontraditional attitudes can foster an equal-power relationship. At the same time, it is also likely that having an egalitarian relationship encourages nontraditional sex-role attitudes. The relationship between these factors can work both ways.

## Imbalance of involvement and resources

Social-psychological theory[9] suggests that power in a couple is affected by each partner's dependence on the relationship. One partner may be passionately in love while the other partner has only a lukewarm interest in the relationship. Such imbalances of involvement are likely to affect the balance of power. Sociologist Willard Waller described this phenomenon as the "principle of least interest," which predicts that the person who is least involved or interested in a relationship will have greater influence. The more involved person, eager to maintain the relationship, will defer to the partner's wishes. Thus the less interested partner is better able to set the terms of the relationship and exert control. Being deeply in love is a wonderful experience. But unless love and commitment are reciprocated, they make a person vulnerable to their partner's influence.

Our questionnaire contained several measures of love and involvement. One question asked straightforwardly, "Who do you think is more involved in your relationship—your partner or you?" Less than half the students reported that their relationship was equal in involvement.

|  | Woman's report | Man's report |
|---|---|---|
| Equal involvement | 48% | 43% |
| Man more involved | 28 | 15 |
| Woman more involved | 24 | 42 |

The "principle of least interest" was strongly supported by our data. In couples where the man was the least involved, it was most common for the man to have more power. In contrast, when the woman was the least involved, nearly half the couples reported that the woman had greater power.

| | Relative involvement | | |
|---|---|---|---|
| Relative power | Woman less involved (60 couples) | Equal (57 couples) | Man less involved (100 couples) |
|---|---|---|---|
| Man more say | 23% | 54% | 70% |
| Equal say | 28 | 20 | 20 |
| Woman more say | 49 | 26 | 10 |

Attraction to a partner and involvement in a relationship are affected by many factors. The degree to which we find our partner highly desirable and rewarding is very important, as is our assessment of the possible alternative relationships available to both of us. If our present partner is more desirable than the available alternatives, our attraction should remain high. Thus such personal resources as physical attractiveness, social skills, prestige, or money affect the balance of power.

Findings concerning physical attractiveness and alternative dating partners illustrate the pattern we found. Although we may like to think that inner qualities are more important than physical appearance, there is ample evidence that beauty can be a valuable resource in interpersonal relations.[10] As part of our study, we took full-length color photos of each participant, and then had these rated on physical attractiveness by a panel of student judges. As predicted, if one person was judged more attractive, she or he was likely to have more say in the relationship.

The more options a person has about alternative dating relationships, the less dependent he or she is on a single partner. We asked students whether they had either dated or had sexual intercourse with someone other than their partner during the past two months. We also inquired if there was a "specific other" they could be dating at present. For both men and women, having dating alternatives was related to having greater power in the current relationship.

Our analysis suggests that a possible way to increase one's relative power in a relationship is to acquire new personal resources or greater options. This message is conveyed, in highly different forms, by both *Fascinating Womanhood* and the Women's Movement. *Fascinating Womanhood* promises women a happier marriage by learning to be more "feminine." Women are encouraged to pay greater attention to their husband, improve their appearance, become better cooks, learn to be more sexually attractive and, in general, improve their "feminine" skills. By increasing her own desirability, the woman may indirectly increase her husband's interest in their relationship. As a result, the husband may be more willing to defer to his wife's wishes and concerns. While endorsing a pattern of male leadership and control, *Fascinating Womanhood* nonetheless suggests ways for women to work within the traditional pattern to achieve their own goals.

Contemporary feminists have rejected inequality between the sexes, and encouraged women to become less dependent on men. This can be achieved by developing closer relationships with other women, and by learning new skills, especially "masculine" skills such as car repair or plumbing. Greatest emphasis has been given to women's gaining financial independence through paid employment. In the next section, data from our study bearing on the impact of women's careers on power in dating relationships will be presented.

### Women's career goals

It is traditionally common for men to divide their interest and energy between personal relationships and work. For women, in contrast, a family and a career have often been viewed as incompatible goals. Typically, women have given far higher priority to personal and family relationships than to paid employment. Many of the college students in our study rejected the idea that the "woman's place" is in the home; both men and women expressed more favorable attitudes toward careers for women. What impact does this have on power in male-female relationships?

Fulltime paid employment makes women more similar to men in several ways. Work provides women with additional skills and expertise, with important interests outside the relationship, and with additional resources such as income or prestige. For all these reasons, it seems likely that a woman's employment might affect power in a dating relationship.

Leonard and Felicia, two of our participants, illustrate this effect. They met and were married in college, where both majored in music. The couple agrees that while Felicia is a competent musician, Leonard is a musical genius on his way to becoming a famous composer. After college, Felicia took a job as a music teacher to put her husband through graduate school. She acknowledged his superior ability, and was willing to support his career by working. But she viewed her job strictly as a necessity. Her primary involvement was in her marriage. Leonard's attitude was completely different. Felicia says bluntly: "For him, music comes first and I'm second. If he had to move to New York to be famous and I wouldn't go, he'd leave me." In part because of this imbalance of involvement, Leonard had greater power in their relationship. He determined where they lived, for instance, and required Felicia to tolerate his sexual infidelities.

During the past year there has been a great deal of strain in the relationship. Partly because of this, Felicia took a summer school course in a new method of teaching music. She found the course exciting, and during the summer she gained greater confidence in her abilities as a music teacher. She became seriously interested in teaching as a career. With the support of other women in the class, Felicia decided to apply for admission to a graduate program in the new instructional method. In long talks with other women, she reexamined her ideas about marriage, sex roles, and her career. She realized that "the fantasy of having a man fulfill a woman is a dangerous myth. You have to fulfill yourself." Despite some objections from Leonard, Felicia intends to start graduate school in the fall. She feels that these changes have already helped her marriage, and changed the balance of power. "If I'd gone on working this year to support him, as Len wanted me to, he'd be the more dominant. . . . If I hadn't decided to go to school, he'd be taking the money and running the show." Having made her decision, Felicia feels less dominated and exploited by her husband. She hopes that as she gains more respect for her own abilities, Len will gain respect for her, too.

This is only an example. We asked all of the couples about their educational and career plans. Nearly 70 percent of both men and women said they planned on going to graduate school. Among those seeking advanced degrees, women were more likely than men to desire only a masters degree (50 percent of women versus 32 percent of men). Men were more likely than women to aspire to a doctorate or the equivalent (38 percent of men versus 19 percent of women). Additional questions probed students' attitudes about fulltime employment for women, and their own support for a dual-career marriage in which both spouses have fulltime careers.

As expected, the woman's educational and career plans were significantly related to the balance of power in the current relationship. For instance, in one analysis we examined the relationship between the highest degree the woman aspired to and the balance of power. The results were striking. When the woman aspired to less than a bachelor's degree, 87 percent of students reported that the man had more power in their relationship. When the woman planned to complete her BA, about half (45 percent) reported that the man had more power. And, among couples where the woman planned on an advanced degree, only about 30 percent reported that the man had more say. As the woman's educational aspirations increased, the likelihood of a male-dominant relationship decreased sharply. In contrast, no relationship was found between the man's educational aspirations or career plans and power.

## OVERVIEW

We have found that power in a dating relationship is related to sex-role attitudes, to the balance of involvement and resources, and to the woman's career plans. For women, these three factors were interrelated. Women who planned on graduate school reported relatively less involvement in their current relationship, had more liberal sex-role attitudes (and tended to date men who were also more liberal), and often planned to make a major commitment to a fulltime career, as well as to marriage.

For men, educational plans, sex-role attitudes, and relative involvement were *not* related. Liberal and traditional men did not differ in their educational goals, nor in their relative involvement in the current relationship. In American society, all men are expected to work. This is as true for men who reject traditional roles as for men who support them. Although the man's educational plans did not affect the balance of power, his own sex-role attitudes and his relative involvement were important determinants of power.

While many women in our sample wanted to pursue a career, they did not see this as a substitute for marriage. About 96 percent of women and 95 percent of men said they expected to marry eventually, although not necessarily this partner. Further, 90 percent of women and 93 percent of men said they wanted to have one or more children. What distinguished traditional and liberal women was not their intention to marry, but rather their orientation toward employment. It remains to be seen, of course, whether the women we studied will follow through on their plans for advanced degrees and fulltime employment.

## POWER TACTICS

Traditional sex roles dictate not only that the man should have more power, but also that the sexes should exert influence in different ways. While men are direct, even bold in their leadership, women are expected to be more subtle and covert. *Fascinating Womanhood* offers several suggestions for giving "feminine advice":

> *Ask leading questions:* A subtle way of giving advice is to ask leading questions, such as "Have you ever thought of doing it this way?"...

The key word is *you*. In this way you bring him into the picture so the ideas will seem like his own.

*Insight:* When expressing your viewpoint use words that indicate insight such as "I feel." Avoid the words "I think" or "I know."

*Don't appear to know more than he does:* Don't be the all-wise, all-knowing wife who has all the answers and surpasses her husband in intelligence.

*Don't talk man to man:* Don't "hash things over" as men do and thereby place yourself on an equal plane with him. . . . Keep him in the dominant position so that he will feel needed and adequate as the leader.[11]

Sociologists have taken note of these differences in male and female styles of power. In fact, Jessie Bernard suggests that in many marriages male control may be only an illusion:

From time immemorial, despite the institutional pattern conferring authority on husbands, whichever spouse had the talent for running the show did so. If the wife was the power in the marriage, she exerted her power in a way that did not show; she did not flaunt it, she was satisfied with the "power-behind-the-throne" position.[12]

This "Lady Macbeth syndrome" is a familiar, and often acceptable, pattern. Jokes about henpecked husbands ridicule not only the man who lacks control but also the wife who foolishly exposes her true power.

Recent research by Paula Johnson[13] has systematically explored sex differences in power strategies. She simulated a work situation in which one student was to supervise the work of a partner. At one point the supervisor was asked to tell the partner to "sort faster," but was given a choice of six ways to make this request. Students conformed to traditional expectations. Women preferred to use "feminine" tactics involving helplessness, giving indirect information, or appealing to a sense of group solidarity. They chose statements such as "Help. Please sort faster. I'm really depending on you." Or, "Please sort faster. I think our group can be one of the best. Let's all try to sort very fast." Although men often used these "feminine" strategies, they were equally likely to use "masculine" strategies that were rejected by women. These included referring to their own expertise, their authority as supervisor, or giving direct information. Statements included, "Please sort faster. I know it's possible to go faster because I've worked on this sort of thing before and you can really go fast." Or, "As your supervisor, I'd like to ask you to sort faster, please."

For women to use direct, authoritative power styles is seen as inappropriate by both women and men. Johnson points out that feminine strategies are often effective, at least in the short run. But they have several disadvantages. First, indirect and manipulative tactics perpetuate women's powerlessness. Such ploys exploit women's subordinate position, in the same way that slaves manipulated their masters. But such manipulation does not challenge the power hierarchy. Feminine styles of influence are designed to conceal women's true influence. As a result, they make women appear helpless and less powerful than they actually are. At the same time, they add to the impression that women are sneaky and devious. Finally, feminine strategies may contribute to women's own feelings of powerlessness and low esteem.

But Jessie Bernard suggests that in recent years, women are increasingly shunning "feminine" styles of power. In describing recent trends, she says:

> The wife was no longer dissembling. She was rejecting the idea of a misfit between the . . . theoretical pattern and the actual pattern. This . . . reflected wives' increasing reluctance to go along with the institutional conception of marriage which put them down and reduced them to manipulative operators. They no longer wanted to be devious, to simulate, to be patronized.[14]

To examine the extent to which boyfriends and girlfriends use different styles of influence, Susan Kaplan[15] invited 59 of our couples to participate in a lab study of couple interaction. Each couple was observed while working together on a series of activities designed to assess different aspects of power. In one part of the study, the couple read brief case histories of hypothetical couples. Each involved some sort of conflict or disagreement. In one case, for instance, David wants to spend a quiet evening with Jane, but she feels they should go to a party given by her friends. For each case, the boyfriend and girlfriend read slightly different accounts of the incident. One version, for instance, would be favorable to Jane's position while the other was more positive to David's point of view. After reading each case, the couple was asked to discuss it and reach a joint decision about whose position in the story was more justified. These discussions were tape-recorded, and later scored by trained coders for twelve different power strategies that men and women might use. Some strategies were more "feminine," such as using an emotional appeal or asking for information. Others, such as taking control or giving an opinion were more stereotypically "masculine." When Kaplan compared the types of strategies used by men and women, she found surprisingly few sex differences. On ten of the twelve measures, men and women did not differ. For instance, men were just as likely as women to use emotional appeals or to ask questions.

The two measures for which sex differences did emerge conformed to sex-role expectations. Men resorted to giving information significantly more often than women did. And women were more likely than men to disagree with an idea or contradict information given by the boyfriend. Kaplan suggests that males take a more assertive stance than females, whose power derives from resisting male assertion. Kaplan sees this as adhering to a traditional pattern in which the man "proposes" and the woman "opposes."

## A HAPPY ENDING?

*Fascinating Womanhood* proposes that the acceptance of traditional sex roles and male leadership are essential to a happy male-female relationship. Feminists argue that traditional sex roles oppress women and make honest male-female relationships difficult. What impact do sex-role attitudes and the balance of power have on the success of a dating relationship? Our surprising answer is that they seem to have little impact on the happiness or survival of dating relationships.

We found no relationship between sex-role attitudes and satisfaction with the current relationship. Liberal and traditional couples rated themselves equally satisfied with their relationships, and indicated that they felt equally close to their partners. Liberals and traditionals did not differ in reports of the likelihood of eventually marrying the current partner, in their love for their partner, or in the number of problems they anticipated in the relationship. Data from our follow-up indicated that liberal and traditional couples were equally likely to stay together or to break up.

To understand these findings, it is important to remember that dating partners usually had similar sex-role beliefs. Having shared attitudes and values may be much more crucial to the success of a relationship than the nature of the attitudes.[16] Mismatching on sex-role attitudes can create problems for couples, and such differences may be most important when a couple first begins to date. Since all the students in our study were already "going with" their partner, we do not have information about the impact of sex roles on first meetings or casual dating. Couples in our study had all survived the beginning of a relationship, perhaps because they agreed about sex roles, or had managed to reconcile their differences.

Since students were nearly unanimous in their endorsement of an egalitarian ideal of power, we might expect the balance of power to affect couple satisfaction or survival. In fact, we found no differences at all between equal-power and male-dominant couples on measures of satisfaction, closeness, or breaking up during the two-year study. In contrast, however, both men and women reported less satisfaction in relationships where the woman had more say. It is apparently easier to follow a traditional pattern or to adhere to the new pattern of equality than to experience a female-dominant relationship.

Currently there is much controversy over proper behavior for men and women. Whether to adopt traditional standards, attempt to modify them, or reject old patterns outright are decisions we all must face. The results of our study suggest that traditional and egalitarian patterns are equally likely to lead to a satisfactory dating relationship, or to a miserable one. Consensus between a man and a woman may be more important for couple happiness than the particular pattern a couple follows.

## NOTES

1   Zick Rubin, *Liking and Loving: An Invitation to Social Psychology* (New York: Holt, Rinehart & Winston, 1973).

2   Jessie Bernard, *The Future of Marriage* (New York: Bantam, 1972); and Margaret Mead, *Male and Female* (New York: Dell, 1968).

3   Kate Millet, *Sexual Politics* (Garden City, N.Y.: Doubleday, 1970).

4   Helen B. Andelin, *Fascinating Womanhood* (New York: Bantam, 1963).

5   *Ibid.*, pp. 134–35.

6   This research is part of a large study of dating relationships. To obtain a representative group of college dating couples, the researchers contacted a random sample of students at four colleges and universities in the Boston area. To be eligible for the study, students had to be "going with" a boyfriend or girlfriend, and both partners had to be willing to participate. A total of 231 couples met these criteria and took

part in the research. Both partners independently responded to lengthy questionnaires concerning their background, attitudes, and current relationship in 1972. Follow-up questionnaires were administered one and two years later.

The typical couple in our study consisted of a sophomore woman dating a junior man. When the study began, the couples had been dating for a median period of eight months. About half the participants' fathers had graduated from college, and about one-fourth held graduate degrees. About 44 percent of the students were Catholic, 26 percent were Protestant, and 25 percent were Jewish, reflecting the religious composition of the colleges in the Boston area. Virtually all participants (97 percent) were white.

Those interested in further papers based on this research should see Letitia A. Peplau, "Impact of Fear of Success and Sex-role Attitudes on Women's Competitive Achievement," *Journal of Personality and Social Psychology*, 34 (1976), 561–68; Charles T. Hill, Zick Rubin, and Letitia A. Peplau, "Breakups before Marriage: The End of 103 Affairs," *Journal of Social Issues*, 32:1 (1976), 147–68; and Letitia A. Peplau, Zick Rubin, and Charles T. Hill, "Sexual Intimacy in Dating Relationships," *Journal of Social Issues*, 33:2 (1977), 86–109.

7   Ronald E. Cromwell and David H. Olson, eds., *Power in Families* (New York: Wiley, 1975).

8   Constantina Safilios-Rothschild, "The Study of Family Power Structure: A Review—1960–1969," *Journal of Marriage and the Family*, 32 (1970), 539–52.

9   Peter M. Blau, *Exchange and Power in Social Life* (New York: Wiley, 1964); and John W. Thibaut and Harold H. Kelley, *The Social Psychology of Groups* (New York: Wiley, 1959).

10   Ellen Berscheid and Elaine Walster, "Physical Attractiveness," in Leonard Berkowitz, ed., *Advances in Experimental Social Psychology*, vol. 7 (New York: Academic Press, 1974).

11   Andelin, *Fascinating Womanhood*, pp. 145–46.

12   Bernard, *The Future of Marriage*, p. 155.

13   Paula B. Johnson, "Women and Power: Toward a Theory of Effectiveness," *Journal of Social Issues*, 32:3 (1976), 99–110; and Paula B. Johnson and Jacqueline D. Goodchilds, "How Women Get Their Way," *Psychology Today*, 10:5 (October 1976) 69–70.

14   Bernard, *The Future of Marriage*, p. 152.

15   Susan L. Kaplan, *The Exercise of Power in Dating Couples*, unpublished doctoral dissertation (Harvard University, 1975).

16   Hill, Rubin, and Peplau, "Breakups before Marriage."

# Jessie Bernard

# The Mother Role*

## A NEW AND UNIQUE INSTITUTION

Motherhood as we know it today is a surprisingly new institution. It is also a unique one, the product of an affluent society. In most of human history and in most parts of the world even today, adult, able-bodied women have been, and still are, too valuable in their productive capacity to be spared for the exclusive care of children. They have been necessary for tilling the fields or fishing or gathering. In a study of six cultures around the world, including our own, for example, a team of anthropologists and psychologists found only our culture following our model.[1]

*Reprinted from Chapter 1, "Mother Is a Role, Women Are Human Beings," in *The Future of Motherhood* by Jessie Bernard. Copyright © 1974 by Jessie Bernard and used by permission of the publisher, The Dial Press.

Among the Nyansongo of Kenya, for example, "during much of the day . . . the mother is working the nearby fields and around the house, and the infant is carried and cared for by a child nurse . . . six to ten years old . . . usually an older sibling . . . who plays an important part in the infant's life."[2] Sometimes co-wives help; sometimes father do also. For "Nyansongo mothers are over-burdened with an agricultural and domestic work load which limits the attention they can pay to their weaned children. In consequence, they delegate a good deal of care-taking and training to older children in the homestead, and they reduce their maternal role to what they consider its bare essentials. . . . Another important consequence of the mother's heavy work load is that she trains the children to share it with her as soon as they are able."[3] Similarly, among the *Rajputs* of India, "during the months when the baby is too old to lie quietly on a cot and too young to walk itself, it is, if possible, turned over to an older girl to carry when the mother is busy working. As a rule, this caretaker will be an older sister, but a cousin may take the child if the sisters-in-law are on good terms."[4] Old men may also help in baby-tending. And once the child begins to walk, if he is a boy, the men—fathers, uncles, or grandfathers—may take over. And so, too, among the villagers of Taira, Okinawa. "From the time he is a month old until shortly before the arrival of the next baby, he [the infant] is constantly carried during the day-time on the back of . . . an adult or an older child. . . . His carriers include parents, paternal grandparents, unmarried aunts and uncles, older siblings in an ex-tended household, and parents and older siblings in a nuclear house-hold."[5] And the Mixtecans of Mexico where "the transference of the primary caretaking responsibilities from the mother to the sibling group . . . takes place . . . about a year after weaning."[6] And among the residents of Tarong, an Ilocos barrio in the Philippines: "in no house-hold did a mother have sole responsibility for her children—it would be unthinkable. . . . If the house is relatively isolated and the family nuclear, the father may well hold the baby whenever he is not in the fields, bathe it, change its clothes, feed it tidbits. If the house has many women or older girls, he will rarely do more than play with the child while it is still young."[7] After weaning, caretakers may be aunts, grandmothers, siblings, or even fathers. "More often than not . . . the child . . . eventually obtains care from the socially approved source— the neighbor-kin group, both adults and peers."[8] For pre-schoolers there are many caretakers, all the children belonging to all in the housing group. "We all help to raise our children."[9] Among the Alors, "since women are primarily responsible for garden work and the subsistence economy, mothers return to regular field work ten days to two weeks after the birth of the child. It is not customary for the mother to work with the child on her back or even near her, as it is in some societies. Instead the infant is left at home in care of some kin, for example the father, an older sibling of either sex, or a grandmother whose field labor is less effective or necessary than that of a younger woman."[10] By way of contrast, we find that in our society today "parents ... generally discourage older siblings ... from assuming responsibility for infants on the grounds that the older child will be irresponsible and that it would also be imposing unduly on him or her. It is thought to be too trying for an older child to face the baby's antisocial behavior and maintain reasonable control over it."[11]

## AND NOT A GOOD ONE

The way we institutionalize motherhood in our society—assigning sole responsibility for child care to the mother, cutting her off from the easy help of others in an isolated household, requiring round-the-clock tender, loving care, and making such care her exclusive activity—is not only new and unique, but not even a good way for either women or—if we accept as a criterion the amount of maternal warmth shown—for children. It may, in fact, be the worst. It is as though we had selected the worst features of all the ways motherhood is structured around the world and combined them to produce our current design.

This charge is based on the findings of the research teams previously quoted. They found that women in cultures where they were given the heaviest load of child care were more changeable in expressing warmth than those in other cultures and more likely to have hostilities not related to the behavior of the children.[12] In fact, the greater the burden of child care assigned to these mothers, the less likely they were to be able to supply the warm care infants require. "Mothers," they reported, "who spend a high proportion of their time caring for children are somewhat more unstable in their emotional reactions to their children than are mothers who do not have such exclusive responsibility."[13] The so-called harassment aspect of child care was also greater among them. Maternal warmth was more likely to occur when there was a grandmother present to spell the mother off. "Mothers who must cope more than others, either with their own children or their children's cousins, are muted in their warmth, while mothers who have the help of a grandmother are free in their expression of affection."[14] Maternal instability likewise decreased when additional caretakers eased the mother's burden and when there were relatively few children requiring her care.

Life-style was also found to be related to maternal warmth. "Mothers who are really isolated from their relatives and substitute caretakers may control expressiveness . . . to avoid further wear and tear on their own frayed nerves and fights among siblings for their own praise and affection."[15] Another study of forty-five cultures for which data were available found a relationship between a high incidence of mother-child households (as, for example, in polygyny) and the inflicting of pain on the child by the nurturant agent. And, conversely, although less markedly, a negative relationship between maternal warmth and incidence of mother-child households.[16]

The two requirements we build into the role of mother—full-time care of children and sole responsibility for them—seem, in brief, to be incompatible with one another, even mutually exclusive. In view of these findings it is sobering to note that in our society we seem to maximize this contradiction in the role so that mothers here "have a significantly heavier burden (or joy) of baby care than the mothers in any other society."[17] Today young mothers who "spend a high proportion of their time caring for children" are corroborating the researchers' report. Yes, they are beginning to tell us, it's true: they find joy in their children, but they do not like motherhood.[18]

## HOME AND MOTHER

The isolated home as we know it, like motherhood with which it is intrinsically related, is also a fairly new institution in human history. The privacy of the home originated as a form of protective isolation, though what it was guarding against changed with time. In the fifteenth century, for example, it was protection against the evils of communal festivities.[19] Later it was protection against too great demands being made upon it:

> In the eighteenth century, the family began to hold society at a distance, to push it back beyond a steadily extending zone of private life. The organization of the house altered in conformity with this new desire to keep the world at bay. . . . People began defending themselves against a society whose constant intercourse

had hitherto been the source of education, reputation and wealth. . . . The history of modern manners can be reduced in part to this long effort to break away from others, to escape from a society whose pressure had become unbearable.[20]

In the nineteenth century the cloistering of the home was a protection against the evils of industrialization and urbanization.

In the new economic order that accompanied the industrial revolution, hard, driving, competitive men were creating a male-oriented civilization in which a dog-eat-dog philosophy prevailed; the survival of the fittest as it was then interpreted, called for an extremely rugged individualism. Let the best man win. It was a world of achievement at almost any human price.

But even for those who could operate successfully in such an atmosphere, as well as for those who could not, there had to be some place where relief was possible. That place was provided by the sheltering home. And it was woman's role to supply the healing balm to the victors as well as to the victims of the cruel outside world. "The Feminine as the giver of shelter and protection" encompassed "the life of the family and group in the symbol of the house."[21]

## THE QUEEN'S WALLED GARDEN

The home was a sacred place. Even for non-believers and agnostics it was a "secular temple," a place for social altruism. In order for the mother to perform her sheltering and protective function she herself had to be protected from the outside world, isolated from it, immured in a walled garden. *Therefore, no career at all.*

> . . . the conception of the home as a source of virtue and emotions which were nowhere else to be found, least of all in business and society . . . made it a place radically different from the surrounding world. It was much more than a house where one stopped at night for temporary rest and recreation—or procreation—in the midst of a busy career. It was a place apart, a walled garden, in which certain virtues too easily crushed by modern life could be preserved and certain desires of the heart too much thwarted be fulfilled.[22]

This isolated home, protected from the outside world for whatever reason, was the mother's responsibility to maintain as a sanctuary. She ruled over it contributing order, arrangement, decision, as well as faithful and wise counseling. In an essay that has been called "the most important single document ... for the characteristic idealization of love, woman, and the home in Victorian thought,"[23] John Ruskin laid out the province of mothers:

> This is the true nature of home—it is the place of Peace; the shelter, not only from all injury, but from all terror, doubt, and division. In so far as it is not this, it is not home; so far as the anxieties of the outer life penetrate into it, and the inconsistently-minded, unknown, unloved, or hostile society of the outer world is allowed by either husband or wife to cross the threshold, it ceases to be home; it is then only a part of that outer world which you have roofed over, and lighted fire in. But so far as it is a sacred place, a vestal temple, a temple of the hearth watched over by Household Gods ... so far as it is this, and roof and fire are types only of a nobler shade and light,—shade as of the rock in a weary land, and light as of the Pharos in the stormy sea;—so far it vindicates the name, and fulfills the praise, of Home.[24]

A man might have to sally forth to meet the perils of the outside world, to struggle on that grim, harsh stage, become hardened, but "he guards the woman from all this; within his house, as ruled by her, unless she herself has sought it, need enter no danger, no temptation, no cause of error or offense."[25] George Eliot put it succinctly: "A loving woman's world lies within the four walls of her own home; and it is only through her husband that she is in any electric communication with the world beyond."[26] Protected, sheltered, isolated, safe within the walls of their gardens, women as mothers became the repositories of all the humane virtues. It was the mother who made of home a school of virtue.

## MOTHER AS SYMBOL

> The idealization of the maternal role in society's taboos indicates that in the interest of the survival of the species the mother-child relationship has to be buttressed by social regulation, and also that this is often not sufficient, and that deficiencies have therefore to be covered up by idealization.[27]

Increasingly idealized—by definition loving, gentle, tender, self-sacrificing, devoted, limited in interests to creating a haven for her family—the mother became in time almost a parody. Mothers have been honored from time immemorial, assessed above rubies in value, as the Proverbial woman was, or as the Roman matron was, or the chatelaine of a medieval castle might be. But the mother adored for her self-abnegation, her "altruistic surrender,"[28] even for her self-immolation, was a nineteenth-century Victorian creation. This image reached its heyday at the turn of the century and lingered on until yesterday.

Even today, in fact, one catches glimpses of the Victorian mother in debates about the place of women.[29] The image still lurks behind the battle cry "A woman's place is in the home." It has retained a tenacious hold on our minds long after the environment that created and supported it has disappeared. And its extension into the future is suggested by its persistence in children's schoolbooks, where mother is still the ever-loving homebody.[30]

It has taken a long time to overcome this concept of the home as a walled garden presided over by a cherishing mother, an isolated, cut-off, protected temple where people could huddle together against a cruel outside world. It may be that only certain members of the post-war generation carry no vestige of it. So far as they are concerned, they want no part of it. For them—and even, increasingly, for their mothers as well—the isolated, walled garden became a prison long ago, keeping them in rather than the world out.

Furthermore, the outside world changed, changing the part played both by the home and by the workshop. The home was no longer a sanctuary for men in a hostile world. They were deriving as much—or as little—satisfaction from their work as from their marriages.[31]

## MOTHERS AS WOMEN

Victorian motherhood was a male—and a middle-class—conception. The more female historians study it from the point of view of the women themselves the less authentic it looks. It was never a genuine portrait even of the Victorian mother, let alone the mother of any other age. Women are just not like that. Now or ever.

Mothers in the home were already becoming a "social problem" a hundred years ago. They were already champing at the bit. They were already compalining of being boxed in. Even then they were fretting and wearied by motherhood's "daily round of trivial tasks, occupying the time and absorbing the energies."[32] Then as now they felt shut in "from the larger life of the world, which courses freshly past the home within which they are imprisoned." Many who "once dreamed of great things" sighed "sadly in the thought of the nursery bondage and . . . looked out wistfully on the noble labors awaiting mind and heart in the outer world."[33] Then, as now, those who fretted "under its [mother-hood's] burdens of care, threw off from them in every way possible their divinely imposed charge" in order to "escape from the home to society, to find for themselves pleasure, or to make for themselves work other than that providentially ordered."[34] As early as 1879, Ibsen's Nora, in reply to her husband's dictum that "before all else" she was "a wife and mother," said: "that I no longer believe. I believe that before all else I am a human being, just as much as you are—or at least that I should try to become one."

⭐ By the turn of the century it was already becoming apparent that there was something wrong about the nineteenth-century model for the role of mother. Women were finding it increasingly difficult to perform it. Invoking the idealized model did no good. "Putting on a Madonna-like pedestal the often impatient, irritable mother who feels chained to her duties, may suffice for the aims of idealism and wishful thinking, but makes life easier neither for mothers nor for children. True, it saves society the feeling that it should change itself."[35] But aggrieved women were not to let "society" spare itself the comfort of standing pat. If they were poor, they were protesting against having too many children;[36] if they were affluent, they were protesting against the confinement of the doll's house. They wanted out.

⭐ But never until this very historical moment have women rebelled as many are now doing against the very way we institutionalize mother-hood. They are daring to say that although they love children, they hate motherhood. That they object to being assigned sole responsibility for child care. That they object to having child care conceived as their only major activity. That they object to the isolation in which they must perform the role of mother, cut off from help, from one another, from the outside world. For the first time they are protesting the false aura of romanticism with which motherhood is endowed, keeping from young women its terrible "hidden underside," which "is hardly talked about." One young mother feels "obsessed with the need to tell people what really happens when you have children," to expose "the terrible weight of responsibility, the way it affects a woman's personality." A group of women, basing their conclusions on their own experiences as participant observers—or, rather, as observant participators—note al-most point for point how the way we institutionalize motherhood is bad for women. They call on women to organize "to fight those aspects of our society that make childbearing and child rearing stressful rather than fulfilling experiences." One young woman speaks of "the baby trap."[37] Another writes a book to tell us that "mother's day is over," to inform us that "until now millions of women have secretly shared, and silently endured, a profound guilt: they love their children, but they do not love being mothers." She hopes her book "will end their solitude and reduce their guilt and make them more dignified human beings."[38]

Nor is motherhood as we institutionalize it good for children. The anger and irritability it fosters in women reverberates on the children. "When it is realized how difficult woman's present situation makes her full self-realization, how many desires, rebellious feelings, just claims she nurses in secret, one is frightened at the thought that defenseless infants are abandoned to her care."[39] It is no less serious because "most women have the morality and decency to repress their spontaneous impulses; nevertheless these impulses suddenly flash out at times in angry scenes, slaps, punishments, and the like." The mother may feel remorse; but the child feels the pain.

The "smother-love" fostered in women with no other channel for self-actualization came in time to be resented by the sons and daughters. These children of the women struggling to fill their lives with the mother role were as much victimized as the women themselves. They began to see their mothers as not all that saintly after all. Sometimes, in fact, they saw them as devouring vultures. Instead of honoring mother they had to fight to rid themselves of their enforced dependencies on her. Mothers were attacked as a generation of vipers[40] who had ruined their sons by their momism[41] and had produced sons full of sexual compulsions.[42] The virtues of the nineteenth-century mother were turned inside out: the angels became monsters. The Great Mother archetype became the Terrible Mother archetype.[43] Once worshipfully hoisted on a pedestal, mothers were now pelted with abuse.

> . . . mothers are held responsible for juvenile delinquency, problem children, neurotic children, vandalism, communism, and the many other woes of society. Now, on bearing a child, one automatically loses any semblance of common sense one may have had earlier when one was in business, in a profession or in some other career. . . . [Mothers] are maligned, insulted, and treated like an evil spirit.[44]

Whether the denigration of the mother resulted, as some alleged, from neglect by working mothers or, as others alleged, from "smother-love" by home-bound mothers, whether too little or too much mothering was the basis of the denigration, it was, in fact, quite real. Whatever was wrong in our society, it had to be the mother's fault.

Role, home, and symbol as components of Victorian motherhood were, then, all relatively new when they arose, but they were already in process of becoming anachronisms when the twentieth century inherited them. What we see today is the tail end of a comet, the tail of a model of motherhood that began to disintegrate as it struck the twentieth century. The comet itself was a model of motherhood that appeared in Victorian times in response to a set of circumstances unique in human history, circumstances that resulted finally in the severance of the two most fundamental aspects of human life, family and work. Two worlds separated out, one an outside work world, one an almost cloistered family world.

It was not the protests of mothers that finally battered down the walls of the queen's garden. It was the outside forces that were taking much of the work of women out of the home and attenuating much that remained within it. The shock waves of industrialization and urbanization that began to break at the end of the eighteenth century were to be felt throughout all of nineteenth-century society. Nothing was to be left untouched, even motherhood. The nature of work, the nature of the home, the nature of all human relations, were all to be transformed. We have to go back more than ten thousand years, to the beginnings of agriculture, to find anything comparable to the events we now call *the* industrial revolution, actually only one of many, before and since.

The walls that had surrounded the home proved unable to withstand the maelstrom of industrialism and urbanism. They crumbled first among the poor. Then among the unmarried daughters of the not-so-poor. Then among the valiant well-to-do, among women who began to see the walls as keeping them in rather than as keeping the world out. Then among wives, even mothers. The walls, however symbolic, remain today as only reminders of the past. They have come to be seen by more and more women as gilded cages, if not as prisons.

The current revolt of many women against the role of mother as institutionalized in our society will no more force us to rethink the structure of motherhood today than did the protests of mothers a century ago. But a host of other forces, including—in addition to continuing technological changes—the antinatalism engendered by the environment movement, are already at work to bring about such a restructuring. We can't go home again. Not, at least, to the Victorian home.

## NOTES

1 Beatrice B. Whiting, ed., *Six Cultures, Studies of Child Rearing* (Wiley, 1963).

2 Robert A. LeVine and Barbara B. LeVine, "Nyansongo: A Gusii Community in Kenya," in Beatrice B. Whiting, ed., *Six Cultures*, p. 139.

3 *Ibid.*, p. 161.

4 Leigh Minturn and John T. Hitchcock, "The Rajputs of Khalapur, India," *Ibid.*, p. 314.

5 Thomas W. Maretzki and Hatsumi Maretzki, "Taira: An Okinawan Village," *Ibid.*, p. 462.

6 Kimball Romney and Romaine Romney, "The Mixtecans of Juxtlahuaca, Mexico," *Ibid.*, p. 650.

7 William F. Mydegger and Corinne Mydegger, "Tarong: An Ilocos Barrio in the Philippines," *Ibid.*, p. 821.

8 *Ibid.*, p. 833.

9 *Ibid.*, p. 834.

10 Cora DuBois, *The People of Alors* (University of Minnesota Press, 1944), p. 36. " 'Lazy' women use the care of the child as an excuse to slight their field work" (p. 34).

11 John L. Fischer and Ann Fischer, "The New Englanders of Orchard Town, U.S.A.," in Beatrice B. Whiting, ed., *Six Cultures*, p. 946. Alorese mothers face the same problem of irresponsibility in older siblings as "baby sitters." It might be noted in passing that despite the much-publicized community child-care facilities in China today a newspaper report in 1972 pointed out that "an older child always seems to be taking care of a younger one" (Wes Gallagher, "Unexpected U.S. Visitors Stir a Tiny Chinese Hamlet," *The Washington Post*, August 17, 1972).

12 Leigh Minturn and William L. Lambert, *Mothers of Six Cultures: Antecedents of Child Rearing* (Wiley, 1964), p. 56.

13 *Ibid.*, p. 66.

14 *Ibid.*, pp. 282–83.

15 *Ibid.*, p. 283.

16 James W. Prescott and Cathy McKay, "Child Abuse and Child Care: Some Cross-Cultural and Anthropological Perspectives," paper prepared for research workshop of the National Institute of Child Health and Human Development, June, 1973, Table 2.

17 Minturn and Lambert, *Mothers of Six Cultures*, p. 97.

18 Shirley Radl, *Mother's Day Is Over* (Charterhouse, 1973), *passim*.

19 Arthur W. Calhoun, *A Social History of the American Family: Volume 1. Colonial Period* (Cleveland: Arthur H. Clark, 1917), pp. 38–40.

20 Philippe Ariès, *Centuries of Childhood* (Knopf, 1962), pp. 398, 406–07.

21 Erich Neumann, *The Great Mother, An Analysis of the Archetype*, trans. Ralph Manheim (Princeton-Bollinger, 1963), p. 137.

22 Walter E. Houghton, *The Victorian Frame of Mind* (Yale University Press, 1957), p. 343.

23  *Ibid.*, p. 343.

24  John Ruskin, "Of Queens' Gardens," Section 68, in *Works*, Vol. 8, p. 122.

25  *Ibid.*, p. 122.

26  George Eliot, "Amos Barton," in *Scenes from Clerical Life,* Vol. 1, p. 85.

27  Alexander Mitscherleck, *Society Without Father, A Contribution to Social Psychology* (Harcourt Brace & World, 1968), p. 56.

28  The concept of altruistic surrender was originally developed by Anna Freud to refer to a form of identification with another person in which one all-but-gave up one's own identity. Arlie Hochschild has developed the concept as a component of the mother role among women sixty-five years of age and older as related to grown sons and daughters *(The Unexpected Community,* Prentice-Hall, 1973, pp. 100 ff.). It may be noted in passing that even Mary, who in the folk mind had been something of a roustabout, became, in effect, a Victorian mother in the nineteenth century, the very model of "the heart of the home." Although she had always been full of maternal warmth and kindness, though amoral, generous with mercy, assistance, and healing even for sinners, she had also been patroness of prostitutes and, in the Mexican folk mind, suspected of promiscuity. Folk tales had her giving milk from her own breast to horribly diseased patients, delivering the baby of a reverend abbess, substituting for a nun who went off to live it up as a prostitute (Wolfgang Lederer, *The Fear of Women,* Harcourt Brace Jovanovich, 1968, pp. 175–77). Not until the middle of the nineteenth century did she become completely domesticated.

29  As late as 1967, 34 percent of the respondents in a Gallup poll believed women's place was in the home. Even among college freshmen, usually an avant garde, 51.9 percent of the men queried in 1971 and 30.6 percent of the women, professed that belief.

30  New Jersey NOW Task Force, *Dick and Jane As Victims* (1972). Published by authors.

31  See Chapter 18.

32  R. Heber Newton, *Womanhood* (Putnam's, 1881), p. 123.

33  *Ibid.*, p. 123.

34  *Ibid.*, p. 123.

35  Alexander Mitscherleck, *Society Without Father*, p. 57.

36  Margaret Sanger, *Motherhood in Bondage* (Brentano's, 1928).

37  Shirley Radl, *Mother's Day Is Over,* p. 10.

38  Simone de Beauvoir, *The Second Sex* (Bantam, 1952), pp. 484–85.

39  *Ibid.*, p. 485.

40  Philip Wylie, *A Generation of Vipers* (Farrar, 1942).

41  William Streckert, *Their Mothers' Sons* (Lippincott, 1956).

42  Philip Roth, *Portnoy's Complaint* (Random House, 1969).

43  Erich Neumann, *The Great Mother,* pp. 148–49. The archetype of the Terrible Mother is the negative side of the Great Mother, witches, vampires, ghouls, specters.

44  Helen E. Peixotto, "Mothers Had Mothers Too," in Edgar J. Schmiedeler, ed., *The Mother the Heart of the Home* (St. Meinard, Ind.: Grail Publications, 1955), pp. 135–36

# Rosalyn F. Baxandall

# Who Shall Care for Our Children? The History and Development of Day Care in the United States

Given America's expressed concern for the well-being of children and the shocking extent of childhood poverty, it is all the more ironical that of all groups among the poor it is children who have been most neglected and most shabbily treated by current social policies.[1] There has been a growing concern for the welfare of children. Many child-care programs are under debate or in the early stages of development. Thus it is important that we should analyze various policies and programs to determine if possible which will be most beneficial over the long haul. Such an analysis, limited to the problem of day care, will be undertaken here with an eye to proposals for an effective and meaningful day-care policy.[2]

In planning a child-care policy for today it is extremely important to examine the programs of yesterday. Much of present day-care policy stems from the idea that the nuclear family ought to be a self-sufficient unit, performing according to its structure a series of economic, educative, protective, recreational, sexual, and biological functions.[3] Moreover, it is considered that a natural division of labor occurs within this family unit, with nurturance allotted to the mother and breadwinning to the father. Provision for early child-care is seen then as a private matter— to be carried out by the nuclear family, and specifically the mother. Yet not so long ago, and not only in rural areas, child-rearing was shared among members of two or more generations, by mothers-in-law and grandmothers, often living under the same roof or nearby, and was not the sole province of the young children's mothers. The situation today is of course much different. Most families live in single-generational units, and usually at some distance from relatives.

At the same time that child-rearing has become chiefly the responsibility of the single-family unit, a tendency toward family breakups has developed. According to 1975 figures, one marriage in three results in divorce.[4] Of public resources allocated to child-welfare services, 70 percent now goes to foster care.[5] Moreover, more than 15.4 million mothers work; and of these more than 5 million have children under six years of age.[6] Even among those whose children are old enough to be in school, few can be home as early as their children. Where the single-family unit no longer exists as a unit, or is overburdened in one way or another, some other solution must be found. Communal living, a return to extended families, and various forms of day care are among the most frequently mentioned solutions, but only the last will concern us here.

## HISTORICAL PERSPECTIVES

The first infant school in the United States seems to have been organized by Robert Owen in New Lanark, Pennsylvania, in the 1830's, after Owen had visited Pestalozzi's infant nursery (modelled on Rousseau's) in Switzerland.[7] Owen's school was, however, a utopian experiment that did not inspire many imitators. The next nursery was opened in 1854 in New York City: the Nursery for Children of the Poor. It was followed by the Virginia Nursery (1872) and the Bethany Day (1887), also in New York.[8] These nurseries provided philanthropic assistance, at first to children of Civil War widows, and later to children who were left during the day by their mothers of immigrant origin while they worked in factories or in domestic service. The care was custodial;

wealthy women performed it. The purpose was described as being to "feed the starving, clothe the naked, enlighten the soul."[9]

Parallel with the growth of the day nurseries was the rise of the kindergarten movement that took its inspiration from Friedrich Froebel. German liberals brought Froebel's thought to the United States after 1848. Froebel stressed the freeing of little children from harsh discipline and fear, and he sought to encourage children's natural development through creative play, nature study, art, and music.[10] Many settlements adopted kindergarten programs. Elizabeth Peabody House in Boston began as a combination settlement and kindergarten. At Hull House in Chicago, the settlement activist Mary McDowell taught kindergarten. Many neighborhood kindergartens established in Boston in the 1840's and 1880's became settlements in the 1890's.

On the whole, the kindergarten tradition, with its stress on education for the normal child, led to the establishment of private nursery schools for the well-to-do. In marked contrast, the day nurseries originated in a welfare tradition that emphasized care and protection for the neglected child and family. Of course, the separation of emphasis was by no means rigid. Day care benefited greatly from improvements in medicine, hygiene, nutrition, and knowledge of child development. Nevertheless, two distinct traditions developed in the field of child care outside the home in this country. This distinction survives today.

In 1896 a National Federation of Day Nurseries was organized to work for higher standards. In 1905 physicians began to inspect day-care facilities and examine the children who used the centers. A new concern for research and experimentation in the area of educational aids for the underprivileged followed from the establishment of special teacher-training schools at Bank Street in New York, Merrill Palmer in Detroit, and elsewhere. These schools, with their emphasis on teacher training, marked the entrance of professionals into the field. Most of these professionals, however, have gone to nurseries and kindergartens rather than into day-care centers. The teachers in day care belong to a *welfare* union, and they are not nearly so well paid as regular teachers who belong to a *teacher's* union.

In 1919 the day nursery was first included in the National Conference of Social Work. By the 1930's, social-work concepts, emphasizing the value of the day nursery in uplifting family life, were particularly being stressed in the day nurseries sponsored by social agencies. For example, Sophie Van S. Theis found "all child caring agencies, irrespective of the particular type of service which they give . . . have come to think in recent years of casework as an essential part of a good child care program."[11] She goes on to say that traditionally, by charter and by history, the day nursery is a social agency. This social-work legacy—not, of course, a part of nursery-school education—led to further emphasis on day care as a welfare service for the unfortunate, deprived, and maladjusted and to further separation between the two traditions.

The major impetus for day-care development in the United States has been furnished by depression and war. Federally financed nursery schools were established in the 1930's—the greatest era of growth for day care—under the Federal Emergency Relief Administration (FERA), later known as the Works Progress Administration (WPA). The primary purpose of federal action in 1933 was to create employment for needy teachers, nutritionists, clerical workers, cooks, and janitors, all part of a larger program to counteract massive unemployment.[12] The WPA spent large sums of public funds on group programs for children aged two to five from welfare-recipient families, and on staff training and parent education. Outstanding people from the child-development field were enlisted for the extensive training programs, which included brief, intensive teacher-training courses to supply immediate staff needs.[13]

WPA day care was conceived primarily as a residual welfare service. The WPA nursery school, by contrast, was identified as an educational service. Nutrition and health services were likewise stressed. Most of the nurseries (except those in New York City) were located in Board of Education facilities and were staffed by jobless school teachers. (In New York City in 1938, of fourteen WPA nurseries only one was located in a public school; the rest were set up in settlements and other social agencies and even in vacant lots, churches, cellars, stores. These were staffed by recreation directors, nurses, and teachers.) By and large the WPA nurseries were kept open ten to twelve hours a day six days a week. By 1937, 40,000 American children were being provided with what most professionals today still consider high standards of care and education.

In October of 1942 the Federal government notified WPA nurseries that they were no longer needed as a source of employment. Therefore, relief-status children need not be served, although children of working mothers might be cared for, so that these mothers could supply the war industries with much-needed womanpower. Also, there were fewer and fewer unemployed teachers to staff the centers; on the contrary, teacher-shortages were beginning to appear.

In 1941 when World War II began, thousands of women entered industrial production to replace the men who had to leave for the armed forces. The demand for women workers was so great that single and childless women alone could not fill it.[14] Women with young children could not work without child care. Consequently in 1941 Congress passed, in a record two weeks, the Community Facilities Act, usually referred to as the Lanham Act. This Act made federal funds available to states on a fifty-fifty matching basis for the expansion of day-care centers and nursery schools in defense areas. These funds could also be used to convert WPA facilities into wartime nurseries. The Children's Bureau was responsible for the development and extension of day-care centers, whereas the United States Office of Education under the aegis of local school boards handled nursery-school operations. Again there was a separation of approaches, with the more well-to-do children getting education and the poorer children receiving therapeutic services. The Children's Bureau proved quite ambivalent about the idea of women at work; it felt that in the long run a mother's absence would be destructive to the family and to basic American values. Most social-work leaders joined the Children's Bureau in the concern that publicly funded nurseries might sanction the employment of women.[15] However, widespread popular acceptance of these day-care centers is indicated by the fact that by July of 1945 the Children's Bureau was responsible for 3,100 day-care centers serving 130,000 children,[16] and about 1,600,000 children were receiving care financed largely by federal funds.[17] Every state except New Mexico had some day-care centers. California supported the most: 392 nurseries.

The purpose of these nurseries was first to relieve unemployment and later to encourage the employment of mothers. When the Second World War ended, and women were no longer wanted in the factories, Congress withdrew the Lanham Act funds for day care. Without funds, most of the nurseries had to close. In Chicago there were 23 wartime centers; in 1968 there were none in the entire state of Illinois. In Detroit during the war there were 80 centers, but by 1957, just three remained. In California, where there was a continued demand for women workers in the electronic and aircraft industries, the Lanham Act funds were not withdrawn, and in fact continue to this day on a "temporary" basis, administered through the State Department of Labor.

New York City has a special history. The Lanham Act did not apply to this city because it was not designated a "war-impact" area. However with the threat of withdrawal of funds to the WPA nurseries, active groups of parents and professionals and labor union representatives sent hundreds of petitions, and publicly pressured Mayor LaGuardia not only to keep open existing city-supported nurseries but also to expand the program. The campaign was successful, and day care survived in New York City.

The 1962 Public Welfare amendments to the Social Security Act mark the first time that day care was included in a federal program that was not part of an emergency or wartime measure. However, the major thrust of these amendments was to be in the direction of rehabilitative social services. Day care was provided to protect children whose parents were unable to provide adequate parental supervision for their children. More money ($800,000) was made available for day-care services under the 1962 amendments, but the sum was still far from adequate. The funds were allotted on a matching basis to the states, and it was up to each state to decide whether, and if so how, to launch or extend a day-care program for children.[18] Unfortunately, the poorest, most conservative states with the greatest need generally make the least provision for child care.

The passage of the Economic Opportunity Act in 1964 was another major step in the history of day care. Project Headstart, as an arm of the Office of Economic Opportunity (OEO), directed specific attention to programs for children. Here again, the program was made available only through the states, and the emphasis was on giving poor, deprived children a "head start" rather than on developing day care as a fundamental development service for all. At least 90 percent of the children in Headstart programs must be from families whose income falls below the poverty line, then defined as $4,000 for a family of four.[19] Many of these programs of the sixties have been cut. In June 1976, 49 day-care centers in New York City closed.[20]

## THE NEED

More mothers are working outside the home now than ever before. In the 1940's only 9 percent of all mothers with children under eighteen worked for wages. In 1977, 51 percent of mothers with minor children worked, including 41 percent with children under six and 35 percent with children under three. The labor-participation rate of mothers has increased two times faster than the participation rate of all women, and the labor-participation rate has increased even more rapidly for mothers of pre-school-age children than it has for mothers of school-age children. More mothers (65 percent) work when the husband has absented himself from the family household than when the husband is present (48 percent).[21]

Day-care facilities have not increased commensurately with the increase in employment of mothers. Licensed public and voluntary day-care centers now care for only one-sixth the number of children cared for at the end of World War II.[22] The gap between availability and need has widened over a period of thirty years. Only in the last few years has the trend been reversed, and that only to a slight degree.[23]

What are the child-care arrangements for these children of working mothers? Of those aged 3 to 13, 83 percent were cared for in their own homes, 70 percent by their parents or other relatives and 9.4 percent by a non-relative. Nearly 10 percent looked after themselves, undoubtedly an underestimate, as most women would hesitate to admit that they have no other alternative. Only 1.7 percent of the children were in group care.[24]

How many parents would use day care if it were available? The figures are of course impossible to provide. An indication of need is that in New York City in 1970 there were 8,000 children on the waiting list for day-care centers operated by the Department of Social Services. No official waiting lists exist or are available from Central Head Start, but many Head Start centers in 1970 recorded waiting lists as long as the lists of those currently enrolled.[25] Many women are known to be unable to take jobs because there is no day care for their children. The Labor Department made a study of underemployment and unemployment in ten high-poverty areas. They found that one out of every five residents who was not in the labor force but who desired a regular job, gave as the principal reason for not looking for work an inability to arrange child care.[26]

Families who can afford to pay for day care do not have enough nursery facilities either. For one thing, the suburban areas where many of them live have health and zoning laws precluding establishment of nursery schools in many residential areas.[27] At private nurseries in

1970, competition for admission was record-high, with applications outnumbering vacancies by as much as 150 to one.[28]

## ATTITUDES TOWARD DAY CARE

Since there seems clearly to be a desperate need for day care, why is the need unmet? Part of the reason is that day care has been stigmatized by its welfare origins. It is thought of as something needed by the problem family. The *Ladies' Home Journal* carried a series on day care from June through November of 1967. One conclusion of this series was that "the concept of day care has not been more widely accepted because it was being presented as something solely for the poor and not for every mother."[29] Day care is often equated with maternal deprivation and emotional problems. Mr. Charles Tobin, secretary of the New York State Welfare Conference, said, "The child who needs day care has a family problem which makes it impossible for his parents to fulfill their parental responsibilities without supplementary help."[30]

Psychiatrists and social workers with their stress on the early mother-child relationship have certainly contributed to the negative attitude toward day care. No one has ever bothered to explore the importance of the *paternal relationship*, or other alternatives to the maternal nexus. As Barbara Wooten, a British sociologist, wrote: "But so long as the study of the role of the father continues to be so much neglected as compared with that of the mother, no opinion on the subject [the emphasis on the young child's need for its mother] can be regarded as more than purely speculative.[31] In the Soviet Union, where group child care from infancy onward is provided for all children as a right, Bronfenbrenner found that not only were the children better socialized, but there was greater companionship between parents and children, and Soviet parents spent even more time with their children than did American parents.[32]

Studies show that there are no detrimental effects on the child if the mother makes an effort to spend an hour or two a day with the child when she is home. Another study illustrates that if a mother enjoys her job, a child benefits from the mother's working. There seems no reason, then, to equate day care with maternal deprivation.[33]

A general prejudice against women's working has also prevented the development of adequate child care facilities outside the home in the United States. A 1960's study that originated in the Child Welfare League found that the average opinionmaker in the community, including the educator and the social worker, does not believe women should work. If they do work, they are working for frivolous reasons and therefore might better take care of their own children.[34] Another kind of negative attitude toward working women is exemplified by Samuel Nocella, International Vice President of the Amalgamated Clothing Workers, who says: "We have looked upon the presence of women in industry a little cynically because years ago we felt that the only way we could solve the problem of unemployment was for women to stay home so that men could have jobs."[35]

The attitude toward women's employment has often been tied in with the general mythology, or conventional wisdom, regarding a nurturing role for women. Part of this myth holds that only the biological mother can effectively "mother," and that a child will obviously therefore be harmed by the mother's absence in a work situation. The welfare mother has been the brunt, then, of contradictory attitudes: on the one hand she is urged to get off the tax rolls and into the job market; on the other hand she is mindful of the approval to be had from staying home to care for her children. Studies show that there is, on the whole, no higher rate of delinquency among the children of working mothers, nor is there evidence that either the husband-wife or the child-parent relationship is impaired.[36] Maternal employment has not been shown to have other harmful consequences for children either.[37] In general, the impact of a mother's employment on her child or children varies with the adequacy of the substitute arrangement, or the mother-child relationship prior to the separation for work, and with the mother's motivation to work and the gratification she receives from her employment.[38] In fact, "group care . . . has positive features. Often those in charge of children's groups are better trained, more patient, and objective in dealing with children than the mothers. A child can be allowed greater freedom to run, climb, and throw in a nursery school than in a home full of breakable objects."[39] "There has been some speculation that greater variety of stimulation provided by several close mother figures may be intellectually stimulating and promote flexibility."[40] Day care in various experiments and full-scale programs in the Soviet Union, East Germany, Czechoslovakia, Hungary, Israel, Greece, and France seems to have benefited children.[41]

Since day care has never been studied from a feminist perspective, there have been few studies on the importance of day care *for the mother.* However, anyone who has been a mother knows that mothers need some kind of break from routine, some breathing spell, and some time for recreation, socializing, and creative pursuits—impossible on any meaningful scale without day care of some kind. In fact, most mothers are better mothers when they have some satisfying independent life of their own.[42] Mothers should not be forced to place their children in day-care centers, but the option should always be present.

Part of the reason why professionals in the child-care field oppose women's working and group care for children of working mothers is that these professionals equate maternal separation, even for a few hours a day, with maternal deprivation. They seem to think that maternal separation for any reason and in any manner has to have traumatic, deleterious effects on young children.[43] This misunderstanding comes out of the Bowlby, Spitz, Roudinesco, and Goldfarb studies showing that children who lived in impersonal institutions and were totally bereft, not only of maternal care but also of adequate maternal substitution, developed irreversible psychopathic or autistic characteristics. But these studies have little bearing on the situation of the child of a working mother generally considered; and they probably have little relevance even to questions of maternal deprivation. Barbara Wooten has questioned the scientific validity of these maternal-deprivation studies, inasmuch as they tended to use only disturbed children in institutions as a sample, never following the subjects into later experiences, whereas their clinical observations and statistics altered with time.[44] Regrettably, these studies are still respected in professional psychological and educational circles. It is true generally that scientific evaluations of the effects of day care on mothers and children are colored by cultural norms. And in a society where one must be considered abnormal in order to qualify for the day-care center, how is the evaluation of such services to be contemplated along guidelines that might with accuracy be termed scientific?

## PERSPECTIVES AND PROBLEMS

Day care can be viewed as a benefit in kind, as opposed to a cash benefit. Benefits in kind are preferred when a quality service is too expensive to be purchased on an individual basis.[45] In 1970 it was estimated that decent day care cost $1,600 per year per child.[46] Together with large sums of money, complex administrative and technological and educational skills are required if the demand for adequate day care is to be met. Individual families cannot be expected to meet these expensive complex demands themselves. Even if they could, there is a view of society whereby the wellbeing of children is too important a priority to be left to individual family discretion; childhood and education are societal rather than individual functions, since they ensure the continuity and survival of the society as a whole.

Day care, then, should be seen as a universal entitlement, like public education, rather than as it is now perceived, as a means-tested provision on the order of welfare. Means tests are not efficient as a way of concentrating help on those in need.[47] Means tests usually degrade and stigmatize and therefore only reinforce the conditions they are intended to alleviate and widen the inequity gap they purport to diminish.[48] In a society such as ours, which sets great emphasis on monetary reward and success, an admission of poverty and failure can prove so detrimental that it outweighs the reward it brings.[49] Many liberal-minded people believe that those who could pay for day care should do so on a sliding scale. However, because of the lingering welfare associations of day care, I feel the only way to make day care available without stigma must be to treat it as an unconditionally free public utility.

One of the problems with benefits in kind, however, is that they are often employed as mechanisms for social control.[50] Day care has in the past been used in this way. At present, day care is made available only on condition that women on welfare become enrolled in special Work Incentive Programs (WIN) and Concentrated Employment Programs (CEPS). Another proposal that would have combined day care with work was the Nixon Administration's Family Assistance Plan (FAP).

In FAP plans, the welfare recipients would be provided vouchers enabling them to purchase day care from government or private profit-making centers. This would constitute a windfall for private, franchised centers that would exist for profit rather than owing to any special evinced vocation for child care. Such centers would naturally seek to cut corners to increase their profits. The existing ones generally are overcrowded, with inadequate equipment and untrained part-time personnel. They are geared not toward child development but rather toward the readiest means to give parents the impression that their children are happy. They also seek to inveigle the parents into purchasing the products made by the day-care franchisers.[51]

The only way to prevent this balance-sheet-dominated kind of day care is to be insistent about having genuine parental control. With this certain criteria and health and education standards should be maintained in day care. Unlike the present Code enforcement, such standards and criteria should not militate against experimentation and innovation. Different communities should be able to develop varying centers to meet their needs. For example: in an area where many parents are employed at night, the day-care center should be open 24 hours a day. In contrast, where parents seek care for half-days only, this too should be made possible, and with due budgetary benefit.

Day care has begun to be a factor in labor-market planning. Recently the AVCO Corporation of Dorchester, Massachusetts, Bell Telephone, Whirlpool, and the Rochester Clothing Company have commenced to use day care as a fringe benefit to attract and attach women workers to relative poorly paid jobs.[52] This is a genuine benefit and may take the place of another $100 or more a month in salary. Moreover, insofar as it succeeds in reducing turnover, it may be taken up by other industries. However, since many of the women in most need of the program would find it difficult to get another job, clearly the plan can also be used to control workers. Women are also less apt to engage in action that threatens the firm: organizing strikes, picketing, etc., when the threat is not only loss of a job, but loss of day care.

Day care should be financed by the federal government. This should be done from general tax revenue, rather than from any wage-related tax. Wage-related taxes are often employed to reinforce a psychological relationship between participation in the labor force and receipt of a benefit.[53] And taxes applied from the general tax revenues are on the whole considered to be of universal benefit. It is true the cost of universal day care stands to be enormous—perhaps as much as 6 to 10 billion dollars annually. The issue, however, is not in fact one of economic feasibility. In the world's wealthiest country the issue is rather one of priorities and readiness. Day-care services might best be administered under a special Early Childhood Agency rather than distributed among the existing (bureaucratic, outmoded, but entrenched) education or welfare systems. It would probably prove simpler to innovate, and to go directly to the task with a new agency structured for it. Early childhood education is a special field, with educational, health, nutritional, developmental, and behavioral components.

Another question often raised when universal day care is proposed is that of work incentive. Will the widespread availability of day care encourage women to engage in economically productive labor? And if so, with what consequences? Already we have explored the social and psychological consequences, and found no necessarily detrimental results, but rather the possibility of beneficial results both for the mother and for the child. As to economic consequences, these might include an even stronger influx of women into the labor market, adding to the unemployment problem. Yet with a growing unemployment among men to match the institutionalized unemployment (housewifery) among women, there might be more incentive for a rethinking of the entire question of the duration and constitution of the work week. Part-time work for all might prove to be a partial solution to unemployment and to family needs alike, especially if men are encouraged to share in housekeeping. Also, it might be argued that day care could in the short run reduce the public assistance rolls, as it would leave welfare mothers free to work. It is estimated that in New York City alone, 250,000 women on welfare would be employable if day-care centers and job training were provided.[54]

At present, the absence of day care operates as a work disincentive. The cost of babysitters and nurseries, transportation, work clothing, and lunches often makes it financially unfeasible for women to work, especially those with low pay. Work-related expenses plus taxes are estimated to take 50 percent of a mother's paycheck.[55]

In the past a combination of voluntary and publicly sponsored day care has been controlled by boards of directors, the welfare apparatus, or the tendencies of the labor market, and shaped to respond to the welfare and therapeutic needs of special families and the labor-productive sector. Yet day care is a unique and invaluable service. It is not interchangeable with other institutions for the structuring of human resources. Obstacles to universal day care seem to consist of its origin in welfare arrangements; negative attitudes on the subject of working women; the psychiatric social-work emphasis on the mother's role in early childhood; the tradition of a single dominant maternal role; the confusion between separation and deprivation; the association of day care with communism;[56] and a general emphasis in our modern psychological and educational theory on individual as opposed to group or contextual development and achievement.[57]

It is time for Americans to face the present realities—the breakdown of the nuclear family, the transformation of women's roles, the new awareness of human (child and parental) needs. It is accordingly time to reorient day-care policy to correspond to this changed reality. This in turn must call forth federally funded, community-controlled, universal day care, under a distinct administration for early childhood purposes.

## NOTES

1 Eveline Burns, "Childhood Poverty and the Children's Allowance," in Eveline Burns, ed., *Children's Allowances and the Economic Welfare of Children* (New York: Citizens' Committee for Children, 1968), p. 3.

2 *New York Times*, Dec. 19 and 29, 1970; Jan. 11, 1971.

3 Alva Myrdal, *Nation and Family* (Cambridge, Mass.: M.I.T. Press, 1941), pp. 3–5.

4 U.S. Bureau of the Census, *Current Population Reports* Series P-20, no. 298, "Daytime Care of Children: October 1974 and February 1975," (Washington, D.C.: Government Printing Office, October 1976), Table 1.

5 Eveline Burns, "The Government's Role in Child and Family Welfare," in *The Nation's Children*, vol. 3, *Problems and Prospects*, ed., Eli Ginzberg (New York: Columbia University Press, 1960), p. 161.

6 U.S. Department of Labor News Release 77–792, September 14, 1977, Table 3.

7 Ethel Beer, *The Day Nursery* (New York: E. P. Dutton & Co., 1930).

8 Bernice Fleiss, "The Relationship of the Mayor's Committee on Wartime Care of Children to Day Care in New York City," doctoral thesis (Education), New York University, 1962; and Mary Bogue and Mary Moran, "Day Nurseries" in *Social Work Yearbook*, vol. 1 (1929), pp. 118–19.

9 Child Welfare League of America, "A Historical Sketch of the Day Nursery Movement," (New York, 1940—typescript in Child Welfare League of America Library).

10 Allen F. Davis, *Spearheads for Reform: The Social Settlements and The Progressive Movement, 1890–1914* (New York: Oxford University Press, 1967), pp. 43–46.

11 Fleiss, who quotes from Sophie Van S. Theis, *The Importance of Casework in the Day Nursery* (New York: National Federation of Day Nurseries, 1935), p. 1.

12 Anna Mayer, *Day Care as a Social Instrument, A Policy Paper*, Columbia University School of Social Work, Jan. 1965, p. 24.

13 Most of my material on the 1930's comes from the Fleiss thesis, and from Gussack Anne LeWine and R. Alice McCabe, *The Public Voluntary Agency-Sponsored Day-Care Program for Children in New York City*, an Administrative Study prepared for the Subcommittee on Day Care of the Committee on Family and Child Welfare, Community Service Society, Dept. of Public Affairs, July 1965.

14 Valerie Oppenheimer, *The Female Labor Force in The United States: Demographic and Economic Factors Governing Its Growth and Changing Composition* (Berkeley: University of California Press, 1970).

15 Mayer, p. 27.

16 Fleiss, p. 82, who quotes Alice Dashiell, "Trends in Day Care," *The Child*, 2 (Sept. 1946), 56.

17   Mayer, p. 27.

18   Katherine Oettinger, "Day Care Today: A Foundation for Progress," in *Report of a Consultation on Working Women and Day-Care Needs* (Washington, D.C.: United States Department of Labor), June 1, 1967 (hereafter, *Report*); Title I, Section 102B, of the Social Security Act as amended in 1962.

19   *Children Are Waiting* (Washington, D.C.: Human Resources Administration, Task Force on Early Childhood Development, July 1970; pamphlet), Appendix A, p. 2.

20   *Liberation News Service* #796, June 19, 1976, p. 4.

21   U.S. Department of Labor News Release 77–792, Table 3.

22   Florence Ruderman, *Child Care and Working Mothers: A Study of Arrangements Made for Daytime Care of Children,* Child Welfare League of America, 1968, p. 10.

23   Mary Keyserling, "Working Mothers and Their Children: The Urgent Need for Day-Care Services," in *Report*, see footnote 20, p. 3.

24   Seth Low and Pearl Spindler, *Child-Care Arrangements of Working Mothers in the United States,* Children's Bureau and Women's Bureau, 1968, pp. 15–16 (based on a study done in 1965).

25   *Children Are Waiting*, p. 8.

26   Keyserling, pp. 5–6.

27   *Ibid.*, p. 6.

28   Martin Tolchin, "Nursery Schools Arouse Rivalry," *New York Times,* Feb. 17, 1964.

29   Keyserling, p. 8.

30   *Guides to State Welfare Agencies for the Development of Day-Care Services,* (Washington, D.C.: United States Dept. of Health, Education and Welfare, Children's Bureau, Welfare Administration, 1963).

31   Barbara Wooton, *Social Science and Social Pathology* (New York: Macmillan, 1959), p. 144.

32   Urie Bronfenbrenner, *Two Worlds of Childhood: U.S. and U.S.S.R.* (New York: Russell Sage Foundation, 1970).

33   F. Ivan Nye and Lois Wladis Hoffman, eds., *The Employed Mother in America* (Chicago: Rand McNally, 1963).

34   Joseph Reid, "Legislation for Day Care," in *Report*, p. 35.

35   "Innovative Approaches—a Panel," *Ibid.*, p. 55.

36   Rose A. John, "Child Development and the Part-Time Mother," *Children* (Nov.–Dec. 1959), 213–18; and Leon Yarrow, "Conceptualizing the Early Environment," in Laura L. Dittman, ed., *Early Child Care: The New Perspectives* (New York: Atherton, 1968), pp. 15–27.

37   Bettye Caldwell and Julius Richmond, "Programmed Day Care for the Very Young Child—A Preliminary Report," *Child Welfare,* 44 (Mar. 1965), 134–42; and Stig Sjolin, "Care of Well Children in Day-Care Centers," *Care of Children in Day Care Centers* (Geneva: World Health Organization, 1964), p. 22.

38   Milton Willner, "Day Care, a Reassessment," *Child Welfare,* 44 (Mar. 1967), 126–27.

39   Eleanor Maccoby, "Children and Working Mothers," *Children,* 5–6 (1958–59), 86.

40  Yarrow, pp. 22–23.

41  Dale Meers and Allen Marans, "Group Care of Infants in Other Countries," in Dittman, pp. 234–82.

42  Willner, p. 129.

43  Julius Richmond, "Twenty Percent of the Nation," *Spotlight on Day Care: Proceedings of the National Conference on Day-Care Services, May 13–15, 1965* (Washington, D.C.: United States Department of Health, Education, and Welfare), p. 45.

44  Wooton, pp. 146, 151, 153.

45  Gerald Holden, "A Consideration of Benefits in Kind for Children," *Children's Allowances and the Economic Welfare of Children* (New York: Citizens' Committee for Children, 1968), pp. 150–52.

46  *New York Times*, Nov. 30, 1970, p. 51.

47  David Bull, "Action for Welfare Rights," in *The Fifth Social Service: Nine Fabian Essays* (London: Fabian Society, May 1970; pamphlet), p. 148.

48  Peter Townsend, Introduction, "Does Selectivity Mean a Nation Divided," *Social Services for All: Eleven Fabian Essays* (London: Fabian Society, Sept. 1968), pp. 1–6.

49  Brian Abel Smith, Conclusion, "The Need for Social Planning," *Ibid.*, p. 114.

50  Holden, p. 151 and Myrdal, p. 150.

51  Joseph Featherstone, "The Day-Care Problem: Kentucky Fried Chicken," *The New Republic*, Sept. 12, 1970, pp. 12–16; and Ann Cook and Herbert Mack, "Business Education, the Discovery Center Hustle," *Social Policy* (Sept.–Oct. 1970), pp. 3–11; *New York Times*, Dec. 27, 1969. For example, if Creative Playthings (a toy corporation) runs a day-care center, they will try to convince the parents of the children that certain Creative Playthings toys are needed for the children's educational development.

52  *New York Times*, Jan. 21, 1970, pp. 59 and 65, and Oct. 29, 1970.

53  Shlakman, p. 28.

54  *New York Times*, Dec. 15 and 29, 1970.

55  Nadine Brozan, "To Many Working Mothers, a Job Is Almost a Losing Proposition," *New York Times*, Jan. 5, 1971, p. 30.

56  Mayer, p. 129, who is quoting Raymond J. Gallagher, Secretary of the National Conference of Catholic Charities, in testimony on Public Welfare Amendments of 1962, Bill No. 10032, *Congressional Record*, 87th Congress, 2d Sess., pp. 578–80.

57  Rochelle Paul Wortis, "Child-Rearing and Women's Liberation," paper delivered at Women's Weekend, Ruskin College, Oxford University, February 28, 1970; pamphlet, p. 1.

# PART 3  GROWING UP FEMALE

# Lenore J. Weitzman*

# Sex-Role Socialization

In our society women are characterized as passive, dependent and emotional in contrast to men, who are considered aggressive, active and instrumental. How can these differences be explained? Are women "naturally" more passive, or are they taught to be more passive? Are men inherently more aggressive, or does our society socialize men into more aggressive roles?

To shed some light on the continued controversy over whether (or to what degree) these

*I wish to thank Susan Feller, Peggy Bernardy, and Kyra Subbotin for their research assistance, and Sheila Tobias for her many helpful suggestions. I am also indebted to William J. Goode, Ruth B. Dixon, Ann Freedman, Jo Freeman, and Sheryl Ruzeck for their comments on the earlier drafts of this article. This paper was revised in 1978, while I was a National Fellow at the Hoover Institute at Stanford University, and I am grateful for the Institution's support. © Lenore J. Weitzman.

observed difference are learned or inherent, this paper will focus on the socialization process. I want to examine how the socialization process shapes the sex roles that women and men come to accept as entirely natural and self-evident.

First, however, let us consider two important and broadly based sources of data which suggest that studying socialization will be fruitful in helping us to understand sex roles as we know them today: data from studies of cross-cultural variation in sex roles, and data from studies of sex roles acquired by persons with biologically ambiguous sexual identities.

Anthropologists who have examined sex roles cross-culturally have found great diversity in the roles assumed "natural" for men and women, and in the extent of differentiation between the sexes. Margaret Mead's classic study of three New Guinea tribes provides impressive evidence of this cross-cultural variation in assigned sex roles.[1] In one tribe, the Arapesh, both men and women were regarded as cooperative, unaggressive, and responsive to the needs of others—characteristics we would normally label as feminine or maternal. In a second society, the Mundugumor, both men and women were aggressive, unresponsive, and individualistic—traits we would normally call masculine. Neither the Arapesh nor the Mundugumor ascribed contrasting personality characteristics to men and women: the Arapesh ideal man, like the ideal woman, was mild and responsive; the Mundugumor ideal for both man and woman was violent and aggressive. In the third society Mead studied, the Tchambuli, there was a reversal of the typical sex roles found in Western cultures. The Tchambuli women were dominant, impersonal and managing; the men were emotionally dependent and less responsible than women.

Cross-cultural data such as those collected by Mead are illuminating because they make us realize that some of our most basic assumptions about what is "natural" are based on cultural beliefs rather than biological necessity. For example, although we have long assumed that women were not fit for war (because they were "naturally" weaker and less aggressive than men) women in other societies, such as Dahomey, were great warriors.* Similarly, we have traditionally regarded women

---

*It should be noted however, that physical strength is almost irrelevant in modern society. No industrial society gives its highest rewards of money, power, or prestige on the basis of physical strength.

as "naturally" more nurturant, and therefore uniquely qualified to rear children: but other societies have assumed males were more nurturant, while still others have regarded child care as so important they have limited it to trained experts.[2]

The varied sex-role assignments given to men and women in different cultures suggest that the basic characteristics of men and women are not biologically determined; rather they are based on cultural definitions of sex-appropriate behavior. Since there is no reason to assume that the biological makeup of men and women in Mead's tribes or in other societies differs from that of men and women in the United States in any basic way, the observed differences between the sexes in these cultures and our own would seem to be culturally determined. The compelling logic of this conclusion becomes more obvious when we consider the alternative: if we hypothetically assume a biological basis for these differences we would then have to conclude that Tchambuli men were dependent because they had more female hormones. This would be akin to concluding that Latin American men are more *macho* than American men because of higher levels of male hormones, or that Oriental women are less aggressive than American women because they have more female hormones.* Since we know that there is no such cross-cultural variation in biological or hormonal sex, we must recognize the great influence of cultural learning in order to explain these differences.

The power of cultural factors is also suggested by a very different line of research: the work of Money, Hampson, and Eckhardt on hermaphrodites.[3] A hermaphrodite is a person who possesses a complete set of both male and female genitalia and reproductive organs. While a complete hermaphrodite is extremely rare, a fair number of babies are born each year whose sex is difficult to determine with certainty. Some of these infants appear to be female, but are biologically male. Others may appear to be male but are biologically female. Dr. John Money and his associates at Johns Hopkins University have spent almost twenty years following the life histories of some of these babies. Of most interest to us here are those babies who were assigned

---

*As the Bems have observed, "If female hormones are responsible for keeping women from high level jobs, we would have to assume that women in the Soviet Union have different hormones, because they comprise 33 percent of the engineers and 75 percent of the doctors." Sandra Bem and Daryl Bem, "Training Woman to Know Her Place: The Power of a Nonconscious Ideology," *Psychology Today*, November, 1970.

one sex at birth but were later found to belong biologically (genetically, gonadally, hormonally) to the opposite sex. In virtually all of these cases, the sex of assignment (and thus of rearing) proved dominant. Thus, babies assigned as males at birth and brought up as boys by their parents (who were unaware of their child's female genetic and hormonal makeup) thereafter thought of themselves as boys, played with boys' toys, enjoyed boys' sports, preferred boy's clothing, developed male sex fantasies, and in due course fell in love with girls. And the reverse was true for babies who were biologically male but reared as girls: they followed the typical feminine pattern of development—they preferred marriage over a career, enjoyed domestic and homemaking duties, and saw their future fulfillment in the traditional woman's role.

This research dramatically illustrates the impact of socialization—even when it contradicts biological sex—and thus further supports the importance of learned differences as powerful determinants of current sex roles. Having indicated the powerful influence of culturally transmitted definitions of sex roles, let us now examine the dynamics of the process by which they are transmitted—the process of socialization.

## EARLY CHILDHOOD SOCIALIZATION

Socialization begins at birth. From the minute a newborn baby girl is wrapped in a pink blanket and her brother in a blue one, the two children are treated differently. The difference starts with the subtle tone of voice of the adults cooing over the two cradles, and continues with the father's mock wrestling with his baby boy and gentler play with his "fragile" daughter.[4] Researchers have observed sex differences in behavior of male and female babies at amazingly young ages, most of it directly traceable to parents' differential treatment of infant boys and girls.

Moss's observations of mothers with infants at three weeks and three months show that even the newborn baby is consistently being given reinforcement for appropriate behavior.[5] Moss, in fact, has tentatively suggested that patterns leading to verbal ability in girls and aggression in boys were being selectively encouraged in the infants he observed.[6]

### Infant socialization

In observing thirteen-month-old babies, Goldberg and Lewis found that the little girls clung to, looked at, and talked to their mothers more often than the little boys.[7] Each of these behavioral differences, however, was linked to differential treatment by the mother when the babies were younger. The researchers had observed the same mothers with their babies when the babies were six months old. At that stage they observed that mothers of girl babies touched their infant girls more often then did mothers of infant boys. They also talked to and handled their daughters more often.[8] By the time these same children were thirteen months old, the researchers observed that the girl babies had learned to respond to the more frequent stimuli they received from their mothers: they reciprocated their mothers' attention, with the result that by thirteen months they talked to and touched their mothers more often than the boys did. In order to establish the causal relationship, i.e., that high frequency of touching at six months causes babies to seek more touching at thirteen months, Goldberg and Lewis reclassified the mothers they had observed at six months into groups with high and low rates of touching. They found that the children (both boys and girls) of mothers with high touching rates at six months sought the most maternal contact at thirteen months.[9]

This research vividly illustrates socialization at its earliest stages. It indicates that sex-role socialization begins before the child is even aware of a sexual identity: before he or she can have an internal motive for conforming to sex-role standards. It also indicates that cultural assumptions about what is "natural" for a boy or for a girl are so deeply ingrained that parents may treat their children differentially without even being aware of it. Presumably, if we interviewed mothers of six-month-old babies, they would not tell us that they expected their young sons to be independent and assertive while still in the cradle. Yet, it appears that at some level mothers do have such expectations, and these expectations are successfully communicated to very young babies. Thus, wittingly or unwittingly, parents encourage and reinforce sex-appropriate behavior, and little boys and little girls respond to parental encouragement and rewards. So little boys learn to be independent, active, and aggressive; their sisters learn to be dependent, verbal, and social.

### Early cognitive socialization

We have been discussing the first type of socialization an infant experiences: simple behavior reinforcement. A second type of socialization begins with cognitive learning—when the child is able to sort out and make conceptual distinctions about the social world and herself or himself. Around the age of three or four, the child begins to make sex-role distinctions and express sex-role preferences. Rabban found that at the age of three both boys and girls still showed incomplete recognition of sex differences and were unaware of the appropriateness of sex-typed toy objects.[10] Each year, however, children's cognitive abilities increase: by age six they are able to distinguish the male and female role clearly, and to identify themselves appropriately. Sex-role learning in these preschool years may be divided into three analytic processes. The child learns:

1 to *distinguish* between men and women and between boys and girls, and to know what kinds of behavior are characteristic of each;
2 to express appropriate sex-role *preferences* for himself or herself;
3 and to *behave* in accordance with sex-role standards.

In labeling these processes I have avoided the term *identification* because of the distinct meaning of this word in the socialization literature. Identification, a frequently used concept in Freudian theory, assumes that sex-role learning is limited to the same-sex parent. This theory will be discussed (and criticized) in the final section of this paper. In the following pages each of these three processes will be discussed separately because each presents a different set of contingencies for the growing boy or girl.

### Distinguishing between male and female roles

Both boys and girls learn to distinguish the male from the female role by observing the men and women around them: their parents, brothers and sisters, neighbors, and friends. In addition to serving as models for the young child, these adults and older boys and girls often provide explicit instructions on proper behavior. Little girls are told what is considered nice and ladylike, and little boys are told what is expected of big strong men.

As already noted, parents are especially influential in defining the male and female role for the young child. They do this both consciously and unconsciously, by example and proscription, by reward and punishment. There is some evidence that fathers are more concerned than mothers with sex-typing in young children. Goodenough's interviews with the parents of two- to four-year-old children indicated that fathers more strictly differentiated sex roles and encouraged stronger sex typing in children than did mothers.[11]

Picture books are another important source of sex-role learning for young children. Through books, children learn about the world outside their immediate environment: they learn what other boys and girls do, say, and feel, and they learn what is expected of children of their age. In a 1972 study of prize-winning pre-school picture books, Weitzman, Eifler, Hokada, and Ross found girls portrayed as passive, doll-like creatures, while the boys were active and adventuresome.[12] Most of the little girls engaged in service activities directed toward pleasing and helping their brothers and fathers. In contrast, the boys were engaged in a variety of tasks requiring independence and self-confidence.

Picture books also provide children with role models—images of what they will be like when they grow up. Weitzman *et al.* found the adult women portrayed in these award-winning books were consistently stereotyped and limited. Most were identified only as wives or mothers. The men were shown in a wide variety of occupations and professions, whereas not one of the adult women had an outside job or profession. The authors conclude that in the world of picture books:

> Little girls receive attention and praise for their attractiveness, while boys are admired for their achievements and cleverness. For girls, achievement is marriage and becoming a mother. Most of the women in picture books have status by virtue of their relationships to specific men—they are the wives of the kings, judges, adventurers and explorers, but they themselves are not the rulers, judges, adventurers and explorers.
>
> Through picture books, girls are taught to have low aspirations because there are so few opportunities portrayed as available to them. The world of picture books never tells little girls that as women they might find fulfillment outside of their homes or through intellectual pursuits. . . .
>
> In a country with over 40 percent of the women in the labor force it is absurd to find that women in picture books remain only mothers and wives. . . .
>
> Their future occupational world is presented as consisting primarily of glamour and service. Women are excluded from the world of sports, politics and science. They can achieve only by being attractive, congenial and serving others.[13]

Another influential source of sex-role socialization for young children is television. Gardner's study of the program *Sesame Street* (another supposed ideal) indicated that television contributes equally to severe sex-role stereotypes:

> On one program, Big Bird (having said that he would like to be a member of a family and having been told that Gordon and Susan would be his family) is told that he will have to help with the work and that since he is a boy bird, he will have to do men's work—the heavy work, the *"important"* work and also that he should get a girl (bird) to help Susan with *her* work of arranging flowers, redecorating, etc. There was more and virtually all of it emphasized that there is men's work and then there is women's work—that men's work is outside the home and women' work is in the home. (This in spite of the fact that 17 *million* children under eighteen have mothers who are employed outside the home; of the 4.5 million are under six.)[14]

Although the images in children's books and TV programs appear to be more stereotyped and rigid than reality, interviews with young children indicate the extent to which these clearly differentiated sex roles are internalized by the child. Hartley asked a sample of young boys what they thought was expected of boys and girls. Her respondents described boys as follows:

> They have to be able to fight in case a bully comes along; they have to be athletic; . . . they must be able to play rough games . . . they need to be smart; they need to be able to take care of themselves; they should know what girls don't know . . . they should have more ability than girls . . . they are expected to get dirty; to mess up the house; to be naughty; to be outside more than girls are; not to be cry babies, not to be softies; and to get into trouble more than girls do.[15]

Girls, according to the boy respondents,

> have to stay close to home; they are expected to play quietly and more gently than boys; they are often afraid; they must not be rough; they have to keep clean; they cry when scared or hurt; their activities consist of "fopperies" like playing with dolls, fussing over babies, and sitting and talking about dresses; they need to know how to cook, sew and take care of children, but spelling and arithmetic are not as important for them as for boys.[16]

When Hartley asked her young respondents about adults, she found their images of the two sexes even more disparate. In the children's eyes men are active and intelligent, strong, ready to make decisions, protect women and children in emergencies. . . . They must be able to fix things, they must get money to support their families, and have a good business head. Men are the boss in the family and have the authority to dispose of money and they get first choice in the use of the most comfortable chair in the house and the daily paper. . . . They laugh and make more jokes than women do. Compared with mothers, fathers are more fun to be with: they are exciting to have around and they have the best ideas.[17]

In contrast, women are seen as a rather tired and unintelligent group.

They are indecisive and they are afraid of many things; they make a fuss over things, they get tired a lot . . . they don't know what to do in an emergency, they cannot do dangerous things, they are scared of getting wet or getting an electric shock, they are not very intelligent. . . . Women do things like cooking and washing and sewing because that's all they can do.[18]

### Expressing sex-role preferences

Once the child has learned to distinguish males from females and has determined the types of behavior that are appropriate for each, he or she may begin to express sex-role preferences. Rabban found that both boys and girls at age three decidedly prefer the mother role when asked to choose which parent they would prefer to be like.[19] Other studies have corroborated this preference of young children for the mother.* According to the reasons the children themselves give for their preference, they like best the parent who caters to their material wants, who expresses affection for them, who plays with them most, and who punishes them least.[20]

But the sex-role preferences of children soon change. By age five most boys, and a significant minority of girls, say they prefer the masculine role. Brown, interviewing five- and six-year-old children, found more cross-sex preferences among girls (indicating a desire to be boys) than among boys.[21] In addition, the boys show a significantly stronger preference for the masculine role than girls reveal for the feminine role.[22] The research of Hartup and Zook corroborates the finding about strength of preference[23] and indicates, further, that with

---

*These preferences of young children challenge Freud's theory of penis envy. They suggest, rather, that young boys may experience something akin to breast envy.

each year more girls prefer to identify with the masculine role than boys with the feminine role.[24]

One explanation for the general preference for the male role is that both boys and girls have learned it is more prestigious in our society. Thus, it is preferable. Hartley's study, cited above, clearly indicates that children perceive the superior status and privileges of the masculine role.[25] They know which sex gets the best chair in the house, and which sex is expected to do the cleaning.[26] Brown, using the values children give to sex-typed toys, also concluded that the children saw the masculine role as having greater prestige and value.[27] Smith has found evidence to suggest that as children grow older, they increasingly learn to give males more prestige.[28] He asked children from eight to fifteen to vote on whether boys or girls have desirable or undesirable traits. With increasing age both boys and girls increasingly ascribed the desirable traits to boys. In addition, boys expressed a progressively better opinion of themselves while self-conceptions of girls progressively weakened.[29]

Thus children learn that it is better to be a male than a female because it is men who exhibit the highly valued traits and are accorded the privilege and prestige in our society.* No wonder, then, that girls are reluctant to express "appropriate" sex-role preferences, and instead continue wishing they were boys. Boys, by contrast, find it easy to express "appropriate" sex role preferences.

It is likely that the preferences of some young girls are different today. The women's liberation movement has brought a heightened awareness of the impact of negative sex-role stereotypes, and conscious attempts to change them. In addition, feminists have encouraged parents to raise their children in a sex-neutral manner and to instill a sense of pride in their daughters.

### Learning sex-role behavior

The third component of the socialization process consists of learning to act like a girl or a boy. Boys appear to have more difficulty learning

---

*Alice Rossi has suggested that girls get a more subtle message with regard to the relative prestige of men and women. They learn that outside the home men are the bosses of women; however, in the home, father does not know best. The message thus communicated to little girls is that women can be important only in the family. Alice Rossi, "Equality Between the Sexes," in *The Woman in America* (Boston: Houghton Mifflin, 1964), p. 105.

appropriate sex-role behavior. Their difficulty stems from three sources: the lack of continuous male role models, the rigidity and harshness of masculine sex-role demands, and the negative nature of male sex-role proscriptions.

Several theorists have suggested that boys know less about the masculine role because of the relative lack of salience of the father as a model. Lynn notes that the father is in the home much less than the mother, and even when he is there, he usually participates in fewer intimate activities with the child than the mother does.[30] Both the amount of time spent with the child, and the intimacy and intensity of parental contact are thought to be important for the child's learning. Since the girl is able to observe her mother throughout the day and has continuous and intimate contact with her, she supposedly finds it easier to use her mother as a model, and to imitate appropriate sex-role behavior.

Lynn has further theorized that because boys have less direct exposure to male models they tend to develop stereotypical images of masculinity.[31] This view has been supported by studies showing that fatherless boys have more exaggerated notions of masculinity than boys who have a father in the home.[32] The tendency of boys to pattern themselves after a male stereotype may help account for the exaggerated forms of masculinity encouraged by male peer groups. In the absence of fuller role models to emulate, boys may view exaggerated "toughness" and aggression as appropriate male behavior.

Hartley has suggested that boys have the additional problem of a more rigorous sex-role definition: "Demands that boys conform to social notions of what is manly come much earlier and are enforced with much more vigor than similar attitudes with respect to girls. These demands are frequently enforced harshly, impressing the small boy with the danger of deviating from them, while he does not quite understand what they are."[33] By contrast, very young girls are allowed a wider range of behavior and are punished less severely for deviation, especially in the middle class. (At young ages it is easier for a girl to be a tomboy than for a boy to be a sissy.) Upon reaching adolescence, however, the behavior of girls is more sharply constricted than is boys'.

In addition to the relative absence of male role models and the rigidity of the male sex role, the socialization of boys is said to be characterized by negative proscriptions.[34] Boys are constantly warned *not* to be sissies, and *not* to engage in other feminine behavior. The literature on learning suggests that it is harder to learn from punishment than from rewards, because the desired behavior is not enunciated in the sanction and therefore remains obscure.[35] Thus some theorists have asserted that the socialization of boys is particularly conducive to anxiety. In Hartley's words,

> the child is asked to do something which is not clearly defined for him, based on reasons he cannot possibly appreciate, and enforced with threats, punishments, and anger by those who are close to him. . . . Anxiety frequently expresses itself in over-straining to be masculine, in virtual panic at being caught doing anything traditionally defined as feminine, and in hostility toward anything even hinting at "femininity," including females themselves.[36]

In contrast to the anxiety-producing sex-role learning of the boy, the socialization literature characterizes the young girl's experiences as easy. She is supposedly provided with more positive opportunities to learn appropriate role behavior through her frequent interaction with her mother* as well as the chance to try out her feminine role in her doll play.[37] This idyllic view of the learning process for girls appears naive to any woman who has been socialized in a middle-class family. It is clear that the sex-role socialization process is equally anxiety-producing for girls, although for somewhat different reasons. The girl is provided with a female model, and is afforded more opportunity to "play out" the "appropriate" behavior, but the role she is asked to play is clearly not a desirable one. As already noted, children understand the relative worth of the two sexes at quite young ages. The little girl is therefore aware of the fact that she is being pushed, albeit gently, into a set of behaviors that are neither considered desirable nor rewarded by the society at large. For example, she is told that it is feminine to play house: to wash dishes, set the table, dress her doll, vacuum the floor, and cook the dinner. In many middle-class homes these activities are delegated to paid domestics, or performed with obvious distaste. Why, then, should the little girl want to imitate those behaviors? I would hypothesize the little girl becomes quite anxious about being encouraged to perform a series of behaviors that are held in low esteem. I would hypothesize further that she experiences considerable internal

---

*This statement presumes a family in which the mother stays at home. It ignores the reality in an increasingly significant number of families in which mothers of preschool children work and may thus have no more frequent contact with their children than working fathers do.

conflict when she realizes that her mother, a loved model, receives neither recognition nor satisfaction for such activities, and yet encourages them in her.

In addition to perceiving the low evaluation of feminine activities, many young girls find boys' activities instrinsically more enjoyable. For example, boys' toys allow a much broader range of activity as well as more active and adventuresome involvement. One study found that the average price of boys' toys was much greater than that of girls' toys for each age group.[38] More girls in Ward's sample preferred boys' toys than preferred girls' toys.[39] Respondents in Komarovsky's study expressed a similar interest in boys' toys—in chemistry sets, baseball gloves, and electric trains. "One of my biggest disappointments as a child," wrote a girl in Komarovsky's study, "happened one Christmas. I asked for a set of tools . . . only to find a sewing set."[40]

Since most growing children enjoy being active, running and playing outside, getting dirty if necessary, and being allowed to explore their own interests, it is not surprising that many girls prefer "boys'" activities, and resent being restricted to being "a sweet little girl." Komarovsky's students reported that they envied the freedom their brothers and other boys were allowed, and resented being constrained to play with "girls' toys," to be sedentary, quiet, and neat in their play.[41]

In reviewing the socialization literature I was struck by the fact that the harsh restrictions placed on boys are often discussed, but those placed on girls are ignored. In fact, there is no reason to believe that the socialization of boys involves greater restrictiveness, control, and protectiveness.[42] Boys may be punished more often, but girls' activities are likely to be so severely constrained to begin with that they never have a chance to engage in punishable behavior. It is also possible that the kinds of sanctions used to socialize women may be more subtle—but no less severe: boys are spanked, but girls may be made to feel unworthy, deviant, guilty, or queer.[43] The following quotes from Komarovsky's study indicate the powerful sanctions and the resulting anguish experienced by girls whose desires conflict with the sex-role preferences of their parents:

> I started life as a little tomboy but as I grew older, Mother got worried about my unladylike ways. She removed my tops, marbles, football, and skates and tried to replace these with dolls, tea sets and sewing games. To interest me in dolls she collected dolls of different nations, dressed exquisitely in their native costumes. . . .

When despite her efforts she caught me one day trying to climb a tree in the park she became thoroughly exasperated and called me a little "freak."

Once I got very dirty playing and Mother told me that if I didn't learn to play quietly and keep myself neat no man would ever want to marry me.

I was a member of a Brownie Troop when I was seven and we were to have a party one day to which each child was to bring her favorite toy. My favorite toy at that time was a set of tin soldiers. Grandmother was shocked and insisted that I would disgrace her by bringing such an unladylike toy. But I refused to take a doll, with the result that I was forced to miss the party. But Grandmother succeeded in making me feel quite "queer" because I didn't like dolls.[44]

These quotes suggest the very real pressures that are brought to bear on the girl whose temperamental preferences do not conform to the feminine stereotype.

In summary, the socialization of boys and of girls may present different sets of difficulties, but difficulties and anxiety in the socialization process are common to both. Typically, girls have more readily available role models, but they probably have less motivation to imitate those models because they (correctly) view the role as more confining and less rewarding than the masculine role. Boys may have less salient role models, and experience more frequent physical punishment, but they have more motivation to learn the masculine role because they (correctly) view it as more highly valued than the feminine role, allowing more exciting and interesting activities.

Consequently, socialization must be understood as an anxiety-producing process for both boys and girls because it requires them both to conform to rigid sex-role standards that are often in conflict with their individual temperaments or preferences. To the extent that we continue to define appropriate sex-role behavior for men and women as polar opposites, we will continue to push many individuals into unnatural molds.

### The learning process: reactions, rewards and punishment

Let us now briefly consider how specific characteristics are encouraged in children of each sex. According to Kagan, the typical child seeks the acceptance of parents and peers and wants to avoid their rejection.

These motives predispose her or him to shun inappropriate activities, and to choose responses that are congruent with sex-role standards.[45]

Parents say that they want their daughters to be passive, nurturing, and dependent and their sons to be aggressive and independent. Therefore, most parents punish aggression in their daughters, and passivity and dependency in their sons.[46] For example, the little girl is allowed to cling to her mother's apron, but her brother is told that he can't be a "sissy" and must go off on his own. The dependency and affection-seeking responses seen as normal for both boys and girls in early childhood become defined as feminine in older children.[47] The result, as Bardwick has noted, is that girls are not separated from their parents as sources of support and nurturance, and they are therefore not forced to develop internal controls and an independent sense of self.[48] Instead, the self that they value is one that emanates from the appraisals of others. Consequently girls develop a greater need for the approval of others and a greater fear of rejection[49] than do boys.

Kagan has observed that our definition of femininity *requires* reactions from other people. The young girl cannot assess whether she is attractive, nurturing, or passive without continual interaction and feedback from others.[50] She is thus forced to be dependent on people and to court their acceptance in order to obtain those experiences that help to establish sex-typed behaviors.[51]

In contrast, the boy is encouraged to be self-reliant. Many masculine sex-typed behaviors, especially those involving physical skills, can be developed alone. A boy is taught to stand up for himself and engage in certain behavior because he, as a person, feels that it is appropriate. In fact, men who stand by their individual principles despite opposition and the scorn of others often become cultural heroes.

According to Bronfenbrenner, different methods of child training are used for boys than for girls. Boys are subjected to more physical punishment, whereas psychological punishments, such as the threat of withdrawal of love, are more frequently used for girls.[52] Children trained with physical punishment have been shown to be more self-reliant and independent.[53] The other method of child training—the love-oriented psychological method—usually produces children who are more obedient and dependent.[54] As girls are most often trained with psychological methods they are exposed to more affection and less punishment than boys. But they are also made more anxious about the withdrawal of love.

Thus, specific methods of child training and the cultural definition of femininity (which necessitates reliance on the approval of others) both encourage dependency in women. Kagan links the crucial significance of others—and their acceptance or rejection—to the finding that girls are often more conforming and more concerned about socially desirable behavior than boys.[55] Another interpretation of female conformity links it to doll-play training. David Matza has hypothesized that girls are taught to be more conforming and concerned with socially acceptable behavior because they are trained to act as socializing agents with their dolls. By talking to, and "training" their dolls to do the right thing, the girls themselves gain a vast amount of experience in articulating and sanctioning the cultural norms.[56]

## VARIATION IN SEX ROLE STANDARDS AND BEHAVIOR

### Individual differences

Thus far we have taken the success of the socialization process for granted and have assumed that most boys and girls eventually adopt the prescribed sex-role behaviors. But most of us can think of exceptions—the self-confident achievement-oriented girl, or the dependent boy who cares very much about others' opinions of him. We all know some people who seem to contradict the stereotypes and others, possibly including ourselves, who conform only to a percentage of them. In fact, we may often feel the pull of the extremes of a single trait within ourselves, wanting to be both independent and dependent at the same time, or feeling that we are at times totally oriented toward achievement and at other times holding back for fear of being too successful.

In an effort to summarize a large body of literature, I have focused on the "average" girl (and boy) and have attempted to describe the "typical" pattern of socialization. As a result, the wide range of variation in individual behavior has been obscured. It is important to pause in this analysis to emphasize the extent of variation among individuals of *both* sexes with regard to personality characteristics, intelligence, and achievement motivation.

The range of differences within each sex is much greater than the differences between the average members of opposite sexes.[57] Whenever we speak of averages, we obscure the great range of variation within each sex. Moreover, after a review of the literature on sex differences, Jo Freeman concluded that what was deemed typical of one sex or the other was based on the average performance of only *two-thirds* of the subjects.[58] But this disregards the behavior of the *remaining one-third* of each sex. Because it is easier to describe the "typical" socialization pattern first, however, we will continue temporarily to "disregard" individual differences. In the final sections of this paper, we will return to the topic of individual behavior variation and examine its implications for socialization theory.

As we continue to describe the "typical" socialization process, the reader should keep in mind the limits of all generalizations. While most descriptions may accurately characterize most boys and girls, there will always be an important minority who "deviate" from the typical pattern. In addition, those who are in the majority and those who are in the minority are always shifting—so that an individual may be "typical" at one point, or in one type of behavior, but "deviant" at other times.

### The continuing research debate

Before we continue, it is important to note that there is still considerable disagreement about the extent to which sex-linked behavioral differences actually exist. Although the earlier research seemed to confirm the existence of differences,[59] many of these findings are now considered open to question. For example, in 1975 Eleanor Maccoby and Carol Jacklin, two Stanford University psychologists, undertook a massive re-evaluation and up-dating of the empirical evidence on sex differences.[60] They reviewed approximately 1,600 studies, published primarily between 1966 and 1973, and concluded that many of the earlier reports of sex differences were unfounded.

Maccoby and Jacklin report that the evidence is equivocal with respect to anxiety, level of activity, competitiveness, dominance, compliance, and nurturance. In addition, although they find fairly solid support for the long-established behavioral differences in verbal ability, spatial ability, and aggressiveness, they do *not* find substantial support for previously reported findings that: (1) girls are more "social" than boys, (2) girls are more "suggestible" than boys, (3) girls have lower self-esteem, or (4) girls are less motivated toward achievement.[61]

Given the political and emotional investments in the debate over sex differences in behavior, it is unlikely that any work on this topic will be accepted as definitive in the near future. Thus it is not surprising that while most scholars have praised the Maccoby-Jacklin effort as the most authoritative analysis in the field, others contend it is biased in the direction of finding no sex differences. For example, one critic has charged that their reliance on studies of very young children (in contrast to older children) has led the authors to underestimate the number of sex differences because some differences do not appear until adolescence.[62] However, the very fact that sex differences do not "appear" until adolescence suggests, at a minimum, that the observed differences between the sexes are likely to be a result of socialization and learning—and are therefore not "inherent."

### Social class variation in sex roles

Sex-role standards also differ by social class and by racial and ethnic group.[63] And even within these large subgroupings, various aspects of family composition affect both the content and the potency of sex-role socialization. Because it is impossible to consider all these factors in each section in a paper of this length, we have focused on the most prevalent section of the population, the broadly defined white middle class. This may have given the reader an erroneous impression of uniformity. Thus, it is important now to consider some of the variations in sex-role standards by social class. In the next section we will consider variation by race.

A parent's social class position is an important determinant of his or her sex-role standards and expectations. Sociologists have generally used a combination of three indicators to measure social class—education, occupation, and income. However, the research on sex-role socialization has been consistent no matter what indicator of class is used. All the studies have found that persons in the higher social classes tend to be less rigid about sex distinctions. In working-class and lower-class families, there is much more concern about different roles for boys and girls and men and women. As Letha and John Scanzoni have pointed out, the theme song of the popular television program "All In The Family" accurately portrays the concern of a working-class father (Archie Bunker) for clear-cut distinctions between the sexes (for the days "when girls were girls and men were men").[64]

As might be expected from these parental expectations, differentiation between boys and girls appears to be sharpest in lower-class families.[65] Rabban found that children from working-class families differentiate sex roles at earlier ages and have more traditional sex-role standards than middle-class children.[66] He showed that working-class boys were aware of the appropriate sex-typed toy choices by age four or five; middle-class boys were not aware of them until age six.[67] The class differences are even greater for girls. Middle-class girls not only showed later awareness of sex-typing than working-class girls, but were less traditional in their sex-role concepts.

Middle-class parents may encourage "traditional feminine behavior" in their daughters, but they also encourage a degree of independence and assertiveness. Not only are middle-class parents willing to "tolerate" daughters who are tomboys, many of them encourage their daughters to do well in sports and to excel in school. Lower-class parents are more likely to view such interests and achievements as "too masculine" and to discourage them.

A similar pattern emerges in the class-related sex-role expectations for boys. Middle-class parents are willing to let their sons be more expressive (to be more nurturant and tender), while working-class parents see these traits as "too feminine" or sissy.[69] Working-class parents want their sons to be instrumental, that is, to be focused on tasks and work.

In summary, then, middle-class parents are interested in seeing both their sons and their daughters develop a greater range of traits along *both* instrumental and expressive lines. In contrast, blue-collar parents encourage traditional sex-role behavior in both boys and girls. These differences are illustrated by Lillian Rubin's comparative interviews with lower- and middle-class families. As Rubin notes, in the homes of the professional middle class, both boys and girls

> have more training in exploring the socio-emotional realm. . . . It's true that for the girls, this usually is the *focus* of their lives, while for the boys, it is not. Nevertheless, compared to childrearing patterns in working-class families, professional middle-class families make fewer and less rigid sex-role distinctions in early childhood. . . .
>
> As small children, therefore, boys in such middle-class homes more often get the message that it's all right to cry, to be nurturant as well as nurtured, to be reflective and introspective, even at times to be passive—in essence, in some small measure, to relate to their expressive side.
>
> Not once in a professional middle-class homes did I see a young boy shake his father's hand in a well-taught "manly" gesture as he bid him good night. Not once did I hear a middle-class parent scornfully—or even sympathetically—call a crying boy a sissy or in

any way reprimand him for his tears. Yet, these were not uncommon observations in the working-class homes I visited. Indeed, I was impressed with the fact that, even as young as six or seven, the working-class boys seemed more emotionally controlled—more like miniature men—than those in the middle-class families.[70]

In later sections of this paper we will trace the ways in which these class differences affect scholastic achievements and the choice of marriage and/or career.

### Ethnic variation in sex roles

Further specification of sex-role standards occurs along ethnic and racial lines. Many people have the impression that Italians, Jews, Asian Americans, Chicanos, Irish, Poles, blacks, and Puerto Ricans have distinctive conceptions of appropriate behavior for men and women.[71] With few exceptions, however, ethnic variation in sex-role standards has been ignored in the socialization literature.[72]

One fascinating study, conducted by Fred Strodbeck, compared the socialization practices of Italian and Jewish mothers in encouraging achievement motivation in their sons.[73] When asked about their aspirations for their sons' achievements, both Italian and Jewish mothers had equally high standards and hopes for their performance. However, when asked how they would respond to their sons' hypothetical failure to meet their high standards, the Italian mothers indicated they would nevertheless love and accept the sons. The Jewish mothers, in contrast, reported they would show displeasure if their sons failed to meet their standards, and moreover they would make their love and acceptance contingent upon the sons' continued striving and eventual success. Strodbeck concluded that the Jewish mothers' "contingent love" was far more powerful in creating high achievement motivation in boys.

Unfortunately, most of the research on achievement motivation and ethnic differences in socialization, like Strodbeck's, focuses exclusively on male samples. As psychologist Matina Horner has noted, most social scientists investigating achievement motivation did not consider women's achievement important enough to investigate.[74] Further, those few who originally included women in their samples later dropped the female respondents from their analysis when they found the females' responses did not conform to the male pattern.

### Racial variation in sex roles: the case of black women

When one first approaches the research literature on black women one cannot help but be puzzled by two seemingly contradictory findings. Some researchers report that black women have adopted a more masculine sex role than white woman and are strong, assertive, and independent. But other studies have shown that their self-images are even more sex-stereotyped than those of white women. In this section we will briefly review the research in support of each of these views, and then try to make some sense of the apparent contradictions.[75] However, it is important to note that sex role research on blacks still remains one of the biggest "blind spots in existing sociology."[76] Clearly, more systematic research in this area is sorely needed.

The sociologists who assert that black women are strong, independent, and dominant trace these attributes to their role in the family and the economy. They point to the legacy of slavery for the roots of the black family structure, and to black woman's historically greater access to occupational opportunities, money, and status.

The black family has frequently been characterized as a matriarchal (mother-headed) extended family with an emphasis on consanguine relationships (i.e., blood ties) rather than the conjugal (husband-wife) relationship.[77] Although sociologists, such as Kandel[78] and Moynihan,[79] have found that there are more female-headed families among blacks even when the socioeconomic status is controlled, the matriarchal family structure is typically a lower-class family pattern.

This lower-class pattern begins, according to Stack, with premarital pregnancy.[80] Since premarital sex is prevalent and parenthood is highly valued (regardless of the child's legitimacy), young women often become pregnant in their teens.[81] However, youth and lack of monetary resources often prevent them from marrying and establishing a separate domicile, so many are unmarried and living in their parents' homes when their first child is born. Thereafter, these unmarried women quickly and accurately assess the relative stability of welfare, as opposed to the extreme economic vulnerability of their male partners, and commonly forgo legal marriage, at least temporarily.[82]

Since these unmarried mothers often stay at home, it is likely that their mothers will play a great role in raising the grandchild. Even married adult children often continue to reside with one or more of their parents, and if a marriage fails, both men and women readily return to their mother's household. Thus the "matriarch" is both the head of the household and the dominant authority figure in many black families. She also provides a female role model.

Stack attributes the lack of permanent husband-wife households to two primary factors. The first is the lack of permanent well-paying jobs for men.[83] The second is the disincentives built into the welfare system.[84] As a result, many researchers report that black women, in contrast to white women, "hold more negative attitudes toward the reliability of men and the security and desirability of marriage."[85] They realize that they cannot rely on men for their support and they socialize their daughters to have the same realistic skepticism. For example, Ladner found that very young black girls originally want to marry a man who is a protector, supporter, and companion. However, with increasing age they come to believe that very few men can fulfill these roles, and they become more ambivalent in their expectations. (Some girls had firmly established the view that men are "no good" by the time they were eight years old.)[86]

Having learned that they cannot count on men or marriage for their future security, black girls realize that they will have to rely on themselves. As a student of mine wrote in an autobiographical socialization paper, "Black girls don't dream of being rescued by 'Prince Charming.' They know that 'Snow White' is White, and that if they want to get something or somewhere, they are going to have to get it themselves."[87] Thus black girls are socialized to become self-sufficient and to rely on their own achievements.

As Ladner notes, the realities of life in the ghetto, where aggressiveness and toughness are requisites for survival, make the ideal of a dependent, passive, middle-class housewife almost unimaginable.[88] The black girl is given responsibility for herself (and sometimes for the home and her younger siblings as well) from an early age and is expected to learn to "fend for herself."

At the same time that the black girl is learning the importance of becoming self-sufficient, her observations of her mother's work role (and her mother's attitude toward work) provide a practical guide toward this end. Because a significant proportion of black women have always worked in the paid labor force, both they and their daughters are more likely to regard work as a normal part of the female role.[89] In fact, employed black women are more likely to hold professional positions than are employed black men, and Epstein has shown that the "double negative" status of being both a woman and a black may actually help a black woman to gain access to the professions that both white women and black men have found difficult to penetrate.[90]

Thus, in contrast to the traditional sex-stereotyped view of work and careers as "masculine" pursuits, in the black community they are seen as natural and acceptable female roles. Work brings money, security, and status—all of which are highly valued by both men and women.

Because black women are more likely to regard work as part of the "normal" female role, they are more likely to encourage and support their daughters' educational and occupational aspirations. Thus, Kandel found that black mothers in female-headed families had higher educational aspirations for their daughters than for their sons.[91]

There are also data to suggest that the daughters absorb their mother's aspirations. Ladner found that young black girls most frequently identify with and aspire to be a "strong black woman"—resourceful, hardworking, and economically independent.[92] The teenage girls she interviewed saw this ideal woman as the one who kept the home intact—by caring for children, carrying out household tasks, and often supporting the family financially. Another popular aspiration was to acquire the skills that would allow the girl to escape from the ghetto and become an educated and upwardly mobile middle-class woman.[93]

Thus, to summarize the first position, there is considerable evidence to support the assertion that young black girls are socialized to become independent, self-reliant, and self-sufficient "strong women." In fact, Ladner has shown that black girls are encouraged to be more independent than white girls, irrespective of social class.[94]

Other research, however, suggests that black women are socialized to accept a traditional female role. For example, Gurin and Gaylord, writing in 1976, found that sex-role influences inhibit the career and educational aspirations of black women in approximately the same ways as white women, and that black and white college women alike continue to be interested in the same traditionally "feminine fields." For example, women of both races are more likely to aspire to be a high school teacher rather than a lawyer. Similarly, for both races, fewer women than men are interested in business or engineering. They conclude that their "results agree with those of earlier studies which indicate that women students of both races tend to have lower aspirations than their male counterparts."[96]

Hershey also reports that black college women ascribe to the same sex-stereotyped identities as white college women.[97] She found that the primary difference in sex-role attitudes among college students is between men and women, not between blacks and whites. Both black and white college women described themselves as tender, gentle, sensitive, and compassionate.* Similarly, both black and white college males described themselves as assertive, having leadership abilities, and having a strong personality. In fact, she found that black men scored higher on masculinity than white men, indicating their "affinity for more traditional patriarchal sex role norms."[98] Thus Hershey concluded that since both black women and black men ascribe to traditional sex-role attitudes, sex is much more important than race in determining sex-role identities.

How can we reconcile these seemingly contradictory findings?

One explanation lies in the social class differences in the research samples. It is possible that lower-class black girls are socialized to be strong and independent but middle-class blacks are not. We know that the mother-headed family, a major source of the strong self-reliant female role, is much more common among the lower classes. This may explain why Stack and Ladner, who studied lower-class girls found them to be self-sufficient and strong. However, Hershey, Gurin and Gaylord, who focused on (mostly middle-class) black college women, found more traditional aspirations and attitudes.**

A second explanation lies in the difference between idealized roles and actual behavior. It is possible that Hershey, Gurin and Gaylord, using questionnaires (which often elicit socially desirable responses), elicited female "ideals," while Stack and Ladner, who conducted lengthy interviews with their respondents "in the field," captured more of their actual behavior. As Hershey herself notes, attitudes and self ratings may not be congruent with behavior.[99] In fact, she suggests that women who take on traditionally masculine tasks may still identify with the ideal-typical female role, and that some would prefer a more sex-stereotyped life if they had the option.[100]

---

*In addition, she found that black women were significantly more stereotyped than white women in their sex-role *attitudes*, although they scored higher than white women on the masculine dimension of the sex-role *identity* scale.

**If black women from lower-class families are being socialized into less traditional sex roles than those from middle-class families, then social class has an opposite effect in black and white families: while white lower-class families are more sex-stereotyped than white middle-class families, black lower-class families may be *less* sex-stereotyped than black middle-class families.

A third way of resolving these findings is to recognize that they are not contradictory at all—each may reflect a different aspect of the black woman's multi-dimensional sex role. Thus black women may be more independent, more self-reliant, and more work-oriented than white women, but, at the same time, they may be as sensitive, nurturant, compassionate, and "feminine." The findings are contradictory only if we assume that "masculinity" and "femininity" are unidimensional.

Women, and black women in particular, may have some "masculine traits" such as independence and self-sufficiency, *and* some traditional "feminine" characteristics, such as warmth and nurturance. For example, in his study of sex roles in the black community Scanzoni found that he had to consider several different role dimensions—each of which varied independently. Thus he found that blacks were more "traditional" with respect to approved behavior for men and women, but were less traditional with respect to women's individualism.[101] In addition, black women were both more nurturant and more task competent, and had more autonomy and power in the family. Thus these findings, like those reviewed above, indicate that "masculine" and "feminine" attributes cannot be viewed as polar opposites.

Similarly, Bem has shown that individuals can score high on both masculinity and femininity, low on both, or some combination of the two.[102] Further, a lot of sex-role behavior is likely to be *situationally specific*—that is, it is likely to depend on the social context. For example, a woman attorney may be assertive with clients, aggressive in court, tender with her husband, and nurturant with her children. In fact, since sex-role attitudes and behaviors are likely to be much more *situationally specific* than the research literature seems to acknowledge, it is surprising that there have not been *more* seemingly contradictory findings—for both blacks and whites.

### Family constellation and sex roles

In addition to class and race, another important variable in sex-role behavior is the family constellation—the number, spacing, and sex ratio of the children in the family. Brim pointed out the importance of siblings in sex-role definitions, finding that children with cross-sex siblings exhibited more traits of the opposite sex than did those with same-sex siblings.[103] This effect was particularly strong when opposite-sex siblings were older. Thus, boys with older sisters and girls with older brothers are more likely to exhibit the traits of the opposite sex.

Another significant aspect of family constellation is the number and presence of adults. Many sociologists have assumed that children who grow up without a father or a mother must be inadequately socialized. However, recent research has indicated that father absence does not affect lower-class boys' occupational achievement, although it may have a depressant effect for middle- and upper-class boys.

On the other hand, the single parent mother-headed family may be a spur to occupational achievement in girls. Hunt and Hunt have found that girls in father-absent families are freed from the ideal-typical female socialization.[104] These families establish a new type of female role model, blurring the traditional distinction between male and female roles and the instrumental/expressive division of labor by sex, because mothers are performing both roles and both types of tasks. Thus, father absence, in conjunction with modifications of the mother role, may remove some of the conventional barriers to female occupational aspirations and achievement. When girls are not socialized into sharply differentiated sex roles, they may be freed from the traditional restraints on female achievement.

## CONTINUING SOCIALIZATION

Although boys and girls learn sex roles early, the definition of appropriate sex-role behavior changes with age. The female sex role at age five is specific to the attributes of a five-year-old, and different from the female sex role at age twenty-five.[105] Sex-role socialization continues throughout the child's life as she or he learns age-specific sex-role behavior.

Thus far we have focused largely on socialization within the family. As the child matures and begins to participate in social relations outside the family, teachers, peers, and other socializing agents become more significant in defining and sanctioning appropriate sex-role behavior.

### The influence of the school

Once the child enters school, her or his experiences there assume great importance. The educational system has generally reinforced sex-role stereotypes. One of the first messages communicated to girls at school is that they are less important than boys. For example, in a 1960 study of all third-grade readers published since 1930, Child, Potter and Levine found 73 percent of the stories were about male characters.[106] Girls' impressions that they are not very important are reinforced by the portrait of the few women who do appear in the texts. Child *et al.* found girls and women shown as timid, inactive, unambitious, and uncreative. Females were not only the moral inferiors of males in these books (they are shown to be lazy twice as often as males), but their intellectual inferiors as well:

> The persons who supply information are predominantly male. . . . Males, in short, are being portrayed as the bearers of knowledge and wisdom, and as the persons through whom knowledge can come to the child.[107]

More recent examinations of elementary school readers indicate that even the newest textbooks retain the same stereotypes.[108] Nor are these stereotypes restricted to readers. Weitzman and Rizzo have found that spelling, mathematics, science, and social studies textbooks purvey an equally limited image of women.[109] Rarely are women mentioned in important roles in history, as government leaders, or as great scientists. This study found the stereotyping to be most extreme in the science textbooks, where only 6 percent of the pictures included adult women. Weitzman and Rizzo hypothesize that the presentation of science as a prototypical masculine endeavor may help to explain how young girls are "cooled out" of science and channeled into more traditional "feminine" fields.[110]

Guidance counselors and teachers can either help to reinforce conformity to the traditional female role, or present exciting new role models to impressionable young girls. In the past they have mostly done the former. Most schools have had a sex-stereotyped tracking system in which girls are channeled into the more "feminine" subjects (English and social studies in academic high schools, typing and bookkeeping in commercial high schools) while boys are encouraged to tackle the "hard sciences." This has not only channeled the two sexes into two different vocational directions, but has further served to keep both boys and girls from learning skills useful in later life. Thus girls who have been excluded from shop have not learned how to fix things around the home, and boys excluded from home economics are kept blissfully ignorant of cooking and other domestic skills.

In the past, girls have also been excluded from most rigorous sports and from school athletic teams. "In fact, the disparity in support for boys' and girls' athletic programs is perhaps the single most visible piece of discrimination in American education. In 1971, boys' participation in high school sports was 12 times that of girls'."[111]

Hopefully, all this is beginning to change with the passage of Title IX (of the Education Amendments of 1972), which forbids all forms of sex-based discrimination in educational institutions. However, a comprehensive report on HEW's progress in enforcing Title IX concludes that as of 1978 "rules and policies that perpetuate unequal treatment of males and females—which are now clearly illegal—are still going on uncorrected in the nation's schools."[112] Some cases cited in this report indicate how far we still have to go:

> A ninth-grader in Livonia, Michigan, wanted to learn how to handle power tools, but shop classes were off limits for girls. "Women," she was told, "should stick to home ec." She wrote the government for help in 1973. Three years later, HEW wrote back, got no answer, and closed the case. The government never checked to find out if girls were still barred from taking shop.

> "Something is wrong! I am doing more work for less pay," a New Jersey woman wrote HEW in September 1973. She was coaching four girls' teams for one-third of what the school paid men to coach the team. HEW left her complaint in limbo for three years before closing it without an investigation.

> One high school senior recounted the way a counselor in Los Angeles tried to discourage her from pursuing a career as a veterinarian. "She said," the girl wrote, "that at our age it's the maternal instinct, and after a few years of college we outgrow it." The worst thing about all these messages is that girls believe them.[113]

### Intellectual and analytic ability

Girls consistently do better than boys in reading, mathematics, and speaking until they reach high school.[114] Then their performance in school and on ability tests begins to drop. Although we have every reason to believe that girls' intellectual achievements do decline during high school, it should be noted that the typical measures of intelligence and scholastic achievement at this age have a strong male bias. Milton found that when adolescent or adult subjects were presented with problems involving primarily mathematical or geometric reasoning, the males consistently obtained higher scores than females.[115] However, if the problem—involving identical logical steps and computations—dealt with feminine content such as cooking and gardening materials, the women scored much better than if the problem dealt with guns, money, or geometric designs. He concluded the typical female believes that the ability to solve problems involving geometry, physics or logic, is a uniquely masculine skill, and her motivation even to attack such problems is low—for unusual excellence in solving them may be equated with loss of femininity.[116]

Since the erroneous finding that women are less analytic than men is often quoted, it deserves some attention here. It has been postulated that analytic thinking is developed by early independence training: how soon a child is encouraged to assume initiative, to take responsibility for herself or himself, and to solve problems alone rather than to rely on others for help or direction.[117] Each of these characteristics, as already reviewed, is encouraged in boys and discouraged in girls. When women are socialized to be dependent and passive, they are supposedly being trained to be more "field-dependent" or "contextual" and less analytic in their thinking.

In a devastating review of the scientific literature on what is usually called analytic ability, Sherman has pointed out that the term analytic ability is misleading.[118] It implies a general intellectual skill, whereas what is apparently being measured in most of the studies is the much more limited ability of spatial perception—the ability to visualize objects out of their context.[119] Boys are generally "field independent" in their spatial perception, whereas girls are more "contextual." Girls score lower on tests of spatial relationships, but in verbal perception— certainly an area that is equally, if not more, important in analytic thinking—they score higher than boys.[120]

It seems ironic that researchers have labeled spatial perception "analytic ability." One might speculate that if women had higher scores on spatial perception and men had higher scores on verbal perception, the latter would have been called analytic ability—for what the researchers have done is to seize upon one of the few traits in which males score higher and label it analytic ability.

Actually, spatial ability has little to do with analytic thinking in any of the usual meanings of that term.[121] Strictly analytic ability has to do with the structure of arguments, the logical closure of propositions and syllogisms, and patterns of logic. Since World War I (in the work of

Whitehead and Russell), and certainly by the 1930's with Wittgenstein's work in modern logic, we generally understand that the underlying structure of logic (and thus of mathematics as well) is ultimately a language pattern, resting on our understanding of linguistic connections. One might therefore argue that people who are best in language and show the most facility in language analysis and construction would potentially have the greatest ability in analytic thinking—in the perception of logical connections and in the understanding of the strength or weakness of arguments.[122] However, this would lead us to conclude that women have superior analytic ability, and the strong anti-female bias pervading the literature on intelligence and analytic thinking precludes this logical conclusion.

It is interesting to note that spatial ability appears to be learned, and is especially strong in individuals who have hobbies or jobs of a mechanical or technical nature. Since the sex disparity in skills related to this ability widens greatly at age seventeen, it is tempting to connect the superior performance of males with the training they receive in high school classes in mechanical drawing, analytic geometry, and shop (as well as with their spare-time activities).

If both spatial and verbal ability can be learned, findings of sex differences in these areas should direct us once again to the socialization process. As Professor William Goode has noted, "Although we encourage the verbal fluency of girls and their ease in writing and speaking, we are more likely to criticize boys for their weakness in logic (we forgive girls that fault; it is an endearing weakness, it is cute). In short, although males have a lower potential we strengthen their (boys') ability in logic. We do not, in contrast, strengthen girls' ability in spatial connections or facilitate girls' growth in the areas in which they appear most talented, i.e., the grasp of language construction, logical progressions, syllogisms, and all the apparatus of clear analytic thinking."[123]

### The influence of parents

It is not the school alone that channels girls and boys in different directions and emphasizes certain skills over others. Parents also have different sex-related expectations. Aberle and Naegele have reported that middle-class fathers show concern over their sons' lack of aggressiveness, good school performance, responsibility, and initiative. In contrast, their concerns for their daughters focus on attractiveness and popularity. As the authors report:

> In all of these categories boys were the object of concern . . . ; satisfaction with girls seemed to focus strongly on their daughters being nice, sweet, pretty, affectionate, and well liked.[124]

With respect to future careers for their daughters, half of the fathers rejected the possibility out of hand. The other half said they would accept the possibility, but preferred and expected their daughters to marry—a career was unnecessary. Only two of the twenty fathers said they wanted their daughters to know how to earn a living.[125]

The Aberle and Naegele study was done in 1952 and may now seem dated. However, more recent studies of parental influence on their children's educational aspirations indicate that girls are still less likely to receive parental support than boys. Sewell and Shah indicate that parents continue to encourage their sons more than their daughters.[126] Similarly, most of Bordua's male adolescents reported that their parents "stress college a lot," whereas most of the girls reported that their parents "don't care one way or the other."[127] Elder suggested that parents put a differential stress on college for boys, and that the financial support that has typically accompanied their concern may have had more of an effect in determining the college plans of adolescents than their own intentions.[128]

Parental pressures to follow a traditional female role are probably greater on the working-class than on the middle-class girl.[129] The working-class girl who aspires to a professional career is seen as especially threatening because her occupational aspirations (if achieved) would result in her being more successful than her father and brothers, in addition to being "unfeminine."

In contrast to lower-class white girls, lower-class black girls may have their educational and occupational aspirations actively supported by their families.[130] There is no difference in aspirations for boys and girls in intact black families, as there is in white families, and we have already noted Kandel's finding that black mothers in single-parent families had higher educational aspirations for their daughters than for their sons.[131]

White parents, in contrast, are more likely to "protect" their daughters and to hold them back, even when they think they are "helping" them. They may think they are treating their sons and daughters equally because they send them to the same schools, camps, etc., but the subtle messages they convey are different. For example, boys are typically allowed more freedom to play away from home, to return home later, and to choose their own activities.[132] As one of Komarovsky's students complained:

> My brother is 15, three years younger than I am. When he goes out after supper, mother calls out, "Where are you going, Jimmy?" "Oh, out." Could I get away with that? Not on your life. I would have to tell them in detail where to, with whom, and if I am half an hour late, mother sits on the edge of the living room sofa watching the door.[133]

Komarovsky concludes that the "risk of this kind of traditional upbringing resides in the failure to develop in the girl independence, inner resources, and that degree of self-assertion which life will demand of her."[134] Thus, both school and parents impede the growing girl's social and intellectual independence.

### The influence of peers

The equation of intellectual success with a loss of femininity appears to be common among high school peer groups. According to the Kennistons, high school girls feel they must hide their intelligence if they are to be popular with boys.

> Girls soon learn that "popularity"—that peculiar American ecstasy from which all other goods flow—accrues to her who hides any intelligence she may have, flatters the often precarious maleness of adolescent boys, and devotes herself to activities that can in no way challenge their sex. The popular girls in high schools are seldom the brilliant girls; or if they are, it is only because they are so brilliant they can hide their brilliance from less brilliant boys. . . . Most American public schools (like many private schools) make a girl with passionate intellectual interests feel a strong sense of her own inadequacy as a woman, feel guilty about these "masculine" outlooks, perhaps even wonder about her own normality.[135]

Thus, school, parents, and peers make it clear to girls that the major criterion for feminine success is attractiveness to men. Pierce found high achievement motivation for women related to success in marriage, not, as for males, to academic success.[136] In Pierce's view, girls see that to achieve in life they need to excel in non-academic ways, i.e., in attaining beauty in person and dress, in finding a desirable social status, and in marrying the right man.[137]

The mass media reinforce this perception and provide explicit instruction on attaining these goals. *Seventeen, Glamour,* and

*Mademoiselle* provide endless pages of fashion, make-up, and dating advice. The girl learns that she must know how to attract, talk to, kiss, keep (or get rid of) a boy, depending on the circumstances, and how to use clothes, cosmetics, and interpersonal skills to accomplish these all-important ends. While fashion magazines tell her how to dress, movies instruct on how to undress—and on the explicit use of sexuality. "On the whole, mass media and popular fiction continue to portray career women as mannish, loose, or both; and the happy ending for working girls still involves abandoning work, marrying, and having many children—and there the story ends."[138]

Just a decade ago one could summarize the three clear lessons that a well-socialized American girl had learned. One concerned her personality, the second her capability, and the third, her future role. With regard to her personality, she had learned to be nurturing, cooperative, sweet, expressive, not too intelligent, and fairly passive. With regard to her capability, she had learned she would always be less capable and less important than most men. With regard to her future, she had learned she would be a wife and mother, and, if she were successful, she would acquire that status soon. Today, as we shall see, the message has become much more complex for the middle-class college girl.

### The "terminal year" of school[139]

The end of high school is a critical juncture at which the lives of girls from lower- and middle-class families diverge. While many middle-class girls will go on to college, the last year in high school is what Sheila Tobias calls "the terminal year" for many lower class girls—their last year in school and their last chance "to find a husband." As Lillian Rubin's interviews with working-class girls reveals, for most of them "getting married was—and probably still is—the singularly most acceptable way out of an oppressive family situation and into a respected social status—the only way to move from girl to woman. Indeed, among working-class girls, being grown up means being married."[140]

Rubin accurately portrays the difference between the perspectives of working-class women and those from middle-class families:

Among the [working-class] women, a few recall girlhood dreams of being a model or an actress, but most remember wanting only to marry and live happily ever after. . . . It's not that the girls from middle-class homes dreamed such different dreams. But along with the marriage fantasy, there was for them some sense of striving for their own development. Even if that were related to enhancing marriage prospects (that is, with a college education a girl can make a "better match"), some aspiration related to self existed alongside it. And, in fact, for those middle-class women, marriage came much later since it was (typically) deferred until after college.[141]

As Rubin notes, the terminal year for most middle-class girls doesn't come until the end of college (and for some it doesn't come until the end of graduate school). But whenever it comes, it brings the same pressures to marry and settle down—to find a husband, to buy a home, to have children—and to fulfill one's role as "a woman."

## SOCIALIZATION PRESSURES IN COLLEGE

For a long time it seemed odd that young women who staunchly resisted the pressures to put social life and popularity above intellectual and vocational achievement during high school, suddenly changed during college. They switched their majors from Economics to English or Art History and decided that they were not really interested in graduate school after all. What happened? It now seems clear that what distinguished them from their working-class sisters was not a stronger commitment to intellectual pursuits, or to feminism, or to a non-traditional lifestyle, but the fact that they did not face the terminal year pressures until the end of college. For them the end of high school was just one more transition point. As long as they continued in school, they were permitted a moratorium on the pressures of "real life." But when these middle-class girls found themselves in their terminal year of school, and thus in the same structural position as their lower-class sisters at the end of high school, their behavior changed.

In the following discussion we shall describe the pressures on college women as if college were the terminal school for all middle-class women. However, women who go into professional or graduate school gain additional moratorium years and thereby further delay the pressures that come with the terminal year of school.

### Peer influences in college

It is now over 30 years since Mirra Komarovsky completed her classic study of sex-role socialization of Barnard College women.[142] At that time (1946), college women reported that they felt caught between the traditional female role and the more modern role—and were constantly pressured by mutually exclusive expectations. For example:

Uncle John telephones every Sunday morning. His first question is: "Did you go out last night?" He would think me a grind if I were to stay home Saturday night to finish a term paper. My father expects me to get an "A" in every subject and is disappointed by a "B." He says I have plenty of time for social life. Mother says, "That 'A' in Philosophy is very nice, dear, but please don't become so deep that no man will be good enough for you."[143]

One might speculate that women in college today are not being subjected to the same pressures. Although their parents may still encourage them to see marriage as the ultimate goal, it is possible that peer definitions of feminine roles are more liberal. The ideology of the current women's liberation movement certainly supports independent achievements for women.

When I first began writing this review paper (in 1972), I did not know of any study that dealt with this possibility in a systematic fashion. So I decided to collect some data from an experiment in my undergraduate course on the family. After a discussion of the ideology and goals of the women's liberation movement, I asked the students to try out the feminist ideals we had discussed in a heterosexual situation of at least one hour's duration.

The most common response encountered by those who completed the assignment, reported by 27 percent of the female students, was a rejection of the feminist behavior by their male companion. In some cases the women were asked to change their behavior: "So after I told him why I was doing it, he said, 'Stop it, please, I don't want you to be a member of women's liberation.' " In other cases, the man treated the woman's ideas or actions as nonserious, tossing them off as a joke or "putting her down as crazy":

I told him I thought being a housewife and a mother was a bore and a lot of shitwork. Well, this really got to him and he said I was crazy. . . . Just then his roommate came in and he related my "weird" ideas to him and they both had a good laugh.

He said it wasn't a man's job to do the housework . . . and that any woman who had decided that she didn't want children was crazy.

In several instances, the friends and boyfriends were so angered or upset by the women's behavior that they refused to deal with it. They tried to terminate the interaction by telling the women they would never attract a man if they continued to act in such an unfeminine manner:

> He told me that if I wanted a man I should start acting like a woman because any man would ball me but if I wanted a husband I'd better do the right things.

In contrast to these emotional reactions, some of the men were more intellectual about their rejection, trying to answer the feminist arguments "rationally" by arguing that motherhood was fulfilling, or that a woman's career was too disruptive to a marriage:

> He said that if I went to law school I'd be challenging him at his own career and would be sacrificing our home life for a materialistic job. . . . He felt women with careers neglected their husbands and children and that they were basically selfish. . . . When I confessed that I was doing a class assignment he seemed relieved but later continued to discuss the disadvantages of a career for a woman.

The second most common reaction (17 percent) was that boyfriends or dates were merely surprised and uncomfortable:

> All of this made him feel uncomfortable, especially when I said this other guy had a good ass.

The third most common response, reported by 12 percent of the students, was subtle resistance by dates and male friends. Although not explicitly challenging the women, the men attempted to regain control of the situation:

> He asked if he could drive instead because he didn't like it to look as if he was being chauffeured around.

> I was sitting on the chair so he came over and handed me the broom, asking me to hold it, but really trying to put me into my proper role.

Most of these men denied trying to regain the dominant position in the relationship, contending that they were "just trying to be helpful."

> He asked how much the dinner cost and told me how much to leave for the tip.

Some of the women (8 percent) reported that their dates or boyfriends did not seem to resent their behavior, but other friends and observers did:

The waiter seemed to feel sympathy for my boyfriend for being with such an assertive, pushy woman, while the cashier sided with me, assuming that by paying my share, I was being taken advantage of. She said sympathetically, "I've got one at home just like him."

These quotes indicate the extent to which third parties observe and try to reinforce conventional behavior, even when the couple is content with new roles.

In contrast to the reactions just described, some 10 percent reported that the males they chose reacted positively to their behavior:

He said he dug me in this particular role and that I should come across like that more often.

He said he admired intelligent women who he could really talk to . . .

He said, "I'd rather have someone who would dig building a cabinet with me instead of worrying about ironing my shirts '

It is interesting to note that 27 percent of the women in the class found they could not carry out the assignment because acting liberated was so normal for them that none of their friends noticed any difference in their conversation or actions:

Since this is the way I always act, no one reacted to anything I did.

I rarely come into contact with people (especially men) who aren't in a liberated circle of people, and when I do, they don't have much to say.

If we combine this 27 percent of the students with the 10 percent who received positive reactions and the 8 percent who were hassled only by outsiders, we find that for almost half of the women in the group, there was positive peer support for rejecting the traditional feminine role. Thus, although a majority of these women university students were still being constrained by male peers to conform to more traditional standards of feminine behavior, change was also evident.*

---

*The class assignment did have an interesting side effect: one-third of the men in the class who did the assignment reported that the experience of articulating the arguments for women's liberation had a positive effect on them:

I think the most significant reaction was within myself. After discussing all the points that were made in class, I became more of a feminist. I think I convinced her about the movement, but I also convinced myself.

When I read the results of this study to my class, several students who had reported they received support for their actions said that this support had definite limits. Many had chosen "low-risk" situations for the class assignments—situations in which neither the man nor the woman had a great stake in the relationship and the woman's behavior was not of critical importance. Both these women and those who had characterized themselves as "already liberated" felt that when they were seriously involved with a man there were more pressures on them to play a more "feminine" role.

Other research on college women similarly suggests that the pressures for more traditional roles may grow especially severe during their junior and senior years in college or with involvement with a particular man. Horner's interviews with Radcliffe students show that parents and boyfriends exert great pressure on them to "return" to traditional feminine roles in their terminal year in the terminal school, and it is at this time that their intellectual performance usually drops.[144]

Another observation of the liberated women in my class was that expressions of peer support for their new role had been exaggerated. Although they themselves felt comfortable in the role, they reported encountering considerable problems in establishing relationships with men. Several felt they were no longer as attractive to men, or that most men did not know how to handle "the new women"—or preferred not to. As one woman reported, "I get a lot of support from both men and women, but most men say something like 'even though I'm really supportive of what you are, I just can't handle it. . . . I'm still hung up on having a more feminine woman who will support *me*'." Thus, although peers may appreciate the independence and intellectual companionship of the liberated woman, they may let her know that they do not consider her "a real woman."

Four years later, in 1976, I tried to repeat this mini-experiment with my undergraduate family class. Both they and I were astonished by how much had changed. The majority of the class reported not only that they were unable to carry out the assignment (because their behavior now seemed "normal"), but they even had difficulty trying to "provoke" a reaction. Some attributed the lack of peer reaction to an increased tolerance for "doing one's own thing." Others, however, felt that a radical change in attitudes had resulted in genuine widespread support for the "new woman."

We will now examine the role expectations for this "new woman."

### Intellectual achievement: the climate of non-expectations

College should present an opportunity for women to broaden their intellectual horizons and to acquire both the background and motivation for occupational success. But in the past women have received less encouragement than men. Women professors have been underrepresented on the faculties of all colleges and universities in the United States, even in fields that were sex-stereotyped as female (such as English or Art History), and women received no more than a passing mention in the intellectual content of most courses.

The predominantly male faculty typically assumed that women came to college to find husbands and become well-rounded individuals. Few professors took their intellectual or occupational aspirations seriously. As Paula Bunting, the former President of Radcliffe College observed, in her day the college environment for even the brightest women was one of "non-expectations." Instead of stimulating the bright young woman's intellectual and political ambitions, college worked as a depressant. Thus many college women came to believe they were less intelligent (or less brilliant or less creative) than their male peers. English Professor Florence Howe describes the internalized inferiority among the women in her creative writing seminar in the 1960s:

> What I learned from listening to my women students was that they consistently considered women writers (and hence themselves) inferior to men. . . . Why should naturally inferior writers attempt anything ambitious? . . . Their comments ranged from "I don't have any ideas" to "I can't write anything really interesting" to "I used to have ideas and imagination but I don't any more."[145]

Although the climate of non-expectations did not make all women doubt their own capacity, it inevitably had a depressant effect on their ambitions. Even those who began college with high aspirations found their expectations for themselves lowered by the time they were ready to graduate: Perhaps they should apply for an M.A. program instead of trying for a Ph.D., or perhaps they should take a year off and decide what they "really" wanted to do.

Even those who did well in school, and who therefore had the external validation of high grades, began to question whether they were "truly" as capable or as committed as their male peers. Of course, those women who got high grades had rarely received the kind of professional encouragement that was lavished on their male peers—a fact which could not have easily escaped their attention. Perhaps some of those male professors had really wanted to encourage their bright women students but feared their interest might be misinterpreted (by their colleagues or their wives, if not by their students). Others may have been concerned about dissuading women from what they assumed was the woman's preferred life pattern, for it was widely assumed that women had to choose between a career and marriage.

In light of these expectations it is not surprising that women college students in the past have always been less likely to graduate from college than men, or that women college graduates have less often gone on to obtain advanced degrees.[146]

It is widely believed that the climate of expectations is now quite different. However, the available data do not yet reflect a major increase in the professional aspirations of college women. For example, while a comparison of the educational expectations of a national sample of college freshmen in 1966 and 1972 indicates that women's expectations for higher education increased more than men's, still, in 1972, only 6.8 percent of the women expected to get a Ph.D. (up from 5.2 percent in 1966), only 4.3 percent expected to get an M.D. (up from 1.9 percent), and only 2.1 expected to get a J.D. (up from .3 percent).[147] These data probably underestimate the aspirations of current college women in two ways. First, they are limited to freshmen and therefore underestimate the percentage of women who will eventually pursue advanced degrees. Second, they end in 1972, and it is likely that the years since 1972 have brought some further changes. For example, the percentage of women enrolled in medical school and business school has increased substantially in recent years, and women now constitute a fourth of the students in law school. Nevertheless, they still do not appear to be choosing and pursuing careers in the high-level professions to the same extent as men.

### Career orientation

It is also widely believed that college women today are much more career oriented than the women who were in college in the 1950's and 1960's. Here the data are less clear, for while the majority of college women now assume they will be employed in the future, their attitudes toward work and family roles suggest that many of them are still thinking in terms of "jobs" rather than "careers." The distinction between a job orientation and a career orientation is one that sociologist Alice Rossi has pinpointed as a critical difference between college men and women in the past.[148] She notes that even though college-educated women might study and prepare for a future occupation, they viewed these occupations as "jobs," not as lifelong vocational commitments. Their middle-class brothers, in contrast, were clearly future oriented, preparing and planning for lifelong careers. (Of course the women's lack of preparation for a lifelong career did not prevent them from working. It did, however, prevent them from organizing their lives for a "career" instead of a "job.")

Elizabeth Douvan has suggested that unmarried college women hold their identities in abeyance, lest premature identity formation reduce their marriage prospects or inhibit their ability to adapt to marriage.[149] It is possible that college women similarly hold back from making lifelong career plans because they expect their careers to be heavily influenced by their future husbands and their family life. If this is so, then the recent upsurge in college women who plan to combine marriage and work does not indicate a fundamental change in women's career orientation. For as long as a woman's work is contingent upon her marriage, or her husband, or her childbearing plans, she is still adhering to women's traditional priorities.

While it was formerly assumed that women had to choose between marriage and work, most college women today plan to combine the two. The shift in attitudes is striking in Cross's data on incoming freshmen women (in one college) between 1964 and 1970. The women were asked what they would like to be doing in fifteen years.[150] In 1964, 65 percent said they would like to be a housewife and mother. Since then, the percentage who express this desire has declined steadily each year—to 60 percent in 1966, to 53 percent in 1967, and to only 31 percent by 1970. In contrast, the percentage who say they want to be a married career woman has doubled; it rose from 20 percent in 1964 to 40 percent in 1970.

Several other studies of college women today confirm that an increasing number plan to combine marriage, family, and a career. Both Cummings (1974) and Parelius (1975) found that almost all students at two women's colleges said they would like to combine the goals of marriage, family, and a career.[151]

Although the word career in these studies may not refer to the lifelong commitment we discussed above, it is clear that the new ideal for college women has become a life of both marriage and work. In addition, this appears to be the preferred life style for at least half of the adult women in the United States. A 1974 Roper poll found that over 50 percent of all adult women in the United States favored combining "marriage, children, and careers" and a 1975 Gallup poll found that 45 percent of women eighteen to twenty-four chose as "the most interesting and satisfying life for [me] personally" the option of "married, children, full-time job."[152]

Despite the widespread acceptance of employment for married women, it is useful to explore two ways in which the college women's traditional socialization may create barriers to her occupational advancement. The first is the psychological fear that if a woman is too achieving or too successful she will not be regarded as feminine and will be rejected by men. The second is the cultural imperative that career women must still "prove" their femininity by being good mothers and wives and by not exceeding their husband's status and achievements.

### Fear of success

Matina Horner's now famous experiment on fear of success was conducted in 1965.[153] At that time Horner found that college women responded with more negative stories (than college men) when presented with the verbal cue, "At the end of the first-term finals, Anne finds herself at the top of her medical school class. . . ." The women associated Anne's success with strong fears of social rejection and unpopularity, doubts about her femininity and normality, and themes of despair or guilt over having achieved too much. Horner concluded that most college women, consciously or unconsciously, equated intellectual achievement with loss of femininity and were therefore caught in a double bind. In testing and other achievement situations they worried not only about failure but also about success, for they feared success might lead to unpopularity and loss of femininity.[154] "Thus women who were otherwise motivated to achieve experienced anxiety in anticipation of success and this may have adversely affected their performance and levels of aspiration."[155]

More recent replications of Horner's original research by Hoffman (in 1974)[156] and by Horner and Walsh (in 1972)[157] indicate that the motive to avoid success continues to be prevalent among college women.* This anxiety about academic success seems to interfere with the task performance of college women. Horner's later work shows that those who were anxious performed more poorly on a competitive task (particularly when the competition was with men) than when a comparable task was performed alone.

Although several researchers have now replicated Horner's experiments (some confirming her findings, others challenging them**) I believe that fear of success, if it does presently exist, is a temporary phenomenon that will soon disappear. When young women have more successful role models and more opportunities to observe how much fun (and power and money) success brings, they will rapidly lose their anxiety about success. Furthermore, in contrast to the current stereotype of successful women as unfeminine, I think they will discover that "success is sexy"—it increases rather than decreases one's attractiveness to the opposite sex. Just as women have always been attracted to powerful men (even though they were not necessarily "handsome") in the past, it is likely that more men will find dynamic and powerful women increasingly attractive in the future.

Nevertheless, the continued anxiety that many college women currently associate with success suggests that the ideal of the wife-mother-career woman is not without its own anxiety. Furthermore, this anxiety may be exacerbated by cultural pressures on the career woman to prove that she is also a good wife and mother.

### The cultural imperatives

The college woman who aspires to a successful career faces two cultural imperatives to prove that she is also a successful woman: one is to bear children; the other, to make sure her occupational achievements do not exceed those of her husband.

Because the belief that the successful career woman is unfeminine is widespread among both men and women,[158] career-oriented women

---

*These studies also reveal that fear of success has increased among college men since 1965. However, among men it seems to take the form of questioning the value of academic success and conventional career goals.

**The details of this fascinating research are beyond the scope of this paper. For a good review of the literature see Mednick et al., *Women and Achievement;* and John Condry and Sharon Dyer, "Fear of Success: Attribution of Cause to the Victim," *Journal of Social Issues,* 32, no. 3 (Summer 1976): 63–83.

may feel under particular pressure to prove their femininity. Lois Hoffman suggests that having a baby may provide the proof the career woman feels she needs.[159] (It may also force her to devote a great deal of time and energy to family roles and thereby reassert their priority in her life.) In a 1971 study of undergraduate women at the University of Michigan, Hoffman's question "What is the most womanly thing you can imagine?" most often elicited the response, "To have a baby."[160] In view of this response, it is not surprising to find that several studies of women in the professions indicate that women in more masculine fields (law, medicine, and the hard sciences), women facing the strongest pressures to prove their femininity, tend to express a desire for more children than women in more conventionally feminine fields (the arts, humanities, education, and nursing.)[161] However, if motherhood solves one set of anxieties, its demands, especially in large families, may easily create other pressures and role conflicts for the young career woman.

A second cultural imperative is that wives should not exceed their husband's status and occupational attainment.[162] In fact, Hoffman suggests that for educated women a successful marital relationship often requires that both partners perceive the husband to be the more intelligent or successful in his career.[163] As Hoffman notes:

any change in this perception may be a threat to the husband's sense of masculinity, the wife's sense of femininity, and thus to the love relationship. In many cases this threat may come simply from a change in the established equilibrium, such as when the career-wife has a success experience, or her husband has a failure; or when the nonworking-wife considers returning to a career or seeking further education.[164]

How can the new woman balance these cultural imperatives with the demands of a career? How can she be and do everything?

One way to resolve the conflict is to have a clear sense of priority. Women's socialization suggests that they should treat work as a "job" and put their responsibilities to husband and family first. Is this what college women are choosing to do?

The limited data on occupational aspirations, career decisions, and dual career marriages suggest that the majority still are.[165] However, sociologist Laurie Cummings has found that a minority of women are beginning to organize their lives differently. Cummings set out to examine the differences among college women who aspired to combine marriage, motherhood, and work. She found that women who are feminists not only express greater confidence in their ability to combine job, family, and marriage, they also make more concrete plans for achieving their aims. They are more likely to plan to go to graduate school, to aspire to a profession, and, most importantly, to plan a continuous rather than an interrupted career.[166] They also seem to have clearer ground rules for an egalitarian marriage. For example, Cummings discusses their responses to the question "How do you feel about women who work to put their husbands through school? Under what circumstances would you be willing to do this?"

> The least feminist women tend either to reject or accept the proposal about putting their husbands through school. . . . The most feminist women were more likely than the other groups to talk about the conditions for considering it. For instance, most either said they would support their husband if he would do the same for them or if it did not interfere with their own plans. In this respect there is evidence that their expectations and ideas of marital and familial duties differ from those of the less feminist women, just as their ideas about a career differ. The more feminist women have some sense of their ground rules for an egalitarian marriage; their answers suggest that they have certain *quid pro quo* established from which they would bargain.[167]

## THE INTERACTION OF SOCIALIZATION INFLUENCES:
## THE CASE STUDY OF MATHEMATICS

Although the previous discussion has focused on each aspect of the socialization process separately, in reality the influence of school, peers, and parents are interactive, and they support and reinforce each other. It is useful to focus on one specific area to illustrate this interactive process. I have chosen mathematics for this case study because of its vital role as a "critical filter" in the selection of college majors. Most of the college majors that readily lead to prestigious occupations—in medicine, chemistry, physics, engineering, computer science, architecture, and even agriculture and business administration—require either college calculus or statistics. But few women have the high school math necessary to take these courses and few colleges offer compensatory math preparation. In 1972, sociologist Lucy Sells found that only 8 percent of the entering female students at the University of California at Berkeley had sufficient math prerequisites (4 years of high school math) to enable them to major in science, engineering, or any of the other math-based subjects.[168] In contrast, 57 percent of the entering male students had sufficient high school math. Thus the potential choice of majors and subsequent career opportunities of 92 percent of the women were severely limited by their lack of mathematical training.*

Let us begin with the question of whether or not there are sex differences in mathematical ability. While many researchers have investigated this subject, the results are mixed and non-conclusive. Further, as Professor John Ernest has observed, there is no consensus as to what "mathematical ability" is: some researchers measure computational proficiency, others geometric or algebraic aptitude, while the psychologists will usually measure some more precise and specific intellectual function.[169]

One comprehensive survey of the research evidence on sex differences in math performance concludes that there are no clear findings: some studies show girls performing better; others, done with students at the same grade level, find boys doing equally well or better.[170] Although it may be premature to conclude that there are no sex differences in mathematical ability and performance, what seems clear in light of the contradictory evidence is that *if* ability differences do exist, they cannot be very strong. Nevertheless, girls seem to get the message that they do not have the same mathematical ability as boys. As a result, they have less confidence in their mathetical skills and screen themselves out of math courses. How do girls come to believe they have less mathematical ability?

Surprisingly, we find no sex differences in *liking* for arithmetic. In a 1973 study of students in grades 2 through 12, John Ernest and his colleagues at U.C. Santa Barbara found that although boys tended to prefer science and girls tended to prefer English, both boys and girls liked mathematics in equal proportions (about 30 percent of both sexes

*In October 1977 Sells replicated her study at the University of Maryland, surveying a stratified sample of incoming freshmen by race and sex. She found the proportions still much the same: 57 percent of the white males had four years of high school math; 20 percent of the black males; 15 percent of the white females (a slight improvement) and only 10 percent of the black females.

said it was their favorite subject; 24 percent liked it second best).[171]

This lack of sex difference in mathematics preference holds true up to the twelfth grade, although its popularity declines in the high school years for both boys and girls. Ernest concludes there is nothing intrinsic about math that makes it more appealing to one sex. Nevertheless, he assumes that boys take more mathematics courses "not for the superficial reason that they like mathematics more than women but because, whether they like it or not, they are aware that such courses are necessary prerequisites to the kinds of future occupations, in medicine, technology or science, they envision for themselves."[172]

Let us examine how parents, peers, and teachers influence this process. With respect to parents, Ernest found that both boys and girls get more help from their mothers with homework in all subjects until the sixth grade. But beginning in the sixth grade, the father helps more in mathematics. The father then is the "authority" on mathematics and continues this role through high school. This fact alone must have its subtle influence on a young girl's (or boy's) attitude.[173]

While peer group attitudes are "sex neutral" in the elementary school years (boys say that boys do better in all subjects while girls say that girls do better in all subjects), by high school a consensus emerges and more students say boys do better than girls in mathematics.[174] (Only 16 percent of all students thought girls did better; 52 percent thought there was no difference.)

Similarly, Lynn Fox, an educator who studied precocious math students for her doctoral thesis at Johns Hopkins University, found that "there are more negative stereotypes for math-gifted girls than boys." Further, mathematically apt girls "seem more willing to sacrifice intellectual stimulation to social stimulation."[175] Other studies have confirmed that girls' performance in math plummets at around age twelve when adolescence makes them more aware of social roles.[176]

Along the same lines, sociologist Sanford Dornbusch reports that when high school students were asked "When you get a poor grade, which reason do you think usually causes the poor grade?", most students gave lack of effort as the reason in every subject. However, when it came to math, 26 percent of the females gave lack of ability as the basis for a poor grade as compared to 15 percent of the males.[177] Female students in every ethnic group in San Francisco were more than three times as likely to say, "I'm not good in math" as the reason for a poor grade as "I'm good in math" as the basis for a good grade.[178] Further, Dornbusch reports, this pattern was found in no other subject for either males or females.

Elizabeth Fennema and Julia Sherman, who have studied how sexual stereotyping affects attitudes and proficiency in mathematics, conclude "there is, then, an accumulation of evidence which points to the conclusion that sexual stereotyping of mathematics as a male domain operates through a myriad of subtle influences from peer to parent and within the girl herself to eventuate in the fulfillment of the stereotyped expectation of a female head that's not much for figures."[179]

Sheila Tobias's book *Overcoming Math Anxiety*, has a section entitled "Street Mathematics," in which she suggests that in addition to negative reinforcement, girls miss learning mathematics naturally at play. For example, she observes that baseball calculations of runs batted in provide challenges in fractions, ratios, and percentages, and throwing and catching a ball involves visualizing a parabolic curve.[180] Similarly, handling a stopwatch and building and taking apart mechanical objects trains boys to think mathematically and, even more important, demonstrates the practical utility of mathematics.

Stereotyped attitudes of peers and students are reinforced by (and are also a result of) the messages they receive in school—both in textbooks and in the expectations of teachers. Weitzman and Rizzo have shown that the most widely used textbooks portray math as a masculine domain.[181] They found males outnumber females 3 to 1 in math textbook illustrations and many of the problems perpetuate extreme sex-role stereotypes. For example, women are shown having trouble counting to three; girls are stereotyped in problems as "girls who cry"; and Alan earns more than Jane for doing the same hourly work.

With regard to teachers' expectations, Ernest reports that 41 percent of the elementary and high school teachers he interviewed felt that boys did better in mathematics, while none of them felt that girls did better.[182] Such expectations may eventually have a "Pygmalion effect"—that is, the student may perform much as the teacher expects. This creates a self-fulfilling prophecy in which those expected to do well perform as expected. Thus, if 41 percent of the teachers expect superior performance from boys, they may, in fact, help to create it. Conversely, however, when teachers expect female students to do poorly in math, they must accordingly affect the girls' performance,* or at least the girls' attitudes and expectations, as well.

For girls, the result of all these socialization pressures—from peers and parents and teachers—is often what Sheila Tobias has labeled "math anxiety."[184] According to Tobias, math anxiety is an

> "I can't" syndrome, and whenever it strikes—for some as early as sixth grade, with word problems; for others, with the first bite of algebra; for still others, not until calculus or linear algebra or statistics, after a high school record of achievement in mathematics—it creates the same symptoms and response. "I can't do this. No amount of practice or trying will make it work for me. I never really understood math. I always memorized and got away with it. Now I've hit the level I always knew was there. I can't do it."
>
> Once a person has become frightened of math, she or he begins to fear all manner of computations, any quantitative data, and words like "proportion," "percentage," "variance," "curve," "exponential."[185]

We began this section by pointing to mathematics as an example of the interactive and cumulative effect of pressures from peers, parents, and teachers—all pointing in the same direction, all telling girls that mathematics is a masculine domain. However, since all the socialization influences point in the same direction, a change in any *one* of them could break the pattern of *consistent* reinforcement. Thus, encouragement from a single parent or teacher, or peer support from just one or two other "math freaks," could break the cycle. One striking example of the impact of a single pro-math influence is provided by Professor Joan Birman of Barnard–Columbia:

> I learned last year, to my astonishment, that for about four years running the honors calculus course had been all male, in spite of the fact that admission was based on an open competitive

---

*Of course there is always the unusual girl who persists despite lack of encouragement. For example, a tiny survey conducted at Stanford revealed that women majoring in natural sciences, mathematics, and engineering had received less encouragement to pursue math studies than had any group of Stanford males, even those males who were majoring in history or the humanities.[183] These "exceptions" will be discussed in the next section.

examination. This fall, one of the senior mathematics majors and myself made an intensive effort to encourage women to *try the exam!* The typical answer was, "I know I won't pass it,"—to which we replied over and over, "Well, if you try it, at worst you will confirm what you already know, and only an hour of time will have been lost." After three days of such advising, the big day came, the exam was given, and this year the class has five men and five women![186]

Birman's experience suggests the powerful potential of a single contrary influence.* This insight leads directly to the next question of how successful women have managed to achieve despite the socialization pressures we've discussed.

## WOMEN'S ACHIEVEMENT

Although this discussion has emphasized formal academic and occupational achievement throughout, it should be clear that there are other areas in which both men and women are motivated to achieve.** For example, some people make lifetime careers of philanthropy or unpaid volunteer work. Some devote their energies to civic affairs. Others aspire to positions of responsibility in religious or recreational organizations. Still others undertake technical or creative pursuits such as photography, rock collecting, or wine-making. And all of these unpaid endeavors may give participants a sense of achievement and success.

Nonetheless, there are limits to the status rewards these activities can bring. For in American society, status is closely related to monetary rewards, which generally come from occupational achievements. And it is clear that men, not women, are socialized to adopt the personality characteristics that are related to success in the more prestigious and financially lucrative occupations.

With the relentless conditioning we have just reviewed, it seems remarkable that some girls do not get the message that they are

---

*Other intervention strategies, such as peer counseling (Mills College, Oakland, California), alternate math curricula for women students (Wellesley College), Math Anxiety Clinics (Wesleyan University, Connecticut), and Adult Group Therapy (Mind Over Math, New York City) operate on the same theoretical assumption. As Tobias states it, "Math Anxiety is probably as much a result, as it a cause of math avoidance in women and girls."[187]

**I am indebted to Sheryl Ruzeck for suggesting this to me.

supposed to be less intelligent and less successful until high school,* and that some escape through their college years. Further, in spite of the overwhelming pressures to conform to the traditional feminine role, many women do aspire to intellectual and professional success, and a significant number of them attain it. How can we account for these women? Are they deviants, or have we presented an over-socialized portrait of women in this essay?

In the statistical sense, women who have attained professional success are deviants in that they are distinctly in the minority; but it is important to realize what a significant minority they are. We have already noted the wide range of individual differences in both sexes and the extent to which our summary has excluded the statistical minority of woman achievers. In this section we shall focus on this "deviant" group, composed of female doctors, lawyers, engineers, architects, professors, scientists, corporation executives, writers, etc., and ask what has been difficult about the socialization of these women. The following discussion will, of necessity, be speculative, because there has not yet been a systematic study of the socialization of high-achieving women. It is meant to be suggestive.

### Family background

One might speculate on various family situations that would encourage a girl's occupational aspirations: being a successful businessman's only child, who has been encouraged to take over her family's business; being the daughter of a female doctor, encouraged to assist in her mother's office; or being the oldest sibling in a large family for whom leadership and authority are natural. Achievement motivation and occupational aspirations may arise from a great variety of sources that are beyond the limited scope of this paper to explore.

Several studies have indicated that the role of the mother is especially important. If the mother works, or has worked, the girl is more likely to see a career as "natural" for a woman. In Hartley's study of girls between the ages of eight and eleven, the girls' future plans were significantly related to their mothers' work roles. When asked what they expected to do when they grew up, significantly more daughters of

---

*This question was raised by Naomi Weisstein in "Kinder, Kuche, Kirche as Scientific Law," *Motive*, April 1969.

nonworking mothers gave "housewife" as their primary choice and more daughters of working mothers mentioned nontraditional professional areas (such as medicine, law, creative work) as their vocational choices. Also, daughters of working mothers were more likely to plan to continue working after marrying and having children.[188]

Traditional identification theory assumed that the same-sex parent was the more crucial in determining the sex-role identity of the child. This theory, which grew out of Freudian theory, asserted that the child must, in order to identify properly as a member of his or her sex, have a same-sex model to imitate.[189] Thus by imitating the father the boy would learn and internalize masculine behavior. Similarly, it was assumed, the girl would learn how to be feminine by imitating the behavior of her mother. According to this theory, the child internalizes not only the particular behavior observed, but a complex integrated pattern of sex-related behavior.[190] I would suggest instead, that a large amount of sex-role behavior can be learned only through interaction with the opposite sex. This is especially true of the "feminine role," which is often defined in terms of relationships with others. It is thus possible that the father teaches the girl how to be feminine as much as the mother does.

Identification theory may be challenged on another ground as well. Identification theorists have assumed that it is necessary for adult role-models to have clearly differentiated sex roles, so that the child can clearly distinguish what is masculine and what is feminine behavior.[191] However, Slater has indicated that adult role-models who exhibit stereotyped sex-role identification may impede, rather than facilitate, the child's sex-role identification. Children may find it easier to identify with less differentiated and less stereotyped parental role models.[192] It is more likely that they will internalize parental values when nurturance (the typically feminine role) and discipline (the typically masculine role) come from the same source.

Both of these challenges to traditional identification theory indicate that the father may play as important a role as the mother in a daughter's socialization. In fact, Heilbrun has shown that highly successful girls tend to have an especially close relationship with, and identify with, a masculine father.[193]

Although there are no direct data, we might speculate that an especially strong stimulus to achievement motivation in women would be a strong father-daughter relationship in which the father encour-

ages his daughter and makes his love and approval dependent on her
performance. Most fathers show unconditional support for their
daughters, whether or not they achieve, because most fathers do not
consider a woman's achievements crucial to her success in life.

The importance of this father-daughter tie has been noted by family
sociologist William J. Goode, who has observed that a large number of
successful women were their fathers' "favorite" child.[194] This can be a
great spur to "masculine" achievement, especially when there are no
sons in the family and the father supports and assists his daughter's
aspirations. This hypothesis has its parallel in research on male
achievement motivation, where McClelland's work has shown that a
strong mother-son relationship (in which the mother bases conditional
love on her son's success) is most conducive to masculine achievement
motivation.[195]

### The oversocialized portrait of women

Thus far, we have considered high occupational achievement and
achievement motivation in women as if it were deviant, and therefore
required a special explanation. However, an alternative view suggests
that, in fact, *most* women are motivated to achieve. This perspective
would lead one to conclude that the socialization literature presents an
oversocialized portrait of women. It is clear that the literature thus far
reviewed in this paper exaggerates in two ways:

  a. Women are assumed to internalize the feminine role *completely*.

  b. The pressures on women are presented as *unidimensional*.

Let us examine each of these.

The socialization literature has probably overestimated the effectiveness of the socialization process. It is assumed that women have
been successfully socialized and have internalized the feminine role.
However, if this were so, women would feel fulfilled within that role,
whereas in fact almost every study of women's fulfillment has shown
that those who conform most closely to the feminine role are least
fulfilled.[196] Both Jessie Bernard[197] and Betty Friedan,[198] after reviewing
the literature on feminine happiness and fulfillment, conclude that
most women are not content with their traditional role.

In addition to exaggerating the effectiveness of the socialization
process for women, the literature incorrectly treats the pressures on
women as unidimensional. Women are viewed as being consistently

rewarded for feminine behavior and consistently punished for or dis couraged from unfeminine behavior. Social learning theory, which is the basis for the bulk of the material presented in this paper, holds that sex-appropriate responses are consistently rewarded and reinforced— and sex-inappropriate behavior consistently discouraged or punished— in the young girl until she comes to learn and internalize the feminine role.[199]

Without denying the pressures on women to conform to the feminine role, one can see that women are socialized in an ambivalent fashion. At the same time that girls are rewarded for typical feminine behavior, they are also rewarded for some types of "masculine" behav- ior. This is because what is labeled masculine behavior is generally highly regarded and rewarded in our society. The girl who excels in school, wins the tennis championship, or fixes a broken car receives approval for each of these activities. Although she may be regarded as too aggressive or masculine, she is also admired for her accomplish- ments. Thus, the feminine role is not consistently reinforced.

Earlier we discussed another aspect of the unidimensional fallacy. When we examined the literature on black women we noted that since many people have some "masculine" traits and some "feminine" traits, and since many of our sex-typed behaviors are situationally specific, it is erroneous to think of individuals as *either* masculine *or* feminine. For example, Tobias notes that women who succeed in math and science, and who therefore might be considered most "deviant" of all, do not score low on *all* feminine characteristics, but only on those feminine characteristics that are inappropriate to their own individual self-image. They are "aggressive" (not passive), but they are also "nurturant" and "caring" (not "cold" and "aloof").[200] Further, Potter found that the women with higher math ability responded positively to a cluster of attributes considered masculine, such as "logical," "persistent" and "intellectual." But this group also scored high on positively-valued feminine attributes, such as "warm," "generous" and so on. What these women seemed to be rejecting, the researcher concluded, was not femininity itself, but the low-valued feminine characteristics such as dependency and passivity. They seemed to have a healthy orientation toward the best of both the male and female worlds.[201]

Similarly, in a study of successful adolescent women, Heilbrun found the subjects both instrumental and expressive; that is, they exhibited the goal-directedness of typically successful males as well as the interpersonal sensitivity of typically successful females.[202] So long as the scoring of sex-role identities is done on an either-or basis, or the "masculine" choices are tallied against the "feminine" choices, these multifaceted combinations of the traits of both sexes are easily overlooked.

If we are correct in asserting that the socialization of women into the traditional female roles is neither totally effective nor totally consistent, then one might legitimately ask why there are not more visible examples of high-achieving women. If, as we have asserted, many women are actually motivated to higher achievement, why has the proportion of women in the professions and in other high-status occupations remained so low?

There are two possible answers to this question. The first is that women's achievement is channeled in a different direction. As noted above, Pierce has shown that women with high achievement motivation are oriented toward finding high-status husbands.[203] Tobias suggests that the women who graduated in the 1950's married the men they themselves wanted to be.[204] Press and Whitney and Lipman-Blumen have also hypothesized that women see success in terms of heterosexual relationships, and that they attain vicarious gratification from the achievements of their husbands and sons.[205] Press and Whitney suggest that women with high achievement motivation pick males who will succeed, so that they may experience success vicariously.[206]

But even though women have been socialized to regard personal occupational success as difficult or undesirable, it seems unlikely that many women with high achievement motivation would be content with vicarious achievement alone. Unless they are allowed to play a significant role in their husbands' or sons' careers, they are likely to channel their energies elsewhere. It is obvious that the energies of many capable women are channeled into volunteer work or into other nonremunerative pursuits. Other high-achievement-oriented women may be found in frustrating jobs that are much below their capability, or in positions that involve power and capabilities that are neither recognized nor rewarded (with either money or position) by their employers.

A second answer to the question of why there are not more visible examples of high-achieving women lies in the structural opportunities available to women in this society. When women are denied real opportunities for advancement and are discriminated against at every stage of the process leading to a professional position, it is not surprising that they have not "made it." Thus, the answer to this question probably lies not so much in the socialization of women as in the structural opportunities available to them in our society.

As long as women are denied real career options, it is a realistic decision not to aim for a career. As long as they lack role models of successful career women, are denied structural supports to aid a career, are told they are neurotic or unfeminine if they are dedicated to an occupation, we cannot expect young women to take the career option seriously. The only way to change their (accurate) perceptions about future options is to create *real options* for them.

## NOTES

1  Margaret Mead, *Sex and Temperament in Three Primitive Societies* (New York: Morrow, 1939; Mentor Books, 1950).

2  Milton Spiro, *Children of the Kibbutz* (New York: Schoken Books, 1960).

3  John Money, *Sex Research: New Developments* (New York: Holt, Rinehart, 1965); "Sex Hormones and Other Variables in Human Eroticism," in William C. Young, ed., *Sex and Internal Secretions*, 3rd ed., vol. 2 (Baltimore: Williams and Wilkins, 1961), pp. 1383–1400; and John L. Hampson and Joan Hampson, "The Ontogenesis of Sexual Behavior in Man," in *ibid.*, pp. 1401–32.

4  Mirra Komarovsky, *Women in the Modern World* (Boston: Little, Brown, 1953).

5  Howard A. Moss, "Sex, Age, and State as Determinants of Mother-Infant Interaction," *Merrill-Palmer Quarterly*, 13, 1 (1967), 19–36, 28, 30.

6  *Ibid.*

7  Susan Goldberg and Michael Lewis, "Play Behavior in the Year-Old Infant; Early Sex Differences," *Child Development*, 40 (1969), 21–30.

8  Jerome Kagan and Michael Lewis, "Studies of Attention in the Human Infant," *Merrill-Palmer Quarterly*, 2 (1965), 95–127.

9  Goldberg and Lewis, "Play Behavior in the Year-Old Infant," p. 29.

10  Meyer L. Rabban, "Sex Role Identification in Young Children in Two Diverse Social Groups," *Genetic Psychological Monographs*, vol. 42 (1950), pp. 81–158.

11  Evelyn Wiltshire Goodenough, "Interests in Persons as an Aspect of Sex Differences in the Early Years," *Genetic Psychological Monographs*, vol. 55 (1957), p. 312.

12  Lenore J. Weitzman, Deborah Eifler, Elizabeth Hokada, and Catherine Ross, "Sex Role Socialization in Picture Books for Pre-School Children," *American Journal of Sociology* (May 1972).

13  *Ibid.* Parts of this quote were paraphrased from the original.

14  Jo Ann Gardner, "*Sesame Street* and Sex Role Stereotypes," in *Women*, 1, 3 (Spring 1970).

15  Ruth E. Hartley, "Sex-Role Pressures and the Socialization of the Male Child," *Psychological Reports*, 5 (1959), 457–68, 461.

16  *Ibid.*

17  *Ibid.*

18  *Ibid.*

19  Rabban, "Sex Role Identification in Young Children," p. 145.

20  M. S. Simpson, "Parent Preferences of Young Children," *Contributing Education*, No. 682 (New York: Teachers College, Columbia University, 1935).

21  Daniel G. Brown, "Sex-Role Preference in Young Children," *Psychological Monographs*, 70, 14 (1956), 1–19.

22  *Ibid.*

23  Willard W. Hartup and Elsie A. Zook, "Sex-Role Preferences in Three- and Four-Year-Old Children," *Journal of Consulting Psychology*, 24 (December 1960), 420–26.

24  Willard W. Hartup, "Some Correlates of Parental Imitation in Young Children," *Child Development*, 33 (1962), 85–96.

25  Hartley, "Sex-Role Pressures."

26  *Ibid.*

27  Brown, "Sex-Role Preference in Young Children."

28  S. Smith, "Age and Sex Differences in Children's Opinion Concerning Sex Differences," *Journal of Genetic Psychology*, 54 (1939), 17–25.

29  *Ibid.*

30  David B. Lynn, *Parental and Sex Role Identification: A Theoretical Formulation* (Berkeley, Calif.: McCrutchan Publishing Corp., 1969), p. 24.

31  *Ibid.*

32  David B. Lynn, "A Note on Sex Differences in the Development of Masculine and Feminine Identification," *Psychological Review*, 66, 2 (1959), 126–35.

33  Hartley, "Sex-Role Pressures," p. 458.

34  *Ibid.*

35  For an excellent review of the learning literatures and the effects of punishment versus rewards, see William J. Goode, "The Uses of Dispraise," in *The Celebration of Heroes* (Berkeley, Calif.: University of California Press, 1978).

36  Hartley, "Sex-Role Pressures."

37  Ruth E. Hartley, "A Developmental View of Female Sex-Role Definition and Identification," *Merrill-Palmer Quarterly*, 10, 1 (Jan. 1964), 3–17, 4.

38  Janet Lever, "Christmas Toys for Girls and Boys," report to Sociology 62a, Sociological Perspectives on Women, Sociology Department, Fall 1970, Yale University, Professor L. Weitzman.

39  William D. Ward, "Variance of Sex-Role Preference Among Boys and Girls," *Psychological Reports*, 23, 2 (1968), 467–70.

40  Komarovsky, *Women in the Modern World*.

41  *Ibid.*

42  Pauline R. Sears, Eleanor Maccoby, and Harry Levin, *Patterns of Child Rearing* (Evanston, Ill.: Row, Peterson, 1957).

43  Urie Bronfenbrenner, "Some Familial Antecedents of Responsibility and Leadership in Adolescents," in Luigi Petrullo, and Bernard M. Bass, eds., *Leadership and Interpersonal Behavior* (New York: Holt, Rinehart, 1961).

44  Komarovsky, *Women in the Modern World*, p. 55.

45  Jerome Kagan, "Acquisition and Significance of Sex Typing and Sex-Role Identity," in Martin Leon Hoffman and Lois Wladis Hoffman, eds., *Review of Child Development Research* (New York: Russell Sage Foundation, 1964), pp. 137–67, 151.

46  David Aberle and Kasper Naegele, "Middle Class Father's Occupational Role and Attitudes Toward Children," in Norman W. Bell and Ezra F. Vogel, eds., *The Family*, rev. ed. (New York: Free Press, 1968); Melvin L. Kohn, "Social Class and Parental Values," *American Journal of Sociology*, 64 (January 1959), 337–51; Sears, Maccoby, and Levin, *Patterns of Child Rearing;* and Paul H. Mussen, John U. Conger, and Jerome Kagan, *Child Development and Personality*, 2d ed. (New York: Harper and Row, 1963).

47  Judith M. Bardwick, Elizabeth Douvan, Matina S. Horner, and David Gutmann, *Feminine Personality and Conflict* (Belmont, Calif.: Brooks/Cole, 1970), p. 4.

48  *Ibid.*

49  *Ibid.*

50  Kagan, "Acquisition and Significance of Sex Typing," p. 151.

51  *Ibid.*

52  Urie Bronfenbrenner, "The Changing American Child: A Speculative Analysis," *Merrill-Palmer Quarterly*, 7 (April 1961), 9, 73–83.

53  Stanley Schachter, *The Psychology of Affiliation* (Stanford, Calif.: Stanford University Press, 1959); Bronfenbrenner, "The Changing American Child."

54  Bronfenbrenner, "The Changing American Child."

55  Kagan, "Acquisition and Significance of Sex Typing," p. 151.

56  Personal conversation, December 1971.

57  Leona E. Tyler, "Sex Differences" under "Individual Differences," in the *International Encyclopedia of the Social Sciences*, vol. 7 (New York: Macmillan, 1968), pp. 207–13.

58  Jo Freeman, "The Social Construction of the Second Sex," in Michele Barskof, ed., *Roles Women Play* (Belmont, Calif.: Brooks/Cole, 1971), p. 127.

59  See, for example, Leona E. Tyler, *The Psychology of Human Differences* (New York: Appleton-Century-Crofts, 1965).

60  Eleanor Maccoby and Carol Jacklin, *The Psychology of Sex Differences* (Stanford, Calif.: Stanford University Press, 1975).

61  *Ibid.*, p. 349.

62  Jeanne H. Block, "Issues, Problems and Pitfalls in Assessing Sex Differences: A Critical Review of the Psychology of Sex Differences," *Merrill-Palmer Quarterly*, 22, 4 (1976), 308.

63  For a more extensive review of the literature, see William J. Goode, Elizabeth Hopkins, and Helen M. McClure, *Social Systems and Family Structures* (Indianapolis: Bobbs-Merrill, 1971).

64  Letha Scanzoni and John Scanzoni, *Men, Women and Change: A Sociology of Marriage and Family* (New York: McGraw-Hill, 1976), p. 30.

65  Goode et al., *Social Systems and Family Structures.*

66  Rabban, "Sex Role Identification in Young Children."

67  *Ibid.*

68  *Ibid.*

69  Scanzoni and Scanzoni, *Men, Women and Change*, p. 35.

70  Lillian Rubin, *Worlds of Pain: Life in the Working Class Family* (New York: Basic Books, 1976), pp. 125–26.

71  See, for example, Herbert Gans, "The Urban Villagers" (New York: Free Press, 1962).

72  Although there has been no systematic study of racial differences in parental treatment of young children, we do know that black mothers, irrespective of class, have much less exposure to child-rearing experts. See, for example, Zena Smith Blau, "Exposure to Child-Rearing Experts: A Structural Interpretation of Class-Color Differences," *American Journal of Sociology*, 69 (May 1964), 596–608.

73  Fred Strodbeck, "Family Interaction, Values, and Achievement," in David McClelland, Alfred Baldwin, Urie Bronfenbrenner, and Fred Strodbeck, eds., *Talent and Society* (Princeton, N.J.: Van Nostrand, 1968), pp. 135–94.

74  Personal conversation, Winter 1971.

75  I am indebted to Marjorie Randon Hershey of the Department of Political Science at Indiana University for her helpful suggestions in a personal conversation in April 1978.

76  Arlie R. Hochschild, "A Review of Sex Role Research," *American Journal of Sociology*, 78 (1973), 1011, 1023.

77  Joyce Aschenbrenner, *Lifelines: Black Families in Chicago* (New York: Holt, Rinehart and Winston, 1975), p. 6.

78  Denise Kandel, "Race, Maternal Authority, and Adolescent Aspiration," *American Journal of Sociology*, 76 (1971), 999–1020.

79  Daniel P. Moynihan, *The Negro Family: The Case for National Action* (Washington, D.C.: U.S. Department of Labor, Office of Policy Planning and Research, 1965).

80  Carol B. Stack, *All Our Kin: Strategies for Survival in a Black Community* (New York: Harper Colophon Books, 1974), p. 121.

81  *Ibid.*, pp. 122–26.

82  *Ibid.*

83  *Ibid.*, p. 112.

84  *Ibid.*, p. 113.

85  Marjorie Randon Hershey, "Racial Differences in Sex Role Identities and Sex Role Stereotyping," *Social Science Quarterly* (1978). See also B. F. Turner and C.B.

Turner, "The Political Implications of Social Stereotyping of Women and Men among Black and White College Students," *Sociology and Social Research*, 58 (1974), 155–62.

86  Joyce A. Ladner, *Tomorrow's Tomorrow: The Black Woman* (Garden City, N.Y.: Doubleday, 1971), pp. 187–88.

87  Tansey Thomas, "Growing Up in the Ghetto," student report, Sociology 131, University of California, Davis, Fall 1971.

88  Ladner, *Tomorrow's Tomorrow*, pp. 120–76.

89  Jo Freeman, personal conversation, April 1978.

90  Cynthia Epstein, "Positive Effects of the Multiple Negative: Explaining the Success of Black Professional Women," *American Journal of Sociology*, 78 (1973), 913–18.

91  Kandel, "Race, Maternal Authority, and Adolescent Aspiration," 1009.

92  Ladner, *Tomorrow's Tomorrow*, pp. 120–76.

93  *Ibid.*

94  *Ibid.*, pp. 187–88.

95  Patricia Gurin and Carolyn Gaylord, "Educational and Occupational Goals of Men and Women at Black Colleges," *Monthly Labor Review* (June 1976), 10.

96  *Ibid.*

97  Hershey, "Racial Differences in Sex Role Identities."

98  *Ibid.*, p. 12.

99  Hershey, personal conversation, April 1978.

100  *Ibid.*

101  John H. Scanzoni, *The Black Family in Modern Society*, Phoenix Edition, (Chicago: University of Chicago Press, 1977), p. 335.

102  See, for example Sandra L. Bem, "Beyond Androgyny: Some Presumptuous Prescriptions for a Liberated Sexual Identity," in J. Sherman and F. Denmark, eds., *Psychology of Women: Future Directions of Research* (New York: Psychological Dimensions, Inc., 1976).

103  Orville G. Brim, "Family Structure and Sex Role Learning by Children," *Sociometry*, 21 (1958), 1–16; Helen L. Koch, "The Relation of Certain Family Constellation Characteristics and the Attitudes of Children Towards Adults," *Child Development*, 26 (March 1955); 13–40.

104  Janet G. Hunt and Larry L. Hunt, "Race, Daughters and Father-Loss: Does Absence Make the Girl Grow Stronger?", *Social Problems*, 25, 1 (1977), p. 91.

105  Hartley, "A Developmental View of Female Sex-Role Definition."

106  Irwin Child, Elmer Potter, and Estelle Levine, "Children's Textbooks and Personality Development: An Exploration in the Social Psychology of Education," in Morris L. Haimowitz and Natalie Reader Haimowitz, eds., *Human Development: Selected Readings* (New York: Thomas Y. Crowell Co., 1960), pp. 292–305.

107  *Ibid.*, p. 302.

108  Women on Words and Images, *Dick and Jane as Victims* (Princeton, N.J., 1972); Marcia Federbush, *"Let Them Aspire,"* (Ann Arbor, Michigan, 1972); and Terry Sario, Carol Nagy Jacklin, and Carol Kehr Tittle, "Sex Role Stereotyping in the

Public Schools," *Harvard Educational Review,* 43, 3 (Aug. 1973).

109   Lenore J. Weitzman and Diane Rizzo, "Images of Males and Females in Elementary School Textbooks," New York, National Organization for Women's Legal Defense and Education Fund, 1974.

110   *Ibid.*

111   "Stalled at the Start: Government Action on Sex Bias in the Schools" (Washington, D.C.: Project on Equal Educational Rights, 1978), p. 13.

112   *Ibid.,* p. 7.

113   *Ibid.,* p. 7, 13, 21.

114   Eleanor E. Maccoby, "Sex Differences in Intellectual Functioning," in Maccoby, ed., *The Development of Sex Differences* (Stanford, Calif.: Stanford University Press, 1966).

115   G. A. Milton, *Five Studies of the Relation Between Sex Role Identification and Achievement in Problem Solving,* Technical Report No. 3, Dept. of Industrial Admin., Department of Psychology, Yale University, Dec. 1958.

116   Kagan, "Acquisition and Significance of Sex Typing," p. 157.

117   Eleanor E. Maccoby, "Woman's Intellect," in *The Potential of Women,* Seymour L. Farber and Roger H. L. Wilson, eds. (New York: McGraw-Hill, 1963), p. 31.

118   Julia A. Sherman, "Problems of Sex Differences in Space Perception and Aspects of Intellectual Functioning," *Psychological Review,* 74, 4 (1967), 290–99.

119   *Ibid.*

120   *Ibid.*

121   The following is paraphrased from comments of Professor William Goode, Jo Freeman, and myself in personal communications, 1971–72.

122   Similar assumptions about the linkage of male abilities and the traits most useful in managerial positions have been challenged in William J. Goode, "Family Life of the Successful Woman" in Eli Ginzberg and Alice Yohalem, eds. *Corporate Lib* (Baltimore: Johns Hopkins University Press, 1973), pp. 97–117.

123   Personal communication, Jan. 1974.

124   Aberle and Naegele, "Middle Class Father's Occupational Role."

125   *Ibid.*

126   This finding is taken from Table 4, p. 569, in William H. Sewell and Vimal P. Shah. "Social Class, Parental Encouragement, and Educational Aspirations," *American Journal of Sociology,* 73, 5 (March 1968), 559–72.

127   David Bordua, "Educational Aspirations and Parental Stress on College," *Social Forces,* 38 (1960), 267.

128   Glen H. Elder, Jr., *Adolescent Achievement and Mobility Aspirations* (Chapel Hill, N.C.: Institute for Research in Social Science, 1962), pp. 159–60.

129   Sex differences in parental encouragement persist even when social class and intelligence are held constant; Sewell and Shah, p. 570.

130   Ladner, *Tomorrow's Tomorrow.*

131   Kandel, "Race, Maternal Authority, and Adolescent Aspiration," p. 1009.

132   Mirra Komarovsky, "Functional Analysis of Sex Roles," *American Sociological Review,* 15 (August 1950), 508–16.

133  *Ibid.*

134  *Ibid.*

135  "An American Anachronism: The Image of Women and Work," *Daedalus* (Summer 1964).

136  James V. Pierce, "Sex Differences in Achievement Motivation of Able High School Students," Cooperative Research Project No. 1097, University of Chicago, December 1961.

137  *Ibid.*

138  Keniston, 1964.

139  I am indebted to Sheila Tobias, Associate Provost of Wesleyan University, for suggesting this term to me.

140  Rubin, *Worlds of Pain,* pp. 40–41.

141  *Ibid.*

142  Mirra Komarovsky, "Cultural Contradictions and Sex Roles," *American Journal of Sociology,* 52 (1946), 184–89.

143  *Ibid.*

144  Personal conversation, Jan. 1971.

145  Florence Howe, "Identity and Expression: A Writing Course for Women," unpublished paper.

146  Lois W. Hoffman "The Employment of Women, Education and Fertility" in Martha Mednick, Sandra Tangri and Lois Hoffman, eds., *Women and Achievement* (New York: John Wiley and Sons, 1975), pp. 110–14.

147  *Ibid.*

148  Rossi, "Equality Between the Sexes."

149  Elizabeth Douvan, "Sex Differences in Adolescent Character Process," *Merrill Palmer Quarterly,* 6 (1960), 203–11.

150  Patricia Cross, *Beyond the Open Door* (San Francisco: Jossey-Bass, 1971), p. 148.

151  Laurie Davidson Cummings, "Value Stretch in Definitions of Career Among College Women: Horatia Alger As Feminist Model," *Social Problems,* 25, 1 (1977), 65–74; and Ann P. Parelius, "Change and Stability in College Women's Orientations toward Education, Family and Work," *Social Problems,* 22 (February 1975), 420–32.

152  Virginia Slims American Women's Opinion Poll, III, n.d., p. 1; and "Women in America," The Gallup Opinion Index, Report 128 (March 1976), p. 30.

153  Matina S. Horner, "Women's Need to Fail," *Psychology Today* (November 1969).

154  *Ibid.,* and "Toward an Understanding of Achievement-Related Conflicts in Women," *The Journal of Social Issues,* 28, 2 (1972), 157–75.

155  Martha Mednick et al., *Women and Achievement,* p. 124.

156  L. W. Hoffman, "Fear of Success in Males and Females: 1965 and 1972," *Journal of Consulting and Clinical Psychology* (1974).

157  M. S. Horner and M. R. Walsh, "Causes and Consequences of the Existence of Psychological Barriers to Self-Actualization," paper presented at the New York Academy of Science Conference, New York, May 1972.

158   See, for example, Cynthia Epstein, *Woman's Place: Options and Limits in Professional Careers* (Berkeley: University of California Press, 1970).

159   Hoffman, "The Employment of Women," p. 114.

160   L. W. Hoffman and M. L. Hoffman, "The Value of Children to Parents," in J. T. Fawcett, ed., *Psychological Perspectives on Population* (New York: Basic Books, 1973).

161   A. G. Levine, "Marital and Occupational Plans of Women in Professional Schools: Law, Medicine, Nursing, Teaching," Ph.D. dissertation, Yale University, 1968.

162   M. Komarovsky, "Cultural Contradictions and Sex Roles: The Masculine Case," *American Journal of Sociology*, 78, 4, (1973), 873–85.

163   Hoffman, "The Employment of Women," p. 115.

164   *Ibid.*

165   See, for example, J. A. Birnbaum, "Life Patterns, Personality Style and Self Esteem in Gifted Family Oriented and Career-Committed Women," Ph.D. dissertation, University of Michigan, 1971; Lynda Lytle Holmstrom, *The Two-Career Family* (Cambridge, Mass.: Schenckman, 1972); and T. N. Garland, "The Better Half? The Male in the Dual Profession Family," in C. Safilios-Rothschild, ed., *Toward a Sociology of Women* (Lexington, Mass.: Xerox College Publishing, 1972).

166   Cummings, "Value Stretch in Career Definitions," 65–74.

167   *Ibid.*, p. 72.

168   Lucy Sells, "Mathematics—A Critical Filter," *The Science Teacher* (February 1978), 28–29.

169   John Ernest, "Mathematics and Sex," April 1976 (preprint of an article to appear in the *American Mathematical Monthly*), p. 6.

170   Elizabeth Fennema, "Mathematics Learning and the Sexes: A Review," *Journal for Research in Mathematics Education*, 5 (1974), 126–39.

171   Ernest, "Mathematics and Sex," p. 3.

172   *Ibid.*, p. 4.

173   *Ibid.*,

174   *Ibid.*, p. 5.

175   Lynn H. Fox, "Facilitating the Development of Mathematical Talent in Young Women," Ph.D. dissertation, Johns Hopkins University, 1974.

176   "Math Mystique: Fear of Figuring," *Time*, March 14, 1977, p. 36.

177   Stanford Dornbusch, "To Try or Not to Try," *Stanford Magazine*, 2, 2 (1974), pp. 50–54.

178   *Ibid.*

179   Elizabeth Fennema and Julia A. Sherman, "Sexual Stereotyping and Mathematics Learning," to appear in *The Arithmetic Teacher*.

180   Sheila Tobias, *Overcoming Math Anxiety* (New York: W. W. Norton, 1978), Chapter 3, "Mathematics and Sex."

181   Lenore J. Weitzman and Diane Rizzo, "Sex Role Stereotypes in Elementary School Textbooks in Five Subject Areas," in *Biased Textbooks* (Washington, D.C.: National Education Association, 1974).

182   Ernest, "Mathematics and Sex," p. 6.

183   Dornbusch, "To Try or Not to Try."

184   Sheila Tobias, "Math Anxiety: Why is a Smart Girl Like You Counting on Your Fingers?", *Ms Magazine*. See also *Overcoming Math Anxiety*, especially Chapter 3.

185   Tobias, "Math Anxiety," p. 57.

186   Quoted in Ernest, "Mathematics and Sex," p. 12.

187   Tobias, *Overcoming Math Anxiety*, Chapter 3.

188   Ruth E. Hartley, "Children's Concept of Male and Female Roles," *Merrill-Palmer Quarterly*, 6 (1960), 83–91.

189   Paul H. Mussen, "Early Sex-Role Development," in David A. Goslin, ed., *Handbook of Socialization Theory and Research* (Chicago: Rand McNally, 1969).

190   *Ibid.*

191   Talcott Parsons, "Family Structure and the Socialization of the Child," in Talcott Parsons and Robert F. Bales, eds., *Family, Socialization, and Interaction Process* (New York: Free Press, 1955), p. 80.

192   Philip Slater, "Parental Role Differentiation," *The American Journal of Sociology*, 47, 3 (November 1961), 296–331.

193   Alfred B. Heilbrun, Jr., "Sex Role, Instrumental-Expressive Behavior, and Psychopathology in Females," *Journal of Abnormal Psychology*, 73, 2 (1958), 131–36.

194   William J. Goode, personal conversation, Dec. 1970.

195   David McClelland, *The Achieving Society* (New York: Free Press, 1964).

196   Abraham H. Maslow, "Dominance, Personality and Social Behavior in Women," *Journal of Social Psychology*, 10 (1942), 259–94.

197   Jessie Bernard, "The Myth of the Happy Marriage," in V. Gornick and R. Morgan, eds., *Women in a Sexist Society* (New York: Basic Books, 1971); and *The Future of Marriage* (New York: World Books, 1972).

198   Betty Friedan, *The Feminine Mystique* (New York: W. W. Norton, 1963).

199   Mussen, "Early Sex-Role Development"; and Walter Mischel, "A Social-Learning View of Sex Differences," in Eleanor E. Maccoby, ed., *The Development of Sex Differences* (Stanford, Calif.: Stanford University Press, 1966).

200   Sheila Tobias, personal conversation, April 1978.

201   Nancy Potter, "Mathematical and Verbal Ability Patterns in Women," Ph.D. dissertation, University of Missouri–Columbia, 1974.

202   Heilbrun, "Sex Role . . . in Females," p. 134.

203   J. Pierce, "Sex Differences in Achievement Motivation."

204   Tobias, personal conversation, April 1978.

205   Jean M. Press and Fraine E. Whitney, "Achievement Syndromes in Women: Vicarious or Conflict-Ridden," paper presented at the Forty-first Annual Meeting of the Eastern Sociological Society, April 1971; and Jean Lippman-Blumen, "How Ideology Shapes Women's Lives," *Scientific American*, 226, 1 (January 1972).

206   Press and Whitney, "Achievement Syndromes in Women."

# Jo Freeman

# How to Discriminate Against Women Without Really Trying

"Any girl who gets this far has got to be a kook" one distinguished (male) member of the University of Chicago faculty told a female graduate student who had come to see him about being on her dissertation committee.

This was just one of many such statements collected by women students at the University in the spring of 1969 to illustrate their contention that "some of our professors have different expectations about our performance than about the performance of male graduate students—expectations based not on our ability as individuals but on the fact that we are women." There were many others. They included:

"The admissions committee didn't do their job. There is not one goodlooking girl in the entering class."

"They've been sending me too many women advisees. I've got to do something about that."

"You have no business looking for work with a child that age."

"I'm sorry you lost your fellowship. You're getting married, aren't you?"

"We expect women who come here to be competent, good students; but we don't expect them to be brilliant or original."

"I see the number of women entering this year has increased. I hope the quality has increased as well."

And most telling of all: "I know you're competent and your thesis advisor knows you're competent. The question in our minds is are you *really serious* about what you're doing." This was said to a young woman who had already spent five years and over $10,000 getting to that point in her Ph.D. program.

These comments hardly contribute to a student's self-image as a scholar. Often made in jest, they are typical of those used by professors on the University of Chicago campus and other campuses to express the only socially acceptable prejudice left—that against women. But if you were to ask these same professors whether they discriminate against women students and colleagues, most would answer that they do not.

Until a few years ago, most women would have agreed with them. Since then, many of the women students and faculty toward whom these comments were aimed have looked at the actions behind the words and concluded that most professors discriminate against women whether they are conscious of it or not.

Women in one social science department openly declared that their professors frequently discouraged them from going to or staying in graduate school. They said the attitude of their professors indicated "that we are expected to be decorative objects in the classroom, that we're not likely to finish a Ph.D. and if we do, there must be something wrong with us." They pointed out that no woman had held a faculty position in their department since the University was founded in 1892 and that this lack of role models was hardly encouraging to women students.

At the time the University community was recovering from a massive sit-in the previous quarter (winter 1969) caused by the firing of Marlene Dixon, the first woman to teach in the Sociology Department in nineteen years. Though women's issues were not the primary concern of the protest, they had been raised publicly for the first time during the course of it, (thanks largely to the efforts of Dixon herself and of the campus women's liberation group), and had generated the greatest response from the University community.

One such response was from the students, who began to organize into departmental caucuses, put out position papers, and confront the faculty with their new feminist consciousness. The other response was from the faculty and the administration. The Committee of the Council of the Academic Senate appointed a Committee on University Women (COUW) to study "the situation and opportunities presently enjoyed by women in the University community." The COUW created a student subcommittee (SCOUW) of six students and three faculty members, of which I was chairperson.

**THE STUDY**

As part of its duties SCOUW developed a detailed, self-administered questionnaire. The design of the study* involved distributing the questionnaire to a sample of approximately 50 male and 50 female respondents from each of the seventeen graduate and undergraduate divisions and professional schools at the University of Chicago at the beginning of the following fall quarter (1969–70). These numbers were chosen to provide adequate samples for comparison. In the final tally each 100-person unit was weighted to represent the actual relative strength of its school or division in the University. The sampling intervals were determined individually for each unit and sex, and the sample was drawn by selecting every $n^{th}$ name from alphabetical lists of students registered that spring.

Although the expected 30 percent loss rate was compensated for, the inevitable elimination of the drop-outs in itself involves a bias: our study excluded the University's casualties, who may well have been those most fruitful to examine. This is analogous to studying the effects of a disease by looking only at its survivors. Although the study no doubt included many who would later drop out, the possibility of bias still exists. One could maintain that those women who perceive discrimination most sharply or get the least support from the University

---

*The study was directed by Ellen Fried, formerly of the National Opinion Research Center, assisted by Nancy Hartsock, then a graduate student in political science at the University of Chicago and now teaching at the Johns Hopkins University. The responses to the questionnaire have been published in *Women in the University of Chicago* (May 1970), available from the Office of Public Information, University of Chicago.

environment are the ones to leave. To a certain extent we are dealing with a group of self-selected women who have at least partially adapted to the system.

The questionnaire took about twenty minutes to complete as most of the questions had precoded answers from which the respondent picked one or more. Students maintained their anonymity by turning in their completed questionnaires separately from a card with their name on it. When a name card was received, the respondent's name was removed from the sample list. Thus at any given moment we had a list of those who had not returned their questionnaires and who could be followed up by phone calls.

The overall response rate was 77 percent. The loss was due partially to non-returning students and partially to failure to turn in the questionnaires. Unfortunately, the rather low response rate was not the only problem the study ran into. Other problems that could bias its results were encountered in three spheres:

1 *The Administration.* The staff had received assurances from intermediate-level administrators that if the questionnaire was not offensive, it would be distributed at registration. Unfortunately, the Provost later decided to avoid any possible complications of the registration procedure and rejected the questionnaire without even looking at it. It might be noted that it is not uncommon for material to be distributed and studies undertaken at registration time. Only four years previously, permission had been given for a study requiring every registering student to fill out a questionnaire on teeth-gnashing. Other studies using the registration handout procedure had been done in the interim. Our low response rate can be attributed largely to this administrative reversal, for the officials of some of the professional schools gave us full cooperation and those units had response rates near 90 percent.

2 *The Faculty.* The study was originally intended to be a far-ranging one that would probe the causes of the problems women students faced in general. Unfortunately, a majority of the faculty members of COUW and SCOUW felt the survey should be used primarily to determine the extent to which women perceived overt discrimination in the classroom and in university services. It was felt that only items leading to explicit recommendations to

the University should be included. For example, questions on the amount of time spent in child care were opposed on the grounds that there was nothing the University could do about any sex differential that might exist here. The Null Environment Hypothesis which will be discussed in detail below, was one of the few nonspecific concerns to survive this weeding out.

3  *The Students.* Members of the campus women's liberation group decided to boycott the questionnaire for political reasons on which they did not elaborate. Most of them were undergraduate women in the social sciences, and this is where we found our lowest return rate—62 percent. Some differences in return rates were certainly due to the different distribution and follow-up methods we had to use. However, the procedures used in this unit were identical for men and women, and the men had a response rate of 81 percent. There is good reason to believe, therefore, that the boycott was effective and that the responses from this unit do not adequately represent the militant feminist viewpoint. Nonetheless, the results were quite striking.

## THE NULL ENVIRONMENT HYPOTHESIS

The Null Environment Hypothesis was a response to the contention of one of the faculty members of SCOUW that the faculty did not discriminate between women and men students—they treated them all poorly. Succinctly put, the hypothesis states that an academic situation that neither encourages nor discourages students of either sex is inherently discriminatory against women because it fails to take into account the differentiating external environments from which women and men students come. As Horner has ,pointed out, many women enter school with a "motive to avoid success" because they fear social rejection or find academic success in conflict with a feminine identity.[1] Even those who have not internalized this notion often find little or no support for intellectual aspirations—particularly at the postgraduate level—because their endeavors are not taken seriously. Thus women enter with a handicap which a "null" academic environment does nothing to decrease and may well reinforce. In other words, professors don't have to make it a specific point to discourage their female students. Society will do that job for them. All they have to do is fail to encourage them. Professors can discriminate against women without really trying.

Obviously, we first had to find out whether the hypothesized null environment existed at the University. Did the faculty provide a supportive environment for the students or did they not? Did they strongly encourage them to develop their potential or did they not?

We asked students how they thought the faculty felt about their going to or being in graduate or professional school and about their having a career. We interpreted a response of "very favorable" to mean that a student felt he or she received positive support. As can be seen in Tables I and II, only 47 percent of the male students and 32 percent of the female students felt they got positive support or encouragement for postgraduate education, either from the male 94 percent or the female 6 percent of the faculty.* Even fewer felt the faculty were very favorable to their having a career. Thus if we define a null academic environment as one with a significant lack of positive support, we can say that such an environment did indeed exist at the University of Chicago. The lack of positive support for women was especially evident. Only a little over two-thirds as many female as male students thought the male faculty were "very favorable" to their having advanced education and a lesser proportion thought they were favorable to their having a career.

If students do not receive support from faculties for going on with their education and careers, where do they get it? Much of it comes from personal commitment. The presence of this internal support mechanism is always assumed in men. Women are supposed to be less deeply committed, and this supposition is often used both as an explanation of their lesser success and as a justification for preferential treatment for men. Ignoring for the moment the self-fulfilling prophecy inherent in such an assumption, we wanted to know exactly how deeply committed our women students were.

We found that they were more deeply committed than the men students. When asked how they themselves felt about having a career, 75 percent of the women as against 60 percent of the men were very favorable. When asked "If you could have a choice, would you choose to have a career at all?" 92 percent of the women compared to 81

---

*Female faculty members scored identically to males, for instance (see Table IV), in the percentage rated "very favorable" to women graduate students' having a career, and only 2.6 percent higher in "very favorable" attitudes toward women's being in graduate or professional school.

TABLE I    Response to: "How do you think these people feel about your going to (being in) graduate or professional school?" by Sex

(Percent Saying Person is "Very Favorable")

| Person | Sex of respondent | |
|---|---|---|
| | Male | Female |
| Male faculty | 47% | 32% |
| Female faculty | 37 | 35 |

TABLE II    Response to: "How do the following people feel about your having a career?" by Sex

(Percent Saying Person is "Very Favorable")

| Person | Sex of respondent | |
|---|---|---|
| | Male | Female |
| Male faculty | 46% | 27% |
| Female faculty | 35 | 27 |

percent of the men said yes. So much for the "women have no career commitment" myth.

There is another myth which says that women will drop out before completing their degree. We had no way to test what our subjects would do in the future, but we could test how strongly they felt about the possibility of dropping out. We discovered that 62 percent of the women said they would be very disappointed if they left school before completing their education, whereas only 53 percent of the men said this; 31.6 percent of the men said they were in school primarily to stay out of the draft.

Further support comes from the external environment, the general atmosphere and mores of the society. We are all aware that our society is more favorable to men's getting advanced education and having a career than to women's doing these things. We also know that we are influenced by these values. But we had no real way of measuring the amount or importance of this influence. This variable had to remain undetermined.

We could, however, measure the perception by our students of positive support by specific people. We could determine whether they felt their relatives, friends, and spouses were very favorable to their

education and their career. This was not adequate to measure the total
influence of the nonacademic environment in which our students lived,
but it did give us some indicators. Therefore we asked the same
questions about the attitudes of these other people as we had about the
attitudes of the faculty.

Here, too, the difference was quite apparent. As seen in Tables III
and IV, men in all cases perceived more support than women—in most
cases considerably more. The difference is greatest of all on the

TABLE III    Response to: "How do you think these people feel about your going to
(being in) graduate or professional school?"

|  |  | Very favorable | Somewhat favorable | Not too favorable | Don't know |
|---|---|---|---|---|---|
| Yourself | M | 66.9% | 24.1% | 6.1% | 2.9% |
|  | W | 67.6 | 23.1 | 4.1 | 5.2 |
| Father | M | 74.6 | 18.7 | 4.6 | 2.0 |
|  | W | 66.8 | 19.4 | 7.4 | 6.4 |
| Mother | M | 77.7 | 19.1 | 2.4 | 0.9 |
|  | W | 62.0 | 27.4 | 5.8 | 4.8 |
| Siblings | M | 58.3 | 26.7 | 1.9 | 13.1 |
|  | W | 44.7 | 26.2 | 4.0 | 25.1 |
| Other relatives | M | 55.2 | 23.5 | 3.4 | 17.9 |
|  | W | 37.5 | 24.6 | 7.9 | 30.0 |
| Most friends of opposite sex | M | 51.4 | 28.5 | 1.4 | 18.7 |
|  | W | 40.0 | 33.1 | 6.3 | 20.6 |
| Most same-sex friends | M | 51.1 | 29.8 | 2.8 | 16.3 |
|  | W | 46.9 | 33.3 | 4.5 | 15.3 |
| Spouse, boy- or girlfriend | M | 64.5 | 26.4 | 2.7 | 6.5 |
|  | W | 62.8 | 23.4 | 6.0 | 7.8 |
| Male faculty member | M | 46.7 | 20.0 | 2.1 | 31.3 |
|  | W | 32.2 | 22.8 | 5.2 | 39.8 |
| Female faculty member | M | 37.1 | 15.8 | 0.9 | 46.2 |
|  | W | 34.8 | 12.7 | 1.0 | 51.4 |
| Any significant older people | M | 56.2 | 19.1 | 1.4 | 23.3 |
|  | W | 44.9 | 21.1 | 3.3 | 30.8 |

question about careers. This should not be surprising: it is much more socially acceptable for a woman to be well educated than for her to earn money with that education.

Much more surprising was a comparison of the attitudes of faculty, nonfaculty, and the students themselves toward their graduate education and career. First, for the most part the weakest support of all came from the faculty—the very people from whom students should have reason to expect the strongest support. Not only is this further

**TABLE IV    Response to: "How do the following people feel about your having a career?" by Sex**

|  |  | Very favorable | Somewhat favorable | Not too favorable | Don't know |
|---|---|---|---|---|---|
| Yourself | M | 60.3% | 24.1% | 11.1% | 4.4% |
|  | W | 75.3 | 15.1 | 6.1 | 3.5 |
| Father | M | 77.0 | 19.0 | 0.8 | 3.1 |
|  | W | 47.5 | 37.0 | 6.1 | 9.4 |
| Mother | M | 79.1 | 17.3 | 1.0 | 2.6 |
|  | W | 49.3 | 33.4 | 10.9 | 6.4 |
| Siblings | M | 52.7 | 31.3 | 1.5 | 14.5 |
|  | W | 33.8 | 27.4 | 5.2 | 33.6 |
| Other relatives | M | 61.1 | 25.2 | 1.1 | 12.6 |
|  | W | 20.8 | 30.6 | 13.7 | 34.9 |
| Most friends of opposite sex | M | 43.4 | 37.6 | 1.7 | 17.3 |
|  | W | 22.9 | 45.8 | 10.8 | 20.5 |
| Most same-sex friends | M | 42.9 | 39.9 | 2.5 | 14.8 |
|  | W | 30.7 | 45.1 | 7.5 | 16.7 |
| Spouse, boy- or girlfriend | M | 62.0 | 29.4 | 2.1 | 6.5 |
|  | W | 51.1 | 32.2 | 7.8 | 8.9 |
| Male faculty member | M | 46.3 | 26.6 | 1.1 | 26.0 |
|  | W | 26.6 | 30.6 | 1.9 | 41.0 |
| Female faculty member | M | 35.3 | 22.3 | 0.7 | 41.6 |
|  | W | 26.6 | 19.5 | 0.6 | 53.3 |
| Any significant older people | M | 53.8 | 25.0 | 0.3 | 21.0 |
|  | W | 35.5 | 28.1 | 1.8 | 34.6 |

confirmation of a tendency toward a null environment at the University of Chicago, but it implies that it is well within the faculty's power to significantly increase the total support students receive for going on with their education.

Second, the men frequently reported more favorable attitudes from others than from themselves. This could imply that the encouragement (or pressure) they receive from parents, spouses, and friends makes up for what they do not receive from the faculty. The women, by contrast, always report a more favorable attitude from themselves, with the difference most noticeable in the case of attitudes toward a career. Obviously women need their higher levels of internal commitment. The cognitive dissonance between their attitudes toward their own potential and the attitudes of others toward it must create a stress endurable only with the help of a strong personal determination to pursue both education and careers.

To test our hypothesis further, we had to know whether the faculty were openly discouraging the students, male and female, or whether their attitude was, in fact, null. The tendency toward the latter was confirmed by the very low percentage of students who felt that the faculty were noticeably unfavorable to their pursuing graduate education or careers and by the very high percentage who answered "Don't know." Among women in particular, this was the most frequent response to the two questions. Among men, however, "favorable," though low, had the highest response rate.

The University of Chicago is essentially a graduate and professional school that prides itself on its low student-faculty ratio. Even undergraduates, less than a third of the student body, are expected to attend mostly small lectures and seminars and do a good deal of guided independent study. Therefore we wanted to check the extent of student-faculty interaction and the effect this interaction had on students. One way we did this was by asking students whether a faculty member had ever revealed to them his/her opinion about the students' seriousness, academic progress, suitability for the field of work, intellectual ability, and the other concerns students have about faculty estimations. From 43 to 93 percent of both women and men students answered that not a single faculty member had expressed an opinion, or implied one, on any of these matters. The intellectual environment was indeed very parched.

**TABLE V**    Response to: "Since you have been at the University of Chicago, has any faculty member in your department (or collegiate division) ever told you or given you the impression that he thought . . . . . ?"

|  |  | No one | Yes, one faculty member | Yes, more than one faculty member |
|---|---|---|---|---|
| That you should apply for a | M | 55.8% | 18.8% | 25.4% |
| scholarship or fellowship | W | 56.4 | 22.2 | 21.4 |
| That the rate at which you are mov- | M | 84.6 | 9.2 | 6.2 |
| ing through the program is too slow | W | 88.4 | 9.7 | 2.7 |
| That you are not working up to | M | 87.0 | 9.7 | 3.3 |
| the University's standards | W | 88.4 | 8.9 | 2.7 |
| That you should switch | M | 93.5 | 5.4 | 1.1 |
| to another field | W | 87.3 | 11.1 | 1.6 |
| That you are well-suited | M | 47.9 | 19.4 | 32.6 |
| for the field you are in | W | 43.6 | 23.8 | 32.7 |
| That you are not a | M | 89.8 | 7.5 | 2.7 |
| serious student | W | 89.3 | 8.5 | 2.1 |
| You are one of the best students in | M | 57.5 | 26.1 | 16.4 |
| one of his classes or department | W | 59.8 | 27.6 | 12.6 |
| That you write well | M | 52.9 | 24.4 | 22.7 |
|  | W | 49.4 | 23.5 | 27.1 |

Yet the overall picture appeared more sterile for women than for men. The number of "don't know" responses given by women indicates that not only do they experience low levels of support, but they do not get enough feedback from the faculty to know where they stand. The University does not care enough about the women within it even to respond negatively. Its discouragement is much more insidious: it fails to respond at all.

This discouragement by default manifests itself in many ways besides lack of faculty encouragement for women students. The very structure of the University is geared to meet the needs of men and those women whose lives most closely resemble men's. Since the lifestyles of the population of intellectually qualified women are more heterogeneous and the demands made upon them more diverse than those of an intellectually similar population of men, fewer can comfortably fit into the University environment.

The two most obvious examples of this are lack of child-care facilities and lack of female role models among the professors. The University will deliberately keep a balance between younger and older faculty because some students relate better to the former and some to the latter. It will also try to have representatives from various fields within a discipline. But it sees no need to provide a sexual representation. The result is that few women have examples before them of how to be a female professional.

The idea of meeting the different needs of different students with different backgrounds is nothing new or radical. Traditionally the Univeristy has provided, within limits, fellowships, loans, and jobs for those who need money; housing for those who are married or are undergraduates and can stand dormitories; jobs for student wives (though seldom for student husbands); remedial courses for those whose academic background is scanty; special programs for those who find the traditional ones too confining; sports programs (primarily for men), recreational facilities; health services (usually without gynecological care); and a host of other opportunities.

What the University fails to acknowledge is that all of these needs are met within the confines of male standards. Because most of academia is male it has never stopped to consider that what is good and necessary for most men is not always good and necessary for most women. Thus the University proved very understanding and flexible in its readiness to accommodate men with draft problems. It gave them draft-exempt jobs, letters of recommendation and standing, showed them as enrolled in courses they were not taking to preserve their deferments, and, if worst came to worst, held their fellowships for them until they came back. But a pregnant woman will often have to drop out—or be forced to leave by losing her fellowship—because the university feels no responsibility to provide child-care centers. Even when she does not leave school, or has her children before she enters, she usually has the major responsibility for their care and this can be quite detrimental to full academic involvement.

This sex-related difference was clearly evident among our students when they were asked how children affected their academic work. Of all those who were parents, 15 percent of the women and only 1 percent of the men said children had a very unfavorable effect. Conversely, 16 percent of the men and a predictable zero percent of the women felt children had a very favorable effect. This is just one example of how the specific needs of women students are not met because the needs of men students provide the standards the university feels obligated to meet.

## THE EXTERNAL ENVIRONMENT

Most important for our study, however, is the fact that students are presumed to come from and exist in a supportive external environment. In reality, that presumption is far more valid for most men than for most women. In many different ways men have been expected and encouraged to go on with their advanced education and need little mental effort to picture themselves in a professional role. Their parents, their undergraduate professors, their friends, their other role models, their spouses, all contribute to this environment. Even if they have neither positive stimulus nor positive goal, their draft boards (at the time of this study) and the gnawing realization that they will, after all, have to do something with their lives, provides a negative spur that is only slightly less effective than a positive one.

For women this is not the case. Instead, the general social atmosphere in which they function tends to work against them. They learn to see women who achieve in the traditional sense of financial success and professional advancement as deviants and correctly perceive that such success often costs more than it gains in personal terms. Several research projects (in addition to the Horner research cited earlier) have documented what most women have always known. Beatrice Lipinski showed that women students think of success as something that is achieved by men but not by women.[2] Others have shown that women are reluctant to violate this social standard. As Kagan and Moss have noted, "The universe of appropriate behaviors for males and females is delineated early in development and it is difficult for the child to cross these culturally given frontiers without considerable conflict and tension."[3] These barriers account for Pierce's finding that high achievement-motivation among high-school women correlates much more closely with early marriage than with success in school.[4] Those women who do cross the frontiers must, according to Maccoby, pay a high price in anxiety and "it is this anxiety which helps to account for the lack of productivity among those women who do make intellectual careers." She feels that "this tells something of a horror story. It would appear that even when a woman is suitably endowed intellectually and develops the right temperament and habits of thought to make use of her endowment, she must be fleet of foot indeed to scale the hurdles society has erected for her and to remain a whole and happy person while continuing to follow her intellectual bent."[5]

Thus it should not be surprising that women tend to aspire at a lower level than men and to require even greater stimulus from the academic environment. As Gropper and Fitzpatrick have pointed out, "Women appear to be less influenced than men by their high grades in deciding *in favor* of advanced education. But they are more influenced than men by their low grades in deciding *against* advanced education."[6] As a group, women are deprived of the rich external environment of high expectations and high encouragement that research indicates is best for personal growth and creative production. Unless they have exceptional backgrounds, they have little to go on but their own internal commitment.

The attrition rates alone testify that this is rarely enough. During the sixties women earned approximately 53 percent of all high school diplomas, 36 percent of all bachelor's degrees, 31 percent of all master's degrees and 10 percent of all doctorates. The greatest drop-off was after the master's degree. Women seemed to lack the stimulus on go on to the doctorate. In retrospect, this was a very logical response to the environment. It is socially expected for women to graduate from high school, generally expected and always acceptable for women to get a B.A. or a B.S., somewhat acceptable and occasionally necessary for a woman to get a master's degree (since many of the professions in which women predominate require it). But Ph.D.'s and some professional degrees are considered unnecessary and often undesirable for a woman to obtain if she is to remain within the purview of social acceptability. And, given the job and salary inequities for holders of such degrees, they are not always economically useful.

The University does little to remedy this situation and much to exacerbate it. It offers virtually no courses on women and there is little material on women in the regular courses. This lack contributes to the feeling that women are not worth studying. There are few women on the faculty—less than half the percentage that prevails in the Ph.D. pool from which the University draws. These are concentrated at the bottom of the academic ladder or are off it entirely, despite the fact that the percentage of women in the older Ph.D. pool is considerably larger than that in the younger and that women Ph.D.'s as a group have higher I.Q.'s, higher grade-point averages, and higher class ranks than their male counterparts. This situation gives many students the idea that high-quality academic women are rare. Some 40 percent of the women students in the SCOUW survey felt that the faculty were less receptive to female students than to male students.

One has only to look at the Rosenthal-Jacobson experiments to see what a depressing effect this environment can have on the aspirations of women students. Although they did not use sex as a salient variable, these experimentors showed that when teachers were told that certain students (actually selected at random) would perform exceptionally well or poorly, those students altered their normal performance in the predicted direction to a significant degree. The teachers stated that they were treating all students exactly alike, yet investigation showed that they were subtly, unconsciously, encouraging or discouraging the chosen ones.[7]

In many ways this environment of subtle discouragement by neglect is more pernicious than a strongly negative one would be. As Eric Berne has theorized, everyone needs "strokes"; and although good strokes are better than bad strokes, bad strokes are better than none. In academic terms, this translates that women will do better when they are pointedly told that their sex makes their abilities and their commitment suspect. At least overt negative response provides women with some interaction and some standards by which they can judge their behavior. It also creates a challenge—something to be overcome. If women are conscious of the roadblocks they face as women at the University and in society they are in a better position to muster the energy to struggle against them. They not only know exactly what they have to face, but by sharing their struggle with other women they can create the context of emotional support that every student needs for high achievement.

Historically it is also evident that overt opposition is preferable to motivational malnutrition. Women did better when things were worse. From the time they first pounded on the doors of higher education their progress was steadily upward until thirty or forty years ago. By then they no longer had to overcome the obstacle of disbelief, but at the same time they no longer had the internal stimulus of knowing they were pioneers. Once women had made it, no one cared—one way or the other. Their place was still seen to be in the home, and the graduate schools did little more than provide a few loopholes for the hardy. The percentage of women earning Ph.D.'s began to go down in the 1920's and has risen only slightly since its nadir in 1950.

In summation, one can say that if the University and the behavior of its faculty do not directly discriminate against women, they indirectly and insidiously discriminate against them. The University is less of an intellectual seedbed than a psychological gauntlet—and it is one that the male students run in full armor, while the women students trip through in their bare skins.

Perhaps the best analogy for understanding the differentiating effect on men and women of the null environment is to be drawn from agriculture. If a farmer transplants into a field two groups of seedlings—one having been nourished thus far in rich, fertilized loam and the other malnourished for having struggled in desert sand—and that farmer then tends all the seedlings with virtually equal lack of care, fertilizer, and water (perhaps favoring the loam-grown seedlings slightly because they look more promising), no one should be surprised if the lesser harvest is reaped from the desert-bred plants. Nor should we, with all the modern farm apparatus and information available, shrug complacently and lament that there is no way to make the desert bloom.

## NOTES

1   Matina Horner, "Why Bright Women Fail" *Psychology Today,* Nov. 1970.

2   Beatrice Lipinski, *Sex-Role Conflict and Achievement Motivation in College Women,* unpublished Ph.D. dissertation, University of Cincinnati, 1965.

3   Jerome Kagan and Howard A. Moss, *Birth to Maturity: A Study in Psychological Development* (New York and London: Wiley 1962), p. 270.

4   James V. Pierce, *Sex Differences in Achievement Motivation of Able High School Students,* Cooperative Research Project No. 1097, University of Chicago, Dec. 1961.

5   Eleanor Maccoby, "Women's Intellect," in Farber and Wilson, eds., *The Potential of Women* (New York: McGraw-Hill, 1963).

6   G. L. Gropper and Robert Fitzpatrick, *Who Goes to Graduate School?* (Pittsburgh: American Institute for Research, 1959).

7   R. Rosenthal and L. Jacobson, *Pygmalion in the Classroom: Teacher Expectations and Pupils' Intellectual Development* (New York: Holt, Rinehart, 1968).

# Inge Powell Bell

# The Double
# Standard: Age*

There is a reason why women are coy about their
age. For most purposes, society pictures them as
"old" ten or 15 years sooner than men. Nobody in
this culture, man or woman, wants to grow old;
age is not honored among us. Yet women must
endure the specter of aging much sooner than
men, and this cultural definition of aging gives
men a decided psychological, sexual and economic
advantage over women.

It is surely a truism of our culture that, except
for a few kinky souls, the inevitable physical
symptoms of aging make women sexually unattractive much earlier than men. The multimillion
dollar cosmetics advertising industry is dedicated
to creating a fear of aging in women, so that it

---

*Reprinted from *Trans-Action* (November–December 1970),
pp. 75–80, by permission of Transaction Inc.

may sell them its emollients of sheep's fat, turtle sweat and synthetic chemicals which claim, falsely, to stem the terrible tide. "Did you panic when you looked into the mirror this morning and noticed that those laugh lines are turning into crow's-feet?" "Don't let your eyes speak your age!" "What a face-life can do for your morale!"

A man's wrinkles will not define him as sexually undesirable until he reaches his late fifties. For him, sexual value is defined much more in terms of personality, intelligence and earning power than physical appearance. Women, however, must rest their case largely on their bodies. Their ability to attain status in other than physical ways and to translate that status into sexual attractiveness is severely limited by the culture. Indeed, what status women have is based almost entirely on their sexuality. The young girl of 18 or 25 may well believe that her position in society is equal to, or even higher than that of men. As she approaches middle age, however, she begins to notice a change in the way people treat her. Reflected in the growing indifference of others toward her looks, toward her sexuality, she can see and measure the decline of her worth, her status in the world. In Simone de Beauvoir's words:

> she has gambled much more heavily than man on the sexual values
> she possesses; to hold her husband and to assure herself of his
> protection, and to keep most of her jobs, it is necessary for her to
> be attractive, to please; she is allowed no hold on the world save
> through the mediation of some man. What is to become of her
> when she no longer has any hold on him: This is what she
> anxiously asks herself while she helplessly looks on the degenera-
> tion of this fleshly object which she identifies with herself.

The middle-aged woman who thickly masks her face with makeup, who submits to surgical face and breast lifting, who dyes her hair and corsets her body is as much a victim of socially instilled self-hatred as the black person who straightens his hair and applies bleaching creams to his skin.

The most dramatic institutionalization of different age definitions for men and women is the cultural rules governing the age at which one can marry. It is perfectly acceptable for men to marry women as much as 15 or 20 years younger than they are, but it is generally unacceptable for them to marry women more than four or five years older. These cultural rules show up very plainly in the marriage statistics gathered by the Department of Health, Education and Welfare. At the time of first marriage the age differential is relatively small; the groom is on the average 1.9 years older than his bride. When widowers remarry, however, the gap is 7.0 years; and when divorced men do, the gap is 3.4 years.

These age differentials put the woman at a disadvantage in several ways. First, whatever may be the truth about age and sexual performance, our culture defines the young as sexually more vigorous and desirable. Thus, the customary age differential means that the man gets the more desirable partner; the woman must settle for the less desirable.

More important, the divorced or widowed woman is severely handicapped when it comes to finding another marital partner. Let us take, for example, a couple who divorce when both are in their thirties. What is the difference in the supply of future marriage partners for the man and for the woman? The man can choose among all women his own age or younger. This includes all those women below 25, many more of whom are as yet unmarried. The woman, by contrast, is limited by custom to men her own age or older. She has access only to age brackets in which most people are married. She is thus reduced to the supply of men who come back on the marriage market as a result of divorce or widowerhood or to those few who have not yet married. It is easy to see which of the two will have an easier time finding companionship or a marriage partner. It is also easy to surmise that the awareness of this difference makes divorce a much more painful option for women than for men and thus puts many women at a continuous disadvantage within a strained marriage.

Statistics bear out our supposition that women have a harder time remarrying than men (see table). It has been estimated that, while

How Many Men and Women in Different Age Groups
Remarry? (Number of Marriages per 1000, 1975)

|  | Women | Men |
|---|---|---|
| Widowed |  |  |
| 45–64 | 14.9 | 71.4 |
| 65 and over | 2.1 | 19.5 |
| Divorced |  |  |
| 25–44 | 158.6 | 278.2 |
| 45–64 | 40.1 | 94.0 |
| 65 and over | 9.1 | 31.4 |

three-quarters of divorced men remarry, only two-thirds of divorced women ever do. In a study of widows and widowers done in 1948, Paul Glick found that half the men who had been widowed during the five years preceding the study had remarried, but three-quarters of the women were still alone. Among those who had been widowed from five to 14 years, two-thirds of the men had remarried, but only one-third of the women had.

Only a small proportion of these discrepancies is due to the shorter life expectancy of men and thus their relative scarcity in the upper-age brackets. For example, in the age brackets 45–64, there are a little over three times as many widowed and divorced women without mates as there are single widowed and divorced men. Yet in the total population the ratio of women to men in that age bracket is only 1.05 to 1. In the over-65 age bracket there are over three and a half times as many divorced and widowed women still alone; yet in the population as a whole, the ratio of women to men in this age bracket is only 1.2 to 1.

Still, the difference in life expectancy between the two sexes does work to a woman's disadvantage in another way. The gentleman in the ad below is making explicit an expectation which is made implicitly by most men:

RECENTLY DIVORCED, 53, affectionate, virile, tall, good-looking, yearns for the one utterly feminine, loving woman in her 30s, 40s with whom he can share a beautiful new life.

At age 50, this gentleman had a life expectancy of 23 years. (It is a little less now.) If he finds a woman of 35, her life expectancy will be 41.27. In other words, he is affectionately offering her a statistical chance of 18 years of widowhood. And she will be widowed at an age when men of her own age will be looking for women in their thirties and forties. At best, he may live to a ripe old age. When he is 75 she will be 57.

Now let us consider the case of a much larger group: women who have husbands. As middle age approaches, many of these married women find that they, too, are vulnerable to the difficulties posed by the different definitions of age in men and women. For them, however devoutly they may wish it as they tidy their homes, take care of their teen-aged children or play bridge, sexual adventure is usually out of the question. This is not just because of the more restrictive mores that bind them to fidelity; their age has already disqualified them for anything else. Not so for the husband. If he is a successful man, his virility will be seen as still intact, if not actually enhanced, and the affair becomes very much the question. Indeed, if he is engaged in a middle-class occupation, he is almost inevitably surrounded by attractive, young females, many of whom—the receptionist, the cocktail waitress at the downtown bar, the airplane hostess—have been deliberately selected to flatter his ego and arouse his fancy. In addition, many of the women hired to fulfill more ordinary functions—the secretaries, typists and the like—find the older man desirable by virtue of his success and wealth. Thus, the middle-aged wife, unless she is one of the statistically few whose husband is truly happy and faithful, is put into competition with the cards stacked against her. And even if her husband doesn't leave her for a younger woman or begin having affairs, she will probably experience anxiety and a sense of diminished self-esteem.

The mass media glamorize and legitimate the older man-younger woman relationship. Successful actors continue to play romantic leads well into their fifties and sometimes sixties (*vide* Cary Grant). Frequently they are cast opposite actresses at least half their age, and the story line rarely even acknowledges the difference. They are simply an "average" romantic couple. The question of whether the 20-year-old heroine is out of her mind to marry the greying 55-year-old hero isn't even raised.

## THE PRESTIGE LOSS

Occupation is man's major role, unemployment or failure in his occupational life the worst disaster than can befall him. The question "What do you do?" is seldom answered, "Well, I'm married and a father. . . ." But because men draw their self-esteem and establish their connections to others very largely through their jobs, retirement is a time of psychic difficulty and discomfort for most men. The woman faces a similar role loss much earlier. Her primary role in life is that of mother: her secondary role is that of homemaker, and her tertiary that of sexual partner. We have already seen that the role of sexual partner, and sexually desirable object, is impaired for many women as middle age approaches. Now we must contemplate the additional fact that the woman's primary role—that of mother—also disappears during middle age.

Indeed, with decreasing family size and increasingly common patterns of early marriage, women are losing their mother role much earlier than formerly. In 1890 the average woman took care of children until her mid-fifties. Today most women see their children leave home when they are in their late forties. Whereas in 1890 the average woman lived 30 years after her last child had entered school and 12 years after her last child married, today, with longer life expectancy, the average woman lives 40 years after her last child enters school and 25 years after her last child marries. Thus, women lose their major role long before the retirement age arrives for men.

Loss of sexual attractiveness and the maternal role comes at a time when the husband is likely to be at the peak of his career and deeply involved in satisfying job activities. Bernice Neugarten, in describing how people become aware of middle age, says:

> Women, but not men, tend to define their age status in terms of timing of events within the family world, and even unmarried career women often discuss middle age in terms of the family they might have had. . . .
>
> Men, on the other hand, perceive the onset of middle age by cues presented outside the family context, often from the deferential behavior accorded them in the work setting. One man described the first time a younger associate helped open a door for him; another, being called by his official title by a newcomer in the company; another, the first time he was ceremoniously asked for advice by a younger man.

Little research has been done on the prestige accorded men and women in different age brackets. The few studies available point to older women as the lowest prestige group in society. In a projective test asking middle-aged persons to make up a story about a picture which showed a young couple and a middle-aged couple in conversation, Neugarten found that the older woman was seen as more uncomfortable in her role than any of the others and was the only figure who was as often described in negative as in positive terms. Mary Laurence found that respondents tended to rate women as having more undesirable personality traits than men through all age ranges, but the age group rated most severely was women over 40.

A study of characters in American magazine fiction from 1890 to 1955 found a decline in the number of older women appearing as characters. By 1955 there were none at all. The middle-aged woman almost never sees herself and her problems depicted in print or on the screen. When they are, she sees mostly negative stereotypes. Her dilemma is very similar to that of the black ghetto child who finds in the

"Dick and Jane" first reader a world that is irrelevant at best, invidious at worst. To have oneself and one's experiences verified in the mythology and art of one's culture is a fundamental psychological need at every stage of the life cycle.

Women's own attitudes toward aging are shown in the interesting finding that, in the listings of the Directory of the American Psychological Association, women are ten times as likely to omit their age as men. Thus, even professional women, who presumably have roles which extend undamaged into middle age, are much more likely than men to feel that their advancing age is a serious impairment.

On the question of whether middle-aged women are actually unhappier or more maladjusted than middle-aged men, the evidence is conflicting and inconclusive. A few studies by various researchers found little or no difference between middle-aged and old men and women on such factors as personality change, engagement with life and reported satisfaction with life. One study found older women more satisfied than older men.

One problem with these efforts, though, is that some of them lump together the middle-aged group with persons past retirement age. Some of the findings may therefore be due to the fact that the retirement age is far more stressful and acute for men than for women. Women have never invested much in careers and have been adjusting to role loss for many years. In old age an additional factor works in favor of women. Women are closer to relatives and thus more sheltered from complete isolation.

The studies present another problem in that the respondents themselves judged how happy or satisfied they were. The trouble with this is that subordinated groups learn to expect less and therefore to be satisfied with less. A middle-aged woman whose husband has had several affairs may report that her marriage has been satisfying because society has taught her to expect infidelity from her husband. A man whose wife had behaved in similar fashion would be less likely to regard his marriage as satisfying. Indeed, social conditioning would probably dictate a more painful crisis for the cuckolded husband. Moreover, measuring the satisfaction levels of people who are already so thoroughly "socialized" doesn't take into account the wife's feelings the first time she saw her own mother experience such treatment from her father and realized that a similar fate was in store for herself. It does not measure the emotional cost of adjusting to the expectation of abuse. In fact, if we were to confine our evidence to degrees of self-reported satisfaction, we might conclude that a great variety of social inequities create no emotional hardships for the subjugated. Elsewhere, however, Pauline Bart shows that middle age is much more stressful for women than for men and this finding corroborates the work of Judd Marmor who has reported that middle-aged women manifest psychiatric disorders three to four times as frequently as middle-aged men.

## THE ECONOMIC LOSS

Discrimination against older women in employment is important because of the large number of people affected. The number of older women in the labor force grew rapidly in the '50's and '60's. By 1977, 56.7 percent of women in the age range of 45 to 54 and 41.0 percent of those 55 to 64 were employed. These percentages had risen sharply from 1940, when they were 24.5 percent and 18 percent respectively.

Discrimination against older workers of both sexes in industry is well documented. A 1965 Department of Labor survey concluded that half the job openings in the private economy are closed to applicants over 55 years of age, and one-fourth are closed to applicants over 45. Women are particularly disadvantaged by this discrimination because, as a result of their typical work and child-rearing cycle, many women come back on the labor market after a long period of absence (and are perhaps entering the market for the first time) during precisely these years. There is very little evidence on the question of whether older women are relatively more disadvantaged than older men. Edwin Lewis states that age is a greater detriment to women than to men but cites no evidence. A Department of Labor publication on age discrimination in employment claims that men are slightly favored, but the evidence is very incomplete. The study found that, compared to the percentage of unemployed older men and women, women were hired in somewhat greater numbers. But unemployment rates are based on self-reporting and are notoriously influenced by the optimism of a given group about the prospects of finding employment. Older women, many of whom are married, are less likely to report themselves as seeking work if they are pessimistic about the possibilities of getting any. The study also surveyed the employment practices of 540 firms and found that, although differences were slight, men were disadvantaged in a larger number of occupational categories. But in clerical work, in which 24 percent of women over 45 are engaged, discrimination against women was decidedly greater.

The problem of discrimination against older men and women is complicated by the fact that a study would have to take into account whether discrimination was practiced because of expected lack of physical strength, long training or internship programs or physical attractiveness. The former two considerations figure much more frequently in the case of men and certainly have more legitimacy as grounds for discriminating than the factor of physical attractiveness, which usually arises solely because the woman is seen as a sex object before she is seen as a productive worker. As long as this is the employer's orientation, it will probably do little good to cite him the studies proving that middle-aged women office workers are superior to young women in work attendance, performance and ability to get along agreeably with others. It would also be necessary to see how much relative discrimination there is within occupational categories. There is little discrimination in certain low-paid, undesirable jobs because the supply of workers in these categories is short. Women tend to be predominantly clustered in precisely these job categories.

A check of one Sunday's *Los Angeles Times* want ads yielded a count of 1,067 jobs advertised for women and 2,272 advertised for men. For both sexes specific upper-age limits or the term "young" were attached to less than 1 percent of the job listings, and there was almost no difference between men and women. However, 97 (or 9 percent) of the female ads used the term "girl" or "gal," while only two of the 2,272 male ads used the term "boy."

To check out my hunch that "girl" is an indirect way of communicating an age limitation, in a state where discrimination by age is supposedly illegal, I called five employment agencies in southern California and asked an interviewer who handles secretarial and clerical placement what he or she thought the term "girl" meant from the employer's side and how it would be interpreted by the average job seeker. Four of the five employment interviewers stated that the term definitely carries an age connotation for employer and job seeker alike. they defined the age implied variously as "under 30"; "under 35—if we were looking in the 35–45 category we would use the term 'mature'; over 45 we don't say anything"; "It means a youngster. I certainly don't think a 45-year-old would go in if she saw that ad"; "It does mean age, which is why we always use the term 'women' in our company's ads (although we may use the term 'girl' on a specific listing)." The last person would not state a specific age because she was obviously worried about being caught in violation of the law, to which she frequently alluded. Only one of the five replied in the negative, saying "to me 'girl' is just another word for 'woman.' You can hardly use the term 'woman' in the wording of an ad." Everyone I questioned agreed that the term "girl Friday" (a tiny proportion of our cases) carries no age connotation. Several, however, mentioned that the terms "trainee," "recent high school grad" and "high school grad" were used to communicate an age limitation.

Along with the term "girl," a number of ads use physical descriptions—almost entirely lacking in men's ads. "Attractive gal for receptionist job" is typical. More specific are the following excerpts from the columns in the *Los Angeles Times:* "Exciting young atty seeks a sharp gal who wants a challenge"; "Young, dynamic contractor who is brilliant but disorganized needs girl he can depend on completely"; and one headlined "Lawyer's Pet" which goes on to say "Looking for a future: want challenge, 'variety,' $$$? Young attorney who handles all phases of 'law' will train you to become his 'right hand.' " Few women over 30 would consider themselves qualified to apply for these jobs.

The use of the term "girl" and the reaction of one employment agency interviewer who considered this as the only proper way to connote "woman" in a want ad underscores the extent to which women's jobs are still considered young girls' jobs, that is, the relatively unimportant work that a girl does before she gets married. One employment agency interviewer stated that his agency frequently had requests for a certain age level because companies want to keep the age range in a certain department homogeneous for the sake of congeniality. It is significant that he mentioned only the "twenties" or "thirties" as examples of such desirable age ranges.

One is tempted to make a comparison between the term "girl" and the insulting racist use of "boy" for all blacks, regardless of age. In both cases, the term indicates that the species under discussion is not considered capable of full adulthood. In both cases, blacks and women are acceptable and even likable when very old, as "uncle" and "grandmother," but somehow both are anachronistic as mature adults.

Given the scarcity and conflicting nature of the data, it is impossible to say with certainty that older women suffer more from discrimination than older men. The question certainly merits further and more systematic exploration.

## CASTE AND CLASS

The division of this article into sexual, prestige and economic loss was taken from John Dollard's analysis of the sexual, prestige and economic gains of whites at the expense of blacks in his classic study, *Caste and Class in a Southern Town*. The choice was not an accident; spokesmen of women's liberation have often drawn heavily on the analogy between the problems of blacks and of women. Yet equally often one hears objections to the analogy. Blacks are, as a group, isolated in the lowest economic strata and physically ghettoed into the worst parts of town, while women, being inextricably connected to men through familial ties, do not share a drastic, common disability. It has also been suggested that to compare the plight of women with that of blacks is to belittle the importance of the need for black liberation. Most of these critics care as little for black liberation as for the liberation of women and need not be taken seriously.

Yet the intellectual objections to the analogy should be discussed. The argument actually rests on the assumption that middle-class status cushions all of life's shocks and that middle-class women are always comfortably embedded in middle-class primary groups. It assumes further that the woes of lower-class women are all essentially class-connected rather than specifically sex-connected. The loneliness of widowhood, the anguish of a woman losing her husband to a younger woman, the perplexity of the woman whose children have left home and who finds herself unwanted on the labor market—these are real hurts, and they go deep, even in the middle class. Further, the notion of the individual as being deeply rooted in his primary groups certainly reflects a partial and outmoded view in a highly individualistic society where the nuclear family, usually the only long-lasting primary group, has become extremely unstable. In our society, men and women are expected to get through life essentially alone. This is true even of the woman who is able to maintain good family ties throughout her life. It is even truer for those who suffer the more common fate of having these ties weakened by discord or severed by death or separation. For the lower-class woman, of course, these difficulties are harsher and more unrelieved, but in every class the woman must bear them alone.

The differential definition of age in men and women represents a
palpable advantage to men at the expense of women. It multiplies the
options for emotional satisfaction on his side while it diminishes them
on hers. It raises his prestige and self-esteem at the expense of hers. All
men in our society benefit to some degree from this custom, while not a
single woman who lives into middle age escapes bearing some of the
cost. If we are ever to restructure this society into one of true equality
for both sexes, this is one of the crucial points at which we must begin.

# Pauline Bart

# The Loneliness of the Long-Distance Mother

*I don't want to be alone, and I'm going to be alone, and my children will go their way and get married . . . of which I'm wishing for it . . . and then I'll still be alone, and I got more and more alone, and more and more alone.*

*—Sara*

Middle age, like adolescence, is a time of physiological as well as sociological changes. At one time the stress often characterizing both these ages was considered physiological in origin and therefore universal. In order to test the so-called "Sturm und Drang" hypothesis concerning adolescents, Margaret Mead went to Samoa, where she found adolescence not stressful at all. As there seemed little reason to assume significant physiological differences between Americans and Samoans, she reasoned that adolescent stress in Western nations had cultural origins. I went to other cultures—unfortunately only through their anthropological records—to learn whether the changes of mid-life were psychologically stressful for women, thus becoming, as it were, the Margaret Mead of the menopause. I studied the roles available to women who were past childbearing and whether women typically had problems with menopause.* I was particularly looking for an absence of depression appearing for the first time in middle age.

Unfortunately, data on the menopause were scarce—available for only five out of the thirty societies I studied. Clearly, anthropologists are generally male and thus not interested in pursuing such information—or unable to, for when the anthropologists were female or when teams included females, information about menopause was reported. Psychiatric data were also scarce, but there was enough information on post-maternal roles and on the relative status of women to allow me to determine whether that status rose or fell in middle age.

It appears that in each culture there is a favored stage in the life cycle of women. For instance, if a woman has high status when she is young, her power and prestige can be expected to decline as she matures, and vice versa. Rather than the usual image of society as a pyramid or ladder, one can think of society as a social ferris wheel.[1] I attempted to correlate these age-related changes in status with cultural and structural factors in the society, paying special attention to roles for post-menopausal women.

Most cultures had definite roles that women were expected to fill after they were through with childbearing and -rearing, but these roles varied from society to society. They included, in addition to the wife role, the roles of grandmother, economic producer, mother and mother-in-law, participant in government, performer of magic and

---

*The cultures and peoples studied were all pre-literate, peasant or traditional: the Andaman Islanders, Serbs, Toda, Twi, Nupe, Tiv, Yoruba, Azande, Bushmen, Lovedu, Bedouin, Wolof, Aleuts, Comanche, Yurok, Navajo, Zuni, Ifugao, Aranda, Trobrianders, Samoans, Marquesans, Pukapukans, Jivaro; and peasant or traditional cultures in Burma, China, rural Ireland, Poland, India, the Soviet Union, and the Philippines. The following aspects of all these cultures were studied: ontogeny, social personality, personality traits, and personality disorders, division of labor by sex, age stratification, sex status, celibacy, family relationships, grandparents and grandchildren, dependency, old-age dependency, adulthood, senescence, and the activities, status, and treatment of the aged.

ritual, and daughter of aged parents. The higher-status roles on the list were those of grandmother, mother-in-law and participator in government, since the available economic role for women was generally limited to performing hard work of little prestige.

Using the following indices for higher status—more freedom (especially from taboos), more respect, special privileges and more power and influence—I found that in seventeen out of the thirty cultures, women registered *higher* status during middle age by at least one index.* In twelve out of the thirty they had more respect, in eight they had more power and influence, in seven they had special privileges, and in four they had more freedom. In eleven cultures middle-aged women registered neither an increase nor a decrease in social status on any of these indices. In only two cultures, those of the Marquesans and the Trobrianders—cultures in a number of ways similar to our own—did women have less power and influence in middle age than when they were younger.

The cross-cultural study therefore indicated that middle age was not usually considered an especially stressful period for women. Consequently, purely biological explanations of the stress felt at this time by Western woman can be rejected. Middle age need not be fraught with difficulty.

It needs to be noted, however, that a major buffer against problems facing women in mid-life has been the kinship group. The literature I surveyed showed that a strong tie to family and kin rather than a strong marital tie, an extended-family system rather than a nuclear-family system, an institutionalized grandmother role, a mother-in-law role rather than no role for a woman in relationship to her son- or daughter-in-law, plus residence patterns keeping one close to one's parents and siblings—all these factors strengthen kinship ties and tend to improve the woman's position in middle age. Thus, very clearly, a woman's status after she stops bearing children can be associated with the structural arrangements and cultural values of her society. Specifically, the associations charted below seem to hold true:

Turning to our own society with this chart in mind, we can begin to see why middle-aged women so often feel stress. In each instance, except for the mother-child bond, which in our society is strong but

---

*Middle age will be defined here as the years from 40 to 65.

| Raised status in middle age | Lowered status in middle age |
|---|---|
| Strong tie to parents, siblings, cousins and other kin | Marital tie stronger that tie to nuclear family |
| Extended-family system | Nuclear-family system |
| Reproduction important | Sex an end in itself |
| Strong mother-child relationship reciprocal in later life | Weak maternal bond, adult-oriented culture |
| Institutionalized grandmother role | Noninstitutionalized grandmother role, grandmother role not important |
| Institutionalized mother-in-law role | Noninstitutionalized mother-in-law role, mother-in-law does not train daughter-in-law |
| Extensive menstrual taboos | Minimal menstrual taboos |
| Matrilocal, patrilocal or duolocal residence pattern | Residence pattern that isolates women from kin and grown children, e.g. neolocal, avuncular |
| Age valued over youth | Youth valued over age |

nonreciprocal, we fall on the right side, where the status of women drops in middle age. For women whose lives have not been child-centered and whose strong marital ties continue, or for those whose children set up residence near them, the transition to middle age may be buffered. But child-centered women note that the relationship with their children is non-reciprocal—that all they are entitled to is "respect." A child once reaching maturity in our culture need honor and look after her/his mother only on Mother's Day, unless she is widowed. And both for these women, and for those who have emphasized the maternal role or the glamour role, middle age may be a difficult stage in the life cycle. Our emphasis on youth and our stipulation that mothers-in-law should not interfere and grandmothers not meddle makes the middle years a time of stress for many thousands, if not millions, of American women.* But let one such woman, one of twenty I interviewed and tested in mental hospitals, speak for herself.

---

*See, however, Neugarten's work on healthy middle-aged women: Bernice Neugarten, ed., *Middle-Aged and Aging: A Reader in Social Psychology* (University of Chicago Press, 1968).

## SARA: THE MARTYR MOTHER

This is Sara's second admission to a mental hospital. The first time, the diagnosis was "psychophysiological gastro-intestinal reaction," but this time, knowing more about her, doctors have diagnosed "involutional depression."

Sara is Jewish. In her early sixties, she is divorced and in what has been called the "empty nest" stage. She represents an amost ideal type of all of the problems that beset an aging woman in our society, in addition to some that began in childhood. Not only did her mother reject her, not only did her husband reject her, but now her children and grandchildren are rejecting her, and she is unable to participate in work or voluntary activities that could give her life meaning because she is physically ill, and transportation is inaccessible. She needs to keep busy, and her activities are severely restricted. She must live alone, and she is phobic about being alone.

Sara has had many physical problems—arthritis, kidney trouble, and, at the time I saw her, severely swollen feet. She has had a hysterectomy and gall bladder surgery. According to her record, her frightened, depressed state was "induced by fear of living in an apartment in Las Vegas where she felt abandoned and unprotected." This feeling has been present "ever since she was asked to move out of her son's home in order to placate the anger of her daughter-in-law who felt she caused trouble by trying to absorb all of her son's time and sympathy." Her (male) psychiatrist characterizes Sara as hypochondriachal and self-pitying.

I asked Sara one question and she immediately launched into a long description of her troubles: her fears of being alone, the failure of medication to alleviate these fears, her physical illnesses, and more:

> I first of all have a lot of fears, and it isn't very easy I guess . . . to do something about it. And . . . these fears just follow me, and just push me in the wrong direction. I'm not really doing what I want to do. I want to go one way, but it just seems to take me the other way and I—can't control them. . . . The minute nobody's here, and those fears start working with me. Everything seems closed up, and everything looks dark.

Sara told me that as a child she felt she was "really nothing." Her Russian-born father died when she was about six, but she always felt close to him. Even now she believes that if he had lived,

He would have always made me feel that I'm not alone, and that
someone loves me. I am very strong for love. . . . This is a very big
thing to me, and I wasn't very fortunate because Mother didn't give
it to me, and I was hungry for it, and when I married I also
thought it was going to be a wonderful thing because somebody is
going to care, but my marriage never turned out good.

While Sara's first child, a son, was a baby, her husband started a
produce store. Sara would go to the store four miles from their home
at four o'clock in the morning in a horse and wagon holding the baby
in her arms, feeding him.

I worked hard my whole life and I thought that if I worked for
him he would—he would be good to me, but he took all that good
[I gave him]. . . . He didn't feel that I was human, too.

A daughter was born, but the marriage continued no better. Her
husband was repeatedly unfaithful, and apparently contracted venereal
disease. Since he needed to work during the night, he refused to let her
have company during the day or evening so that he could rest and
sleep. He was rude to her friends. And "even with sex he was very, very
rude about it."

Me: How was he rude with sex?
Sara: Very much so. He was concerned . . . about himself,
nothing about me. . . . He had another woman that he took out,
and I found out about it, but I didn't let on. I thought, well, if
that's a weakness, maybe he'll overcome it. Let me try and, uh, cope
with it enough to see if I couldn't get him to reason . . . maybe later
I could. But I couldn't. He would always run away when I wanted
to reason with him. He would slam the door and go away for a few
days, come back and throw the dirty clothes into the bathroom
hamper, and everything was coming to him, but nothing was
coming to me.
Me: Were you ever able to have sex satisfactory for you?
Sara: I say no. He—he always felt that he was tired and it was
"necessary" and it "wasn't necessary" when he thought it was. [What
she apparently means is that he had sexual relations with her only
when he wanted to.]

Years later, with her son in the army and her daughter still at home,
Sara decided she could not "take" her marriage anymore. She divorced
her husband. But after the divorce she became very frightened about

having to be on her own. Although she had a job at the time, this did little to lessen her insecurity. In addition, she was "very hurt" at having had to get a divorce. This feeling was heightened whenever she sublet her apartment; her tenants made her feel it wasn't "nice" to divorce. It never occurred to her to consult a psychiatrist, either during her marriage or immediately after her divorce because "At those times if you went to a psychiatrist people thought you were insane."

She became physically ill immediately after the divorce. She had to have gall bladder surgery. Then she became anemic and had to be under a doctor's care. Then, nine years after the divorce, a hysterectomy was necessary. Ever since this operation she believes she has been "entirely different." "To me it feels like Sara died."

Sara has four grandchildren. When they were very small she took care of them, but now that they are older she is expected to leave them alone. Their lack of concern and respect hurts her, although she loves them "very dearly." Some years ago on the advice of her doctor and at the invitation of her daughter-in-law she left her home in New Jersey and went to Las Vegas to reap the benefits of the Nevada climate and to live with and help take care of her son's family. But when the grandchildren matured, Sara was no longer needed. Rather than tell her this, the daughter-in-law tried to drive Sara out with unkind treatment: "She just treated me so that—it just made me go. You know what I mean? You can treat a person enough to make them feel they want to go."

At that time her daughter in New Jersey was expecting a baby and so Sara seized the chance to go and help her. Before she left, her son told her that if she wanted to return to Las Vegas she would have to find another place to live. He pointed out that perhaps she hadn't realized that living with them was a "temporary thing." Sara believes her daughter-in-law pressured him to do this. In New Jersey, she contacted friends to see whether she could remain in the East, but no one was willing to help her.

She returned to Las Vegas and tried to find work as a saleslady, but this was possible only during the Christmas rush.

> It's very difficult in that town to get a job at my age, because it's considered as attraction and they—hire the young girls. . . . I couldn't get no work and I was pretty disappointed because I felt that there was nothing else in this Vegas that I could do.

She had belonged to the Sisterhood of the local temple and enjoyed attending services, being present at meetings and doing volunteer work. Now living alone, she needed transportation so that she could participate in these activities. When her son did take her to services, he would rush her home as soon as possible after they were over, saying, "I'm not going to stay here all night, you know."

She asked her daughter-in-law, who was active in the Sisterhood, to inform the temple that she would be willing to help with any work that needed to be done. Her daughter-in-law said,

> "They don't want people like you. Our organization wants young people . . . they want young blood that can do things. . . . What can you do?"

Not only was Sara unable to do volunteer work, she was no longer permitted to sing in the choir. When the synagogue had been small the cantor had asked her to sing. Then the Jewish community had built a larger temple and hired a new cantor who limited participation to people who could read music. Sara asked for a chance to learn how, but the cantor never offered to teach her or have anyone else teach her.

I asked Sara if she had been happier before her children left home, and she said, "Yes and no. Because my husband never let any of us enjoy it." When I asked specifically what changes in her own feelings of self-worth she had noticed since her children left, she replied: "I don't . . . I don't feel like . . . I don't feel at all that I'm wanted. I just feel like nothing."

Then I asked Sara what was the worst thing that had ever happened to her.

> When I had to break up and be by myself, and be alone, and I'm just—I really feel that I'm not—not only not loved but not even liked sometimes by my own children. . . . They could respect me. If—they can't say good why should they . . . hurt my feelings and make me cry, and then call me a crybaby, or tell me that I ought to know better or something like that. My worst thing is that I'm alone, I'm not wanted, nobody interested themselves in me. Nobody cares.

Sara couldn't think of the best thing that had ever happened to her, but the best times of her life, she said, were when she was pregnant and when her children were babies.

I was glad that God gave me . . . the privilege of being a mother and—and I loved them. In fact, I wrapped my love so much around them.

She felt grateful to her husband, since "if it weren't for him it wouldn't be the children. *They were my whole life, that was it.*"

## ROLE LOSS, RELIGION, AND DEPRESSION; OR WHY NOT TO BE A JEWISH MOTHER

Sara was typical in many ways of the twenty middle-aged women I interviewed in mental hospitals,* all but one of whom were or had been married and had children. All but two of these women were depressed, and eleven were Jewish. I had predicted that the Jewish mother, especially if she had limited herself to being a housewife, would be the one to find the departure of children most stressful, since this departure, according to my hypothesis, is most difficult for women whose primary role is that of mother. The devotion of the Jewish woman to her children is legendary, eulogized in songs and stories and more recently satirized by comedians and writers. From the widely selling books of such prominent Jewish sons as Phillip Roth (*Portnoy's Complaint,* 1967), Bruce J. Friedman (*A Mother's Kisses,* 1964), and Dan Greenburg (*How to Be A Jewish Mother,* 1965) we have been led to see that the other side of the coin of extreme devotion to children is overprotection, controlling behavior, and the development of a "martyr complex" by the mother.

When some crucial items in the interview protocols were analyzed, certain factors reminiscent of the cross-cultural survey began to emerge. These women did not have a kinship network to whom they could turn in times of trouble (here it should be noted that my data were gathered in Los Angeles, where this lack is probably more

---

*Of the women interviewed eleven were married, one separated, six divorced, one widowed and one single. Of the eight women whose children had all departed (the empty-nest women), four were married, and four divorced, widowed, or separated. Of those who had at least one child out of the home but at least one child still at home (partially empty-nest) three were married and none were divorced, widowed, or separated. Four women had marital but not maternal role loss, one had partial marital role loss but not maternal role loss, and four had no role loss. Eighteen of the twenty were diagnosed depressed. Eleven women were Jewish and nine women were housewives.

prevalent than in many other areas of the country). Though they did not believe that their children "owed" them anything, it was clear from the interviews that the Jewish women in particular had expectations of their children that were not being met. None of the women were spending time caring for their grandchildren, but several had done so when the grandchildren were younger, and these women had had to cope with the loss of both mother and grandmother roles. When asked what they were most proud of, the women said their children. In general, they were least proud of their failure to have happy homes. Most of the women felt they were expected to keep busy and not "interfere" once their children were raised. They considered their lives lonelier now than when they were younger, and mentioned that they were less busy. This decline in activity, however, was not an asset, since it gave them more time to ruminate on their problems.

Perhaps the interview item most relevant for this essay was the one asking the women to rank in order of importance seven possible roles. These were: being a homemaker; taking part in church, club, and community activities; being a companion to my husband; helping my parents; being a sexual partner to my husband; my paying job; and helping my children.

Significantly, the mother role—"helping my children"—was most frequently ranked first or second. The role of homemaker was also ranked high. Roles such as "my paying job" and "taking part in church, club, and community activities" were considered unimportant. Thus, precisely those roles that become constricted with age were viewed as important, whereas the roles that could be expanded—the occupational and the organizational roles—were dismissed as unimportant.

All the Jewish women interviewed (but see below for epidemiological data), as expected, had had overprotective or overinvolved relationships with their children, and had experienced feelings of depression when the children left. My analysis of the interviews also showed that many of the women had severe physical illnesses before their hospitalization for depression and that in some cases the physical illness was associated with the failure of their marriages, since when ill they could not meet the expectations of their husbands. A strikingly high proportion of the women had lost their fathers at an early age. This loss deprived them of the opportunity to learn role relationships in an intact family, and therefore may have led to an over-involvement in the maternal role and to depression when the role was lost.

The departure of their children seemed related to the depression of all of the empty-nest mothers, Jewish and non-Jewish alike. The major difference appeared to be that the non-Jewish mothers "keep a stiff upper lip"—they do not complain about their children, they do not express a desire to see them more often or state that they want to live with them—whereas two of the Jewish "empty-nest" mothers I interviewed said openly that they wanted to live with their children. They also talked about wanting a grandmother role.

The interview material lent support to the epidemiological data I had gathered earlier from the records of 533 women between the ages of 40 and 59, hospitalized for the first time for mental illness. The five hospitals varied from an upper-class private hospital to two state hospitals. Among these women, maternal role-loss seemed important only for those in the empty-nest stage. For women with some children still at home, depression seemed associated with other factors. On the basis of the epidemiological data the women with more than one role-loss—for example, both marital and maternal—did not have a higher rate of depression than the women with only one role-loss. However, these data showed only the presence or absence of depression, and nothing about the severity or intensity of the depression where present.* When the intensity of depression could be observed, as in the interviews, those women with a multiple role-loss did appear to be in a worse situation than those with a single loss.

The epidemiological data did not support the hypothesis that maternal role loss would be especially stressful for Jewish women, primarily because the Jewish women in this group were found to be more likely to be depressed whatever their role state. Indeed, one of the most striking relationships to come to light is the high degree of association between being Jewish and being depressed. When ethnicity was cross-tabulated with depression, Jews had a higher rate than any other group—84 percent; Wasps had 47 percent and blacks 22 percent. In other words, whereas more than four out of every five of the Jewish women patients studied were diagnosed as depressed, less than half the non-Jewish sample had this diagnosis. If this high incidence of depression originates in the traditional Jewish socialization process, which makes aggression taboo and uses guilt as a means of social control, then

---

*I did not find that women diagnosed as psychotic had more severe symptoms than those with "neurotic" depression. Diagnosis depended primarily on hospital.

depression should be less common among Jews from less traditional homes. Indeed, evidence to support this hypothesis was found, in the higher rate of depression among Jewish women with foreign-born mothers—only 67 percent of those with native-born mothers were depressed, as compared with 92 percent of those with foreign-born mothers (but the numbers were small).

All in all, however, the Jewish women were more depressed than the non-Jewish women for whatever category they were compared, although significantly, the difference in depression between Jews and non-Jews was markedly reduced when *only housewives with overprotective relationships with their children were studied.* Non-Jews in this category also had an extremely high rate of depression. So you don't have to be Jewish to be a Jewish mother. The pathological effect of an overprotective mother on her children has been discussed by clinicians for many years. This investigation demonstrated that overprotection can be pathological for the mother. And Jews are more likely to have overinvolved relationships with their children than are non-Jews.

Contrary to my original hypothesis that women in high-status occupations would be relatively mildly affected by the loss of the maternal role, the epidemiological data showed that women with professional or managerial occupations had a high rate of depression. (The interview material bore less directly on this question, for the one woman among the twenty with role-loss who had had a job considered professional— she was a nurse—was not greatly involved in her profession. Far from considering it a "calling," she had become a nurse only after her first divorce and had stopped working outside the home during her first marriage.) The norms of our society are such that a woman is not expected to "fulfill" herself through an occupational role, but rather through the traditional feminine roles of housewife and mother. In addition, many women in high-status occupations suffer because of double messages about achievement, nonegalitarian marriages in which the wife's job is considered less important than the husband's and she is responsible for the housework, and the discrimination they experience at work. The fourteen women in the epidemiological sample with high-status occupations and maternal role-loss were also found to be either unhappily married or divorced. In view of a woman's cultural

---

*But in this comparison 80 percent of the Jewish women had such a relationship while only 48 percent of the non-Jewish women did.

expectations and the considerable stresses and role contradictions she may face in a high-status occupation in a sexist society, it is not surprising that the occupational role could not be expanded to compensate for a lost maternal or marital role.

Nevertheless, my study did not support the theory advanced by a number of psychiatrists, most notably Helene Deutsch and Theresa Benedek,[2] that it is the so-called feminine and mothering woman who has the easiest time during the menopause and that it is the—in Deutsch's phrase—"masculine protester" who has the most difficulty. On the contrary, my findings indicate tnat it is the women who play the traditional feminine role—who are housewives, are not aggressive, are centered on their children, who in short, have "bought" the cultural proscriptions—who are most prone to depression when their children leave. The depressed women I studied, far from being masculine protesters, were half a standard deviation more "feminine" on the MMPI test than the mean for the criterion group.

This is not to say that all housewives who are overinvolved or overprotective with their children are hospitalized when their children leave home, or that all housewives become depressed in middle age. Under the following conditions the women would continue to receive vicarious gratification.

1  Their husbands are financially successful
2  Their husbands do not become interested in other women, nor want a divorce, nor die
3  Their children fulfill their expectations, i.e.,
    a  The son obtains a good job
    b  The daughter makes a "good" marriage
    c  The mother-child relationship can continue through frequent phone calls and visits

If these conditions are met, then women of the type we have been discussing need not become depressed. But if any one of these conditions is not fulfilled, then such a woman may be in a dangerous situation. All of these cases depend on the actions of other people rather than the woman herself.

## INTEGRATION OF PSYCHIATRIC AND SOCIOLOGICAL THEORY
Both the psychodynamic and the existential theories of depression state that depression is a result of loss. Psychodynamically oriented psychia-

trists consider the loss that of an ambivalently loved object, whereas existentialists, such as Ernest Becker, consider the loss to be a loss of meaning. In Freudian terms, depressives are understood as individuals who, instead of expressing anger toward the ambivalently loved lost object, turn the anger inward, against themselves. One possible way of combining the Freudian and existentialist views is as follows:

People who are intrapunitive, who do not express their anger, especially if they are women, are conforming to the cultural norms. Since they are "good," they expect to be rewarded. Should their husbands or children leave them, their life may seem meaningless; their world may no longer "make sense." Their introjected anger has led to "proper" behavior, which in turn has led to expectations of reward. If the reward does not materialize, but in fact tragedy strikes, they will suffer from a loss of meaning and become depressed.

The loss that was the independent variable for this study was role-loss, especially the loss of the maternal role for middle-aged women who had overinvolved or overprotective relationships with their children. There is no direct evidence that the "lost" children were ambivalently loved, although some of the interviews I held might suggest that ambivalence was present. It was, however, quite clear that both the interviewees and the epidemiological sample were made up of "norm-following" women.

In *The Revolution in Psychiatry*, Ernest Becker says that it is the women who have been too closely integrated into the social structure who become depressed when they find that their "sacrifice," their exemplary behavior, has been in vain. They discover that it is the exploiters rather than the martyrs who are rewarded, contrary to what they have always believed. They were told that as women they should live for their children. They did so. Their husbands became interested in other women or preoccupied with their jobs, or they died. Their children left home. Since their feeling of being useful stemmed primarily from husband and children, these losses left them with no sense of worth.[3]

Durkheim's work is also relevant to the stresses a mother may feel when her children leave, particularly his concepts of *egoistic* and *anomic* suicide. According to Durkheim it is not marriage that protects a woman from egoistic suicide, as it is for men. Rather it is the birth of children that reduces the suicide rate for women, and immunity to suicide increases with the "density" of the family. This density diminishes, needless to say, when the children mature and leave.

Durkheim focused on problems stemming from normlessness, from anomie. There are indeed few norms governing the relationship between an American woman and her adult children. When the children leave, the woman's situation is consequently normless. There would be, for example, no folkway, no pattern, no mores that could indicate to Sara just what she should expect from her children, just what their relationship should be with her.[4]

All the women I interviewed said their children "owed" them nothing. But there was an additional element of normative confusion faced by the Jewish women. The norms considered appropriate in parent-child relationships in traditional Jewish culture—and therefore adhered to by the women—may not have been completely internalized by their children. The children were also exposed to Anglo-Saxon parent-child relationships, which are more restrained and place more emphasis, at least on the verbal level, on the parent's desire for independence, both for her child and for nerself.

## WHAT NEEDS TO BE DONE

The cross-cultural study, showing the multiplicity of possible roles for middle-aged women, made it clear that not only need status not drop in mid-life, but in most cultures it actually rises. That fact, however, would be cold comfort to the American women we have studied who are already depressed. It is unreasonable to expect them to change their value systems or personality structures of characteristic patterns of interaction at this stage of the game. These women are not psychotic, if by psychotic we mean the patient does not know what reality is. They know exactly what their reality is: that is why they are depressed. We must change society so that these tragedies will not be repeated. More basic changes are required than the "band-aid" reforms making it easier for older women to re-enter the labor force. The entire system of sex roles should be changed so that women could, if they chose, remain in the labor force after childbearing. (This is particularly important for professional women and those whose occupations have changing skills.) Not only should there be adequate 24-hour-a-day, parent-controlled day-care centers, but men whould share the child-care and housekeeping responsibilities. The value system should change so that a man's "masculinity" will not be measured by his occupational achievement, freeing him then to devote more time and energy to his family; and a woman's sense of adequacy should not be dependent on her fulfilling the traditional female roles of wife and mother in the traditional manner. She should have other options, such as not being considered a failure if she does not marry, and deciding not to have children even if she does marry. There are many industrialized societies—such as the Soviet Union, Poland, Sweden, and Finland—where women play a vital part in the economy. Our record on the participation of women in the professions is shameful when we look at that of these other countries. It is interesting to note, however, that even there, when professions (e.g., medicine or pharmacy) have changed from primarily masculine to primarily feminine, they are redefined so as to require "naturally feminine" qualities and skills.

Age discrimination as well as sex discrimination and sexism should be overcome. Although both older men and older women are discriminated against, such discrimination hurts women earlier because of the double standard in aging. A woman's physical attractiveness is one of her assets and a requirement for certain jobs, such as receptionist, hostess, waitress.

The increasing participation of women in the labor force (if not prevented by a decreased demand for workers in the 1970's), declining desired and actual fecundity, the power of the women's movement in fighting sex discrimination and loosening sex role stereotypes, and the increasing self-esteem and self-confidence of women in general should improve the situation of middle-aged women.

Most imperative of all, we must nurture a new sense of worth in the girls of our society, to ensure that as women they will not feel useless when their children or their husbands leave them. If one's satisfaction, one's sense of value, comes from other people rather than from one's own accomplishments, it follows that when these people depart, one is left with an empty shell in place of self. On the other hand, if one's sense of self comes from her own accomplishments, one is not so vulnerable to breakdown when significant others leave.

The woman's liberation movement, by pointing out alternative life styles, by providing the emotional support necessary for deviating from the conventional sex roles, and by emphasizing the importance of women actualizing their own selves, fulfilling their own potentials, can aid in the development of personhood for both men and women.

## NOTES

1   Pauline Bart, Why Women's Status Changes in Middle Age: The Turns of the Social Ferris Wheel," *Sociological Symposium,* Fall 1969, p. 1.

2   Helen Deutsch, *The Psychology of Women: A Psychoanalytic Interpretation* (New York: Grune and Stratton, 1945), vol. 2; Theresa Benedek and Boris Rubenstein, *Psychosexual Functions in Women* (New York: Ronald Press, 1952), pp. 1–11.

3   Ernest Becker, *The Revolution in Psychiatry* (Glencoe, Ill.: Free Press, 1964).

4   Emile Durkheim, *Suicide,* tr. John A. Spaulding and George Simpson (Glencoe, Ill.: Free Press, 1951).

# PART 4 THE WORKING WOMAN

# Francine D. Blau

# Women in the Labor Force: An Overview

Women have traditionally engaged in three types of economically productive work. First, they have produced goods and services for their family's own consumption; second, they have engaged in household production for sale or exchange on the market; third, they have worked for pay outside the home. The process of industrialization has brought about a reallocation in the relative importance of these three types of economic activities, greatly increasing the absolute and relative number of women who seek and obtain paid employment. In this chapter we trace this evolution in the working woman's role, examine the status of women in the labor market in terms of their employment and earnings, and draw some conclusions regarding the changes that must be made in their employment patterns if women are to gain equality in the labor market.

## HISTORICAL PERSPECTIVES

In the preindustrial economy of the American Colonial period, work was frequently allocated on the basis of sex, but there could be little question that the work of women was as essential to the survival of the community as that of men. Unlike England and the Continental countries, where women were routinely employed as reapers, mowers, and haymakers, the Colonies left their agricultural work mostly to the men, at least among the nonslave population.[1] This departure from the customs of the mother country may have been due to the economic importance of the household industries carried on primarily by women and children, who produced most of the manufactured goods for the Colonies. In addition to cleaning, cooking, and caring for their children, colonial women considered spinning, weaving, and making lace, soap, shoes, and candles part of their ordinary housekeeping duties, for the colonial economy at first provided no other source for these goods and services.[2]

Moreover, the pressures of a struggling frontier society, faced with a continual labor shortage and imbued with a puritanical abhorrence of idleness, opened up a wide range of business activities to women. They could be found working as tavern keepers, store managers, traders, speculators, printers and publishers, as well as in the more traditional women's occupations of domestic servant, seamstress, and tailor.[3] But many of the colonial businesswomen were widows, frequently with small children to provide for, who carried on their husband's enterprise after his death.[4] In some cases opportunities for women to remain single and self-supporting were curtailed, perhaps because of women's economic value in the home. For example, in early New England female family heads were given their proportion of planting land, and in Salem even unmarried women at first also received a small allotment. "The custom of granting 'maid's lotts,' however, was soon discontinued in order to avoid 'all presidents and evil events of graunting lotts unto single maidens not disposed of.' "[5]

Although conditions peculiar to the Colonies may have contributed to the relatively high status of American women, the more general point has been made that before the Industrial Revolution separated the home from the place of work, women were able to take a more active role in the economic life of the community.[6] The broad thrust of industrialization may indeed have diminished the participation of women in certain kinds of economically productive work. But in

America women played a crucial role in the development of the first important manufacturing industry, the textile industry.

During the seventeenth century, when spinning and weaving were household industries done primarily by women and children, each household provided its own raw materials and produced chiefly to meet its own needs. But it was not uncommon for women to market part of their output, selling it directly to customers or shopkeepers for credit against their account.[7] With the expansion of the industry in the latter half of the eighteenth century, it became more common for women to be employed by merchants to spin yarn in their own home. Under this commission system the merchants would sell the yarn or put it out again to be woven into cloth. The first factories in America embodied no new technology. They were "merely rooms where several looms were gathered and where a place of business could be maintained." Women delivered yarn they had spun at home to these establishments and were paid for it there.[8]

The first textile factory to incorporate power machinery was established in Pawtucket, Rhode Island, in 1789 by Samuel Slater, a British immigrant. By 1800, fifteen mills had been established in New England for the carding and spinning of yarn. When the power loom was introduced in 1814, the whole process of cloth manufacture could be carried on in the new factories.[9] But cloth was still made primarily by women and children, who constituted the bulk of the new industrial work force.

> The earliest factories did not open any new occupations to women. So long as they were only "spinning mills" there was merely a transferring of women's work from the home to the factory, and by the time that the establishment of the power loom had made weaving also a profitable factory operation, women had become so largely employed as weavers that they were only following this occupation, too, as it left the home. It may, in brief, be said that the result of the introduction of the factory system in the textile industries was that the work which women had been doing in the home could be done more efficiently outside of the home, but women were carrying on the same processes in the making of yarn or cloth.[10]

Perhaps even more interesting than the pioneering role of women in the industry is the reaction of illustrious contemporaries to it. Alexander Hamilton, for example, claimed that one of the great advantages of the establishment of manufacturing was "the employment of persons who would otherwise be idle (and in many cases a burthen on the community). . . . It is worthy of particular remark, that, in general, women and children are rendered more useful, and the latter more early useful, by the manufacturing establishments, than they would otherwise be."[11] The notion that a farmer's masculinity might be threatened by the entry of his wife or children into paid employment apparently did not trouble American men of the time. Hamilton noted, on the contrary, that men would benefit from having a new source of income in the family.[12] Others claimed that the new factories not only opened up a new source of income but also built character in their employees:

> The rise of manufactures was said to have "elevated the females belonging to the families of the cultivators of the soil from a state of penury and idleness to competence and industry.". . . In the same spirit of unreasoning exaggeration the women in villages remote from manufacturing centers were described as "doomed to idleness and its inseparable attendants, vice and guilt."[13]

Since the economy of the United States during this period was predominantly agricultural, with an extremely favorable land-to-labor ratio, women and children were virtually the only readily available source of labor for the infant manufacturing industry. This would seem to be an important factor in the approval accorded the entry of women into the wage-labor force. The existence of a factor of production, women, which was more productive in the new industrial pursuits than in the home, was cited as an argument for the passage of protective tariffs to encourage the development of the textile industry in a country that appeared to have a clear comparative advantage in agriculture.*

Of course, later attitudes toward women working outside the home were not nearly as encouraging. While a careful investigation of the

---

*"To the 'Friends of Industry,' as the early protectionists loved to call themselves, it was . . . a useful argument to be able to say that of all the employees in our manufacturing establishments not one fourth were ablebodied men fit for farming." Edith Abbott, *Women in Industry* (New York: Appleton, 1910), p. 51. The same author noted (p. 52, n. 1) that "manufactures are lauded because of their 'subserviency to the public defense; their employment of women and children, machinery, cattle, fire, fuel, steam, water, and even wind—instead of our ploughmen and male laborers.'"

causes for this change remains to be undertaken, it seems reasonable to suggest that the gradual dwindling of the supply of unsettled land coupled with the waves of immigrants that provided a more abundant source of labor shifted public concern to the problem of providing sufficient employment for men. In any case, by the turn of the twentieth century sentiment against the "intrusion" of women into the industrial work force was strong enough to compel Edith Abbott to answer this charge specifically in her classic study, *Women in Industry*. Her words add a valuable perspective to contemporary discussions of the issue as well:

> Women have been from the beginning of our history an important factor in American industry. In the early days of the factory system they were an indispensable factor. Any theory, therefore, that women are a new element in our industrial life, or that they are doing "men's work," or that they have "driven out the men," is a theory unsupported by the facts.[14]

A careful investigation of the facts also leads us to further qualify the statement that the separation of the home from the place of work during the Industrial Revolution tended to reduce the participation of American women, particularly married women, in many kinds of economically productive work. For one thing, though it is estimated that in 1890 only five percent of married women had jobs outside the home,[15] this pattern did not prevail among all groups in the female population. For another, various types of work done in the home continued to be important in the economy throughout the nineteenth century.

The two major groups of married women for whom work outside the home was fairly common were black women, the majority of whom still lived in the South, and immigrant women in the textile-manufacturing towns of New England. In 1890 one quarter of black wives and two-thirds of the large number of black widows were gainfully employed. Most of these women worked either as field hands or as domestic servants, the same kinds of jobs black women had always done under slavery.[16] Undoubtedly the greater tendency of black wives to engage in market activity can be explained in large part by the low incomes of black men.

The women who worked in the New England textile mills were carrying on the long tradition of the participation of women in this industry. In two Massachusetts towns, Fall River and Lowell, for example, nearly one-fifth of all married women worked outside the home in 1890. Most were first- or second-generation immigrants of French-Canadian or Irish ancestry. The low wages of men working in the textile mills frequently made it necessary for other family members, including children, to work in the mills too. Thus, Robert Smuts has suggested that it was for family reasons as well as financial ones that married women went to work: "Since many of the older children worked in the mills mothers were not needed at home to care for them. Indeed, a mother whose children worked could look after them better if she went to work in the same mill."[17]

In addition to women from these two groups, married women from other sectors of the population were forced to seek market work when they suffered misfortunes against which there was little social protection in the nineteenth and early twentieth centuries. Some indication of the kinds of problems these women faced can be gained from the results of a study conducted by the United States Bureau of Labor Statistics in 1908:

> Among one group of 140 wives and widows who were employed in the glass industry, 94 were widows, or had been deserted, or were married to men who were permanently disabled. Thirteen were married to drunkards or loafers who would not work. The husbands of ten were temporarily unable to work because of sickness or injury. Seventeen were married to unskilled laborers who received minimum wages for uncertain employment. Only six were married to regularly employed workers above the grade of unskilled labor.[18]

As noted earlier, some women contributed to the incomes of their families by earning money for work performed in their own homes. The types of employment and working conditions of this group varied widely. Some women took in boarders or did laundry or sewing. Others, in New York, Chicago, and other major cities, eked out a meager existence doing home work in the garmet industry, while Bohemian and German women in New York's upper East Side tenements provided a cheap source of labor for the cigar industry.[19]

Another element of home work, the production of goods and services for the family's own use, remained extremely important throughout the nineteenth century, even in urban areas. Women frequently kept livestock and poultry and raised fruits and vegetables in small home gardens. Even foodstuffs bought at the market were usually in their natural, unprocessed form. Preserving, pickling, canning, and jelly making, as well as baking the family bread, were normal household duties. Much of the family's clothing, curtains, and linens were sewn or knit in the home. And, of course, the housekeeping tasks of cleaning, washing, and cooking were all undertaken without the benefit of modern appliances.[20] In sum, women have consistently played a major role in the American economy.

## THE FEMALE LABOR FORCE SINCE 1890

While the process of industrialization took production of many goods and services out of the home and into the market, it also incorporated ever-increasing numbers of women into the paid labor force. Since fairly reliable data on the female labor force did not become available until 1890, we shall confine our discussion of the trends in female labor force participation to the period 1890–1977. The figures in Table 1

TABLE 1   Women in the Civilian Labor Force, Selected Years, 1890–1977

| Year | Number (in thousands) | As percentage of all workers | As percentage of female population |
|------|-----------------------|------------------------------|-----------------------------------|
| 1890 | 3,704 | 17.0 | 18.2 |
| 1900 | 4,999 | 18.1 | 20.0 |
| 1920 | 8,229 | 20.4 | 22.7 |
| 1930 | 10,396 | 21.9 | 23.6 |
| 1940 | 13,783 | 25.4 | 28.6 |
| 1945 | 19,290 | 36.1 | 38.1 |
| 1947 | 16,664 | 27.9 | 30.8 |
| 1950 | 18,389 | 29.6 | 33.9 |
| 1955 | 20,548 | 31.6 | 35.7 |
| 1960 | 23,240 | 33.4 | 37.7 |
| 1965 | 26,200 | 35.2 | 39.2 |
| 1970 | 31,520 | 38.1 | 43.3 |
| 1975 | 36,998 | 39.9 | 46.3 |
| 1977 | 39,952 | 41.0 | 48.4 |

SOURCES: U.S Dept. of Labor, Women's Bureau, *1969 Handbook on Women Workers*, p. 10; U.S. Dept. of Labor, Bureau of Labor Statistics, *U.S. Working Women—A Data Book*, Bulletin 1977, (Washington, D.C.: U.S. Government Printing Office, 1977), p. 5; *Employment and Earnings*, January 1978, Tables A-1, A-2.

NOTE: Pre-1940 figures include women 14 years of age and over; figures for 1940 and after include women 16 years of age and over.

indicate a relatively slow rate of increase in the proportion of women of working age that were in the labor force in the early decades of this period.[21] Between 1940 and 1977, however, more dramatic changes in women's labor force status occurred. In 1940 less than 29 percent of the female population 16 years of age and over was in the labor force. By 1977 the figure had risen to over 48 percent, and well over half of all women between the ages of 16 and 64 were working or seeking work. Women workers increased from one quarter to over two-fifths of the civilian labor force.

When we take into account the World War II experience, however, these changes look less impressive. Between 1940 and 1945 the female labor force expanded by 5.5 million, and 38 percent of all women 16 years of age and over were working. As the 1947 figures indicate, considerable ground was lost in the immediate postwar period. In fact, it was not until 1953 that the absolute number of women workers surpassed its wartime peak. Participation rates did not regain their 1945 levels until 1961.[22]

The long-term growth in the female labor force that has occurred since 1940 was accomplished primarily by the entry of new groups of women into the labor market. Before 1940 the typical female worker was young and single. The peak age-specific participation rate occurred among women 20 to 24 years of age, as Figure 1 shows. In the next twenty years older married women entered or reentered the labor force in increasing numbers, while the labor force participation rates of women between 20 and 34 years of age remained relatively constant. Since 1960 there has been a sizable increase in the participation rates of all women under 65. The fastest increase, however, has occurred among women aged 20 to 34, many of whom are mothers of preschool-age children. For example, the labor force participation rate of married women with children under six years old rose from 18.6 percent in 1960 to 39.3 percent in 1977.[23]

Valerie Oppenheimer has identified the growth in the sex-specific demand for women workers as an important factor in the increase in the female labor force and in its changing composition. The growing importance of service industries and white-collar work has provided greatly expanded employment opportunities for women, within the framework of the sexually segregated labor market. Moreover, the increase in these jobs, coupled with the appearance of new female occupations between 1940 and 1960, created a demand that greatly

**FIGURE 1**    Labor Force Participation Rates of Women by Age, 1940–77

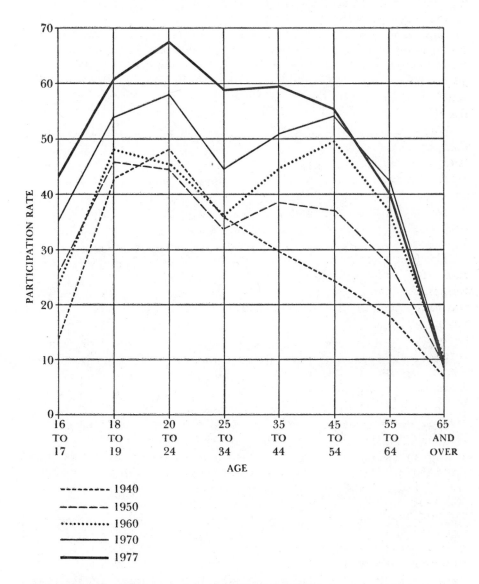

SOURCES: *Employment and Earnings*, January 1978, p. 141, and U.S. Department of Labor, Woman's Bureau, *1975 Handbook on Women Workers*, p. 12.

exceeded the supply of young single women workers, once the backbone of the female labor force. Thus, as Oppenheimer concludes,

> The combination of the rising demand for female labor and the declining supply of the typical worker opened up job opportunities for married women and older women that had not previously existed. . . . The great influx of older married women into the labor force, was, in good part a *response* to increased job opportunities—not the creator of such opportunities.[24]

Oppenheimer also points out that under the pressures of labor shortages, employers were forced to abandon their prejudices against employing older married women.[25] Further research may show that a similar process has operated to the benefit of young married women in the period since 1960. There is some evidence that employers have been reluctant to hire married women with young children, either because they feared such women would have high rates of absenteeism or because they made a moralistic judgment that mothers of preschool-age children should remain at home.[26] Some employers may have been forced to discard these concerns in order to meet their demand for female labor, thus making possible the rapid increase in the labor force participation of women in this group that has occurred in recent years.

If, as Oppenheimer contends, the growing demand for women workers was a crucial factor in the expansion of the female labor force, the question arises whether large numbers of women are outside the labor force simply because sufficient opportunities for work have not been present. The extreme responsiveness of women to the demands created by the emergency conditions of World War II and the evidence that the female labor force tends to grow more quickly during upswings in the business cycle than during recession would support this view.[27] If we further take into account the extremely limited availability of child care centers and the narrow range of jobs open to women, it becomes difficult to regard the decision whether or not to seek paid employment solely as a matter of free choice or personal preference for many women.

## WHICH WOMEN WORK
The result of the sequential entry into the labor force of black and immigrant women, young single women from all ethnic groups, older married women, and most recently the increased labor force particpa-

tion of the younger group of married women, is that the female labor force has come to resemble much more closely the total female population. Women who engage in market work have been drawing closer to the total female population in terms of their racial composition, age, educational attainment, marital and family status and other characteristics. For example, in 1977, the median age of working women was 35, six years younger than the median of 41 for the entire female population. In that year, 51 percent of ever-married working women and 45 percent of all ever-married women had children under 18, while 18 percent of ever-married women workers and 19 percent of all ever-married women had children under six.[28] Thus, it is rapidly becoming more difficult to consider working women an unrepresentative or atypical group.

Nonetheless, it is clear that most women work from financial necessity. Of the women in the labor force in March 1977, 24 percent were single, 19 percent were widowed, divorced, or separated from their husbands.[29] Thus, a substantial proportion of the female labor force has little or no alternative means of support for themselves or their dependents. Further, the contribution to family income of working wives is often of critical importance for the economic welfare of the family.

The economic plight of families headed solely by women is particularly serious. In March 1977, 7.7 million American families, 1 in 7 of all the families in the population, were headed by women.[30] Female-headed families constitute a large and growing proportion of the poverty population. In 1976, one-third of the families headed solely by women lived in poverty, while one-twentieth of the families headed by men or with two parents had incomes below the poverty threshold.[31] Over 60 percent of all poor families with children are now headed solely by women.[32]

While single, widowed, divorced, and separated women are still more likely to work than married women, since married women are the largest group in the adult female population, the postwar increases in their labor market activity mean that the majority of working women are now married. Married women living with their husbands comprised 30 percent of the female labor force in 1940 and 57 percent in 1977.[33]

Education is a major factor in determining whether a married woman will seek employment. In March 1977, 33 percent of wives with less than four years of high school, 50 percent of wives who had graduated from high school, and 60 percent of wives with four or more years of college were in the labor force.[34]

Among both male and female workers, educational attainment generally affects employment opportunities and pay scales. Although the educated woman often meets with discrimination that keeps her from better-paid, more prestigious jobs, her opportunities are still greater than those of a less educated woman. Thus, the more education a woman has, the higher the "opportunity cost" to her (the level of her foregone earnings) of remaining out of the paid labor force. The attraction of market work is therefore greater for more educated women. It may also be more feasible for such women to participate in the labor force, since the better a woman's educational credentials, the greater her chances of finding a job that pays enough to enable her to purchase those goods and services to ease the "double burden" of home and work. The correlation between educational attainment and employment may also reflect a process of self-selection; those women who earn diplomas may be more strongly motivated, ambitious, and career-oriented than those who do not.

In recent years, the observed inverse relationship between husband's income and wife's labor force participation has become less consistent. For example, in 1951, participation rates of married women were highest among those whose husbands earned less than $3,000 (in 1973 dollars). By 1960, wives whose husbands' earnings were in the $5,000–$6,999 category (in 1973 dollars) were the most likely group to be in the labor force. And, by 1977, the highest participation rates were found among wives with husbands earning between $13,000 and $14,999.[35] Increased earnings and employment opportunities for married women with higher levels of education has eroded the simple inverse relationship between husband's income and wife's labor force participation. Now the relationship is curvilinear—with middle-income men more likely to have working wives than either low- or high-income men.

Proportionately more black women than white particpate in the labor force, although the differential has been declining in recent years. In 1948, 31 percent of all white women and 46 percent of all nonwhite women sixteen years of age and over were working. By 1977, 48 percent of white women and 51 percent of nonwhite women were in the labor force.[36] A primary factor in the racial differential in labor force participation rates is the greater financial necessity of market work among black women. A higher proportion of black women are widowed, divorced, or separated from their husbands. These women must rely heavily on their own earnings to support themselves and their families. Furthermore, the lower average earnings of black men increase the importance of a wife's contribution to family income.

## OCCUPATIONAL DISTRIBUTION

As seen in Table 2, the distribution of female and male workers by major occupation group reveals striking differences. In 1977 almost 70

TABLE 2  Occupational Distribution of the Labor Force by Sex and Race, 1977

| | Percentage of employed labor force | | |
| | Males | Females | |
| Major occupation group | | Total | Nonwhite |
| --- | --- | --- | --- |
| White-collar workers[a] | 40.9 | 63.2 | 5.8 |
|   Professional and technical | 14.6 | 15.9 | · 14.3 |
|   Manager, officials | | | |
|     and proprietors | 13.9 | 5.9 | 2.9 |
|   Clerical | 6.3 | 34.7 | 26.0 |
|   Sales | 6.0 | 6.8 | 2.6 |
| Blue-collar workers[a] | 46.1 | 14.6 | 18.4 |
|   Craftsmen and foremen | 20.9 | 1.6 | 1.3 |
|   Operatives | 11.6 | 11.2 | 15.5 |
|   Transportation equipment | | | |
|     operatives | 6.0 | 0.6 | 0.4 |
|   Nonfarm laborers | 7.6 | 1.2 | 1.2 |
| Service workers[a] | 8.8 | 20.9 | 34.9 |
|   Private household | 0.1 | 3.1 | 8.9 |
|   Other | 8.7 | 17.9 | 26.0 |
| Farm workers[a] | 4.2 | 1.3 | 0.9 |
|   Farmers and | | | |
|     farm managers | 2.5 | 0.3 | b |
|   Farm laborers | | | |
|     and foremen | 1.7 | 1.0 | 0.9 |

[a]Figures may not add to totals because of rounding.
[b]Less than 0.05 percent.
SOURCE: *Employment and Earnings*, January 1978, p. 152.

percent of male white-collar workers (29 percent of all working men) were in either professional and technical or managerial jobs, whereas only about 34 percent of female white-collar workers (22 percent of all working women) were in one of these categories. Furthermore, while a somewhat higher proportion of women than men were employed as professional or technical workers, the majority of the women in this category were concentrated in the two traditionally female professions of school teacher and nurse.[37] In 1977, 55 percent of female white-collar workers (35 percent of all employed women) were working in clerical jobs.

Since 1960 women have been entering the skilled trades at a faster rate than men. There were nearly twice as many women in these trades in 1970 as in 1960.[38] Yet men continue to hold a disproportionate share of the highest-status, highest-paying blue-collar jobs. Only 11 percent of women blue-collar workers (1.6 percent of employed women) were craftsmen or foremen in 1977. Yet 45 percent of the men in this group (21 percent of the male labor force) were categorized as craftsmen and foremen. Data collected by the Equal Employment Opportunity Commission indicate that even in industries where women represent a large proportion of operatives, they may be excluded from craft jobs. For example, in 1971, women comprised 66 percent of the operatives employed in the electronics industry in Boston, but were only 7 percent of the craftsmen. Similarly, in the instruments industry of that city, 44 percent of the operatives, but only 8 percent of the craftsmen, were women.[39]

While there has been considerable improvement in the occupational status of nonwhite women workers in recent years, their employment distribution remains skewed toward the lower rungs of the occupational ladder. Thirty-five percent of nonwhite working women were employed in service jobs in 1977, compared to 21 percent of all women workers. Nine percent of nonwhite women workers were in the lowest-paying occupation of private household worker; they comprised nearly two-fifths of all women in this occupation. While 46 percent of nonwhite women held white-collar jobs, 57 percent of this group were clerical workers.

Examination of the detailed occupational distribution of female employees highlights two aspects of the position of women in the labor market. First, women workers are heavily concentrated in an extremely small number of occupations. Half of all working women were employed in just 21 of the 250 detailed occupations listed by the Bureau of the Census in 1969. Just five occupations—secretary-stenographer, household worker, bookkeeper, elementary school teacher, and waitress—accounted for one quarter of all employed women. Men workers were much more widely distributed throughout the occupational structure, with half of them employed in 65 occupations.[40] Second, most women work in predominantly female jobs. A list of the occupations in which 70 percent or more of the workers were women was compiled by Oppenheimer from 1900 and 1960 census figures. She found that in both years well over half of all working women were in these "women's jobs."[41] The only major change over the period was an increase in the number of occupations on the list.

Another way of approaching the issue of the concentration of women in sex-segregated occupational categories is to construct an "index of segregation" based on the percentage of women in the labor force who would have to change jobs in order for the occupational distribution of women workers to match that of men. This index of segregation has remained virtually the same since 1900; it was 66.9 in 1900 and 65.8 in 1970, suggesting that sex segregation has been virtually unaffected by the vast social and economic changes of the present century.[42] Indeed, a detailed analysis of employment data from the 1950 and 1970 Censuses reveals that over the twenty year period there was a larger net inflow of men into predominantly female occupational categories than of women into predominantly male occupations. For the most part this was the result of an increase in the participation of men in such predominantly female professions as elementary school teacher, librarian, nurse, and social worker.[43]

In light of the magnitude and stability of the degree of occupational segregation by sex, one can only concur with Edward Gross' conclusion:

> Those concerned with sexual segregation as a social problem can take small comfort from these figures. They suggest that the movement of women into the labor market has not meant the disappearance of sexual typing in occupation. Rather, the great expansion in female employment has been accomplished through the expansion of occupations that were already heavily female, through the emergence of wholly new occupations (such as that of key punch operator) which were defined as female from the start, and through females taking over previously male occupations. This last may be compared to the process of racial invasion in American

cities. From the group's point of view, such invasion provides new opportunities but still in a segregated context.[44]

A number of variations on the theme of sex segregation are worth noting. The sex composition of occupations is subject to variation by region and industry. This may be illustrated by data collected by the Equal Employment Opportunity Commission. In 1971, women comprised 25 percent of insurance sales personnel in Boston, but less than 5 percent in New York City. Moreover, the mere representation of women in an industry is frequently not a very good predictor of their access to higher-level jobs. In the Detroit electronics industry, 21 percent of all workers and 46 percent of sales workers were women; in Boston, although 38 percent of electronics workers were women, they held only 16 percent of sales positions. It is doubtful that such large differences can be explained in terms of differences among the cities in personnel needs or in the availability of qualified women.[45]

The sex typing of a job often may even vary from one business establishment to another. One firm may hire only men as elevator operators, while another may hire only women; many restaurants employ either waiters or waitresses, but not both. A recent study of employment patterns of male and female office workers in three large Northeastern cities revealed a strong and consistent pattern of sex segregation by establishment among workers employed in the same occupational categories.[46]

These variations in the sex composition of occupations by region, industry, and firm reveal the extremely arbitrary way in which many jobs are sex-typed. Efforts to justify the exclusion of one sex from a job on the basis of differences in training or ability will have to be reconciled with the evidence that in different locales, industries, or companies, a "man's job" may be a "women's job."

## EARNINGS

In 1976 the annual median earnings of women who worked full-time, year-round were $8,099, only 60 percent of the annual median earnings of working men. Nonwhite women were even more disadvantaged. The median earnings of those who were full-time, year-round workers was only $7,831 in 1976, or 54 percent of the median income of white men.[47] In 1955, women earned 64 percent the income of men, but the gap between the earnings of women and men increased between 1956 and 1967, and has fluctuated between 57 and 60 percent since then.[48] A large difference in earnings between male and female workers is found even when adjustments are made for sex differences in hours of work and educational attainment.[49]

A further measure of the problem can be gained by comparing the earnings distribution of female and male workers. In 1976, 26 percent of all year-round, full-time working women earned less than $6,000 as compared to 9 percent of working men, while only 7 percent of the women, as compared to 42 percent of the men, earned $15,000 or more.[50]

A growing body of research into the question of male-female pay differences supports the view that discrimination accounts for a significant share of the differential. After controlling for education, experience, and other factors that might tend to cause productivity differences between men and women, the proportion of the sex differential attributable to pure discrimination has been estimated at between 29 and 43 percent of male earnings.[51]

Earnings differentials by sex persist even when we control for major occupation group. In 1977, the ratio of the median earnings of full-time, year-round women workers to those of full-time, year-round men workers was 65 percent for professional and technical workers; 59 percent for managers, officials, and proprietors; 63 percent for clerical workers; 43 percent for sales workers; 57 percent for craftsmen and foremen; 57 percent for operatives; and 57 percent for service workers.[52] These pay differences are in large part due to sex segregation in employment, which means that even within broad occupational groups, men and women tend to be concentrated in different detailed occupational categories or to work in different industries.

Since earnings are directly tied to both work experience and job tenure, the intermittent labor force participation of many women workers and their shorter average length of time on a particular job would lead us to expect some differences in median earnings between women and men workers.[53] The observed earnings differentials, however, exceed what could be expected to result from these factors. These extremely high differentials can best be understood in terms of the sexual segregation of the labor market discussed in the preceeding section. At the risk of some oversimplification, the effect of the resulting "dual labor market" on women's earnings can be explained in terms of supply and demand.

The demand for women workers is mainly restricted to a small number of sex segregated occupations. At the same time, the supply of women available for work is highly responsive to small changes in the wages offered as well as to employment opportunities in general. Moreover, employers can attract more women into a job simply by increasing the flexibility of work schedules. Thus, in most predominantly female jobs, there exists a reserve pool of qualified women outside the labor market who would be willing to enter it if the price or the job were right. The abundance of supply relative to demand, or what has been termed the "over-crowding" of female occupations, results in lower earnings for women's jobs.[54]

Thus it is not surprising that the rapid expansion of the female work force corresponded with an increasing gap between the earnings of women and men, as larger numbers of women crowd into the same limited set of occupations. Of course, this is not to suggest that women and men never work together on the same job in the same establishment, or that in those cases wage differentials do not exist. Rather it suggests that the practice of unequal pay for equal work is made possible by the limited job opportunities open to women, who have little choice but to accept the disparity. Moreover, nominal differences in job definitions sometimes provide a further excuse for unequal pay even in the case of comparable work.

There are some who argue that women do not need to earn as much as men, and hence that the low earning power of working women is not a significant social problem. Single women who work are only biding their time before marriage, so the argument goes, and married women are only supplementing their husbands' already ample incomes. The assumptions underlying this view—that single women do not need to make a living wage or to be able to save for the future, and that all husbands earn enough to provide adequately for their wives and children—are left unexamined.

It has been shown that work is a financial necessity for most women, but two additional points need to be made. First, in a society in which value often means monetary value, it is extremely unlikely that women can attain "equality," however that may be defined, without equal earning opportunities. Second, a significant change in women's social status will require the real possibility of economic independence for women, and not simply limited earning opportunities at low income levels.

### Prospects for the future employment of women

Because we are in a period of less than full employment, the question is often raised as to whether or not the economy can generate enough jobs to absorb the anticipated increase in the number of women seeking work. This ability to provide employment for a larger female work force depends on two factors. First is the aggregate level of economic activity. To a great extent, this is within the control of our policy makers. Thus, it is extremely important that full-employment be made a national goal of the highest priority and that the government pursue the necessary measures to assure a full-employment economy in the coming years.

Second, since women are heavily concentrated in a limited number of occupational categories, the ability of women to find employment depends not only on the aggregate number of jobs available, but on the structure of demand as well. The Bureau of Labor Statistics projections of the occupational distribution of the work force in 1980 indicate that the structure of demand will continue to favor the employment of women, even if the present uneven distribution of women among occupations persists into the future. Above average rates of increase in employment are anticipated in the professional and technical, clerical and service categories[55] that accounted for 71 percent of women workers in 1977.

The aggregate statistics do, however, conceal certain problem areas. For example, employment in elementary and secondary school teaching, in which 36 percent of all professional women were engaged in 1969, is not expected to grow as rapidly as it has in the past. The Bureau of Labor Statistics projections indicate that the number of people seeking to enter the noncollege teaching profession could be as much as 75 percent above projected requirements.[56] Such shifts in demand are not unusual in a dynamic and changing economy. Under conditions of full employment, the decline in the need for teachers would be offset by expanding employment opportunities in other areas. However, given the sex segregation of the labor market and the long period of training required for most professional jobs, this shift in demand could pose serious problems for college-educated women. Present projections indicate that other traditionally female professions will not expand sufficiently to compensate for the poor prospects in elementary and secondary education. Those professions in which demand is expected to expand rapidly—medicine, dentistry, architecture, science, and engineering—have not traditionally employed large numbers of women.[57] If no efforts are made to encourage a substantial change in the type of training acquired by women at the college and graduate level, the consequence could well be serious underemployment of college-trained women.[58] If, in the absence of sufficient professional opportunities, women college graduates begin to compete for jobs that have in the past been held by women with less education, the latter group will be adversely affected as well.

While the continued trend toward a service economy and white-collar employment does not in general indicate a worsening of the economic position of women, it does not necessarily imply an improvement. Lower earnings and higher unemployment rates will probably continue to plague the female work force as long as occupational segregation by sex persists. For this reason, the goal of equal employment opportunity is crucial to the economic welfare of women.

The evidence presented in the preceding sections shows that until women have more occupational mobility, it is extremely unlikely that the pay differentials between female and male workers will be substantially reduced. Although it is not possible to predict exactly what the distribution of female employment would be if there were complete equality of opportunity in the labor market, it can reasonably be expected that women would be much more evenly distributed throughout the occupational structure.

The size of the effort needed to make substantial changes in the occupational distribution of women workers should not be underestimated. Not only are women heavily concentrated in a small number of occupations, they comprise 41 percent of the civilian labor force. Nonetheless, a great deal can be accomplished by concentrating on the *new* jobs created by the growth and replacement needs of the economy. This is illustrated by the results of a simulation experiment shown in Figure 2. The 1980 figures show what the sex composition of employment in each occupation would be if, between 1969 and 1980, 40 percent of the new jobs in each category had been allocated to women and 60 percent to men. The particular ratio employed is, of course, purely illustrative, but the results give some indication of the impact a different distribution of job opportunities could have on the occupational distribution of women workers.

It appears as though fairly large changes would have been forthcoming. The female proportion of those employed as managers, officials, and proprietors would have increased from 16 to 26 percent, the

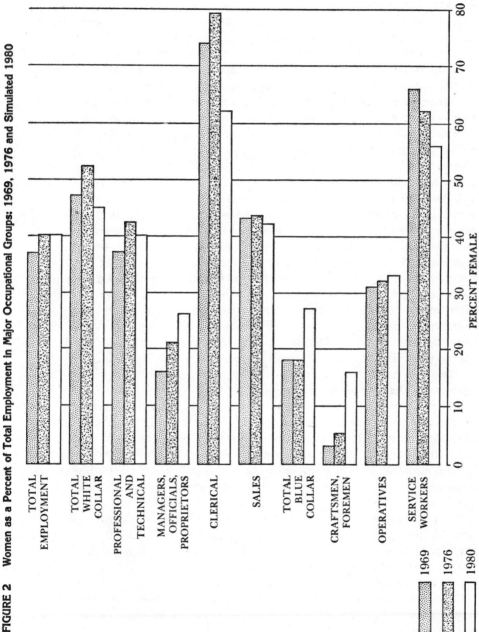

**FIGURE 2    Women as a Percent of Total Employment in Major Occupational Groups: 1969, 1976 and Simulated 1980**

female proportion of craftsmen and foremen from 3 to 16 percent. Similarly, women would have declined from 74 to 61 percent of all clerical employees and from 66 to 56 percent of service workers.

However, the actual figures for 1976, nearly two-thirds of the way through the eleven-year period, indicate that, in many cases, progress fell short of what was possible. Although in 1976 women comprised 21 percent of managers, officials and proprietors, they were less than 5 percent of craftsmen and foremen. While the female proportion of service workers did decline by 4 percentage points between 1969 and 1974, women's share of clerical jobs increased by 5 percentage points. Thus, in 1976, the skewed occupational distribution of women workers continued to be a serious barrier to the economic equality of women.

An assessment of the future prospects of women in the labor market would be incomplete without some consideration of the impact of the level of unemployment on women's economic status. The adverse effect of periods of high unemployment on women cannot be overemphasized. First, since the unemployment rate of women is generally higher than that of men, women bear a disproportionate share of unemployment. Second, in times of high unemployment, many women become discouraged and drop out of the labor force; others postpone their entry until economic conditions improve. This kind of "hidden unemployment" is a particular problem for women. Finally, the level of unemployment will undoubtedly affect the social acceptance of programs designed to increase the opportunities for women in what are presently predominantly male jobs.

An unavoidable consequence of the effort to expand the employment opportunities open to women is that men will face a new source of competition. Thus, some men may find that they are unable to obtain employment in their preferred occupation. However, under conditions of full employment, they can always find employment elsewhere. Further, buoyant demand conditions combined with a new occupational mobility for women workers would tend to reduce earnings differentials between jobs that were once predominantly male or female. Thus, the price paid by men for being unable to enter the occupation of their choice might not prove to be very great. On the other hand, during a period of high unemployment, public support for a fundamental change in women's employment status may diminish. Moreover, since it is the new jobs that become available in a growing, healthy economy that are most likely to become available to women, the maintenance of full employment is important if we are to move *rapidly* toward the goal of economic equality for women.

## NOTES

1   Edith Abbott, *Women in Industry* (New York: Appleton, 1910), pp. 11–12.

2   Eleanor Flexner, *Century of Struggle: The Women's Rights Movement in the United States* (New York: Atheneum, 1968), p. 9.

3   Abbott, *Women in Industry*, pp. 13–18. "It should be noted that the domestic servant in the seventeenth and eighteenth centuries was employed for a considerable part of her time in processes of manufacture and that, without going far wrong, one might classify this as an industrial occupation." *Ibid.*, p. 16.

4   Flexner, *Century of Struggle*, p. 9.

5   Abbott, *Women in Industry*, pp. 11–12.

6   Viola Klein and Alva Myrdal, *Women's Two Roles* (London: Routledge and Kegan Paul, 1956), p. 1.

7   Abbott, *Women in Industry*, pp. 18–19.

8   *Ibid.*, p. 19, and for quote, p. 37.

9   Elizabeth Faulkner Baker, *Technology and Women's Work* (New York: Columbia University Press, 1964), p. 5.

10   Abbott, *Women in Industry*, p. 14.

11   Alexander Hamilton, *Report on Manufactures*, vol. 1, cited in Baker, p. 6.

12   Hamilton, *Report on Manufactures*, cited in Abbott, p. 50.

13   Abbott, *Women in Industry*, p. 57.

14   *Ibid.*, p. 317.

15   Robert W. Smuts, *Women and Work in America* (New York: Columbia University Press, 1959), p. 23.

16   *Ibid.*, pp. 10, 56.

17   *Ibid.*, p. 57.

18   *Ibid.*, p. 51.

19   *Ibid.*, pp. 14–17.

20   *Ibid.*, pp. 11–13.

21   There is some question whether there was any increase at all in female labor force participation during the 1890–1930 period. The 1910 census, in which enumerators were given special instructions *not* to overlook women workers, especially unpaid family workers, yielded a participation rate of 25 percent. Robert W. Smuts has argued that women workers were undercounted in the 1900, the 1920, and perhaps the 1930 census as well, but that over the period, gradual improvements in technique, broader definitions of labor force status, and a redistribution of the female work force from unpaid farm work to paid employment resulted in an apparent rather than a true increase in the female participation rate. Smuts, "The Female Labor Force," *Journal of the American Statistical Association*, LV (March 1960), pp.

71–79. For a discussion of this issue see Valerie Kincade Oppenheimer, *The Female Labor Force in the United States* (Berkeley, University of California, Institute of International Studies, 1970), pp. 3–5.

22  U.S. Department of Labor, Manpower Administration, *Manpower Report of the President,* March 1970 (Washington, D.C.: U.S. Government Printing Office), p. 217.

23  U.S. Department of Labor, Manpower Administration, *Manpower Report of the President,* April 1975 (Washington, D.C.: U.S. Government Printing Office) and U.S. Department of Labor, News Release 77-792 (September 14, 1977), p. 1.

24  Oppenheimer, *Female Labor Force,* p. 187.

25  *Ibid.,* p. 188.

26  See for example, Georgina M. Smith, *Help Wanted—Female: A Study of Demand and Supply in a Local Job Market for Women* (Rutgers, N.J.: Rutgers University, Institute of Management and Labor Relations, 1964), pp. 18–19.

27  See Gertrude Bancroft McNally, "Patterns of Female Labor Force Activity," *Industrial Relations* (May 1968), pp. 204–18.

28  U.S. Department of Labor, News Release 77-792 (September 14, 1977), Table III.

29  U.S. Department of Labor, News Release 77–792, Table I.

30  *Ibid.,* Table V.

31  U.S. Department of Commerce, *Money Income and Poverty Status of Families and Persons in the United States: 1976 (Advance Report),* Bureau of the Census, Current Population Reports Series P–60, No. 107 (Washington, D.C.: U.S. Government Printing Office, September 1977), Table 16.

32  *Ibid.,* Table 20.

33  U.S. Department of Labor, News Release 77–927, Table I.

34  U.S. Department of Labor, Michelotti Kopp, "Educational Attainment of Workers, March 1977," Special Labor Force Report No. 209, Bureau of Labor Statistics (Washington, D.C.: U.S. Government Printing Office, 1978).

35  U.S. Department of Labor, "Marital and Family Characteristics of the Labor Force, March 1977," Special Labor Force Report No. [unassigned], Bureau of Labor Statistics (Washington, D.C.: U.S. Government Printing Office, 1978).

36  *Employment and Earnings,* January 1978, p. 139.

37  *Ibid.,* p. 153.

38  Janet Neipert Hedges and Stephen Beims, "Sex Stereotyping in the Skilled Trades," *Monthly Labor Review,* 97 (May 1974), 16.

39  U.S. Equal Employment Opportunity Commission, *Research Report No. 43: Employment Profiles of Minorities and Women in the SMSA's of 20 Large Cities, 1971* (July 1974).

40  Janice Neipert Hedges, "Women Workers and Manpower Demands in the 1970's," *Monthly Labor Review,* 93 (June 1970), 19.

41  Valerie Kincade Oppenheimer, "The Sex-Labeling of Jobs," *Industrial Relations* (May 1968), 220, Table 6.

42  The source for the 1900 figure was Edward Gross, "Plus Ça Change. . . ? The Sexual Structure of Occupation Over Time," *Social Problems,* 16 (Fall 1965), 202. The 1970 figure was computed from U.S. Department of Commerce, *U.S. Census of the*

*Population, Detailed Characteristics,* Bureau of the Census, final report PC(1)–D1, U.S. Summary (Washington, D.C.: U.S. Government Printing Office, 1973), Table 221, pp. 718–24.

43   Francine D. Blau, *Equal Pay in the Office* (Lexington, Mass.: Lexington Books, D. C. Heath & Co., 1977), pp. 10–18.

44   Gross, "Plus Ça Change. . . ?," pp. 202.

45   U.S. Equal Employment Opportunity Commission, *Research Report No. 43: Employment Profiles of Minorities and Women.*

46   Francine D. Blau, "Sex Segregation of Workers by Enterprise in Clerical Occupations," *Labor Market Segmentation,* Richard C. Edwards, Michael Reich, and David M. Gordon, eds. (Lexington, Mass.: Lexington Books, 1975). See also, John B. Buckley, "Pay Differences between Men and Women in the Same Job," *Monthly Labor Review,* 94 (November 1971), 36–39.

47   U.S. Department of Commerce, Bureau of the Census, Current Population Reports, Series P-60, no. 114, *"Money Income and Poverty Status of Families and Persons in the United States: 1976,"* (Washington, D.C.: U.S. Government Printing Office, July 1978), Table 58.

48   U.S. Department of Labor, *U.S. Working Women: A Databook,* Bureau of Labor Statistics, Bulletin 1977 (Washington, D.C.: U.S. Government Printing Office, 1977), Table 37, p. 35.

49   *Manpower Report of the President* (April 1975), p. 62.

50   U.S. Department of Commerce, Bureau of the Census, Current Population Reports Series P-60, no. 114, *Money Income and Poverty Status of Families and Persons in the United States: 1976* (Washington, D.C.: U.S. Government Printing Office, July 1978) Table 58.

51   See Isabel Sawhill, "The Economics of Discrimination Against Women: Some New Findings," *Journal of Human Resources,* 8 (Summer 1973), for a review of this research.

52   "Money Income and Poverty Status of Families and Persons in the United States 1976," Table 7.

53   In addition, full-time hours for women tend to be less than those of men on the average. For the effect of adjustment for this factor on the earnings differential, see *Economic Report of the President* (January 1973), p. 104.

54   Barbara R. Bergmann, "Occupational Segregation, Wages and Profits When Employers Discriminate by Race or Sex," *Eastern Economic Journal,* 1 (April and July 1974), 103–10. See also Francine D. Blau, "Women's Place in the Labor Market," *American Economic Review,* 62 (May 1972), 161–66.

55   U.S. Department of Labor, Bureau of Labor Statistics, "The U.S. Economy in 1980: A Preview of BLS Projections," *Monthly Labor Review,* 93 (April 1970), 21–24.

56   Hedges, "Women Workers and Manpower Demands in the 1970's," p. 22.

57   *Ibid.*

58   Current trends in female enrollment in professional training appear to point in the right direction. See John B. Parrish, "Women in Professional Training—an Update," *Monthly Labor Review,* 98 (November 1975), 49.

# Kay Lehman Schlozman

# Women and Unemployment: Assessing the Biggest Myths

LEMONT, ILL.—Sandy and Ed Biggest like to fly for fun and last spring they bought their second two-seater airplane. The Biggests, both 33 years old, also own two cars and a comfortable six-room house, fully paid for, in this pleasant suburb of Chicago. Their two children, aged nine and fourteen, attend Catholic school.

Ed is an $18,000-a-year mechanic for Amoco Chemical Co. Sandy is a housewife. The couple currently has no outside income, but in the early days of their marriage Sandy worked and Ed put in many seven-day weeks, allowing them to build a respectable nest egg. They still consider themselves quite comfortable financially.

Yet Sandy, an attractive and energetic woman, is an unemployment statistic because she's bored with housework and has been looking for a job. And not just any job, mind you. Despite the fact that she has only a high school education, she says she won't settle for less than a position selling sophisticated business machines at a salary of $15,000 a year.

"I'd be working right now if I wasn't so fussy about the kind of work I'd take," she admits. "I'm not looking for a job because we need the money, so why shouldn't I be choosy?"

Sandy Biggest's attitudes about work may not be universal, but they surely shed some light on a sizable and often overlooked component of the nation's unemployment picture: housewives who are looking for jobs but don't "need" them by most economic standards. . .

. . . it has come to be widely recognized that many women who don't have to work to survive approach job hunting in a different way than do men and women who must work to live, and that their inclusion among the jobless might make the overall rates seem more alarming than they actually are.

Christopher A. Evans in The Wall Street Journal[1]

In mid-1975 there were more Americans out of work than there were in the depression year of 1931. Yet widespread unemployment in the 1970's has largely been ignored by opinion leaders in politics and the media. Many of those who actually have paid attention to the problem have tended to minimize it, using two arguments, both of which rest on false premises and draw false conclusions about the role of women in the economy. First, it is argued that the inflated rate of unemployment in recent years is primarily a function of various changes in the composition of the labor force, among them the entry into the labor force of unprecedented numbers of married women. Second, it is implied that both because government and union benefits provide a financial cushion to the unemployed and because so many of the unemployed are not main wage earners for their households, unemployment does not necessarily imply suffering and hardship, especially for women. Those who advance these positions are not especially concerned with the welfare of women. Their interest is in explaining unemployment, and especially in diminishing the seriousness attached to current high rates of unemployment. Still, their arguments rest on certain widely held assumptions about the economic needs and behavior of women.

Because these two arguments have consequences both for the seriousness with which women are taken as members of the labor force and for the gravity attributed to women's unemployment as a problem, they deserve more detailed consideration. When examined in the light of current data about unemployment, neither the contention that high unemployment rates are a function of the entry into the work force of large numbers of women nor the assertion that women do not undergo hardship when they are unemployed is supported. Thus, current analysts have misunderstood both the role of women in causing unemployment in the 1970's and the consequences of this unemployment.

### How do we know about the unemployed?

Before examining the prevailing myths about the causes and consequences of contemporary unemployment, we must first understand how unemployment is defined and how we know about the unemployed. One obvious way to find out about the unemployed is simply to do what Mr. Evans of the *Wall Street Journal* did before he wrote the lines cited above—find some unemployed people and talk to them. Although this method has the advantage of being simple and direct, it will probably produce biased results. Those interviewed may not be typical of the unemployed at all. As a matter of fact, there may be no typical unemployed person.

The unemployed are a diverse group. The engineer fired in the face of cutbacks in defense expenditures, the high school dropout hanging out on a street corner, the auto assembly line worker laid off when business is sluggish, and the recent college graduate searching for a first job have little in common except their joblessness. Thus to get an accurate picture of the unemployed as a group, it is important both to speak to a relatively large number of the unemployed and to make sure that they are selected *randomly* so that the resulting sample includes all kinds of people—black and white, carpenters and clerks, men and women, household heads and secondary earners, and so on—and will reflect in an unbiased way the composition of the much larger group of the over seven million unemployed Americans.

Fortunately, we do have access to such information. The most important source of such information is the Bureau of Labor Statistics of the United States Department of Labor. Each month the government surveys roughly 47,000 households and, on the basis of detailed questions, classifies each household member aged 16 and over as employed, unemployed, or not in the labor force. On the basis of the data collected, the Bureau of Labor Statistics is able to make inferences with remarkable accuracy about the employment status of members of the work force as a whole or of any sub-group within it—for example, women, teenagers, or construction workers.

Although there is no controversy over the way in which the government collects this information and, hence, no dispute over the accuracy of the statistics themselves, there has been debate over the government's definition of unemployment. The government considers as employed any person who had a job during the preceding week, even if that person did no work because he or she was ill, on vacation, or out on strike. On the other hand, the government considers as unemployed any person who was without a job during the past week, who is currently available for work, and who has made active efforts to find work during the past four weeks.[2] Conservatives argue that this definition inflates the unemployment rate because it gives the same weight to the unemployment of a teenager making occasional, half-hearted attempts to find a job or a housewife looking for part-time work as it does to the unemployment of a household head seeking full-time work. They urge that those who live with a parent or spouse who has a full-time job, those who are insufficiently skilled or educated to qualify for most jobs, and those who are not making serious efforts to find work not be counted as unemployed. Liberals, on the other hand, argue that the government's definition actually understates the amount of unemployment because it does not consider as unemployed part-time workers who would prefer full-time work and "discouraged workers" who want jobs but are so pessimistic about their chances of finding work that they have given up looking.[3] For our purposes it is less important to evaluate these alternative definitions than it is to understand how the government collects information about the unemployed and whom it considers to be unemployed.

The data collected by the Bureau of Labor Statistics have certain shortcomings: although they contain valuable information about the objective characteristics of the unemployed—their previous occupations, the length of their unemployment, and so on—they contain no information about how the unemployed feel about their situation. In order to compensate, we will also examine the data we collected in an April, 1976 metropolitan work force survey.[4]

## WOMEN AND UNEMPLOYMENT

Having done the preliminary ground work to understand who is considered unemployed and how we get information about them, let us return to Sandy Biggest. Because she is currently jobless, actively looking for work, and available to take a job should the right one materialize, Sandy is considered unemployed by the government. According to Evans, women like Sandy Biggest form a substantial contingent within the nation's unemployed and, thus, artificially increase the unemployment rate. Those complacent about unemployment argue that the entry into the labor market of large numbers of housewives returning to work—who have the financial security to be picky about just what jobs they will take and who do not need the money anyway—has inflated the current unemployment rate artificially. Further, they conclude, although the unemployment rate seems uncooperatively reluctant to dip back to the levels deemed acceptable in the decades of the fifties and sixties, there is no reason to panic; after all, it's all because Sandy Biggest and her kind are being so fussy, and nobody is really suffering.

Clearly, this is an unnecessarily flippant summary of a complicated analysis. If we are to understand both the relationship between women's work force behavior and unemployment, and the effects of unemployment on women, we must examine critically the components of this analysis. Our discussion will focus on two questions: To what extent has the entry of women into the labor force contributed to current high unemployment rates? Does unemployment imply suffering and hardship for women?

### Are women responsible for high unemployment?

To what degree does the unemployment rate of the mid-seventies reflect the inability of the economy to absorb the unprecedented number of women who have entered the work force in recent years? That more and more women work is undeniable. As shown in Table 1, since the depression women's work force participation—that is, the percentage of adult women who are either working or unemployed, as opposed to keeping house, going to school, or retired—has nearly doubled: in 1940 only a quarter of all women were in the labor force; by 1976 nearly half were.[5] What is less certain is whether it is the inability of the economy to absorb these new and renewed workers that has raised unemployment rates in recent years to levels substantially above what was considered tolerable in the fifties and sixties. A quick look at the data in Table 2 casts doubt on this conclusion. As shown in

**TABLE 1    Work Force Participation by Women[a]**

|                   | 1940  | 1950  | 1960  | 1970  | 1976  |
|-------------------|-------|-------|-------|-------|-------|
| 16–19 years       | 18.9% | 41.0% | 39.4% | 44.0% | 50.1% |
| 20–24 years       | 45.6  | 46.1  | 46.2  | 57.8  | 65.2  |
| 25–44 years       | 30.5  | 36.4  | 39.9  | 47.9  | 57.4  |
| 45–64 years       | 20.2  | 33.2  | 44.3  | 49.3  | 48.6  |
| 65 years and over | 6.1   | 9.7   | 10.8  | 9.7   | 8.2   |
| Total             | 25.8% | 33.9% | 37.8% | 43.4% | 47.4% |

[a]Percentage of all women 16 years and over (14 years and over in 1940) who are either working or unemployed and looking for work. Housewives, students, and retirees are not labor force participants.

SOURCE: U.S. Department of Commerce, Bureau of the Census, *Historical Statistics of the United States: Part I*, pp. 131–32; U.S. Department of Labor, Bureau of Labor Statistics, *Employment and Earnings*, January 1977, p. 139.

**TABLE 2    Work Force Participation by Women and Average Annual Unemployment Rate: 1967–76**

|      | Work force participation by women[a] | Unemployment rate[b] |
|------|--------------------------------------|----------------------|
| 1967 | 41.2% | 3.8% |
| 1968 | 41.6  | 3.6  |
| 1969 | 42.7  | 3.5  |
| 1970 | 43.4  | 4.9  |
| 1971 | 43.4  | 5.9  |
| 1972 | 43.9  | 5.6  |
| 1973 | 44.7  | 4.9  |
| 1974 | 45.7  | 5.6  |
| 1975 | 46.4  | 8.5  |
| 1976 | 47.4  | 7.7  |

[a]Percentage of all women 16 and over who are either working or unemployed and looking for work

[b]Percentage of all work force members, male and female, who are unemployed and looking for work

SOURCE: Department of Labor, Bureau of Labor Statistics, *Employment and Earnings*, February 1977, pp. 22–23.

Table 2, women's labor force participation has risen slowly but steadily during the past decade until, in 1976, 47.4 percent of all females sixteen years and over were in the labor force.

If those who blame the current high unemployment rates on the entry into the labor force of large numbers of women are correct, then we would expect the unemployment rate to climb equally steadily, though probably at a different rate. Clearly, this is not the case. The data in Table 2 show that, while the portion of adult women in the work force has climbed at the steady rate of one percent or less each year for the last decade, the average annual unemployment rate has bounced around quite a bit, achieving a low of 3.5 percent in 1969 and reaching a high of 8.5 percent in 1975, presumably rising and falling in response to other factors than the number of women in the labor force.

Figure 1 presents these data in a somewhat different fashion and casts further suspicion on the hypothesized links between the number of women entering the labor force and high rates of unemployment. In this case we compare the growth rate of the female labor force from year to year with the growth rate of the unemployed of both sexes. Looking at the dotted line, we see once again that the female work force has grown slowly, but steadily, over the past decade. In 1967, there were 3.9 percent more women in the work force than in 1966; in 1968, 3.0 percent more than in 1967; and so on. With only two exceptions, in each of the past ten years the number of women who are either working or unemployed and looking for work is three to four percent higher than it was the year before. If those who posit a relationship between growing work force participation by women and high rates of unemployment are correct, we would expect the number of unemployed to grow in a similarly steady fashion—the number of unemployed growing at some unknown, but more or less constant rate. However, Figure 1 shows that this is hardly the case. Looking at the solid line, we see that the number of unemployed workers of both sexes has often fluctuated substantially from year to year. In 1967, there were 3.5 percent more people out of work than in 1966. In 1968, there were actually 5.3 percent *fewer* unemployed people than in 1967; therefore, for that year the growth rate was negative. The following year the number of jobless people was virtually unchanged; there were .5 percent more unemployed in 1969 than in 1968. Thus, from year to year the number of unemployed has sometimes increased dramatically, sometimes decreased, and sometimes stayed about the same. In contrast to the steady growth of the female work force, these shifts are

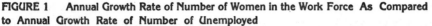

**FIGURE 1    Annual Growth Rate of Number of Women in the Work Force As Compared to Annual Growth Rate of Number of Unemployed**

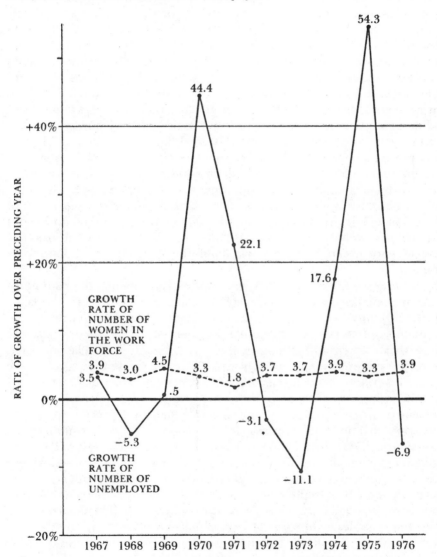

SOURCE: U.S. Dehartment of Labor, Bureau of Labor Statistics, *Employment and Earnings,* February 1977, pp. 23–24.

clearly too dramatic to be a function solely of the increased number of women who are looking for jobs. Obviously, Sandy Biggest and her sisters are not singlehandedly responsible for the high levels of unemployment that have characterized the American economy in the mid-seventies.

Before we completely reject the supposed relationship between women's increased labor force participation and high rates of unemployment, we should consider a more sophisticated version of that argument. This variant suggests that it is not the increasing numbers of working women but the changing composition of the labor force that is swelling the unemployment rate. According to this position, higher unemployment is inevitable in the mid-seventies because groups with traditionally high rates of unemployment—namely, women and teenagers—form a much larger component of the labor force than they did during the past two decades. Thus, higher unemployment rates are inevitable. To give a caricature of this position, if more and more people who don't need to work and are very fussy about what jobs they will accept begin to look for work, unemployment rates are bound to be high.

It certainly is the case that with earlier retirements, the coming of age of the large group of post-war babies, and the entry into the labor force of many women, the work force is somewhat younger and more female than it was in the low unemployment year of 1969. It is also the case that women and teenagers have traditionally had relatively high rates of unemployment (though whether it is because these groups are "hard-to-employ" is a matter of some controversy).[6] But these demographic changes hardly account for the persistently high rates of unemployment in recent years. Using a simple statistical procedure we can ascertain just how much impact these changes in the composition of the work force have had on overall unemployment. The overall rate of unemployment at any time reflects different rates of unemployment for various subgroups in the population. In April, 1969, when the overall rate of unemployment was 3.2 percent, 11.9 percent of work force females aged 16 to 19 were unemployed; at that time only 1.5 percent of males aged 45 to 54 were unemployed. In April of 1976, the rates were 17.1 and 4.3 for these groups respectively. If we take the April, 1969 unemployment rates for each of the age-sex groups in the work force (males—16 to 19; males—20 to 24; and so on) and apply them to the analogous groups in the labor force of April, 1976, we can arrive at a hypothetical figure that shows how much of the increase in the unemployment rate over the seven-year period is a function of the demographic change in the composition of the work force.[7] This number gives an estimate of how much unemployment there would have been if the economic conditions prevailing in 1969 had obtained for the unemployment-prone work force of 1976.

This comparison indicates that relatively little of the increase in unemployment between 1969 and 1976 can be accounted for by the increase in the number of women and teenagers in the work force. In 1969, the unemployment rate was 3.2 percent. If each of the age-sex sub-groups in the work force had maintained its 1969 rate of unemployment while changing in size, the unemployment rate in April, 1976 would have been 3.4 percent.[8] However, the actual average unemployment rate for 1976 was 7.4 percent. Thus, only a small amount of the increase in unemployment can be attributed to demographic changes in the shape of the work force.[9]

### Do women undergo hardship when unemployed?

The second assumption minimizing the seriousness of the unemployment problem holds that just because there are a lot of unemployed people these days it doesn't mean there is a lot of hardship like there was when people sold apples on the streets during the thirties; many of the unemployed, especially women, don't really need to work for economic reasons; besides, what with unemployment benefits and welfare, the government is so generous that nobody really suffers anyway. This general, if somewhat flippant, statement of a commonly held view once again calls to mind Sandy Biggest. Sandy is quite unabashed in admitting that her primary motivations in looking for work are not financial. With her twin airplanes and autos, she is hardly standing in soup lines because she is unemployed.

**Hardship and unemployment—the case of Marilyn Wilson**   If the *Wall Street Journal* had interviewed Marilyn Wilson, one of the respondents interviewed in our April, 1976 metropolitan work force survey, the story would have been very different. Ms. Wilson was laid off from her job as an assembler in a Los Angeles electronics plant. Although she had finished two years of college, she was making only $3.00 an hour at the time she was laid off—an annual salary $1,672 less than the 1974 average for an adult man who had never gone past eighth grade.[10] A thirty-five-year-old widow with three children, she has been unemployed before, once for nine months. This time she was unemployed for a shorter period of time, but even this was a harrowing experience. She describes her heroic efforts to cope financially—cutting down on necessities like food and luxuries like her automobile—and concludes ruefully, "Our standard of living isn't too high so there's not too much to cut out." Her suffering is not merely financial, but psychological as well. She recalls her insomnia, her peevishness toward her children when they would ask for a forbidden luxury like an ice cream cone, her anxiety about how she would be able to pay the rent and whether she would be evicted. She describes the process of looking for a job as an assault on her sense of herself—"A single woman with three children is not considered responsible." Although she had hoped to get into something demanding more skill, she ultimately accepted another menial job as an assembler doing precisely what she had been doing before.

Marilyn Wilson's is hardly the only case of hardship. Dolores Jones, a twenty-seven-year old switchboard operator from Chicago describes her feeling during the eight months she was unemployed: "I was depressed and irritable. I wanted to stay in the house all the time. I didn't want to be around my friends because I felt inferior and had no money to spend with them. . . . You lose all hope for the future. Everything comes to a standstill and you are afraid of tomorrow." For Margaret Wells, a divorced woman in her fifties who has been out of work for two years and barely scrapes by on welfare, it is the loneliness that is excruciating. And for Agnes Little, a fifty-year-old housekeeper who is "too old to do hard work and too young to get senior citizens benefits," the psychological burden has been so devastating that she says she has been constantly depressed and has even contemplated suicide—"I can't see no use for living." Although she has done volunteer work at a hospital in the past, she can no longer do even this because she is afraid to walk alone on the streets of Chicago's West Side and can't afford the fare on the bus.

### Hardships and unemployment—a more systematic assessment

Although the hardships these women have undergone contrast sharply with the fun and security of Sandy Biggest's life, they are isolated cases and are perhaps no more representative than that of our unemployed aviatrix. We can, however, make a more systematic assessment of the assertion that, because so many unemployed women do not actually need to work, and because unemployment insurance and welfare offer financial protection to the economically needy, women do not suffer when they are out of work.

In the course of our analysis we will make an unusual sort of feminist argument. Ordinarily, the task of a feminist analysis is to show that—contrary to the prevailing mythology that the sexes are equally well, or badly, off—women are in some respect worse off then men. So, for example, a feminist might demonstrate that, in general, women are paid less than men with comparable qualifications. In our case, however, the feminist project is somewhat different. When it comes to unemployment, the common wisdom is that women are in better shape than men. In discrediting this myth we shall show that jobless women have no advantage over jobless men; they suffer exactly the same hardships as men do when they are out of work.[11]

### Why do women work?

The contention that most women do not need to work because they are supported by their husbands requires examination. Figure 2 shows that it is indeed the case that in 1975 most work force women were married and living with their husbands. However, 45 percent of these married women, or 26 percent of all work force women, were married to men who earned less than $10,000 in the preceding year, which is just about what the Bureau of Labor Statistics had estimated was necessary for an urban family of four to maintain a low standard of living at the time. If we add these women—who, although living with their husbands, presumably are in the work force out of economic need—to the 42 percent of women who are either single, separated, divorced, or widowed, we find that over two-thirds, 68 percent, of all labor force women work out of economic necessity. These figures are for all work force women, not just unemployed women. Although the government does not publish analogous figures broken down by employment status, we can infer from the fact that unemployment rates for female family heads are disproportionately high, that an even greater share of unemployed women are seeking work out of sheer economic need, rather than out of boredom or a search for fulfillment.[12]

### Do government benefits protect the unemployed from hardship?

Although the majority of women who work do so out of need, there are those who argue that women out of work do not suffer a hardship because government benefits provide a financial cushion to the un-

FIGURE 2    Marital Status and Husband's 1974 Income of Working Women—1975

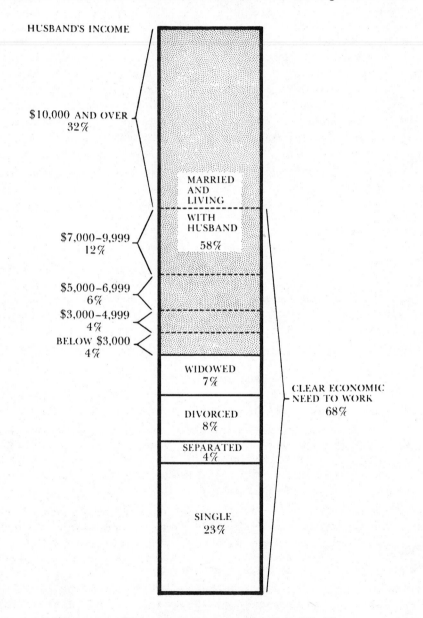

SOURCE: U.S. Department of Labor, Women's Bureau, "Why Women Work."

employed. This contention requires reevaluation. Not all those who are unemployed are entitled to unemployment compensation. Since unemployment compensation, like Social Security, is seen as a form of social insurance for which a worker has paid indirect "premiums" (in the form of a tax on wages paid by his employer), rather than as a form of subsidy like welfare, those who have never worked before or are re-entering the labor force after a hiatus—for example, to raise children or to go back to school—usually do not qualify.

Given this and the added fact that certain categories of workers—such as private household workers—usually do not qualify, we would expect that unemployed men would be more likely than unemployed women to qualify for unemployment compensation. Unfortunately, the government does not break down insured unemployment by sex. However, data from our 1976 unemployment study do lend some confirmation to our expectation. Respondents were asked whether anybody in the household had received either unemployment compensation or one of the forms of government subsidy—welfare or food stamps. As shown in Figure 3-a, unemployed women were less likely than their male counterparts to live in households in which somebody had received benefits from unemployment insurance and more likely to be in households in which somebody had benefited from government subsidies, either welfare or food stamps. Forty-nine percent of the jobless men, but only 36 percent of the unemployed women dwelled in households in which somebody had collected unemployment compensation; on the other hand, 15 percent of the unemployed men, as opposed to 25 percent of the unemployed women lived in households in which somebody had collected welfare or food stamps. When we consider those whose economic needs are greatest—main wage earners with dependent children[13]—the differences between unemployed men and women are even more dramatic: among main wage earners with dependent children, 65 percent of the men, but only 33 percent of the women, lived in households in which somebody had collected unemployment compensation; on the other hand, only 19 percent of the men, but 67 percent of the women, lived in households in which somebody had received food stamps or welfare (see Figure 3-b).[14]

It should be noted that the figures from our study are about households, not individual respondents, and, thus, do not permit us to make inferences about how many unemployed women collect unemployment compensation. Still, the differences between the sexes are sufficiently striking that we can conclude that unemployed women are

**FIGURE 3  Government Benefits Received in Households of Unemployed**

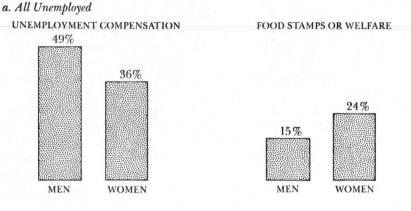

*a. All Unemployed*

UNEMPLOYMENT COMPENSATION      FOOD STAMPS OR WELFARE

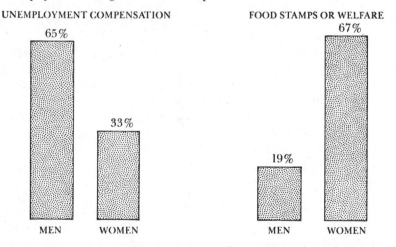

*b. Unemployed Main Wage Earners with Dependent Children*

UNEMPLOYMENT COMPENSATION      FOOD STAMPS OR WELFARE

less likely to be cushioned financially, at least by the insurance forms of unemployment coverage, and are thus more likely to be forced to depend on the subsidy forms of government aid.

**How much hardship do women experience when out of work?**

Using the data from our unemployment study, however, we can test much more directly the propositions that unemployment is no longer

accompanied by deprivation and unhappiness and that whatever suffering occurs is borne by the male unemployed. Those who would
minimize the significance of unemployment among women would
expect unemployment to have less impact on the lives of women than
on the lives of men. Once again, the data do not confirm the expectation. With one significant exception, which will be discussed, the responses of women to unemployment are virtually identical to those
of men.

The data in Figure 4, for example, dispute the notion that unemployment is an experience of no great consequence for women. Unemployed respondents were asked whether, when they considered their
predicament, they got angry or they just thought that that's how life is
sometimes. Presumably, if unemployment were an experience with
greater consequences for men than for women, we would expect a
higher percentage of the men to express anger. We found that, in fact,
there is virtually no difference between the sexes in their propensity to
indicate feelings of anger. If anything, a few more of the unemployed
women, 24 percent, than of the unemployed men, 22 percent, give
voice to feelings of anger.

Respondents were also asked about both their financial and
psychological well-being: satisfaction with income and with life in
general.[15] Two conclusions are immediately apparent from Figure 5-a.
The first is that unemployment is an experience that has a major
impact on people's personal lives: the unemployed are substantially less

**FIGURE 4    Responses to Unemployment**

*When you think about the fact that other people have jobs and you
are out of work, do you get angry or do you think that that is just
how life is sometimes?*

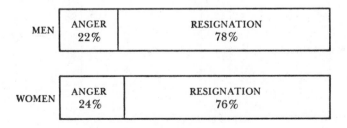

**FIGURE 5**  Dissatisfaction with "Life as a Whole" and with Income

*a. Entire Work Force–Percent Dissatisfied*

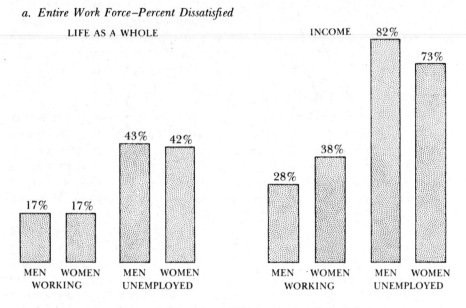

*b. Main Wage Earners with Dependent Children–Percent Dissatisfied*

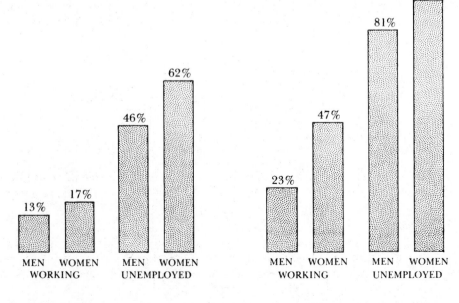

satisfied with both their incomes and their lives in general than are those who are working. Second, it is clear that the effects of unemployment are as significant for women as they are for men. The level of dissatisfaction with life in general is much higher for the unemployed than for those with jobs, but the difference between males and females is nil or minimal.[16] The data on satisfaction with income are slightly more complicated, but the same patterns are apparent. In this case the differences between the sexes are a bit larger: working women are slightly more dissatisfied with their incomes than are working men; unemployed women are somewhat less dissatisfied with their incomes than unemployed men.

When we consider those with the greatest financial needs and responsibilities, main wage earners with dependent children, we see that the women in this group face particularly difficult circumstances. Granted, relatively few of the women in our sample have these responsibilities. (Fourteen percent of the working women, as opposed to 54 percent of the employed men, and 15 percent of the unemployed women, as opposed to 26 percent of the jobless men, are main wage earners with dependent children.) However, as shown in Table 3, these women are likely to be economically pressed. Both employed and unemployed, female chief earners with dependent children have family incomes substantially below those of their male counterparts. As a matter of fact the average family income of households in which an *employed* woman is the main wage earner is actually lower than the

TABLE 3    Average 1975 Family Income: Main Wage Earners with Dependent Children

|  | Men | Women |
|---|---|---|
| Employed | $18,300 | $12,200 |
| Unemployed | 12,900 | 5,900 |

average family income of households in which an *unemployed* man is the main wage earner.[17] In the case of unemployed women in this group, their family incomes are well below the poverty level.

As shown in Figure 5-b, these differences in objective economic circumstances are, not surprisingly, reflected in subjective expressions of dissatisfaction. Among main wage earners with dependent children, the unemployed, regardless of sex, are much more dissatisfied with both their lives in general and their incomes than are those with jobs. In this case, however, there is a difference between the men and the women. Unemployed women who support families are especially unhappy, both financially and psychologically. In addition, working female main earners with dependent children are substantially less satisfied with their incomes, though no less unhappy with their lives in general, than their male counterparts. Once again, this is hardly surprising, given the substantial differences in the real economic circumstances of the men and the women in this category.

What we have found so far is that while the unemployed express far more dissatisfaction with their lives and their incomes than those who are working, there is virtually no difference between the degree of hardship borne by the men and the women, except in the case of main wage earners with dependent children, in which case the women suffer a special disadvantage. There is, however, one respect in which unemployment seems to be a relatively more difficult experience for men than for women. Unemployed respondents were asked whether there had been more tension in the family since they had been unemployed. Respondents were surprisingly frank in saying that there was more family tension as a result of their unemployment. However, in this case there was a difference between the men and the women. As shown in Figure 6, 50 percent of the men, as opposed to 35 percent of the

**FIGURE 6    Unemployment and Family Tension**

*Many people who have been out of work have found that when they were around the house more, there was more family tension. Since you have been unemployed, has there been more tension, less tension, or hasn't it made any difference?*

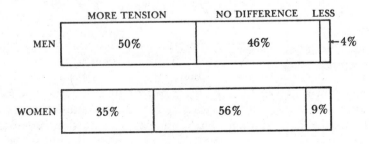

women, indicated that there was more tension. Furthermore, twice as many unemployed women, 9 percent, as unemployed men, 4 percent, said that there was actually less tension in the house. This difference in the response of men and women to the experience of unemployment is quite consistent with the traditional division of labor between men and women. In view of the traditional female role as the keeper of the hearth, it is hardly surprising that, even among women who are used to working, the experience of being around the house all day is less likely to be a difficult one.

## SUMMARY

On the basis of our discussion, it seems that the description of Sandy Biggest as a typical unemployed woman—the affluent and secure suburbanite who seeks fulfillment in the workplace—conveys several misconceptions that distort the interpretation of both unemployment and the motivations and needs of work force women. We have seen that explanations of high unemployment rates in the mid-seventies which rest on the increased number of women in the work force are not satisfactory. Neither the entry into the work force of large numbers of women nor the changing composition of the labor force—the increase in the proportion of so-called "hard-to-employ" women and teenagers—is sufficient to explain the jump in overall unemployment rates in recent years.

Furthermore, the consequences of unemployment for women cannot be dismissed lightly. We examined the contention that unemployment in an era of the welfare state is not accompanied by hardship—especially among women, who are accused of seeking work primarily for psychological rather than economic rewards. We saw that this perspective simply cannot be substantiated. First of all, the majority of women work for precisely the same reason that men do: they need money. Second, we saw that unemployment insurance may not provide the kind of economic protection it is assumed to give. Eligibility for unemployment compensation is by no means universal among the unemployed and, for various reasons, unemployed women are less likely to qualify than unemployed men. Finally, and most importantly, when hardship and dissatisfaction are measured directly, it becomes clear that male and female unemployed suffer equally. With the single exception of increased family tension for unemployed men—a difference readily comprehended given the traditional female role of homemaker—there is virtually no difference between the responses of men and women to the experience of unemployment. Further, the relatively small group of unemployed women who are main wage earners with dependent children seem to suffer special hardship. Thus, once again, it seems clear that unemployment in the 1970's is a serious problem with serious consequences for the men and women who experience it and that it is folly to underestimate its significance for either sex.

## NOTES

1 Christopher A. Evans, *The Wall Street Journal*, February 7, 1977, p. 12.

2 A more detailed account of the government's sampling procedures and the definitions used to classify members of the work force can be found in the Bureau of Labor Statistics pamphlet *How the Government Measures Unemployment*, Report 418 (Washington, D.C.: U.S. Department of Labor, 1973). The report also makes clear how ambiguous cases, such as workers who are waiting to be recalled from layoff, are handled.

3 For an account of this debate see Eileen Shanahan, "Study on Definitions of Jobless Is Urged," *New York Times*, January 11, 1976, p. 36.

4 These data were collected in conjunction with a study at the Center for International Affairs at Harvard University being conducted by Professor Sidney Verba and myself, and were analyzed at the Boston College Computation Center. These data differ in important ways from those collected by the government: They are based on a smaller number of interviews (about 1,350 respondents of whom 550 were unemployed); the respondents were selected from the urban work force and, thus, none lived in small towns or on farms; interviews were conducted over the telephone rather than in person; respondents answered questions for themselves only, whereas in the government's monthly surveys, one member of the household answers for all the others. These differences should be borne in mind because they render these data not strictly comparable to those collected by the government. However, these differences in no way diminish the utility of these data for helping us to understand the experiences of the unemployed.

5 Table 1 also shows that—with the exception of older women, who, like their male counterparts, are retiring at earlier and earlier ages—the trend holds for women of all ages.

6 The controversy about why women have high unemployment rates is too complicated to summarize in this context. It is clear, however, that it is simplistic to assert that it is simply a function of the fact that women like Sandy Biggest who are financially secure can afford to be choosy about what jobs they will accept. First of all, when women are unemployed, the average duration of their unemployment is shorter than it is for men. Also, women are concentrated in occupations for which the pay is low and the working conditions undesirable compared with those occupa-

tions dominated by men of similar educational attainment. Thus, on the face of it, it would not seem that women are fussier than men when they search for a job. For a detailed account of the various explanations that have been advanced for the high rates of unemployment women have traditionally suffered, see Marianne A. Ferber and Helen M. Lowry, "Women: The New Reserve Army of the Unemployed," in *Women and the Workplace*, Martha Blaxall and Barbara Reagan, eds. (Chicago: University of Chicago Press, 1976), pp. 213–32.

7   The technique was suggested by Robert M. Solow, "Macro-Policy and Full Employment," in *Jobs for Americans*, Eli Ginzberg, ed. (Englewood Cliffs, N.J.: Prentice-Hall, Inc., 1976), p. 41.

8   This estimate is based on data from the U.S. Department of Labor, Bureau of Labor Statistics, *Employment and Earnings*, (Washington, D.C.: U.S. Government Printing Office, May 1969), p. 37 and (May 1976), pp. 22–23.

9   Using somewhat different techinques, Kenneth W. Clarkson and Roger E. Meiners reach the same conclusion. "The Spurious Increase in Unemployment Rates," *Policy Review*, 1 (Summer 1977), 30.

10  Based on data in U.S. Department of Labor, Employment Standards Administration—Women's Bureau, "The Earnings Gap between Women and Men" (Washington, D.C.: U.S. Government Printing Office, 1976), p. 10.

11  Obviously, we cannot undertake such an analysis without making comparisons between men and women. Thus, although our interest is in jobless women, we can only understand the degree of their hardship by comparing them with jobless men.

12  Figures about unemployment among household heads are reported in Stephen M. St. Marie and Robert W. Bednarzik, "Employment and Unemployment during 1975," *Monthly Labor Review* (Washington, D.C.: U.S. Government Printing Office, February 1976), 16.

13  The Census Bureau automatically designates the husband as the head of the household of a married couple. But we asked each respondent "Who is usually the main wage earner for this household?" Only a handful of respondents had difficulty choosing a main wage earner. In the overwhelming majority of cases, if a male adult was present he was so designated. In a few cases, married women were chosen as main wage earners. In all cases, however, the designations are the respondents', not ours.

14  The differences between unemployed men and women are even more striking when another form of unemployment insurance—supplemental unemployment benefits (SUB's) from a company or union—is considered. Fifty-two percent of the unemployed men, as opposed to 37 percent of the unemployed women, lived in households in which somebody received one of the automatic forms of benefits— unemployment compensation or SUB's. The analogous figures for main wage earners with dependent children are 70 percent of the men and 33 percent of the women.

15  Respondents were asked the following questions: "Thinking about your life as a whole, would you say that you are very satisfied, somewhat satisfied, somewhat dissatisfied, or very dissatisfied? What about your income, are you very satisfied, somewhat satisfied, somewhat dissatisfied, or very dissatisfied?"

16   In her study of blue-collar workers, Rachelle B. Warren also found unemployment to be as psychologically stressful for women as for men. "The Troubles of Blue Collar Women," *Behavior Today*, 6 (April 14, 1975), 1.

17   This discrepancy in incomes is a function of many factors, among them: the greater availability of unemployment compensation to unemployed men; the higher wages paid to men when they do work; the greater likelihood that a household headed by a man will have a second adult wage earner.

# Evelyn Nakano Glenn and Roslyn L. Feldberg

# Clerical Work: The Female Occupation

## INTRODUCTION

Every weekday, from nine in the morning until five in the evening, in offices all over the country, accounts are checked, correspondence typed, inventories tallied, bills prepared, appointments booked, records filed, and documents reproduced. This "paper work" is carried out in small offices of one or two persons and in corporate headquarters with hundreds of workers; in private industry and in public agencies. Some of the people are all-around workers, carrying out a myriad of different activities each day; others are single-function clerks, repeating the same small task over and over. Some work with paper, pencil and perhaps a manual typewriter; others with highly sophisticated equipment that automatically handles many complex clerical operations.

The ten most frequently found titles of the sixteen million people engaged in clerical activities are secretary, bookkeeper, typist, cashier, receptionist, telephone operator, bank teller, counter clerk, file clerk, and keypunch operator. There are numerous other titles classified as "clerical and kindred" occupations.

All of them are engaged in what is called "white collar" work (to contrast it with blue collar manual labor). Traditional features that have characterized clerical occupations include the following: The work is "clean"—it takes place indoors in relatively safe, clean, and comfortable surroundings and involves no great physical exertion; it is "mental"—it relies to some extent on workers' judgment and requires a literate work force that is able to read, write, and manipulate symbols; it lacks a distinctive product—its outcome is not a concrete commodity, but a flow of documents and communication. In addition, the clerical worker has traditionally enjoyed certain advantages in work life over the factory employee: a fixed weekly salary rather than hourly wages, more regular hours, greater job security, smaller fluctuations in salary during hard times, and greater opportunities for advancement.[1] These supposed advantages conferred on clerical work a status above blue collar, sales, and service occupations. At the same time, clerical work was looked down on from the other white collar occupations—managerial and professional ranks—as more routine, offering less scope for independent decisions. In addition, the workers' hours, movements, and work patterns were subject to closer controls. Although there have been many changes (which will be described later), these traditional features are still prominent in popular conceptions of clerical work.

### Clerical work as a female occupation

Aside from the work itself, the most distinctive feature of clerical work is the gender of the people who do it: They are overwhelmingly female. In the United States in 1977, nearly four out of five (78.9 percent) clerical workers were women. In the two largest categories, secretaries and typists, the proportion rises to 99.1 percent and 96.3 percent. Overall, 12.7 million women were engaged in clerical work in 1977. Over one third (34.7 percent) of all employed women were in this category.[2] Clerical work is therefore, absolutely and proportionally, the largest single occupation for women. The degree to which clerical work is common to women can be confirmed by personal experience. Recently in an all-female discussion section of a sex roles course, the instructors asked how many students had *ever* done office work. Out of 25 women present, 23 raised their hands, including the two instructors.

Considering these numbers and percentages, it can be argued that clerical work represents the *prototypical* female employment experience. We shall explore this tie between women and clerical work by examining a set of inter-related questions: How did clerical work become a large and predominantly female occupation? What have been the consequences on wages, status, and working conditions of women being concentrated in this occupation? What have been the impacts of economic and organizational changes on the role and function of clerical work? What effects have these factors had on the quality of work life for this group of women workers? What is the outlook for, and what are the possible outcomes of, organizing clerical workers? What form might a largely woman-based organizing movement take?

In addressing these questions, the following line of argument is developed. There have been two seemingly contradictory trends in clerical work. The increased size and complexity of organizations mean that internal control, coordination, and communications become increasingly critical for organizational survival. Since these activities rely largely on clerical labor, clerical work takes on a more central role in the economy. But while clerical work has become more important, organizations have pushed toward streamlining and mechanizing the work to increase efficiency in and control over the work process. This has degraded the work, caused the status of clerical workers to fall, and further restricted opportunities for advancement. In summary, clerical workers as a group have become a large and important part of the economy, while their jobs and status have become less desirable. The combination of these two trends can be expected to strengthen the impetus for worker organizing—to use the untapped power of clerical workers as leverage to improve their wages and conditions relative to other groups.

## THE FEMINIZATION OF CLERICAL WORK

Let us now look more closely at the office set-up of a typical large organization. At the top, occupying the highest positions, are the officers and top managers, all men. Each has at least one private secretary and/or administrative assistant. Below them are other managers, mostly men, graded into many levels. Several of them may share the services of a single secretary or call on a common pool of typists and/or clerks. Below them are several specialized sections, divided according to function—for example, accounting, billing, inventory control and so forth. Each section has many woman clerks engaged in routine tasks of record-keeping and communication. The supervisor of each section is frequently a woman promoted from the ranks. In addition there may be a xerox or reproduction unit made up of a mixed group of young men and women, and a computer section made up of women clerks and keypunchers and a male programmer. An office manager, usually a man, may be responsible for overall office organization.

In short, we observe two separate groups of office jobs, divided by sex. Some jobs are clearly "female" (typists, secretaries, keypunchers); others are clearly "male" (vice-president, product manager, sales manager). Furthermore, groups of jobs organized into a hierarchy are also sex-typed. "Management" is a male hierarchy and "clerical" staff is a largely female hierarchy. Each hierarchy is made up of jobs graded by level, representing steps in a career. When a person takes a job she/he occupies not only that particular job, but also a step on a particular career ladder.[3] A person who starts on the clerical career ladder may move up the ranks as she/he gains experience, but she/he rarely is allowed to cross over into a different ladder. Occasionally one hears of a clerk or secretary who becomes an officer in the company. Such stories generate excitement precisely because each is a freak occurrence.

The segregation of jobs by sex is so universal that the office structure is frequently viewed as a "natural" situation. Does not having men in authority and women in subordinate positions reflect their places in society as a whole? Moreover, don't the requirements for clerical and managerial jobs fit the stereotypes for feminine and masculine traits? Women are said to make good clerks because they are conscientious about details, have nimble hands for operating office machines, and are sufficiently submissive to take orders well. In contrast managerial traits—rationality, decisiveness, objectivity and assertiveness—are seen as exclusively masculine qualities.

The appearance of "naturalness" is shattered by an historical survey, which reveals that the sex composition of jobs shifts over time. Jobs that were once predominantly male sometimes come to be occupied primarily by women, and vice versa. When the work force of an occupation changes from largely male or mixed-sex to predominantly female, the process is called *feminization.* Accompanying the shift in sex may be a change in the actual activities of the job or in the traits that are seen as necessary for the job.

Changes in both sex composition and job activities have taken place in the office. The present division of labor in the large office is a fairly recent phenomenon. Until 1910, office work was done almost exclusively by men. Clerks were few in number, constituting only 2.6 percent of the labor force in 1900.[4] Until the last years of the nineteenth century, most businesses were small, local family-owned enterprises.[5] The offices were made up of, at most, a handful of clerks. The head clerk had extensive responsibilities, many of which would be labelled managerial today.[6] His advice might be sought by his employer, because of his familiarity with the details of the business. He might be expected to carry on the business when the owner was absent or away. Braverman notes:

> This picture of the clerk as assistant manager, retainer, confidant, management trainee, and prospective son-in-law can of course be overdrawn. There were clerks—hard-driven copyists in law offices, for example—whose condition and prospects in life were little better than those of dock workers. But by and large, in terms of function, authority, pay, tenure of employment (a clerical position was usually a lifetime post), prospects, not to mention status and even dress, the clerks stood much closer to the employer than to factory labor.[7]

The ground for women's entrance into the offices was prepared during the Civil War, when women were hired to work in the government due to the shortage of male labor. The "experiment" was successful, for the women proved to be good workers and economical, working for only two-thirds to one-half the wages paid to men.[8]

The large-scale entry of women into offices, however, did not begin until the last years of the nineteenth century. This period was one of rapid growth and consolidation of corporations.[9] The economy came to be dominated by enterprises with national markets and substantial financing by banks. The size of organizations mushroomed and with it the volume of communication, record-keeping, and related activities. Hence there was a burgeoning demand for clerical labor, met by an influx of workers into the field. As shown in Table 1, the clerical work force grew from an estimated 91,000 in 1870 to more than 770,000 by 1900, doubling in the next ten-year period to 1,885,000. Except for 1929–35, during the depression, the clerical work force has grown substantially every decade. As impressive as the overall growth was, the most striking trend was the increasing proportion of women. While the size of the occupation increased eightfold between 1870 and 1900, the proportion of women increased 340-fold. The number of women entering clerical work then began to exceed the number of men, so that by the late 1920's a tipping point was reached when over half of all clerical workers were women.

Women, far from being seen as "naturally" suited to office work, were at first considered an oddity. An 1875 engraving depicts the ludicrousness of women in offices by showing them crocheting, dressing each other's hair, reading Harper's Bazaar and spilling ink; a man, presumably the owner, has just walked in and is dumbstruck. A lively debate was carried on in the pages of popular and business magazines from the 1890's through the 1920's by attackers and defenders of women in offices.[10] During the 1920's and 1930's many popular novels and short stories depicted the lives and loves of the "office girl," in which the principal conflict was between romance and marriage vs. career and spinsterhood.[11]

Faced with this skepticism about their desirability, why did increasing numbers of women go into clerical work rather than other occupations? Clearly the large number of jobs created by changes in corporate structure was one necessary condition. In addition, some writers have emphasized the impact of the typewriter, which was invented in 1873.[12] The Remington Company trained women to demonstrate the new machines so that, from the beginning, the machines were operated by women. Typing in offices became identified as a feminine specialty.

Although this may have facilitated women's entry into the field, it would not have made a difference if there were not a large supply of available women to do the work.[13] Women constituted an untapped reservoir of educated and cheap labor. Women in that era were more likely to have finished high school (a requisite) than men.[14] And those men who had the requisite education could find better opportunities elsewhere. In contrast, women with high school educations had few options that were more attractive. Factory and sales jobs were lower in status and in pay.[15] There is also scattered evidence that clerical workers received higher wages, particularly in the early period, than did teachers.[16]

**TABLE 1  Growth of the Clerical Force: 1870–1977 (in thousands)**

|  | 1870 | 1880 | 1890 | 1900 | 1910 | 1920 | 1930 | 1940 | 1950 | 1960 | 1970 | 1977 |
|---|---|---|---|---|---|---|---|---|---|---|---|---|
| Total clerical workers | 91 | 186 | 490 | 770 | 1,885 | 3,311 | 4,274 | 4,847 | 7,635 | 9,783 | 13,714 | 16,106 |
| As % of employed persons | .7% | 1.1% | 2.1% | 2.6% | 5.1% | 8.0% | 9.0% | 9.1% | 12.8% | 14.7% | 17.4% | 17.8% |
| Female clerical workers | 2 | 8 | 83 | 204 | 677 | 1,601 | 2,223 | 2,549 | 4,597 | 6,629 | 10,233 | 12,715 |
| As % of all clerical | 2.4% | 4.3% | 16.9% | 26.5% | 35.9% | 48.4% | 52.0% | 52.6% | 60.2% | 67.8% | 74.6% | 78.9% |

Figures are not strictly comparable due to minor reclassifications of occupational categories.

SOURCES: For the years 1870–1940 total clerical workers and female clerical workers, compiled from Janet M. Hooks, *Women's Occupations Through Seven Decades*, U.S. Department of Labor, Women's Bureau, Bulletin No. 218, Washington D.C., 1947. Table 11A: Occupations of Women Workers, 1870–1940; Table 11B: Occupations of All Workers, 1870–1940.

1870–1940 employed persons from U.S. Bureau of the Census, *Historical Statistics, Abstracts of the U.S.*, Series D57–71.

For the years 1950–1970, U.S. Bureau of the Census, *Statistical Abstract of the U.S.*, 1972 Table 366: "Employed Persons, by Major Occupation Group and Sex: 1950–1972".

For 1977, U.S. Department of Labor, Bureau of Labor Statistics, *Employment and Earnings*, 25 (January, 1978) Table 21: "Employed Persons by Occupation, Sex, and Age".

Part of the reason men had better opportunities was that while clerks were growing more numerous, another category was also increasing in size. Managers were needed to help coordinate the diverse activities and departments of the new organizations. A new stratum of hired managers, replacing the old-style owner-manager, was inserted between the top officers and the clerks. Henceforth this new stratum became the dominant group in the office, taking over the planning and decision making, leading one observer to call this the era of the "managerial revolution."[17]

The rise of managers and the feminization of clerical work fundamentally altered the meaning and status of clerical work. Increasingly, it meant the carrying out of routine tasks planned, set up, and supervised by others. A clerical job came to be viewed less and less as a stepping stone to business success. A survey conducted in the late 1920's showed that 88 percent of the office managers "felt they needed 'clerks who are satisfied to remain clerks'."[18] Thus, women entered the work force in occupations that no longer offered the traditional advantages of white collar jobs: they found themselves in dead-end occupations that were declining in status, and, to make matters worse, wages did not rise as many had expected.

In fact, most writers argue that the wages of clerical workers actually declined in relation to manual labor, both in the early period and in the years after World War II.[19] Evidence on this point is scattered. Although available data indicate a fall in *average* office wages compared to *average* factory wages over the last 90 years, the degree and timing of the fall are difficult to pin down. Data from different historical periods are not comparable because the definitions of office work sometimes differ and men's and women's wages are not reported separately.

Prior to 1920, we find no systematic evidence of decline. National wage data for the years 1890 to 1926 (shown in Table 2) indicate marked fluctuations in the relative wage advantage of clerical workers in manufacturing and steam railways over other wage earners in those industries. Overall, however, the clerical workers earned substantially more than other wage earners during the entire 36-year period.[20] Data on postal employees and government employees (not shown in the table) indirectly confirm the relatively higher clerical salaries during this same period.

It is only after 1920 that there are systematic data that separate men's and women's wages. For the period from 1920 through World War II,

**TABLE 2**  Average Yearly Wages for Clerical and Wage Workers in Manufacturing and Steam Railways, 1890–1926

|  | 1890 | 1900 | 1910 | 1920 | 1926 |
|---|---|---|---|---|---|
| Clerical workers in manufacturing and steam railways | 848 | 1011 | 1156 | 2160 | 2310 |
| Wage earners in manufacturing | 439 | 435 | 558 | 1358 | 1309 |
| Wage earners in steam railways | 560 | 548 | 677 | 1817 | 1613 |
| Clerical wages as proportion of manufacturing | 193.2% | 232.4% | 207.2% | 159.0% | 176.5% |

SOURCE: U.S. Bureau of the Census, *Historical Statistics of the United States, Colonial Times to 1970*, Bicentennial Edition, Part 2, (Washington, D.C.: U.S. Government Printing Office, 1975), Series D, pp. 779–793.

**TABLE 3**  Average Weekly Wages for Office Workers and All Workers* in New York Manufacturing Industries, 1914–1947

|  | 1914 | 1924 | 1934 | 1944†† | 1947 |
|---|---|---|---|---|---|
| Office worker | $19.18 | $33.58 | $32.45 | $42.99 | $47.74 |
| Women office workers | ** | 21.29 | 21.15 | 34.60 | 40.76 |
| All factory workers | 11.82† | 26.22 | 21.97 | 47.71 | 53.96 |
| All women factory workers | ** | 16.65 | 14.90 | 38.46 | 39.62 |

* Including office workers
**Breakdown by sex not available
† Average for last 7 months of the year
††Wages for years after 1939 are not comparable with earlier years because of some changes in classification.
SOURCE: New York State Department of Labor, *Handbook of New York Labor Statistics 1948*, Special Bulletin No. 226, 1949, Tables D4 and D12.

the most systematic data were collected by New York State, which surveyed office workers employed in factories as well as all workers employed by these establishments. Table 3 presents information for five representative years. Note that clerical women during the entire period earned much less than clerical men (usually 50 to 60 percent) and somewhat less than factory men. The only group over which they have an advantage is factory women, and this declines over time.

In the post World War II era, there is much clearer evidence of an overall decline (not due to a greater proportion of low-wage women). As Table 4 shows, clerical women's wages declined markedly in relation to men's blue collar wages. Their advantage over blue collar women was also reduced. As a result, by the 1970's the average combined

TABLE 4    Median Yearly Wage or Salary Income for Full Year Clerical Workers and Operatives by Sex, 1939–1976

|  | 1939 | 1949 | 1960 | 1970 | 1976 |
|---|---|---|---|---|---|
| Clerical workers: Women | $1072 | $2235 | $3586 | $5539 | $8128 |
| Clerical workers: Men | 1564 | 3136 | 5247 | 8652 | 12843 |
| Operatives: Women | 742 | 1920 | 2970 | 4465 | 6649 |
| Operatives: Men | 1268 | 2924 | 4977 | 7644 | 11688 |
| Women clerical workers: Wages as percent of men operatives | 84% | 76% | 72% | 72% | 69% |
| Women clerical workers: Wages as percent of women operatives | 144% | 116% | 121% | 124% | 122% |

SOURCES: For 1949, U.S. Bureau of the Census, *1950 Census of the Population of the United States: Special Reports*, Vol. 4, P-E No. 1B, Table 20: "Income in 1949 of the Experienced Civilian Labor Force Who Worked 50–52 Weeks."

For all other years, U.S. Bureau of the Census, *Current Population Reports*, Series P-60, No. 69, Table A-10 (for 1939 and 1960), No. 80, Table 55 (for 1970), and No. 107 (Advance Report), Table 7 (for 1976).

The figures given for all years except 1949 are for *full-time*, full-year workers. Those for 1949 are for all full-year workers.

male-female clerical wages were lower than the average combined male-female blue collar wages. The consequences of this erosion in wages for clerical workers is discussed later in this article.

## THE FUNCTIONS OF CLERICAL WORK

The role of clerical work in organizations and in the economy has been altered as well as increased over time. In the early stages of industrialization, the accounting, record keeping, and other office operations were incidental to the main productive activities of a company. The amount of clerical labor expended for a given unit of goods produced was relatively small. In more advanced stages of capitalism, however, the accounting and record keeping functions become much more complex. The number of intermediate stages between production and consumption—wholesaling, transportation, advertising, marketing—increased and at each stage clerical operations need to be performed. Finally:

> Just as in some industries the labor expended upon marketing begins to approach the amount expended upon the production of the commodities being sold, so in some industries the labor expended upon the mere transformation of the form of value (from the commodity form into the form of money or credit)—including the policing, the cashiers and collection work, the recordkeeping, the accounting, etc.—begins to approach or surpass the labor used in producing the underlying commodity or service.[21]

In short, in large-scale modern organizations, clerical operations are no longer incidental functions, but important processes in their own right.

An equally important trend in the past quarter century has been a shift of economic growth from manufacturing to the service and financial sectors. These sectors rely on clerical labor in the same way that manufacturing industries rely on blue collar labor—for the production of the main goods for exchange. The so-called "office industries" (principally banking, insurance and finance) deal almost solely with the accounting and transfer of values. To a lesser, but still considerable extent, service industries and public agencies—such as educational institutions and auto registration bureaus—rely heavily on office functions to do their work. Thus they become "semi-clerical" industries. The office and "semi-clerical" industries together now employ a larger and larger share of the work force.

The sheer numbers of workers employed in clerical work have made it important to the economy. But the services the "office" and "semi-clerical" industries provide to other sectors of the economy have made these industries vital even for basic production activity. The net result is that clerical work is increasingly central to the operation of the economy as a whole.

These developments constitute what has been called a paper work revolution. The incredible growth of these clerical occupations in turn has significance for issues of gender equality. Women have traditionally been seen as an auxiliary work force, a secondary group of workers who carry out the least essential activities, while men carry out the central ones. The paper work revolution changes that pattern. Functions previously seen as auxiliary are now central to the running of industrial organizations, and it is women who are carrying out these functions. For the first time since the early 1800's women predominate in a job category that is central to the industrial economy. They can no longer be viewed simply as auxiliary workers. As a collectivity, therefore, women clerical workers have a great deal of potential—but as yet unrealized—power, perhaps equal to that of male production workers.

## THE CHANGING CONDITIONS IN THE OFFICE

The realization of this potential power is made problematic, however, by a second and related trend. The very size and centrality of clerical operations has made managers eager to bring office work under closer managerial control.[22] As a result of their efforts to do so, the features once distinctive to clerical work are being eroded and the line between it and manual work is being blurred.[23]

Most people are aware of the principle of subdivision as it applies to the organization of blue collar production. Tasks are broken down into small segments so that each worker does one part of the overall work. An unskilled worker can be trained quickly to carry out these narrow tasks and should the worker leave, she/he can be easily replaced by another unskilled worker. Mechanization speeds up the work by substituting machine power for human energy. The pace of the machine controls the pace of the work. With more sophisticated machinery, many operations can be carried out automatically.

These same principles of subdivision and mechanization can be applied to paper work, and have been since the rise of the large office. The initial thrust for reorganization of clerical work occurred in the "office" industries. Operations such as handling correspondence were studied and then standardized. Where possible the operation was divided into sub-tasks assigned to different pools of workers. By the second decade of the century scientific management was introduced into office routines.[24] Extensive time and motion studies were conducted on the minutest details—opening file drawers, taking off a paper clip, and so forth. Office machines, both simple and complex, were also introduced, but more slowly. Extensive mechanization and automation occurred after World War II.[25]

These changes in the office have been uneven. There are numerous small offices today that scarcely differ from their nineteenth-century counterparts. Even in large corporations, pockets of the "preindustrial office" have survived. The private secretaries have been largely exempt from the rationalizing trend, performing a variety of tasks from composing letters and answering the telephone to running personal errands. They have frequent personal contact with their superiors. Since the secretary's whole position is defined by her attachment to a particular person, some observers have labelled her the "office wife".[26] This personal tie to her boss effectively screens her from organizational scrutiny of her activities. Until recently corporations were willing to tolerate this situation, even encouraging it for the sake of managerial morale. Having a secretary to carry out time-wasting routine chores was a perquisite of executive status.

In recent years the drive for control over employees' time and output has taken on added momentum. The first step in control is to gather the scattered secretaries and place them in a pool where they can be centrally supervised. Private secretaries are increasingly reserved for the highest ranks of managers. Lesser lights must make do with the shared services of pools.

Pools of typists and clerks have existed for some time, but now their use is more extensive and they are more highly organized. We observed an example of the new pooling system in a branch office of a firm we will call Public Utility. The office was reorganized when an IBM word processing system was installed.

Middle level managers (called clients in this system) share the services of two major pools of clerks. The Word Processing unit, made up of 10 to 12 women, does all typing. Clients submit material to be typed on dial dictation equipment; the word processing clerks transcribe the material into typed form, using semi-automatic machines. The work flow is continuous, unvaried and fast. The Administrative Service Center performs all non-typing services, such as answering phones and scheduling appointments. Instructions for carrying out tasks are written in manuals. For example, precise instructions are given for routing phone calls and delivering the mail. A third group does all copying and reproduction work.

These new pooling arrangements have been facilitated by technological advancements. For example, output machines with memory capacities can type over a hundred form letters an hour, inserting names, addresses and greetings from a computer list. However, the impetus to subdivide the work process can best be understood not as a response to technological possibilities but as part of a drive to attain control over the cost of clerical services and to assure reliability and standardization in the work process. Since the automated systems require workers to use standard forms, they also make it easier for management to trace errors and assess each worker's productivity, whether it be lines typed or phone calls answered.

## THE EXPERIENCES OF CLERICAL WORKERS

What impact do conditions have on the workers themselves? How do the women feel about their jobs? In 1975 and 1976 we conducted in-depth interviews of 30 clerical workers in a variety of jobs in many different organizations. Their responses were as varied as their own situations.

**Pay**  Women clerical workers are not poorly paid in comparison to other women workers, but their wages reflect the disadvantaged position of women in relation to men. In 1975, the median wages for women clerical workers employed full-time year round was $7,562. This figure was only 68.0 percent of the median wages for male factory operatives whose jobs require less education and training; and it was only 62.3 percent of that earned by male clerical workers.[27] Another important yardstick is the standard of living made possible by wages. According to U.S. Department of Labor estimates, in 1975 a single person in the urban United States spent between $5,668 and $5,821 to live on an intermediate budget.[28] This figure excluded state and local taxes and disability payments. If these expenditures are added in, we see that median clerical salaries were sufficient to maintain a moderate standard of living for a single individual. They were clearly inadequate for a woman head of household with two dependents, who needed between $10,416 and $11,795 on an intermediate budget.[29] Thus, most clerical women with families are dependent on another person's income to maintain a moderate standard of living.

The salaries among the women we interviewed in the Boston area ranged from $5,000 and $13,600 with a mean of $8,998 and a median of $9,074. These figures are higher than the national average. However, the cost of living in Boston is also higher. The intermediate budget for a single individual took from $6,693 to $6,874, and a head of household with two dependents needed from $12,301 to $13,929.[30] Thus, the women we interviewed were representative, vis-a-vis the cost of living, of women nationally. It is also important to note that five of the thirty women (17.7 percent) earned *below* the intermediate standard for single individuals. Half of all the women felt their wages should be higher, primarily because they felt their work was worth more. The responses of the women who judged their salaries appropriate were interesting. Nine said that the work they did or their own qualifications were not worth more, and five that other women doing comparable work received similar wages. Perhaps these workers internalized the low value accorded their work by society and the company, accepted other women's low wages as the appropriate comparison, or realized that they had little hope of earning more. Whatever the reason, their acceptance dissipated the feeling that they deserved a living wage.

**Deskilled jobs**    Clerical jobs have been deskilled in two ways. First, the *variety* of skills required in all-around jobs is not needed in the growing number of limited function jobs. An Administrative Services clerk, who had formerly worked in smaller offices, complained that she was unable to keep up her typing skills. All typing was done in the Word Processing Unit. She did not want to type fulltime, so she did not get to type at all. Second, the *level* of skills required is degraded. Complete accuracy is not essential in typing because the new equipment corrects errors semi-automatically. Even literacy, long a hallmark of clerical occupations, is being programmed out of some traditional specialties. The file clerk in automated systems does not need to know the sequence of the alphabet or numbers. She simply places the documents to be filed on the plate of the machine as quickly as possible.

**Over-qualified workers**  A related outcome is that many women feel they have abilities and skills that go unused. Many women are simply *over-educated.* Our sample of 30 women included 16 with at least some college. This proportion is much higher than in the general clerical population; nevertheless, nationally, 28.4 percent of all clerical workers do have at least some college and 6.7 percent of them have four or more years (Table 5). As one of the college-educated women in our sample noted "the things on the job description, any sixth grader could do." College-educated women are not alone in feeling their jobs are too limited. Many of the non-college women are *over-skilled.* They've received training in stenography or other specialties in high school or vocational institutions. These skills are either obsolete or in limited demand because of the new systems. The women expressed their convictions of being underused by such statements as "I could do more"; "I can handle more responsibility"; "There's no way I would not welcome more challenging work"; or "I feel misplaced."

**TABLE 5**   **Educational Attainment of Women Clerical Workers, March 1977**

| | Total employed (thousands) | Less than 12 years | 12 years | 1-3 years college | 4 years college | 5 or more years college |
|---|---|---|---|---|---|---|
| | | | Years of school completed | | | |
| Number | 12,487 | 1,372 | 7,492 | 2,790 | 696 | 136 |
| Percent | 100.0 | 11.0 | 60.0 | 22.3 | 5.6 | 1.1 |

SOURCE: U.S. Department of Labor, Bureau of Statistics, *Educational Attainment of Workers, March, 1977*, Special Labor Force Report 209 (Washington, D.C.: U.S. Government Printing Office, 1977), Table J.

**Career ladders**

Because of the sex-segregated office hierarchies described previously, clerical jobs do not link up to professional or managerial ladders. Many workers find themselves at the tops of their ladders in a few years, with nowhere to go. Although there are few advantages to staying in the job, there are also few benefits from changing. The worker typically finds she can only move horizontally or downward. One woman expressed frustration that she was at a dead-end in her current job, then concluded "It took me ten years of seniority to get a month's vacation. If I left and went to another job, I don't know how long it would take."

### Job security

Just as a blue collar assembly line worker can be easily replaced, the clerical worker in a highly rationalized clerical job finds she has a precarious hold on her position. Caplow points out the basic similarities of semiskilled factory work and clerical jobs in large offices in this regard:

> The modern technics (sic) of job classification and personnel selection, developed in connection with large-scale production, are designed above all to facilitate the interchangeability of personnel. One method of ensuring interchangeability is to reduce each complex operation to a series of simple operations which require no extraordinary ability. . . . At the same time, the formal qualifications required for employment are standardized by the educational process, so that there are comparatively few differences that matter between one worker and another.[31]

Many clerical workers are acutely aware that they are expendable. A worker notes "We laugh around here and say 'Clericals? They're the throw-aways.' I feel like clerical workers are like machines. When the machines break down, you just replace them." An insurance company clerk says, "I'm a number. That's all anybody is at X. If you die, they replace you the next day. You can always be replaced." A clerk in Administrative Services describes the manuals the clerks are required to write, listing their duties and specifying exactly how each of her clients likes to have his mail delivered. She says "If I'm out, my fill-in should be able to do what I do. . . . It's like writing yourself out of a job."

### Control over the worker

The private secretary and limited function clerk illustrate the two main forms of control over the office worker. The secretary experiences personal control by her immediate boss. By definition, she is doing a good job if he is pleased by her performance. By the same token, the boss screens the secretary from direct company control. Several secretaries mentioned that their bosses safeguarded their time or protected them from unpleasant company assignments. The basis of control, therefore, is highly personal, with all of the problems of arbitrariness that this entails.

In contrast, clerks in pooled arrangements are subject primarily to impersonal controls. By this we mean that formal rules are applied (e.g. clocking in) and external checks of performance are built into the work routine. The supervisor makes no special effort to keep track of workers' performance—the worker is, for example, simply visible at her designated post. A supervisor at a large insurance company claims she can tell at a glance whether one of her charges is doing her assigned task. The total output of a clerk is automatically counted by her machine.

While the secretary can get angry at her boss for exercising control, a word processing clerk cannot easily target her resentment. She may be angry at her supervisor, while realizing that the supervisor has no real power, or feel generally angry at "them" (the anonymous big bosses). Frequently, the anger is experienced as a pervasive sense of tension or a feeling of being in a fishbowl.

### The meaning of work

The many negative job conditions do not mean women find no meaning or satisfaction in their jobs. We found that, on the whole, the women were committed to working, if not to their specific jobs. In addition to the income, which they clearly saw as most important, the women found meaning in three areas. First, work provided opportunities to form and maintain social connections. Second, it gave direction and purpose to their lives by structuring their time and getting them involved in "useful" activity. Third, for some women, particularly married women with children, it provided an identity separate from their family roles.[37]

### Coping

Since the women sought meaning in their work, which their particular jobs sometimes frustrated, they responded in a number of ways. A few, whose jobs allowed the latitude, informally expanded their jobs, gradually taking over added responsibilities. (They were not given titles or salaries commensurate with their actual activities). Some, particularly the college graduates, intended to leave the clerical field altogether. The majority, however, felt they had limited options and tried to find what satisfactions they could on the job—by being particularly "nice" to each other, by viewing the materials they typed as critical to the company, or by simply doing their often limited jobs well. At the same time, they protected themselves from attempts to exploit their eagerness to do something meaningful. They shrugged off compliments and rejected ploys designed to get them to do extra work.

## ORGANIZING

None of the women in our study spontaneously suggested organizing or unionization as a possible strategy for dealing with her problems. Clerical work is the largest category of wage workers who remain non-unionized. Experienced labor organizers generally consider clerical workers the most difficult segment of labor to organize, and have made relatively little effort to do so. A variety of arguments have been put forward to explain the difficulties of organizing them. Most explanations focus on two characteristics: their gender and their lack of worker consciousness.

1. One line of argument is that women see themselves as secondary workers. Their primary commitment is to their present or future family roles. Therefore, their wages and working conditions are not of sufficient importance to motivate them to join unions.[33]

2. A second line of argument focuses on women's socialization. Women are trained to take a subordinate position to men. Their situation in the office does not strike them as unfair, thus they are unlikely to organize in opposition to authority.[34]

A related argument is that, also as a result of socialization, women accept exploitation because they've been trained to think it unladylike to fight back. According to one writer:

> . . . a great majority of office workers are female and have been socialized into anti-militant values, militancy having been equated by their parents with unfeminine attitudes. Furthermore, the single office girl might prefer the prestige of a white collar job to the demotion in status involved in joining a union and thereby becoming less attractive (perhaps even declasse) to the young executive she had her eye on.[35]

The above quote also illustrates the common view that clerks fail to identify as workers because they identify with management. In the case of men, it is because they aspire to managerial positions;[36] in the case of women, it is because they hope to *marry* into management.[37] Lockwood cites a union official who says the personal relations between managers and clerical workers make it unlikely that they will unite to oppose management.[38] In addition, common dress and working conditions, and overlapping job activities encourage clerks to see themselves as part of management.

A further belief illustrated by the above quote and elaborated by Lockwood is that clerical workers are particularly status conscious.[39] Their marginal social positions make them snobbish and anxious about their status. To protect themselves they set up artificial barriers between themselves and the working class.

More and more women see themselves as serious, long-term workers. Out of the 30 women we interviewed, 27 planned to be working five years in the future, some outside of clerical work, but most within it. This is a realistic expectation, given the emerging pattern for women of more continuous participation in the labor force. More than half of all women between the ages of 18 and 64 are employed.[40] Several trends point to women spending more years in the labor force. First, single women have traditionally high rates of employment and more young women are remaining single today. Second, labor force participation among married women with children has increased phenomenally over the past 15 years. Thirdly, women are having fewer children, which means they will be taking fewer years out for child-bearing and child-rearing.[41] In fact, a special study of work life expectancies indicated that the work life of women born in 1970 can be expected to average 22.9 years.[42] Certainly the women we interviewed took their earning power seriously. Being able to make a living, being economically independent, were important sources of pride and self esteem.

Whether women consider union activity "unfeminine" is harder to determine directly. What is clear is that about half of the women we interviewed, when asked directly, supported the idea of a union. Those who opposed the idea expressed concern that the unions represented another outside force, another "they," who would impose conditions they themselves might not want. Such an expression can hardly be taken to mean that women accept subordination easily. Finally we note that nationally 61 percent of clerical workers in 1970 were married.[43] It is unlikely that they reject union activity for the sake of snaring a manager into marriage.

We found little evidence that clerks identify with management in opposition to their own self-interest. To be sure, private secretaries took personal pride in their bosses' successes. However, clerks in other categories were keenly aware of the dichotomy between boss and worker. Many of them resented what they perceived as attempts by management to manipulate them through false compliments. Others complained about having no say over where they worked or what they did. They could be transferred from one section to another, or their jobs changed at will. This powerlessness of the individual worker was one of the main reasons given for supporting a union. As one worker said, "If we had unions, we could stick together and help each other instead of one person defending herself." Another woman displayed a wily cynicism about managerial pronouncements. She said that when the company instituted pools, workers were told that the new systems would be more democratic. She shrewdly pointed out that while a secretary received $150 a week, a pool clerk got only $120.

We would argue, therefore, that female character and false consciousness are not impenetrable barriers to organizing. The fact remains that clerical workers have not been organized. Why? An important part of the answer is that not much effort has been put into organizing them. Many are employed in sectors of the economy that are newer and not unionized—for example, service industries.[44] Unions have generally concentrated on improving wages and benefits and increasing membership in industries in which they are already established, rather than organizing new industries.

Another part of the answer lies in the labor market situation faced by women. Most explanations of the absence of unions overlook this factor. Women confront a sex-segregated labor market. They are crowded into a few sex-typed occupations. The occupations dominated by women are those in which it is difficult to control entry (i.e., monopolize jobs) and in which there is a surplus of qualified workers who are not in the labor force at a given time.[45] Any worker can be easily replaced from this available labor pool. Under these conditions it is difficult for women to develop collective strength.

Still another part of the answer lies in the composition of the clerical work force. Clerical workers are extremely diverse; they come from widely varied educational and social backgrounds. Our own sample reflects the range: father's occupations covered the 13 major groupings used by the U.S. Census. Their own educations varied from less than high school to postgraduate college degrees. Because of the limited job options open to women, due to sex-typing of jobs, women with diverse qualification end up in a common occupation. Their current situations were equally varied. Among the married women in our study, some were married to professionals, others to semi-skilled or unskilled workers. This fits the national picture. Nationally, of all married female clerical workers with employed husbands, 52 percent have white collar husbands and 41 percent have blue collar husbands.[46] Since they lack a shared class situation, it should not be surprising that they lack a sense of common identity.

Despite the barriers to organizing, we end with the prediction that clerical workers will organize on a large scale. Our prediction is based partly on the changes in the office we described. The common disadvantages that women face in the office may become more important than the lack of common class background. There is some evidence that employed women come to judge their social class from their own occupations, rather than their husband's or their father's.[47]

In addition, there has been a general trend toward unionization among white collar workers, and growing efforts have been made to organize clerical workers. Organized labor has stepped up its campaign to organize state and municipal employees. They have also begun making in-roads in the private sector. In January, 1978 more than 1200 members of Local 29 of the Office and Professional Employees Union in Oakland, California ended a three-month strike against a major insurance company after obtaining a satisfactory settlement on work conditions.[48] Grassroots groups have sprung up among women office and service workers in the larger cities. Active groups include Nine-to-Five in Boston; Women Office Workers in New York; Women Employed in Chicago, and Union Wage and Women Organized for Employment in San Francisco. Some of these grassroots groups have evolved a second structure, locals of established unions or separate unions affiliated with internationals. In Boston, Local 925 of the Service Employees International Union was a spin-off of the original Nine-to-Five group. However, Nine-to-Five continues as a separate organization that focuses on politicizing activities.

There are two possible, but not mutually exclusive, outcomes of clerical organizing. One is that clerical workers will receive increased material benefits in the form of higher wages, shorter hours, better medical insurance, and other traditional union goals. Another is that the quality of work life will be improved through, for example, changes in the organization of work activities.

The history of organized labor would indicate that the first set of goals is likely to be achieved, but not the second. However, the degree to which issues of quality of work life are addressed will depend partly on which forms of organizing predominate. The fact that most of the workers in this case are women and that there is a women's movement to provide a model offers some possibilities. The women's movement has given women a degree of common consciousness never before reached—an awareness of oppression based on gender. It has provided many women with an experience of collective struggle that can be directly transferred to worker organizing. The most successful grassroots organizing—which might best be called preunionizing movements—borrow heavily from the techniques of the women's movement. These include the use of group support to help women identify common problems; consciousness raising activities such as public speak-outs; and interpersonal strategies for changing worker-boss relationships. Organizing based on women's movement techniques and some of its ideology is more likely to lead to demands for fundamental changes in the work place than if more traditional approaches are used.

It is an exciting future to contemplate. When clerical women organize widely, they will become one of the largest groups within the union movement. They may well alter the issues and concerns addressed by organized labor.

**NOTES**

1   U.S. Department of Labor, *Trends of Earnings Among White Collar Workers During the War*, Bureau of Labor Statistics Bulletin No. 783 (Washington, D.C.: U.S. Government Printing Office, 1944). Also Grace Coyle, "Women in the Clerical Occupations," *The Annals,* American Academy of Political and Social Sciences 143 (1929), 180–87.

2   *Employment and Earnings*, January 1978, pp. 151–53.

3   See Rosabeth Kanter, "Women and the Structure of Organizations," in Marcia Millman and Rosabeth Kanter, eds., *Another Voice* (New York: Anchor Books, 1975). Also, Rosabeth Kanter, *Men and Women of the Corporation* (New York: Basic Books, 1977).

4   The best descriptions of the historical changes in office work are: Margery Davies, "Women's Place Is at the Typewriter: The Feminization of the Clerical Labor Force," *Radical America*, 8 (1974), 1–28; Harry Braverman, *Labor and Monopoly Capital* (New York: Monthly Review Press, 1974), Chapter 15; C. Wright Mills, *White Collar* (New York: Oxford University Press, 1956).

5 Daniel Bell, "The Breakup of Family Capitalism," in *The End of Ideology*, rev. ed. (New York: Collier Books, 1961).

6 Mary Kathleen Benet, *The Secretarial Ghetto* (New York: McGraw-Hill, 1972).

7 Braverman, *Labor and Monopoly Capital*, p. 294.

8 Davies, "Women's Place Is at the Typewriter."

9 Bell, "The Breakup of Family Capitalism."

10 Davies, "Women's Place Is at the Typewriter."

11 Judith Smith, "The New Woman Knows How to Type: Some Connections Between Sexual Ideology and Clerical Work, 1900–1930," paper presented at the Berkshire Conference on the History of Women, Radcliffe College, 1974.

12 Writers who have made this point include: Coyle, "Women in the Clerical Occupations"; Davies, "Women's Place Is at the Typewriter"; Janet Hooks in *Women's Occupations Through Seven Decades*, Women's Bureau Bulletin No. 218 (Washington, D.C.: U.S. Government Printing Office, 1944); Bruce Bliven, Jr. in *The Wonderful Writing Machine* (New York: Random House, 1954); and Elizabeth F. Baker in *Technology and Woman's Work* (New York: Columbia University Press, 1964).

13 The introduction of new technologies is often related to changes in the sex composition of an occupation. Jo Freeman (personal communication) points out that sometimes a new labor force is introduced because the older group of workers will not or cannot use the new technology. We would argue against strictly technological determination, however. The replacement of frame-spinning machinery with mule-spinning machinery in the 1840's coincided with a changeover from a predominately female to a predominately male labor force in textiles. Mule-spinning equipment was considered unsuitable for women, partly because it was awkward to use with long skirts. Mule spinning had been widely used for many years in England prior to its use in the U.S. Due to the shortage of male labor, its introduction into American factories was delayed for many years. Thus, we would argue that a changeover in labor force accompanying technological change occurs only when there is an available alternate labor pool. See Edith Abbot, *Women in Industry* (New York: D. Appleton and Company, 1910), especially pp. 91–92.

14 Valerie K. Oppenheimer. *The Female Labor Force in the United States: Demographic and Economic Factors Governing Its Growth and Changing Composition*, Population Monograph Series No. 5 (Berkeley: University of California, 1970).

15 Robert Smuts, *Women and Work in America*, rev. ed. (New York: Schocken Books, 1971).

16 U.S. Bureau of the Census, *Historical Statistics of the United States, Colonial Times to 1970*, Bicentennial Edition, Part 2 (Washington, D.C.: U.S. Government Printing Office, 1975), 168. Also Elyce Rotella, "Occupational Segregation and the Supply of Women to the American Clerical Labor Force, 1870–1930," paper presented at the Berkshire Conference on the History of Women, Radcliffe College, 1974.

17 James Burnham, *The Managerial Revolution* (New York: John Day, 1941).

18 Coyle, "Women in the Clerical Occupations."

19 For example, Braverman, *Labor and Monopoly Capital*; Mills, *White Collar*; and Coyle, "Women in the Clerical Occupations."

20   Braverman (*Labor and Monopoly Capital*) uses tne 1900 data on manufacturing and steam railway workers and contrasts it with 1971 data on clerical and manual wages to illustrate the erosion of clerical wages. The contrast implies a dramatic decline over the 70 years. As Table 2 shows, the 1900 figures are the point of maximum difference, 56 percent greater than 1890, thus accentuating the apparent decline of clerical wages.

21   Braverman, *Labor and Monopoly Capital*, p 302.

22   Alfred Vogel, "Your Clerical Workers Are Ripe for Unionism," *Harvard Business Review*, 49 (1971), 48–54.

23   Evelyn N. Glenn and Roslyn L. Feldberg, "Degraded and Deskilled: The Proletarianization of Clerical Work," *Social Problems*, 25 (1977), 52–64.

24   Influential proponents of scientific management in offices were William Henry Leffingwell (*Scientific Office Management* (Chicago: A. W. Shaw Company, 1917)), and Lee Galloway (*Office Management: Its Principals and Practices*. (New York: The Ronald Press Company, 1918)).

25   Jon M. Shepard, *Automation and Alienation: A Study of Office and Factory Workers* (Cambridge, Mass.: M.I.T. Press, 1972).

26   Benet, *The Secretarial Ghetto* and Kanter, *Men and Women of the Corporation*.

27   U.S. Department of Labor, Bureau of Labor Statistics, *U.S. Working Women: A Databook*, Bulletin 1977 (Washington, D.C.: U.S. Government Printing Office, 1977), Table 39.

28   See U.S. Department of Labor, Bureau of Labor Statistics, *Autumn 1975 Urban Family Budgets and Comparative Indexes for Selected Urban Areas* (Boston, Mass., May 1976). Budget figures are presented for lower, intermediate, and higher budgets for families of four. Figures for single individuals and single heads of families are computed from these basic figures using equivalence scales from Table A-1, *Revised Scale of Equivalent Income for Urban Families of Different Size, Age, and Composition* which is available from regional Bureau of Labor Statistics offices.

29   *Ibid.*

30   *Ibid.*

31   Theodore Caplow, *The Sociology of Work* (New York: McGraw-Hill, 1954), p. 85.

32   Roslyn L. Feldberg and Evelyn N. Glenn, "Category or Collectivity: The Consciousness of Clerical Workers," paper presented at the Meetings of the Society for the Study of Social Problems, Chicago, 1977.

33   Albert Blum, *Management and the White Collar Union* (New York: American Management Association, 1964).

34   *Ibid.*

35   Elliot Krause, *The Sociology of Occupations* (Boston: Little-Brown, 1971), p. 86.

36   Mills, *White Collar*.

37   Krause, *The Sociology of Occupations*.

38   David Lockwood, *The Black-coated Worker* (London: Unwin University Books, George Allen & Unwin, Ltd., 1958).

39   *Ibid.*

40   *1975 Handbook of Women Workers,* p. 3.

41   Allyson Sherman Grossman, "Women in the Labor Force: The Early Years," *Monthly Labor Review,* 98 (1975), 3–9.

42   Howard N. Fullerton and James J. Byrne, "Length of Working Life for Men and Women, 1970," *Monthly Labor Review,* 99 (1976), 31–35.

43   U.S. Bureau of the Census (1973), Table 31.

44   Martin Oppenheimer, "Women Office Workers: Petty-Bourgeoisie or New Proletarians?", *Social Scientist,* Monthly Journal of the Indian School of Social Sciences, Trivandrum, Kerala, #40–41.

45   See Caplow, *The Sociology of Work,* Chapter 10, for a discussion of these and related points. An economist, Mary Stevenson, in "Wage Differences Between Men and Women: Economic Theories," in Ann H. Stromberg and Shirley Harkess, eds., *Women Working* (Palo Alto, Ca.: Mayfield Publishing Company, 1978) analyzes the impacts of occupational segregation and consequent crowding of women's occupations on women's wages.

46   Unpublished data for 1977 from the Bureau of Labor Statistics. The remaining 7 percent of the husbands are either service or farm workers. However, of all named female clerical workers only 89.4 percent have husbands who were employed in the civilian labor force in 1977.

47   Kathleen Ritter and Lowell Hargens, "Occupational Positions and Class Identifications of Married Women: A Test of the Asymmetry Hypothesis," *American Journal of Sociology,* 80 (January 1975), 934–48.

48   Reported in *Seven Days,* January 1978, p. 4.

# Barbara M. Wertheimer

# "Union Is Power": Sketches from Women's Labor History

### EARLY ATTEMPTS TO UNIONIZE

Women have always worked, in the paid as well as the unpaid workforce. Wherever this work has been for pay, their labor has been valued at less than a man's. In the 1847 mill town of Lowell, Massachusetts, an activist group of women textile workers played a major role as writers and editors of the *Voice of Industry*. One edition carried an article that summed up the problem then. Its theme continues to the present.

> It is well known that labor performed by females commands but little when compared to that what is paid to men—though the work may be of the same character. Why is this? What possible difference can it make to the employer whether he pays A or B one dollar for accomplishing a piece of work, so that it

be done equally as well by one as the other? A female generally receives but about one-half as much as is paid to a man for doing the same amount of labor. It has been urged that they are the weaker sex, and are dependent upon us for resistance, and per consequence this difference in the price of labor should be made. But this very dependence is the result of inequality, and would not exist were the proper remedy applied. There are, it is well known, hundreds of families in our cities supported solely by females, who are obliged to labor with the needle twelve to fourteen hours out of the twenty-four, to gain hardly a comfortable subsistence for themselves and those dependent upon them, so trifling is the compensation they receive.[1]

In 1814 the first power loom went into operation, and a year later the first mill opened in Waltham, Massachusetts. Women and children made up the first factory population of the United States in the early nineteenth century. The agricultural sector suffered from an acute labor shortage, and every able-bodied man was needed to work the land. The new industrialists gave assurances that, indeed, they did not mean to lure men off the land but rather to take advantage of "six hundred thousand girls in the country between the ages of ten and sixteen," not fit for agriculture because they were too young or too weak, but good candidates for work in the mill.[2]

By 1830, some 55,000 workers, most of them women, worked in the growing number of mills dotting the New England landscape along the rushing streams that provided the necessary water power. By mid-century, close to 100,000 were employed by the textile industry. Home production of textiles was a thing of the past: the time of the wage-earning woman was at hand.

As early as 1824, women began to organize to fight wage cuts, the speeding up of their increasingly larger and noisier machines, and the relentless stretch-out where each worker had to tend more machines for less money. "Our present object is to have union," proclaimed striking Lowell mill workers in 1834.[3] Walking out to protest another wage cut, the women vowed to "have their own way if they died for it." As in so many other turnouts (as strikes were called then), the women lost.

Organizing was difficult for men in the nineteenth century (and labor organizations invariably went under with each of the country's frequent economic downturns), but it was doubly hard for women. Striking against their employer violated every code society had established for women's behavior. It was daring to act in concert, to parade in the street, to protest conditions, to make demands of an employer. Newspapers berated the women; ministers pressured them to return to work.

In addition, unions of the first half of the nineteenth century, primarily for craft and skilled workers, neither organized nor accepted women members. The women who struck had no national organizations to turn to for help, and no prior union experience. In forming trade unions they were pioneers in uncharted territory. Moreover, their pay was so meager that they could neither withstand long strikes nor pay dues to support an organization that could make strike benefits available in time of need.

Since society frowned on women participating in labor organizations or even in making public speeches, women rarely could count on the public for support. Furthermore, companies did not recognize their unions. Strike leaders not only were fired, but also blacklisted, and found themselves unable to find work in any mill throughout New England. Courts, too, sided with the employers. The wonder is that women organized at all.

About the year 1836 a mystery woman traveled from the hills of New Hampshire to the Lowell mills to become one of the most dynamic labor leaders in American history, though we know about her for only ten short years of her life. The job of labor organizing was a lonely one. Sarah Bagley spent several years laying the groundwork, training a corps of young women like herself, conducting classes in her boarding-house room. Together, in 1845 these women formed the Lowell Female Labor Reform Association with their motto "Try Again!", which is just what the women had to do. Their turnouts failed, as they had a decade earlier, but these women did not stop there. Through the labor paper *Voice of Industry,* they publicized the worsening conditions in the mills. Failing to win improvements through their strikes, the women tried to shorten their 14-hour workday through joining the 10-hour day movement. The Lowell Female Labor Reform Association succeeded in pressuring the Massachusetts state legislature to hold this country's first public hearings on factory conditions, at which mill women became the first to testify about the health hazards, low pay, and long hours of factory work.

As suddenly as she appeared, Sarah Bagley—labor educator, journalist, orator, public activist, organizer, and the country's first woman telegrapher—vanished. After 1846 there is no record of her life or whereabouts. But her active years in the Lowell mills, defying society's sanctions on women's proper place, attest to her courage. Criticized for speaking in public (and she could hold a crowd of 2,000 in a pre-microphone era) she responded:

> For the last half a century, it has been deemed a violation of woman's sphere to appear before the public as a speaker; but when our rights are trampled upon and we appeal in vain to legislators, what shall we do but appeal to the people?[4]

By mid-century the character of the mill workforce changed; immigrant families replaced the farm women to form a permanent factory population. Newly arrived in a strange land, penniless, they were forced to take jobs at any wages to support themselves. They were victims not only of low pay and long hours, but of increasingly unsafe working conditions: machines with no safety guards, buildings without fire escapes or proper ventilation, poor sanitary facilities. Conditions were no better for the growing numbers of women who worked in city tenements sewing shirts, umbrellas, making flowers, or rolling cigars for a pittance. Neither group was able to organize successfully, though they tried repeatedly to raise their wages even to subsistence levels.

As early as 1831, Lavinia Waight, New York tailoress and secretary of her union, openly talked of female oppression. Tailors and tailoresses in Boston tried to organize in 1844. That same year in New York, Elizabeth Gray spoke to some seven hundred women and publicly named employers who were paying ten to eighteen cents a day to their workers. The Female Industry Association grew out of that New York meeting, taking in book folders, stitchers, straw hat workers, lace makers, and sewing workers of all kinds. But again the women found themselves powerless against the employers, while their meetings drew men who circulated among them with offers of an easier life through prostitution.[5]

## ADVANCES IN WARTIME

Ironically, wartime has always meant the expansion of job opportunities for women. The Civil War saw nursing established as a profession, through the remarkable women who served on both sides.[6] On the home front, new factories in the North opened almost overnight, employing thousands of women workers to produce the uniforms and munitions the army needed. The government, giving job preference to war widows and children of soldiers who had been killed in action, hired women as clerks and copyists for the first time. Congress recognized that this was not a temporary phenomenon and in 1866 set wages for them at $900 a year, while men doing the same work earned $1,800. The reforms of 1870 set equal wages for men and women in each job category. This made little difference, however, since men and women rarely performed the same work.

It was not long after the war that the first national union of women workers was formed, short lived but successful for a time. The Daughters of St. Crispin, organized in 1869, united women shoebinders from Lynn, Massachusetts, to San Francisco, California, and included more than 40 lodges at its height. At its second convention the organization adopted this resolution on equal pay:

> Whereas the common idea among employers has been and still is that woman's labor should receive a less remuneration, even though equally valuable and efficient, than is paid men even on the same qualities of work; and
>
> Whereas in every field of human effort the value and power of organization is fully recognized: Therefore be it
>
> Resolved by this national Grand Lodge . . . that we demand for our labor the same rate of compensation for equal skill displayed, or the same hours of toil, as is paid other laborers in the same branches of business; and we regard a denial of this right by anyone as a usurpation and a fraud. . . .[7]

Only a few years earlier in Troy, New York, shirt and collar manufactur'ng center of the country, the Troy Collar Laundry Union was organizing. For several years this union was one of the most successful of the period, even sending donations to unions of men on strike. Fiery Kate Mullaney, the leader, also was active in the National Labor Union, and an advocate of women's suffrage. She saw in the ballot a political tool that would win for women the respect of the local press which, she noted, backed the men's organizing efforts while belittling those of the women. However, after a long strike that proved disastrous for the Collar Laundry Union, the women were forced to sign a pledge to give up their union in return for their jobs. In 1869, after a short but glorious six years, the Troy Collar Laundry Union folded.

## CHANGES FOLLOWING THE WAR

In the decades following the Civil War a few unions, faced with growing numbers of women in their trade, began to support the admission of women to membership. The first to do so was the National Union of Cigar Makers, which opened its doors to women and black workers in 1867. Eight years later it added a clause to its constitution forbidding any local to refuse membership to a worker because of sex. In one of the early public tributes to women as union members, the Cigar Makers *Journal* in 1878 declared that women were as loyal to the union as any men, stating:

> [Women] picketed the factories faithfully, from early morning
> till late in the evening, in stormy weather, rain and snow, and
> piercing cold.[8]

Nonetheless, locals of the national union dragged their heels about admitting women and blacks to equal membership and some went to great lengths to discourage their entrance into the industry. Since many women produced cigars in the home rather than in the factory, the "system of working" was an important union issue as well as a human one. The conditions of homeworkers were described in an 1885 study by New York City:

> These people worked till twelve p.m. or one o'clock a.m., then slept
> by the machine a few hours, and commenced work again. [Women
> sat] surrounded by filth with children waddling in it, whose hands,
> faces and bodies were covered with sores . . . even on the lips of
> the workers.[9]

Organizing these tenement shops was close to impossible. At the same time, the union saw the homeworkers as a major threat to its pay scale. Adolph Strasser, union president, turned to protective legislation to keep down the numbers of women in cigarmaking. He urged passage of laws restricting women under eighteen to no more than eight hours of work a day with no overtime allowed, and prohibiting women from working six weeks before or after giving birth to a child. These laws cut with more than one edge. Good as they might seem in themselves, employers forced to follow these strict rules regarding their female employees would simply not hire them, and would employ men instead. For women dependent on even the few cents they could earn at cigarmaking to feed their families, it spelled disaster. Even so, by the turn of the century more than one-third of all cigar workers were women, up from 10 percent in 1870.

The second union to admit women was the International Typographical Union, which helped young Augusta Lewis organize International Typographical Union Local No. 1 for women compositors. In 1870 Lewis was elected corresponding secretary for the entire union, the first woman ever to be elected a national officer of a union made up predominantly of men. In her post as secretary she surveyed conditions in the printing industry and organized, as well as making the usual reports of that post. She tried to use her position to appeal to the men for greater acceptance of union women in the trade. Often the women could not find work because union foremen would not hire them, nor would union printers back them up. While Women's Typographical Union No. 1, never very large, lasted just nine years, by the time it disbanded the doors to union membership had been opened to women in printing on an equal basis with the men.[10]

## BLACK WOMEN WORKERS

Black women in America have always worked, since 1619 when the first three arrived in the colony of Virginia on a Dutch frigate along with seventeen black men. If life was difficult for white women, how much more so for black, most of whom were slaves until the Civil War. Sharing the long hours of work in the fields with the men, women carried the additional burden of cooking and child care. After the official end to the slave trade in 1808, owners saw black women slaves as breeders of more slaves and often used them as such.

After the Civil War, slaves who could do so migrated to the North or the West to escape the tenant and sharecropping systems that virtually enslaved them anew. They were not welcomed in the cities by white workers, who feared—with some justification—that employers would use them as strikebreakers. In all but a very few unions they were refused membership. Black men had such a difficult time finding employment in the cities that it often was the black woman, working at housework and taking in laundry, who kept the family from starvation. Black laundresses are credited with forming Mississippi's first labor organization, the Washerwomen of Jackson. In June, 1866, they organized to set prices for their work that were uniform throughout the city, and fined members who violated the code and charged less.

That same year the National Labor Union, a loose association of local unions and lodges, voted to admit black workers (and women). However, since few member locals in fact admitted blacks, not many black workers actually joined. Toward the end of 1869 the National Colored Labor Union was founded, from the start admitting both unskilled workers and women to membership. One woman, Mary A. S. Carey, was elected to the NCLU's first executive committee and women attended the Union's first convention. Included in convention reports was that of the committee on women's labor, which urged the new organization to profit from "the mistakes heretofore made by our white fellow citizens in omitting women . . . that women be cordially included in the invitation to further and organize cooperative societies."[11] The report was adopted unanimously, including its endorsement of equal rights for women workers. Unfortunately, the NCLU had a brief life.

## KNIGHTS OF LABOR

In 1881 the first national labor federation of any substance, the Noble Order of the Knights of Labor, opened its doors to women and to black workers, and called for equal pay for equal work. It was a federation made up of lodges across the country and their favorite anthem, sung at every assembly, voiced their philosophy:

> Storm the fort, ye Knights of Labor,
>     Battle for your cause;
> Equal rights for every neighbor—
>     Down with tyrant laws!

Among the women who joined the Knights was Leonora Barry, a widow trying to support two children through her work in a hosiery mill in Amsterdam, New York. She rose rapidly to leadership, soon heading an assembly of almost 1,000 women. At the 1886 convention of the Knights in Richmond, Virginia, she met and worked closely with the 15 other women delegates to put forward a motion, unanimously passed by what must have been a startled group of male delegates, calling for the appointment of a full-time paid woman organizer (general investigator) and a secretary to assist her. Barry was chosen for the job, a new one for a woman in labor history. Her energy, enthusiasm, and zeal show in the report of her activities for the next year. In a time when communications were slow and travel painful, she answered 537 requests for help from women wanting to organize; filled 213 appointments; visited almost 100 towns and cities; filled 100 speaking engagements; answered 789 letters seeking advice or information; distributed some 2,000 leaflets; and answered 97 telegrams.[12]

Barry charted a new course. With no road maps to guide her, she became organizer, business agent, and labor educator all in one. When women wrote to Knights' headquarters to request that a man be assigned as their president because they found they could not conduct meetings, she ran classes in parliamentary procedure. She worked for passage of state factory inspection laws, and helped set up two cooperative shirt factories, in line with Knights of Labor philosophy that cooperatives were an alternative to the wage system. She launched an insurance department to help women in need, and initiated boycotts of non-union products. A dynamic speaker, she was much in demand on the women's suffrage platform and in support of temperance. The causes for which she worked included industrial education to enable women to find jobs in other than traditionally low-paid women's work; abolition of the tenement system of labor; and prohibition of child labor. She was one of the first to point out the movement of northern mills south in order to escape new northern laws limiting employment of children . . . and the need for wider passage of legislation protecting children from exploitation.

While a traditionalist in some ways (she believed it unladylike to lobby by buttonholing state assemblymen and left paid employment herself when she remarried), she was far ahead of her time. Many of her conclusions about women's role in unions anticipated problems that women union leaders discuss today: poor meeting attendance, low self-confidence of women members, the role of encouragement in stimulating greater involvement of women in their assemblies, and women's reluctance to try better jobs even when they had the training for them. She was discouraged when she found women earning good wages who failed to extend a helping hand to other women. She came to believe that women should be organized in one "industrial hive" rather than in separate women's assemblies; she saw, too, that the indifference of the men in the Knights played an important part in discouraging women's participation.

Like Sarah Bagley and other women union leaders before her, Barry suffered the wrath of society for her non-traditional role in a period when it was still deemed unladylike for women to travel unaccompanied on the railroads or to speak out on behalf of workers. When priests of the Catholic Church dubbed her a "lady Tramp," it hurt her as much as it angered her, and she lashed back, proclaiming her right "as an Irishwoman, a Catholic, and an honest woman" to come to the support of working women.[13]

One of the most significant women of her day, she remained active in those causes in which she believed even after she remarried, left her job, and moved to St. Louis. For example, she took an active part in the campaign for state suffrage in Colorado (1893) and continued as a popular speaker until 1928, when mouth cancer forced her to retire.

Yet history books rarely record her contributions, just as labor history texts ignore the strikes of women members of the Knights of Labor, such as that of the Yonkers (New York) carpet weavers in 1885. Here 2,500 women walked off the job and formed a mass picket line around the mill. This time police violence against the strikers backfired and the women found public support for their struggle. The New York labor movement joined forces to honor the bravery of the women, who held out for six months. While they did not win the union recognition they sought, they did get important grievances resolved and a wage cut rescinded.

At its peak, 50,000 women belonged to the Knights, out of a total claimed membership of 700,000. This marked a new phase in women workers' organizing. For the first time a labor federation had recognized the importance of its women members and established a woman's department, elevating its director to a post as a general officer in 1887. While individual men in the Knights often failed to cooperate with the women's department—or did so reluctantly—the Knights openly supported equal pay for equal work, in some cases with considerable success. After 1890 the Knights of Labor declined. It would be many years before women found the same welcome and support in a labor federation again.

## THE WOMEN'S TRADE UNION LEAGUE

As the Knights declined, a new labor organization rose to take its place: the American Federation of Labor. In 1890 when the Federation was in ascendance, close to four million women were employed outside the home in a total work force of 22 million. One in four of these working women was non-white, and most of the non-white women still lived and worked in the South.

New jobs were opening for white women as several occupations became established as "women's work": retail sales, telephone switchboard operation, clerical and secretarial work, and garment sewing. By 1895, although many unions still refused to admit women, 5 percent of all union members were female. Officially the policy of the AFofL was to organize women and to urge equal pay. In practice, the Federation did not have the power to enforce this policy on member unions and exerted little pressure on them to conform. In some cases the AFofL chartered federal locals of women workers, allowing direct affiliation with the Federation, but these small, independent locals had a low survival rate.

Nonetheless, by the turn of the century women made up more than half of all union members in five industries: women's clothing, gloves, hat and cap, shirtwaist and laundry, and tobacco. Women's wages averaged little more than half of men's, and black women, few of whom were in any industrial or office jobs, earned only half of what white women made.

Women needed to unionize. In 1903 an organization was launched that officially and unequivocally investigated conditions of women workers and sought to help them organize. The National Women's Trade Union League for the first time joined to this goal the expertise and funds of middle-class women with a social conscience and the energy and dedication of rank-and-file women workers. Together they exerted an influence far in excess of the organization's always modest membership.

In 1909 the League issued a *Handbook* that described the industries it had investigated, those in which most women worked. This publication underscored the need for collective action to improve working conditions. For example, in describing women in steam laundries the *Handbook* reported:

> How would you like to iron a shirt a minute? Think of standing at a mangle just above the washroom with the hot steam pouring up through the floor for 10, 12, 14 and sometimes 17 hours a day! Sometimes the floors are made of cement and then it seems as though one were standing on hot coals, and the workers are dripping with perspiration. Perhaps you have complained about the chemicals used in the washing of your clothes, which cause them to wear out quickly, but what do you suppose is the effect of these chemicals upon the workers? They are . . breathing air laden with

particles of soda, ammonia, and other chemicals! The Laundry Workers Union . . . in one city reduced this long day to 9 hours, and has increased the wages 50 percent. . . .[14]

The first major test for the League came that same year, when 20,000 New York City shirtwaist workers walked off their jobs to begin a winter-long strike that would result in shaping a major labor union— the International Ladies' Garment Workers' Union. This union today remains one of the top two unions in number of women members. Pauline Newman, veteran ILGWU organizer, was among those who walked out of the Triangle Shirtwaist Company in November, 1909. She describes that day:

> Thousands upon thousands left the factories from every side, all of them walking down toward Union Square. It was November, the cold winter was just around the corner. We had no fur coats to keep warm, and yet there was the spirit that led us on. . . .
>
> I can see the young people, mostly women, walking down and not caring what might happen. The spirit, I think the spirit of a conqueror led them on. They didn't know what was in store for them, didn't really think of the hunger, cold, loneliness and what could happen to them. They just didn't care on that particular day; that was *their* day.[15]

The story of the strike is well known: the arrests; the days and nights women strikers spent in the workhouse; the weeks of cold and hunger; and the victories as shop after shop finally recognized the union, 339 shops in all. Some shops, including the notorious Triangle Shirtwaist Company, did not. To these the workers drifted back in defeat.

Though union conditions proved hard to maintain, still the strike, viewed in context, was a great achievement. Thousands of immigrant workers, mostly women, stood firm against employers who had all the force of law behind them. Out of their struggle and sacrifice, with the active support of the Women's Trade Union League, they laid the foundation for a strong international union that could endure.

Just a year later these same workers would rally again following the tragic Triangle Shirtwaist Company fire in which 146 of their number lost their lives. This time the struggle was for factory legislation. The owners of the Triangle Company had locked the factory doors so that there was no escape for the women trapped in the burning building. They also had never checked the fire escapes, which crumpled under the weight of workers fleeing the fire. Nevertheless, they were found innocent when brought to trial. An aroused public and a determined union and factory commission (whose chief investigator was Frances Perkins) finally succeeded in getting the New York legislature to pass factory safety and inspection laws. Again the Women's Trade Union League played an important role.

Two other major labor struggles in the first two decades of the twentieth century involved women workers: the strike of men's clothing workers in Chicago in 1910 and the Lawrence textile workers' strike of 1912. In the first, the WTUL again was prominent. The second remains one of the triumphs of the Industrial Workers of the World. This loose-knit union organized industrially, opening its doors to women and blacks and unskilled workers that the craft unions would not take in. However, while it encouraged women to join its staff as organizers, no women ever held key leadership positions although several, including Elizabeth Gurley Flynn, achieved a national reputation.

The Chicago clothing workers' strike resulted, four years later, in the birth of the Amalgamated Clothing Workers of America, a union whose membership today still is over 75 percent female. Here, as in the ILGWU, no woman has ever held a top office at the international level, and women remain a small minority of both unions' executive boards, although many women hold local and regional positions of considerable responsibility.

## UNION DOORS OPEN TO WOMEN

As women moved into the same unions as men, unions of women workers became a thing of the past. What did women win or lose through this change? Unions of women workers invariably were small, independent, and financially weak. They had no long staying power, were limited in scope, and operated in isolation from the rest of the labor movement. Women needed to join with men. The combined strengths of both were necessary in the struggle to organize at a time when there were no labor laws that gave workers the right to form unions or protected them against job loss for doing so. There was no such thing as unemployment insurance, food stamps, or welfare programs to assist workers who might face weeks of joblessness through blacklisting.

On the other hand, unions of women workers had provided a chance for women to develop leadership skills, to set forth their own bargaining demands that represented their interests, and to have what one labor historian has called their "moment in the sun."[16] In unions run by men, women would for almost three generations, and with few exceptions, take a back seat, only gradually asserting their rights to major union leadership positions.

In 1920 women at last won the right to vote. It did not alter the political direction of the country, however, and the decade that followed World War I was difficult for men and women workers alike. The employer-sponsored American Plan to crush unions and the government's anti-Red Palmer raids combined to make the period preceding the Great Depression one of intense hostility to labor organizations. Union membership, not surprisingly, declined drastically. The depression that hit the southern textile industry in the later years of the decade should have served as a barometer of the unhealthy state of the economy, but not many noticed. Four major—and unsuccessful—strikes of southern textile workers in Tennessee, North Carolina, and Virginia against low wages, the stretch out and speed up, and the harassing conditions of mill life, led thousands of workers, many of them women, to endure months of violence, only to return in defeat to the mills. In the Gastonia (North Carolina) strike, Ella May Wiggins, mother, worker, union activist, and song writer, was shot and killed. Elizabethton, Marion, Greensboro, and Danville are southern towns, too, that join Gastonia as names in labor history. In 1934, just four years later, textile workers struck again, but even in a general strike workers could not match the strength of employer might.

With the Great Depression, however, came the election of Franklin D. Roosevelt and the New Deal. The National Labor Relations Act, passed in 1935, for the first time wrote into law the right of workers to organize into unions of their own choosing. Out of this new spirit industrial unionism was born: one union for all workers in the same plant or mill rather than many separate craft unions. Breaking away from the AFofL, a number of unions that sought to organize this way formed the Committee for Industrial Organization (later the Congress of Industrial Organizations or CIO). The cry "The President wants you to join the union" swept the country as thousands of workers rushed to sign up in the new CIO. Shirtworkers in Pennsylvania, store workers in Five-and-Dimes, "baby" strikers fourteen years of age or younger who worked for as little as five cents a week, sat in where they worked or marched on picket lines until union recognition was won.

One of the most famous of the sit-down strikes, that of auto workers in Flint, Michigan, owed its success in part to the Women's Emergency Brigade headed by Genora Johnson, wife of a sit-down striker and mother of two young boys. When the Brigade was organized to give active support to sit-down strikers in the plant, Johnson told the women: "Don't sign up for this unless you are prepared to stand in the front line against the onslaughts of the police."[17] Five hundred women responded, donning red berets and armbands with white letters E.B., and organizing in almost a military fashion with five lieutenants working under Johnson. These were women, as Johnson put it, who "could be called out of bed at any hour, if necessary, or sleep on a cot at the union hall."[18]

All through the strike the women saw to it that the men inside the plant got the food they needed. When the National Guard threw tear gas into the factory to force the men out, it was the Emergency Brigade that smashed the windows to let in the fresh air that, some say, saved the strike. Those who were there remember to this day the sight and the sound of the Emergency Brigade as it marched over the hill and down the street to the plant singing:

> Hold the fort, for we are coming,
> Union men be strong,
> Side by side we battle onward
> Victory will come!

## THE COALITION OF LABOR UNION WOMEN

World War II, like the first world war just a generation earlier, brought new numbers of women into the work force—six million women who had not previously been employed. In 1940 women in the work force numbered 13 million; by 1944 that number was up to 19 million, three million of whom were members of labor unions, many for the first time. Jobs opened to women that they had never had the chance to perform before, and most women wanted to keep on working in those jobs. As in the past, however, they were thanked for their services when the war ended, and encouraged to return to the kitchen. For many the return was only temporary; others returned not to the kitchen but to the less skilled, lower paying jobs they had held before.

The numbers of women seeking work outside the home has continued to grow. By 1960 fully one-third of the work force was female.

Today more than two out of every five workers are women, over 40 million in number, with some five and one-half million women now members of labor unions or employee organizations.

Partly as a result of the women's movement, partly because of their increasing numbers in the work force and in unions, women workers gradually have assumed a new role. Equal pay for equal work and opportunities for job mobility have come to mean as much to employed women as to men. Increasingly women are using Title VII of the Civil Rights Act and the Equal Pay Act as vehicles to achieve these goals if they cannot do so through their unions.

Union women, however, are entitled to turn first to their labor organizations for support, for enforcement of anti-discrimination clauses in their contracts, for maternity leave without loss of seniority, for the negotiation of parental leave clauses, and for medical plans that cover the cost of abortion. They can expect their unions to insist on job posting, to back them when they bid for jobs not traditionally thought of as women's work, and to work for passage of laws providing more extensive child care, tax reform, and equal coverage of pensions and social security programs. They expect, too, that their unions will support the Equal Rights Amendment and work actively for its passage.

As an outgrowth of this new awareness on the part of trade union women, 3,500 of them from across the country, from a wide spectrum of unions, gathered in Chicago in March, 1974, to found a new organization, the Coalition of Labor Union Women (CLUW). Its purpose was to move more women into leadership roles in the labor union structure, and to work within the framework of the labor movement to achieve four major goals:

- To increase afirmative action on the job and women's involvement in their unions at all levels;
- To work for legislation important to women workers, both on federal and state levels;
- To encourage women's participation in the political process, including more women running for office;
- To help organize the many millions of unorganized women workers in the United States, without which the labor movement, which has been at a membership standstill, cannot grow.

In structure, CLUW to some extent parallels the labor movement itself. It has an elected executive board on which city chapter organizations are represented, as are the unions themselves, through their members who participate in CLUW.

For all the initial enthusiasm that surrounded CLUW, the organization has not grown much beyond its 1974 membership level. Even with its modest numbers, however, hovering around 5,000, CLUW has spoken out effectively as the new voice of union women. It has been instrumental, for example, in moving the policy of the AFL–CIO to support the Equal Rights Amendment. It has achieved the appointment of a woman as associate director of the Civil Rights Department of the merged federation with responsibility for Women's Activities. It has attained the naming of four union women leaders as members of the Civil Rights Committee of the AFL–CIO where, in the past, only national union presidents held these committee posts.

Nonetheless, statistics indicate how far union women still must go. Only two small unions of the federation have women presidents. No woman sits on the AFL–CIO Executive Council. The only woman to head a department in the federation is the librarian. Although women compose 25 percent of all members of unions affiliated with the AFL–CIO, they hold only 7 percent of the key elected or appointed posts—and these include few policy making positions.

How much real change can CLUW effect? Union women organizing as women are news today, and CLUW has received considerable publicity and its leaders a great deal of visibility in the few years since its founding in 1974. George Meany, AFL–CIO President, has met with CLUW officers, as have the heads of the giant Teamsters and Auto Workers unions. CLUW has received financial support from a number of unions, enabling it to maintain its low dues. One of CLUW's most publicized achievements was a study tour, foundation-funded, that sent 19 CLUW leaders to three countries to examine child care programs and, on their return, to promote increased support for child care legislation. But all this is only a beginning, and the handful of women who have achieved prominence have an awesome responsibility to bring numbers of other women along with them.

CLUW has a potential for effecting change not only through its chapters but through its conventions. These provide education on key union and working women's issues and enable union women to cooperate more effectively with other women's groups, such as the National Organization for Women, on campaigns of general interest to women, such as the drive for passage of the Equal Rights Amendment. CLUW was well represented at the Houston International Women's Year conclave as well as at the state IWY meetings, and CLUW leaders saw to it that union women in general were involved in these events.

CLUW has provided new opportunities for participation, new chances for union women to meet and learn about other women who have had little prior contact with the labor movement. CLUW members meet women from unions other than their own, also important. CLUW chapters provide a political rough-and-tumble where members gain leadership skills that are transferable to their own unions. Here is a chance to practice speaking in public, to run for office, to chair committees, to conduct chapter business—all necessary skills for the woman who wants to move up the leadership ladder in her own union. In sum, CLUW rationalizes and legitimizes union women's focus on issues related to equality. Within CLUW these large issues become less threatening because here they are kept within the boundaries of the labor movement and endowed with the familiar perspectives of unions to which women members are extremely loyal.

Only time will reveal whether CLUW, for all these pluses, will siphon off the energies of capable union women and thus succeed mainly in taking pressure off the men who now hold so many of the critical union posts. Does CLUW, which adheres closely to the programs and policies of the AFL–CIO, channel women's energies away from the organization of women's caucuses in their own unions and into more accepted areas that do not conflict with union policies? Clearly, it is important for union workers to present a united front when dealing with employers and with issues of concern to all workers: full employment, labor law reforms that will improve the chances of organizing the unorganized, national health insurance legislation, and contending with today's swing to the right. Would a woman's caucus in local unions, not always concurring with the union's leadership, be a liability, or would it make union leaders more responsive? If CLUW grows, as it gets stronger, will it as a matter of course serve *this* role?

The Coalition of Labor Union Women is a product of our times, a result of the impact of the women's movement, of equal pay and antidiscrimination laws of the 1960's, and of the influx of new millions in the work force. Women look around them and see other women who combine homes, families, jobs, and union responsibilities. Those who are members of CLUW are part of an organization alert to the realities of job discrimination and the ways they can use their unions to combat it. For example, a National CLUW Model Contracts Task Force provides valuable guidelines for local and perhaps even national bargaining on women's issues. The political and legislative experience in which CLUW members participate with other union women is quite different from stamp-licking, coffee-pouring roles of women of the past. Self-confidence, motivation, the desire to see competent women in political and community and union offices, all grow out of these experiences.

But even this renascence owes its existence to the working women of the past. The Lowell women held high their banners reading "Try Again!" The strike signs of the Lynn shoebinders in 1860 stated: "American Ladies Will Not Be Slaves!" Leonora Barry, Pauline Newman, and countless others traveled a lonely road that women today travel together. True, equal pay for work of equal value is still in the future. Twenty-eight unions as yet have no women members. But job areas are opening for women that will change that. There is no turning back. Women in this country and in countries around the world today seek a full partnership role in the work force, in labor unions, and in political and community life.

## NOTES

1  Philip Foner, *The Factory Girls* (Champaign-Urbana: The University of Illinois Press, 1977), p. 309.

2  Barbara Wertheimer, *We Were There: The Story of Working Women in America* (New York: Pantheon, 1977), p. 56; Edith Abbott, *Women in Industry* (New York: D. Appleton & Co., 1910), pp. 51–59.

3  John B. Andrews and W. D. P. Bliss, *History of Women in Trade Unions*, Bureau of Labor Report on Conditions of Women and Child Wage-Earners in the United States, Vol. 10 (Washington, D.C.: U.S. Government Printing Office, 1911), p. 24. Quote is from *The Man*, Feb. 22, 1834.

4  *Ibid.*, p. 71. From *Voice of Industry*, June 5, 1845. For a fuller account of the early mill women see Wertheimer, *We Were There*, Chapter 5.

5  Wertheimer, *We Were There*, p. 99.

6  A number of books have been written by and about Civil War nurses. For suggestions see Bibliography of *We Were There*, pp. 408–10.

7  Andrews and Bliss, *History of Women in Trade Unions*, p. 109, quoting the *American Workman*, April 30, 1870.

8  Cigar Makers' *Journal*, May 10, 1878.

9  Annie Nathan Meyer, *Women's Work in America* (New York: Henry Holt & Co., 1891), p. 308.

10  For a fuller account see Wertheimer, *We Were There*, pp. 166–69.

11   Philip Foner, *Organized Labor and the Black Worker, 1619–1973* (New York: Praeger, 1974), p. 34.

12   Andrews and Bliss, *History of Women in Trade Unions,* pp. 118–19.

13   Philip Foner, *The History of the Labor Movement in the United States,* vol. 2 (New York: International Publishers, 1947–65), p. 65.

14   *Handbook,* National Women's Trade Union League, 1909, as quoted in *Toward Better Working Conditions for Women,* Women's Bureau Bulletin #252 (Washington, D.C.: U.S. Department of Labor, 1953), p. 14.

15   Pauline Newman, talk to Trade Union Women's Studies students, New York State School of Industrial and Labor Relations, Cornell University, March 1975. Quoted in Wertheimer, *We Were There,* p. 301.

16   Connie Kopelov, *Women in American Labor History,* New York, Trade Union Women's Studies (course module) (New York State School of Industrial and Labor Relations, Cornell University, March 1976), p. 16a.

17   Jeane Westin, *Making Do* (Chicago: Follett Publishing Company, 1976), p. 310.

18   *Ibid.,* p. 315.

# Martha S. White

# Women in the Professions: Psychological and Social Barriers to Women in Science

Talented and educated women with family responsibilities often face special problems of identity and self-esteem when they attempt to continue their professional activity. Although many do so successfully and encounter few problems, others find it more difficult. I first became aware of some special aspects of these problems when I interviewed women scholars at the Radcliffe Institute—women with outstanding intellectual and creative ability who had been awarded fellowships so that they might continue their professional interests on a part-time basis.[1]

The Institute members were particularly ques-

Reprinted from *Science* 170 (October 23, 1970), 413–16. Copyright 1970 by the American Association for the Advancement of Science. Published originally under the title "Psychological and Social Barriers to Women in Science."

tioned about their feelings of identity as a professional. Did they feel any more professional as a result of their fellowship at the Institute? What made a person feel professional? Had their commitment to their work changed as a result of their Institute experience? At the time, I hypothesized that one outcome of the fellowship, of the opportunity to work deeply and seriously on a project, would be a greater sense of competence. The greater the sense of inner competence, my reasoning went, the greater would be the sense of commitment on future productive work. This proved to be only partially true.

Many indicated that the fellowship program had resulted in a genuine change in the conceptions of themselves as professionals, but their responses suggested that this change was rarely due solely to the opportunity to work on their projects. Although this was important, equally significant was the access to stimulating colleagues, both within and outside the Institute, which the special status conferred by the fellowship made possible. Appraisals of their work by others, coupled with acceptance and recognition by people whose professional opinions were relevant and appropriate, made a significant difference in determining whether a woman felt like a professional, and whether she in turn had a strong sense of commitment to future work.

Challenging interaction with other professionals is frequently as necessary to creative work as is the opportunity for solitude and thought.[2] Yet comments from many women indicate that it is particularly difficult for them to attain, especially for the woman who seeks reentry. As one woman astutely noted:

> Those of us who have interrupted our careers because of children or moving with our husbands across the country have special difficulties. Our departments maintain no ties with us. Often no one knows us, and the articles and books on which we are working may not be published for another three to five years. Meanwhile, if we are to be productive, we need to be professionally involved again.

Although women offer unique qualities to intellectual and creative endeavors, one of the main barriers to women's achievement of excellence and commitment is the expectation that women's career patterns and motivation will be the same as men's. When they are not, there are many phrases ("lost to marriage," "didn't pan out," "dropped out") which indicate the disappointing nature of their acts, the hopelessness of their making choices which are uniquely theirs as women. Many, possessing energy and talent, will choose the same career paths and find great personal satisfaction in meeting the same demands as many men. But others who live life differently, and who may choose differently from the traditional career pattern, also have much to offer, and our gain is greater if we can include their talents among those which society and science utilize. Attracted to scholarship and scientific research, they continue on to graduate school or professional school after college because of their deep interest in a field. Many have clear and well-defined plans for a career, while others wish to combine "worthwhile work" with homemaking. Because of their serious intellectual interest and involvement, such women usually do well academically and are excellent students. Yet they find that their interest in learning and in excellence does not receive the same recognition after college or graduate school as it did before unless they determinedly indicate that they plan a full-time uninterrupted career. But clearly the dominant (and in many cases preferred) life pattern for many a highly trained woman still includes multiple roles, dual commitments, and occasional interruptions. If she wishes to continue her professional activity on a flexible or modified schedule, or faces temporal or geographic discontinuities, she is frequently excluded from important aspects of what the sociologists call "socialization into a profession."

## PROFESSIONAL SOCIALIZATION

In the normal course of men's and women's professional careers, only a part of their professional training takes place in college, in graduate or professional schools, or in a training program. Many professions and occupations have periods analogous to that of the medical intern or resident (though these stages are frequently informal and rarely explicitly recognized) during which the individual learns to behave in ways which other people in the field regard as "professional." Such "socialization" usually occurs during graduate school as well as during the first decade of employment after one is launched on a career, and consists of learning the roles, the informal values and attitudes, and the expectations which are an important part of real professional life. During this stage of a career, the person not only learns occupational roles and skills, but gains a firmer image of himself as competent and adequate. Appraisals of his work by others permit self-criticism to grow and standards of judgment to develop. Such a sense of competence may come quickly and early for some, but develop slowly and gradually for others. Once a person has this sense of competence and regards himself as a professional, it is probable that he has less need to learn from colleagues and indeed may have greater freedom to diverge from the accepted way of doing things, seeking his own pathway instead. It is this firm sense of professional identity and capability which women, regardless of their ability, may find difficult to achieve, or achieve only at a high personal price.

Many people are unaware of this period of role learning in scholarly, scientific or academic professions and fail to realize how important such a stage is and how lengthy it has become because of the increased complexity of professional life. Everett Hughes, the sociologist, has noted that many still think of professions as they were in the nineteenth century, although they have vastly changed since then.[3] Many professions are practiced in complicated organizations, with consequent nuances of status and levels of organization to contend with. There are elaborate social systems in all parts of academic and business life, and purely technical training is rarely enough. The aspiring young scientist must be knowledgeable about many aspects of institutions, journals, professional meetings, methods of obtaining source materials, and funding grant applications. Knowing how to command these technical and institutional facilities requires numerous skills, many unanticipated by the young student. But once gained, such skills often seem very simple in retrospect and even thoughtful professionals forget that they were once not second nature. This is the kind of learning we speak of as "caught," not "taught," and it is a valued by-product of acceptance and challenging association with other professionals.

## SPONSORSHIP

Studies of professions and professional identity have also stressed the importance of sponsorship as a device for influencing commitment and affecting the self-image. Referred to by some writers[4] as the "protégé system," sponsorship is common to the upper echelons of almost all professions, including the scientific fields. One must be "in" both to learn crucial trade secrets and to advance within the field. Unfortunately a man may be hesitant about encouraging a woman as a protégé. He may be delighted to have her as an assistant, but he may not see her as his successor, or as one who will carry on his ideas, or as a colleague. He may believe that she is less likely to be a good gamble, a risk for him to exert himself for, or that she is financially less dependent upon a job. Because of subtle pressures from his wife, he may temper his publicly expressed enthusiasm or interest. He may fail to introduce her to colleagues or sponsor her for jobs. And as one of Ann Roe's studies of eminent scientists indicated,[5] the advancement and success of protégés are important to the sponsor's own feelings of satisfaction in his professional efforts; nonachieving protégés reflect on the sponsor's public and private image.

In addition, sponsorship affects the recognition an individual receives. One might assume (or hope) that excellence and productivity in scientific work is all that is needed for recognition, but in reality ideas are more likely to be accepted if they are promoted or mentioned by eminent sponsors, or if they are the products of joint authorship with a well-known professional or derive from a well-known laboratory or university. Whether a woman is "sponsored" in these ways will partially determine who reads her work, listens to her reports, or even offers friendly comments on the draft of a paper. Such informal signs of recognition increase motivation and affect one's subjective feelings of commitment to a field, as well as feelings of professional identity.

## ARE WOMEN IN THE CLUB?

A recent study of women Ph.D.'s[6] showed that the full-time employed woman Ph.D. published as much as her male colleagues and was more likely than the average male scientist to be in research. She was involved in the activities of her professional organization, was sought out as a consultant, and was more likely to be awarded fellowships and be accepted in honorary societies. Despite all this evidence of productivity and commitment, the authors of the study noted that the women often felt left out, and suggested that

> the problem which bothers the woman Ph.D. who is a full-time contributor to her profession is that she is denied many of the informal signs of belonging and recognition. These women report that even on such daily activities as finding someone to have lunch or take a coffee break with, or finding someone with whom she can chew over an idea, or on larger issues such as finding a partner with whom she can share a research interest, the woman Ph.D. has a special and lower status.

This exclusion from the informal channels of communication is of particular importance in fast-moving science, where, as Sir Alfred

Egerton has noted, "of the total information extant, only part is in the literature. Much of it is sorted in the many brains of scientists and technologists. We are as dependent on biological storage as on mechanical or library storage." Jessie Bernard astutely comments: "It is this access—[to] the brains of fellow scientists—that may be more limited for women than for men."[7]

The need for stimulating colleagues was also attested to in a study by Perrucci of women engineers and scientists.[8] She found that women were more apt than men to endorse as important the opportunity "to work with colleagues who are interested in the latest developments in their field" and "to associate with other engineers and scientists of recognized ability." Interestingly enough, no differences appeared between men and women of comparable education as to whether they desired challenging work or work involving "people versus things."

The evidence also seems to indicate, however, that in many cases women are reluctant to put themselves forward or to protest their being left out. It is a vicious circle: men indifferent or unaware of excluding women; women insecure and hesitant of intruding. The remedy is not necessarily more individual boldness, but must include new institutional arrangements and programs which do not depend on individual initiative.[9] However, as the Radcliffe data indicated, such arrangements and programs are not too difficult to achieve.

There have been lone individuals who have flourished on society's neglect and produced great ideas or masterpieces, but this is not characteristic of those in the professions or the majority of people. For most people, acceptance by others and interaction with challenging groups or organizations are a source of deep personal significance and of creative energy as well. Yet it is this acceptance and this interaction which are often denied, both purposefully and inadvertently, to women, whether they participate full time or on a flexible schedule, whether they remain continously in the field or seek reentry.

## A NEW CAREER CONCEPT

Because of their life patterns, many women with scientific training have nonprofessional roles and identifications to which they are deeply committed. They seek an occupational or professional identity which recognizes and takes into account this dual commitment. For women with these values, a new concept of professional "career" may be necessary.

Numerous women, either because of their own inclination or their personal situations, enjoy and competently manage full-time work and a full-time career. Others, however, seem to be seeking to invent for themselves a new and more varied conception of career, one which has not existed before and for which there are few models or patterns available. They have a full-time commitment, but do not always plan to work on a full-time basis; their lives and where they work are governed to a greater degree by nonoccupational factors. As a result of the smaller size of families, and the shorter span of child-rearing, few of these women see their maternal role as bringing their professional life to an end. They think of themselves as a permanent part of the working force, and regard flexible schedules and part-time work as a necessary part of the solution. Some seem to be seeking an alternative career model which is neither upward-moving nor "success-oriented," but which recognizes their commitment to family responsibilities as an important part of their choice. To accommodate this lateral career, or "career of limited ambition,"[10] they seek to improvise a new professional role which is more differentiated and diversified than the accepted pattern. (I should note parenthetically that this interest in new career patterns is by no means limited to women.) Such an alternative mode might be represented schematically by an ascending spiral movement, indicating career choices which are upward in direction but slowly paced, with long horizontal stopovers. Deeper knowledge or more varied experience would be the goals of such a career: not greater status, but greater esteem; not primarily extrinsic rewards, but intrinsic satisfactions.[11]

Such new models are long overdue. Almost a century of experimentation has been spent in attempting to fit women's career patterns into those followed by most men, and the result has not been phenomenally successful. If such alternative career patterns can gain general recognition, the result may be more productive, creative work. As Epstein[12] has so succinctly noted, the barriers to women's advancement and achievement are not merely a function of prejudice or incapacity. The structures of professions, narrow and inflexible as they often are, may create limits which are largely unintended. But groups and colleagues are powerful forces in shaping attitudes and behavior; the institutional settings and social mechanisms which inhibit commitment and identity can also be used to promote change and to encourage different consequences.

## SUGGESTIONS

What can women do to cope with these barriers and discriminatory practices which intensify the effects of discontinuity in their lives? How can they fully utilize their talents, yet make choices that are suitable to their goals and life styles? What constructive action can be taken to remedy the inadequate socialization which the current structure of the professions makes inevitable for many women?

In overcoming the barriers, the importance of sponsorship and the maintenance of communication with stimulating colleagues should not be underestimated. When a woman has to interrupt her training, graduate study, or employment, she should talk over future alternatives or avenues of return with an adviser and ask for letters of recommendation which may be used when a return is contemplated. She can seek ways to keep in touch with her department or work group. As one successful woman observed, "She should leave no gap unfilled."

Women with similar fields of interest can often profit by forming or joining other women in associations which provide professional stimulation and motivation, as well as information and access to new opportunities. Such groups can be particularly effective in assisting women who have temporarily retired to return to or keep up with their field. Several studies[13] suggest the possibility that women who are more ambitious in the traditional male-career sense may be more stimulated to achieve by the presence of men who are achieving, while women who regard intellectual achievement as part of the feminine role may react more favorably to the presence of capable women colleagues. This at least suggests that many talented younger women might be more encouraged by knowing and observing in the professional role other women who value the feminine family role. Such models are still too often a rarity.

Part-time work has only begun to be utilized effectively. Many men have long known that they are most productive when they engage in a variety of functions, carrying out activities which complement but may have very little immediate relation to each other. Although the initial stages of learning how to accomplish this are not easy, many women are discovering that such juggling can work even in complex and demanding scientific and engineering fields. Pilot projects using women scientists in the federal government have found both a shorter week and a shorter day successful.[14] Enthusiastic women report that they get almost as much done, while employers note that they get more than their money's worth, since there is little wasted time and important thinking time often comes free. In fields with hard-to-find skills such as data processing, part-time job opportunities may make it easier to recruit employees. An innovation which has been used with great success in education, social work, library work and medical residencies is to have two women share one job. Thoughtfully and carefully planned, the partnership job has proved not only eminently suitable to the needs of women, but of benefit to employers as well.[15] Partnership teaching has proved so useful in education that one wonders why it was not thought of before.

Sometimes women create their own part-time opportunities. In the San Francisco area, a group of women biologists found they lacked opportunities for part-time work and for keeping up with their fields while their children were small. They organized a talent pool, incorporating as an educational group, Natural Science Education Resources. They have since offered a unique series of classes on plants and animals to mothers and their preschool children, served as consultants to teachers and schools, developed new ecology programs, presented adult education courses, and obtained a pilot National Science Foundation grant. Several women have now moved on to other jobs, leaving a vacant place which is eagerly taken by someone else seeking such a part-time opportunity.

Although all of these part-time approaches serve to prevent technical obsolescence, retraining programs and reentry techniques are also needed. Although some writers counsel noninterruption as the only answer, it seems more realistic to assume that discontinuity will continue to be a fact of life for many women. A woman's interests change between the time she is in college and the point at which she decides to involve herself more deeply again. Fortunately mid-career retraining is becoming mandatory for many scientific fields; if reentry opportunities for women can only be included by companies, universities, and professional societies along with the continuing education programs for full-time professionals, these transitions can be more easily accomplished.

Some women have planned their own transitional reentry programs. One woman chemist talked to a local college professor and offered to assist him in his laboratory courses during the year in order to bring her knowledge up to date. She proved so capable that he admitted her to advanced seminars, supervised her in tutorial reading, and is now working to retain her in a permanent capacity in the department.

Master's degree programs aimed at updating skills are particularly promising. Rutgers University has had one for mathematicians, and Wellesley College has had a two-year program for chemists.

Some may raise the question: Aren't women now insisting on the same opportunities as men? Do women want the same opportunities or do they want special opportunities? The answer is simply that they need both. Career commitment takes a variety of forms for women and may increasingly do so for men. Longevity, population pressures, and the explosion of knowledge have created new needs and life stages for us all. If we become obsessed with simply giving women the same opportunities as men (important though this may be), we not only obstruct effective recognition of the differences in women's lives, but may fail to note what is already a trend—more complex educational and occupational patterns for both men and women. Many of the programs and innovations developed to suit women's needs are needed for men as well. They too are feeling the impact of new knowledge, the expectation of intellectual retooling every decade, and the need for part-time refresher courses to update proficiency. They too have discovered that interests change after twenty years in a field, that challenge can outweigh security, and that mid-life may bring a desire to shift the focus of a career. And surely we are all learning the lesson that education is most useful when one is most ready for it. Many young students are no longer so eager to cram all their education and professional training into the beginning of their adult years.

While the patterns of women's lives may be more varied, the interruptions more pronounced and profound, and possibly the needs for guidance greater, our attempts to foster a social climate which meets the complex needs of women today may well be pointing the way toward meeting the diverse needs of both the men and the women of tomorrow.

## SUMMARY

Commitment and creativity in science are not merely a function of an individual's competence or excellence, but are a product of the social environment as well. Acceptance and recognition from significant other people (one's peers and other professionals) and opportunities for stimulating and challenging interaction are essential for developing a strong occupational or professional identity, and for creating the inner sense of role competence which can lead to greater commitment and productivity in professional work. Unfortunately women, especially those who have experienced interrupted or discontinuous careers, find such opportunities and acceptance difficult to obtain.

The scientific community can foster the professional development and effectiveness of women in science by permitting women more flexible opportunities for professional participation, by being more aware of practices which exclude women on the basis of gender rather than ability, and by separating standards of excellence from time schedules.

Women can help themselves by keeping up contacts with others in their fields, partipating in professional groups, becoming familiar with new part-time approaches and reentry skills, creating their own retraining and employment opportunities, and instituting new programs appropriate to their needs.

"Restriction of opportunity not only blights hope; it excludes the person from the chance to acquire the knowledge and skill that would in turn enable him to surmount the barriers to effectiveness."[16]

## NOTES

1   M. S. White, "Conversations with the Scholars" (report submitted to the Radcliffe Institute, 1966). The Radcliffe Institute supports part-time scholars, provides funds for domestic and child care help, a place to work and access to the library and intellectual resources of Radcliffe and Harvard. The scholars neither work for a degree nor take courses, but engage in creative or scholarly work within their fields. Many already have their doctorate, or its equivalent in achievement. In addition, the Institute sponsors other fellowship programs for part-time graduate study and medical residency training, and conducts a research program.

2   D. C. Pelz, "Creative Tensions in the Research and Development Climate," *Science* 157 (1967), 160; H. S. Becker and J. W. Carper, *American Journal of Sociology*, 41 (1956) 289; J. J. Sherwood, "Self-Identity and Referent Others," *Sociometry*, 28 (1965), 66.

3   E. C. Hughes, "Professions," *Daedalus*, 92 (1963), 655.

4   C. F. Epstein, *Woman's Place* (Berkeley: University of California Press, 1970).

5   A. Roe, "Women in Science," *Personnel and Guidance Journal*, 54 (1966), 784.

6   R. J. Simon, S. M. Clark, and K. Galway, "The Woman Ph.D.: A Recent Profile," *Social Problems*, 15 (1967), 221.

7   J. Bernard, *Academic Women* (University Park, Pa.: State College, The Pennsylvania Press, 1964), p. 303.

8 C. C. Perrucci, "The Female Engineer and Scientist: Factors Associated with the Pursuit of a Professional Career" (unpub. report, 1968).

9 See U.S. Civil Service Commission, *Changing Patterns: A Report on the Federal Women's Program Review Seminar* (Washington, D.C.: U.S. Government Printing Office, 1969); A. L. Dement, "The College Woman as a Science Major," *Journal of Higher Education*, 33 (1962), 487.

10 M. K. Sanders, "The New American Female: Demi-Feminism Takes Over," *Harper's*, 231 (1965), 37.

11 R. H. Turner, "Some Aspects of Women's Ambition," *American Journal of Sociology*, 70 (1964), 271.

12 Epstein, *Woman's Place.*

13 E. G. French and G. S. Lesser, "Some Characteristics of the Achievement Motive in Women," *Journal of Abnormal Social Psychology*, 68 (1964), 119; C. A. Leland and M. M. Lozoff, *College Influences on the Role Development of Undergraduates* (Stanford, Calif.: Institute for the Study of Human Problems, Stanford University, 1969), pp. 46–90.

14 U.S. Civil Service Commission, *Changing Patterns;* Dement.

15 I. Zwerling, "Part-Time Insured Staff," *Hospital and Community Psychiatry*, 21 (1970), 59; W. A. Thompson et al., "An Answer to the Computer Programmer Shortage." *Adult Leadership*, vol. 18, no. 7 (Jan. 1970), p. 213.

16 M. B. Smith, in *Socialization and Society*, ed. J. A. Clausen (Boston: Little, Brown, 1968), p. 313.

Judith Lorber*

# Trust, Loyalty, and the Place of Women in the Informal Organization of Work

When a student walks into a classroom, he or she is not likely to make a particular effort to find a same-sex person to sit near, unless they are friends. On most college campuses today, class-rooms, dormitories, extracurricular activities, and social groups are mixed by sex. Yet in the work world, job titles, work sites, promotion tracks, unions, lunch groups, coffee-break groups, and after-work leisure groups all tend to be sex-segregated. Even when sex discrimination is made illegal, the informal aspects of work perpetuate and support occupational segregation. In order to understand the social pressures of the informal organization of work, we must understand the power of the colleague peer group.

*I would like to thank Arlene Kaplan Daniels for her helpful comments.

## THE COLLEAGUE PEER GROUP

Two seemingly opposing social-psychological tendencies shape work life in male-dominated American occupations and professions. The first is individual competitiveness—often fierce, bitter, and personal, even in areas supposedly objective and dispassionate.[1] The second is the development of team cohesiveness or esprit de corps. The development of the colleague peer group is not really an opposite tendency to aggressive individualism, since informal colleague groups as well as formally structured teams frequently compete with each other. As Maccoby and Jacklin state:

> Male competition in real-life settings frequently takes the form of groups competing against groups (as in team sports), an activity that involves within-group cooperation as well as between-group competition, so that cooperative behavior is frequently not the antithesis of competitiveness.[2]

Except where the occupation is almost exclusively female, women have been excluded from most individual and team competition. The major role of women at work has been to be either docile, silent handmaidens or one of the prizes of success. As handmaidens, women keep the operation going smoothly for men;[3] as sexual prizes, they enhance and validate the successfulness of men.[4] In this paper, I shall examine this systematic exclusion of women from the peer groups that dominate all but the almost totally female occupations and professions in American society.

## A BAND OF BROTHERS

In most occupations, the organization of work is supposed to be based either on notions of bureaucratic rationality and efficiency or on universalistic professional standards of competence. However, the shared norms of informal work groups are equally, if not more, significant in determining job performance. These informal shared norms determine what is proper and improper behavior in many areas of work, such as rate of production, attitudes toward clients or customers, demeanor toward superiors and inferiors, dress, and major and minor rule violations. The norms are rooted in trust in the members of one's group, an exchange of favors among peers, and loyalty to those who bestow sponsorship and patronage. Thus, in bureaucratic organizations, the formal organization of work is strongly influenced by entrenched peer work groups and empire builders with their loyal followers; in professional organizations careers are shaped through the patronage and standards of exclusive inner circles; and in blue-collar work, the peer group determines which of management's rules are to be obeyed and which ignored.

While universalistic standards imply an acceptance of any and all who are qualified to do the work, the informal norms serve as open or subtle bases for inclusion or exclusion of novices from the inner circles of work life. Those who are excluded are felt to be not quite trustworthy—that is, it is felt they will be unreliable as colleagues or work partners. As Hughes has said, "The colleague group is ideally a brotherhood; to have within it people who cannot, given one another's attitudes, be accepted as brothers is very uncomfortable."[5]

Those who are excluded from informal work groups are at a disadvantage in filling the true requirements of their jobs, since important aspects of the work experience are not shared with them. Additionally, they are not sponsored for promotion and, should they gain a formal position of power, they discover it is extremely difficult to find loyal subordinates or exert their authority.[6] Therefore, they rarely rise to truly high levels of power and prestige within their work organizations. As a result, they have fewer resources to offer their colleagues, which further perpetuates their exclusion from the colleague peer groups.[7] To cite Hughes again, the first of their kind to attain a certain status are forever marginal because they are not invited to participate in "the informal brotherhood in which experiences are exchanged, competence built up, and the formal code elaborated and enforced."[8]

Davis, in his essay on the problems the visibly disabled have in group situations, discusses how the handicap becomes the focal point of the interaction, excluding the true focus.[9] Embarrassment is barely contained, stereotypical characteristics are attributed to the deviant, and the "normals" are not sure what can and cannot be expected of the different one. As a result, the deviant is never fully included as a normal participant. Rather, as Davis says, "The interaction is kept starved at a bare subsistence level of sociability. As with the poor relation at the wedding party . . . sufficient that he is here, he should not expect to dance with the bride."[10] For women breaking into male occupations, who also have a visible handicap, the line would go—sufficient we gave her a job, she shouldn't expect to go out to lunch with the boys.[11]

For the woman at work, it is important to know why it is so easy for men to find reasons to exclude women from their inner circles and work peer groups, in what ways this exclusion does or doesn't resemble the exclusion of some men, and how women can counteract this process.

## REASONS FOR LACK OF TRUST OF WOMEN BY MALE COLLEAGUES

### Like trusts like

Men and women in America are brought up in different cultural worlds. American boys are raised in a world filled with machinery, sports, and superheroes, with the goal of successful conquest; American girls are raised in a world filled with doll babies and doll houses, clothes, cosmetics, and the goal of successful marriage. They may even be brought up in different *moral* worlds—most American males learn the ideal is to curse, drink, smoke, gamble, and sleep around; most American females learn the ideal is to act virtuously and interest themselves in higher things, such as art, music, dance, literature, religion, and the social welfare of the downtrodden. So, in adulthood, we find men making policy, enforcing work norms, and deciding on sponsorship in smoke-filled rooms, over the three-martini lunch, at poker games, and at parties with prostitutes. As brother breakers of the moral code, men learn to look the other way, and this enforces their trust in each other.[12]

Examples of similar colleague protectiveness can be found in other Westernized countries. In Japan, for instance, the all-male after-work bar is the only place a man can go to unburden himself, knowing his colleagues will console him. According to Shaplen, ". . . [T]hey protect him and side with him, whether he is right or wrong, in his personal and sometimes his professional affairs."[13] Other examples that come to mind are the working-class pubs and saloons of the British and Irish, and the English upper-class exclusive clubs, where the members belong to similar occupations or have gone to the same school. Jan Morris can provide some interesting examples of male cohesiveness. Once a male member of a close-knit, homogeneous army unit, she has undergone a sex-change operation and is living as a female. She says,

> Sometimes nowadays I hear a party of men sharing a joke or an experience which, though not necessarily prurient, they would not think of sharing with a woman; and I think to myself not without a

wry nostalgia that once long ago, in the tented mess of the 9th Queen's Royal Lancers, they would have unhesitatingly shared it with me.[14]

As upholders of the moral code and traditional moral entrepreneurs,[15] women are not to be trusted to look the other way unless they are the subordinates of men. Secretaries, file clerks, typists and receptionists know that if they publicize their boss's dirty secrets, they will be out of a job.[16] As Szymanski[17] points out, because they have access to the details of corporate deals, women must be thoroughly subordinate and loyal. Kanter[18] calls the traditional secretary-manager relationship "patrimonial."

Even as equals women's moral stance will set them apart from their colleagues. Thus, Mary Anne Krupsak, past Lieutenant Governor of New York State, described herself in her 1974 election campaign as "not just one of the boys"—an emphasis on both her femaleness and her political purity. Another woman politician, New Jersey State Senator Alene S. Amond, had to file suit because she was barred from party caucuses after she reported to the press secret deliberations that fostered her fellow legislators' interests at the expense of their constituents.[19]

Similarly, men who come from a different cultural background or who are felt to have a different moral code have frequently been excluded from inner circles by those men already entrenched in a particular occupation or profession.[20] The police provide an excellent example of peer-group loyalty based on shared norms of sometimes doubtful morality. According to Stoddard,[21] the police "code" of semilegal and illegal practices is taught to new recruits in informal interaction. At the same time, the "old hands" carefully test the discretion and loyalty of the newcomers to see if they can be trusted. In his words,

> . . . [A]ll "code" practitioners have the responsibility of screening new recruits at various times to determine whether they are "alright guys," and to teach by example and mutual involvement the limitations of "code" practices. If the recruit accepts such training, he is welcomed into the group and given the rights and privileges commensurate with this new status. If he does not, he is classified as a "goof" and avoided by all the rest.[22]

At present, according to Tyree and Treas,[23] women more frequently than men are found in jobs where they do not share the social background of their peers. Whether the inclusion of women in colleague groups will lead to different attitudes and practices at work or whether they will gradually assimilate the norms of male old hands probably depends on their numbers, the homogeneity of their other social characteristics, and the extent to which they form an in-group of their own.[24]

## Sex games

The second reason women are felt to be disruptive of male inner circles is sex. (The same attitude is held about homosexuals.) When sexual relations are a possibility, the comfortable intimacy of colleague relations is disrupted by the threat of seductions, pursuits, rivalries, jealousies, and the private intimacy of the couple.[25]

The prime loyalty of the couple is to each other, not to the group. They can talk intimately about the others, and share opinions. They themselves in turn are not treated as individuals, but as a team. They are liked or disliked in tandem. They cannot dispense favors as individuals, or enter another inner circle as an individual, because the others will mentally include the partner in their calculations of trust and loyalty. Thus, the loyalties and enmities of one usually become the loyalties and enmities of the other. Even if they emphasize their individuality, unless they work in widely separated spheres, they may find it easier to operate openly as a team.

Whether membership in a male-female team is advantageous to women is questionable. Epstein[26] feels that because of incipient jealousy on the part of spouses, women are not likely to be chosen by men as proteges. If they are chosen, she feels that they are not likely to be designated as successors who can attain individual recognition. Rather, they are likely to become identified with a particular person and paid off in affection rather than in promotion, salary, or co-authorship.[27] Wilkie and Allen[28] found, however, that while male-female pairs were less likely to rotate the order of names on papers than single-sex pairs, the man was not significantly more likely than the woman to be the senior author. As they put it, "Perhaps traditional roles, which characteristically define, if not the man as the principal, at least one of the pair as the principal, play some part in hampering the development of equal collaboration between professionals of different sexes."[29]

The growing casualness about sex relations in general may soon permit long- and short-term coupling to be compatible with colleague cohesiveness. We may soon see the day when going to bed with a fellow worker will be no more remarked on, should it become known, than going out to lunch. But in order for that to happen, the norms will have to be such that male-female relations do not necessarily imply a special social relationship. In short, women will have to be invited out to lunch in the first place.

### Untrustworthy mothers

The last reason for men's lack of trust in women as colleagues is peculiar only to women, since it concerns their role as mothers. A very long time ago, working women were usually unmarried, childless, or beyond child-bearing age.[30] They were thus considered free of the possibility of getting inconveniently pregnant and disrupting the work team. Later, married women left work immediately on becoming impregnated, or, if they were "career women" who planned to continue working, they carefully limited and timed their pregnancies to be least disruptive of work schedules. Today, such timing is even easier, since a contraceptive failure can be corrected by a legal abortion at an early date.

However, while women may be relied on to use contraception fairly efficiently, will they be willing to have an abortion to interrupt an ill-timed pregnancy? Men may feel (or want to believe) that women are not that "cold-blooded,"[31] even though Guttmacher[32] and Rosen and Martindale[33] found that women with feminist orientations are quite willing to have abortions should an accidental pregnancy interfere with career goals.

Women are not expected to be able to put their work before their child's welfare. They are pressured to be available during vacations, and when a child is ill, emotionally troubled, or mentally retarded, to an extent men are not. Duberman[34] suggests that women do not want to relinquish or truly share their household responsibilities because it is part of their pride in being a woman to be able both to work and take care of their families. She cites one professional woman who felt that by being good at *all* her jobs—teaching, mothering, and housewifery—she showed up men, who were successful only in their occupational role.

Yet, by refusing to give up their prime directive, women place themselves in a position of being not quite reliable colleagues to men, who doubt they can do it all—or who want to make sure they do *not* do it all. As Coser and Rokoff[35] have shown, as long as women are the responsible parents, their loyalties to their families will be considered potentially disruptive of colleague relationships.

## PRIMARY LOYALTIES: MALE AND FEMALE

The question of primary loyalty goes to the heart of the problem of women and the informal organization of work. If there is a conflict, where should a working woman's loyalties lie—with her colleagues or her love partner? With her work team or her family? With her professional equals or with all women employees?

The traditional sexual division of labor has kept most colleague groups unisex, eliminating to a great extent the disruptive possibilities of sexual relations among colleagues. Formerly, it was a common norm that sexual couples did not work in the same place, so that the open admission of a love relationship between co-workers meant that one person left—usually the one who was lower in status. Thus, the conflict between loyalty to the love partner and loyalty to colleagues was eliminated by written or unwritten anti-nepotism rules.

Up to now, male colleague loyalties have been part of their main role of economic provider and have enhanced their possibilities of individual success, while female colleague loyalties in industrial society have been secondary to their main role of mother-wife. Is there a way that women can develop colleague loyalties that permit them to succeed as individuals and do not exacerbate interpersonal conflicts? I suggest that there is. Women must develop or strengthen inner circles of their own within male-dominated occupations and professions.

## CREATING A BAND OF SISTERS

The present composition of inner circles cannot be combatted by strict credentialism. The application of universalistic standards of training and experience to the formerly excluded will only perpetuate their exclusion, since the inner-circle principle starts in training and educational institutions. Since it is a fact of work life that colleagues band together to shape their work roles and for patronage, sponsorship, and mutual help up the ladder, the formerly excluded must form inner circles of their own and expand their power through their own selective recruitment and sponsorship. Groups of women students in medical and law schools have already successfully expanded the recruitment of women and also changed modes of teaching and curriculum to meet their own needs.[36] In the academic world, and in the professions, women have used women's caucuses in lieu of individual patrons to find jobs for available women and women for available jobs.[37]

Given the low number of women likely to be found in most male-dominated occupations, women must cast a wide net to form a band of sisters. They must cut across status hierarchies or extend their contacts outside their own particular organizations. Even if their day-to-day commitment is to their immediate workplace and colleague groups, the ultimate commitment of women who want to advance the cause of women must be to other competent, able women.

This process of women developing loyalty to women may become the "new credentialism" of the Insider, as Merton[38] claims, but I feel it is a political necessity at present.[39] Indeed, it seems to have been a political necessity since 1840, when Margaret Fuller advocated that rather than joining with men, women should themselves take up weapons and mutually help each other.[40]

## NOTES

1  Ian I. Mitroff, "Norms and Counter-norms in a Select Group of the Apollo Moon Scientists: a Case Study of the Ambivalence of Scientists," *American Sociological Review*, 39 (1974), 579–95.

2  Eleanor Emmons Maccoby and Carol Nagy Jacklin, *The Psychology of Sex Differences* (Stanford, Cal.: Stanford University Press, 1974), p. 274.

3  Albert Szymanski, "Race, Sex, and the U.S. Working Class," *Social Problems* 21 (1974), 724; and Rosabeth Moss Kanter, *Men and Women of the Corporation* (New York: Basic Books, 1977), pp. 69–103.

4  Robert Seidenberg, *Corporate Wives—Corporate Casualties?* (Garden City, N.Y.: Anchor, 1975), pp. 143, 147.

5  Everett Cherrington Hughes, "Dilemmas and Contradictions of Status," in Lewis A. Coser and Bernard Rosenberg, eds., *Sociological Theory* (New York: Macmillan, 1969), p. 362.

6  Rosabeth Moss Kanter, "Women and the Structure of Organizations: Explorations in Theory and Behavior," in Marcia Milman and Rosabeth Moss Kanter, eds., *Another Voice: Feminist Perspectives on Social Life and Social Science* (Garden City, N.Y.: Anchor, 1975), pp. 60–63.

7  Jean Lipman-Blumen, "Toward a Homosocial Theory of Sex Roles: an Explanation of the Sex Segregation of Social Institutions," *Signs*, 1 (Spring 1976 Supplement), 15–31.

8  Hughes, p. 360.

9  Fred Davis, *Illness, Interaction, and the Self* (Belmont, Cal.: Wadsworth, 1972), pp. 130–49.

10  *Ibid.*, p. 140.

11  For analyses of the subsequent effects of tokenism, see Kanter, "Some Effects of Proportions on Group Life: Skewed Sex Ratios and Responses to Token Women," *American Journal of Sociology*, 82 (1977), 965–90; and Judith Long Laws, "The Psychology of Tokenism: an Analysis," *Sex Roles*, 1 (1975), 51–67.

12  Kanter, *Men and Women of the Corporation*, pp. 49–67. She argues that it is the "uncertainty quotient" in managerial decision-making that necessitates trust and therefore social homogeneity among corporation managers.

13  Robert Shaplen, "A Reporter at Large. From MacArthur to Miki—III," *New Yorker Magazine*, August 18, 1975, 38–65.

14  Jan Morris, *Conundrum* (New York: New American Library, 1974), p. 34.

15  Herman P. Lantz, Jane Keyes, and Martin Schultz, "The American Family in the Preindustrial Period: from Base Lines in History to Change," *American Sociological Review*, 40 (1975), 21–36.

16  B. J. Phillips, "The Secretary's Dilemma," *Ms. Magazine*, 3 (1975), 66–67, 120.

17  Szymanski, "Race, Sex, and the U.S. Working Class," p. 724.

18  Kanter, *Men and Women of the Corporation*, pp. 69–103.

19  Donald Janson, "28 New Jersey Senators Ordered to Trial for Closing Caucus to Women Colleague," *New York Times*, February 19, 1975, 1,39. See also Kristen Amundsen, *A New Look at the Silenced Majority* (Englewood Cliffs, N.J.: Prentice-Hall, 1977), pp. 67–68.

20  David N. Solomon, "Ethnic and Class Differences among Hospitals as Contingencies in Medical Careers," *American Journal of Sociology*, 61 (1961), 463–71.

21  Ellwyn Stoddard, "The Informal 'Code' of Police Deviancy: a Group Approach to 'Blue-coat' Crime," in Clifton D. Bryant, ed., *Deviant Behavior: Occupational and Organizational Bases* (Chicago: Rand McNally, 1974), pp. 218–38.

22  *Ibid.*, p. 229.

23  Andrea Tyree and Judith Treas, "The Occupational and Marital Mobility of Women," *American Sociological Review*, 39 (1974), 293–302.

24  Kanter, "Some Effects of Proportions on Group Life"; and Judith Lorber, "Women and Medical Sociology: Invisible Professionals and Ubiquitous Patients," in Marcia Milman and Rosabeth Kanter, eds., *Another Voice: Feminist Perspective on Social Life and Social Science* (Garden City, N.Y.: Anchor, 1975), pp. 75–105.

25  Donald Roy, "Sex in the Factory: Informal Heterosexual Relations between Supervisors and Work Groups," in Clifton D. Bryant, ed., *Deviant Behavior: Occupational and Organizational Bases* (Chicago: Rand McNally, 1974).

26  Cynthia Fuchs Epstein, *Women's Place* (Berkeley: University of California Press, 1971), p. 169; and Epstein, "Bringing Women In: Rewards, Punishments, and the Structure of Achievement," in Ruth B. Kundsin, ed., *Women and Success: The Anatomy of Achievement* (New York: Morrow, 1974), pp. 13–21.

27  Epstein, "Ambiguity as Social Control: Consequences for the Integration of Women in Professional Elites," in Phyllis L. Steward and Muriel G. Cantor, eds., *Varieties of Work Experience: The Social Control of Occupational Groups and Roles* (Cambridge, Mass.: Schenckman, 1974), p. 32.

28  Jane Riblett Wilkie and Irving Lewis Allen, "Women Sociologists and Co-Authorship with Men," *The American Sociologist,* 10 (1975), 19–24.

29  *Ibid.,* p. 24.

30  Valerie Kincade Oppenheimer, "Demographic Influence on Female Employment and the Status of Women," *American Journal of Sociology,* 78 (1973), 946–61.

31  For limited recent data on male attitudes, see Bernard M. Bass, Judith Krusell, and Ralph A. Alexander, "Male Managers' Attitudes toward Working Women," in Linda S. Fidell and John DeLamater, eds., *Women in the Professions: What's All the Fuss About?* (Beverly Hills, Cal.: Sage Publications, 1971), pp. 63–78; and Kanter, *Men and Women of the Corporation,* pp. 106–07.

32  Sally Guttmacher and Dolores Kreisman, "Women's Work, Woman's Role, and Delay in Securing an Abortion," paper presented at Annual Meeting, American Public Health Association, Chicago, 1975.

33  R. A. Hudson Rosen and Lois J. Martindale, "Abortion as 'Deviance': Traditional Female Roles vs. the Feminist Perspective," paper presented at American Sociological Association Annual Meetings, San Francisco, 1975.

34  Lucile Duberman, *Gender and Sex in Society* (New York: Praeger, 1975), p. 128.

35  Rose Laub Coser and Gerald Rokoff, "Women in the Occupational World: Social Disruption and Conflict," *Social Problems,* 18 (1971), 535–54.

36  Margaret A. Campbell, *Why Would a Girl Go into Medicine? Medical Education in the United States: a Guide for Women* (Old Westbury, N.Y.: Feminist Press, 1973); and Elaine Hilberman *et al.,* "Support Groups for Women in Medical School: a First-year Program," *Journal of Medical Education,* 50 (1975), 867–75.

37  Ruth M. Oltman, "Women in the Professional Caucuses," in Linda S. Fidell and John DeLamater, eds., *Women in the Professions: What's All the Fuss About?* (Beverly Hills, Cal.: Sage Publications, 1971), pp. 123–44.

38  Robert K. Merton, "Insiders and Outsiders: a Chapter in the Sociology of Knowledge," *American Journal of Sociology,* 78 (1972), 9–47.

39  For similar sentiments, see Arlie Hochschild, "Making It: Marginality and Obstacles to Minority Consciousness," in Ruth B. Kundsin, ed., *Women and Success: The Anatomy of Achievement* (New York: Morrow, 1974), pp. 194–99; and Cynthia Secor, "Androgyny: an Early Reappraisal," *Women's Studies,* 2 (1974), 161–69.

40  Secor, "Androgyny," p. 169.

# PART 5 INSTITUTIONS OF SOCIAL CONTROL

# Mary Eastwood

# Feminism and the Law

The women's movement has sought to achieve four major goals: (1) equal treatment under the law; (2) protection from discrimination on the basis of sex; (3) physical self-determination; and (4) political and economic power for women as a class. The tactics for achieving the first three goals are, respectively: (1) litigation under the Constitution and ratification of the proposed Equal Rights Amendment; (2) the enactment and enforcement of laws and regulations prohibiting discrimination because of sex; and (3) abortion litigation and abortion law repeal, efforts to reform laws pertaining to rape and other sexual assaults, and increased concern for protection against wife beating.

With the achievement of the first three, the limitations imposed on women because of their sex will be lifted and the fourth goal should automatically follow if women fully utilize their rights. This article summarizes some of the cases and laws relevant to the first two goals.[1]

In pursuit of these goals, the women's movement has brought about a veritable revolution in women's legal status. Although women still experience discrimination and do not yet have complete equality under the law, most sex discrimination is now illegal and court decisions of the past decade have had a significantly different orientation than those of the preceding century.

## EQUAL TREATMENT UNDER THE CONSTITUTION

### Historical background

The Fourteenth Amendment to the United States Constitution provides that no state shall "deprive any person of life, liberty, or property; nor deny to any person within its jurisdiction the equal protection of the laws." The same basic prohibitions apply to the federal government under the due process clause of the Fifth Amendment. Despite the protective purpose of these amendments, courts in the past generally have found laws treating women as an inferior class to be constitutional.

In 1872, three Supreme Court justices, in a concurring opinion upholding the refusal of the State of Illinois to allow women to practice law, offered this reasoning:

> The natural and proper timidity and delicacy which belongs to the female sex evidently unfits it for many of the occupations of civil life. The constitution of the family organization, which is founded in the divine ordinance, as well as in the nature of things, indicates the domestic sphere as that which properly belongs to the domain and functions of womanhood. . . . The paramount destiny and mission of woman are to fulfill the noble and benign offices of wife and mother. This is the law of the Creator.[2]

In other words, "the woman's place is in the home" because that is where God intended her to be.

In 1908, in the famous case of *Muller v. Oregon*,[3] the Supreme Court held that an Oregon law establishing maximum hours of work only for women did not violate the Fourteenth Amendment Due Process Clause. Three years earlier the Court had declared unconstitutional a New York law limiting the hours of work for both men and women on the ground it violated the right of liberty to contract for employment.[4]

Consequently, the *Muller* decision was regarded as a major victory for those seeking decent standards of labor, even though the Court sustained special laws for women in the belief that women were an inferior class of persons needing special protection: "[Woman] is properly placed in a class by herself, and legislation designed for her protection may be sustained. It is impossible to close one's eyes to the fact that she still looks to her brother and depends upon him."[5] The Court reasoned, in effect, that women are reproductive instruments of the state; which therefore has an interest in controlling their activity and protecting their health:

> That woman's physical structure and the performance of maternal functions place her at a disadvantage in the struggle for subsistence is obvious. This is especially true when the burdens of motherhood are upon her. . . . As healthy mothers are essential to vigorous offspring, the physical well-being of woman becomes an object of public interest and care in order to preserve the strength and vigor of the race.[6]

In 1917, legislation restricting hours of work for both sexes was upheld by the Supreme Court in *Bunting v. Oregon*,[7] so there was no longer a need for the *Muller* rationale to uphold the constitutionality of labor standards legislation. Nevertheless, the theory in *Muller* that women may be treated differently than men for purposes of legislation became precedent for numerous cases restricting women's activities in other areas unrelated to employment. For example, *Muller* was cited to justify exclusion of women from jury service,[8] different treatment of women in licensing occupations,[9] and the exclusion of women from a state-supported college.[10]

The attitude that women's legal status should be determined by her idealized family status was expressed by the Court as late as 1961, in *Hoyt v. Florida*,[11] when it upheld the conviction by an all-male jury of a woman for murdering her husband. To the argument that she was denied her Fourteenth Amendment rights by a Florida law providing that no woman be selected to serve on a jury unless she registers her willingness to do so with the circuit court clerk—which virtually insured exclusion of women from the jury pool—the Court stated:

> Despite the enlightened emancipation of women from the restrictions and protections of bygone years, . . . woman is still regarded as the center of home and family life. . . . a State [may]

conclude that a woman should be relieved from the civic duty of jury service unless she herself determines that such service is consistent with her own special responsibilities.[12]

The designation of women's function in the home as a basis for treating men and women differently under the law in reality has relegated women to a service class. Regardless of a woman's economic position, her status under the Constitution has been that of a servant—to men and to the state.

### The current situation

In the 1970's, the Supreme Court has begun to take a more enlightened view of the position of women under the Constitution. Cases challenging laws that differentiate on the basis of sex have either been found to be unconstitutional or have been upheld on the ground that more favored treatment of women in the law is justified to compensate for other discrimination against women. Those cases in which the Court found sex distinctions unconstitutional are discussed first.

*Reed v. Reed*[13] involved an Idaho statute that gave preference to male relatives in the appointment of administrators of decedents' estates. The purpose of the statute was to eliminate the need for a probate court determination as to which of two relatives, otherwise equally entitled, should be appointed as administrator. The Court stated that "[t]o give a mandatory preference to members of either sex over members of the other, merely to accomplish the elimination of hearings on the merits, is to make the very kind of arbitrary legislative choice forbidden by the Equal Protection Clause of the Fourteenth Amendment . . . ."[14] *Reed* is important because it was the first case in which the Court found unconstitutional a law differentiating on the basis of sex.

In a 1973 decision, *Frontiero v. Richardson*,[15] the Court held that federal statutes that permitted a male member of the uniformed services to claim his wife as a dependent without a showing that she was in fact dependent upon him for her support, but denied a female member dependency benefits for her husband unless he was in fact dependent upon her for over one-half of his support, violated the rights of female members under the Due Process Clause of the Fifth Amendment. The opinion of four of the justices in *Frontiero* represents a more current view of the status of women under the Constitution:

It is true, of course, that the position of women in America has improved markedly in recent decades. Nevertheless, it can hardly be doubted that, in part because of the high visibility of the sex characteristic, women still face pervasive, although at times more subtle, discrimination in our educational institutions, in the job market and, perhaps most conspicuously, in the political arena.[16]

*Frontiero* is also significant because it represents the first time the Court considered sex discrimination as comparable to racial or ethnic discrimination. The courts have used different tests to determine whether a law that differentiates between classes of persons violates the constitutional requirement of equal protection of the laws. The standard traditionally applied in sex discrimination cases has been to uphold the law if the difference in treatment is reasonable and bears a rational relationship to the purpose of the legislation. The courts have applied a stricter test for constitutionality in cases involving discrimination because of race or national origin. Such classifications have been regarded as inherently suspect and violative of the Constitution unless it can be shown that the government has a compelling interest in maintaining the class distinction. In comparing sex with race and national origin in *Frontiero,* the Court stated:

> Moreover, since sex, like race and national origin, is an immutable characteristic determined solely by the accident of birth, the imposition of special disabilities upon the members of a particular sex because of their sex would seem to violate "the basic concept of our system that legal burdens should bear some relationship to individual responsibility . . ." [citation omitted]. And what differentiates sex from such nonsuspect statutes as intelligence or physical disability, and aligns it with the recognized suspect criteria, is that the sex characteristic frequently bears no relation to ability to perform or contribute to society. As a result, statutory distinctions between the sexes often have the effect of invidiously relegating the entire class of females to inferior legal status without regard to the actual capabilities of its individual members. . . .
> With these considerations in mind, we can only conclude that classifications based upon sex, like classifications based upon race, alienage, or national origin, are inherently suspect, and must therefore be subjected to strict judicial scrutiny.[17]

Although the Court has declined to adopt the stricter test of constitutionality in subsequent cases, this has not prevented the Court from striking down other sex distinctions in the law.

Two years later, in *Taylor v. Louisiana,*[18] the Supreme Court held that women as a class may not be excluded from jury service or given automatic exemptions based solely on sex if this results in jury lists that are almost all male. The Court expressly rejected the woman's-place-is-in-the-home rationale of *Hoyt v. Florida*,[19] although the case was based primarily on the defendant's "Sixth Amendment right to be tried by a jury drawn from a fair cross section of the community."[20]

Gender-based distinctions were directly involved in two cases challenging the constitutionality of provisions of the Social Security Act. In *Weinberger v. Weisenfeld*,[21] the Court held unconstitutional a provision in that Act[22] that provided benefits for the surviving widow and minor children of a working man covered by the Act, but provided benefits only for the minor children and not the widower upon the death of a working woman covered by the Act. Weisenfeld's wife died in childbirth and he was left with the sole care of their infant son. The Court held that the denial of benefits to Weisenfeld violated his right to equal protection of the laws secured by the Constitution, stating:

> Obviously, the notion that men are more likely than women to be the primary supporters of their spouses and children is not entirely without empirical support. . . But such a gender-based generalization cannot suffice to justify the denigration of the efforts of women who do work and whose earnings contribute significantly to their families' support.[23]

The Court stated further that the Constitution forbids sex distinctions that give lesser benefits to families of female workers who pay Social Security taxes than to the families of male workers, and recognized the father's as well as the mother's responsibility for child care:

> Given the purpose of enabling the surviving parent to remain at home to care for a child, the gender-based distinction of sec. 402(g) is entirely irrational. The classification discriminates among surviving children solely on the basis of the sex of the surviving parent. . . . The fact that a man is working while there is a wife at home does not mean that he would, or should be required to, continue to work if his wife dies. It is no less important for a child to be cared for by its sole surviving parent when the parent is male rather than female. And a father, no less than a mother, has a constitutionally protected right to the "companionship, care, custody, and management" of "the children he has sired and raised. . . ."[24]

The other case, *Califano v. Goldfarb*,[25] involved a provision of the Social Security Act[26] that differentiated on the basis of sex in the payment of survivor's benefits. Goldfarb's wife had worked as a secretary for almost 25 years. When she died, Goldfarb applied for widowers' benefits, but his application was denied because benefits were payable to a husband on the basis of earnings of a deceased wife only if he was receiving at least half of his support from her when she died. A surviving wife did not have to prove such dependency. The Court held that because the sex differentiation "results in the efforts of female workers required to pay social security taxes producing less protection for their spouses than is produced by the efforts of men," it is "forbidden by the Constitution."[27] One justice concurring in the decision thought it was the widower-beneficiaries who were discriminated against by the statute and that "this discrimination against a group of males is merely the accidental byproduct of a traditional way of thinking about females."[28] The four dissenting justices also thought it was the men who were being discriminated against but did not feel it was unconstitutional to do so.

Cases involving state laws providing different age limits for men and women present a clearer picture of which sex is being discriminated against. In *Stanton v. Stanton*,[29] the Court held that a Utah statute providing for parental support for male children to age 21 and for female children to age 18 denies females the equal protection of the laws, stating:

> If a specified age of minority is required for the boy in order to assure him parental support while he attains his education and training, so, too, is it for the girl.[30]

*Craig v. Boren*[31] involved an Oklahoma statute that prohibited the selling of 3.2 percent beer to males under 21 but allowed its sale to women over 18. The state's rationale for this law was that it wanted to cut down on drunken driving and men between ages 18 and 21 were more likely to be arrested for this crime than women. The Court held that the statute denied to males aged 18–21 the equal protection of the laws. In that case, the Court enunciated an equal protection test somewhere in between the two tests discussed above, stating:

> To withstand constitutional challenge, previous cases establish that classifications by gender must serve important governmental

objectives and must be substantially related to achievement of those objectives.[32]

A now-superseded New Hampshire statute that punished men who had sexual intercourse with consenting females under age 15 but imposed no penalty on normal sexual intercourse between a woman and a male under 15 was held unconstitutional by the U.S. Court of Appeals for the First Circuit in *Helgemoe* v. *Meloon.* The Supreme Court denied review of the case on June 5, 1978.*

Vestiges of *Muller v. Oregon* are evident in those recent Supreme Court decisions upholding the constitutionality of differences in treatment based on sex. In *Muller,* restrictions on hours of work for women were justified in part on the theory that legislation to protect women is "necessary to secure a real equality of right" in the unequal struggle for subsistence.[33] A concept of compensatory discrimination was suggested by the Court in that case:

> This difference [between men and women] justifies a difference in legislation and upholds that which is designed to compensate for some of the burdens which rest upon her.[34]

A similar theory of compensating women for discrimination was used by the Court in *Kahn v. Shevin,* upholding a Florida statute that granted widows, but not widowers, an annual $500 property tax exemption:

> There can be no dispute that the financial difficulties confronting the lone woman in Florida or in any other State exceeded those facing the man.[35]

In *Schlesinger v. Ballard,*[36] federal statutes providing longer tenure (before mandatory discharge) for female than for male naval officers who are not promoted[37] were held not violative of the due process rights of male officers. The Court reasoned that the longer period of tenure for women is consistent with the goal of providing women officers with fair and equitable career advancement programs.

Similarly, a formula for computing Social Security retirement benefits that was more advantageous to women was upheld in *Califano v. Webster.*[38] In finding constitutional the preferential treatment of women, the Court stated:

---

*Helgemoe* v. *Meloon,* 564 F.2d 602 (1st Cir. 1977), cert. denied 46 L.W. 3751.

The challenged statute operated directly to compensate women for past economic discrimination. . . . Thus, allowing women, who as such have been unfairly hindered from earning as much as men, to eliminate additional low-earning years from the calculation of their retirement benefits works directly to remedy some part of the effect of past discrimination.[39]

The cases discussed above all involved differences in treatment based on sex. During the 1970's the Court also considered the constitutional implications of differences in treatment based on child bearing (a function exercised by some women but no men). School board practices of requiring pregnant schoolteachers to take leave without pay after their fourth and fifth months of pregnancy were challenged by teachers in Virginia and Ohio. The Supreme Court held that mandatory termination of employment in those cases was unconstitutional under the Due Process Clause of the Fourteenth Amendment, stating:

> This Court has long recognized that freedom of personal choice in matters of marriage and family life is one of the liberties protected by the Due Process Clause of the Fourteenth Amendment. . . . [N]either the necessity for continuity of instruction nor the state interest in keeping physically unfit teachers out of the classroom can justify the sweeping mandatory leave regulations that the Cleveland and Chesterfield County School Boards have adopted. While the regulations no doubt represent a good-faith attempt to achieve a laudable goal, they cannot pass muster under the Due Process of the Fourteenth Amendment, because they employ irrebuttable presumptions that unduly penalize a female teacher for deciding to bear a child.[40]

The Court did not deal with the issue of discrimination on the basis of sex, in that the termination policy could apply only to female and not to male teachers.

Although a woman may not be arbitrarily removed from her job because of pregnancy, the Court has held that the Constitution does not require that she be paid for the time she takes off from work due to pregnancy and childbirth, even though such benefits are paid for workers disabled for other reasons. In *Geduldig v. Aiello*,[41] the Court upheld a California disability insurance system that provided benefits for employees temporarily disabled from work but denied benefits to pregnant women unable to work because of normal pregnancy and childbirth. Benefits were allowed, however, where the pregnancy involved medial complications. The Court held that California's insurance system did not violate the Fourteenth Amendment Equal Protection Clause, and discussed the sex discrimination issue in a footnote:

> The California insurance program does not exclude anyone from benefit eligibility because of gender but merely removes one physical condition—pregnancy—from the list of compensable disabilities. While it is true that only women can become pregnant, it does not follow that every legislative classification concerning pregnancy is a sex-based classification. . . . Normal pregnancy is an objectively identifiable physical condition with unique characteristics. Absent a showing that distinctions involving pregnancy are mere pretexts designed to effect an invidious discrimination against one sex or the other, lawmakers are constitutionally free to include or exclude pregnancy from the coverage of legislation such as this on any reasonable basis, just as with respect to any other physical condition. . . . The program divides potential recipients into two groups—pregnant women and nonpregnant persons. While the first group is exclusively female, the second includes members of both sexes. The fiscal and actuarial benefits of the program thus accrue to members of both sexes.[42]

Sex segregation, as distinguished from different or unequal treatment, was involved in a 1977 case in which the Court affirmed (by an equally divided court) a decision of the U.S. Court of Appeals for the Third Circuit, holding that a teenage girl could be excluded from an all-male public high school where the school system provided a comparable all-female public high school.[43] In this area, the courts clearly have not regarded sex classification as being as invidious as racial discrimination.

Nevertheless, in the majority of cases involving women's rights during the past decade, the Supreme Court has interpreted the Fifth and Fourteenth Amendments to the Constitution as requiring equal treatment, or has permitted distinctions for purposes of compensating women for discrimination in society at large. To insure equal rights under the Constitution, however, the women's movement has given priority to securing ratification of the proposed Equal Rights Amendment to make complete equality mandatory in all cases.

### The Equal Rights Amendment

The proposed Equal Rights Amendment to the Constitution provides that "Equality of rights under the law shall not be denied or abridged by the United States or by any State on account of sex." An equal rights amendment was first proposed in 1923 by Dr. Alice Paul and the National Women's Party as a response to the Court decisions emanating from *Muller*. The ERA was finally passed by the Congress on March 22, 1972. It must be ratified by three-fourths of the states within seven years, unless Congress votes to extend the time for ratification. If it comes into effect, such a constitutional requirement of absolute equality of the sexes would result in changes in the application of any laws differentiating on the basis of sex.

The 1972 Senate Judiciary Committee report on the proposed Equal Rights Amendment attempted to explain the effect the amendment would have.[44] As in the case of the Fourteenth Amendment, it would apply only to governmental action and not to purely private action. The ERA would not limit the power of the states to regulate cohabitation and sexual activity—such as requiring sex-segregated sleeping quarters in college dormitories, prison dormitories, and military barracks. The ERA would also require that men and women be treated equally with respect to the draft. If there were compulsory military conscription, women as well as men who meet the physical and other requirements would be subject to the draft and would be assigned to duties based on their qualifications and the needs of the services, rather than on sex.

The ERA would require equal treatment of men and women in state laws and regulations governing employment. Laws which apply only to one sex or which differentiate on the basis of sex would either be held unconstitutional or extended to the other sex. Single-sex state schools and colleges, but not necessarily private schools, would have to change their admission policies to admit both sexes.

Laws relating to domestic relations—marriage, divorce, alimony, child support, custody, and visitation—"will have to be based on individual circumstances and needs, and not on sexual stereotypes."[45] For example, alimony would not be awarded to a divorced wife on the basis of her sex, but could be awarded to either spouse based on contribution to the marriage or financial need. Neither parent would be preferred because of his or her sex in awarding child custody—the best interests of the child would control. Under the ERA support obligations would be based not on the sex of the spouse but on earning power and nonmonetary contributions to the family.

The adoption of the ERA would give women a new constitutional base upon which to challenge discriminatory laws and official practices.

It would limit the power of government—the Congress and state legislatures, federal and state executive agencies, and the courts—to adopt or approve laws and policies that provide different treatment of men and women. However, if the ERA fails to be ratified, it does not mean that difference in treatment will continue. Effective challenges to discrimination through litigation under the Fifth and Fourteenth Amendments would become even more important to women.

## LEGAL PROTECTION AGAINST SEX DISCRIMINATION

During the past 15 years, a number of federal laws have been enacted that affirmatively prohibit discrimination against women (and in most instances minorities).

1  The Equal Pay Act[46] prohibits paying a woman at a lower rate than a man who is doing substantially the same work if the jobs require equal skill, effort, and responsibility. Different pay rates are allowed if they are based on a nondiscriminatory seniority or merit system, or a system that measures earnings by quality or quantity of production.

2  Title VII of the Civil Rights Act of 1964, as amended,[47] prohibits discrimination on the basis of race, color, religion, sex, or national origin in all aspects of employment by employers covered by the Act. It also prohibits the segregation or classification of employees in any way that would tend to deprive an individual of employment opportunities, and covers employment agencies and labor organizations as well as employers. The 1972 amendments to Title VII of the Civil Rights Act of 1964[48] permit federal employees and applicants, as well as employees in the private sector and state and local employees, to file suit in federal district court if they are not satisfied with the disposition of their complaints by the agencies.

3  Executive Order No. 11246 of September 24, 1965, as amended by Executive Order No. 11375 of October 13, 1967,[49] prohibits discrimination in employment under federal contracts. Each federal contract must contain a nondiscrimination clause in which the contractor agrees not to discriminate in any aspect of employment. The government has the power to enforce the nondiscrimination clause by cancelling, terminating, suspending, or delaying the contract if the contractor discriminates.

4 Executive Order No. 11478 of August 8, 1969, prohibits discrimination in employment by the federal government itself and by the District of Columbia government.

5 Title IX of the Education Amendments of 1972[50] prohibits discrimination on the basis of sex under educational programs or activities receiving federal financial assistance, with certain exceptions. The prohibition covers discrimination in employment of teachers and other school personnel, and discrimination in admissions, financial aid, and access to educational programs and activities.

6. The Equal Credit Opportunity Act[51] makes it unlawful for any creditor to discriminate against any applicant on the basis of sex or marital status with respect to any aspect of a credit transaction.

7. The State and Local Fiscal Assistance Act of 1972[52] (Revenue Sharing) prohibits exclusion of any person, on the grounds of race, color, national origin, or sex, from participation in or enjoyment of the benefits of any program or activity whose funding is in whole or in part provided by the Act.

A similar prohibition against discrimination in connection with federal grants for law enforcement and criminal justice purposes was included in the Crime Control Act of 1973.[53] A prohibition against sex discrimination was added to the Fair Housing Act in 1974[54] and nondiscrimination clauses have been included in numerous other federal statutes as well.[55]

### Title VII litigation

The sex discrimination provisions of Title VII of the Civil Rights Act of 1964 have been the subject of considerable litigation. An important effect of the law was to invalidate restrictive state labor laws and employer practices that preserved the better paying and otherwise more desirable jobs for men. In a 1971 case, *Mengelkoch* v. *Industrial Welfare Commission*,[56] women employees challenged the consistency with Title VII (and the constitutionality) of California's restrictions on hours of work, which applied to women only. The effect of the restrictions was to deprive women of access to the higher paid jobs, which might occasionally require some overtime work, and of the opportunity to earn overtime pay. A restraining order was entered against the company and the state, prohibiting discrimination against women on the basis of the state hours laws.

In *Bowe v. Colgate-Palmolive Co.*[57] (1969), the United States Court of Appeals for the Seventh Circuit held that an employer-imposed practice at Colgate's Jeffersonville, Indiana, plant, allowing only men to work on jobs requiring the lifting of 35 pounds or more, was unlawful under Title VII. The court stated that Colgate must give all of its workers the opportunity to demonstrate their ability to perform more strenuous jobs, and then permit those who could to apply for any position to which their seniority entitled them. The rule that purported to protect women at the Colgate plant from lifting more than 35 pounds had resulted in the top pay rate for women employees equaling the bottom rate for men. The 35-pound rule also meant that some of the more tiring and difficult jobs were women's jobs; one such job required the worker to spend the day lifting filled bottles of liquid Ajax, so that by quitting time she had lifted over 17 tons.

Also in 1969, in *Weeks v. Southern Bell Telephone & Telegraph Co.,*[58] the United States Court of Appeals for the Fifth Circuit similarly held that a 30-pound weight-lifting limitation on women workers was unlawful under Title VII, as was the exclusion of women from jobs in order to protect them from having to work at night. The court pointed out:

> Title VII rejects just this type of romantic paternalism as unduly Victorian and instead vests individual women with the power to decide whether or not to take on unromantic tasks. Men have always had the right to determine whether the incremental increase in remuneration for strenuous, dangerous, obnoxious, boring or unromantic tasks is worth the candle. The promise of Title VII is that women are now to be on an equal footing.[59]

These and other early appellate court decisions in Title VII cases are important because they insured that the new law was properly interpreted to require equal employment opportunity for women. The employers involved did not appeal them to the Supreme Court.

The first sex discrimination case to be heard by the Supreme Court under Title VII was *Phillips v. Martin Marietta Corporation* in 1971.[60] It involved the question of whether an employer's policy of not hiring women with pre-school age children constituted illegal sex discrimination. The Court of Appeals for the Fifth Circuit had held that it did not because the "discrimination was based on a two-pronged qualification, *i.e.* a woman with pre-school age children," rather than on sex alone.[61] The Supreme Court reversed the decision, stating in part: "The Civil Rights Act of 1964 requires that persons of like qualifications be given employment opportunities irrespective of their sex. The Court of Appeals therefore erred in reading this section as permitting one hiring policy for women and another for men—each having pre-school age children."[62]

The *Phillips* case involved an employment policy that obviously treated men and women differently. In a 1977 case, *Dothard v. Rawlinson*,[63] the Supreme Court considered the question of an Alabama statute requiring applicants for jobs as prison guards to weigh at least 120 pounds and be at least 5 feet 2 inches tall, regardless of sex. The Court found that although the qualification was ostensibly neutral as to sex, it operated disproportionately to exclude women from eligibility for jobs as prison guards, denying them equal employment opportunity. However, the Court upheld an Alabama regulation that excluded women from correctional positions involving contact with prisoners in all male maximum security institutions. Being male was considered a bona fide occupational qualification for such positions.

The effect of pregnancy on working women's employment rights was the subject of two other Supreme Court decisions. In *General Electric Company v. Gilbert*,[64] the Supreme Court held that an employer's disability insurance plan excluding pregnancy-related disabilities from coverage does not violate the Title VII prohibition against sex discrimination. The Court reasoned that sex discrimination means difference in treatment between men and women. Difference in treatment based on pregnancy, which is a temporary function of only some women, does not itself constitute discrimination unless the exclusion of pregnancy benefits is shown to be a "mere pretext" designed to discriminate against women. The facts in the case indicated that female employees of General Electric already were securing greater monetary benefits from the insurance system than were male employees, so that no adverse impact on women as a class resulted from the exclusion of pregnancy benefits.

However, the Court ruled in *Nashville Gas Company v. Satty*,[65] that Title VII is violated if an employer denies seniority rights to female employees who return to work after pregnancy leave. The Court held that such an employer policy imposes a burden on women that men do not suffer. A second issue in that case involved the denial of sick pay to female employees absent from work due to pregnancy. Following its decision in the *Gilbert* case, the Court pointed out that exclusion of sick pay for pregnancy is a violation of Title VII only if it is shown that the exclusion in a mere pretext for discriminating against women.

On April 25, 1978 the Supreme Court held that Title VII prohibits an employer from requiring female employees to pay more than male employees for equal retirement benefits. Although women live longer than men, Title VII prohibits the use of such class generalizations when it works to the detriment of individual employees because of their sex.[66]

## CONCLUSION

In recent years there has been dramatic improvement in the law affecting women as a class. However, it may take women several decades before these improvements will have a real effect on their lives. A 55-year-old woman who has been denied educational or employment opportunities because of sex discrimination cannot make up for it now. It is too late for the 35-year-old welfare mother with nine children to benefit much from the Supreme Court's abortion rulings.

It should also be noted that although the courts that ruled on the cases and the Congress that enacted the laws consist predominantly of men, their actions were not the result of benevolent paternalism. Women litigants with women lawyers brought many of the key cases, feminist organizations lobbied for the legislation and women in Congress helped push it through, and the activities of the women's movement generally have helped educate the lawmakers and judges.[67]

Finally, there are other legal issues that the women's movement is, or should be, addressing itself to. Is it possible to reform marriage and divorce laws so as to be consistent with feminist philosophy? Is the concept of adult dependency—imbedded in our income tax, Social Security, retirement, and other laws providing social benefits—consistent with feminist goals? Do our laws and public policies on the family inhibit equality between the sexes? Can reform of the rape laws protect women from violent sexual assaults? Are the legal issues respecting homosexuality, and particularly lesbianism, relevant to feminism? How should the law deal with prostitution and pornography, if at all? If the next ten years are to show as much progress for women as the last ten, these are some of the issues that need to be debated

## NOTES

1 The Supreme Court decisions on abortion are discussed in the article by Nadean Bishop, elsewhere in this book.
2 *Bradwell v. Illinois*, 83 U.S. (16 Wall.) 130, 141 (1872).
3 *Muller v. Oregon*, 208 U.S. 412 (1908).
4 *Lochner v. New York*, 198 U.S. 45 (1905).
5 *Muller v. Oregon*, 208 U.S. at 422.
6 Id. at 421.
7 *Bunting v. Oregon*, 243 U.S. 426 (1917).
8 *Commonwealth v. Welosky*. 276 Mass. 398, 177 N.E. 656, 664 (1931), *cert. denied*, 284 U.S. 684 (1932).
9 *Quong Wing v. Kirkendall*, 223 U.S. 59, 63 (1912); *People v. Case*, 153 Mich. 98, 101, 116 N.W. 558, 560 (1908); *State v. Hunter*, 208 Ore. 282, 288, 300 P.2d 455, 458 (1956).
10 *Allred v. Heaton*, 336 S.W.2d 251 (Tex. Civ. App.), *cert. denied*, 364 U.S. 517 (1960); *Heaton v. Bristol*, 317 S.W.2d 86 (Tex. Civ. App.), *cert. denied*, 359 U.S. 230 (1958).
11 *Hoyt v. Florida*, 368 U.S. 57 62 (1961).
12 Id. at 61–62.
13 *Reed v. Reed*, 404 U.S. 71 (1971).
14 Id. at 76.
15 *Frontiero v. Richardson*, 411 U.S. 677 (1973).
16 Id. at 685–686.
17 Id. at 686–687.
18 *Taylor v. Louisiana*, 419 U.S. 522 (1975).
19 *Hoyt v. Florida*, 368 U.S. 57 (1961).
20 419 U.S. at 534.
21 *Weinberger v. Weisenfeld*, 420 U.S. 636 (1975).
22 42 U.S.C. 402(g).
23 *Weinberger v. Weisenfeld*, 420 U.S. at 645.
24 Id. at 651–52.
25 *Califano v. Goldfarb*, 430 U.S. 199 (1977).
26 42 U.S.C. 402(f)(1).
27 *Califano v. Goldfarb*, 430 U.S. at 206–207.
28 Justice Stevens, concurring, 430 U.S. at 223.
29 *Stanton v. Stanton*, 421 U.S. 7 (1975).
30 Id. at 15.
31 *Craig v. Boren*, 429 U.S. 190 (1976).
32 Id. at 197.
33 *Muller v. Oregon*, 208 U.S. 412, 42 (1908).
34 Id. at 422–423.

35  *Kahn v. Shevin*, 416 U.S. 351 (1974).

36  *Schlesinger v. Ballard*, 419 U.S. 498 (1975).

37  10 U.S.C. 6382, 6401.

38  *Califano v. Webster*, 430 U.S. 313 (1977).

39  Id. at 318. In 1972, Congress amended the Social Security Act to make the benefits formula equal for men and women. 86 Stat. 1340 (1972).

40  *Cleveland Board of Educ. v. La Fleur*, 414 U.S. 632, 639–40 and 647–48 (1974).

41  *Geduldig v. Aiello*, 417 U.S. 484 (1974).

42  Id. at 496–97.

43  *Vorchheimer v. Philadelphia School District*, 45 L.W. 4378 (April 19, 1977), affirming 532 F.2d 880 (3rd Cir., 1976). See also *Williams v. McNair*, 316 F.Supp. 134 (D.S.C., 1970), *aff'd*, 401 U.S. 951 (1971).

44.  S. Rep. No. 92–689, 92d Cong., 2d Sess. (1972), pp. 11–18.

45  Id. p. 17.

46  29 U.S.C. 206(d).

47  42 U.S.C. 2000e.

48  86 Stat. 103 (1972); 42 U.S.C. 2000e–16.

49  The 1967 Executive Order extended the 1965 order to include sex discrimination. Executive orders are published in Title 3 of the Code of Federal Regulations, in chronological and numerical order.

50  20 U.S.C. 1681.

51  15 U.S.C. 1691.

52  31 U.S.C. 1242.

53  42 U.S.C. 3766.

54  42 U.S.C. 3604–3606.

55  For example, 8 U.S.C. 1152, 1422 (immigration and naturalization); 12 U.S.C. 1735f-5 (federal mortgage loan assistance); 15 U.S.C. 775 (Federal Energy Administration programs); 20 U.S.C. 1866 (Women's Educational Equity Act of 1974); 20 U.S.C. 1078a, 1087-2 (student loans); 20 U.S.C. 2504 (Peace Corps volunteers); 23 U.S.C. 324 (federal highway assistance); 28 U.S.C. 1862, 1867 (federal jury service); 29 U.S.C. 848, 983, 991 (comprehensive employment and training programs administered by the Labor Department); 33 U.S.C. 1251 note (federal assistance for water pollution control); 42 U.S.C. 295h-9, 298b-2 (federally assisted training for health professions); 42 U.S.C. 2985g (federal assistance for community economic development programs); 42 U.S.C. 5057 (domestic volunteer services programs); 42 U.S.C. 5151 (disaster assistance); 42 U.S.C. 5672 (federal assistance for juvenile justice and delinquency prevention); 42 U.S.C. 5891 (Energy Research and Development Administration programs); 43 U.S.C. 1651 note (Trans-Alaska Pipeline); 48 U.S.C. 1708 (rights of access to and benefits from submerged lands conveyed to territories); 49 U.S.C. 1608 (federally assisted urban mass transit programs); 31 U.S.C. 1242 (State and Local Fiscal Assistance Act of 1972).

56  *Mengelkoch v. Industrial Welfare Commission*, 442 F.2d. 1119 (9th Cir., 1971).

57  *Bowe v. Colgate-Palmolive Co.*, 416 F.2d 711 (7th Cir., 1969); 489 F.2d 896 (7th Cir. 1973).

58  *Weeks v. Southern Bell Telephone & Telegraph Co.*, 408 F.2d 228 (5th Cir., 1969).

59  Id. at 236.

60  *Phillips v. Martin Marietta Corporation*, 400 U.S. 542 (1971).

61  411 F.2d 1, rehearing denied 416 F.2d 1257 (5th Cir., 1969).

62  400 U.S. at 544.

63  *Dothard v. Rawlinson*, 45 L.W. 4888, decided June 27, 1977.

64  *General Electric Company v. Gilbert*, 45 L.W. 4031, decided Dec. 7, 1976.

65  *Nashville Gas Company v. Satty*, 46 L.W. 4026, decided Dec. 6, 1977.

66  *City of Los Angeles v. Manhart*, 46 L.W. 4347.

67  Jo Freeman, *The Politics of Women's Liberation* (New York: Longman, Inc., 1975).

# Naomi B. Lynn

# American Women and the Political Process

The political activities of American women comprise a mixed record that ranges from minimal tokenism to limited achievement. Politics has strategic importance for women because the ultimate success of the women's movement will rest heavily on effective use of the political process. Women will never achieve political equality until women are found in powerful decision-making positions in numbers that reflect their approximate percentage of the total population. Furthermore, women's present status is incompatible with the democratic norms used to justify the very existence of American society.

Women are relatively inactive in politics because they are denied the opportunities to develop the self-confidence that political scientists have found to characterize the active citizen in a democratic society. Duverger points out:

If the majority of women are little attracted to political careers, it
is because everything tends to turn them away from them; if they
allow politics to remain essentially a man's business, it is because
everything is conducive to this belief: tradition, family life,
education, religion and literature. . . . The small part played by
women in politics merely reflects and results from the secondary
place to which they are assigned by the customs and attitudes of
our society and which their education and training tend to make
them accept as the natural order of things.[1]

## WOMEN AS VOTERS

### The women's suffrage movement

A major turning point for women came in the 1830's, when the early
efforts of northern women to secure the abolition of slavery demonstrated the effectiveness of agitation for human rights.[2] Soon after
slavery was abolished, the issue of women's suffrage came to the fore.
The first victories came in areas where women represented a minority
of the population, such as the American West and New Zealand. In
1869 the territory of Wyoming gave women the right to vote. Three
years later Susan B. Anthony voted illegally in the presidential election,
and she was later convicted in court. She drafted the Women Suffrage
Amendment, which was finally ratified in 1920.

After 1920 the women's suffrage movement was faced with a decision. Should it exert its considerable influence in active politics, or
should it shift to nonpartisan efforts? The National American Woman's
Suffrage Association decided on the second route, and such groups as
the League of Women Voters became a main focus of women's political
attention for decades.[3] The move was justified by a desire to keep
women united and to hold all officeholders accountable to all women,
but it did dilute the force of women's political power. As one observer
has said, "Looking back across the years since the 19th Amendment we
can see where women erred. Winning the vote was accepted as an end
in itself, which it was not. Having won political power, women have
never used it. Therein lies our failure."[4]

### Women's voting patterns

Voting, like any other behavior, can become a habit, but it must be
supported by norms and expectations regarding legitimate behavior.

Women who were not involved in the consciousness-raising efforts of the suffrage movement were uncomfortable about exercising their new voting right.[5] A 1924 study of Chicago women revealed that 11.4 percent of them still did not believe women should vote.[6]

Social norms were quite effective in shaping voting patterns: immigrant women and southern women were tied to the traditional view that political affairs were a man's purview. In the West, women had been forced by the realities of frontier life to take an active part in the social and economic life of the community. John Stucker found in his study that when barriers to voting were lifted, immigrant and white southern women had a much lower voting turnout than women in the West.[7] Women's suffrage in the South was further complicated by efforts to disenfranchise blacks. Poll taxes, literacy tests, and long residence requirements made it almost impossible for black women to vote.[8]

The gradual increase in women voters can be accounted for in part by the fact that the older generations, who had been brought up with the idea that voting was a man's prerogative, were gradually replaced by later generations who grew up after women's suffrage had become a fact of life. The civil rights legislation of the 1960's has also facilitated black female voting. Table 1 shows the overall record of voting by men and women from 1948 to 1976. A gap has persisted, the men's voting percentages remaining higher than women's. Yet more total votes are cast by women, owing to their greater numbers in the population.

TABLE 1    Percentages of Men and Women Voting in Elections 1948–1976

|       | 1948 | 1952 | 1956 | 1960 | 1964 | 1968 | 1972 | 1976 |
|-------|------|------|------|------|------|------|------|------|
| Men   | 69   | 72   | 80   | 80   | 73   | 69   | 76   | 78   |
| Women | 59   | 62   | 69   | 69   | 60   | 66   | 70   | 69   |

SOURCE: Center for Political Studies, Inter-University Consortium, University of Michigan. These percentages are estimates subject to normal sampling errors.

A closer look at the 1976 election shows that age makes a difference: in this election persons under 30 had a lower voting turnout, but the difference between men and women was less than 6 percent (64 percent for males and 58 for females). It is among those over 50, raised in the more traditional environment, that we find the biggest male-female difference in voting—86 percent for males and 70 percent for females. But the most critical variable is education. Women in the lowest education group were least likely to vote—74 percent of males in this group voted, but only 51 percent of the women. Of those with at least a high school education, 71 percent of males and 66 percent of females voted. And of those with college educations, 87 percent of the men and 84 percent of the women voted.[9] As more women move into the higher education category, more should be voting. A pioneer suffragette once said that if men wanted to keep women down, they made their first mistake when they taught them their ABC's.[10]

The authors of *The American Voter* found that mothers of young children were less likely to vote than fathers of young children, regardless of educational level. The researchers suggested that the demands of child care could keep the women from voting, but their political involvement could still be higher than the voting turnout alone would indicate.[11] However, sociologists have noted the primacy of the role of mother in the identification of the adult female, and this author's own research suggests that among women with education above the high school level, motherhood tends to lower their sense of political efficacy and hence their political participation.[12] Further research is needed to examine the full impact that motherhood has on the development of women's political sense of self.

## Party identification

Before 1948 women apparently did not identify with a particular party as strongly as men, though survey data are not available to prove this point. Since 1948 the party identification of men and women has become generally similar. In 1976, 47 percent of the men and 51 percent of the women considered themselves Democrats and 34 percent of the men and 33 percent of the women considered themselves Republicans. As Table 2 shows, the strength of the party identification is also similar.

Data on the question of how presidential preferences of men and women differ are inconsistent. As Table 3 reflects, women voted more heavily for Eisenhower than men did in both 1952 and 1956. More women also voted for Nixon than Kennedy in 1960, despite the myth that women voters are swayed more than men by a candidate's physical appearance. But in the following three elections women supported Democratic candidates at a slightly higher percentage than men. Women switched again in 1976, but in all these cases the close results may be attributed to sampling errors.

**TABLE 2** Party Identification by Sex 1968–1976

| Year and sex | Strong Democrat | Weak Democrat | Independent Democrat | Independent | Independent Republican | Weak Republican | Strong Republican |
|---|---|---|---|---|---|---|---|
| **1968** | | | | | | | |
| Men | 21% | 23% | 11% | 9% | 10% | 17% | 9% |
| Women | 20 | 27 | 9 | 11 | 8 | 14 | 11 |
| **1972** | | | | | | | |
| Men | 15 | 22 | 11 | 13 | 13 | 14 | 10 |
| Women | 14 | 29 | 11 | 9 | 9 | 14 | 12 |
| **1976** | | | | | | | |
| Men | 13 | 22 | 13 | 16 | 13 | 14 | 7 |
| Women | 15 | 26 | 10 | 13 | 8 | 15 | 10 |

SOURCE: Center for Political Studies, Inter-University Consortium, University of Michigan.

**TABLE 3    The Vote by Sex in Presidential Elections, 1952–1976**

| Year and candidate | Men | Women |
|---|---|---|
| 1952 | | |
| Eisenhower | 53% | 58% |
| Stevenson | 47 | 42 |
| 1956 | | |
| Eisenhower | 55 | 61 |
| Stevenson | 45 | 39 |
| 1960 | | |
| Kennedy | 52 | 49 |
| Nixon | 48 | 51 |
| 1964 | | |
| Johnson | 60 | 62 |
| Goldwater | 40 | 38 |
| 1968 | | |
| Nixon | 43 | 43 |
| Humphrey | 41 | 45 |
| Wallace | 16 | 13 |
| 1972 | | |
| McGovern | 37 | 38 |
| Nixon | 63 | 62 |
| 1976 | | |
| Carter | 53 | 48 |
| Ford | 45 | 51 |

SOURCE: Gallup Opinion Index, Dec. 1976, report no. 137.

### Women and the issues

Early voting data on women's stands on issues have been scanty and have emphasized women's moralistic orientation as revealed in their strong stand on prohibition. Women are also described as generally more conservative than men. However, as has been mentioned, women have voted more heavily for Democratic presidential candidates in the last three out of four elections than men have. Recent and more thorough studies have shown that women do differ from men in their stand on some issues. Gallup data and the 1972 Virginia Slims Poll, conducted by Louis Harris, show that women are less likely to seek military solutions to international problems. On the issue of Vietnam more women classified themselves as doves. The greater value women apparently place on human life goes beyond war to the issues of capital punishment and social welfare.[13] Only on issues where their own children were involved, such as busing, were women more conservative than men.

Whether or not a women's bloc vote will materialize remains to be seen. In close elections, such as the 1976 presidential race, a difference of a few percentage points in the voting choices of men and women could make the critical difference. A real voting bloc has yet to be seen even on issues dealing with women's rights, since no candidate has sought election on a primarily feminist platform (although a significantly higher number of female voters voted for N.Y. Lt. Governor Mary Ann Krupsak in 1974 and Bella Abzug in her 1976 Senate race. Virginia legislator Jim Thompson lost his seat in 1977 when feminist groups organized to oust him because of his long-standing opposition to ratification of the ERA). It must always be remembered that women differ in ideology, personality, education, income, and social class, and that these variables will continue to affect their political choices.

## POLITICAL PARTICIPATION

The questions about women's political participation are made more difficult because what we consider "political" has been based mainly on male models. Many of the questions about political participation do not even consider some of the political activities that may occupy a woman's time. Getting a stop sign put up in front of a school may involve organizing, petitioning, lobbying, bargaining, and various other kinds of political pressure and yet researchers may neglect to classify this as "political" activity. With this in mind, we will look at women's political activities using Milbrath's traditional hierarchy of political involvement.[14] A hierarchy is used because political participation is assumed to be cumulative—that is, persons who engage in the higher level activities are likely to also perform those lower in rank. The lowest rank are what Milbrath calls "spectator activities." These include voting and wearing a button or putting a sticker on the car. "Transitional activities" are on a higher level and include contacting a public official, contributing money to a party, or attending a political meeting or rally. "Gladiator activities" include contributing time to a campaign, becoming active in a party and at the highest level being a candidate or holding public office (see Table 4).

The biggest and most consistent difference between men and women is in giving money. Women do not contribute to campaigns as much as men. This could be a result of their lower incomes and less control over monies, but it is also true that women have not been socialized to make contributions. Men are more likely to be in occupations and organizations where political contributions are expected and asked for. At other levels, there are minimal differences between the percentage participation of men and women and in some years women were *more* actively involved than men. It is apparent that women have been more active than generally assumed.

**TABLE 4**    Hierarchy of Political Involvement—Women and Men 1968–1976

| Activity and year | Men | Women |
|---|---|---|
| Gladiator activity | | |
| Working for a party or candidate | | |
| 1968 | 5.3 | 6.1 |
| 1972 | 4.2 | 5.7 |
| 1976 | 4.4 | 4.5 |
| Transitional activities | | |
| Attending a political meeting | | |
| 1968 | 4.5 | 4.8 |
| 1972 | 9.8 | 8.2 |
| 1976 | 5.7 | 6.8 |
| Giving money to a party | | |
| 1968 | Not available | Not available |
| 1972 | 12.0 | 9.2 |
| 1976 | 11.1 | 6.9 |
| Spectator activity | | |
| Wear a button or put sticker on car | | |
| 1968 | 15.8 | 14.1 |
| 1972 | 14.0 | 14.1 |
| 1976 | 7.0 | 8.1 |

SOURCE: Center for Political Studies, Inter-University Consortium, University of Michigan.

## Party work

Modern government is party government. Political power must rest on party power. As women's political activities increase they must necessarily play a greater role in party affairs, and this partisanship presents an important area for women. The parties have admitted women as workers on various levels, but they have not yet received them on a level approaching equality.

Women's motives for political participation appear to be similar to men's. They are motivated by the desire to support particular candidates and issues. Women are more likely to mention family and friends as initial reasons for political activity. Once they get involved in politics, affiliation needs become less strong. When desire for political power is measured by political ambition and political achievement need, women scored lower than men.[15]

Partisanship and party activity, however, lead to little power for women. Women find ready employment as stuffers and doorbell ringers. They are less likely to find themselves in a position of responsibility or decision making. Even when a woman does reach high party office, she is likely to find herself treated like a precocious child when she sits in the party councils—an object of benevolent amusement or perhaps pride, but hardly a source of wisdom or power.

While men who get into party activities are praised for assuming their proper civic responsibilities, the active woman may be chastised for leaving her home. Even such a scholarly observer as Robert E. Lane revealed this bias when he wrote,

> It is too seldom remembered in the American society that working girls and career women, and women who insistently serve the community in volunteer capacities, and women with extra-curricular interests of an absorbing kind are often borrowing their time and attention and capacity for relaxed play and love from their children to whom it rightfully belongs. As Kardiner points out, the rise of juvenile delinquency (and, he says, homosexuality) is partly to be attributed to the feminist movement and what it did to the American mother.[16]

Women also face the problem of discrimination in staff jobs. A survey of 1976 presidential candidates' campaigns found that women held only ten of the 69 most important jobs on the campaign staffs of eleven major presidential candidates. Even these top ten women held limited policy and decision-making power, and their salaries were consistently found to be about half of those of their male counterparts.[17] One party worker recalled a high-level party meeting at which she was present: "The press secretary sent out for cokes, it was a very hot and muggy night. There were six of us in the room, and he came back in with five cokes. I will never forget that small, petty way of telling me that I didn't really belong."[18] Women are learning to be more aggressive and to insist on fairness, refusing jobs at salaries lower than their male counterparts. Says experienced New York political activist Carol Opton, "Salary is the key. There may be times when you'll have to make coffee, and you can grit your teeth once or twice on that fight. But you must stick to your guns on salary."[19]

### The woman convention delegate

Party conventions are an integral part of the American political system. It is at party conventions that the decision is made about the choices the American people will have when they vote in November. In addition to nominating candidates for President and Vice-President, the parties also ratify the party platform which spells out the party's position on public issues. At conventions various factions come together to discuss common problems and to indulge in the bargaining and compromising which makes possible the coalitions which comprise our national parties. At conventions party leaders interact with rank and file members and learn about concerns and potential troublespots in the coming election. For many party workers, attending a convention is viewed as a reward for years of faithful service. Conventions provide political scientists with data on party elites. Much of what we know about party activists (both male and female) comes from delegate studies.

A few women were delegates to the national party conventions prior to suffrage, but there was a notable jump after the right to vote was secured. Additionally the Democratic National Committee was expanded to include one woman as well as one man from each state and the Republicans followed suit in 1924. No effort was made to require equal representation of the sexes at the national party conventions prior to 1976.[20] The number of women at these conventions fluctuated between ten and seventeen percent until the 1972 Democratic National Convention saw the application of new rules requiring affirmative action to encourage proportionate representation of minorities, youth and women in each state delegation. They did not set quotas, but they

TABLE 5   Percent Women Delegates at Major Party Conventions

| Year | 1952 | 1956 | 1960 | 1964 | 1968 | 1972 | 1976 |
|---|---|---|---|---|---|---|---|
| Democratic | 12.5% | 11.6% | 11.1% | 14.2% | 13.3% | 39.9% | 33.7% |
| Republican | 10.5 | 15.7 | 15.1 | 17.8 | 16.7 | 29.8 | 31.5 |

SOURCE: Compiled by Martin Gruberg and Jo Freeman with assistance from Christine Way Lynn and various staff members of the Democratic and Republican National Committees.

did put out guidelines specifying that if the state delegation was challenged, the lack of proportional representation would be viewed as *prima facie* evidence of violation of the guidelines.

The result of these guidelines and of activities of women's movement organizations such as the National Women's Political Caucus was an enormous jump in female delegates to 40 percent of the total. The Republicans had no such compelling rules, but were under pressure internally to follow the Democratic example. Thirty percent of the delegates at their 1972 convention were women. By 1976, there was a backlash "of the regulars who had felt excluded in 1972 and wanted back in. They blamed 'quotas' at the convention for defeat in the election. The rules were changed for 1976 to emphasize good intentions rather than good results. They still required affirmative action, but if a state party submitted and followed an approved plan, it was not really held responsible for inadequate results."[21] Only 34 percent of the Democratic delegates were women in 1976. The Republicans had not had any major fight over their delegate selection rule, which emphasized state's rights and only said, "Each state shall endeavor to have equal representation of men and women in its delegation." Almost 32 percent of the Republican delegates were women in 1976.[22]

The drop in the percentage of women at the 1976 Democratic convention led the Democratic Women's Caucus to attempt to obtain a guarantee of equal representation at the 1980 convention from the Democratic nominee Jimmy Carter. They received only the commitment that future conventions would "*promote* equal division between delegate men and delegate women from each state and territory" and that the "national party shall encourage and assist state parties to adapt provisions to achieve this goal."[23] In addition, the women received Carter's pledge to increase the number of women appointed to high political office. Although the compromise on delegates lacked the *required* equal representation wanted by feminists, it was obvious that women would continue pressure for political power and would never again be satisfied with the tokenism that typified earlier party conventions.

## THE FEMALE CANDIDATE

Candidacy for public office is an important threshold for the woman with a strong interest in politics. A woman who runs for office appears to have about the same chance of being elected as a man running for similar office. Getting women to seek public office is therefore critical.

### Prejudice

Shirley Chisholm, member of the U.S. House of Representatives from New York, has summed up the prejudice a woman faces when she seeks public office:

> When I decided to run for Congress I knew I would encounter both antiblack and antifeminist sentiments. What surprised me was the much greater virulence of the sex discrimination. I was constantly bombarded by both men and women exclaiming that I should return to teaching, a woman's vocation, and leave politics to the men.[24]

A 1969 Gallup Poll showed that 67 percent of the electorate would vote for a black man for President of the United States. Only 54 percent said they would vote for a woman, regardless of her race.[25] But this prejudice appears to be breaking down. A 1976 Gallup Poll found that 73 percent of those surveyed said they would vote for a woman for president if she were nominated by their party. Eighty-eight percent said they would vote for a woman for Congress.[26]

However, the women running for office in the early 1970's were often those who were equipped by experience and expectation to deal with discrimination. A special survey found that of fifteen female candidates for various offices, five were black and six of the fifteen were running on "woman power" platforms.[27]

### Additional barriers

The woman who wants to run for office might emulate the model of Patsy Mink, Congresswoman from Hawaii. Mink worked behind the scenes in Democratic politics, doing the dull work of running party headquarters and ringing doorbells. Ultimately she chose to run for territorial office, and though her name was not well known, by her own hard work and that of her supporters she was elected to the House and served six terms before resigning to make an unsuccessful bid for the U.S. Senate in 1976.[28] This sort of story would be easy to duplicate among male members of the House of Representatives, but Mink is one of the few women who have been able to follow it to a successful conclusion.

By and large, party leaders are even more prejudiced than voters and rival candidates. They often permit women to run only in situations where they are certain to lose.[29] Then when the inevitable happens, all that may be remembered is that a woman lost.

There are other myths and preconceptions that plague women candidates. It is said that women cannot take the time away from their children that candidacy and public office require. A seat in the state legislature, to cite a common first-rung office, may require two to three months away from home every winter. But this argument does not explain the lack of women candidates from areas near the state capital. Political leaders also argue that it is a waste of time, effort, and money to promote a young woman for office when she is liable to become pregnant at any time. The fact that modern birth control techniques render the pregnancy of a serious candidate highly unlikely may serve to dispel this myth in time. In any event, the election in 1972 to the House of Representatives of a young mother (Patricia Schroeder, D. Colo.) and the 1973 birth of a daughter to another Congresswoman (Yvonne Braithwaite Burke, D. Calif.) may defuse this argument.

If the barriers of family responsibilities, myths, party organization, and prejudiced voters are not enough, the female candidate often finds that her means of making a living is a barrier too. Proportionately, more women than men are in civil service or teaching jobs that are not conducive to office seeking. The woman who must go off the payroll to have the privilege of spending large sums of money campaigning is at a disadvantage compared to a business or professional man whose income continues. The legal profession contributes more office holders than any other, and in 1970–71 only 7.8 percent of the students entering law school were women.[30] In 1977 women accounted for 25.2 percent of law school students—a significant increase in the pool of potential female politicians.[31]

Another barrier faced by many women is their relationship with their husband. In 1968 three female lawyers, Martha W. Griffiths (D. Mich.), Patsy Mink (D. Hawaii), and Margaret M. Heckler (R. Mass.) had reached the House of Representatives. In her study of these three, Lamson found that each had an unusual degree of solidarity in her relationship with her husband, and each husband played a vital role in prompting and even managing his wife's campaign. In the present cultural context few husbands are prepared or equipped to do this.[32] When Kansas Representative Martha Keys married Indiana Representative Andrew Jacobs, she found that her marriage and its potential implications for her district were a major issue in her re-election campaign. Some voters questioned her legal residence and doubted that her loyalties and political independence would remain intact when she was married to a representative from another state. No such concerns were raised about Jacobs.

Still another barrier the female candidate faces is that male politicians are used to dealing with other men. Congresswoman Margaret Heckler has stated that party leaders do not enjoy drinking with women and sharing with them the sort of camaraderie they have in a stag group.[33] This socializing (it might be termed cronyism) often serves as the foundation for relationships that lead to the selection of candidates. Many young men are identified with powerful political leaders and under their guidance and tutelage go on to successful political careers, but women generally lack this support.

Even more serious is the fund-raising problem. Congresswoman Heckler points out that the big givers, who like to back a winner, consider a female candidate a poor investment. Former Senator Maureen Neuberger of Oregon has also emphasized that raising money poses an especially difficult challenge for the female candidate.[34] Women tend not to be highly confident fund raisers, since they lack the business experience of most men. All these elements combine to thin the ranks of female candidates.

## WOMEN IN PUBLIC OFFICE

The number of women holding public office is incredibly low, especially when you consider that women comprise more than 51 percent of the population. Even in areas of traditional female interest, such as school boards, women fill only 13 percent of the positions. At the county level they hold less than three percent of the positions. Only 5 percent of mayors and members of municipal and township councils are women.[35]

Women in public office have very high visibility. They are constantly identified as women, and men may act self-conscious or patronizing in their presence. When a woman officeholder makes mistakes, they are usually attributed to her sex. Instead of saying "Nobody's perfect," people are likely to say, "Just like a woman."[36]

### State offices

Women are making the biggest advances in state legislatures. In 1963 there were 351 women legislators (141 Democrats, 206 Republicans, 4 independents). The figure dropped back to 318 in 1967.[37] Before the 1972 election there were 344 women in state legislatures. As a result of that election, the figure went up to 424, representing an increase of 18.8 percent.[38] In 1974 the figure was 615. And in 1976 it reached 685, 9.1 percent of the total. California made the biggest increase in percentage, from three to six, including the first woman elected to the state senate. By the beginning of 1978 women were 9.3 percent of all state legislators.[39]

Women's progress in state legislatures is concentrated in the smaller states of the Northeast and in the West. New Hampshire alone accounts for 20 percent of all women in lower houses. Connecticut, Maine, and Vermont are next highest in percentage of women in the legislature. All of these states rank in the lower half of the states in population. Emmy E. Werner attributes the success of women candidates in the smaller, nonurbanized states to the easy accessibility campaigners have to voters, the low cost of campaigning in these areas, and the small districts that exist in New England legislatures.[40]

Pay and political pay-off are often lowest in positions where the highest percentages of women are found. In 1975 the New Hampshire legislature paid $100 per year. California paid $19,500. There were 24 women in the New Hampshire legislature and two in California's.

Until 1974 only three women had been elected state governors, and all of them came to office largely or entirely in their capacity as wives. Miriam A. ("Ma") Ferguson of Texas was elected in 1924 and 1932; her husband was the former governor and had been impeached. Nellie Taylor Ross was elected in 1925 to serve her dead husband's unexpired term in Wyoming. Lurleen Wallace was elected in Alabama in 1966, when her husband, George, was prohibited by the state constitution from succeeding himself in office. In 1974 Ella T. Grasso, a Democrat, was elected governor of Connecticut, the first woman governor to be chosen in her own right. Grasso had a long political career in Connecticut, having served in the General Assembly, as Secretary of State, and in the U.S. Congress. The second woman governor to be elected in her own right, Dixie Lee Ray of the state of Washington, had a very different political career. Her election as governor was her first entry into partisan politics. She was on the faculty of the University of Washington until appointed chairperson of the Atomic Energy Commission and then Assistant Secretary of State for Scientific Affairs under Henry Kissinger. These two backgrounds point out that there is no one road to political success.

## Congress

The first woman to be elected to the United States House of Representatives was Jeanette Rankin of Montana in 1916.* Throughout a long life she kept up her interest in public affairs. Although her last term in the House was over thirty years ago, she led an antiwar march in Washington in 1968 at the age of 87. The first woman who actually served in the Senate was Hattie W. Caraway of Arkansas, who was appointed in 1932 to fill her dead husband's unexpired term. Later she won election to a six-year term, the first of only three women ever to do this.

Caraway's record is part of a pattern that characterized women in Congress before 1949: they entered via "widow's succession." Since then this pattern has broken down. Margaret Mead has pointed out that widows are the only women society allows to be both dominant and respectable at the same time. If power is thrust upon a woman by her husband's death, she may accept it without blame.[41]

In the Senate a woman is more likely to enter by appointment than by election, even when the vacancy is caused by something other than her husband's death. Of the 11 women who served in the Senate between 1917 and 1978, 7 were appointed to fill a vacancy. Of these vacancies, 4 were caused by the death or resignation of a non-relative.

---

*EDITOR'S NOTE: Jeanette Rankin was the only representative to vote against U.S. entry into both World Wars I and II.

Table 6 shows the number of women members of the House and Senate from 1947 to 1978. There is certainly no very clear growth pattern. The total rose from 8 in the 80th Congress to 19 in the 87th, then dropped to 11 before rising again to 19 in the 95th.

TABLE 6   Number of Women Members of Congress, 1947–1978

| Congress | Year | Senate | House |
|----------|------|--------|-------|
| 80th | 1947–48 | 0 | 8 |
| 81st | 1949–50 | 1 | 9 |
| 82nd | 1951–52 | 1 | 10 |
| 83rd | 1953–54 | 2 | 11 |
| 84th | 1955–56 | 1 | 16 |
| 85th | 1957–58 | 1 | 15 |
| 86th | 1959–60 | 1 | 16 |
| 87th | 1961–62 | 2 | 17 |
| 88th | 1963–64 | 2 | 11 |
| 89th | 1965–66 | 2 | 10 |
| 90th | 1967–68 | 1 | 11 |
| 91st | 1969–70 | 1 | 10 |
| 92nd | 1971–72 | 1 | 12[a] |
| 93rd | 1973–74 | 0 | 16[b] |
| 94th | 1975–76 | 0 | 19[c] |
| 95th | 1977–78 | 2[d] | 18 |

[a]Charlotte Reid left Congress to accept a Presidential appointment.

[b]Two widows, Lindy Boggs and Cardiff Collins, were elected in special elections in 1973 to succeed their late husbands.

[c]Shirley Pettis was elected in a special election in 1975 to succeed her late husband.

[d]In 1978 Muriel Humphrey and Maryon Allen were appointed to the Senate to succeed their late husbands.

During the entire 1917–78 period, 38 of the 50 states sent women to Congress. Table 7 shows the record of all the states. Despite New York's leading position with 10, the Western states have sent more women relative to their populations. It is interesting to note that Vermont and New Hampshire, the states with the largest number of women in state legislatures, had no women in Congress in the entire 60-year period.

**TABLE 7**    States Represented by Women in Congress, 1917–1978

| State | Number of Congresswomen | State | Number of Congresswomen |
|---|---|---|---|
| North Atlantic | | North Central | |
| Maine | 1 | Ohio | 2 |
| New Hampshire | 0 | Indiana | 2 |
| Vermont | 0 | Illinois | 8 |
| Massachusetts | 3 | Michigan | 2 |
| Rhode Island | 0 | Wisconsin | 0 |
| Connecticut | 3 | Minnesota | 2 |
| New York | 10 | Iowa | 0 |
| New Jersey | 4 | Missouri | 1 |
| Pennsylvania | 3 | North Dakota | 0 |
| | 24 | South Dakota | 2 |
| | | Nebraska | 3 |
| | | Kansas | 2 |
| South Atlantic | | | 24 |
| Delaware | 0 | | |
| Maryland | 4 | | |
| Virginia | 0 | Western | |
| West Virginia | 1 | Montana | 1 |
| North Carolina | 1 | Wyoming | 0 |
| South Carolina | 3 | Colorado | 1 |
| Georgia | 4 | New Mexico | 1 |
| Florida | 1 | Arizona | 1 |
| | 14 | Utah | 1 |
| | | Nevada | 0 |
| | | Idaho | 1 |
| South Central | | Washington | 2 |
| Kentucky | 1 | Oregon | 3 |
| Tennessee | 3 | California | 5 |
| Alabama | 3 | Hawaii | 1 |
| Mississippi | 0 | Alaska | 0 |
| Louisiana | 2 | | 17 |
| Texas | 1 | | |
| Oklahoma | 4 | | |
| Arkansas | 4 | | |
| | 18 | | |

The modal age at which Congresswomen began their service is 50. A study of Congresswomen during the 1917–78 period indicates that over half of them were college graduates. Some 90 percent were wives or widows, and 39 percent of their husbands had also served in Congress. Twenty-one percent of the women in Congress had been teachers, and 16 percent had been lawyers. No other occupation was shared by as many as 10 percent. The prior political activity listed most often was service in a state House of Representatives. It is interesting to note that all 5 of the Congresswomen newly elected in 1972 were lawyers. All 5 also ran as professional politicians and not on the basis of familial connections. In the 1974 and 1976 elections no newly elected Congresswomen were lawyers.

It is well known that the secret of success in Congress is to acquire seniority. The freshman legislator is expected to serve inconspicuously, his/her only hope of wielding influence being to keep winning re-election until he/she inevitably becomes a committee chairman. Unfortunately, few of the women who have served in Congress have been reelected enough times to reach this level. From 1918 to 1978 only 18 Congresswomen served five or more terms, the minimum length of time generally required to gain power in the House. The only woman Senator to gain extensive seniority was Margaret Chase Smith of Maine. Senator Smith was elected to the House in 1940 when her Congressman husband was seriously ill from a heart attack, from which he later died.[42] She was elected to the Senate for the first time in 1948 and served until she was defeated in 1972. She was renowned for her service to her constituents, her independence of thought, and her record of never missing a roll call.

In Congress, women are not accepted in the "club," an informal organization that can have considerable influence. Another traditional gathering in the House was known as the "Board of Education"; in the "Board" the Speaker and a chosen few compared notes and had a few drinks. It was used informally to plan strategy and occasionally to educate new members in the ways of the House. One Congresswoman with twenty years' seniority had never heard of it when asked by a researcher.[43] The male administrative aide to a Congresswoman summed up the problem this way: "No woman can quite make it. The power structure doesn't operate that way. So much of the power structure is built around the golf course, the bar, over cards, in the gym shower room, etc. I doubt that the best or most able women can ever get to the inner circle where there is complete acceptance."[44]

No woman has ever been elected to any of the party leadership roles, which are sources of considerable power. These would include Speaker of the House, Majority Leader, and party whips. Women who have shown competence and who have received recognition, such as choice committee posts, have tended to adopt role behavior more like that ascribed to the male stereotype.[45] Despite such successes, a woman is never accepted as fully as a man might be. We must conclude, then, that the overall record is one of stagnation. A token degree of representation has occurred, but there has not been continuing progress.

## The political woman

From studies based on convention delegates, party activists and officeholders, a profile of the political woman is beginning to emerge. Compared to women in the general population, the political woman has been found to be "more intelligent, more assertive, more venturesome, more imaginative and unconventional, and more liberal in their attitudes."[46] Comparing males to females, Constantini and Craik found that political leaders of both sexes were "outgoing, socially skilled, and persistent." Relatively higher scores were recorded for females on self control, projecting a less easy-going and direct style of expression. Women are characterized as different from their male counterparts in their "tendency toward a serious and dutiful manner and in a fretful uncertainty about themselves and their situation, which is accompanied by a greater degree of anxiety and readiness for psychological change."[47] The latter analysis should not be surprising when one considers the change in role and break from traditionally expected behavior which political activity demands for some women.

Jeane Kirpatrick found many psychological similarities between the sexes. Both male and female legislators in her study had "strong egos, high self-esteem and a high sense of personal effectiveness and political efficacy."[48] In short, women political leaders have personality characteristics, such as feelings of competence and self-confidence, which are similar to those found in male politicos.

Studies of women officeholders at all levels of government indicate that their backgrounds are similar to other women in the general population.[49] Only among those seeking the highest office do we find that their parents showed unusually high interest in politics. Most have lived in their communities for a long time. They are somewhat older than the general population—a likely result of waiting until their children were older before running for public office. Like most political leaders they have higher educational and occupational status than the average. In every office except U.S. Representative and governor, women officeholders are as likely to be married and no more likely to be divorced, widowed, or single. Except in Congress and as governor, the majority of women are serving their first term. They are more likely to be Democrats than Republicans.

## THE FEMALE ADMINISTRATOR

Women's progress in attaining high appointive posts and administrative jobs in government has been spotty. The record reveals areas of no progress at all, areas where there has been retrogression, and areas where advances have taken place in spite of prejudice.

### High appointive posts

Certain appointive posts have never been held by women. The most conspicuous example is that no women has ever been appointed to the United States Supreme Court. In 1978 there were only 9 female federal judges. Five Cabinet members have also been women: Frances Perkins, Secretary of Labor from 1933 to 1945; Oveta Culp Hobby, Secretary of Health, Education, and Welfare from 1953 to 1955; Carla Hills, Secretary of Housing and Urban Development from 1975 to 1977; and two Carter appointees, Secretary of Commerce Juanita M. Kreps and Patricia Roberts Harris at HUD. By the beginning of 1978, the Carter administration had appointed only 11 percent women to the posts of undersecretary, deputy secretary, assistant secretary, general counsel, or their equivalents. Ford's appointments to the equivalent positions were 14 percent female.[50]

However, Carter had a better record in appointments to executive non-career positions in the Civil Service (GS 16-18), whose occupants also turn over with a new administration. Women in these "super-grade" jobs more than doubled in Carter's first year.

**TABLE 8   Women in Non-career "Supergrade" Jobs**

|          | 12/30/75 | 12/30/76 | 12/30/77 |
|----------|----------|----------|----------|
| Total    | 472      | 438      | 497      |
| Women    | 21       | 29       | 66       |
| % Women  | 4.4%     | 6.6%     | 13.3%    |

SOURCE: Memo of April 7, 1978 to President Carter from Alan K. Campbell, Chair, United States Civil Service Commission.

## Government employment

The federal government is expected to set an example for other employers in breaking down employment restrictions based on sex. Studies indicate that federally employed women earn higher salaries than women in the private sector doing similar work, but they still tend to cluster in the lower GS grades. Approximately 94 percent of all female employees are in grades below those designated management levels. Only 48 percent of the men are in these grades. (See Table 9.)

**TABLE 9**    Women Employed in the Federal Government: Full-time White Collar Civilian Employment in the Federal Government—Total and Women by Grade Levels (In thousands unless otherwise indicated; as of October 31 for each year)

| Grade grouping | | 1969 | 1970 | 1972 | 1973 | 1974 | 1975 |
|---|---|---|---|---|---|---|---|
| 1–6 | Total | 546 | 531 | 555 | 554 | 574 | 568 |
| | Women | 399 | 384 | 393 | 395 | 410 | 409 |
| | % Women | 73.1 | 72.3 | 70.8 | 71.4 | 71.5 | 72.0 |
| 7–12 | Total | 433 | 563 | 574 | 567 | 579 | 598 |
| | Women | 113 | 117 | 122 | 123 | 134 | 146 |
| | % Women | 25.6 | 20.8 | 21.1 | 21.7 | 23.2 | 24.4 |
| 13 and above | Total | 278 | 165 | 174 | 174 | 179 | 184 |
| | Women | 6 | 6 | 7 | 7 | 8 | 9 |
| | % Women | 2.0 | 3.6 | 4.0 | 4.3 | 4.6 | 5.0 |
| Total | Total | 1990 | 1982 | 1992 | 1894 | 1957 | 1976 |
| | Women | 665 | 657 | 671 | 644 | 682 | 697 |
| | % Women | 33.4 | 33.2 | 33.7 | 34.0 | 34.9 | 35.3 |

GS 1–6 = $5,000 – 12,000
GS 7–12 = $10,000 – 23,000
GS 13 = $21,000+

SOURCE: *Statistical Abstract of U.S. 1977*, U.S. Department of Commerce, Social and Economic Statistics Admin., Bureau of the Census, Table 448.

Women should not expect redress from individual members of Congress whose own records deserve closer scrutiny. Senators have been hiring women for professional jobs but still pay them less than their male counterparts.[51] A recent survey shows that Representatives were paying high-ranking male employees from 18 to 129 percent more than women in similar jobs.[52]

When a woman gets an administrative post, she must contend with the problem posed by the many men who find it hard to work under a woman. These feelings were well expressed by Herbert A. Miller, who testified for the National Woman's Party on behalf of the Equal Rights Amendment in 1970:

> The difficulties I had working under a woman largely stemmed from my own feelings concerning her status in a bureaucratic hierarchy. Many men for whom I have worked, frankly, have been more difficult to please than the woman for whom I worked, but I accepted the difficulties of working for a man as part of the working world in which I lived. . . .
>
> The cause of my difficulty was not so much the woman under whom I worked, but my own feelings of resentment and unwillingness to accept a woman as a professional equal or superior.[53]

Meeting this problem remains a major challenge.

## CONCLUSION

Our level of understanding of "political women" is still at the seminal stage. We are not certain if our political status is a product of socialization, motivation or structural limitations. We suspect it is a product of all three forces, but we don't know the relative causal effect of each. We are not even sure that our attempts to understand female political behavior are not plagued by sexism and too much reliance on male models, male assumptions and male expectations. We do know that there is no turning back. Women are beginning to experience the first stirrings of political equality and they like it. In the future they will demand more.

## NOTES

1   Maurice Duverger, *The Political Role of Women* (Paris: UNESCO, 1975), pp. 129, 130.

2   Andrew Sinclair, *The Emancipation of the American Woman* (New York: Harper and Row, 1965), p. 39.

3   *Ibid.*, pp. 326–27.

4   Mrs. Gladys O'Donnell, President, National Federation of Republican Women, in a statement before the Constitutional Amendments Subcommittee of the Judiciary Committee, U.S. Congress, Senate, Committee on the Judiciary, *The "Equal Rights"*

*Amendment,* Hearings before the Subcommittee on Constitutional Amendments, Senate, on S. J. Res. 61, 91st Cong., 5th sess., May 1970, p. 664.

5  John J. Stucker, "Women as Voters: Their Maturations as Political Persons in American Society," in Marianne Githens and Jewel L. Prestage, eds., *A Portrait of Marginality: The Political Behavior of the American Woman* (New York: David McKay, 1977), pp. 271–73.

6  Charles E. Merriam and Harold F. Gosnell, *Non-Voting* (Chicago: University of Chicago Press, 1924), p. 47.

7  Stucker, "Women as Voters," pp. 270–78.

8  *Ibid.,* p. 271.

9  Center for Political Studies, Inter-University Consortium, University of Michigan. The author wishes to thank Barbara Farah of CPS for help in obtaining data.

10  Sinclair, *Emancipation of the American Woman,* p. 92.

11  Angus Campbell, Philip E. Converse, Warren E. Miller, and Donald E. Stokes, *The American Voter* (New York: Wiley and Sons, 1964), pp. 487–88.

12  Naomi B. Lynn and Cornelia B. Flora, "Child-Rearing and Political Participation: The Changing Sense of Self," *Journal of Military and Political Sociology* (Spring 1973) 91–103.

13  *The 1972 Virginia Slims American Women's Opinion Poll,* conducted by Louis Harris and Associates; Gallup Opinion Index, Sept. 1970, report no. 63; Gallup Opinion Index, April 1972, report no. 82.

14  Lester W. Milbrath, *Political Participation* (Chicago: Rand McNally & Company, 1965), especially pp. 16–22.

15  Jeane J. Kirkpatrick, "Incentives to Participation: The Presidential Elite," paper presented at the Annual Meeting of the Southwestern Political Science Association, San Antonio, Texas, March, 1975. See also, Naomi B. Lynn and Cornelia B. Flora, "Societal Punishment and Aspects of Female Political Participation: 1972 National Convention Delegations," in Marianne Githens and Jewel L. Prestage, (eds.), *A Portrait of Marginality: The Political Behavior of the American Woman* (New York: David McKay, 1977), pp. 143, 144.

16  Robert E. Lane, *Political Life* (New York: Free Press, 1959), p. 355.

17  *Christian Science Monitor,* May 5, 1976, p. 23.

18  Jeff Greenfield, "Ms. Smith Goes to Washington, Part II," *Wichita Eagle,* Feb. 23, 1976, p. 28.

19  *Ibid.*

20  Paul T. David, Ralph M. Goldman, and Richard C. Bain, *The Politics of National Party Conventions* (Washington, D.C.: The Brookings Institution, 1960), pp. 327–28.

21  Jo Freeman, "Something DID Happen at the Democratic Convention," *Ms.,* 5, 4 (November 1976), 75.

22  In 1976 the Republicans had 710 women delegates out of 2,259 (31.4 percent); 856 alternates were women, making the combined total percentage 47.9. The Democrats had 1,036 women out of 3,075 (34 percent), 740 alternates out of 1,902, making the combined percentage 39.

23 Freeman, "Something DID Happen," 75–76.

24 U.S. Congress, House of Representatives, Committee on Education and Labor, *Discrimination Against Women,* Hearings before the Special Subcommittee on Education on Section 805 of H.R. 16098, 91st Cong., 2d sess., July 1970, pt. 2, p. 913.

25 Gallup Opinion Index, April 1968, report no. 46.

26 Gallup Opinion Index, March 1976, report no. 128.

27 *The Spokeswoman,* 1, 14 (June 1, 1971), 12.

28 Peggy Lamson, *Few Are Chosen: American Women in Political Life Today* (Boston: Houghton Mifflin, 1968), pp. 98–109.

29 *Ibid.,* p. xxii. Lamson quotes both the chairman and the second vice-chairman of the Democratic National Committee on this point.

30 "Appendix: The Status of Women in American Law Schools," *Rutgers Law Review,* 25 (Fall 1970), 77.

31 "Law School Enrollment Steadies but Number of Women Students Increase," *American Bar Association Journal,* 63 (August 1977), 1134.

32 Lamson, *Few are Chosen,* pp. 87–123.

33 "How Women Are Doing in Politics," *U.S. News and World Report,* Aug. 31, 1970, p. 26.

34 "Increase in Female House Members in 1971 Expected," *Congressional Quarterly Weekly Report,* 28 (July 10, 1970), 1746.

35 Marilyn Johnson and Kathy Stanwick, *Profile of Women Holding Office* (New Brunswick, N.J.: Center for the American Woman and Politics, Eagleton Institute of Politics, 1976), pp. xxi, xxii.

36 U.S. Congress, Senate, Committee on the Judiciary, *Equal Rights, 1970,* Hearings on S.J. Res. 61 and S.J. Res. 231, 91st Cong., 2d sess., Sept. 1970, p. 243.

37 Emmy E. Werner, "Women in the State Legislatures," *Western Political Quarterly,* 21 (March 1968), 42–46; *Discrimination Against Women,* Hearings, pt. 2, pp. 912–13.

38 *The Spokeswoman,* 3, 6 (December 1, 1972), 4.

39 Figures compiled by The National Women's Educational Fund, 1532 16th St. N.W., Washington, D.C. 20036.

40 Werner, "Women in the State Legislatures," 43–45.

41 *Discrimination Against Women,* Hearings, pt. 2, p. 1058.

42 Lamson, *Few Are Chosen,* p. 10.

43 Frieda L. Gehlen, "Women in Congress," *Trans-action,* 6 (October 1969), 38.

44 *Ibid.,* p. 39.

45 *Ibid.*

46 Emmy E. Werner and Louise M. Bachtold, "Personality Characteristics of Women in American Politics," in Jane S. Jaquette, ed., *Women in Politics* (New York: John Wiley & Son, 1974), pp. 79–83.

47 Edmond Constantini and Kenneth H. Craik, "Women as Politicians: The Social Backgrounds, Personality, and Political Careers of Female Party Leaders," *Journal of Social Issues,* 28, 2 (1972), 226.

48  Jeane J. Kirkpatrick, *Political Woman* (New York: Basic Books, Inc., 1974), p. 220.
49  The following discussion is based on data contained in Johnson and Stanwick.
50  Steve Hess, "Carter Lags in Naming Women," *Washington Star*, Oct. 23, 1977, p. E-5.
51  *New York Times*, Aug. 5, 1977, sec. II, p. 4.
52  *New York Times*, Aug. 13, 1977, p. 7.
53  *Equal Rights*, 1970, Hearings, p. 266.

# Elizabeth M. Almquist

# Black Women and the Pursuit of Equality*

We sometimes forget that black women are women as well as black, that they are deeply concerned about women's issues, and that they are frequently front-line activists in the battle for women's rights. We forget because an image prevails that black women are unconcerned and uninvolved with the women's movement. This image stems from the mass media's selective focus on white women, the early anti-female statements of some black activists, and the common perception that black women are concerned only with racial issues. The evidence belies the image. For some time black women have been speaking out against chauvinism and stereotyping. Recall 1972 presi-

*Research for this essay was supported in part by a multi-disciplinary grant from the Administration on Aging to the Center for Studies in Aging of North Texas State University.

dential candidate Shirley Chisholm's statement: "I have pointed out time and time again that the harshest discrimination I have encountered in the political arena is anti-feminism."[1] In national surveys, black women express positive attitudes toward the feminist movement.[2] Marjorie Lansing finds that black women believe that sex discrimination affects them seriously and that this belief is an important factor in their recent increases in political activity.[3] Black women make their presence felt in feminist groups. Seventeen percent of the elected state delegates to the 1977 National Women's Conference in Houston were black women, 7 percent more than are in the adult female population.[4] And most national feminist groups have had at least one black president.[5] In addition, there are two national organizations of black feminists—the National Black Feminist Organization (headquartered in New York City) and Black Women Organized for Action (headquartered in San Francisco).

The facts have also been overlooked by social scientists who have paid little attention to the specific problems of black women. When they have looked at black women, they have tended to stress differences between black and white women, thereby conveying the idea that race is the only important issue. But very recent research reveals that black women and white women are in fact very similar to one another and are becoming more so every year, especially in the areas of education, jobs and earnings. One section of this essay describes the enormous similarities between black and white women, showing that they are the common victims of sex discrimination in employment and wages. In the field of employment, sexual barriers to equality are much stronger than racial barriers.

The following pages highlight the unique version of the black woman's role that emerged during slavery, the long slow climb away from that degraded position, and the ways in which black women have been blamed for the problems heaped upon blacks in an oppressive society. This necessarily selective presentation is a prelude to describing a few of the many ways in which black women cope with the burdens they face as women. Black women meet parallel versions of all the dilemmas white women encounter, and in most instances these problems are exacerbated because they cannot tap the greater economic resources of white men. After reviewing the evidence concerning sex discrimination in the labor market, the essay concludes with a brief acknowledgement of black women's achievements in their efforts to overcome the dual barriers of sex and race.

## SLAVERY CREATES A UNIQUE ROLE FOR BLACK WOMEN

In their push for freedom, dignity, and equality, black women confront the same barriers that white women do, plus the extra hardships imposed on them by racism. The racial barriers originated with slavery, when black women were allotted a peculiar version of the female role. This version included all of the burdens and few of the privileges of womanhood. One of the unique features of our society's form of slavery was the extent to which slave status and racial status were linked together—being black became synonymous with being a slave. A slave was regarded as an inferior creature, incapable of being educated, unlike anything except property, and unworthy of receiving the simplest kind of human respect. These definitions of black women lingered on long after the Civil War.

During slavery, black women were used as field hands, house servants, forced breeders of new generations of slaves, and as sexual objects. All black women were vulnerable to being sexually used and discarded by the master or his sons. Female field hands had a dual role. They did harsh physical labor by day and returned to the quarters at night to do the "woman's work" of maintaining a family. Since slave marriages were not officially recognized and any slave—woman, man or child—could be sold at the owner's whim, family stability was precarious at best.

House servants confronted another duality. They wet-nursed and raised the master's children, thereby gaining affection but not respect. They were always "mammies" and never mothers. They groomed, coiffed and dressed the master's wife, but they could never attend the fancy dinners or wear the pretty clothes themselves. Black women cooked and cleaned so that some whites could enjoy a luxurious life style, but the only rights they had were to the leftovers from the master's table.

Sojourner Truth, a former slave and activist in both the abolition and the women's rights movements, spoke of the double jeopardy that black women faced. Her words describe the indignity of working like a man while being denied the rights that a man has, and the pain of being a woman but not having the courtesies or security that many white women could command. At an 1851 Women's Rights Convention in Ohio, she said:

> Well children, where there is so much racket there must be
> something out of kilter. I think that between the Negroes of the

South and the women of the North all talking about rights, the white men will be in a fix pretty soon. But what's all this talking about? That man over there says that women need to be helped into carriages and lifted over ditches, and to have the best place everywhere. Nobody ever helped me into carriages, or over mud puddles, or gives me any best place . . . and ain't I a woman? Look at me! Look at my arm! . . . I have plowed, and planted and gathered into barns, and no man could head me—and ain't I a woman? I could work as much and eat as much as a man—when I could get it—and bear the lash as well—and ain't I a woman? I have borne thirteen children and seen most all sold off into slavery, and when I cried out with my mother's grief, none but Jesus heard—and ain't I a woman?[6]

When emancipation came, it brought little change in black women's status. They continued to work as servants in the homes where they had previously been slaves and to toil in the fields as farm laborers. During slavery, black women usually had not been taught to sew.[7] Afterward they were denied work in the textile and clothing factories that employed many white women. When black women moved off the farms they were allowed only the meanest of "women's" jobs— laundress, janitress, dishwasher. By 1910, 97 percent of black women were still classified as farm laborers, domestics, and unskilled service workers.[8]

Even after slavery was abolished, education was still a scarce commodity for blacks, and women's rights to education were not fully established either. Therefore black women had a doubly difficult time obtaining schooling. The earliest attempts to establish schools for black girls met with violent resistance even in the North. In 1834, Prudence Crandall opened a school in Connecticut for free Negro girls. She was harassed, jailed on a vagrancy charge, and stoned. The school windows were broken and the building defaced. In 1851 the first school to train black women as teachers was opened in Washington, D.C. The school had 40 students, "despite a host of tribulations similar to those endured by Prudence Crandall: repeated evictions, arson and other forms of mob violence."[9] By 1890 only 30 Negro women had received college degrees.

The same movement that gained black men the right to vote still denied the same right to all women, black or white. The women's movement and the abolition movement had been intertwined for years. After the war, women were asked to put aside their cause to work for

Negro suffrage. In 1867, Sojourner Truth, now 80 years old, addressed the convention of the American Equal Rights Association:

> There is a great stir about colored men getting their rights, and not a word about the colored women; and if colored men get their rights and not colored women theirs, you see the colored men will be masters over the women, and it will be just as bad as it was before. . . .
>
> I have done a great deal of work; as much as a man, but did not get so much pay. . . . We do as much, we eat as much, we want as much. . . .
>
> I own a little house in Battle Creek, Michigan. Well every year I got a tax to pay. Taxes, you see, be taxes. . . . There was women there that had a house as well as I. They taxed them to build a road, and they went on the road and worked. It took 'em a good while to get a stump up. Now, that shows that women can work. If they can dig up stumps they can vote. It is easier to vote than dig stumps.[10]

The Fifteenth Amendment granting Negro men the franchise was ratified in 1870. It would be 50 more years before women won the vote for themselves.

### THE SO-CALLED MATRIARCHY

Black men fared only a little better after the Civil War than did black women. By 1910, 56 percent of black males were still farm tenants and laborers, and another 38 percent were semiskilled factory workers or unskilled laborers.[11] Throughout the first five decades of the twentieth century, minority people of both sexes were destined to take mainly the jobs that white people left behind on their upward climb into business and the professions. The jobs left over for blacks were carefully segregated by sex, just as were "white" jobs. Women were the hotel maids and the dishwashers but not the waiters and doormen who at least got some tips to supplement their meager wages. After 1930, when black leaders began urging men to join the unions they had formerly shunned, black women were simply not included in the jobs that were becoming unionized.[12]

There is some evidence that men migrated to the North and to the cities at a faster rate than women did.[13] In any case, women in the rural South could not always count on having a man for a mate, and many of the available men were unable to obtain a living wage. For these and other reasons, a sizeable number of black women formed households composed of an older woman, her grown daughters and several grandchildren. This arrangement is a remarkably flexible one, with the grandmother caring for the children while the younger adults go out to work for pay. A single woman with children probably could not survive on the low wages she received; by combining the resources of several wage earners, the family could "get by." E. Franklin Frazier, a black sociologist, was among the first to label such families as matriarchal and he described them in generally positive terms.[14] Unfortunately, contemporary social scientists who analyze such arrangements have not stressed the flexibilities or the advantages of such adaptive strategies. Instead they have tended to see the female-headed family as a deficient unit, incapable of properly providing for the well-being of children.

The matriarchal label acquired new significance in 1965 with the publication of the Moynihan Report.[15] This report was titled "The Negro Family: The Case for National Action," and it received an enormous amount of media attention. The Report made many Americans aware that more black than white families (21 vs. 9 percent at the time of the report; 33 vs. 10 percent today) are headed solely by women. It pointed out that severe and unrelenting discrimination against black men creates both economic instability for blacks *and* a large number of female-headed families. The report concludes that mother-centered families and the lack of job prospects for black youth leave children unmotivated to achieve, so that black children perform poorly in school, drop out, and become delinquents more often than whites. In the discussion of the problems of young people, males receive a great deal more attention than females. The report contains not a word about employment discrimination against black women.

The Report can be criticized for many reasons—it contains the false assumption that black women fare better in the labor force than black men do and it implies that black women reject the financially dependent male—but at least it does point to white racism as an important determinant of economic and social problems for blacks. Nonetheless, most people did not read the actual report.[16] Instead they read the publicity surrounding the report, which emphasized the father-absence syndrome and boldly proclaimed that black women are matriarchs who are responsible for emasculating black men.

The Moynihan Report is not the first to label black women as matriarchs, nor probably will it be the last.[17] But the Report acquired a special significance because it was government sponsored and therefore replete with authoritative statistics, because it received so much publicity, and because members of the public too quickly assumed that all black families are female dominated and that female domination is the source of severe problems in the family. Members of the public could not acknowledge the severity of discrimination against blacks, they could not realize that discrimination is the precursor of social problems, and they could not imagine the bleak labor market situation for black women. But many readily assimilated the idea of matriarchy. In this way, black women became the scapegoats for white hostility. They were branded as emasculating matriarchs who were responsible for the general plight of blacks. Instead of being praised for the courage that they displayed in caring for their children under the most difficult circumstances, black women were denounced for the very strengths they had exhibited.

## STEREOTYPES AND REALITIES

Black women face problems as women that are not simply the result of white oppression. Throughout history, black women have been assigned roles and stereotypes that resemble those of white women and that are just as damaging in their effects on the person. Toni Cade describes the stereotypes of black women, how the stereotypes prevent real communication and sharing between men and women, and the pain of breaking through the stereotypes to confront each other honestly. She writes "It seems to me that you find your Self in destroying illusions, smashing myths, laundering the head of whitewash, being loyal to some truth, to the struggle. That entails at the very least cracking through the veneer of this sick society's definition of 'masculine' and 'feminine.' "[18]

The stereotypes of black women are not always carbon copies of those applied to whites, but they are parallel. One important parallel is that the stereotypes carry contradictory images of what a woman is. The Sapphire version portrays women as immoral, cold, hard, bitter, dominating and self-serving.[19] On the other hand the Good Mother image depicts woman as a virtuous, gentle, loving, nurturant, and stoical individual who seeks nothing for herself but only to protect her children. These images are but elaborated versions of the old dichotomy between the Madonna Virgin Mary and the Temptress Eve.[20] Both are negative. The Sapphire version is unpalatable and the

Good Mother version means virtually complete self-negation. The truth is that black women conform to neither image.

Nevertheless, black women are subject to cultural pressures to conform to certain ideals. One that all women confront is the demand to be beautiful. Not long ago, black women used bleaching creams and hair straighteners in an attempt to emulate the light-skinned straight-haired stereotype of beauty. Fortunately, black women ultimately rejected this stereotype, and began selecting black styles. The fashion and cosmetic industries seized on the trend, giving women a larger array of fashion items to choose from. Magazines now show black models and give advice on make-up and hair styles for black women. Yet these changes put even more pressure on black women to strive for beauty, and as the products are expensive, few black women can afford the cost.[21]

The cultural pressure for beauty and style is linked with another sexist maxim: A woman is nothing if she does not have a man. This dictate hits black women particularly hard because there are too few black men available. The sex ratio (number of men per 100 women) has been dropping steadily since 1940. By 1977, the sex ratio among blacks aged 25–44 was only 80 while among whites the ratio was approximately 100. This means that there are only 4 black men for every 5 black women. The total figures are staggering. In round numbers, there are 700,000 more black women than men in this age group. These figures help explain why a lower percentage of black than white women (38 vs. 61 percent of all women 14 and over) are married and living with their husbands.[22]

As they grow up, black girls learn that they cannot rely on marriage to produce a secure life. At the same time, their own career prospects are not very rosy. Merely getting a job is tenuous—black women have consistently had higher unemployment rates than any other group. The unemployment rate for teen-aged girls is alarmingly high and climbing. It rose from 17.6 percent in 1950 to 43.6 percent in 1977.[23]

Higher unemployment rates are one reason that black women and their families are more likely to be living in poverty than black men or white women. In 1976, 31.3 percent of all black women over age 16 were impoverished, compared to 19.6 percent of similar black men, 9.8 percent of white women and 6.2 percent of white men.[24] Moreover, while the poverty rate has declined for all families in the last twenty years, it has declined least of all for those families headed by black women (see Table 1).

TABLE 1   Percent of Families in Poverty, 1959 and 1976

| | Female headed families | | Husband/wife and male headed families | |
| --- | --- | --- | --- | --- |
| | Black | White | Black | White |
| 1959 | 65.4 | 34.8 | 43.3 | 13.3 |
| 1976 | 52.2 | 25.2 | 13.5 | 4.9 |
| % decline | 20.1 | 27.6 | 68.8 | 63.2 |

SOURCE: Bureau of the Census, *Money and Income and Poverty Status of Families and Persons in the United States: 1976 (Advance Report)* Current Population Reports Series P-60, No. 107, Sept. 1977, Table 16, pp. 22–23.

The extra impact of being black and poor is apparent in the lack of personal as well as economic security. For example, black women are raped more often than white women (blacks report 158 rapes per 100,000 population each year while whites report 90 per 100,000) and are more often victims of robbery and aggravated assault (but not larceny). Rape occurs more frequently among those with low incomes.[25]

Partly because black girls face uncertain futures in both marriage and work, they are also more vulnerable to other kinds of sexual exploitation. Some are persuaded that submitting to pressures for sexual intercourse may be the only hope for "catching" a man. The "finance-romance" equation is not unique to the black community; white girls are also pressured to trade sexual favors for the promise of financial support.[26] But in any case, black women have slightly more children than whites, and they begin childbearing at an earlier age. For example, in 1976, married black women between ages 15 and 24 had an average of 1.4 children while white women had .8 children. Among those aged 35 to 44, blacks had 3.8 children and whites had 3.0 children.[27] Early motherhood is often a link in a long chain of economic and social difficulties. Fewer than one-third of the high schools in the country have programs for pregnant teenagers.[28] The younger a woman is at the birth of her first child, the more likely she is to become divorced, drop out of school, and be living in poverty.[29]

Compared to other industrial nations, the United States has high infant and maternal mortality rates. The United States ranks fifteenth among the industrial nations of the world in infant mortality rates.[30] While our medical technology is very advanced, our medical services are very unevenly distributed. Relatively affluent people can secure health care from a private physician while medical services and adequate nutrition are not available to large numbers of non-affluent women. Because blacks are more often poor, they meet the hazards of childbearing too often. The infant death rates were about 23 per 1000 black baby girls and 12 per 1000 white baby girls in 1976. In addition, black women are even more likely than white women to die from causes related to childbirth. There were 29.5 deaths per 100,000 live births for blacks and 9.0 per 100,000 for whites in 1976.[31]

Women have had to fight for the right to control their own bodies and to determine whether and when they will have children. This battle is two-edged. While there are no official statistics to record the number of forced sterilizations performed on black women, any number is too large. Pregnant women are sometimes told that the physician will not deliver the baby unless they consent to a tubal ligation, and even that the tubes will come "untied" in five years.[32] On the other side of the battle, the controversy over abortion continues. Today women can have an abortion *if* they can pay for it. Congress has banned the use of Medicaid Funds for "elective" abortions; President Carter and Health, Education and Welfare Secretary Joseph A. Califano are opposed to the use of federal funds for abortion; and the Supreme Court has upheld the decisions of Connecticut and Pennsylvania to use state funds for childbirth but not for abortions. This means that all three branches of the federal government have acted to prevent women of meager means from securing medically safe abortions. Since black women are too often poor, they are heavily represented among the many women who face the "choice" between seeking a risky, not-so-cheap illegal abortion and bearing an unwanted child.

## DISCRIMINATION IN THE LABOR MARKET IS BASED ON SEX

Social scientists who study employment patterns have rarely considered the situation of black women. Even the very recent research that measures sex discrimination tends to overlook black women.[33] In the past, researchers have compared black women to white women and black men to white men. This stress on racial factors that hamper achievement obscures the sex discrimination that affects black women very seriously. The material that follows (1) compares employed black and white women to show the increasing similarity between their patterns of labor force participation and the way in which they are the common victims of sex discrimination at work; (2) compares black women with black men to indicate the extent to which black women are disadvantaged in relation to their brothers and husbands; and (3) compares all three groups of minority workers to white men to show that the disadvantaged position of black women is currently more a function of their being female than of being black.

In the stress on racial differences, the many similarities between black and white women have gone unrecognized. In reality, black and white women today have nearly identical patterns of labor force participation. Changes over the last 25 years have brought them ever closer together. The similarities between the two groups occur in several areas: rates of labor force participation, occupational prestige, education, and earnings. In most of these, black women have been improving their status while white women have changed very little. For labor force participation rates, however, the situation is reversed: white women are becoming similar to black women. Twenty-five years ago, all categories of black women had markedly higher labor force participation rates than white women did. While the rates of all women have been increasing, so many more white women than black are entering the labor force that their rates are approaching parity. By 1977, 48 percent of whites and 51 percent of blacks were paid employees.[34]

Increasing similarities are most apparent in occupations. Black women are now entering jobs that white women have long dominated. In 1965, only 24 percent of employed black women but 62 percent of employed white women were white collar workers. In 1977, the figures were 46 and 66 percent respectively. In 1965, 55 percent of black women were service workers (including 30 percent who were private household workers) and only 12 percent were secretaries or clerks. Twelve years later, black service workers had declined to 35 percent (only 9 percent remained as household domestics), while 26 percent were clerical workers.[35]

Another way to illustrate the growing similarity between black and white women is to consider the degree of overlap between their distributions in the eleven major occupational categories. In 1965, the overlap was small; 60 percent of black women were in the same occupational categories as white women and 40 percent were in different ones. By 1977, 79 percent were in the same categories and only 21 percent were in different categories.[36] Again, this change was achieved mainly by black women moving into jobs traditionally held by white women.

Black women are also closing the gaps between themselves and white women in earnings. In 1959, prime age black women workers (25–54 years) earned only 62 percent of the amount white women did; by 1974, the figure had risen to 98 percent (see Tables 2 and 3). In 1974, white women earned just $108 more per year than black women. Reynolds Farley[37] found that this very small difference is more than accounted for by three facts: more black women than white live in the South where wages are lower than in other regions; black women have completed fewer years of schooling (11.9 vs. 12.6); and they have lower occupational prestige than whites (33 vs. 45 on a 100 point scale of prestige). These gaps are somewhat larger than the gap in earnings between black and white women. How then do black women manage to come so close to white women when they bring home the paychecks?

Paula Hudis[38] also found regional, occupational, and educational differences between the two groups of women, but she argued that black women compensate by working longer hours and by remaining in the labor force steadily rather than interrupting employment for long periods after childbearing. Hudis also suggests that black women may travel further to work and search more aggressively for jobs that yield higher pay.

Black women are closing the gaps between themselves and white women because they are achieving progress while white women are virtually standing still. Between 1959 and 1974, white women made the smallest gains in education, occupational prestige, and earnings of the four race-sex groups. Black women made the largest gains of any of the four groups in occupational prestige, but they were considerably outdistanced by black males in education and by both black and white males in earnings increases (see Table 2).

In 1974, black women still had slightly higher educational attainment and job prestige than black men, but the distance between them was smaller than in 1959. Yet in 1974, women were earning only 62 percent as much as black men were earning in terms of annual earnings and 71 percent as much as black men in hourly earnings. How can this paradox be true? Why do women who have higher educations and higher occupational prestige earn so much less than black men? There are several reasons. One is that occupational prestige is a relatively poor predictor of earnings. A high prestige score does not necessarily produce a large paycheck. More importantly, segregation of jobs by sex and the consequent crowding of women into a smaller

TABLE 2    Indicators of Labor Force Status by Sex and Race

| Race-sex group | Average in 1959 | Average in 1974 | Increase 1959–1974 |
|---|---|---|---|
| | Years of school completed | | |
| White males | 11.2 | 12.9 | + 1.7 |
| Black males | 8.5 | 11.2 | + 2.7 |
| White females | 11.4 | 12.6 | + 1.2 |
| Black females | 9.5 | 11.4 | + 1.9 |
| | Occupational prestige* | | |
| White males | 37.2 | 44.3 | + 7.1 |
| Black males | 18.9 | 27.7 | + 8.8 |
| White females | 38.1 | 44.8 | + 6.7 |
| Black females | 20.1 | 33.3 | +13.3 |
| | Annual earnings | | |
| White males | $10,638 | $13,432 | +2794 |
| Black males | 5,473 | 9,137 | +3664 |
| White females | 4,762 | 5,760 | + 998 |
| Black females | 2,954 | 5,652 | +2698 |
| | Hours worked per year | | |
| White males | 2,145 | 2,184 | + 39 |
| Black males | 1,852 | 1,910 | + 58 |
| White females | 1,614 | 1,617 | + 3 |
| Black females | 1,453 | 1,651 | +198 |
| | Hourly earnings | | |
| White males | $4.96 | $6.15 | +$1.19 |
| Black males | 2.96 | 4.78 | + 1.82 |
| White females | 2.95 | 3.56 | + .61 |
| Black females | 2.03 | 3.42 | + 1.39 |

SOURCE: Adapted from Reynolds Farley, "Trends in Racial Inequalities: Have the Gains of the 1960s Disappeared in the 1970s?", *American Sociological Review*, 42 (1977), 422–30. Data refer only to persons aged 25 to 54 who reported earnings and hours worked per year.

*Occupational prestige scores are derived by asking people to evaluate individual occupations according to how "good" or "poor" they think the job is. Many female occupations may receive high prestige scores because respondents believe the occupation is "good" for a woman's job.

**TABLE 3**   Black Women's Labor Force Status Expressed as a Percentage of the Labor Force Status of White Men, Black Men and White Women

| Race-sex group used in comparison | Percentage in 1959 | Percentage in 1974 | Percent change 1959–1974 |
|---|---|---|---|
| *Years of school completed* | | | |
| White males | 85% | 92% | + 7 |
| Black males | 112 | 106 | – 6 |
| White females | 83 | 94 | +11 |
| *Occupational prestige* | | | |
| White males | 54% | 75% | +21 |
| Black males | 131 | 126 | –11 |
| White females | 53 | 74 | +21 |
| *Annual earnings* | | | |
| White males | 28% | 42% | +14 |
| Black males | 54 | 62 | + 8 |
| White females | 62 | 98 | +36 |
| *Hours worked per year* | | | |
| White males | 68% | 76% | + 8 |
| Black males | 78 | 86 | + 8 |
| White females | 90 | 102 | +12 |
| *Hourly earnings* | | | |
| White males | 41% | 56% | +15 |
| Black males | 69 | 71 | + 2 |
| White females | 69 | 96 | +27 |

SOURCE: Adopted from Reynolds Farley, "Trends in Racial Inequalities: Have the Gains of the 1960s Disappeared in the 1970s?", *American Sociological Review*, 42 (1977), 422–30. Data refer only to persons aged 25 to 54 who reported earnings and hours worked per year.

number of occupations means that black women are concentrated in lower paying jobs than are black men. Black men are much more likely to be high status professionals, business executives, and crafts workers than black women are. These occupations pay more than the secretarial and service jobs in which women are concentrated. Overall, black women are much more similar to white women in occupational distribution than they are to black men. Again using the eleven major occupational categories, the overlap between black women and black men is only 58 percent. Fully 42 percent of the women are in different job categories from black men.[39]

Sex segregation and the subsequent low pay of black women is especially apparent in the professional fields. Like white women, black women are underrepresented in the high paying professions and over-represented in the low paying professions. Women are 46 percent of the total black professionals, yet they are only 7 percent of the engineers, 14 percent of the lawyers, 24 percent of the physicians and dentists, and 25 percent of the life and physical scientists. On the other hand, women are 79 percent of the black librarians, 97 percent of the nurses, and 78 percent of the non-college teachers.[40]

The other important reason that black women have lower wages than black men is sex discrimination in pay. In the workplace, discrimination against black women is much more sexual than racial. This point has been demonstrated statistically in other pieces of research, but it is an idea that is strongly resisted, even by trained social scientists.[41]

The impact of sex discrimination on black women can best be seen by including white men and making comparisons among the four race-sex groups. In one study based on 1970 statistics,[42] the earnings that were lost due to wage discrimination were estimated by controlling for education, occupation and region. The first two comparisons involved race discrimination. It was found that black males lost $1,772 in comparison to white males and that black women lost nothing because of wage discrimination when compared to white females. These racial comparisons show that black males, but not females, suffer earnings losses when compared with their white counterparts. The second set of comparisons involved sex discrimination. When compared to black males, black women lost $2,501 while white women lost $4,570 when compared to white males. These losses from sex discrimination clearly exceed those from racial discrimination. These findings point to a very clear conclusion: To the extent that we can disentangle racial and sexual components in black women's employment status, the sexual component is the more decisive one.

When we look at the labor force patterns over the past 25 years, another conclusion seems well established: Racial inequalities have declined over time, but sexual inequalities have persisted or even increased. While black women's status has improved both relatively and in absolute terms, black male status has improved even faster. Black women have very nearly caught up with white women. The major question is whether black women will be stopped in their progress and stay at the same level that white women have now achieved or whether both groups of women will surge ahead to achieve equality with men. The outlook is not optimistic. With racial barriers to equality crumbling, sexual barriers seem to be standing firm.

Much of the material discussed thus far has presented only the average characteristics of black women as a group, and most of the detailed labor force data pertains only to women aged 25–54. There are enormous variations around the average—not all black women are poor and not all black women work for pay. For example, age is a critical factor. The increasing similarity between black and white women is especially strong for those under 35. Concomitantly, there are major generational differences among blacks. The 70-year-old woman who had only a few years of schooling, who spent her entire working life as a domestic and who now subsists on the minimal benefits from old-age assistance has different needs and interests than the highly educated, 30-year-old lawyer who is a political activist and community organizer.

The special age-occupation mix for black women becomes especially poignant when we recognize that historically black women were confined to few roles other than that of domestic worker. That black women have only recently begun to escape this confinement is revealed in these figures: In 1970, among black women workers who were 65 years old or older, one-half were domestics. Among those aged 45–64, one out of three were maids. Among those who are 35–44 years old, one out of six; among those aged 25–34, one out of ten; and finally among those aged 20–24, only one out of eighteen.[43] It is apparent that when we speak of changes in the labor force—occupational upgrading, the movement of black women into white collar jobs, increases in earnings—it is primarily younger women who are reaping these benefits. In the meantime, there remains a large cadre of older black women whose lives are scarcely improved by the changes that are occurring now.

## THE PUSH FOR CHANGE CONTINUES

Despite the age variations, black women as a group are experiencing change in many areas. One dramatic case is in the area of political participation. In 1956, only 29 percent of eligible black women voted in the presidential election compared with 46 percent of black men, 72 percent of white women and 82 percent of white men. A few years later, the proportion of black women who voted in the presidential election had more than doubled: In 1972, 63 percent voted in the presidential election. Although this increase was in part due to the 1965 Voting Rights Act, it was larger than the increase among black men, bringing black women's voting rates to within 5 percent of black men, 8 percent of white women and 13 percent of white men.[44] However, in 1976, the gap in voting rates between black men and women widened as only 56.6 percent of the latter, compared to 83 percent of the former, voted.[45] Black women are also increasing their share of elected offices. There are four black women in Congress and women now hold about 12 percent of the state legislative seats held by blacks, while women as a whole are only 9 percent of the total state legislators.[46]

Black women are also very active in protest politics. Pierce and his colleagues[47] studied both traditional political activity (registering, voting, discussing politics, attending meetings, campaigning, contacting public officials) and protest activity (talking protest, boycotting, marching, picketing and sitting in). Women were no less active than men in either type of activity. However among higher income blacks, men predominate in political activity, and among lower income groups, women were more active than men, especially in protest politics.

Throughout history, black women's dual victimization in a racist, sexist society has meant that they have had fewer resources and more barriers than any of the other groups. But black women have survived this adversity, and in some cases have achieved more with their meager resources than anyone would have predicted. Today black women are becoming better educated, more active and more outspoken than ever before. They continue to press for civil rights for blacks, to reject the labels applied to them by white society, and to work hard for a black revolution that recognizes and rewards them for their participation. Spurred on by feminism, they are reorienting their relationships to black men, rejecting the notion that a woman is incomplete without a man. As the competition for scarce black males decreases, so does the vulnerability to sexual exploitation. Black women are cooperating with white women to make the government, the courts, and employers recognize women's rights and respond to women's needs. Meanwhile, since black women have always been fighting back in the face of severe oppression—both sexual and racial—we can expect that they will continue to devise inventive solutions to the dilemmas they face by being both female and black.

## NOTES

1   Speech delivered at the Conference on Women's Employment. Hearings before the Special Subcommittee on Education of the Committee on Education and Labor, House of Representatives, Ninety-First Congress, Second Session (Washington, D.C.: U.S. Government Printing Office, 1970), pp. 909–15.

2   In a national survey conducted in 1972, 58 percent of black women and 42 percent of white women reported that they felt "warm" toward the women's movement. Reported in JoAnn Reynolds, "That the Women's Movement is a Middle Class Movement is Bunk," unpublished paper based on data from the National Opinion Research Center. See also the Virginia Slims American Women's Opinion Polls, conducted in 1970 and 1972 by Louis Harris, and in 1974 by the Roper Organization.

3   Marjorie Lansing, "The Voting Patterns of American Black Women," in Marianne Githens and Jewel Prestage, eds., *A Portrait of Marginality: The Political Behavior of the American Woman* (New York: David McKay, 1977), pp. 379–94.

4   News Release of October 3, 1977, IWY Office of Public Information. Figure based on a return of 1341 questionnaires from 1442 elected delegates.

5   NOW, Aileen Hernandez, 1970–1971; NWPC, Audry Colom, 1975–1977; FEW was founded by Allie Latimer-Weeden, 1968.

6   This statement comes from impressions of the convention written down by Frances D. Gage and published in *History of Woman Suffrage*, Vol. 1, pp. 515–17. This excerpt is from *Women Together* by Judith Papachristou, (New York: Alfred E. Knopf, 1976), p. 36.

7   Julia C. Spruill, *Women's Life and Work in the Southern Colonies* (New York: W. W. Norton, 1972).

8   Dale H. Hiestand, *Economic Growth and Employment Opportunities for Minorities* (New York: Columbia University Press, 1964).

9   Eleanor Flexner, *Century of Struggle* (New York: Atheneum, 1972), p. 99.

10  Quoted in Gerda Lerner, ed., *Black Women in White America: A Documentary History* (New York: Random House, 1973), pp. 569–71.

11  Hiestand, *Economic Growth.*

12  Edna Bonacich, "A Theory of Ethnic Antagonism: The Split Labor Market," *American Sociological Review*, 37 (1972), 547–59. See also Ray Marshall, *The Negro and Organized Labor* (New York: Wiley, 1966).

13  See Jacquelyne Jackson, "But Where Are the Men?", *The Black Scholar*, 3 (1971), 30–41.

14  E. Franklin Frazier, *The Negro Family in the United States* (Chicago: The University of Chicago Press, 1939).

15 Daniel Patrick Moynihan, "The Negro Family: The Case for National Action," in Lee Rainwater and William L. Yancey, *The Moynihan Report and The Politics of Controversy* (Cambridge, Mass.: M.I.T. Press, 1967), pp. 39–124.

16 Among eight people teaching social problems courses in my department, I found *none* who had read the text of the report.

17 One of the best critiques of the matriarchal concept is found in Robert N. Staples, "The Myth of the Black Matriarchy," *The Black Scholar*, 1 (1970), 8–16.

18 Toni Cade, ed., *The Black Woman: An Anthology* (New York: New Amerian Library, 1970), pp. 101–10.

19 Renee Ferguson, "Women's Liberation Has a Different Meaning for Blacks," in Gerda Lerner, ed., *Black Women in White America*, pp. 587–91.

20 See Section V on "The Double Image" in the first edition of this book.

21 Several of the authors in Toni Cade, ed., *The Black Woman*, address this issue.

22 U.S. Department of Labor, "Marital and Family Characteristics of the Labor Force, March 1977," Special Labor Force Report [unassigned], Bureau of Labor Statistics (Washington, D.C.: U.S. Government Printing Office, 1978). There are no clear-cut answers to the question of why there are so few men. Jacquelyne Jackson describes higher male death rates from childhood diseases, violence (including police-induced violence) in the community, death in the armed services, and selective migration. Even if black men are present and are simply not counted in the census, the simple fact that they are not enumerated means that they are not functioning enough to play roles as providers and husbands. See, Jackson, "But Where are the Men?"

23 Data derived from *Employment and Earnings,* January 1978, p. 142; and U.S. Bureau of the Census, *A Statistical Portrait of Women in the United States*, Current Population Reports: Special Studies Series P–23, No. 58 (Washington, D.C.: U.S. Government Printing Office, 1976), pp. 72 and 67. This volume is hereafter referred to as *"A Statistical Portrait."*

24 Bureau of the Census, *Money Income and Poverty Status of Families and Persons in the United States: 1976 (Advance Report)* Current Population Reports Series P–60, No. 107 (Washington, D.C.: U.S. Government Printing Office, September 1977), Table 10, p. 25.

25 Michael J. Hindelang, Christopher S. Dunn, Alison L. Armick, and L. Paul Sutton, *Sourcebook of Criminal Justice Statistics, 1974* (Albany, N.Y.: Criminal Justice Research Center, 1975).

26 "The few semi-permanent (male-female) relationships that do develop are invariably built on some shaky finance-romance basis, her trying to get into his pockets, him trying to get into her drawers. Our blues singers have chronicled that madness for generations. But only lately has there developed something saner. And it's developed through the Struggle." Toni Cade, *The Black Woman*, p. 106.

27 U.S. Bureau of the Census, *Current Population Reports*, Series P–20, No. 388, "Fertility of American Women: June 1976," Tables 22 and 23.

28 Nancy Frazier and Myra Sadker, *Sexism in School and Society* (New York: Harper and Row, 1973).

29   Lloyd Bacon, "Early Motherhood, Accelerated Role Transition, and Social Pathologies," *Social Forces*, 52 (1974), 333–41. Only 12 percent of the women who became mothers before age 15 ever graduated from high school compared to 62 percent of the women who postponed their first child until age 22. Thirty percent of the women who had children very early in life were living in poverty compared to 11 percent of the women who postponed childbirth until age 22.

30   *U.N. Demographic Yearbook*, 1974.

31   Department of Health, Education and Welfare, National Center for Health Statistics, *Vital Statistics of the United States: 1976* (Washington, D.C.: U.S. Government Printing Office, 1979). Infant death rates in Vol. 2, *Mortality*, Table 2–3. White maternal mortality rates in Vol. 2, *Mortality*, Table 1–16. Black maternal mortality rates computed from Vol. 2, *Mortality*, Table 1–25 and Vol. 1, *Natality*, Table 2–1.

32   One young lawyer, Edna Primus, has been publicly reprimanded by the South Carolina Supreme Court for assisting a woman who had been sterilized to understand her rights and advising her of the legal assistance the American Civil Liberties Union would provide. The reprimand was on a charge of soliciting clients. Primus appealed the case to the U.S. Supreme Court which overturned her reprimand. Details in *Civil Liberties*, No. 320, November, 1977.

33   When such research is based on sample surveys, the numbers of black women included are often too small to yield reliable conclusions. But in other cases, where appropriate numbers were available, researchers have simply avoided making comparisons among groups that would reveal the seriousness of sex discrimination. Several of the issues are described in Elizabeth M. Almquist, "Social Science Research on Women and Wage Discrimination: The Missing 40 Percent and the Missing Perspective," paper presented at the American Sociological Association Annual Meetings, Chicago (1977).

34   *Employment and Earnings*, January 1978, p. 142.

35   The 1965 figures are from *A Statistical Portrait*, Table 13–16, p. 74: and the 1977 figures are from *Ibid*., p. 152.

36   *Ibid*.

37   "Trends in Racial Inequalities: Have the Gains of the 1960s Disappeared in the 1970s?" *American Sociological Review*, 42 (1977), 422–30. Data based on people who were employed and between ages 25 and 54.

38   "Commitment to Work and Wages: Earnings Differences of Black and White Women," *Sociology of Work and Occupations*, 3 (1976), 127–45.

39   *Employment and Earnings*, January 1978, p. 152.

40   Unpublished data for 1977 annual averages, Bureau of Labor Statistics.

41   More details are included in Almquist, "Social Science Research on Women and Wage Discrimination," but see also Elizabeth M. Almquist, "Women in the Labor Force," *Signs: Journal of Women in Culture and Society*, 2 (1977), 843–55.

42   Elizabeth M. Almquist, "Untangling the Effects of Race and Sex: The Disadvantaged Status of Black Women," *Social Science Quarterly*, 56 (1975), 116–28.

43   U.S. Bureau of the Census, 1973, *Census of Population: 1970*, Subject Reports, Final Report PC(2)–1B, *Negro Population*.

44   Lansing, "The Voting Patterns of American Black Women."

45   Data supplied by Barbara Farah, Center for Political Studies, University of Michigan.

46   Estimate derived by combining figures from Jewell Prestage, "Black Women State Legislators: A Profile," in Githens and Prestage, *A Portrait of Marginality,* pp. 401–18, and Naomi Lynn's article in this volume.

47   John C. Pierce, William P. Avery, and Addison Carey, Jr., "Sex Differences in Black Political Beliefs and Behavior," *American Journal of Political Science,* 17 (1973), 422–30.

# Mary Nelson

# Why Witches Were Women

Misplacement of one social order by another leads
inevitably to a set of issues and conflicts. These
arise like sparks at each point where the new and
the old make contact, where they treat the same
phenomenon differently. The crime of witchcraft
in Renaissance Europe arose at the points in time
and space where the new industrial order was
displacing the old feudal order.

One issue that arose was whether the Church
or the State is the final judge of human behavior.
This materialized as a jurisdictional dispute between ecclesiastical courts (the Inquisition) and
secular courts. A second issue was whether the
feudal family or the industrial job should have
first claim on human energies. This materialized
as a dispute over the proper place of women. In
the language of the time, it became the question
of who is a witch.

The practice of sorcery by the various European tribes was probably a relic of the Stone Age, but the crime of witchcraft was invented by the Inquisition in the late fifteenth century. The Inquisitors' notions of witchcraft, such as their belief that witches ride broomsticks at night to orgiastic black masses in the forest where they fornicate with the Devil and feast on roasted children, was a mixture of archaic beliefs about sorcerers and contemporary fears of evil in women.* It was no harmless fantasy. Between the years 1400 and 1700 approximately half a million people, most of them women, were burned as witches.[1] The interest of the Inquisition and its successors in spreading a mortal fear of witches throughout western Europe and in developing a science for finding and punishing them is the first concern of this paper. The second is to explain why witches were women.

During the early Middle Ages, when western Europe was a disorganized backwash of the thriving Middle Eastern kingdoms, the magical arts were treated with leniency by Church and State. Sorcery was punished only by the State, and only when it had resulted in loss of life or the destruction of property.[2] In these cases the sorcerer was punished for the fruits of his craft, not for sorcery itself. The Church, for its part, maintained that witchcraft was an illusion.[3] Missionaries to the northern tribes hoped that as their charges became fully Christianized, the pagan lore would fall into disuse and be forgotten.[4] But it was not. Persons skilled in casting spells and concocting herbal medicines continued to be feared and employed at all levels of medieval society.[5]

Early in the thirteenth century a train of events began that eventually resulted in the creation of the crime of witchcraft and the burning

---

*In the Teutonic tradition there was a belief that witches were cannibals and that once a year, on the first of May or Saint Walpurgis's night, there was a nocturnal gathering of witches called the *trolla-thing*, where they ate and sang. What the Dominican Inquisitors added was the belief that witches made a pact with the Devil, that they ate specifically children at their nocturnal gathering, and that the primary activity at the gathering was fornication with the Devil. Whereas the traditional witch was something of a power unto herself because of her knowledge of herbs and potions, the witch of the Dominicans was merely a tool of the Devil, who possessed and controlled her. For a fuller description of the traditional beliefs, see H. C. Lea, *A History of the Inquisition of the Middle Ages*, 3 vols. (New York: Russell, 2d printing, 1956), III, 401–8. For a crosscultural and historical discussion of fertility cults, see J. L. Henderson and M. Oakes, *The Wisdom of the Serpent: The Myths of Death, Rebirth, and Resurrection* (New York: Collier, 1963).

of thousands of witches. It began in Toulouse, in southern France. The revival of trade on the Mediterranean had fostered there the growth of a tolerant and cosmopolitan society, in which painting and chivalrous poetry flourished.[6] Within this society an ascetic, dualistic sect from Bulgaria, known as the Cathars, made converts not only among the townsfolk but also among the nobility and the clergy.[7] Even the bishop was known to be interested in their views. Pope Innocent III was displeased by these developments, as one might expect. Fearing that the heretics would create a breach in the otherwise solid monarchy—Christendom—over which he ruled,[8] he sought first to lure them back into the fold with the gentle preaching of ascetic preachers who differed from the heretics only in that they remained loyal to the Church. The Dominican Order was created for this purpose; their emblem shows two dogs shepherding an unruly flock.[9] When their preaching failed to have the desired effect, Innocent called for a military crusade against the heretical province, much like the Crusades he and others before him had sent against the infidels in the Holy Land. The knights of northern France, who long had coveted the lands to the south, responded to Innocent's call.[10] Their victory was swift and bloody, but the heretics remained heretical and the local populace became still more united against the invaders from the north.

Innocent made one last effort to bring the heretics back to the Church and ensure the loyalty of the southerners to their new seignior, the King of France. He created the Inquisition, an ecclesiastical court answerable only to himself. The inquisitorial procedure was modeled after the Roman trial procedures for treason.[11] Inquisitors, most of whom were recruited from the Dominican Order, were empowered to search out offenders, use torture to obtain confessions, deny legal advisers to the accused, and confiscate the property of the convicted. Their goal was to persuade heretics to repent. If, however, they decided that a heretic was irretrievably lost to God, he was handed over to the State to be executed.*

The new court proved to be an effective tool for handling the problems of disloyalty and heresy. In 1245 the last stronghold of the Cathars fell and two hundred were executed in a single day.[12] Sur-

---

*J. Madaule, *The Albigensian Crusade: An Historical Essay,* trans. B. Wall (New York: Fordham University Press, 1967). The Church dealt only with spiritual matters. The disposition of the heretic's body thus fell to the State.

vivors fled to Normandy or went underground to be periodically discovered by the Inquisition throughout the next century.[13] By 1250, however, the Inquisitors found themselves without heretics and began searching for new unruly flocks to shepherd. In 1257 they petitioned Pope Alexander IV to extend their jurisdiction to sorcery, but he refused.[14] He reaffirmed the official Church policy of treating witchcraft and sorcery as an illusion and urged the Inquisitors not to be distracted from their true work, that of recalling heretics to the Church. Subsequent popes were similarly petitioned, and they responded in the same way. During this time the Inquisitor Bernard Gui published a handbook for interrogating sorcerers and a guide for recognizing magical practices.[15] Similar inquisitorial handbooks had previously appeared as guides to the prosecution of earlier heresies, such as Catharism and Waldensianism. Gui's guidelines make no mention of night-flying, which later became the inspiration for the Inquisitors' belief in the Sabat, as the black mass was called; nor do they mention the pact with the Devil and the sexual practices that later provided the basis for most of the accusations against witches. From this we may surmise that the Inquisitors did not yet hold these beliefs.

Despite official discouragement, the Inquisition conducted a small number of witch trials in the Pyrenees during this period.[16] Finally, in 1326, Pope John XXII provided the sanction the Inquisitors had sought for nearly seventy years. He had a personal stake in the issue because he feared that there were conspirators in his own palace who plotted to poison him using witchcraft. He issued a bull, the *Super illius specula,* which declared that although witchcraft is an illusion all who *used the services* of sorcerers were to be punished as heretics and all books on the subject were to be burned.[17] Armed with this authority, the Inquisition launched a witch craze in Toulouse and Normandy that continued for a full century, until the 1430's, and resulted in the execution of several hundred persons, mostly peasant women.[18] At the close of this period, more inquisitorial handbooks for witch hunting appeared, written by Inquisitors who participated in the craze in Toulouse.

The most important document to appear at this time was a paper issued in 1458 by the Inquisitor Nicholas Jaquerius,[19] who argued that the existing sect of witches was *different* from the traditional variety. Thus traditional Church policy, which held that witchcraft was an illusion, was no longer applicable. According to Jaquerius the new breed of witches all attended the Sabat, where they copulated with demons, desecrated Christian symbols, and feasted on unbaptized infants. Moreover, they were certainly heretics, for even if the Sabat were an illusion, the witches' belief in it indicated that they were followers of the Devil and pagan goddesses even in their waking hours.

The final victory of the Inquisition followed shortly. In 1451 the pope had appointed Hugh le Noir Inquisitor General in France, and he had already prosecuted a number of peasant women in the northern town of Arras.[20] In 1484 two Inquisitors, Jakob Sprenger and Henry Krämer, petitioned Pope Innocent VIII for a similar appointment to the Rhineland. He replied with the bull *Summis desiderantes,* which not only granted their petition but also affirmed the Church's belief in the heresy of witchcraft and in its responsibility, through the Inquisition, to remove that foul cancer from Christendom. The bull was published at the front of a handbook for witch hunters called the *Malleus Maleficarum (The Witches' Hammer).* Sprenger and Krämer wrote the *Malleus* a few years after they obtained the bull, but by placing the bull in the front they gave the appearance that the handbook had been commissioned by Innocent.[21]

Of all the witch hunters' handbooks written, the *Malleus* was the most widely used. It appeared to be authoritative, and since it was printed on the newly invented printing press, it was more widely distributed than any of the earlier handbooks could have been.[22] Even so, the *Malleus* contained little that was new. It reiterated exhaustively the arguments of previous handbooks and restated Jaquerius's observations about the practices of the "new" witch cult. But an important section was added to explain why witches were women, or rather, why women were witches. The *Malleus* was thereby transformed into a classic statement of misogyny. How did a woman become a witch? Through demonic possession. How did the Devil come to possess a woman? According to the authors of the *Malleus,* her soul was persuaded to shift its allegiance from God to the Devil. A strong spirit could not be conned into such a bad bargain, but women were thought to have weak, frivolous, even malicious natures. Any woman was an easy mark for the Devil, while demonic possession remained rare, they believed, among men. Furthermore, since the Devil's ace in the hole was free sex, women were expected to be more prone to go over to his side because they were simply more lustful. As our authors explained:

> All witchcraft comes from carnal lust, which is in women insatiable. See Proverbs xxx: There are three things that are never satisfied, yea, a fourth thing which say not, It is enough; that is, the mouth of the womb. Wherefore for the sake of fulfilling their lusts they consort even with devils. More such reasons could be brought forward, but to the understanding it is sufficiently clear that it is no matter for wonder that there are more women than men found infected with the heresy of witchcraft. And in consequence of this, it is better called the heresy of witches than of wizards, since the name is taken from the more powerful party. And blessed be the Highest Who has so far preserved the male sex from so great a crime: for since He was willing to be born and to suffer for us, therefore He has granted to men this privilege.[23]

No doubt the Inquisitors rejoiced at Innocent's bull, for it condoned and even encouraged the witch hunting they had furtively engaged in already and promised to keep them in business a while longer. Ironically, however, it brought their demise, for the secular authorities would not tolerate the use of such a powerful political tool as witch trials by anyone but themselves. The Inquisition was expelled from the Tyrol in 1485 and from France in 1491.[24] In both cases, Inquisitors had inadvisedly interfered with important persons of state by bringing them to trial for witchcraft. The Italian cities also refused to give the Inquisitors free rein. Most of the papal bulls dealing with witchcraft following the *Summis desiderantes* consisted of appointments of Inquisitors to uncooperative Italian cities.[25] Spain had succeeded in making the Inquisition a state institution just a few years before Innocent issued his bull. The Spanish Inquisitors were more interested in *conversos* than witches, but the principle was the same.* Isabel and Ferdinand allowed the Inquisition to function in their realm only while it remained under royal control.[26] In Germany the Inquisition had never been very active, and by 1517 it was unable to silence Martin Luther.**

---

*The Inquisition concerned itself only with wayward Christians. Nonchristians were not under its jurisdiction. In Spain large numbers of Jews and Moors were registered with the State as converts to Christianity (*conversos*), and then accused of irregularities in the practice of their religion. In this way they became subject to the Inquisition.

**Lea, *History of the Inquisition*, II. 420–26. The Inquisition was finally discredited in Germany because of its participation in feuds among the theologians at the University of Cologne.

In short, just at the time the Inquisition was in a position to hunt witches in the grand style, it was dismantled by the secular authorities, who took the task upon themselves. The witch craze the Inquisition had initiated continued for two more centuries and became far more brutal than it had ever been before.

During the 1500's the persecution of witches was conducted in connection with the Reformation and the Counter Reformation.[27] The Protestants found scriptural support for their witch hunting in Exodus 22: "Thou shalt not suffer a witch to live." They also relied on most of the Dominican demonology, even though they rejected the rest of Catholic doctrine.[28] Luther himself believed in witches and thought that his mother had been bewitched. He attributed the fact that he often felt sick when he visited Wartburg to spells cast by his adversaries there.[29] Like his Dominican predecessors, he believed that all witches attended the Sabat, that they made pacts with the Devil, and that they were lustful and prone to sexual misbehavior. Many of the persons who were actually executed as witches in Luther's Saxony were members of a rival Protestant sect, the Anabaptists, and particularly Anabaptist women preachers.[30] The Anabaptist men were generally accused of heresy instead. This practice was consistent with Luther's view that women should remain at home caring for their husbands and raising their children to be proper members of the Elect.[31] Marriage, he felt, was a holy vocation. He closed convents and brothels alike and sent the inmates out to marry. Witchcraft became a crime in Saxony in 1572.[32]

Calvin was more skeptical of the Dominican witch beliefs than Luther. He believed that the Devil could do nothing without the permission of God and that he could never conquer the faithful. Nevertheless, Calvin regarded the Devil as an alert and energetic enemy.[33] In 1545 he led a campaign against witchcraft in Geneva that resulted in the execution of 31 witches. Calvinist missionaries succeeded in spreading the craze to Scotland in 1563. When James VI of Scotland, a Calvinist, became King of England, he revised the lenient statutes dealing with witchcraft and wrote his own handbook for witch hunters, the *Demonologie*. Under Queen Elizabeth the English witch craze became specifically anti-Catholic. Bishop Jewel of Switzerland demanded that Elizabeth take action against the witches lest they take over her kingdom. The witch craze that followed was worst in the Catholic counties of Essex and Lancashire. Calvinist missionaries from England also spread the craze to Bavaria, Baden, Württemberg, and

Mecklenberg. Bishop Palladius, the Reformer of Denmark, declared that all who used Catholic prayers were witches and must be burned.[34]

During the Catholic reconquests beginning in the 1580's, the Jesuits were highly active at ferreting out witches. Many of the accused were obstinate Protestants. In France witches were found primarily in Huguenot areas, such as Orleans, Languedoc, Normandy, and Navarre. Up to that time France had remained relatively free of witch trials, in part because the monarchy wished to protect the good name of Joan of Arc,[35] who was burned by the Inquisition as a witch. But in the 1590's whole villages accused of witchcraft were burned in the Rhineland, and the Spanish bishops of Flanders launched an anti-Protestant witch craze there.[36]

Throughout both the Protestant and Catholic witch crazes, a large number of peasant women who were not particularly involved in the political conflicts at the root of the accusations found themselves accused nonetheless, for it was common practice to first accuse a few women and then, through the use of torture, elicit the names of suspected (male) political enemies or rivals from them.[37] The enemies were thus indicted and brought to trial not as Catholics or Protestants but as witches, making it nearly impossible for them to defend themselves. The continued execution of women along with political enemies served to reaffirm the validity of the fundamental witch beliefs. If all witchcraft accusations had been brought against political rivals, the political motivation of the trials would soon have become too transparent for the populace to tolerate, which in fact happened in the Tyrol in the 1520's.[38] As it was, the major critics of the witch hunts confined their remarks to the injustices in the trial procedures, particularly the use of torture, and never attacked the fundamental beliefs that supported the demonology. The critics sought to prevent the use of witch trials to harass the innocent, but they left intact the belief in the reality of demons and the possibility of demonic possession.[39] They did not question the misogyny of those beliefs. So long as witchcraft was seen as a preeminently female crime, it remained credible, since to their way of thinking it was in the nature of women to commit such atrocities. Thus, despite the fact that women were not the actual target of the Reformation and Counter Reformation witch hunts, they remained the inspiration for the underlying beliefs and continued to be the victims as well.

The final chapter in the witch craze was the worst of all. During the closing years of the Thirty Years' War there appeared a number of "burning judges" who grew rich from the property confiscated from the witches they had burned. A fairly large proportion of the persons accused of witchcraft during this period were men, especially wealthy men.[40] As many as fifty to one hundred were burned each year in villages in Bavaria and along the Rhine between 1620 and 1630,[41] and the judges who had condemned them subsequently appeared in fine carriages with their wives dressed in the most expensive gowns.[42] During these years the local princes and their small bureaucracies were hard-pressed for funds to maintain the machinery of government.[43] The Thirty Years' War had depleted their cash reserves, and often the surrounding land was ruined as well. Witch trials constituted a convenient and lucrative source of income.

The witch craze ended when it was suppressed. In Mecklenberg the trials were halted by the Swedes, who invaded in the 1630's. Frederick II halted the trials in Germany following the Thirty Years' War in order to establish some semblance of order and peace in his empire. The Anglican nobility of England had never been convinced of the need for witch trials and simply revoked the witch statutes of the Calvinist James VI after there had been no accusations of witchcraft for several decades.[44] Some students of the witch craze have argued that by the seventeenth century the witch trials had to end because the new spirit of science and progress made believing in witchcraft ludicrous.[45] It is possible that a growing habit of skepticism contributed to the final end of the craze, but the critics who wrote at the end of the period added virtually nothing to what the earliest critics of witch trials had written.[46] It appears more likely that the witch craze ended because the institutions that had found it advantageous to persecute witches no longer had the power to do so. The Inquisition was dismantled by the monarchs. The local judges, who once were the most active in burning witches in the Holy Roman Empire, were not able to continue after the Thirty Years' War because the legal system was centralized and kept under the control of the Emperor.

We have seen that there were three fairly distinct periods in the European witch craze. The first, the ecclesiastical period, began approximately in the 1320's and continued intermittently until the 1490's, when the Inquisition was expelled from France and captured in Spain. The second was the period of the Reformation and Counter Reformation, during the 1560's through the 1590's, in which the craze was an extension of the religio-political conflicts of the time. This was followed by a short but essentially secular period in which the officers of the courts sought to profit personally from the conviction of witches. These "burning judges" appeared at the close of the Thirty Years' War. Throughout the witch craze the vast majority of the accused were women, particularly peasant women. The theme of the witch hunts from the beginning was the culpability of women. Some other equally disliked and defenseless group, such as Jews, lepers, or children, could have played the role just as well. The question that remains, then is why witches were women.

The Dominican Inquisitors who wrote the *Malleus* and other related demonologies saw witches—and women, the two being inseparable—as a true threat to the survival of Christendom. Witches not only destroyed crops and sent storms to sailing expeditions, but threatened to destroy the whole population by killing infants in the womb and taking away men's generative powers. These fears were not entirely fantasy. At the time the Inquisitors were formulating their witch beliefs, enormous changes were taking place in the relationship of women to the social order. The development of an industrial system of producing goods and urban living patterns made the medieval family structure obsolete and required changes in the make-up of the labor force. Both of these new conditions made it necessary for women to step outside their traditional social roles. The medieval family was primarily a property-holding institution,[47] in which the wife's main duty was to provide male heirs for the family holdings, if any, and to add to her husband's fortunes through her dowry.[48] A woman who did not marry commonly entered a convent,[49] if her family was rich; otherwise she stayed home to help work the family land. When a family moved to the city, however, it became a buying unit dependent on a cash income. Members of the family accordingly sought employment in the guilds or with the large industrial manufacturers. Daughters who did not marry and could not afford to enter convents were either apprenticed to a trade or sent out to fend for themselves,[50] since very few urban-industrial families could afford to support unemployed members.

These new conditions raised the basic issues of women's participation in the industrial-urban labor force and the desirability of using various methods of birth control to limit family size. These may be reduced to a single issue: what is the proper relationship of a woman to the institution of the family? Medieval society gave two cultural responses. The first was to glorify woman's traditional role. In the fourteenth century (but beginning earlier in Languedoc, before the Crusade against the Cathars) woman became an object of respect, even of worship.[51] The Troubadors developed a poetry that consisted almost entirely of praise for the chaste lady locked in her castle tower.[52] At the same time there arose the cult of the Virgin Mary, in which the Virgin was worshipped as the ideal woman. She was viewed as entirely sexless (clerics argued about whether even her conception was immaculate, just as Christ's was)[53] and devoted to helping others. Numerous legends appeared at the time in which the Virgin intervened to protect mortals from assailants, Satan, and even the judgment of God.[54]

The second response to changes in women's role was the development of the witch beliefs, in which women were portrayed as the polar opposite of the Virgin. To understand this response fully, we must take a closer look at the economic and social conditions that faced women at the time.

The pressure on women to enter the labor force resulted not only from their dependence on cash income, mentioned earlier, but from the considerable hurdles to marriage in the new industrial society. To put it simply, marriageable men were in short supply.[55] Guild rules forbade members who had not yet reached the status of master to marry, and as the population increased in the late 1200's and again in the 1400's, a journeyman's prospects of becoming a master became poorer and poorer. At the same time, and this was perhaps more important than the problem of guild restrictions, men who were employed by the large manufacturers (usually in the textile and mining industries) lived too close to starvation to be able to marry. The new urban proletariat was drawn mainly from peasant families who could no longer support their children on the family land holdings. The rural emigrants to the cities were so plentiful that urban wages remained extremely low, and business fluctuations created chronic insecurity among the hordes of urban laborers.[56]

What was to become of women in the cities who could not find husbands? Very few had parents who were able to continue supporting them, in the traditional pattern. There are numerous records of the daughters of tradesmen being apprenticed to the family trade. Many were also apprenticed to enter the traditional female trades of spinning and weaving. However, if the family was unable to provide for an unmarried daughter in this way, she either became a prostitute or found employment with one of the large manufacturers, or both.[57]

There are records of contemporary laborers complaining that employers used rural workers, women, and the foreign-born to break strikes and keep wages low.[58] There is some evidence, though records are understandably poor, that the number of prostitutes increased rapidly during the period of early industrial development.[59] In the late 1200's, in some towns, new laws were passed imposing stiff fines or public punishment for slandering a chaste woman by calling her a prostitute.[60] During the early 1300's the towns along the Rhine and in Alsace-Lorraine, where new industries were rapidly developing, passed laws aimed at confining prostitution to certain streets and houses.

There were some efforts to develop more acceptable alternatives for unmarried women than prostitution or entering the labor force. In the 1200's and 1300's a number of daughters of rich bourgeois families used their personal wealth to establish secular convents. If their families had been more wealthy, they would have bought their daughters' entrance into convents, as the aristocracy did. The secular convents they established, called Beguine houses, were open to all women who wished to remain chaste and earn their living by manual labor, usually spinning and weaving. The Beguines encountered enormous difficulties because the Church accused them of heresy and sought to place them under the supervision of the male clerical orders, the Dominicans and Franciscans. This proved unsatisfactory to the Beguines because they were harassed by monks seeking sexual favors from them. When they complained to the pope about these abuses, he responded by requiring all new members of the organization to be over forty years old. The Beguines were also harassed by the guilds, which considered them a source of economic competition and invoked city ordinances forbidding nonguild craft work to close the Beguine houses.[61] Most of the Beguines eventually became absorbed into the ecclesiastical structure as tertiaries (clerics who live in the world rather than the monastery and have no office in the Church). The few houses that survived became hospitals or poorhouses, primarily because the need for such institutions was very great.[62]

The economic expansion of the 1200's, as we have seen, created new work patterns and living arrangements for the peasantry and especially for women. It also led to the growth of numerous new cities along the Rhine, in Flanders, and in England, a substantial increase in population, the perfection of the money system, and even the settling of new lands.[63] It was interrupted in the 1300's by two serious natural disasters. The first was a terrible famine from 1315 to 1317, which appears to have taken a greater toll on the population than any previous European famine on record. Much more devastating was the second disaster, an epidemic of the Plague that killed about a third of the European population between 1347 and 1350. The disease reappeared in localized outbreaks until the end of the century. The death toll was especially high in the cities, though city dwellers escaping to the countryside succeeded in bringing the Plague there too.[64]

In the aftermath of the Plague, surviving peasants and wage laborers found themselves in an advantageous position. The labor shortage produced by the drop in population created a substantial increase both in real wages and in the prices peasants could command for the food they brought into the cities. For the first time they were able to include meat regularly in their own diets, and the economic insecurity they had experienced for nearly two centuries was alleviated. Under such favorable conditions, we might expect the population to increase rapidly to its former size. But it did not. In fact, the population of Europe did not begin its next growth spurt—one that extends to our own time—until the 1700's. This lag can be partly accounted for by the periodic return of the Plague and by the continuation of the Hundred Years' War in France and England. These factors were insufficient, however, to maintain the depressed level of the population. There is evidence that a third and more important factor was at work. During the second half of the fourteenth century, the reduction of the birth rate was considerably greater than the loss of population (i.e., potential parents). This indicates that some form of contraception or infanticide or both was being practiced.[65]

It is not difficult to account for the use of birth control at that time. A large part of the population had suddenly been introduced to a higher standard of living as a result of high wages. They did not wish to jeopardize their new prosperity by raising large families and were no longer on the land where they needed them. Many did not marry, and those who did limited the number of children they had. The Church complained of the widespread use of *coitus interruptus* by married and unmarried persons to prevent pregnancy,[66] which suggests that this was the most commonly used method of contraception. There is also evidence that infanticide was being practiced.[67] In England during the

1300's and 1400's, there was an "unmistakeable deficiency in the number of female children born, both among the more prosperous landholding groups and in servile families."[68]

Thus, during the century preceding the witch craze, when the demonology and witch beliefs of the Dominican Inquisitors were being formulated, women were responding to the demands of urban-industrial life by stepping outside the traditional female role. Owing to the shortage of available men, many were entering the labor market or turning to prostitution instead of marrying. Moreover, many were apparently using contraception and infanticide during the late 1300's and into the 1400's to limit the size of their families, against the teachings of the Churches. Seen in this context, the Dominicans' charge that witches took away men's generative powers, killed infants, and publicly indulged their sexual lust with no eye to childbearing do not appear so bizarre. It is also reasonable that the Dominicans should have been especially suspicious of midwives, since they were experts in methods of birth control, and most likely cooperated in abortions and infanticides. The demonologists were mistaken in their belief that these acts were committed for the purposes of demonic ritual; but it should not surprise us that the Dominicans responded to social innovations in religious terms.

The witch is the medieval stereotype of the "bad woman." She personally is sexually unproductive, and she destroys the fruit of other women's wombs. In addition, she is an adultress in the most fundamental way. Unlike the Virgin and the nun, who give themselves to God, the witch has turned from God to take another lover, the Devil. Some males were also accused of witchcraft, but the witch was preeminently female because of her special association with birth and the cycle of nature. From this perspective, we may see the witch beliefs as a backlash that occurred within a highly conventional and invested part of the feudal order in response to changes in the social function and behavior of a problematic but relatively powerless group—women. The *Malleus Maleficarum* and similar works on witchcraft were highly scholarly manifestations of a general fear of the changes taking place in the medieval social order, particularly in the medieval family. The witch was an excellent symbolic vehicle for expressing those fears. The Dominicans shared these fears even with the Humanists of the day, who showed great concern for the proper education of children and the need for women to remain good wives and mothers. Luther, as we saw earlier, was particularly eager that women should marry and find their true vocation in caring for their husbands and children.

In the fifteenth century the Dominicans needed new kinds of heresy to give their organization a purpose for continuing. They found that witchcraft was just the heresy they needed. In Spain, where industrialization had not begun, the Jews, an indigenous minority group that a large part of the Spanish population was eager to persecute, were selected as the target rather than women. Eventually the trials came to be used by other organizations to persecute their own demons. The Protestants killed Catholics as witches, the Catholics burned the Protestants, and certain enterprising judges burned whole villages, male and female, in order to confiscate their victims' wealth. In the end, the witch trials became a secular political tool.

The disjunctions in the female role that inspired the witch craze are still with us. We have yet to resolve the issues of birth control and the participation of women in the labor market. Clearly, the displacement of the feudal social order by the industrial order remains unfinished. Meanwhile, the industrial and urban system that precipitated the events we have discussed is itself being replaced by a highly centralized, cosmopolitan, bureaucratic, communications-oriented system that makes the familiar form of the debate on the viability of the family and the proper place of women in society obsolete. As the new order becomes stronger and displaces more and more of the old industrial order, new issues built into this new displacement process will replace the old ones.

## NOTES

1  G. L. Kittredge, *Notes on Witchcraft* (1907), as cited by E. P. Currie in "Crimes Without Criminals: Witchcraft and Its Controls in Renaissance Europe," *Law and Society Review*, III (1968), 10.

2  H. C. Lea, *A History of the Inquisition of the Middle Ages*, 3 vols. (New York: Russell, 2d printing, 1956), III, 408.

3  *Ibid.*, p. 494. Church policy was contained in the *capitulum Episcopi*, which is attributed to an obscure church council called the Council of Anquira.

4  *Ibid.*, pp. 485–96.

5  J. Michelet, *Satanism and Witchcraft: A Study in Medieval Superstition*, trans. A. R. Allison (New York: Citadel Press, 1939), pp. 86–87.

6  J. Madaule, *The Albigensian Crusade: An Historical Essay*, trans. B. Wall (New York: Fordham University Press, 1967).

7   W. Wakefield and A. Evans, eds., *Heresies of the High Middle Ages* (New York: Columbia University Press, 1969), p. 36.

8   Madaule, *Albigensian Crusade.*

9   P. Mandonnet, *St. Dominic and His Work,* trans. M. B. Larkin (St. Louis, Mo.: Herder Book Co., 1944).

10  Madaule, *Albigensian Crusade.*

11  Lea, *History of the Inquisition,* I, 151.

12  T. Szasz, *The Manufacture of Madness: A Comparative Study of the Inquisition and the Mental Health Movement* (New York: Harper and Row, 1970), p. 294.

13  H. Trevor-Roper, *The European Witch-Craze of the Sixteenth and Seventeenth Centuries* (New York: Harper and Row, 1969), p. 175. Note discussion of G. L. Burr.

14  *Ibid.,* p. 103.

15  Lea, *History of the Inquisition,* III, 449.

16  Trevor-Roper, *European Witch-Craze,* p. 102.

17  Lea, *History of the Inquisition,* III, 452–53.

18  Trevor-Roper, *European Witch-Craze,* p. 103.

19  Lea, *History of the Inquisition,* III, p. 497.

20  *Ibid.,* pp. 519–30.

21  Trevor-Roper, *European Witch-Craze,* p. 101.

22  *Ibid.,* p. 102.

23  J. Sprenger and H. Krämer, *Malleus Maleficarum,* trans. M. Summers (Suffolk, Eng.: John Rodker, 1928), p. 47.

24  Lea, *History of the Inquisition,* III, 530, 541.

25  H. C. Lea, *Materials Toward a History of Witchcraft,* ed. A. C. Howland, 3 vols. (New York: Thomas Yoseloff, 1957), pp. 220–29.

26  H. C. Lea, *A History of the Inquisition in Spain* (London: Macmillan, 1906).

27  See G. Länglin, as cited in Lea, *Materials,* III, 1079.

28  Trevor-Roper, *European Witch-Craze,* p. 137.

29  Lea, *Materials,* III, 417.

30  R. Clifford, University of Chicago School of Divinity, personal communication, March 1969.

31  R. Bainton, *Women of the Reformation in Germany and Italy* (Minneapolis: Augsberg Pub. House, 1971), p. 10.

32  Lea, *Materials,* I, 417.

33  *Ibid.,* p. 428.

34  Trevor-Roper, *European Witch-Craze,* p. 143.

35  Lea, *History of the Inquisition,* III, 530.

36  Trevor-Roper, *European Witch-Craze,* p. 139.

37  Lea, *History of the Inquisition,* III; see the discussion of the treatment of the witches of Arras, beginning p. 519, and for a discussion of the use of torture, see pp. 513–14.

38  Trevor-Roper, *Eurpean Witch-Craze*, p. 135

39  *Ibid.*, p. 148.

40  E. P. Currie, "Crimes Without Criminals: Witchcraft and Its Controls in Renaissance Europe," *Law and Society Review*, III (1968), 25.

41  Trevor-Roper, *European Witch-Craze*, p. 156.

42  Currie, "Crimes Without Criminals," p. 22.

43  Trevor-Roper, *European Witch-Craze*, pp. 67–77.

44  Curie, "Crimes Without Criminals," p. 32.

45  For example, H. C. Lea, in the works cited above; Andrew Dickson White, *A History of the Warfare Between Science and Theology in Christendom* (New York: Appleton, 1896); and Joseph Hansen, *Quellen und Untersuchungen zur geschichte des hexenwahns* (Bonn, Germany: C. Georgi, 1901).

46  Trevor-Roper, *European Witch-Craze*, p. 161.

47  P. G. Aries, *Centuries of Childhood: A Social History of Family Life* (New York: Knopf, 1962). See also W. Goodsell, *History of the Family as a Social and Educational Institution* (New York: Macmillan, 1915).

48  B. Jarrett, *Social Theories of the Middle Ages, 1200–1500* (London: Ernest Benn, 1926), p. 57.

49  E. W. McDonnell, *The Beguines and Beghards in Medieval Culture* (New Brunswick, N.J.: Rutgers University Press, 1954), p. 83.

50  *Ibid.*, p. 87.

51  Editors of *Life*, *Epic of Man* (New York: Time, 1961). See also Michelet, *Satanism and Witchcraft*, p. 102.

52  Denis de Rougement, *Love in the Western World*, trans. M. Belgion (New York: Pantheon, 1956).

53  Lea, *History of the Inquisition*, III, 597–610.

54  Editors of *Life*, *Epic of Man*.

55  McDonnell, *Beguines and Beghards*, p. 84.

56  N. Cohn, *The Pursuit of the Millennium* (New York: Oxford University Press, 1970). See also R. F. Heilleiner, "The Population of Europe from the Black Death to the Eve of the Vital Revolution," in E. E. Rich and C. H. Wilson, eds., *The Cambridge Economic History of Europe* (Cambridge, Eng.: Cambridge University Press, 1967), IV, 84.

57  McDonnell, *Beguines and Beghards*, p. 86.

58  P. Boissonnade, *Life and Work in Medieval Europe*, trans. E. Power (London: Routledge and Kegan Paul, 1927), p. 205.

59  Heilleiner, "Population of Europe," p. 72.

60  P. La Crois, *History of Prostitution*, trans. S. Putnam (Chicago: Pascal Covici, 1926), II, 113

61  McDonnell, *Beguines and Beghards*, pp. 270–77.

62  *Ibid.*, p. 82.

63  H. Pirenne, *Economic and Social History of Medieval Europe* (New York: Harcourt, Brace, and World, 1937).

64  Heilleiner, "Population of Europe," p. 6.

65  *Ibid.*, p. 71.

66  *Ibid.*, p. 70.

67  W. Goodsell, *A History of the Family as a Social and Educational Institution* (New York: Macmillan, 1915), p. 212.

68  Heilleiner, "Population of Europe," p. 71.

# Laura Shapiro

## Violence: The Most Obscene Fantasy*

There is a widespread notion that violence against women is abnormal. Rapists and murderers constantly have their backgrounds, their relationships with mothers, wives and lovers, analyzed in detail to uncover the incident that will explain their hatred. Yet attacks on women are as certain in American life as death and taxes—more certain than taxes, since some people manage not to pay. In the climate of anti-female violence that hangs over our lives, all women pay.

The Bronx postal worker admitted to be "Son of Sam," who shot eight women with no apparent motive, need only have been born a male to be encouraged to despise women; and the little boy

*Reprinted, with minor revisions, from *Mother Jones* (December 1977), pp. 11–12, by permission of the publisher and the author.

eyeing the cover of *Hustler* at the corner store is getting the same encouragement. Murder is a somewhat narrower and more extreme response than most, but it differs only in degree from the assaults on women that are supported by law, custom, social policy and enlightened contemporary thought.

Strangling old ladies with nylon stockings is probably the only interaction with women that is generally considered wrong. The younger the woman, and the more the attack can be seen as encompassing sexuality in any form, the more it approaches the acceptable. The fantasy of "complicity" dominates nearly all traditional thinking about rape and sexual assault. The recent California case in which a judge decided a woman who hitchhikes "advertises" her willingness to be raped was a classic in this field of thinking.

But the most damning evidence of "complicity" is a marriage license. Wife-beating is estimated by the FBI to be the most frequently occurring crime in the country. It is standard practice in families of every race and class and community: 45 percent of the women in a Hartford, Connecticut, survey had been abused; 18,000 cases of "family offense" were filed in New York state between 1973 and 1974; in a nine-month period, a thousand women in Dade County, Florida—the heartland of healthy sexuality, according to Anita Bryant—reported being beaten; and in wealthy Montgomery County, Maryland, about 650 women came forward for help one year.

A handful of homes and refuges for battered women now exist, and they're jammed full; the hotlines are busy continually. Women who can run away and get help, do. But even after a few years of news reports and some creeping legislation, belief remains firm that brutality against wives is as fully sanctified as the rest of the marriage sacrament. As recently as June 1976, a woman in Brooklyn filed for divorce because her husband had beaten her. The judge decided that two beatings in four years weren't sufficient cause to demand divorce, and he refused to grant one. When she appealed, the higher court agreed with the judge by a vote of four to one.

The police, welfare departments and other legal agencies usually don't intervene in "domestic quarrels," no matter what the result. In Washington, D.C., for example, it was discovered that as many as 11 women eventually *murdered* by their husbands tried to obtain warrants for their husband's arrest from lawyers at the local Citizens' Complaint Center. Unfortunately, the lawyers at the center didn't think the assaults the women described sounded very serious—until the women turned up dead.

Most men aren't rapists and killers, and most violence against women isn't especially dramatic. A far more common way of attacking women is for a man to stick his head out of a car window and shout remarks about breasts and vaginas to women walking by, or to stand on the sidewalk and hiss suggestions about sex and fellatio. Verbal rape doesn't leave any cuts or bruises; however, it's a marvelously effective way of humiliating women, and the rapists who fall into this category are assured that their actions are not only unpunishable but officially encouraged.

It has been a matter of unquestioned fact for many centuries that women's bodies aren't attached to human beings; they simply exist as public property, much like the deer and ducks who populate the woods every autumn for hunters. Currently, it's common to see blank-eyed, bloodless female bodies splayed against concrete walls or collapsed at the feet of sullen-faced men; this sells clothing and music. All manner of degradation, from meaningless nudity to rape to dismemberment, goes under the heading of "art" in the movie business. But these are only the latest variations on an ancient theme. A society that supports and enjoys the dehumanization of females on such a massive scale nurtures the streetcorner obscenities that follow women everywhere and reaffirms the universal premise that sex is all women are about.

The bridge between the use of women's bodies in popular culture and the use of women's bodies by rapists and sadists is a short one and easily crossed: the way is paved with pornography. Magazines featuring four-color layouts of nude dental hygienists vacuuming their living rooms or practicing yoga gave way long ago to a whole range of grotesqueries and brutality. The discovery of ten-year-old participants in peep shows and cheap films shocks the readers of *The New York Times,* but a few inches away on the newsstand *Penthouse* caters to the same taste by painting up its models to look like young girls, albeit grossly well-developed ones. As it happens, the largest group of rape victims are girls between the ages of ten and 19.

Most people confuse the graphic show of genitals accompanying the usual harsh witless fantasies—pornography—with sex. Pornography in truth is only secondarily concerned with sex; its main function is to be a vehicle for male power. Men have always been awed and terrorized by what happens in the female body, for its sexuality is all secrets, and its mysterious possibilities are demonstrated in blood and birth.

The outlandish scenarios and vivid crotch displays in the men's magazines—the reader of an average issue nowadays must feel like a gynecologist by the time he's done—are designed to make men believe that a woman is under control, submissive, willing to be dominated. Pornography feeds on frustrations; it helps build them, too. And, as the social taboos fall away and the portrayals become more and more desperately explicit, violence lunges in.

Most men, and a regrettable number of women, are so well-conditioned to living in a world that endangers and degrades women that they can't take it seriously. Nothing arouses more sneers and jeers and accusations of paranoia than when a woman objects to being manhandled on the street or complains about the glorification of rape on every newsstand. Women who are unable to walk to the corner mailbox at night, whose stomachs clench when they see a man on the sidewalk ahead walking straight toward them, who take more taxis than they can afford and who live behind four sets of locks, are not especially comforted to remember that the civil rights of a crotch-peddler like Larry Flynt are under constant vigilance by anxious liberals. In the sacred hierarchy of defensible rights, a woman's physical freedom ranks low, and the preservation of her self-respect has no place at all.

But there is no way to circulate a petition for that freedom or to hire famous lawyers to defend her right to peace on the streets and safety at home. Legislation against "dirty books" is notoriously difficult to write without banning *Lady Chatterley's Lover* at the same time, although it does seem that the old legal demand for "redeeming social value" protected artists and women more effectively than the current muddle of "community standards." The real problem, of course, is the rigid belief of generations that masculinity is dominance, and, despite the remarkable permeation of the ideas of the women's movement into the most unlikely hearts and minds, that belief in dominance will be the last to go.

In the meantime, there seems to be at least one way to build up one's sense of personal strength and to actively resist the invitations to victimization that surround women—and that is to learn self-defense. The martial arts may get a woman out of a tight spot if properly applied, but they also offer a chance to feel physically in control, to feel that your body is yours for a change, to rip yourself sharply away from the malignant images of women that blind both sexes. The hardest thing about self-defense is learning to hit back; nothing contradicts a woman's cultural training more dramatically than retaliation. But women who study self-defense usually find that harassment on the street decreases significantly, simply because they don't carry themselves like victims anymore. Men tend to attack women who look vulnerable. Rapists, like millions of other outstanding citizens, are fully convinced that women "want it," from anyone at any time.

Dismantling that fantasy means dismantling a large proportion of the psychological foundation of our society, but, for millions of women who resent being subjected to cruel and insane definitions of sexuality, the wrecking crews won't arrive a moment too soon.

# Nancy Henley and Jo Freeman

# The Sexual Politics of Interpersonal Behavior

Social interaction is the battlefield where the daily war between the sexes is fought. It is here that women are constantly reminded where their "place" is and that they are put back in their place, should they venture out. Thus, social interaction serves as the most common means of social control employed against women. By being continually reminded of their inferior status in their interactions with others, and continually compelled to acknowledge that status in their own patterns of behavior, women learn to internalize society's definition of them as inferior so thoroughly that they are often unaware of what their status is. Inferiority becomes habitual, and the inferior place assumes the familiarity—and even desirability—of home.

Different sorts of cues in social interaction aid this enforcement of one's social definition, particularly the verbal message, the nonverbal message transmitted within a social relationship, and the nonverbal message transmitted by the environment. Our educational system emphasizes the verbal message and teaches us next to nothing about how we interpret and react to the nonverbal ones. Just how important nonverbal messages are, however, is shown by the finding of Argyle et al.[1] that nonverbal cues have over four times the impact of verbal ones when both verbal and nonverbal cues are used. Even more important for women, Argyle found that female subjects were more responsive to nonverbal cues (compared with verbal ones) than male subjects. If women are to understand how the subtle forces of social control work in their lives, they must learn as much as possible about how nonverbal cues affect people, and particularly about how they perpetuate the power and superior status enjoyed by men.

Even if a woman encounters no one else directly in her day, visual status reminders are a ubiquitous part of her environment. As she moves through the day, she absorbs many variations of the same status theme, whether or not she is aware of it: male bosses dictate while female secretaries bend over their steno pads; male doctors operate while female nurses assist; restaurants are populated with waitresses serving men; magazine and billboard ads remind the woman that home maintenance and child care are her foremost responsibilities and that being a sex object for male voyeurs is her greatest asset. If she is married, her mail reminds her that she is a mere "Mrs." appended to her husband's name. When she is introduced to others or fills out a form, the first thing she must do is divulge her marital status acknowledging the social rule that the most important information anyone can know about her is her legal relationship to a man.

These environmental cues set the stage on which the power relationships of the sexes are acted out, and the assigned status of each sex is reinforced. Though studies have been made of the several means by which status inequalities are communicated in interpersonal behavior, they do not usually deal with power relationships between men and women. Goffman has pointed to many characteristics associated with status:

> Between status equals we may expect to find interaction guided by symmetrical familiarity. Between superordinate and subordinate we may expect to find assymetrical relations, the superordinate having the right to exercise certain familiarities which the subordinate is

not allowed to reciprocate. Thus, in the research hospital, doctors tended to call nurses by their first names, while nurses responded with "polite" or "formal" address. Similarly, in American business organizations the boss may thoughtfully ask the elevator man how his children are, but this entrance into another's life may be blocked to the elevator man, who can appreciate the concern but not return it. Perhaps the clearest form of this is found in the psychiatrist-patient relation, where the psychiatrist has a right to touch on aspects of the patient's life that the patient might not even allow himself to touch upon, while of course this privilege is not reciprocated.

Rules of demeanor, like rules of deference, can be symmetrical or assymetrical. Between social equals, symmetrical rules of demeanor seem often to be prescribed. Between unequals many variations can be found. For example, at staff meetings on the psychiatric units of the hospital, medical doctors had the privilege of swearing, changing the topic of conversation, and sitting in undignified positions; attendants, on the other hand, had the right to attend staff meetings and to ask questions during them . . . but were implicitly expected to conduct themselves with greater circumspection than was required of doctors. . . . Similarly, doctors had the right to saunter into the nurses' station, lounge on the station's dispensing counter, and engage in joking with the nurses; other ranks participated in this informal interaction with doctors, but only after doctors had initiated it.[2]

A status variable widely studied by Brown and others[3] is the use of terms of address. In languages that have both familiar and polite forms of the second person singular ("you"), asymmetrical use of the two forms invariably indicates a status difference, and it always follows the same pattern. The person using the familiar form is always the superior to the person using the polite form. In English, the only major European language not to have dual forms of address, status differences are similarly indicated by the right of first-naming; the status superior can first-name the inferior in situations where the inferior must use the superior's title and last name. An inferior who breaks this rule by inappropriately using a superior's first name is considered insolent.[4]

According to Brown, the pattern evident in the use of forms of address applies to a very wide range of interpersonal behavior and invariably has two other components: (1) whatever form is used by a superior in situations of status inequality can be used reciprocally by intimates, and whatever form is used by an inferior is the socially prescribed usage for nonintimates; (2) initiation or increase of intimacy is the right of the superior. To use the example of naming again to illustrate the first component, friends use first names with each other, while strangers use titles and last names (though "instant" intimacy is considered proper in some cultures, such as our own, among status equals in informal settings). As an example of the second component, status superiors, such as professors, specifically tell status inferiors, such as students, when they can use the first name, and often rebuff them if they assume such a right unilaterally.

Although Brown did not apply these patterns to status differences between the sexes, their relevance is readily seen. The social rules say that all moves to greater intimacy are a male prerogative: It is boys who are supposed to call girls for dates, men who are supposed to propose marriage to women, and males who are supposed to initiate sexual activity with females. Females who make "advances" are considered improper, forward, aggressive, brassy, or otherwise "unladylike." By initiating intimacy they have stepped out of their place and usurped a status prerogative. The value of such a prerogative is that it is a form of power. Between the sexes, as in other human interaction, the one who has the right to initiate greater intimacy has more control over the relationship. Superior status brings with it not only greater prestige and greater privileges, but greater power.

These advantages are exemplified in many of the various means of communicating status. Like the doctors in Goffman's research hospital, men are allowed such privileges as swearing and sitting in undignified positions, but women are denied them. Though the male privilege of swearing is curtailed in mixed company, the body movement permitted to women is circumscribed even in all-woman groups. It is considered unladylike for a woman to use her body too forcefully, to sprawl, to stand with her legs widely spread, to sit with her feet up, or to cross the ankle of one leg over the knee of the other. Many of these positions are ones of strength or dominance. The more "feminine" a woman's clothes are, the more circumscribed the use of her body. Depending on her clothes, she may be expected to sit with her knees together, not to sit cross-legged, or not even to bend over. Though these taboos seem to have lessened in recent years, how much so is unknown, and there are recurring social pressures for a "return to femininity," while etiquette arbiters assert that women must retain feminine posture no matter what their clothing.

Prior to the 1920's women's clothes were designed to be confining and cumbersome. The dress reform movement, which disposed of corsets and long skirts, was considered by many to have more significance for female emancipation than women's suffrage.[5] Today women's clothes are designed to be revealing, but women are expected to restrict their body movements to avoid revealing too much. Furthermore, because women's clothes are contrived to reveal women's physical features, rather than being loose like men's, women must resort to purses instead of pockets to carry their belongings. These "conveniences" have become, in a time of blurred sex distinctions, one of the surest signs of sex, and thus have developed the character of stigma, a sign of woman's shame, as when they are used by comics to ridicule both women and transvestites.

Women in our society are expected to reveal not only more of their bodies than men but also more of themselves. Female socialization encourages greater expression of emotion than does that of the male. Whereas men are expected to be stolid and impassive, and not to disclose their feelings beyond certain limits, women are expected to express their *selves*. Such self-expression can disclose a lot of oneself, and, as Jourard and Lasakow[6] found, females are more self-disclosing to others than males are. This puts them at an immediate disadvantage.

The inverse relationship between disclosure and power has been reported by other studies in addition to Goffman's earlier cited investigation into a research hospital. Slobin, Miller, and Porter[7] stated that individuals in a business organization are "more self-disclosing to their immediate superior than to their immediate subordinates." Self-disclosure is a means of enhancing another's power. When one has greater access to information about another person, one has a resource the other person does not have. Thus not only does power give status, but status gives power. And those possessing neither must contribute to the power and status of others continuously.

Another factor adding to women's vulnerability is that they are socialized to *care* more than men—especially about personal relationships. This puts them at a disadvantage, as Ross articulated in what he called the "Law of Personal Exploitation": "In any sentimental relation the one who cares less can exploit the one who cares more."[8] The same idea was put more broadly by Waller and Hill as the "Principle of Least Interest": "That person is able to dictate the conditions of association whose interest in the continuation of the affair is least."[9] In other words, women's caring, like their openness, gives them less power in a relationship.

One way of indicating acceptance of one's place and deference to those of superior status is by following the rules of "personal space." Sommer has observed that dominant animals and human beings have a larger envelope of inviolability surrounding them—i.e., are approached less closely—than those of a lower status.[10] Willis made a study of the initial speaking distance set by an approaching person as a function of the speakers' relationship.[11] His finding that women were approached more closely than men—i.e., their personal space was smaller or more likely to be breached—is consistent with their lower status.

Touching is one of the closer invasions of one's personal space, and in our low-contact culture it implies privileged access to another person. People who accidentally touch other people generally take great pains to apologize; people forced into close proximity, as in a crowded elevator, often go to extreme lengths to avoid touching. Even the figurative meanings of the word convey a notion of access to privileged areas—e.g., to one's emotions (one is "touched" by a sad story), or to one's purse (one is "touched" for ten dollars). In addition, the act of touching can be a subtle physical threat.

Remembering the patterns that Brown found in terms of address, consider the interactions between pairs of persons of different status, and picture who would be more likely to touch the other (put an arm around the shoulder or a hand on the back, tap the chest, hold the arm, or the like): teacher and student; master and servant; policeman and accused; doctor and patient; minister and parishioner; adviser and advisee; foreman and worker; businessman and secretary. As with first-naming, it is considered presumptuous for a person of low status to initiate touch with a person of higher status.

There has been little investigation of touching by social scientists, but the few studies made so far indicate that females are touched more than males are. Goldberg and Lewis[12] and Lewis[13] report that from six months on, girl babies are touched more than boy babies. The data reported in Jourard[14] and Jourard and Rubin[15] show that sons and fathers tend to refrain from touching each other and that "when it comes to physical contact within the family, it is the daughters who are the favored ones."[16] An examination of the number of different regions in which subjects were touched showed that mothers and fathers touch their daughters in more regions than they do their sons; that daughters touch their fathers in more regions than sons do; and that males touch their opposite-sex best friends in more regions than females do. Over-all, women's mean total "being-touched" score was higher than men's.

Jourard and Rubin take the view that "touching is equated with sexual interest, either consciously, or at a less-conscious level,"[17] but it would seem that there is a sex difference in the interpretation of touch. Lewis reflects this when he writes, "In general, for men in our culture, proximity (touching) is restricted to the opposite sex and its function is primarily sexual in nature."[18] Waitresses, secretaries, and women students are quite used to being touched by their male superordinates, but they are expected not to "misinterpret" such gestures. However, women who touch men are often interpreted as conveying sexual intent, as they have often found out when their intentions were quite otherwise. Such different interpretations are consistent with the status patterns found earlier. If touching indicates either power or intimacy, and women are deemed by men to be status inferiors, touching by women will be perceived as a gesture of intimacy, since it would be inconceivable for them to be exercising power.

A study by Henley puts forward this hypothesis.[19] Observations of incidents of touch in public urban places were made by a white male research assistant, naive to the uses of his data. Age, sex, and approximate socioeconomic status were recorded, and the results indicated that higher-status persons do touch lower-status persons significantly more. In particular, men touched women more, even when all other variables were held constant. When the settings of the observations were differentially examined, the pattern showed up primarily in the outdoor setting, with indoor interaction being more evenly spread over sex combinations. Henley has also reported observations of greater touching by higher status persons (including males) in the popular culture media; and a questionnaire study in which both females and males indicated greater expectancies of being touched by higher status persons, and of touching lower status and female ones, than vice versa.[20]

The other nonverbal cues by which status is indicated have likewise not been adequately researched—for humans. But O'Connor argues that many of the gestures of dominance and submission that have been noted in the primates are equally present in humans.[21] They are used to maintain and reinforce the status hierarchy by reassuring those of higher status that those of lower status accept their place in the human pecking order.

The most studied nonverbal communication among humans is probably eye contact, and here too one finds a sex difference. It has repeatedly been found that women look more at another in a dyad than men do.[22] Exline, Gray, and Schuette suggest that "willingness to engage in mutual visual interaction is more characteristic of those who are oriented towards inclusive and affectionate interpersonal relations,"[23] but Rubin concludes that while "gazing may serve as a vehicle of emotional expression for women, [it] in addition may allow women to obtain cues from their male partners concerning the appropriateness of their behavior."[24] This interpretation is supported by Efran and Broughton's data showing that even male subjects "maintain more eye contact with individuals toward whom they have developed higher expectancies for social approval."[25]

Another possible reason why women gaze more at men is that men talk more,[26] and there is a tendency for the listener to look more at the speaker than vice versa.[27]

It is especially illuminating to look at the power relationships established and maintained by the manipulation of eye contact. The mutual glance can be seen as a sign of union, but when intensified into a stare it may become a way of doing battle.[28] Research reported by Ellsworth, Carlsmith, and Henson supports the notion that the stare can be interpreted as an aggressive gesture. These authors write, "Staring at humans can elicit the same sort of responses that are common in primates; that is, staring can act like a primate threat display."[29]

Though women engage in mutual visual interaction in its intimate form to a high degree, they may back down when looking becomes a gesture of dominance. O'Connor[30] points out, "The direct stare or glare is a common human gesture of dominance. Women use the gesture as well as men, but often in modified form. While looking directly at a man, a woman usually has her head slightly tilted, implying the beginning of a presenting gesture or enough submission to render the stare ambivalent if not actually submissive."*

---

*"Presenting" is the term for the submissive gesture seen in primates, of presenting the rump to a dominant animal; O'Connor also points out that it is a human female submissive gesture as well, seen, for example, in the can-can.

The idea that the averted glance is a gesture of submission is supported by the research of Hutt and Ounsted into the characteristic gaze aversion of autistic children. They remark that "these children were never attacked [by peers] despite the fact that to a naive observer they appeared to be easy targets; this indicated that their gaze aversion had some signalling function similar to 'facing away' in the kittiwake or 'head-flagging' in the herring gull—behavior patterns which Tinbergen has termed 'appeasement postures.' In other words, gaze aversion inhibited any aggressive or threat behavior on the part of other conspecifics."[31]

Gestures of dominance and submission can be verbal as well as nonverbal. In fact, the sheer use of verbalization is a form of dominance because it can quite literally render someone speechless by preventing one from "getting a word in edgewise." As noted earlier, contrary to popular myth, men do talk more than women, both in single-sex and in mixed-sex groups. Within a group a major means of asserting dominance is to interrupt. Those who want to dominate others interrupt more; those speaking will not permit themselves to be interrupted by their inferiors, but they will give way to those they consider their superiors. Zimmerman and West found in a sample of 11 natural conversations between women and men that 46 of the 48 interruptions were by males.[32]

Other characteristics of persons in inferior status positions are the tendencies to hesitate and apologize, often offered as submissive gestures in the face of threats or potential threats. If staring directly, pointing, and touching can be subtle nonverbal threats, the corresponding gestures of submission seem to be lowering the eyes from another's gaze, falling silent (or not speaking at all) when interrupted or pointed at, and cuddling to the touch. Many of these nonverbal gestures of submission are very familiar. They are the traits our society assigns as desirable secondary characteristics of the female role. Girls who have properly learned to be "feminine" have learned to lower their eyes, remain silent, back down, and cuddle at the appropriate times. There is even a word for this syndrome that is applied only to females: coy.

In verbal communication one finds a similar pattern of differences between the sexes. As mentioned earlier, men have the privilege of swearing, and hence access to a vocabulary not customarily available to women. On the surface this seems like an innocuous limitation, until one realizes the psychological function of swearing: it is one of the most harmless and effective ways of expressing anger The alternatives are to express one's feelings with physical violence or to suppress them and by so doing turn one's anger in on oneself. The former is prohibited to both sexes (to different degrees) but the latter is decisively encouraged in women. The result is that women are "intropunitive"; they punish themselves for their own anger rather than somehow dissipating it. Since anger turned inward is commonly viewed as the basis for depression, we should not be surprised that depression is considerably more common in women than in men, and in fact is the most prevalent form of "mental illness" among women. Obviously, the causes of female depression are complex.[33]

Swearing is only the most obvious sex difference in language. Key has noted that sex differences are to be found in phonological, semantic, and grammatical aspects of language as well as in word use.[34] In one example, Austin has commented that "in our culture little boys tend to be nasal . . . and little girls, oral," but that in the "final stages" of courtship the voices of both men and women are low and nasal.[35] The pattern cited by Brown,[36] in which the form appropriately used by status superiors is used between status equals in intimate situations, is again visible: in the intimate situation the female adopts the vocal style of the male.

In situations where intimacy is not a possible interpretation, it is not power but abnormality that is the usual interpretation. Female voices are expected to be soft and quiet—even when men are using loud voices. Yet it is only the "lady" whose speech is refined. Women who do not fit this stereotype are often called loud—a word commonly applied derogatorily to other minority groups or out-groups.[37] One of the most popular derogatory terms for women is "shrill," which, after all, simply means loud (out of place) and high-pitched (female).

In language, as in touch and most other aspects of interpersonal behavior, status differences between the sexes mean that the same traits are differently interpreted when displayed by each sex. A man's behavior toward a woman might be interpreted as an expression of either power or intimacy, depending on the situation. When the same behavior is engaged in by a woman and directed toward a man, it is interpreted only as a gesture of intimacy—and intimacy between the sexes is always seen as sexual in nature. Because our society's values say that women should not have power over men, women's nonverbal communication is rarely interpreted as an expression of power. If the situation precludes a sexual interpretation, women's assumption of the male prerogative is dismissed as deviant (castrating, domineering, unfeminine, or the like).*

Of course, if women do not wish to be classified either as deviant or as perpetually sexy, then they must persist in playing the proper role by following the interpersonal behavior pattern prescribed for them. Followed repeatedly, these patterns function as a means of control. What is merely habitual is often seen as desirable. The more men and women interact in the way they have been trained to from birth without considering the meaning of what they do, the more they become dulled to the significance of their actions. Just as outsiders observing a new society are more aware of the status differences of that society than its members are, so those who play the sexual politics of interpersonal behavior are usually not conscious of what they do. Instead they continue to wonder that feminists make such a mountain out of such a "trivial" molehill.

## NOTES

1   M. Argyle, V. Salter, H. Nicholson, M. Williams, and P. Burgess, "The Communication of Inferior and Superior Attitudes by Verbal and Non-verbal Signals," *British Journal of Social and Clinical Psychology*, 9 (1970), 222–31.

2   Goffman, "The Nature of Deference and Demeanor," *American Anthropologist*, 58 (1956), 473–502

3   R. Brown, *Social Psychology* (Glencoe, Ill.: Free Press, 1965). See also R. Brown and M. Ford, "Address in American English," *Journal of Abnormal and Social Psychology*, 62 (1961), 375–85; R. Brown and A. Gilman, "The Pronouns of Power and Solidarity," in T. A. Sebeak, ed., *Style in Language* (Cambridge, Mass.: M.I.T. Press, 1960).

4   Brown, *Social Psychology*, pp. 92–97.

5   W. L. O'Neill, *Everyone Was Brave: The Rise and Fall of Feminism* (Chicago: Quadrangle, 1969), p. 270.

---

*We are not suggesting that just because certain gestures associated with males are responded to as powerful, women should automatically adopt them. Rather than accepting male values without question, individual women will want to consider what they wish to express and how, and will determine whether to adopt particular gestures or to insist that their own be responded to appropriately meanwhile.

6   S. M. Jourard and P. Lasakow, "Some Factors in Self-Disclosure," *Journal of Abnormal and Social Psychology,* 56 (1958), 91–98.

7   D. I. Slobin, S. H. Miller, and L. W. Porter, "Forms of Address and Social Relations in a Business Organization," *Journal of Personality and Social Psychology,* 8 (1968), 289–93.

8   E. A. Ross, *Principles of Sociology* (New York: Century, 1921), p. 136.

9   W. W. Waller and R. Hill, *The Family: A Dynamic Interpretation* (New York: Dryden, 1951), p. 191.

10  R. Sommer, *Personal Space* (Englewood Cliffs, N.J.: Prentice-Hall, 1969), Chap. 2.

11  F. N. Willis, Jr., "Initial Speaking Distance as a Function of the Speakers' Relationship," *Psychonomic Science,* 5 (1966), 221–22.

12  S. Goldberg and M. Lewis, "Play Behavior in the Year-old Infant: Early Sex Differences," *Child Development,* 40 (1969), 21–31.

13  M. Lewis, "Parents and Children: Sex-role Development," *School Review,* 80 (1972), 229–40.

14  S. M. Jourard, "An Exploratory Study of Body Accessibility," *British Journal of Social and Clinical Psychology,* 5 (1966), 221–31.

15  S. M. Jourard and J. E. Rubin, "Self-disclosure and Touching: A Study of Two Modes of Interpersonal Encounter and Their Interrelation," *Journal of Humanistic Psychology,* 8 (1968), 39–48.

16  Jourard, "Exploratory Study," p. 224.

17  Jourard and Rubin, "Self-disclosure and Touching," p. 47.

18  Lewis, "Parents and Children," p. 237.

19  N. Henley, "The Politics of Touch," American Psychological Association, 1970. In P. Brown, ed., *Radical Psychology* (New York: Harper & Row, 1973).

20  N. Henley, *Body Politics: Sex, Power and Nonverbal Communication* (Englewood Cliffs, N.J.: Prentice-Hall, 1977).

21  L. O'Connor, "Male Dominance: The Nitty Gritty of Oppression," *It Ain't Me Babe,* 1 (1970), 9.

22  R. Exline, "Explorations in the Process of Person Perception: Visual Interaction in Relation to Competition, Sex, and Need for Affiliation," *Journal of Personality,* 31 (1963), 1–20; R. Exline, D. Gray, and D. Schutte, "Visual Behavior in a Dyad as Affected by Interview Control and Sex of Respondent," *Journal of Personality and Social Psychology,* 1, (1965), 201–09; and Z. Rubin, "Measurement of Romantic Love," *Journal of Personality and Social Psychology,* 16 (1970), 265–73.

23  Exline, Gray, and Schuette, "Visual Behavior in a Dyad," p. 207.

24  Rubin, "Measurement of Romantic Love," p. 272.

25  J. S. Efran and A. Broughton, "Effect of Expectancies for Social Approval on Visual Behavior," *Journal of Personality and Social Psychology,* 4 (1966), p. 103.

26  M. Argyle, M. Lalljee, and M. Cook, "The Effects of Visibility on Interaction in a Dyad," *Human Relations,* 21 (1968), 3–17.

27 Exline, Gray, and Schuette, "Visual Behavior in a Dyad."

28 Exline, "Explorations in the Process of Person Perception."

29 P. C. Ellsworth, J. M. Carlsmith, and A. Henson, "The Stare as a Stimulus to Flight in Human Subjects: A Series of Field Experiments," *Journal of Personality and Social Psychology*, 21 (1972), p. 310.

30 O'Connor, "Male Dominance."

31 C. Hutt and C. Ounsted, "The Biological Significance of Gaze Aversion with Particular Reference to the Syndrome of Infantile Autism," *Behavioral Science*, 11 (1966), p. 154.

32 D. Zimmerman and C. West, "Sex Roles, Interruptions and Silences in Conversation," in B. Thorne and N. Henley, *Language and Sex* (Rowley, Mass.: Newbury House, 1975).

33 For more on this see P. B. Bart, "Depression in Middle-aged Women," in V. Gornick and B. K. Moran, *Woman in Sexist Society* (New York: Basic Books, 1971); and P. Chesler, *Women and Madness* (New York: Doubleday, 1972).

34 See also M. R. Key, *Male/Female Language* (Metucnen, N.J.: Scarecrow, 1975); R. Lakoff, *Language and Woman's Place* (New York: Harper & Row, 1975); C. Miller and K. Swift, *Words and Women* (New York: Doubleday, 1976); B. Thorne and N. Henley, *Language and Sex: Difference and Dominance* (Rowley, Mass.: Newbury House, 1975).

35 W. M. Austin, "Some Social Aspects of Paralanguage," *Canadian Journal of Linguistics*, 11 (1965), pp. 34, 37.

36 Brown, *Social Psychology*.

37 Austin, "Some Social Aspects of Paralanguage," p. 38.

# Karen L. Adams and Norma C. Ware

# Sexism and the English Language: The Linguistic Implications of Being a Woman

## INTRODUCTION

This article is intended as an introduction to the problem of sexism in English—what it looks like, and how it affects the way women think, feel and act in our society. It is divided into three parts. The first looks at how female human beings are referred to in English, the cultural attitudes these kinds of references suggest, and what the implications are for the ways women see themselves and their role in society. In the second part, the emphasis shifts to language use. The characteristic speech habits of both women and men are examined, along with their effects on the way women lead their lives. The third part of the article takes up the question of change—what is being done to combat linguistic sexism, and what more *could* be done.[1]

## REFERRING TO WOMEN

One of the most intriguing characteristics of language is that it acts as a kind of "social mirror," reflecting the organization and dynamics of the society of which it is a part. Because of this, we can learn a great deal about a society by analyzing the structure of the language its members speak. Since our purpose here is to improve our understanding of the situation of women in *this* society, let's look at some of the words used to refer to women in English.

### The sexualization of women

English words used to refer to women are often "sexually weighted." This is evident in some sex specific pairs of nouns which are similar in meaning, but where the female form has taken on sexual overtones. A prime example of this is the supposedly parallel set of terms *master* and *mistress*. Both of these words refer to someone who possesses and/or has power over someone or something else, as in "He is the *master* of his fate," or "She is the *mistress* of a great fortune." However, as Lakoff has pointed out, it is also true that the word *mistress* has acquired a sexual connotation its masculine counterpart has not.[2] Thus we can use a sentence like "Jane is Tom's *mistress*" to report the fact that Jane and Tom are sleeping together and be understood perfectly, while to attempt to describe the same situation with the expression "Tom is Jane's *master*" is to invite communicational disaster. The latter sentence fails to express its intended meaning because the word *master* is devoid of sexual connotations.

The existence of this kind of asymmetrical relationship between what are ostensibly simple male/female equivalents is not restricted to a single example, however. Consider the pair *sir* and *madam,* where the latter refers to the proprietor of a brothel as well as serving as a term of address. Even the words *man* and *woman* may be seen to conform to this pattern. The sexual overtones inherent in the word woman show through clearly in sentences such as:

> "Girl, you'll be a *woman* soon. Soon you'll need
> a man." (from a popular song)

> "After six months at sea, the first thing Bill
> wanted to do on leave was to find a *woman.*"

Then there is the case of the male academician who objected to the title of a new course on the grounds that it was "too suggestive." The title in question was, quite simply, "Women in the Social Order."[3]

Another indication of the sexualization of women in English is the many more ways of describing women than men, in terms of their sexuality, that the language seems to have. Schulz reports the findings of two investigators who, as part of a larger study of slang, managed to collect over 500 synonyms for *prostitute*, but only 65 for the masculine sexual term *whoremonger*.[4] She also states that she herself has "located roughly a thousand words and phrases describing women in sexually derogatory ways. There is nothing approaching this multitude for describing men."[5]

Schulz also points out the degeneration of what were once quite neutral terms relating to women into terms that have sexual or negative connotations or both. She explains how the word *hussy*, for example, is derived from the Old English *huswif* (*housewife*), whose meaning was simply "female head of the household." A *spinster* was originally someone who operated a spinning wheel. A *broad* was simply a young woman, and *tart* and *biddy* were terms of endearment![6]

Linguists generally agree that the fact that a language has an elaborate vocabulary on a given topic means that this topic is somehow of particular concern or importance to the society as a whole. What, then, shall we conclude from the fact that English has so many terms describing women in specifically sexual ways? Is a woman's sexuality considered the most salient aspect of her being, rivaling or even outweighing her humanity in importance? Furthermore, why are so many of these terms pejorative? Is it due to the well-known "sex is dirty" attitude that is characteristic of our culture? If this is true, notice where it leaves women—in the position of having their entire existence defined in terms of something that is considered unclean, distasteful. The implications of this are sobering at best.

### The trivialization of women

A look at the kinds of people and things women tend to be grouped with in the English language can also tell us a great deal about how our culture regards the female sex. Consider, for example, stock phrases like *women and children first,* or *wine, women and song.* And then there are the less proverbial but no less significant classifications offered by various prominent individuals in recent years. For instance, before the draft was eliminated, President Nathan Pusey of Harvard is reputed to have lamented its draining effect on male brainpower at the University with the words "We shall be left with *the blind, the lame and the women.*"[7]

Examples like these are not difficult to find. The question is, what do these sorts of groupings imply about the kind of people women are considered to be? For us, at least, the implication is that women are immature (like children), frivolous (to be indulged in for entertainment purposes, like wine and "song"), and handicapped (like the blind and the lame). Singly or in combination, these presumed female attributes provide a convenient excuse for not taking women seriously; they serve to trivialize the female sex.

This "trivialization effect" appears elsewhere in the language as well. For instance, it is common practice to refer to adult females as "girls." Although it is probably true that the suggestion of youth it brings is in some sense a desirable one (in this society, after all, we admire and envy the young, while the old are considered worthless) it is nevertheless also true that the association carries with it certain decidedly negative connotations—irresponsibility, immaturity, "smallness" of body or mind, etc. What is associated with youth tends to "lack stature," and therefore importance, almost by definition. A simple experiment should help make this clear. In reading the following sentences, notice whether your mental image of the person being referred to changes in any way when the word *girl* is replaced by *woman:*

1. A *girl* friend of mine once told me. . . .
   *woman*
2. A *girl* I know was just appointed president of Bryn Mawr.
   *woman*
3. I can't tonight. I'm playing cards with some of the *girls.*
   *women.*
4. (One female doctor to two others) I've just diagnosed a very rare disease and I can't wait to talk to you *girls* about it!
   *women*

What do the kinds of changes you notice suggest to you?

The words *man* and *boy* could also be used in some of the above sentences and the substitution of *boy* for *man* would have the same sort of trivializing effect. However, the issue here is one of frequency. Males are referred to as "boys" much less often than females are called "girls."[8]

### Woman in terms of man

The English language also has a tendency to define women as a sort of male appendage. A woman's linguistic existence is in many cases expressed in essentially male terms, from a male point of view, and/or with male interests in mind. One example of this tendency is the fact that many of the nouns that refer to women performing various activities or roles are linguistically marked as derivatives of the basic (male) form. Thus we have poet*ess* and actr*ess*, songstr*ess* and stewar*dess*, usher*ette* and major*ette*, not to mention proper names like Jeanette and Henriette. Only in matters of marriage and the few, female-dominated professions, is the female form the primary one. Thus we have widow*er*, *male* nurse and *male* prostitute.

Another example of the way English tends to classify women in essentially male terms is the case of social titles that make the declaration of a woman's marital status (i.e., her relationship to a man) obligatory. Until very recently at least, women had no choice but to reveal whether they were single or (ever) married every time they wanted to refer to themselves in the conventional title-plus-last-name manner. One was either *Miss* Somebody-or-Other, or *Mrs.* Somebody-or-Other.[9] Now, of course, one can be *Ms.* Somebody-or-Other and supposedly avoid the whole issue. That this is not always the case, however, is suggested by the fact that the use of *Ms.* is often interpreted to mean "unmarried, and slightly ashamed of the fact." As one writer reports, "After four attempts to convince a travel agent that I was not 'Miss' or 'Mrs.' but 'Ms.,' she finally responded with 'Oh, I'm not married either, but it doesn't bother me'."[10]

One of the more subtle ways in which the English language represents the female as a derivative, or sub-set, of the male is by means of the linguistic convention known as "generic Man." In English, the same word that is used to refer to "male human beings" is also used in the generic sense, to refer to "all human beings." That word is, of course, *Man.* Our English grammar books assure us that persons of both sexes are meant to be included in expressions like *Man, the Hunter, the Man in the street, good-will to Men, all Men are created equal,* etc. But is this really the case? For example, if all "men" were really created equal, then presumably neither the women's suffrage movement nor the more recent struggle over the Equal Rights Amendment would have taken place. And if *Man* is really generic, why is there something decidedly funny about a sentence like "My brother married a spaceman who works for NASA"?[11] Furthermore, as one author is quick to point out, any woman encountering "a threshold marked 'Men Only,' . . . knows that the admonition is not intended to bar animals or plants or inanimate objects. It is meant for her."[12]

That generic Man is not always quite what he appears to be is particularly well-illustrated by the following incident: At the end of one of the hour-long segments of Jacob Bronowski's highly acclaimed T.V. series. *The Ascent of Man,* ". . . the host of the series chatted for a few minutes with a guest anthropologist about what women were doing during this early period in the ascent of man."[13]

The same generic principle that makes *Man* both male and female is supposed to apply to pronouns as well. We have all been taught that the third person singular pronoun *he* is both masculine and sex indefinite. But again, if this is true shouldn't the following statement sound perfectly natural?

No person may require another person to perform, participate in, or undergo an abortion against *his* will.[14]

Experimental evidence of the male bias in generic Man has been provided by recent research. For example, Linda Harrison of Western Michigan University reports she compared junior high school students' interpretations of a series of seven statements in which the physical appearance and activities of early human beings were described. The series of statements was presented in three different forms to separate groups of students. On one, the terms referring to people were *man, men, mankind* and *he.* On the second form, they were *humans, people* and *they.* On the third, *men and women* and *they* were used. All of the students were asked to draw the people described in the statements, and to give each person a modern first name (for easy reference). Statistical analysis of the data revealed that students of both sexes drew only male figures more often in response to the generic Man terms.[15] This study offers clear evidence that despite what the grammar books tell us, in actual usage generic Man does not apply equally to men and women, but suggests that the person being referred to is male.

All this is not to say, however, that generic terms are never interpreted generically. Grammar-book definitions and years of English composition classes have presumably had some impact, and sentences such as the following may well be taken as referring to both sexes.

1  *Man* the lifeboats!
2  A dog is *man's* best friend.
3  The essence of a human being is *his* sense of Self.
4  Each student should pick up *his* paper upon entering
   the room.

The point is that this exacerbates, rather than solves, the problem. Insofar as *Man* is both generic and non-generic, women find themselves caught in a linguistic contradiction of rather formidable proportions, as they discover that they are being defined as both *Man* and *Not Man* at the same time.[16] Precisely because the word is used to mean both male people and people in general, being *included* under the rubric of *Man* means losing their "linguistic identity" as women. By the same token, not to be included amounts, linguistically speaking, to being defined out of the human race. The generic Man convention sets up a linguistic structure whereby women can be portrayed in English *either* as women, *or* as people, but not both.

Finally, we note that the practice of excluding females from human groups that are supposedly made up of people of both sexes is not limited to the generic Man case alone. Miller and Swift supply us with sobering evidence of this fact when they quote a television commentator as saying, "People won't give up power. They'll give up anything else first—money, home, *wife*, children—but not power."[17]

### Implications and consequences (or, so what?)

How does all this effect the way women live in the world? There are two views of the relationship of language to society and its effect thereon. Some people maintain that the relationship between language and society is one of representation, and representation only. According to this point of view, language serves as a social mirror, reflecting the implicit values, attitudes and prejudices of the society in which it is embedded, but having no power to influence the perceptions and/or interactions of the people in that society. From this argument it follows that while we may find the picture the English language paints of women distasteful, it has no real effect on the way they think and feel about themselves or the way they lead their lives.

A considerable number of people disagree with this position, however. They maintain that language not only *reflects* social values, attitudes, etc., but *reinforces* them as well. In any language, it is easier to talk about some things than others. We have seen, for example, that many of the words that English offers us as ways of referring to women are also words having sexual connotations. Thus the language in some sense makes it easy to talk about women in a sexual way, and provides the basis for the formation of a habit.

With the habit of talking about things in certain ways comes the habit of thinking about them in those same ways. Thus the language-based predisposition to talk about women in sexual terms makes it more likely that a speaker will think about them in those terms. Result? The well-known tendency of this society to view women as "sex objects" is lent additional support. It is in this sense, then, that language may be said to reinforce, as well as reflect prevailing social opinion.

One implication of this argument is that this ability of language to reinforce the status quo will facilitate the perpetuation of sexist attitudes and practices, and inhibit social change. Another is the possibility that, according to this theory, women are liable to come to "see themselves as the language sees them." For if the tendency to talk about things in certain ways leads to the tendency to think about them in those same ways, it follows that women speaking the English language will be encouraged to view themselves as sex objects, as trivial, as ambivalent about their status as complete human beings, etc. It seems fairly clear that the net result of either or both of these possibilities is in some sense to help "keep women in their place."

## FEMALE AND MALE DIFFERENCES IN USAGE

Just as there are differences in the words that refer to women and men, so are there differences in the ways that women and men talk. In English the same words, the same grammatical forms and the same conversational strategies can be and are used by both sexes. However, the frequency of the usage of these words and strategies and the situations in which they are used differ depending on the speaker's and listener's sex.[18] This section describes examples of these differences and how they relate to control and dominance in verbal interaction.

### Sex roles and speaking "proper" English

In the society at large the manner in which some people talk is more "prestigious" than the way that others do. In America, as in other countries, it is generally the language of the urban, well-educated, and wealthier speakers that is held in higher esteem. It is their upper class speech that is the most acceptable and carries the label of "Standard English." It is this "standard" language that is taught in schools and used by TV broadcasters and newspaper reporters.

The acknowledged existence of a standard language would lead one to expect that all speakers of English would strive to speak this more "esteemed" style in an effort to sound more like those who have prestige. However, one of the most consistent findings of those who have studied sex-based variation in English has been that women, no matter what their socio-economic level, their race, or their age, use more grammatically "correct" forms than men, and pronounce words in more "acceptable" ways. This means that they succeed in sounding more like Standard English speakers than men do.

Trudgill, in a study of Norwich English (a form of British English), found that, as in American English, women employed prestigious speech forms more often than men.[19] He also found that when speakers were asked about their utilization of standard and non-standard forms, differences between actual and perceived behavior appeared. Speakers "perceive their own speech in terms of the norms at which they were aiming rather than the sound actually produced,"[20] so that there were always cases of "over-reporting" and "under-reporting" of actual usages. These instances were strongly correlated with sex differences no matter what the class of the speaker. Women claimed that they used standard forms more frequently than they actually did and men reported that they employed them less frequently than they actually did. As Trudgill convincingly argues, the *actual* speech differences between female and male speech, combined with the differences in reporting indicate that women and men identify with different role models and seek to talk like these models.

One explanation of the "correctness" of women's speech is presented by Thorne and Henley.[21] They point to research by Goffman,[22] which demonstrates that inferior status leads to careful and circumscribed behavior. They claim that women's usage of Standard English is an example of this circumscribed behavior. A related argument is presented in Trudgill.[23] He characterizes women as "status conscious." Thus, he says, they act in ways that will improve their status. They seize on language as a way to do this because for women the only readily available sources of prestige are those that have to do with appearance.

But what of the male usage of less standard forms? Why does behaving like a man mean employing lower class speech? One of the ways of explaining this is that the prevalent socialization of males, because it is mostly peer oriented, leads to the development of a male sex role that includes competitiveness, independence and toughness. In our society it seems that working class males are thought of as having a life style that embodies these characteristics. Speaking the "less acceptable" or "non-standard" language associated with working class males then becomes a way for all males to appear tough and independent.

There are other methods by which female and male sex roles are verbally distinguished. For example, swearing is a way of shocking and antagonizing others, in addition to being a way to release anger. Its usage is more frequent in the speech of males, and observation indicates that many of the forms used for swearing, such as *son of a bitch*, vilify women. Swearing is considered improper in female speech when it occurs, and Jespersen, a well known linguist, also claims that women themselves object to its usage.[24] If women do swear they tend to limit themselves to milder forms like *shit, hell, damn.* Personal observation of the rather strong reactions that can occur when a woman curses—dropped jaws, expressions of disgust, turning aside in horror—testify to the fact that it is still a strongly tabooed behavior for women.

### Weakness and women's speech

It has been argued that women more frequently employ certain language patterns that make their speech sound weak. Some examples of these are the use of fillers and hesitation markers such as *ah, well, um-m-m*, and the use of phrases such as *I think, ya know,* and *I guess.* Unfortunately there has been little reliable sampling of these claims. However, Dubois and Crouch[25] did one such study of the use of tag questions, as in "It's a nice day, *isn't it?*" It had previously been argued by Lakoff[26] and others that women used tag questions to weaken assertions. However, the Dubois and Crouch study of the differences in the use of tag questions among participants in an academic discussion did not corroborate this claim. In their sample men used them more than women. It seems the male speakers used them to make a question sound more like an assertion so as not to appear uninformed, thus conveying the opposite effect of what Lakoff had suggested. In addition others have found tag questions to be used as veiled threats by males, e.g. "You agree with me, don't you?". The results of the Dubois and Crouch study indicate that the identification of "weak" forms in women's speech is more complicated than has been suggested and is an area in need of more investigation.

Another attribute of women's speech that is associated with weakness involves voice quality or intonation. Intonation can be thought of as a musical scale, with a high point, a low point, and steps between. Women's intonation range is wider than men's, sometimes giving what is interpreted as an emotional, and therefore weak, quality to their voice. This characterization comes about because large fluctuations in voice level can be used to convey emotion, and being emotional is a devalued behavior in our society. An additional difference in women's and men's intonation patterns is that women use more patterns that end at higher levels, as do intonation patterns for questions, thus giving a hesitant quality to their speech. Men rarely use these forms.[27]

### Differences in conversational strategies and their effect on women

Another category of linguistic behavior that is relevant here is conversational interaction. Sacks, Schegloff and Jefferson[28] refer to conversation as a system that is "party administered" and "interactionally managed." This means that speech exchanges are under the control of the individuals participating in them, and the interaction that arises is a consequence of the relationship between the speakers. It is not unexpected then that the disparate status of females and males in our society shows in these exchanges.

**Interruptions**    One characteristic of conversations is speaker-change or "turn-taking." A speaker signals the finish of her or his turn in various ways: through eye contact, lowering the voice level, or calling on someone else to take over. The general strategy in conversation is for the listener to wait for one of these signals and then start talking. However, there is another way to gain the floor—to interrupt.[29] This is considered impolite but, as we found earlier, where proper speech behavior is concerned, women and men act differently.

Zimmerman and West,[30] in a study of two-person conversations between twenty white, 20–30 year old, college educated people, found that in same sex conversations (10 female/female and 10 male/male), interruptions were about the same. These break-ins occurred in about 15 percent of the conversations. However, in mixed sex conversations (11 of them) this picture changed radically. In these cases interruptions turned up in 99 percent of the conversations, and, except for two instances in one conversation, males were the guilty parties. This incredibly large difference in the frequency of interruptions in same sex versus mixed sex exchanges, and the discrepancy in the sex of the interruptors, suggest different motivations in the two cases. In same sex exchanges, Zimmerman and West suggest interruptions are idiosyncratic. However, we feel they may also be related to the parties' emotional involvement in the exchange. While these factors may affect interactions between the sexes as well, interruptions in this case seem to be a systematic strategy designed to limit women's access to conversation. Moreover, this pattern is parallel to the interruptions found in adult-child interactions, where it is overwhelmingly the adult that interrupts the child.[31]

**Selective reinforcement**   Women and men also handle the role of listener differently. A listener is expected to signal attentiveness in any of several ways: head nodding, interjecting such words as *right, um-hmm,* or making more extensive verbal comment. Inadequate response from a listener can bring about a cessation in the exchange or at least a question such as "Are you listening?".

Evidence that men listen differently from women is reported in Fishman[32] and Hirschman.[33] Both found that males use significantly fewer interjections like *um-hmm* than females in both same sex and mixed sex verbal exchanges.[34] This lack of reinforcement by males can be seen as part of the competitive style that the male sex role in this culture prescribes for them. In conversations, this competitive style is manifested as a desire to dominate the exchange. One way of accomplishing this is by interrupting. Another way is by this limited reinforcement. As Aries reports in her data on all-male small group interactions,[35] rather than encouraging each other, males concern themselves with establishing a hierarchy. They accomplish this by "brain-picking" to see who knows the most, by telling jokes at each other's expense, and by telling stories about such physically threatening topics as castration and riots. It is easy to see how this difference in the use of reinforcers could make a woman, used to a supportive interaction style with other women, feel off-balance in mixed-sex interactions.

Another male strategy is to make a minimal or delayed response in an exchange. Speakers can infer from these kinds of responses that the listener thinks what they have to say is of little interest, and therefore, switch topics in an effort to engage the listener. In Zimmerman and West's data this was the effect in three of the ten mixed exchanges. These results suggest that males use the strategy at least partially as a way to control the topic, changing it to one they can talk on freely.

**Amount of talk**   Another difference between women and men in conversations is the length of the turn at talking. We all know the stereotype of the talkative woman and the strong, silent man. However, data from a variety of sources invalidate this stereotype. The finding is generally that men talk longer during their turns than women. This substantially larger volume of speech affords them a dominant position in an interaction. For example, Aries found that in groups comprised of both males and females (mixed sex groups) the males initiated 66 percent of the conversations compared to 34 percent for women. In her data, those who initiated talk were also the ones who took up more of the available time for talk and were also the ones considered as leaders by the others. Also, men were the recipients of more of the talk. The women in the groups oriented toward the males, rather than the other females, and drew them out.

## MAKING CHANGES

As far as reference or representation is concerned, the logical solution to the problem of sexism in English is to change the language to eliminate it. As a matter of fact, many such changes have already been proposed. Best known among them is the highly-controversial *Ms.* Most of us are also aware that words and phrases that are clearly sex indefinite are being recommended as substitutes for the ambiguous generic Man constructions (sales*person,* spokes*person, human*kind, mail *carrier,* etc.). Where no appropriate expression exists in the language, new forms are being coined to fill the gaps, hence the recent appearance of *chairperson, anchorperson, freshperson,* etc. That there is also a movement afoot to do away with generic *he* is not surprising, either. Extension of the use of *they* to the singular, alternation of *she or he* with *he or she,* and the newly coined *s/he,* all occupy prominent positions on the rather long list of suggestions for its replacement.

Some of these proposed changes are already well on their way to institutionalization. One of the first major efforts in this direction was undertaken by the editors of the American Heritage School Dictionary in the late sixties. It became the first of its kind to be made up of definitions and sample sentences premeditatedly non-sexist in nature. The editors of the dictionary have made a conscious effort both to represent women in equal numbers with men and to break down traditional sex-role stereotypes. Thus we find in the pages of the dictionary references to women of "dedicated political principles," who "pride themselves on their eloquence," who "make names for themselves," whose "minds begin to percolate," and who just generally have a lot of "brains and courage," at the same time that we are reading about men who "strive to attain mastery over their emotions," whose "resolve begins to waver," who "study typing at night," and who are known to have "tears well up in their eyes."[36]

Since the publication of the American Heritage School Dictionary in 1972, efforts to eliminate sexism from the country's reading matter have grown steadily in number and proportion. Major textbook publishers have distributed sets of guidelines to their authors and editors, encouraging them to use only non-sexist language in their writing and providing specific examples as to how this is to be done. Library cataloguers are calling for the eradication of sexism in both the language and conceptualization of card cataloguing systems, while various religious organizations are in the process of re-wording the texts of materials used in their services.[37]

Along with these institutional efforts, the on-going, day-to-day struggle of individual women themselves to combat sexist language must be recognized. More and more women are refusing to be called, or to call themselves, *girls*. More and more actors and poets are objecting to having their sex indicated by the *-ess* ending, arguing that unlike who they *are*, what they *do* has no sex. Finally, it seems reasonable to suppose that the fact that terms like *chairperson, freshperson,* and *Ms.* are becoming increasingly more familiar and acceptable to our ears is due in large part to efforts on the part of women to introduce them into the language. (The title of *Ms.* magazine, for example, seems to have been chosen with this in mind.)

A few years ago the principal question being asked by those who recognized and objected to the presence of sexism in the English language was can it be changed? Is it in fact possible to legislate the changes necessary to wipe out language's sexist bias? It should be clear from the preceding discussion that this question is now well on its way to being answered in the affirmative. The fact that many such changes are actually underway, however, only gives rise to another, equally important question: Will the eradication of sexism in the English language help eliminate it from other parts of society? We think language does indeed have the power to influence other parts of society and can work to facilitate change.

The attack on the problems that women encounter in their usage of language has also begun at both institutional and personal levels. For example, there exist more and more assertiveness training groups that have as their goals (but ones not often presented as such) changing the kinds of linguistic habits that we have described in this article. We find these groups in all kinds of settings, from large corporations to informally sponsored workshops.

Assertiveness training attempts to define a new category of interactional behavior. It rejects the one-up/one-down (i.e. aggressive vs. passive) interaction style that has been traditional in our society, for one that is balanced (i.e. assertive). Understanding the difference between these styles is essential for determining the changes women need to make to become assertive. There has been a tendency to label women's language as "weak," "hesitant," "correct," and "polite," as though all these words were equivalent. However, in becoming assertive there should be no reason to lose politeness. As Bloom, Coburn, and Pearlman report, "characteristics of assertive behavior include expressing your feelings, needs, and ideas and standing up for your legitimate rights in ways that don't violate the rights of others."[38] Being assertive means retaining concern and respect for others and their needs without losing respect for oneself. This means politeness or concern for others from a position of strength not weakness.

An awareness of sexist language is the first step toward reaching this position. Exactly what assertive vs. passive and aggressive speech will sound like remains to be seen. However, once we know the rules of the game we can work to modify them, to defy them, and to use them to our own advantage. We all can only benefit from the eradication of sexism in the English language.

**NOTES**

1  This article does not include information on the relationships between women and language in other societies and what is true of English may not necessarily be true of other languages. Also, most of the data on usage that we describe are for white middle and upper-class speakers. Descriptions of the interaction styles of other groups, such as Mexican-Americans and Blacks, are lacking in the sources available to us.

2  Robin Lakoff, *Language and Woman's Place* (New York: Harper and Row, 1975), p. 29. The extent to which the original meaning of mistress is still in use is open to question. Lakoff, for example, argues that the word is "practically restricted to its sexual sense." On the other hand, one of the present authors maintains that she quite comfortably refers to herself as *mistress* of her pet dog and cat. Also, Dubois and Crouch include in their article criticizing Lakoff's work the following actual quotes in which the word is used in a non-sexual sense:

"It was not that she would make any demonstration; she just did not want to be looked at when she was not quite *mistress* of herself." O. LaFarge, *Laughing Boy* (Boston: Houghton Mifflin, 1927, reprinted 1957.) (Italics added.)

"The walls are full of pictures of famous people, from President Nixon to President Sadat of Egypt, all of them autographed to the *mistress* of the house—former movie star Shirley Temple Black." P. J. Oppenheimer, "Shirley Temple Black Talks About Her Times of Tears, Her Times of Triumph," *Family Weekly,* Nov., 1974, pp. 9–11. (Italics added.)

Betty Lou Dubois and Isabel Crouch, "The Question of Tag Questions in Women's Speech: They Don't Really Use More of Them, Do They?", *Language in Society,* 4 (1975), 289–94.

3   Laurel Richardson Walum, *The Dynamics of Sex and Gender: A Sociological Perspective* (Chicago: Rand McNally College Publishing Co., 1977), p. 18. Walum also notes in her discussion the fact that the same word can have both sexual and non-sexual meanings, depending on whether it is used to refer to a male or to a female. She points out that "a male *tramp* is simply a hobo but a female *tramp* is a slut . . ." (*Ibid.*)

4   A whoremonger, according to Webster's Third New International Dictionary (unabridged version, 1966), is an archaic term meaning "a man consorting with whores or given to lechery. Synonyms: *Whoremaster, Fornicator,*" p. 2612.

5   Muriel R. Schulz, "The Semantic Derogation of Women," in Barrie Thorne and Nancy Henley, eds., *Language and Sex: Difference and Dominance* (Rowley, Mass.: Newbury House Publishers, Inc., 1975), pp. 64–75.

6   *Ibid.,* pp. 66–68.

7   This example appears in Mary Ritchie Key, *Male/Female Language* (Metuchen, N.J.: The Scarecrow Press, 1975), p. 82.

8   What is more likely to happen we think, is that men will be referred to as *guys,* rather than *boys*—a term that seems distinctly less trivializing somehow. Could this be one reason why young women seem so often to refer to each other as *guys* as well?

9   Even more striking in this regard is the fact that a woman is expected to take her husband's name upon marriage, so that she becomes not only *Mrs.* Somebody-or-Other, but *Mrs. John* Somebody-or-Other. Related also is the familiar practice of referring to a married couple as *man and wife,* now rapidly becoming obsolete.

10   Walum, *The Dynamics of Sex and Gender,* p. 19, footnote 2.

11   This example originally appeared in A. P. Nilsen, "Grammatical Gender and its Relationship to the Equal Treatment of Males and Females in Children's Books" (Ph.D. dissertation, College of Education in the Graduate College, University of Iowa, 1973), pp. 86–87. We discovered it in Casey Miller and Kate Swift, *Words and Women* (Garden City, N.Y.: Anchor Press/Doubleday, 1976), p. 29.

12   Alma Graham, "The Making of a Non-Sexist Dictionary," in Thorne and Henley, eds. *Language and Sex,* p. 62.

13   Miller and Swift, *Words and Women,* p. 20.

14   This example appears in Key, *Male/Female Language,* p. 89. Italics added. It is interesting to note that *he* has not always been considered the correct third-person pronoun for referring to a single human being of indeterminate sex. Until about the eighteenth century, the correct choice of pronoun for such a purpose was *they.* It was only when certain eighteenth-century grammarians decided that there was something inherently plural about *they,* and so prescribed a substitute for use in the singular, that our present "generic He" was born.

15 Linda Harrison, "Cro-Magnon Woman—In Eclipse," *The Science Teacher*, April, 1975, pp. 8–11.

16 Note that this same contradictory quality could also conceivably serve as a convenient way of covering up the exclusion of women. One can always claim to be using *Man* in the generic sense, whether one actually is or not. Thus the ambiguity inherent in the meaning and the usage of the word *Man* effectively turns it into yet another weapon in the arsenal of those who have an interest, for whatever reason, in keeping women in the social backwaters and out of the mainstream.

17 The late Frank McGee on the "Today Show," NBC-TV, June 19, 1972. Italics added. In Miller and Swift, *Words and Women*, p. 37.

18 While this article focuses on speech differences that vary according to sex, the way one talks is affected by numerous other things. Some of the other factors are: a person's socio-economic level, including education and occupation; the speaker's age; how well the conversants know each other; the topic under discussion; the location, such as at a church or at home; the method of communication, such as writing versus speaking; the speaker's personality; and finally, the linguistic form being used.

19 Peter Trudgill, "Sex, Covert Prestige and Linguistic Change in the Urban British English of Norwich," *Language in Society*, 1 (1972), pp. 179–95. Reprinted in Thorne and Henley, eds., *Language and Sex*, pp. 88–104.

20 William Labov, *The Social Stratification of English in New York City*, (Washington, D.C.: Center for Applied Linguistics, 1966), p. 455.

21 Barrie Thorne and Nancy Henley, "Difference and Dominance: An Overview of Language, Gender and Society," in Thorne and Henley, eds., *Language and Sex*, pp. 17–18.

22 Erving Goffman, "The Nature of Deference and Demeanor," *American Anthropologist*, 58 (1956), 473–502. Reprinted in Goffman, *Interaction Ritual* (New York: Anchor Books, 1967), pp. 47–95.

23 Trudgill, *Language in Society*, 1 (1972), pp. 91–92.

24 Otto Jespersen, *Language, Its Nature, Development and Origin*, (New York: Macmillan, 1922), Chapter 11, pp. 237–54.

25 Dubois and Crouch, *Language in Society*, 4 (1975).

26 Lakoff, *Language and Woman's Place*, pp. 14–17.

27 For further discussion of this see Ruth Brend, "Male-Female Intonation Patterns in American English," *Proceedings of the Seventh International Congress of Phonetic Sciences*, 1971, (The Hague: Mouton, 1972), pp. 866–69. Reprinted in Thorne and Henley, eds., *Language and Sex*, pp. 84–87.

28 Harvey Sacks, Emmanuel Schegloff and Gail Jefferson, "A Simplest Systematics for the Organization of Turn-taking in Conversation," *Language*, 50:4 (1974), 696–735.

29 Interrupting is different from overlapping another's speech. Overlaps are instances where the listener starts before the speaker concludes, but the new speaker begins at or nearly at a signaled transition point. Interruptions, however, don't occur at these signaled transition points for speaker alternation and therefore are a disruption.

30 Donald Zimmerman and Candace West, "Sex Roles, Interruptions and Silences in Conversation," in Thorne and Henley, eds., *Language and Sex*, pp. 105–29.

31  Candace West and Donald Zimmerman, "Women's Place in Everyday Talk: Reflections on Parent-Child Interaction," *Social Problems*, 24:5 (June 1977), 521–29.

32  Pamela Fishman, "Interactional Shitwork," *Heresies*, 2 (May 1977), 99–101.

33  Lynette Hirschman, "Analysis of Support and Assertive Behavior in Conversations," Paper presented at the Linguistic Society of America, summer meeting, July 1974.

34  Interestingly enough, in mixed sex exchanges, Hirschman found that both sexes use support forms less than when they are in same sex situations. This is an indication that conversations do not flow as easily across sex boundaries.

35  Elizabeth Aries, "Interaction Patterns and Themes of Males, Females, and Mixed Groups," *Small Group Behavior*, 7:1 (1976), 1–18.

36  Graham, in Thorne and Henley, eds., *Language and Sex*, pp. 59–60.

37  Miller and Swift, *Words and Women*, pp. 145–47.

38  Lynn Bloom, Karen Coburn and Joan Pearlman, *The New Assertive Woman*, (New York: Delacorte Press, 1975), p. 9.

# Helen Mayer Hacker

# Women as a Minority Group*

Although sociological literature reveals scattered references to women as a minority group, comparable in certain respects to racial, ethnic, and national minorities, no systematic investigation has been undertaken as to what extent the term "minority group" is applicable to women. . . .

Yet it may well be that regarding women as a minority group may be productive of fresh insights and suggest leads for further research. The purpose of this paper is to apply to women some portion of that body of sociological theory and methodology customarily used for investigating such minority groups as Negroes, Jews, immigrants, etc. It may be anticipated that not only will

*Reprinted from *Social Forces*, 30 (October 1951): 60–69, by permission of the University of North Carolina Press.

principles already established in the field of intergroup relations contribute to our understanding of women, but in the process of modifying traditional concepts and theories to fit the special case of women, new viewpoints for the fruitful reexamination of other minority groups will emerge.

In defining the term "minority group," the presence of discrimination is the identifying factor. As Louis Wirth has pointed out, "minority group" is not a statistical concept, nor need it denote an alien group. Indeed for the present discussion I have adopted his definition: "A minority group is any group of people who because of their physical or cultural characteristics, are singled out from the others in the society in which they live for differential and unequal treatment, and who therefore regard themselves as objects of collective discrimination." It is apparent that this definition includes both objective and subjective characteristics of a minority group: the fact of discrimination and the awareness of discrimination, with attendant reactions to that awareness. A person who on the basis of his group affiliation is denied full participation in those opportunities which the value system of his culture extends to all members of the society satisfies the objective criterion, but there are various circumstances which may prevent him from fulfilling the subjective criterion.

In the first place, a person may be unaware of the extent to which his group membership influences the way others treat him. He may have formally dissolved all ties with the group in question and fondly imagine his identity is different from what others hold it to be. Consequently, he interprets their behavior toward him solely in terms of his individual characteristics. Or, less likely, he may be conscious of his membership in a certain group but not be aware of the general disesteem with which the group is regarded. A final possibility is that he may belong in a category which he does not realize has group significance. An example here might be a speech peculiarity which has come to have unpleasant connotations in the minds of others. Or a lower-class child with no conception of "class as culture" may not understand how his manners act as cues in eliciting the dislike of his middle-class teacher. The foregoing cases all assume that the person believes in equal opportunities for all in the sense that one's group affiliation should not affect his role in the larger society. We turn now to a consideration of situations in which this assumption is not made.

It is frequently the case that a person knows that because of his group affiliation he receives differential treatment, but feels that this treatment is warranted by the distinctive characteristics of his group. A Negro may believe that there are significant differences between whites and Negroes which justify a different role in life for the Negro. A child may accept the fact that physical differences between him and an adult require his going to bed earlier than they do. A Sudra knows that his lot in life has been cast by divine fiat, and he does not expect the perquisites of a Brahmin. A woman does not wish for the rights and duties of men. In all these situations, clearly, the person does not regard himself as an "object of collective discrimination."

For the two types presented above: (1) those who do not know that they are being discriminated against on a group basis; and (2) those who acknowledge the propriety of differential treatment on a group basis, the subjective attributes of a minority-group member are lacking. They feel no minority-group consciousness, harbor no resentment, and, hence, cannot properly be said to belong in a minority group. Although the term "minority group" is inapplicable to both types, the term "minority-group status" may be substituted. This term is used to categorize persons who are denied rights to which they are entitled according to the value system of the observer. An observer, who is a firm adherent of the democratic ideology, will often consider persons to occupy a minority-group status who are well accommodated to their subordinate roles.

No empirical study of the frequency of minority-group feelings among women has yet been made, but common observation would suggest that, consciously at least, few women believe themselves to be members of a minority group in the way in which some Negroes, Jews, Italians, etc., may so conceive themselves. There are, of course, many sex-conscious women, known to a past generation as feminists, who are filled with resentment at the discriminations they fancy are directed against their sex. . . . Yet the number of women who participate in "women's affairs" even in the United States, the classic land of association, is so small that one cannot easily say that the majority of women display minority group consciousness. . . .

Still, women often manifest many of the psychological characteristics which have been imputed to self-conscious minority groups. Kurt Lewin[1] has pointed to group self-hatred as a frequent reaction of the minority-group member to his group affiliation. This feeling is exhibited in the person's tendency to denigrate other members of the group, to accept the dominant group's stereotyped conception of them, and to indulge in "mea culpa" breast-beating. He may seek to exclude himself from the average of his group, or he may point the finger of scorn at himself. Since a person's conception of himself is based on the defining gestures of others, it is unlikely that members of a minority group can wholly escape personality distortion. Constant reiteration of one's inferiority must often lead to its acceptance as a fact.

Certainly women have not been immune to the formulations of the "female character" throughout the ages. From those (to us) deluded creatures who confessed to witchcraft to the modern sophisticates who speak disparagingly of the cattiness and disloyalty of women, women reveal their introjection of prevailing attitudes toward them. Like those minority groups whose self-castigation outdoes dominant-group derision of them, women frequently exceed men in the violence of their vituperations of their sex. They are more severe in moral judgments, especially in sexual matters. A line of self-criticism may be traced from Hannah More, a blue-stocking herself, to Dr. Marynia Farnham, who lays most of the world's ills at women's door. Women express themselves as disliking other women, as preferring to work under men, and as finding exclusively female gatherings repugnant. The *Fortune* polls conducted in 1946 show that women, more than men, hve misgivings concerning women's participation in industry, the professions, and civic life. And more than one-fourth of women wish they had been born in the opposite sex.[2]

Militating against a feeling of group identification on the part of women is a differential factor in their socialization. Members of a minority group are frequently socialized within their own group. Personality development is more largely a resultant of intra- than intergroup interaction. The conception of his role formed by a Negro or a Jew or a second-generation immigrant is greatly dependent upon the definitions offered by members of his own group, or their attitudes and behavior toward him. Ignoring for the moment class differences within the group, the minority-group person does not suffer discrimination from members of his own group. But only rarely does a woman experience this type of group belongingness. Her interactions with members of the opposite sex may be as frequent as her relationships with members of her own sex. Women's conceptions of themselves, therefore, spring as much from their intimate relationships with men as with women. . . .

Even though the sense of group identification is not so conspicuous in women as in racial and ethnic minorities, they, like these others, tend to develop a separate subculture. Women have their own language, comparable to the argot of the underworld and professional groups. It may not extend to a completely separate dialect [such] as has been discovered in some preliterate groups, but there are words and idioms employed chiefly by women. Only the acculturated male can enter into the conversation of the beauty parlor, the exclusive shop, the bridge table, or the kitchen. In contrast to men's interest in physical health, safety, money, and sex, women attach greater importance to attractiveness, personality, home, family, and other people. . . .

We must return now to the original question of the aptness of the designation of minority group for women. . . . Formal discriminations against women are too well-known for any but the most summary description. In general they take the form of being barred from certain activities or, if admitted, being treated unequally. Discriminations against women may be viewed as arising from the generally ascribed status "female" and from the specially ascribed statuses of "wife," "mother," and "sister.". . .

As females, in the economic sphere, women are largely confined to sedentary, monotonous work under the supervision of men, and are treated unequally with regard to pay, promotion, and responsibility. With the exceptions of teaching, nursing, social service, and library work, in which they do not hold a proportionate number of supervisory positions and are often occupationally segregated from men, they make a poor showing in the professions. Although they own 80 percent of the nation's wealth, they do not sit on the boards of directors of great corporations. Educational opportunities are likewise unequal. Professional schools, such as [those of] architecture and medicine, apply quotas. Women's colleges are frequently inferior to men's. In co-educational schools women's participation in campus activities is limited. As citizens, women are often barred from jury service and public office. Even when they are admitted to the apparatus of political parties, they are subordinated to men. Socially, women have less freedom of movement, and are permitted fewer deviations in the proprieties of dress, speech, manners. In social intercourse they are confined to a narrower range of personality expression.

In the specially ascribed status of wife, a woman—in several states—has no exclusive right to her earnings, is discriminated against in employment, must take the domicile of her husband, and in general must meet the social expectation of subordination to her husband's interests. As a mother, she may not have the guardianship of her children, bears the chief stigma in the case of an illegitimate child, is rarely given leave of absence for pregnancy. As a sister, she suffers unequal distribution of domestic duties between herself and her brother, must yield preference to him in obtaining an education, and in such other psychic and material gratifications as cars, trips, and living away from home.

If it is conceded that women have a minority-group status, what may be learned from applying to women various theoretical constructs in the field of intergroup relations?

One instrument of diagnostic value is the measurement of social distance between dominant and minority groups. But we have seen that one important difference between women and other minorities is that women's attitudes and self-conceptions are conditioned more largely by interaction with both minority- and dominant group members. Before measuring social distance, therefore, a continuum might be constructed of the frequency and extent of women's interaction with men, with the poles conceptualized as ideal types. One extreme would represent a complete "ghetto" status, the woman whose contacts with men were of the most secondary kind. At the other extreme shall we put the woman who has prolonged and repeated associations with men, but only in those situations in which sex-awareness plays a prominent role, or the woman who enters into a variety of relationships with men in which her sex identity is to a large extent irrelevant? . . .

Social distance tests as applied to relationships between other dominant and minority groups have for the most part adopted prestige criteria as their basis. The assumption is that the type of situation into which one is willing to enter with average members of another group reflects one's estimate of the status of the group relative to one's own. When the tested group is a sex-group rather than a racial, national, religious, or economic one, several important differences in the use and interpretation of the scale must be noted.

1. Only two groups are involved: men and women. Thus, the test indicates the amount of homogeneity or we-feeling only according to the attribute of sex. If men are a primary group, there are not many

groups to be ranked secondary, tertiary, etc., with respect to them, but only one group, women whose social distance cannot be calculated relative to other groups.

2. Lundberg[3] suggests the possibility of a group of Catholics registering a smaller social distance to Moslems than to Catholics. In such an event the group of Catholics, from any sociological viewpoint, would be classified as Moslems. If women expressed less social distance to men than to women, should they then be classified sociologically as men? Perhaps no more so than the legendary Negro who, when requested to move to the colored section of the train, replied, "Boss, I'se done resigned from the colored race," should be classified as white. It is likely, however, that the group identification of many women in our society is with men. The feminists were charged with wanting to be men, since they associated male physical characteristics with masculine social privileges. A similar statement can be made about men who show greater social distance to other men than to women.

Social distance may be measured from the standpoint of the minority group or the dominant group with different results. In point of fact, tension often arises when one group feels less social distance than the other. A type case here is the persistent suitor who underestimates his desired sweetheart's feeling of social distance toward him.

3. In social distance tests the assumption is made of an orderly progression—although not necessarily by equal intervals—in the scale. That is, it is not likely that a person would express willingness to have members of a given group as his neighbors, while simultaneously voicing the desire to have them excluded from his country. On all scales marriage represents the minimum social distance, and implies willingness for associations on all levels of lesser intimacy. May the customary scale be applied to men and women? If we take the expressed attitude of many men and women not to marry, we may say that they have feelings of social distance toward the opposite sex, and in this situation the usual order of the scale may be preserved.

In our culture, however, men who wish to marry must perforce marry women, and even if they accept this relationship, they may still wish to limit their association with women in other situations. The male physician may not care for the addition of female physicians to his hospital staff. The male poker player may be thrown off his game if women participate. A damper may be put upon the hunting expedition if women come along. The average man may not wish to consult a woman lawyer. And so on. In these cases it seems apparent that the steps in the social-distance scale must be reversed. Men will accept women at the supposed level of greatest intimacy while rejecting them at lower levels.

But before concluding that a different scale must be constructed when the dominant-group attitude ... being tested is that of men toward women, the question may be raised as to whether marriage in fact represents the point of minimum social distance. It may not imply anything but physical intimacy and work accommodation, as was frequently true in nonindividuated societies, such as preliterate groups and the household economy of the Middle Ages, or marriages of convenience in the European upper class. Even in our own democratic society where marriage is supposedly based on romantic love there may be little communication between the partners of marriage. The Lynds[4] report the absence of real companionship between husband and wife in Middletown. Women have been known to say that although they have been married for twenty years, their husband is still a stranger to them. ... Part of the explanation may be found in the subordination of wives to husbands in our culture which is expressed in the separate spheres of activity for men and women. A recent advertisement in a magazine of national circulation depicts a pensive husband seated by his knitting wife with the caption, "Sometimes a man has moods his wife cannot understand." In this case the husband is worried about a pension plan for his employees. The assumption is that the wife, knowing nothing of the business world, cannot take the role of her husband in this matter.

The presence of love does not in itself argue for either equality of status nor fullness of communication. We may love those who are either inferior or superior to us, and we may love persons whom we do not understand. The supreme literary examples of passion without communication are found in Proust's portrayal of Swann's obsession with Odette, the narrator's infatuation with the elusive Albertine, and, of course, Dante's longing for Beatrice.

In the light of these considerations concerning the relationships between men and women, some doubt may be cast on the propriety of placing marriage on the positive extreme of the social distance scale with respect to ethnic and religious minority groups. Since inequalities of status are preserved in marriage, a dominant-group member may be willing to marry a member of a group which, in general, he would not wish admitted to his club. The social-distance scale which uses marriage as a sign of an extreme degree of acceptance is inadequate for appreciating the position of women, and perhaps for other minority groups as well. The relationships among similarity of status, communication as a measure of intimacy, and love must be clarified before social distance tests can be applied usefully to attitudes between men and women.

Is the separation between males and females in our society a caste line? Folsom[5] suggests that it is, and Myrdal[6] in his well-known Appendix 5 considers the parallel between the position of and feelings toward women and Negroes in our society. The relation between women and Negroes is historical, as well as analogical. In the seventeenth century the legal status of Negro servants was borrowed from that of women and children, who were under the *patria potestas,* and until the Civil War there was considerable cooperation between the Abolitionist and women suffrage movements. According to Myrdal, the problems of both groups are resultants of the transition from a pre-industrial, paternalistic scheme of life to individualistic, industrial capitalism. Obvious similarities in the status of women and Negroes are indicated in Chart 1.

While these similarities in the situation of women and Negroes may lead to increased understanding of their social roles, account must also be taken of differences which impose qualifications on the comparison of the two groups. Most importantly, the influence of marriage as a social elevator for women, but not for Negroes, must be considered. Obvious, too, is the greater importance of women to the dominant group, despite the economic, sexual, and prestige gains which Negroes afford the white South. Ambivalence is probably more marked in the attitude of white males toward women than toward Negroes. The "war of the sexes" is only an expression of men's and women's vital need of each other. Again, there is greater polarization in the relationship between men and women. Negroes, although they have borne the brunt of anti-minority-group feeling in this country, do not constitute the only racial or ethnic minority, but there are only two sexes. And, although we have seen that social distance exists between men and women, it is not to be compared with the social segregation of Negroes.

At the present time, of course, Negroes suffer far greater discrimination than women, but since the latter's problems are rooted in a biological reality less susceptible to cultural manipulation, they prove

**CHART 1    Castelike Status of Women and Negroes**

| Negroes | Women |
|---|---|
| **1. High social visibility** ||
| a. Skin color, other "racial" characteristics | a. Secondary sex characteristics |
| b. (Sometimes) distinctive dress-bandana, flashy clothes | b. Distinctive dress, skirts, etc. |
| **2. Ascribed attributes** ||
| a. Inferior intelligence, smaller brain, less convoluted, scarcity of geniuses | a. ditto |
| b. More free in instinctual gratificatons. More emotional, "primitive" and childlike. Imagined sexual prowess envied. | b. Irresponsible, inconsistent, emotionally unstable. Lack strong super-ego. Women as "temptresses." |
| c. Common stereotype, "inferior" | c. "Weaker" |
| **3. Rationalizations of status** ||
| a. Thought all right in his place | a. Woman's place is in the home |
| b. Myth of contented Negro | b. Myth of contented women—"feminine" woman is happy in subordinate role |
| **4. Accommodation attitudes** ||
| a. Supplicatory whining intonation of voice | a. Rising inflection, smiles, laughs, downward glances |
| b. Deferential manner | b. Flattering manner |
| c. Concealment of real feelings | c. "Feminine wiles" |
| d. Outwit "white folks" | d. Outwit "men-folk" |
| e. Careful study of points at which dominant group is susceptible to influence | e. ditto |
| f. Fake appeals for directives; show of ignorance | f. Appearance of helplessness |
| **5. Discriminations** ||
| a. Limitations on education—should fit "place" in society | a. ditto |

**CHART 1    Continued**

| Negroes | Women |
| --- | --- |
| b. Confined to traditional jobs—barred from supervisory positions. Their competition feared. No family precedents for new aspirations. | b. ditto |
| c. Deprived of political importance | c. ditto |
| d. Social and professional segregation | d. ditto |
| e. More vulnerable to criticism | e. e.g., conduct in bars [women drivers] |

6. Similar problems

a. Roles not clearly defined, but in flux as result of social change. Conflict between achieved status and ascribed status.

more lasting. Women's privileges exceed those of Negroes. Protective attitude of white males toward women than toward Negroes. The "war but most boys are still taught to take care of girls, and many evidences of male chivalry remain. The factor of class introduces variations here. The middle-class Negro endures frustrations largely without the rewards of his white class-peer, but the lower-class Negro is still absolved from many responsibilities. The reverse holds true for women. Notwithstanding these and other differences between the position of women and Negroes, the similarities are sufficient to render research on either group applicable in some fashion to the other.

Exemplary of the possible usefulness of applying the caste principle to women is viewing some of the confusion surrounding women's roles as reflecting a conflict between class and caste status. Such a conflict is present in the thinking and feeling of both dominant and minority groups toward upper-class Negroes and educated women. Should a woman judge be treated with the respect due a judge or the gallantry accorded a woman? The extent to which the rights and duties of one role permeate other roles so as to cause a role conflict has been treated elsewhere by the writer. Lower-class Negroes who have acquired dominant-group attitudes toward the Negro resent upper-class Negro pretensions to superiority. Similarly, domestic women may feel the career woman is neglecting the duties of her proper station.

Parallels in adjustment of women and Negroes to the class-caste conflict may also be noted. Point 4 "Accommodation Attitudes" of the foregoing chart indicates the kinds of behavior displayed by members of both groups who accept their caste status. Many "sophisticated" women are retreating from emancipation with the support of psycho-analytic derivations.[7] David Riesman has recently provided an interesting discussion of changes "in the denigration by American women of their own sex" in which he explains their new submissiveness as in part a reaction to the weakness of men in the contemporary world.[8] "Parallelism" and "Negroidism" which accept a racially restricted economy reflect allied tendencies in the Negro group.

Role segmentation as a mode of adjustment is illustrated by Negroes who indulge in occasional passing and women who vary their behavior according to their definition of the situation. An example of the latter is the case of the woman lawyer who, after losing a case before a judge who was also her husband, said she would appeal the case, and added, "The judge can lay down the law at home, but I'll argue with him in court."

A third type of reaction is to fight for recognition of class status. Negro race leaders seek greater prerogatives for Negroes. Feminist women, acting either through organizations or as individuals, push for public disavowal of any differential treatment of men and women.

The "race relations cycle," as defined by Robert E. Park,[9] describes the social processes of reduction in tension and increase of communication in the relations between two or more groups who are living in a common territory under a single political or economic system. The sequence of competition, conflict, accommodation, and assimilation may also occur when social change introduces dissociative forces into an assimilated group or causes accommodated groups to seek new definitions of the situation. The ethnic or nationality characteristics of the groups involved are not essential to the cycle. In a complex industrialized society, groups are constantly forming and reforming on the basis of new interests and new identities. Women, of course, have always possessed a sex-identification though perhaps not a group awareness. Today they represent a previously accommodated group which is endeavoring to modify the relationships between the sexes in the home, in work, and in the community.

The sex-relations cycle bears important similarities to the race-relation cycle. In the wake of the Industrial Revolution, as women acquired industrial, business, and professional skills, they increasingly sought employment in competition with men. Men were quick to perceive them as a rival group and made use of economic, legal, and ideological weapons to eliminate or reduce their competition. They excluded women from the trade unions, made contracts with employers to prevent their hiring women, passed laws restricting the employment of married women, caricatured the working woman, and carried on ceaseless propaganda to return women to the home or keep them there. Since the days of the suffragettes there has been no overt conflict between men and women on a group basis. Rather than conflict, the dissociative process between the sexes is that of contravention, a type of opposition intermediate between competition and conflict. . . . It includes rebuffing, repulsing, working against, hindering, protesting, obstructing, restraining, and upsetting another's plans.

The present contravention of the sexes, arising from women's competition with men, is manifested in the discriminations against women, as well as in the doubts and uncertainties expressed concerning women's character, abilities, motives. The processes of competition and contravention are continually giving way to accommodation in the relationships between men and women. Like other minority groups, women have sought a protected position, a niche in the economy which they could occupy, and, like other minority groups, they have found these positions in new occupations in which dominant-group members had not yet established themselves and in old occupations which they no longer wanted. When women entered fields which represented an extension of services in the home (except medicine!), they encountered least opposition. Evidence is accumulating, however, that women are becoming dissatisfied with the employment conditions of the great women-employing occupations and present accommodations are threatened.

What would assimilation of men and women mean? Park and Burgess in their classic text define assimilation as "a process of interpenetration and fusion in which persons and groups acquire the memories, sentiments, and attitudes of other persons or groups, and. by sharing their experiences and history, are incorporated with them in a cultural life." If accommodation is characterized by secondary contacts, assimilation holds the promise of primary contacts. If men and women were truly assimilated, we would find no cleavages of interest along sex lines. The special provinces of men and women would be abolished. Women's pages would disappear from the newspaper and women's organizations would pass into limbo. The sports page and racing news would be read indifferently by men and women. Interest in cookery and interior decoration would follow individual rather than sex lines. Women's talk would be no different from men's talk, and frank and full communication would obtain between the sexes.

Group relationships are reflected in personal adjustments. Arising out of the present contravention of the sexes is the marginal woman, torn between rejection and acceptance of traditional roles and attributes. Uncertain of the ground on which she stands, subjected to conflicting cultural expectations, the marginal woman suffers the psychological ravages of instability, conflict, self-hate, anxiety, and resentment.

In applying the concept of marginality to women, the term "role" must be substituted for that of "group." Many of the traditional devices for creating role differentiation among boys and girls, such as dress, manners, activities, have been de-emphasized in modern urban middle-class homes. The small girl who wears a playsuit, plays games with boys and girls together, attends a co-educational school, may have little awareness of sexual differentiation until the approach of adolescence. Parental expectations in the matters of scholarship, conduct toward others, duties in the home may have differed little for herself and her brother. But in high school or perhaps not until college, she finds herself called upon to play a new role. Benedict[10] has called attention to discontinuities in the life cycle, and the fact that these continuities in cultural conditioning take a greater toll of girls than of boys is revealed in test scores showing neuroticism and introversion. In adolescence girls find frank, spontaneous behavior toward the neighboring sex no longer rewarding. High grades are more likely to elicit anxiety than praise from parents, especially mothers, who seem more pleased if male callers are frequent. There are subtle indications that to remain home with a good book on a Saturday night is a fate worse than death. But even if the die is successfully cast for popularity, not all problems are solved. Girls are encouraged to heighten their sexual attractiveness, but to abjure sexual expression.

Assuming new roles in adolescence does not mean the complete relinquishing of old ones. Scholarship, while not so vital as for the boy, is still important, but must be maintained discreetly and without obvious effort. Komarovsky[11] has supplied statements by Barnard College girls of the conflicting expectations of their elders. Even more than to the boy is the "allround" ideal held up to girls, and it is not always possible to integrate the roles of good date, good daughter, good sorority sister, good student, good friend, and good citizen. The superior achievements of college men over college women bear witness to the crippling division of energies among women. Part of the explanation may lie in women having interiorized cultural notions of feminine inferiority in certain fields, and even the most self-confident or most defensive woman may be filled with doubt as to whether she can do productive work.

It may be expected that as differences in privileges between men and women decrease, the frequency of marginal women will increase. Widening opportunities for women will call forth a growing number of women capable of performing roles formerly reserved for men, but whose acceptance in these new roles may well remain uncertain and problematic. This hypothesis is in accord with Arnold Green's[12] recent critical re-examination of the marginal-man concept in which he points out that it is those Negroes and second-generation immigrants whose values and behavior most approximate those of the dominant majority who experience the most severe personal crises. He believes that the classical marginal-man symptoms appear only when a person striving to leave the racial or ethnic group into which he was born is deeply identified with the family of orientation and is met with grudging, uncertain, and unpredictable aceptance, rather than with absolute rejection by the group he is attempting to join. [He must also be] committed to success-careerism. Analogically, one would expect to find that women who display marginal symptoms are psychologically bound to the family of orientation in which they experience the imperatives of both the traditional and new feminine roles, and are seeking to expand the occupational (or other) areas open to women rather than ... content themselves with established fields. Concretely, one might suppose women engineers to have greater personality problems than women librarians.

Other avenues of investigation suggested by the minority-group approach can only be mentioned. What social types arise as personal adjustments to sex status? What can be done in the way of experimental modification of the attitudes of men and women toward each other and themselves? What hypotheses of inter-group relations may be tested in regard to men and women? For example, is it true that as women approach the cultural standards of men, they are perceived as a threat and tensions increase? Of what significance are regional and community variations in the treatment of and degree of participation permitted women, mindful here that women share responsibility with men for the perpetuation of attitudes toward women? This paper is exploratory in suggesting the enhanced possibilities of fruitful analysis if women are included in the minority-group corpus, particularly with reference to such concepts and techniques as group belongingness, socialization of the minority-group child, cultural differences, social-distance tests, conflict between class and caste status, race-relations cycle, and marginality. I believe that the concept of the marginal woman should be especially productive [as a subject for scholarly investigation].

## NOTES

1  Kurt Lewin, "Self-Hatred Among Jews," *Contemporary Jewish Record*, 4 (1941): 219–32.

2  *Fortune*, Sept. 1946. p. 5.

3  George A. Lundberg, *Foundations of Sociology* (New York: McKay, 1939), p. 319.

4  Robert S. and Helen Merrell Lynd, *Middletown* (Cambridge, Mass.: Harvard University Press, 1929), p. 120; and *Middletown in Transition* (Cambridge, Mass.: Harvard University Press, 1937), p. 176.

5  Joseph Kirk Folsom, *The Family and Democratic Society* (London: Routledge, 1948), pp. 623–24.

6  Gunnar Myrdal, *An American Dilemma* (New York: Harper, 1944), pp. 1073–78.

7  As furnished by such books as Helene Deutsch, *The Psychology of Women* (New York: Grune & Stratton, 1944–45); and Ferdinand Lundberg and Marynia F. Farnham, *Modern Woman: The Lost Sex* (New York: Harper, 1947).

8  David Riesman, "The Saving Remnant: An Examination of Character Structure," in John W. Chase, ed., *Years of the Modern: An American Appraisal* (New York: Longmans, Green, 1949), pp. 139–40.

9  Robert E. Park, "Our Racial Frontier on the Pacific," *The Survey Graphic*, 56 (May 1, 1926): 192–96.

10  Ruth Benedict, "Continuities and Discontinuities in Cultural Conditioning," *Psychiatry*, 1 (1938): 161–67.

11  Mirra Komarovsky, "Cultural Contradictions and Sex Roles," *The American Journal of Sociology*, 52 (Nov. 1946): 184–89.

12  Arnold Green, "A Re-Examination of the Marginal Man Concept," *Social Forces*, 26 (Dec. 1947): 167–71.

# PART 6  FEMINISM

NAN GOLUB

# Viola Klein

# The Historical Background

Our historical memory is so short, and our imagination so limited, that we fail to be sufficiently
aware of the striking contrast between our present
attitudes and those of, say, a hundred years ago.
[Since we are unaware that women who were not
slaves could be sold in the open market, it is with]
amazement [that] we read the following note in
*The Times* of July 22, 1797: "The increasing value
of the fair sex is regarded by many writers as
the certain index of a growing civilization.[1]
Smithfield[2] may for this reason claim to be a
contributor to particular progress in finesse, for in
the market the price was again raised from one
half a guinea to three-and-one half." This trend

Reprinted with permission of the publisher from Viola Klein,
*Feminine Character: History of an Ideology* (Urbana: University of
Illinois Press, 1973), chapter 2.

in the "progress of finesse" (to adopt for a moment the standard of *The Times* of 1797) does not seem to have persisted, as the following story indicates:[3]

> In 1814 Henry Cook of Effingham, Surrey, was forced under the bastardy laws to marry a woman of Slinfold, Sussex, and six months after the marriage she and her child were removed to the Effingham workhouse. The governor there, having contracted to maintain all the poor for the specific sum of £210, complained of the new arrivals, whereupon *the parish officer to Effingham prevailed on Cook to sell his wife.* The master of the workhouse, Chippen, was directed to take the woman to Croydon market and there, on June 17, 1815, *she was sold to John Earl for the sum of one shilling* which had been given to Earl for the purchase. To bind the bargain the following receipt was made out:
>
> 5/—stamp
>
> June 17, 1815
>
> Received of John Earl the sum of one shilling, in full, for my lawful wife, by me,
>
> HENRY COOK.
>
> Daniel Cook  
> John Chippen } Witnesses.
>
> In their satisfaction of having got rid of the chargeability of the woman the parish officers of Effingham paid the expenses of the journey to Croydon, including refreshments there, and also allowed a leg of mutton for the wedding dinner which took place in Earl's parish of Dorking . . ."

Miss Pinchbeck rightly remarks: "That the expenses incurred by such transaction could be entered up in the parish accounts and regularly passed by a parish vestry, is sufficient evidence, not only of the futility of parish administration under the old Poor Laws, but also of the straits to which women were reduced by the weakness of their economic and social position."

These instances do not seem to be isolated cases. More examples are recorded in the "Sale of Wives in England in 1823," by H. W. V. Temperley (in *History Teachers' Miscellany* for May 1925), and as late as 1856 such a benevolent critic of this country as R. W. Emerson has to report, in his *English Traits:* "The right of the husband to sell his wife has been retained down to our times." All this in England, a country which was proverbially called a "Wives' Paradise," and of which Defoe had said in 1725 that, if there were only a bridge between the continent and England, all Continental women would like to come across the Straits.

Judging this situation from our distant point of observation we must not, however, adopt an attitude of righteous indignation and fail to see the facts in their correct perspective. We must not overlook the fact that we are dealing with a pre-individualistic period: and although women's lot no doubt was, in every respect, harder than men's, woman was no more than one stage behind man in the social evolution. We should misrepresent the situation if we conceived of the "Subjection of Women" as the submission of the weaker sex to the superior physical and economic power of free and independent males. It would seem more exact to say that women remained serfs after men had already outgrown the state of serfdom. If we adopt Muller-Lyer's[4] classification of the historic development into three main phases—the Clan Epoch, the Family Epoch, and the Individual Epoch—according to the social unit which ideologically forms the basic element of the social organization, and which is felt to be the ultimate "end in itself" at a given period, we should say that the capitalist period marks the transition from the family phase to the individual phase generally, but that this transition was delayed in the case of women. Keeping in mind the power of persistence of all those attitudes, customs, and traditions which are linked with the family and handed down by the very personal, very emotional contact within the primary groups, we cannot be surprised at the retarded social development in the case of women.

Another error ... is the idea that women were, of old, excluded from the economic life of society, and are only now reluctantly and gradually being admitted into the masculine sphere of work. This is a misrepresentation of facts. Before the agricultural and industrial revolution there was hardly any job which was not also performed by women. No work was too hard, no labour too strenuous, to exclude them. In fields and mines, manufactories and shops, on markets and roads as well as in workshops and in their homes, women were busy, assisting their men or replacing them in their absence or after their death, or contributing by their own labour to the family income. Before technical inventions revolutionized the methods of production the family was, first of all, an economic unit in which all members, men, women, and children, played their part. The advice given in *A Present for a Servant Maid* in 1743: "You cannot expect to marry in such a manner as neither of you shall have occasion to work, and none but a fool will take a wife whose bread must be earned solely by his labour and who will contribute nothing towards it herself,"[5] expresses a general attitude. Society as a whole was not rich enough, and the methods of work not sufficiently productive individually to admit of dispensing with anyone on the score of age or sex. Marriage, at that time, was not looked on, as it was later, as a liability for the man and as a sort of favour conferred upon woman, involving for her a life insurance for a minimum premium, but was regarded as a necessity for all, both for their personal fulfillment and their economic benefit. Only when growing industrialization transferred more and more productive activities from the home to the factory, when machines relieved woman of a great part of her household duties, and schools took over the education of her children, woman's economic value as a contributor to the family income declined, particularly in the middle classes. Where before women and children had assisted in providing for the needs of the family, this responsibility now devolved upon one man. Women and children became an economic liability rather than an asset, and marriage was increasingly felt to be a burden for the man. The emotional satisfaction which it may have offered to both, man and woman, was not enough to make good the loss of self-respect incurred by women by the knowledge of their economic uselessness. The endeavour to reinstate women in the economic process, on the one hand, and to restrict the size of families, on the other, has continued from then on up to the present day.

At all times, however, the common characteristic of women's work, as contrasted with men's was, first of all, that it was subsidiary, i.e. that it involved assisting the men of the family—fathers, husbands, brothers—rather than independent; secondly, and closely connected with this fact, that it was paid at a lower rate, if it received any payment at all and was not included in the family wage; and, thirdly, that it was mostly unskilled. Although they were accepted as members by some guilds and apprenticed in their crafts, women generally played the part of odd hands, doing useful work of many kinds, but acquiring their skill in a casual way rather than by systematic training. Here we find one of the reasons for the emphasis on education which was so prominent in the feminist movement ever since Mary Wollstonecraft first raised her voice in support of the emancipation of women. It seems significant that prior to her famous *Vindication of the Rights of Women* (1792) she should have published her *Thoughts on the Education of Daughters* (1786). The lack of sufficient training was felt to be one of the major disabilities in women's struggle for independence.

For her personal happiness, her social status, and her economic prosperity, marriage was for woman an indispensable condition. But it was left to a later period, when all the economic and social advantages of marriage seemed to have weighed in her favor alone, that she had to develop the "clinging vine" type as a feminine ideal in order to "appease" men. Only by flattering his vanity could she make up for the loss of the practical contribution she had to offer in the matrimonial relation.

> A good woman has no desire to rule [says Mrs. Graves] where she feels it to be her duty, as it is her highest pleasure "to love, honour and obey"; and she submits with cheerful acquiescence to that order in the conjugal relation which God and nature have established. Woman feels she is not made for command, and finds her truest happiness in submitting to those who wield a rightful sceptre in justice, mercy and love.[6]

"Nothing is so likely to conciliate the affection of the other sex," advises Mrs. Sandford, "as the feeling that women look to them for guidance and support."[7] In other words, nothing befits the slave so well as servility.

To win a husband—woman's only aim and preoccupation—must, in fact, have been a formidable job at that time, if we keep in mind what enormous obstacles Victorian morality put in the way of the only end they thought worth achieving. "Acquaintances with the other sex should be formed with excessive caution"[8] was the general opinion held at the time, and everything was done to prevent free association of the sexes. "It would be improper, nay, indecorous, to correspond with the gentleman unknown to your father," an anxious questioner is warned. Young ladies were, however, protected not only from contact with "gentlemen unknown to their father," but from their brothers' friends and all other men who were not selected as prospective husbands by their parents.

> J. should not walk with a gentleman much her superior in life, unless she is well assured that he seeks her society with a view to marriage, and she has her parents' approbation of her conduct. All

young girls should study so to conduct themselves that not even the whisper of envy or scandal should be heard in connection with their names.

Moreover, apart from seclusion, her job of finding a husband was rendered more difficult by the "maidenly reserve" enjoined on her which forbade her to seek a man's attention or to show him signs of sympathy.

All the poets and prose-writers who have written upon love are agreed upon one point [is one advice given in the correspondence column of the *London Journal*], and that is that delicate reserve, a rosy diffidence, and sweetly chastened deportment are precisely the qualities in a woman that mostly win upon the attention of men, whether young or old. The moment she begins to seek attention, she sinks in the esteem of any man with an opinion worth having.

A few more quotations from the same source will make it clear with what immense difficulties, imposed by etiquette, the Victorian girl had to struggle in her main pursuit of captivating a husband.

We cannot lend any countenance to such glaring impropriety as trying to "catch the gentleman's attention!" It is his duty to try to catch yours; so preserve your dignity and the decorum due to your sex, position and usages of society.

Violet must wait. Is she not aware of the motto *Il faut me chercher* (I must be sought after)? The gentleman will propose when he finds Violet is really a timid, bashful girl.

Mary F. is deeply in love with a young gentleman and wishes to know the best way to make him propose; she thinks he is fond of her, but is rather bashful. The best way is to wait. He will propose quite time enough. If Fanny were to give him a hint, he might run away. Some men are very fastidious on the subject of feminine propriety.

Lavina wants to be married—but cannot obtain even a sweetheart. She is afraid her commanding appearance intimidates the young gentlemen of her acquaintance. Nothing of the kind. It is her anxiety, her feverish stepping out of her maidenly reserve, which has shocked their preconceived notions of feminine propriety—and so frightened them into dumb significance. Lavina must be more retiring, think less of herself, and learn to spell better.

The number of quotations, all in the same vein, could be increased indefinitely. They go to show that almost insuperable obstacles were laid on the Victorian girl's only road to happiness, and it seems as if the peculiar feminine affliction called "decline," which consisted in "a form of suicide by acute auto-suggestion,"[9] was by no means only a matter of fashion and a "desire for ethereality." "It might be said of a large number of Victorian ladies that there was, literally, 'no health in them.' The ideal of a fair young maiden wasting away for no apparent reason or from love unrequited was universally upheld in polite literature," says C. J. Furness in his interesting book. But, considering the inner conflicts and the shattering frustration which must have resulted from the circumstances just described, it is questionable whether the melancholy and "decline" of so many Victorian girls were entirely due to fashion and literary model (the two classic examples quoted by Furness are Dicken's "little Nell" and "little Eva" in *Uncle Tom's Cabin*). It is probable that they were at least partly the outcome of a situation which made marriage for woman the only career and purpose in life, while at the same time depriving her both of the sense of social usefulness and of the means of successfully pursuing her interests or of expressing her emotions. Frailness and disease were, moreover, the only means by which a woman could "catch" attention without offending contemporary morality.

> The number of characters in Victorian fiction—sometimes meant to be touching, sometimes not (but always tiresome viewed from the standpoint of today)—who could not put a foot on the ground for weakness and yet had no actual disease is amazing. To most Victorian women, this type of invalidism appeared not merely interesting but attractive: it was almost the only way in which they could attract attention to themselves, while remaining models of propriety, in a world indifferent to their potential intellectual or athletic endowments; and the fancies of young girls who would nowadays see themselves pleading at the bar or playing championship tennis at Wimbledon, dwelt then on pictures of themselves as pathetically helpless creatures in the grip of lingering (but not painful) illness and the objects of the constant concern of their doting families.[10]

A radical change in the life of Western society had been brought about in the second half of the eighteenth and in the beginning of the nineteenth century by new technical inventions which caused an entire reorganization of the productive process. The economic and social effects of the Industrial Revolution are familiar enough to everyone for a brief summary to suffice. Not at once but gradually

> the industrial revolution cast out of our rural and urban life the yeoman cultivator and the copyholder, the domestic manufacturer and the independent handicraftsman, all of whom owned the instruments by which they earned their livelihood; and gradually substituted for them a relatively small body of capitalist entrepreneurs employing at wages an always multiplying mass of propertyless men, women and children, struggling like rats in a bag, for the right to live. This bold venture in economic reconstruction had now been proved to have been, so it seemed to me, at one and the same time, a stupendous success and a tragic failure. The accepted purpose of the pioneers of the new power-driven machine industry was the making of pecuniary profit; a purpose which had been fulfilled, as Dr. Johnson observed about his friend Thrale's brewery, "beyond the dreams of avarice." Commodities of all sorts and kinds rolled out from the new factories at an always accelerating speed with an always falling cost of production, thereby promoting what Adam Smith had idealized as "The Wealth of Nations." . . . On the other hand, that same revolution had deprived the manual workers—that is, four-fifths of the people of England—of their opportunity for spontaneity and freedom of initiative in production. It had transformed such of them as had been independent producers into hirelings and servants of another social class; and, as the East End of London in my time only too vividly demonstrated, it had thrust hundreds of thousands of families into the physical horrors and moral debasement of chronic destitution in crowded tenements in the midst of mean streets.[11]

The decline of domestic industries deeply affected the life of women. While the increasing specialization of labor created a multitude of new jobs in factories and homes with very low wages for the women of the new proletariat, it narrowed the lives of the middle-class women and robbed them of their economic usefulness. Not only industrial activities, but more and more of the specifically feminine types of work formerly connected with household duties, were carried out on an increasing scale by the factories, e.g. bread-baking, beer-brewing, soap-making, tailoring, etc. Moreover, the enormous prosperity created by the new industrial organization produced a growing veneration of wealth (now no longer expressed in terms of landed property but of the more flexible commodities of money, shares, factories, and interest-bearing securities). It produced, in the new upper and middle classes, an ambition to compete with each other in the outward signs of prosperity; in consumption, in finery, in the idleness of women. A man's prestige required that his wife and daughters did not do any profitable work. The education of girls was aimed at producing accomplished ladies, not educated women. Frances Power Cobbe recalls in her memoirs:[12]

> Nobody dreamed that any of us could, in later life, be more or less than an ornament to society. That a pupil in that school should become an artist or authoress would have been regarded as a deplorable dereliction. Not that which was good and useful to the community, or even that which would be delightful to ourselves, but that which would make us admired in society was the *raison d'etre* of such a requirement. The education of women was probably at its lowest ebb about half a century ago. It was at that period more pretentious than it had even been before, and infinitely more costly, and it was likewise more shallow and senseless than can easily be believed.

If by ill chance the daughter of a middle-class family had to earn her living, there were only two possible careers open to her: that of the much-despised governess, or that of needlewoman. Both involved a loss of caste, and, besides, were not sufficiently remunerative to make her self-supporting.

Under these circumstances it was not surprising that, among the women of the middle classes, more and more voices were clamoring for equal opportunities and higher education.

It is worth recalling that these were aspirations of the upper and middle classes. They were not identical with the interests of the working women. Whereas the women of the upper and middle classes claimed political freedom, the right to work, and improved educational facilities, working women wanted protection; while middle-class women were fighting for equality, working-class women demanded differential treatment. This claim for differential treatment of women in industry has been recognized by everyone except the doctrinaire feminists and the rigid free-trade economists, and, in fact, the first historic examples of State interference in private enterprise are those laws protecting women and children: the Factory Acts applying to the cotton industry, from 1802 onwards; the Mines Act in 1842 which made illegal the employment underground of women and children under the age of seven; and the Ten Hours Act (1847), which limited the working hours of women and children in industry. The flogging of women had been prohibited in the eighteen-twenties.

The appalling conditions of the industrial proletariat on one side, the increase of wealth on the other, gave rise to a growing concern about social problems. The poverty of the masses gradually penetrated public consciousness and created among the ruling classes of Victorian England what Beatrice Webb characterizes as a collective "sense of sin." No longer was poverty accepted as a necessary evil with devout resignation. It was realized more and more that the misery of the poor was not unavoidable and, therefore, that it should be remedied. Charles Booth's extensive investigation into the *Life and Labour of the People* and Karl Marx's *Kapital* are two outstanding examples of this development.

The decline of Christianity, brought about by the unprecedented progress of physical science during the nineteenth century, no longer admitted of the passive acquiescence in the state of affairs as being ordained by God. No longer was one satisfied that human suffering would be rewarded by heavenly bliss beyond the grave, but one asked for remedy here and now. The poverty of the poor—and, to some extent, also the "Subjection of Women"—were no longer considered as irremediable natural states, but as the result of social institutions for which Man and not God was responsible. The following quotation from John Stuart Mill's *Utilitarianism*[13] gives a very good illustration of this new attitude towards human misery and the prevailing optimism with regard to the power of science and education:

> No one whose opinion deserves a moment's consideration can doubt that most of the great positive evils of the world are in themselves removable, and will, if human affairs continue to improve, be in the end reduced within narrow limits. Poverty in any sense implying suffering, may be completely extinguished by the wisdom of society, combined with the good sense and providence of individuals. Even that most intractable of enemies, disease, may be infinitely reduced in dimensions by good physical and moral education and proper control of noxious influences; while the progress of science holds out a promise for the future of still more direct conquests over this detestable foe.

The characteristic state of mind of that period cannot be better summed up than in Beatrice Webb's words:

> It seems to me that two outstanding tenets, some would say, two idols of the mind, were united in this mid-Victorian trend of thought and feeling. There was the current belief in the scientific method, in that intellectual synthesis of observation and experiment, hypothesis and verification, by means of which alone all mundane problems were to be solved. And added to this belief in science was the consciousness of a new motive; the transference of the emotions of self-sacrificing service from God to man.[14]

Philanthropic activities expanded on an increasing scale, and, in keeping with the scientific spirit of the time, systematic investigations were made into the conditions of the poor, investigations which mark the beginning of social science. Underlying, and partly motivating, these activities were the prevailing optimism of the period, created by the success of expanding capitalism, and the almost naive belief in the power and possibilities of science.

> It was a forward looking age, simple and serious, believing in the worthwhileness of things. The reigning theory still regarded the removal of restrictions as the one thing needful; it trusted human character and intellect to dominate their environment and achieve continued progress. It was an age content with its ideals, if not with its achievements, confident that it was moving on, under the guidance of Providence, to the mastery of the material world and the creation of certain nobler races, now very dimly imagined.[15]

There is a peculiar affinity between the fate of women and the origin of social science, and it is no mere coincidence that the emancipation of women should have started at the same time as the birth of sociology. Both are the result of a break in the established social order and of radical changes in the structure of society; and, in fact, the general interest in social problems to which these changes gave rise did much to assist the cause of women. Both, too, were made possible by the relaxation of the hold which the Christian Churches had for centuries exercised over people's minds. But the relation of woman's emancipation to social science does not only spring from a common origin; it is more direct: the humanitarian interests which formed the starting-point of social research, and practical social work itself, actually provided the back door through which women slipped into public life.

Owing, presumably, to the emotional character of philanthropic work and to the absence of pecuniary profit attaching to it, it did not seem "improper" for women of standing to engage in charitable activities, and soon we find ladies of rank and consequence running charity organizations, working for prison reform, collecting rent in the slums of the East End of London, embarking on propaganda for the abolition of slavery, against cruelty to children, against alcoholism and prostitution, and for the emancipation of women. The social history of the nineteenth century is full of women pioneers in all fields of social reform. [The American] *Frances Wright*, a disciple of Robert Owen, who worked for the practical solution of the slavery problem; *Harriet Martineau*, the political economist, translator of Auguste Comte, who became one of the most distinguished publicists and political leader-writers of her day and who worked for the Reform Bill; *Octavia Hill*, one of the founders and leading spirits of the Charity Organization Society, who became famous by her work for the improvement of working-class houses; *Elizabeth Fry*, the Quaker, who worked for prison reform, founded committees of visiting ladies to care for the prisoners, and who made missionary journeys for her cause all over Europe; *Florence Nightingale*, who during the Crimean War reorganized the military health services after their complete breakdown under the military authorities and who created a new career for women as hospital nurses and probationers; *Louisa Twining*, one of the most active pioneers in Poor Law Reform and in improving the lot of the inmates of workhouses; *Frances Power Cobbe* and *Mary Carpenter*, who tried in Ragged Schools and Reformatories to promote the welfare of neglected children; *Beatrice* and *Katherine Potter*, who were rent collectors in the east End of London and social investigators into the living and working conditions of the poor (Beatrice, later married to Sidney Webb, becoming one of the outstanding social investigators of our time); the Baroness *Angela Burdett-Coutts*, who with money and influence, actively supported most of the charitable organizations; *Josephine Butler*, reputed for her agitation for the repeal of the Contagious Diseases Acts, but equally active in promoting better education for women—these are only a few selected names, and do not include those who worked more directly as the propagandists of the women's cause: for their parliamentary suffrage, their university education and occupational equality, and against discrimination in moral questions.

All this work helped, first, to demonstrate women's ability to organize, to investigate, to do administrative and all kinds of intellectual work; and, second, to create a new feminine type, distinct from the prevailing Victorian ideal of the submissive and "respectable" wife whose sphere of activities and interests was circumscribed by the triad Church, Child, Kitchen.

Speaking of Miss Cons, another social worker in the East End slums, Beatrice Webb notes in her diary (1885): "To her people she spoke with that peculiar *combination of sympathy and authority which characterized the modern type of governing women*," and she prophetically adds: "These governing and guiding women may become important factors if they increase as they have done lately." As distinctive characteristics of this new type of women she stresses their "eyes clear of self-consciousness" and their "dignity of habitual authority."

Not a few of these women were aware of the fact that, while they were fighting poverty, slavery, and disease, they were, at the same time, fighting in the cause of women. And many of them had consciously accepted this as a secondary aim. They felt that, by creating new openings for women and by furnishing evidence of their ability to work, they contributed to the future improvement of women's position, and they preferred their method of missionary work to the political and journalistic activities of their feminist sisters. As Harriet Martineau put it in a refutation of feminist polemics: "The best advocates are yet to come—in the persons of women who are obtaining access to real social business—the female physicians and other professors in America, the women of business and the female artists in France; and the hospital administrators, the nurses, the educators and substantially successful authoresses of our own country."[16] This prognosis seems to be essentially correct.

The fact that women entered "social business" by way of public relief work, as journalists, and as "substantially successful authoresses of novels," illustrates an interesting sociological phenomenon: the fact, namely, that new crafts, new industries, or new arts afford the opportunities for hitherto excluded social groups to take part in the life of the community and to rise in the social scale. It is not by admittance to the traditionally established professions that newcomers are accepted. The old taboos excluding specific groups from certain spheres of work live on in the form of prejudices and are an effective barrier to their admission. It is the development of new branches of trade, of art, or industry, which enables outsiders to force their way, or to slip, into the established system. Once they are settled there they may have a chance of making an entry into the formerly reserved occupations if they have succeeded by their skill, their acknowledged character, or the power that they have meanwhile accumulated, in conquering old prejudices. The same process may be observed in the case of women, of Jews, of foreign immigrants. In the case of women it was the spheres of social investigation, of charity organization, of the expanding educational system, and of social health services which were the places of least resistance through which the bastion of masculine business was penetrated. The expansion of industry further increased the scope of possible work and created new types of occupation. In the same way, for instance, shorthand typing has today replaced the needlework of times past as a characteristic feminine occupation.

In the arts it was the novel, developing during the nineteenth century as a new literary form, which attracted women and in which some of them won fame as writers of the first rank. One has only to mention the names of Jane Austen, the three Bronte sisters, George Eliot, and Olive Schreiner, to illustrate this point. Among the lower ranks of fiction the number of successful women authors was legion.

Women thus began, by their achievements, to make themselves conspicuous. The fact could no longer be overlooked that there were a number of women—a small minority still, but an impressive *elite* which could be increased—who did not conform to the traditional definition of the type. There was in consequence a feeling among some contemporaries that the definition needed readjustment. In this way women became a problem for philosophers, psychologists and sociologists.

Women themselves became restless. Some of them felt frustrated by the lack of useful work and did not think, with Dr. Gregory, that passing their time with "needlework, knitting and such like" was a sufficiently agreeable way of "filling up their many solitary hours."[17] Even more of them felt humiliated by the fact that their sex was their only means of getting a livelihood and thought it a degradation of marriage that it should, first of all, have to be considered a business arrangement securing their income and social status. Love and marriage being the main concern of women, it was only natural that their revolt should not have sprung from thirst for knowledge or a desire for freedom or adventures, but that, first of all, it should have been expressed as a protest against the humiliation of having to barter their love for support. As Olive Schreiner said in *The Story of an African Farm:*[18]

> It is for love's sake yet more than for any other that we look for that new time. . . . When love is no more bought or sold, when it is not a means of making bread, when each woman's life is filled with earnest, independent labour, then love will come to her, a strange sudden sweetness breaking in upon her earnest work; not sought for, but found.

Moreover, the chances of marriage were more uncertain than they had ever been before, owing, partly, to the increased economic difficulties arising from a social ideal which required the dependence of a whole family on the remunerative work of one member only, partly to the greater liabilities involved in rising social standards, and partly to a growing individualism. The number of people remaining single became large enough to permit their being termed, as a group, "protestants of marriage" and for these to become a social problem. Contrary to the general assumption, however, the surplus of women which would at any rate have deprived a number of them of the chances of getting married, and which as a serious problem was very much on women's minds at the time, was not a new phenomenon. Although the data available are incomplete it appears, according to Karl Bucher,[19] that during the Middle Ages the numerical superiority of women was even greater, varying from 10 percent to 25 percent (the present rate is on an average 7.5 percent in most European countries). But owing to the fact that most industrial activities were carried out in the house the chances of female employment then were bigger. Women were admitted to a number of trades, such as woolen and linen weaving, braiding, tailoring, fur-dressing and tanning, baking, leather-cutting and armorial embroidery, goldsmith's work and gold-spinning. In addition they worked in trades not submitted to regulations, in marketing, huckstering, copying, as musicians in taverns, as nurses, doctors, midwives, as sutler-women accompanying armies and crusades, as porters, gaolers, in the excise, in money-changing, in herding, and in many other professions. Living in homes of relatives they were no useless addition to the household. Moreover, various institutions were provided—apart from nunneries—where single women or widows found board and accommodation. It was industrialization with its separation of home and work, and with its improvement in the social standards of the middle and upper classes, which made the fate of the unmarriageable woman so acute a problem from the nineteenth century onward.

In this way it happened that

> middle class women, by force of circumstances, were being more and more compelled to seek a greater development of their powers in order to become better able to maintain themselves in an honourable independence in case of need. . . . Great numbers of women have, of course, aimed at higher education who are in no possible need of it for the purposes of gaining a livelihood thereby; but the incentive spoken of has been one of the strongest factors in the situation. As large numbers of women became more and more dependent on their own exertions for self-maintenance they found that school French, and school music, dancing, flower-painting, needlework, and a diligent use of the back-board, did not necessarily qualify them to undertake remunerative employment, and play their part in the struggle for existence; while as for the old tradition that anything more than elementary education might unfit a woman for becoming a wife and mother, that was set aside by the stern logic of statistics, which proved that there were many thousands of women who could not hope to enter the matrimonial state at all or who became widows and self-dependent after doing so.[20]

The need for making some provision in the event of their having to depend on their own resources was felt by women to be imperative. The following quotation from a report on the "Emigration of Educated Women" read by Miss Rye at a meeting of the Social Science Congress in Dublin in 1861 will shed some light on the urgency of the problem:

> My office is besieged every day by applicants for work, and there is scarcely a county or city in the United Kingdom that has not sent some anxious enquiries to me. Unfortunately my experience on this point is not singular: Miss Faithfull at the Printing Press, Miss Crowe at the Register Office, Mrs. Craig at the Telegraph Station, have all a surplus list of applicants. A short time since 810 women applied for one situation of £15 per annum; still later (only ten days ago) 250 women applied for another vacancy worth only £12 a year (the daughters of many professional men being among the numbers); and, on the authority of Mrs. Denison, lady superior of the Welbeck Street Home, London, I may state that at an office similar to those already alluded to 120 women applied in *one day* to find that there was literally *not one situation for any one of them.*[21]

The demand not only for a better general education, but for such special training as would enable women to take up independent careers, had its root in the practial necessity of not having to rely on one's feminine charm only in providing for one's future.

In addition, ideological factors played an important part in creating a "Women's Cause." The contrast between their position as the dependents of men and the prevalent individualist philosophy was one of the things which gave women most cause and most incitement to protest. The spreading democratic ideology taught that all human beings had equal rights by nature; that man must never be used as a means to anything else but is to be considered an "end in himself"; and that everyone should have an equal chance of free development as an individual.

Although the ideal of the Rights of Man did not explicitly include the rights of women (and these were certainly not endorsed by all who stood up for the democratic ideal), they may be assumed to be implicit. The demands for women's emancipation, i.e. for their equal citizenship and rights to education, were engendered by the democratic propaganda for equality and liberty and were its logical consequence. Women's struggle for enfranchisement, for equal opportunities, and for full legal rights were incidental to the struggle of the rising bourgeoisie for political power and social ascendancy.

Whether they fought for a reform of the marriage laws on the ground that no one should have property rights over other persons, whether they fought for equal educational facilities, or whether they emphasized the importance of the suffrage as a means and the expression of their equality, the trend of thought behind all shades of feminist opinion was the democratic ideology. (The same is true with regard to the illusion, held by a section of feminists, that the vote was the key to the earthly paradise.)

The opposition to feminist claims was strong and bitter not only among those who had vested interests in the legal, political and personal submission of women. It was at least equally strong among the majority of women themselves. While the claim to equality challenged the masculine feeling of power and superiority, it attacked, in women, those symbols which they had developed as substitute gratifications for their lack of real power, and which were no less close to their hearts than the feeling of superiority was to man's. Queen Victoria's appeal to all women of good will "to join in checking this mad, wicked folly of Women's Rights with all its attendant horrors, on which my poor feeble sex is bent, forgetting every sense of womanly feeling and propriety"[22]—certainly found a readier emotional response among the majority than the unorthodox claim of the feminists. Queen Victoria was not the only eminent woman who, though by her own character and achievement defying the familiar notion of the weak and mentally inferior female, objected to the equalitarian claims of Feminism. Hannah More, the moral writer, for instance, held that "that providential economy which has clearly determined that women were born to share with men the duties of private life, has clearly demonstrated that they were not born to divide with them its public administration,"[23] and although "pestered to read the *Rights of Women*," Mary Wollstonecraft's famous book, she was "invincibly resolved not to do it."

Caroline Norton, known for her struggle to secure for mothers some rights over their children, wrote in 1838: "The wild and stupid theories advanced by a few women of 'equal rights' and 'equal intelligence' are not the opinion of their sex. I, for one (I, with millions more), believe in the natural superiority of man, as I do in the existence of God. The natural position of woman is inferiority to man." And Beatrice Webb (who, however, later regretted this action) signed a manifesto in 1889, drafted by Mrs. Humphry Ward and some other distinguished ladies, against the enfranchisement of women, and in indignant protest against the suffragettes she allowed herself to be carried away at a public luncheon to make the statement: "I have never met a man, however inferior, whom I do not consider to be my superior."[24]

Nowhere were feminists more than a small, much-despised, and even more ridiculed minority. Their unpopularity resulted in part from their militant methods of agitation; in part from their over-emphasis on enfranchisement, which was a repetition of the struggle for the Reform Bill, with similar methods and bound to have the similar result described (with regard to the workers) by Esme Wingfield-Stratford in these words: "They had roared for the Bill, the whole Bill and nothing but the Bill, and it took them a little time to discover that what they had got was—nothing but the Bill."[25] But the main shortcoming of Feminism was that, a child of the Victorian era, it presented woman as a sort of sexless creature, a mere abstraction without flesh and blood. The suffragettes' exaltation of woman into a rational super-person "beyond the coarseness of animal instincts," their hatred of Man as their Enemy Number One, their contempt of his unsatiable sensuality, were the weakest points in their theory. It laid feminists open to ridicule and attack, and deprived them of the sympathy of the younger generation of women who, in the dilemma between "Rights" and emotions, would always be prepared to sacrifice abstract principles to emotional satisfaction. In spite of all its revolutionary *elan* the feminist movement had but little appeal to youth, and the report published in the *Vossische Zeitung* in 1932 is probably characteristic not only for Germany but to some extent of other countries as well: "Almost all meetings of women's organizations . . . show the same picture. At least three-fourths of the women present are over forty. The generation between twenty and thirty is almost completely lacking; that between thirty and forty is sparsely represented."[26]

It is the more remarkable that in spite of all their failings feminists saw almost all their demands gradually realized—in several instances by frankly anti-feminist statesmen (such as Asquith in this country or President Wilson in the United States, who, himself an anti-suffragist, enfranchised the women of his country in 1917 [sic])—simply by force of practical necessity, and because their claims were in accordance with the general trend of social development.

**NOTES**

1 Quoted from S. D. Schmalhausen and V. Calverton, eds., *Woman's Coming of Age: A Symposium* (New York: Liveright, 1931).

2 A market particularly reputed for its sales of women.

3 Recorded by Ivy Pinchbeck in *Women Workers and the Industrial Revolution* (London: George Routledge & Sons, 1930), p. 83.

4 E. Muller-Lyer, *The Evolution of Modern Marriage* (London: Allen & Unwin, 1930), from *Phasen der Liebe*, first pub. in Munich, 1913.

5 Quoted in Dorothy George, *London Life in the 18th Century* (London: Kegan Paul, 1925).

6 A. J. Graves, *Women in America* (New York: Harper Bros., 1858), quoted from Schmalhausen and Calverton, eds.

7 Quoted from *Ibid.*

8 This and the following quotations are taken from *Advice to Young Ladies*, a collection of answers to correspondents published in the *London Journal* between 1855 and 1862 (London: Methuen, 1933).

9 Clifton J. Furness, ed., *The Genteel Female: An Anthology* (New York: Knopf, 1931).

10 Irene Clephane, *Towards Sex Freedom* (London: John Lane, 1935).

11 Beatrice Webb, *My Apprenticeship* (London: Longmans, 1926).

12  *The Life of Frances Power Cobbe as Told by Herself* (London· Swan Sonnenschein & Co., 1904).

13  Chapter 2.

14  Webb, *My Apprenticeship.*

15  R. M. Butler, *A History of England, 1815–1918* (London: Home University Library, 1928).

16  Quoted from Janet E. Courtney, *The Adventurous Thirties: A Chapter in the Women's Movement* (Oxford: Oxford University Press, 1933).

17  The pertinent paragraph in Dr. John Gregory's *A Father's Legacy to His Daughters* runs: "The intention of your being taught needlework, knitting and such like is not on account of the intrinsic value of all you can do with your hands, which is trifling, but . . . to enable you to fill up, in a tolerably agreeable way, some of the many solitary hours you must necessarily pass at home." (Quoted from John Langdon-Davies, *A Short History of Women* (London: Cape, 1928.)

18  First published in London, 1833.

19  Karl Bucher, *Die Frauenfrage im Mittelalter* (Tubingen, 1882).

20  Edwin A. Pratt, *Pioneer Women in Victoria's Reign* (London: Newnes, 1897).

21  *Ibid.*

22  Quoted from Courtney, ed.

23  Quoted from Clephane.

24  Webb, *My Apprenticeship.*

25  Esme Wingfield-Stratford, *The Victorian Tragedy* (London: Routeledge, 1930).

26  Hiltgunde Graef, "Die vergreiste Frauenbewegung" (The senile feminist movement), *Vossische Zeitung,* Nov. 20, 1932.

# Judith Hole and Ellen Levine

# The First Feminists*

The contemporary women's movement is not the first such movement in American history to offer a wide-ranging feminist critique of society. In fact, much of what seems "radical" in contemporary feminist analysis parallels the critique made by the feminists of the nineteenth century. Both the early and the contemporary feminists have engaged in a fundamental reexamination of the role of women in all spheres of life, and of the relationships of men and women in all social, political, economic and cultural institutions. Both have defined women as an oppressed group and have traced the origin of women's subjugation to

---

*Reprinted from Judith Hole and Ellen Levine, *Rebirth of Feminism* (New York: Quadrangle, 1971), pp. 1–14 with permission of the publisher.

male-defined and male-dominated social institutions and value systems.

When the early feminist movement emerged in the nineteenth century, the "woman issue" was extensively debated in the national press, in political gatherings, and from church pulpits. The women's groups, their platforms, and their leaders, although not always well received or understood, were extremely well known. Until recently, however, that early feminist movement has been only cursorily discussed in American history textbooks, and then only in terms of the drive for suffrage. Even a brief reading of early feminist writings and of the few histories that have dealt specifically with the woman movement (as it was called then) reveals that the drive for suffrage became the single focus of the movement only after several decades of a more multi-issued campaign for women's equality.

The woman movement emerged during the 1800's. It was a time of geographic expansion, industrial development, growth of social reform movements, and a general intellectual ferment with a philosophical emphasis on individual freedom, the "rights of man," and universal education. In fact, some of the earliest efforts to extend opportunities to women were made in the field of education. In 1833, Oberlin became the first college to open its doors to both men and women. Although female education at Oberlin was regarded as necessary to ensure the development of good and proper wives and mothers, the open admission policy paved the way for the founding of other schools, some devoted entirely to women's education.[1] Much of the groundbreaking work in education was done by Emma Willard, who had campaigned vigorously for educational facilities for women beginning in the early 1820's. Frances Wright, one of the first women orators, was also a strong advocate of education for women. She viewed women as an oppressed group and argued that, "Until women assume the place in society which good sense and good feeling alike assign to them, human improvement must advance but feebly."[2] Central to her discussion of the inequalities between the sexes was a particular concern with the need for equal educational training for women.

In was in the abolition movement of the 1830's, however, that the woman's rights movement as such had its political origins. When women began working in earnest for the abolition of slavery, they quickly learned that they could not function as political equals with their male abolitionist friends. Not only were they barred from membership in some organizations, but they had to wage an uphill battle for the right simply to speak in public. Sarah and Angelina Grimke, daughters of a South Carolina slaveholding family, were among the first to fight this battle. Early in their lives the sisters left South Carolina, moved north, and began to speak out publicly on the abolition issue. Within a short time they drew the wrath of different sectors of society. A Pastoral letter from the Council of the Congregationalist Ministers of Massachusetts typified the attack:

> The appropriate duties and influence of woman are clearly stated in the New Testament. . . . The power of woman is her dependence, flowing from the consciousness of that weakness which God has given her for her protection. . . . When she assumes the place and tone of man as a public reformer . . . she yields the power which God has given her . . . and her character becomes unnatural.[3]

The brutal and unceasing attacks (sometimes physical) on the women convinced the Grimkes that the issues of freedom for slaves and freedom for women were inextricably linked. The women began to speak about both issues, but because of the objections from male abolitionists who were afraid that discussions of woman's rights would "muddy the waters," they often spoke about the "woman question" as a separate issue. (In fact, Lucy Stone, an early feminist and abolitionist, lectured on abolition on Saturdays and Sundays and on women's rights during the week.)

In an 1837 letter to the President of the Boston Female Anti-Slavery Society—by that time many female anti-slavery societies had been established in response to the exclusionary policy of the male abolitionist groups—Sarah Grimke addressed herself directly to the question of woman's status:

> All history attests that man has subjugated woman to his will, used her as a means to promote his selfish gratification, to minister to his sensual pleasure, to be instrumental in promoting his comfort; but never has he desired to elevate her to that rank she was created to fill. He has done all he could to debase and enslave her mind; and now he looks triumphantly on the ruin he has wrought, and says, the being he has thus deeply injured is his inferior. . . . But I ask no favors for my sex. . . . All I ask of our brethren is, that they will take their feet from off our necks and permit us to stand upright on that ground which God designed us to occupy.[4]

The Grimkes challenged both the assumption of the "natural superiority of man" and the social institutions predicated on that assumption.

For example, in her *Letters on the Equality of the Sexes* . . . Sarah Grimke argued against both religious dogma and the institution of marriage. Two brief examples are indicative:

> . . . Adam's ready acquiescence with his wife's proposal, does not savor much of that superiority *in strength of mind*, which is arrogated by man.[5]
>
> . . . [M]an has exercised the most unlimited and brutal power over woman, in the peculiar character of husband—a word in most countries synonymous with tyrant. . . . Woman, instead of being elevated by her union with man, which might be expected from an alliance with a superior being, is in reality lowered. She generally loses her individuality, her independent character, her moral being. She becomes absorbed into him, and henceforth is looked at, and acts through the medium of her husband.[6]

They attacked as well the manifestations of "male superiority" in the employment market. In a letter "On the Condition of Women in the United States" Sarah Grimke wrote of:

> . . . the disproportionate value set on the time and labor of men and of women. A man who is engaged in teaching, can always, I believe, command a higher price for tuition than a woman—even when he teaches the same branches, and is not in any respect superior to the woman. . . . [Or] for example, in tailoring, a man has twice, or three times as much for making a waistcoat or pantaloons as a woman, although the work done by each may be equally good.[7]

The abolition movement continued to expand, and in 1840 a World Anti-Slavery Convention was held in London. The American delegation included a group of women, among them Lucretia Mott and Elizabeth Cady Stanton. In Volume I of the *History of Woman Suffrage*, written and edited by Stanton, Susan B. Anthony, and Matilda Joslyn Gage, the authors note that the mere presence of women delegates produced an "excitement and vehemence of protest and denunciation [that] could not have been greater, if the news had come that the French were about to invade England."[8] The women were relegated to the galleries and prohibited from participating in any of the proceedings. That society at large frowned upon women participating in political activities was one thing; that the leading male radicals, those most concerned with social inequalities, should also discriminate against

women was quite another. The events at the world conference reinforced the women's growing awareness that the battle for the abolition
of Negro slavery could never be won without a battle for the abolition
of woman's slavery:

> As Lucretia Mott and Elizabeth Cady Stanton wended their way
> arm in arm down Great Queen Street that night, reviewing the
> exciting scenes of the day, they agreed to hold a woman's rights
> convention on their return to America, as the men to whom they
> had just listened had manifested their great need of some
> education on that question.[9]

Mott and Stanton returned to America and continued their abolitionist
work as well as pressing for state legislative reforms on woman's
property and family rights. Although the women had discussed the
idea of calling a public meeting on woman's rights, the possibility did not
materialize until eight years after the London Convention. On July 14,
1848, they placed a small notice in the *Seneca* (New York) *Country
Courier* announcing a "Woman's Rights Convention." Five days later, on
July 19 and 20, some three hundred interested women and men,
coming from as far as fifty miles, crowded into the small Wesleyan
Chapel (now a gas station) and approved a Declaration of Sentiments
(modeled on the Declaration of Independence) and twelve Resolutions.
The delineation of issues in the Declaration bears a startling re-
semblance to contemporary feminist writings  Some excerpts are illustrative:[10]

> We hold these truths to be self-evident: that all men and women
> are created equal; that they are endowed by their Creator with
> certain inalienable rights; that among these are life, liberty, and the
> pursuit of happiness. . . .
> The history of mankind is a history of repeated injuries and
> usurpations on the part of man toward woman, having in direct
> object the establishment of an absolute tyranny over her. To prove
> this, let facts be submitted to a candid world. . . .
> He has compelled her to submit to laws, in the formation of
> which she has no voice. . . .
> He has made her, if married, in the eye of the law, civilly
> dead. . . .
> He has monopolized nearly all the profitable employments, and
> from those she is permitted to follow, she receives but a scanty
> remuneration. He closes against her all the avenues to wealth and

distinction which he considers most honorable to himself. As a teacher of theology, medicine, or law, she is not known.

He allows her in church, as well as State, but a subordinate position, claiming Apostolic authority for her exclusion from the ministry, and, with some exceptions, from any public participation in the affairs of the Church.

He has created a false public sentiment by giving to the world a different code of morals for men and women, by which moral delinquencies which exclude women from society, are not only tolerated, but deemed of little account in man.

He has usurped the prerogative of Jehovah himself, claiming it as his right to assign for her a sphere of action, when that belongs to her conscience and to her God.

He has endeavored, in every way that he could, to destroy her confidence in her own powers, to lessen her self-respect, and to make her willing to lead a dependent and abject life.

Included in the list of twelve resolutions was one which read: "*Resolved,* That it is the duty of the women of this country to secure to themselves their sacred right to the elective franchise."

Although the Seneca Falls Convention is considered the official beginning of the woman's suffrage movement, it is important to reiterate that the goal of the early woman's rights movement was not limited to the demand for suffrage. In fact, the suffrage resolution was included only after lengthy debate, and was the only resolution not accepted unanimously. Those participants at the Convention who actively opposed the inclusion of the suffrage resolution:

... feared a demand for the right to vote would defeat others they deemed more rational, and make the whole movement ridiculous. But Mrs. Stanton and Frederick Douglass seeing that the power to choose rulers and make laws, was the right by which all others could be secured, persistently advocated the resolution. . . .[11]

Far more important to most of the women at the Convention was their desire to gain control of their property and earnings, guardianship of their children, rights to divorce, etc. Notwithstanding the disagreements at the Convention, the Seneca Falls meeting was of great historical significance. As Flexner has noted:

[The women] themselves were fully aware of the nature of the step they were taking; today's debt to them has been inadequately acknowledged. . . . Beginning in 1848 it was possible for women who rebelled against the circumstances of their lives, to know that they were not alone—although often the news reached them only through a vitriolic sermon or an abusive newspaper editorial. But a movement had been launched which they could either join, or ignore, that would leave its imprint on the lives of their daughters and of women throughout the world.[12]

From 1848 until the beginning of the Civil War, Woman's Rights Conventions were held nearly every year in different cities in the East and Midwest. The 1850 Convention in Salem, Ohio:

> . . . had one peculiar characteristic. It was officered entirely by women; not a man was allowed to sit on the platform, to speak, or vote. *Never did men so suffer.* They implored just to say a word; but no; the President was inflexible—no man should be heard. If one meekly arose to make a suggestion he was at once ruled out of order. For the first time in the world's history, men learned how it felt to sit in silence when questions in which they were interested were under discussion.[13]

As the woman's movement gained in strength, attacks upon it became more vitriolic. In newspaper editorials and church sermons anti-feminists argued vociferously that the public arena was not the proper place for women. In response to such criticism, Stanton wrote in an article in the Rochester, New York, *National Reformer:*

> If God has assigned a sphere to man and one to woman, we claim the right to judge ourselves of His design in reference to *us,* and we accord to man the same privilege. . . . We have all seen a man making a jackass of himself in the pulpit, at the bar, or in our legislative halls. . . . Now, is it to be wondered at that woman has some doubts about the present position assigned her being the true one, when her every-day experience shows her that man makes such fatal mistakes in regard to himself.[14]

It was abundantly clear to the women that they could not rely on the pulpit or the "establishment" press for either factual or sympathetic reportage; nor could they use the press as a means to disseminate their ideas. As a result they depended on the abolitionist papers of the day, and in addition founded a number of independent women's journals including *The Lily, The Una, Woman's Advocate, Pittsburgh Visiter* [sic], etc.

One of the many issues with which the women activists were concerned was dress reform. Some began to wear the "bloomer" costume (a misnomer since Amelia Bloomer, although an advocate of the loose-fitting dress, was neither its originator nor the first to wear it) in protest against the tight-fitting and singularly uncomfortable cinched-waisted stays and layers of petticoats. However, as Flexner has noted, "The attempt at dress reform, although badly needed, was not only unsuccessful but boomeranged and had to be abandoned."[15] Women's rights advocates became known as "bloomers" and the movement for equal rights as well as the individual women were subjected to increasing ridicule. Elizabeth Cady Stanton, one of the earliest to wear the more comfortable outfit, was one of the first to suggest its rejection. In a letter to Susan B. Anthony she wrote:

> We put the dress on for greater freedom, but what is physical freedom compared with mental bondage? . . . It is not wise, Susan, to use up so much energy and feeling that way. You can put them to better use. I speak from experience.[16]

When the Civil War began in 1861, woman's rights advocates were urged to abandon their cause and support the war effort. Although Anthony and Stanton continued arguing that any battle for freedom must include woman's freedom, the woman's movement activities essentially stopped for the duration of the war. After the war and the ratification of the Thirteenth Amendment abolishing slavery (for which the woman activists had campaigned vigorously), the abolitionists began to press for passage of a Fourteenth Amendment to secure the rights, privileges, and immunities of citizens (the new freedmen) under the law. In the second section of the proposed Amendment, however, the word "male" appeared, introducing a sex distinction into the Constitution for the first time. Shocked and enraged by the introduction of the word "male," the women activists mounted an extensive campaign to eliminate it. They were dismayed to find that no one, neither the Republican administration nor their old abolitionist allies, had any intention of "complicating" the campaign for Negroes' rights by advocating women's rights as well. Over and over again the women were told, "This is the Negroes' hour." The authors of *History of Woman Suffrage* analyzed the women's situation:

> During the six years they held their own claims in abeyance to the slaves of the South, and labored to inspire the people with

enthusiasm for the great measures of the Republican party, they were highly honored as "wise, loyal, and clear-sighted." But again when the slaves were emancipated and they asked that women should be recognized in the reconstruction as citizens of the Republic, equal before the law, all these transcendent virtues vanished like dew before the morning sun. And thus it ever is so long as woman labors to second man's endeavors and exalt *his* sex above her own, her virtues pass unquestioned; but when she dares to demand rights and privileges for herself, her motives, manners, dress, personal appearance, character, are subjects for ridicule and detraction.[17]

The women met with the same response when they campaigned to get the word "sex" added to the proposed Fifteenth Amendment which would prohibit the denial of suffrage on account of race.[18]

As a result of these setbacks, the woman's movement assumed as its first priority the drive for woman's suffrage. It must be noted, however, that while nearly all the women activists agreed on the need for suffrage, in 1869 the movement split over ideological and tactical questions into major factions. In May of that year, Susan B. Anthony and Elizabeth Cady Stanton organized the National Woman Suffrage Association. Six months later, Lucy Stone and others organized the American Woman Suffrage Association. The American, in an attempt to make the idea of woman's suffrage "respectable," limited its activities to that issue, and refused to address itself to any of the more "controversial" subjects such as marriage or the church. The National, on the other hand, embraced the broad cause of woman's rights of which the vote was seen primarily as a *means* of achieving those rights. During this time Anthony and Stanton founded *The Revolution,* which became one of the best known of the independent women's newspapers. The weekly journal began in January, 1868, and took as its motto, "Men, their rights and nothing more; women, their rights and nothing less." In addition to discussion of suffrage, *The Revolution* examined the institutions of marriage, the law, organized religion, etc. Moreover, the newspaper touched on "such incendiary topics as the double standard and prostitution."[19] Flexner describes the paper:

[It] made a contribution to the women's cause out of all proportion to either its size, brief lifespan, or modest circulation. . . . Here was news not to be found elsewhere—of the organization of women typesetters, tailoresses, and laundry workers, of the first women's clubs, of pioneers in the professions, of women abroad. But *The*

*Revolution* did more than just carry news, or set a new standard for professionalism for papers edited by and for women. It gave their movement a forum, focus, and direction. It pointed, it led, and it fought, with vigor and vehemence.[20]

The two suffrage organizations coexisted for over twenty years and used some of the same tactics in their campaigns for suffrage: lecture tours, lobbying activities, petition campaigns, etc. The American, however, focused exclusively on state-by-state action, while the National in addition pushed for a woman suffrage Amendment to the Constitution. Susan B. Anthony and others also attempted to gain the vote through court decisions. The Supreme Court, however, held in 1875[21] that suffrage was not necessarily one of the privileges and immunities of citizens protected by the Fourteenth Amendment. Thus, although women were *citizens* it was nonetheless permissible, according to the Court, to constitutionally limit the right to vote to males.

During this same period, a strong temperance movement had also emerged. Large numbers of women, including some suffragists, became actively involved in the temperance cause. It is important to note that one of the main reasons women became involved in pressing for laws restricting the sale and consumption of alcohol was that their legal status as married women offered them no protection against either physical abuse or abandonment by a drunken husband. It might be added that the reason separate women's temperance organizations were formed was that women were not permitted to participate in the men's groups. In spite of the fact that temperance was in "woman's interests," the growth of the women's temperance movement solidified the liquor and brewing industries' opposition to woman suffrage. As a result, suffrage leaders became convinced of the necessity of keeping the two issues separate.

As the campaign for woman suffrage grew, more and more sympathizers were attracted to the conservative and "respectable" American Association which, as noted above, deliberately limited its work to the single issue of suffrage. After two decades "respectability" won out, and the broad-ranging issues of the earlier movement had been largely subsumed by suffrage. (Even the Stanton-Anthony forces had somewhat redefined their goals and were focusing primarily on suffrage.) By 1890, when the American and the National merged to become the National American Woman Suffrage Association, the woman's movement had, in fact, been transformed into the single-issue suffrage movement. Moreover, although Elizabeth Cady Stanton, NAWSA's first president, was succeeded two years later by Susan B. Anthony, the first women activists, with their catholic range of concerns, were slowly being replaced by a second group far more limited in their political analysis. It should be noted that Stanton herself, after her two-year term as president of the new organization, withdrew from active work in the suffrage campaign. Although [she had been] one of the earliest feminist leaders to understand the need for woman suffrage, by this time Stanton believed that the main obstacle to woman's equality was the church and organized religion.

During the entire development of the woman's movement, perhaps the argument most often used by anti-feminists was that the subjugation of women was divinely ordained as written in the Bible. Stanton attacked the argument head-on. She and a group of twenty-three women, including three ordained ministers, produced *The Woman's Bible*[22] which presented a systematic feminist critique of woman's role and image in the Bible. Some Biblical chapters were presented as proof that the Scripture itself was the source of woman's subjugation; others to show that, if reinterpreted, men and women were indeed equals in the Bible, not superior and inferior beings. "We have made a fetich [*sic*] of the Bible long enough. The time has come to read it as we do all other books, accepting the good and rejecting the evil it teaches."[23] Dismissing the "rib story" as a "petty surgical operation," Stanton argued further that the entire structure of the Bible was predicated on the notion of Eve's (woman's) corruption:

> Take the snake, the fruit-tree and the woman from the tableau,
> and we have no fall, nor frowning Judge, no Inferno, no
> everlasting punishment;—hence no need of a Savior. Thus the
> bottom falls out of the whole Christian theology. Here is the reason
> why in all the Biblical researches and higher criticisms, the scholars
> never touch the position of women.[24]

Not surprisingly, *The Woman's Bible* was considered scandalous and sacrilegious by most. The Suffrage Association members themselves, with the exception of Anthony and a few others, publicly disavowed Stanton and her work. They feared that the image of the already controversial suffrage movement would be irreparably damaged if the public were to associate it with Stanton's radical tract.

Shortly after the turn of the century, the second generation of woman suffragists came of age and new leaders replaced the old.

Carrie Chapman Catt is perhaps the best known; she succeeded Anthony as president of the National American Woman Suffrage Association, which by then had become a large and somewhat unwieldy organization. Although limited gains were achieved (a number of western states had enfranchised women), no major progress was made in the campaign for suffrage until Alice Paul, a young and extremely militant suffragist, became active in the movement. In April, 1913, she formed a small radical group known as the Congressional Union (later reorganized as the Woman's Party) to work exclusively on a campaign for a *federal* woman's suffrage Amendment using any tactics necessary, no matter how unorthodox. Her group organized parades, mass demonstrations, hunger strikes, and its members were on several occasions arrested and jailed.[25] Although many suffragists rejected both the militant style and tactics of the Congressional Union, they nonetheless did consider Paul and her followers in large part responsible for "shocking" the languishing movement into activity pressuring for the federal Amendment. The woman suffrage Amendment (known as the "Anthony Amendment"), introduced into every session of Congress from 1878 on, was finally ratified on August 26, 1920.

Nearly three-quarters of a century had passed since the demand for woman suffrage had first been made at the Seneca Falls Convention. By 1920, so much energy had been expended in achieving the right to vote that the woman's movement virtually collapsed from exhaustion. To achieve the vote alone, as Carrie Chapman Catt had computed, took:

> . . . fifty-two years of pauseless campaign . . . fifty-six campaigns of referenda to male voters; 480 campaigns to get Legislatures to submit suffrage amendments to votes; 47 campaigns to get State constitutional conventions to write woman suffrage into state consitutions; 277 campaigns to get State party conventions to include woman suffrage planks; 30 campaigns to get presidential party conventions to adopt woman suffrage planks in party platforms, and 19 campaigns with 19 successive Congresses.[26]

With the passage of the Nineteenth Amendment the majority of women activists as well as the public at large assumed that having gained the vote woman's complete equality had been virtually obtained.

It must be remembered, however, that for most of the period that the woman's movement existed, suffrage had not been seen as an all-inclusive goal, but as a means of achieving equality—suffrage was only one element in the wide-ranging feminist critique questioning the fundamental organization of society. Historians, however, have for the most part ignored this radical critique and focused exclusively on the suffrage campaign. By virtue of this omission they have, to all intents and purposes, denied the political significance of the early feminist analysis. Moreover, the summary treatment by historians of the nineteenth and twentieth-century drive for woman's suffrage has made that campaign almost a footnote to the abolitionist movement and the campaign for Negro suffrage. In addition, the traditional textbook image of the early feminists—if not wild-eyed women waving placards for the vote, then wild-eyed women swinging axes at saloon doors—has further demeaned the importance of their philosophical analysis.

The woman's movement virtually died in 1920 and, with the exception of a few organizations, feminism was to lie dormant for forty years.

## NOTES

1  Mount Holyoke opened in 1837; Vassar, 1865; Smith and Wellesley, 1875; Radcliffe, 1879; Bryn Mawr, 1885.

2  Quoted in Eleanor Flexner, *Century of Struggle: The Woman's Rights Movement in the United States* (Cambridge, Mass.: The Belknap Press of Harvard University Press, 1959), p. 27.

3  *History of Woman Suffrage* (republished by Arno Press and *The New York Times*, New York, 1969), Vol. 1, p. 81. Hereafter cited as *HWS*. Volumes I–III were edited by Elizabeth Cady Stanton, Susan B. Anthony, and Matilda Joslyn Gage. The first two volumes were published in 1881, the third in 1886. Volume IV was edited by Susan B. Anthony and Ida Husted Harper and was published in 1902. Volumes V and VI were edited by Ida Husted Harper and published in 1922.

4  Sarah M. Grimke, *Letters on the Equality of the Sexes and the Condition of Woman* (Boston: Issac Knapp, 1838, reprinted by Source Book Press, New York, 1970), p. 10ff.

5  *Ibid.*, pp. 9–10.

6  *Ibid.*, pp. 85–86.

7  *Ibid.*, p. 51.

8  *HWS*, p. 54.

9  *Ibid.*, p. 61.

10  *Ibid.*, pp. 70–73.

11  *HWS*, p. 73.

12  Flexner, p. 77.

13  *HWS*, p. 110.

14  *Ibid.*, p. 806.

15  Flexner, p. 83.

16  *Ibid.*, p. 84.

17  *HWS*, Vol. II, p. 51.

18  The Thirteenth Amendment was ratified in 1865; the Fourteenth in 1868; the Fifteenth in 1870.

19  Flexner, p. 151.

20  Flexner, p. 151.

21  *Minor v. Happersett*, 21 Wall. 162, 22 L. Ed. 627 (1875).

22  (New York: European Publishing Company, 1895 and 1898. Two Parts.)

23  *Ibid.*, Part II, pp. 7–8.

24  Stanton, letter to the editor of *The Critic* (New York), March 28, 1896, quoted in Aileen S. Kraditor, *The Ideas of the Woman Suffrage Movement, 1890–1920* (New York: Columbia University Press, 1965), n. 11, p. 86.

25  A total of 218 women from 26 states were arrested during the first session of the Sixty-fifth Congress (1917). Ninety-seven went to prison.

26  Carrie Chapman Catt and Nettie Rogers Shuler, *Woman Suffrage and Politics* (New York, 1923), p. 107. Quoted in Flexner, p. 173.

# Jo Freeman

# The Women's Liberation Movement: Its Origins, Organizations, Activities, and Ideas

Sometime during the 1920's, feminism died in the United States. It was a premature death—feminists had just obtained that long-sought tool, the vote, with which they had hoped to make an equal place for women in this society—but it seemed an irreversible one. By the time the suffragists' granddaughters were old enough to vote, social mythology had firmly ensconced women in the home, and the very term "feminist" had become an insult.

Social mythology, however, did not always coincide with social fact. Even during the era of the "feminine mystique," the 1940's and 1950's, when the relative numbers of academic degrees given to women were dropping, the absolute numbers of such degrees were rising astronomically. Women's participation in the labor force was also rising, even while women's position within it was declining. Opportunities to work, the trend toward smaller families, plus a change in preferred status symbols from a leisured wife at home to a second car and a color television set, helped transform the female labor force from one of primarily single women under 25, as it was in 1940, to one of married women and mothers over 40, as it was by 1950. Simultaneously, the job market became even more rigidly segregated, with the exception of female professional jobs, such as teaching and social work, which were flooded by men. Thus women's share of professional and technical jobs declined by a third, with a commensurate decline in women's relative income. The result of all this was the creation of a class of highly educated, underemployed, and underpaid women.

## ORIGINS IN THE 60's

In the early 1960's, feminism was still an unmentionable, but it was slowly awakening from the dead. The first sign of new life was President Kennedy's establishment of a national Commission on the Status of Women in 1961. Created at the urging of Esther Petersen of the Women's Bureau, the short-lived Commission thoroughly documented women's second-class status. It was followed by the formation of a citizen's advisory council and fifty state commissions. Many of the people involved in these commissions, dissatisfied with the lack of progress made on their recommendations, joined with Betty Friedan in 1966 to found the National Organization for Women (NOW).

NOW was the first new feminist organization in almost fifty years, but it was not the sole beginning of the organized expression of the movement. The movement actually has two origins, from two different strata of society, with two different styles, orientations, values, and forms of organization. In many ways there have been two separate movements that have not entirely merged. Although the composition of both branches tends to be predominantly white, middle-class, and college-educated, initially the median age of the activists in what I call the older branch of the movement was higher. Too, it began first. In addition to NOW, this branch contains such organizations as the National Women's Political Caucus, Women's Equity Action League, Federally Employed Women (FEW), and almost 100 different organizations and caucuses of professional women. Their style of organization has tended to be traditionally formal, with elected officers, boards of directors, bylaws, and the other trappings of democratic procedure. All started as top-down organizations lacking a mass base. Some have subsequently developed a mass base, some have not yet done so, and others don't want to.

In 1967 and 1968, unaware of and unknown to NOW or to the state commissions, the other branch of the movement was taking shape. While it did not begin on the campuses, its activators were on the younger side of the generation gap. Although few were students, all were under 30 and had received their political education as participants in or concerned observers of the social-action projects of the preceding decade. Many came direct from New Left and civil rights organizations where they had been shunted into traditional roles and faced with the contradiction of working in a freedom movement but not being very free. Others had attended various courses on women in the multitude of free universitites springing up around the country during those years.

During 1967 and 1968 at least five groups formed spontaneously and independently of each other in five different cities—Chicago, Toronto, Detroit, Seattle, and Gainesville, Florida. They arose at a very auspicious moment. The blacks had just kicked the whites out of the civil rights movement, student power had been discredited by SDS, and the organized New Left was on the wane. Only draft-resistance activities were on the rise, and for women whose consciousness was sufficiently advanced, this movement more than any other movement of its time exemplified the social inequities of the sexes. Men could resist the draft. Women could only counsel resistance.

There had been individual temporary caucuses and conferences of women as early as 1964 when Stokeley Carmichael of the Student Nonviolent Coordinating Committee made his infamous remark that "the only position for women in SNCC is prone." But it was not until 1967 that the groups developed a determined, if cautious, continuity and began to expand. In 1968 they held a national conference, attended by over 200 women from around this country and Canada on less than a month's notice. For the next few years they expanded exponentially.

This expansion was more amoebic than organized, because the younger branch of the movement prides itself on its lack of organization. Eschewing structure and damning leadership, it has carried the concept of "everyone doing her own thing" almost to its logical extreme. The thousands of sister chapters around the country are virtually independent of each other, linked only by journals, newsletters, and cross-country travelers. Some cities have a coordinating committee that tries to maintain communication among local groups and to channel newcomers into appropriate ones, but none of these committees has any power over the activities, let alone the ideas, of any of the groups it serves. One result of this style is a very broadly based, creative movement, to which individuals can relate as they desire, with no concern for orthodoxy or doctrine.

Another result is political impotence. It would be virtually impossible for this branch of the movement to join together in a nation-wide action, even assuming there could be an agreement on issues. Fortunately, the older branch of the movement does have the structure necessary to coordinate such actions, and is usually the one to initiate them.

## ACTIVITIES

It is a common mistake to try to place the various feminist organizations on the traditional left/right spectrum. The terms "reformist" and "radical" are convenient and fit into our preconceived notions about the nature of political organization, but they tell us nothing relevant. As with most other kinds of categories, feminism cuts across the normal political categories and demands new perspectives in order to be understood. Some groups often called reformist have a platform that would so completely change our society it would be unrecognizable. Other groups called radical concentrate on the traditional female concerns of love, sex, children, and interpersonal relationships (although with nontraditional views). The activities of the organizations are similarly incongruous. The most typical division of labor, ironically, is that those groups labeled radical engage primarily in educational work whereas the so-called reformist ones are the activists. It is structure and style of action rather than ideology that more accurately differentiates the various groups, and even here there has been much borrowing on both sides.

The activities of the two branches have been significantly different. In general, the older branch has stayed with the traditional forms, creating a national structure prepared to use the legal, political, and media institutions of our country. NOW and its subsequent sister organizations have done this with great skill. The Equal Employment Opportunity Commission has changed many of its prejudicial attitudes toward women in its rulings of the last few years. Numerous lawsuits have been filed under the sex provision of Title VII of the 1964 Civil Rights Act. The Equal Rights Amendment has passed Congress. The Supreme Court has legalized some abortions. Complaints have been filed against more than 400 colleges and universities, as well as many businesses, charging sex discrimination. Articles on feminism have appeared in virtually every news medium, and a whole host of new laws have been passed prohibiting sex discrimination in a variety of areas.

The younger branch has been more experimental. Its most prevalent innovation was the development of the "rap group." Essentially an educational technique, it spread far beyond its origins and became a major organizational unit of the whole movement. From a sociological perspective the rap group is probably the most valuable contribution by the women's liberation movement to the tools for social change. As such it deserves some extended attention here.

The rap group serves two main functions. One is simply bringing women together in a situation of structured interaction. It has long been known that people can be kept down as long as they are kept divided from each other, relating more to their social superiors than to their social equals. It is when social development creates natural structures in which people can interact with one another and compare their common concerns that social movements take place. This is the function that the factory served for the workers, the church for the Southern civil rights movement, the campus for students and the ghetto for urban blacks. Women have generally been deprived of structured interaction and been kept isolated in their individual homes, relating more to men than to each other. Natural structures for interaction are still largely lacking, although they have begun to develop. But the rap group has provided an artificial structure that does much the same thing.

The second function of the rap groups is to serve as a mechanism for social change in and of themselves. They are structures created specifically for the purpose of altering the participants' perceptions and conceptions of themselves and of society at large. The process is known as "consciousness-raising" and is very simple. Women come together in groups of five to fifteen and talk to one another about their personal problems, personal experiences, personal feelings, and personal concerns. From this public sharing of experiences comes the realization that what was thought to be individual is in fact common; that what was considered a personal problem has a social cause and probably a political solution. Women see how social structures and attitudes have limited their opportunities and molded them from birth. They ascertain the extent to which women have been denigrated in this society and how they have developed prejudices against themselves and other women.

It is this process of deeply personal attitude change that makes the rap group such a powerful tool. The need for any movement to develop "correct consciousness" has long been known. But usually this consciousness is not developed by means intrinsic to the structure of the movement and does not require such a profound resocialization of one's self-concept. This experience is both irreversible and contagious. Once women have gone through such a resocialization, their views of themselves and the world are never the same again even if they stop participating actively in the movement. Those who do drop out rarely do so without spreading feminist ideas among their own friends and colleagues. All who undergo consciousness-raising feel compelled themselves to seek out other women with whom to share the experience.

There are several personal results from this process. The initial one is a decrease in self- and group-depreciation. Women come to see themselves and other women as essentially worthwhile and interesting. With this realization, the myth of the individual solution explodes. Women come to believe that if they are the way they are because of society, they can change their lives significantly only by changing society. These feelings in turn create a consciousness of oneself as a member of a group and the feeling of solidarity so necessary to any social movement. From this awareness comes the concept of "sisterhood."

The need for group solidarity explains why men have been largely excluded from women's rap groups. Sisterhood was not the initial goal of these groups, but it has been one of the more beneficial by-products. Originally, the idea of exclusion was borrowed from the Black Power movement, which was much in the public consciousness when the women's liberation movement began. It was reinforced by the unremitting hostility of most of the New Left men at the prospect of an independent women's movement not tied to radical ideology. Even when this hostility was not evident, women in virtually every group in the United States, Canada, and Europe soon discovered that when men were present, the traditional sex roles reasserted themselves regardless of the good intentions of the participants. Men inevitably dominated the discussion, and usually would talk only about how women's liberation related to men, or how men were oppressed by the sex roles. In all-female groups women found the discussions to be more open, honest, and extensive. They could learn how to relate to other *women,* not just to men.

Unlike the male exclusion policy, the rap groups did not develop spontaneously or without a struggle. The political background of many of the early feminists of the younger branch predisposed them against the rap group as "unpolitical" and they would condemn discussion meetings which "degenerated" into "bitch sessions." This trend was particularly strong in centers of New Left activity. Meanwhile, other feminists, usually with a civil rights or apolitical background, saw that the "bitch session" obviously met a basic need. They seized upon it and created the consciousness raising rap group. Developed initially in New York and Gainesville, Fla., the idea soon spread throughout the country, becoming the paradigm for most movement organization.

### NOW and NWPC

These national organizations have and continue to function primarily as pressure groups within the limits of traditional political activity. Diversification in the older branch of the movement has been largely along occupational lines and primarily within the professions. This branch has stressed using the tools for change provided by the system, however limited these may be. It emphasizes short-range goals and does not attempt to place them within a broader ideological framework.

Initially, this structure hampered the development of older branch organizations. NOW suffered three splits between 1967 and 1968. As the only action organization concerned with women's rights, it had attracted many different kinds of people with many different views on what to do and how to do it. With only a national structure and, at that point, no local base, individuals found it difficult to pursue their particular concerns on a local level; they had to persuade the whole organization to support them. This top-down structure, combined with limited resources, placed severe restrictions on diversity and, in turn, severe strains on the organization. Local chapters were also hampered by a lack of organizers to develop new chapters and the lack of a program into which they could fit.

These initial difficulties were overcome as NOW grew to become the largest single feminist organization. While it never hired organizers to develop chapters, the enormous geographical mobility of its members and their desire to create chapters wherever they moved had the same results. Too, NOW benefited greatly from the publicity the movement received in the early seventies. While much of that publicity was a response to the eye-catching tactics of the younger branch, or was aimed at creating "media stars" (none of whom were NOW leaders), NOW was often the only organization with a telephone and a stable address that incipient movement participants could find. Consequently, its membership grew at the same exponential rate the younger branch had experienced in the late sixties.

As the membership grew, the organization became highly decentralized. In 1973, NOW had three national offices with different functions: Administrative in Chicago, Legislative in Washington, D.C., and Public Relations in New York. Its 40,000 members were organized into 700 relatively autonomous chapters and numerous topical task forces. Although it consistently moved in a more radical direction, it had yet to experience another major split.

Within two years, all this changed. With its first contested presidential election in 1974, NOW developed two major factions that fought for control of the organization and very nearly split it into two. Although these factions articulated their concerns ideologically, the fight in fact was not over issues but was a very ordinary attempt by "outs" to become "ins." By 1975 the "insurgent" faction had established solid control, and over the next few years this faction began to centralize NOW. A single office was located in Washington, the national by-laws were re-written to provide for five paid officers, and state organizations were created which deprived local chapters of much of their autonomy.

While this centralization did drain resources and energy from the chapters, it allowed the national office to focus the organization's efforts and thus, on the national level, to increase its power. In the meantime, the issues surrounding the Equal Rights Amendment acquired a national prominence that had not developed when the amendment emerged from Congress in 1972. Under assault from the right wing, who saw the ERA, along with abortion, busing, and gay rights, as leading to the destruction of the family and the American way of life, the Amendment became symbolic of a national struggle unwarranted by its real potential impact. Therefore, when the ERA still lacked three states necessary for ratification one year from the March 22, 1979, deadline, NOW declared it would focus its efforts on the ERA to the virtual exclusion of anything else. In doing so, it repeated the history of the nineteenth-century Woman Movement, which after years of fighting for women's rights on many fronts focused all its efforts on gaining suffrage. With this change, NOW virtually completed its transformation from a social movement organization into an interest group.

The other major national feminist organization, the National Women's Political Caucus, has always been primarily an interest group, even though it emerged out of the women's liberation movement. Formed in 1971 by prominent female politicians, its major aim has been to get more women elected and appointed to public office. Its organization mirrors that of the typical political party, with the effective unit being the state organization and the national office primarily servicing rather than directing the local chapters. Although it has a decidedly feminist bias, its membership is exceedingly diverse with large numbers concerned chiefly with gaining office rather than pushing issues. Without the context of a movement to maintain feminist standards, it would be very easy for the NWPC to become an interest group dedicated solely to the upward mobility of female politicians.

## THE SMALL GROUPS

The younger branch has had an entirely different history and faces different prospects. It was able to expand rapidly in the beginning because it could capitalize on the New Left's infrastructure of organizations and media and because its initiators were skilled in local community organizing. Since the primary unit was the small group and no need for national cooperation was perceived, multitudinous splits increased its strength rather than drained its resources. Such fission was often "friendly" in nature, and even when not, served to bring ever-increasing numbers of women under the movement's umbrella.

Unfortunately, these newly recruited masses lacked the organizing skills of the initiators, and, because the very ideas of "leadership" and "organization" were in disrepute, they made no attempt to acquire them. They did not want to deal with traditional political institutions and abjured all traditional political skills. Consequently, the growth of the movement institutions did not go beyond the local level, and they were often inadequate to handle the accelerating influx of new people into the movement. Although these small groups were diverse in kind and responsible to no one for their focus, their nature determined both the structure and the strategy of the movement. To date, the major, though hardly exclusive, activities of the younger branch have been organizing rap groups, putting on conferences, putting out educational literature, and running service projects such as bookstores and health centers. This branch's contribution has lain more in the impact of its new ideas than in its activities. It has developed several ideological perspectives, much of the terminology of the movement, an amazing number of publications and "counter-institutions," numerous new issues, and even new techniques for social change.

Nonetheless, this loose structure is flexible only within certain limits, and the movement has not yet shown a propensity to transcend them. The rap groups have afforded excellent techniques for changing individual attitudes, but they have not been very successful in dealing with social institutions. Their loose, informal structure encourages participation in discussion, and their supportive atmosphere elicits personal insight; but neither is very efficient in handling specific tasks. Thus, although they have been of fundamental value to the development of the movement it is the more structured groups that are the more politically effective.

Individual rap groups tend to flounder when their members have exhausted the virtues of consciousness-raising and decide they want to do something more concrete. The problem is that most groups are unwilling to change their structure when they change their tasks. They have accepted the ideology of "structurelessness" without recognizing the limitations of its uses.

Because "structurelessness" provided no means of resolving political disputes or carrying on ideological debates, the younger branch was racked by several major crises during the early seventies. The two most significant ones were an attempt by the Young Socialist Alliance, youth group of the Socialist Workers' Party, to take over the movement, and the so-called gay/straight split. The Trotskyist YSA saw the younger branch of the movement as a potential recruiting ground for socialist converts, and directed its members to join with that purpose in mind. Although YSA members were never numerous, their enormous dedication and their contributions of time and energy enabled them to quickly achieve positions of power in many small groups whose lack of structure provided no means of resisting. However, many New Left women had remained within the younger branch, and their past experience with YSA predisposed them to mistrust it. Not only did they disagree with YSA politics, but they recognized that because YSA members owed their primary allegiance to a centralized national party they had the potential to control the entire movement. The battle that ensued can euphemistically be described as vicious, and it resulted in YSA being largely driven from the younger branch of the movement. (Several years later, in their SWP guise, YSA members began to join NOW, but NOW's structure makes it more difficult to control.) However, the alienation and fragmentation this struggle left in its wake made the movement ill prepared to meet its next major crisis.

The gay/straight split occurred not because of the mere presence of lesbians in feminist groups, but because a vocal group of those present articulated lesbianism as the essential feminist idea. It was argued first that women should identify with, live with, and associate with women only, and eventually that a woman who actually slept with a man was clearly consorting with the enemy and could not be trusted. When this view met the fear and hostility many straight women felt toward homosexuality, the results were explosive.

The gay/straight struggle raged for several years and consumed most of the time and energy of the younger branch. By the time the tensions eased, most straight women had either become gay or left the younger branch. Some joined NOW, some rejoined the New Left, and many simply dropped out of women's groups altogether. Once gay women predominated (by about four to one) in the small groups, their anger toward straight women began to moderate. However, the focus of both the gay and straight women remaining was no longer directed at educating or recruiting non-feminists into the movement, but at building a "women's culture" for those that remained. While a few groups engaged in outreach through public action on issues of concern to all women (e.g., rape) or even on issues concerning straight women exclusively (e.g., wife-beating), most of the small groups concerned themselves with maintaining a comfortable niche for "women-identified women" and with insulating themselves from the damnation of the outside world. Consequently, while the small groups still exist throughout the country, most are hard for the uninitiated to locate and thus their impact on the outside world is now limited.

Their impact on the organizations of the older branch is also limited, as the networks which formerly existed were largely demolished by these crises. A major impetus for NOW's movement in a more radical direction during the early seventies was the pressure it received from the small groups, which frequently accused it of being part of the establishment. The insurgent faction that took control of NOW in the mid-seventies did so on the platform of "out of the mainstream and into the revolution." Once this faction attained power, however, it proceeded to go in the opposite direction, becoming more concerned with respectability in order to appeal to a wide spectrum of women than with developing a consistent feminist interpretation on issues. Without pressure from the younger branch, it found the mainstream more appealing than revolution.

## IDEAS

Initially, there was little ideology in the movement beyond a gut feeling that something was wrong. NOW was formed under the slogan "full equality for women in a truly equal partnership with men," and in 1967 the organization specified eight demands in a "Bill of Rights." It and the other organizations of the older branch have largely concluded that attempts at a comprehensive ideology have little to offer beyond internal conflict.

In the younger branch a basic difference of opinion developed quite early. It was disguised as a philosophical difference, was articulated and acted on as a strategic one, but actually was more of a political disagreement than anything else. The two sides involved were essentially the same people who differed over the rap groups, but the split endured long after the groups became ubiquitous. The original issue was whether the fledgling women's liberation movement should remain a branch of the radical left movement or become an independent women's movement. Proponents of the two positions became known as "politicos" and "feminists," respectively, and traded arguments about whether the enemy was "capitalism" or male-dominated social institutions and values. They also traded a few epithets, with politicos calling feminists politically unsophisticated and elitist, and in turn being accused of subservience to the interests of left-wing men. With the influx of large numbers of previously apolitical women, an independent, autonomous women's liberation movement became a reality instead of an argument. The spectrum shifted toward the feminist direction, but the basic difference in orientation remained until wiped out by the debate over lesbian feminism. Those women who maintained their allegiance to the Left then created their own socialist feminist groups or united in feminist caucuses within Left organizations.

Socialist feminism and lesbian feminism are just two of the many different interpretations of women's status that have been developed. Some are more sophisticated than others, and some are better publicized, yet there is no single comprehensive interpretation that can accurately be labeled *the* women's-liberationist, feminist, neofeminist, or radical feminist analysis. At best one can say there is general agreement on two theoretical concerns. The first is the feminist critique of society, and the second is the idea of oppression.

The traditional view of society assumes that men and women are essentially different and should serve different social functions; their diverse roles and statuses simply reflect these essential differences. The feminist perspective starts from the premise that women and men are constitutionally equal and share the same human capabilities; observed differences therefore demand a critical analysis of the social institutions that cause them. Since these two views start from different premises, neither can refute the other in logical terms.

The term "oppression" was long avoided by feminists out of a feeling that it was too rhetorical. But there was no convenient euphemism, and "discrimination" was inadequate to describe what happens to women and what they have in common with other disadvantaged groups. As long as the word remained illegitimate, so did the idea, and that was too valuable not to use. Oppression is still largely an undeveloped concept in which the details have not been sketched, but it appears to have two aspects related much as the two sides of a coin—distinct, yet inseparable. The sociostructural manifestations are easily visible as they are reflected in the legal, economic, social, and political institutions. The sociopsychological ones are often intangible; hard to grasp and hard to alter. Group self-hate and distortion of perceptions to justify a preconceived interpretation of reality are just some of the factors being teased out.

Sexism is the word used to describe the particular kind of oppression that women experience. Starting from the traditional belief of the difference between the sexes, sexism embodies two core concepts. The first is that men are more important than women. Not necessarily superior—we are far too sophisticated these days to use that tainted term—but more important, more significant, more valuable, more worthwhile. This presumption justifies the idea that it is more important for a man, the "breadwinner," to have a job or a promotion, to be paid well, to have an education, and in general to have preference over a woman. It is the basis of men's feeling that if women enter a particular occupation they will degrade it and that men must then leave it or be themselves degraded; it is also at the root of women's feeling that they can raise the prestige of their professions by recruiting men, which they can do only by giving men the better jobs. From this value comes the attitude that a husband must earn more than his wife or suffer a loss of personal status and a wife must subsume her interests to his or be socially castigated. The first core concept of sexist thought, then, is that men do the important work in the world, and the work done by men is what is important.

The second core concept is that women are here for the pleasure and assistance of men. This is what is implied when women are told that their role is complementary to that of men; that they should fulfill their natural "feminine" functions; that they are "different" from men and should not compete with them. From this concept comes the attitude that women are and should be dependent on men for everything, especially their identities, the social definition of who they are. It defines the few roles for which women are socially rewarded—wife, mother, mistress; all pleasing or beneficial to men—and leads directly to the Pedestal theory that extols women who stay in their place as good helpmates to men.

It is this attitude that stigmatizes those women who do not marry or who do not devote their primary energies to the care of men and their children. Association with a man is the basic criterion for a woman's participation in this society, and one who does not seek her identity through a man is a threat to the social values. It is similarly this attitude that causes women's-liberation activists to be labeled as manhaters for exposing the nature of sexism. People feel that a woman not devoted to looking after a man must hate men or be unable to "catch" one. The effect of this second core concept of sexist thought, then, is that women's identities are defined by their relationship to men, and their social value is determined by that of the men they are related to.

The sexism of our society is so pervasive that we are not even aware of all its manifestations. Unless one has developed a sensitivity to its workings, by adopting a self-consciously contrary view, its activities are accepted with little question as "normal" and justified. People are said to "choose" what in fact they never thought about. A good example of sexism is what happened during and after World War II. The sudden onslaught of the war radically changed the whole structure of American social relationships as well as the American economy. Men were drafted into the army and women into the labor force. Now desperately needed, women had their wants provided for as were those of the boys at the front. Federal financing of day-care centers in the form of the Lanham Act passed Congress in a record two weeks. Special crash training programs were provided for the new women workers to give them skills they were not previously thought capable of exercising. Women instantly assumed positions of authority and responsibility unavailable to them only the year before.

But what happened when the war ended? Both men and women had heeded their country's call to duty to bring the struggle to a successful conclusion. Yet men were rewarded for their efforts and women punished for theirs. The returning soldiers were given the G.I. Bill and other veteran's benefits. They got their old jobs back and a disproportionate share of the new ones created by the war economy. Women, on the other hand, saw their child-care centers dismantled and their training programs cease. They were fired or demoted in droves and often found it difficult to enter colleges flooded with ex-GIs matriculating on government money. Is it any wonder that they heard the message that their place was in the home? Where else could they go?

The eradication of sexism, and of sexist practices like those described above, is obviously one of the major goals of the women's-liberation movement. But it is not enough to destroy a set of values and leave a normative vacuum. The old values have to be replaced with something. A movement can begin by declaring its opposition to the status quo, but eventually, if it is to succeed, it has to propose an alternative.

I cannot pretend to be definitive about the possible alternatives contemplated by the numerous participants in the women's liberation movement. Yet from the plethora of ideas and visions feminists have thought, discussed, and written about, I think that two predominant ideas have emerged. I call these the Egalitarian Ethic and the Liberation Ethic. They are closely related and merge into what can only be described as a feminist humanism.

The Egalitarian Ethic means exactly what it says. The sexes are equal; therefore sex roles must go. Our history has proven that institutionalized difference inevitably means inequity, and sex-role stereotypes have long since become anachronistic. Strongly differentiated sex roles were rooted in the ancient division of labor; their basis has been torn apart by modern technology. Their justification was rooted in the subjection of women to the reproductive cycle. That has already been destroyed by modern pharmacology. The cramped little boxes of personality and social function to which we assign people from birth must be broken open so that all people can develop independently, as individuals. This means that there will be an integration of social functions and life-styles of men and women as groups until, ideally, one cannot tell anything relevant about a person's social role by knowing that person's sex. But this greater similarity of the two groups also means more options for individuals and more diversity in the human race. No longer will there be men's work and women's work. No longer will humanity suffer a schizophrenic personality desperately trying to reconcile its "masculine" and "feminine" parts. No longer will marriage be an institution in which two half-people come together in hopes of making a whole.

The Liberation Ethic says this is not enough. Not only the limits of the roles must be changed, but their content as well. The Liberation Ethic looks at the kinds of lives currently being led by men as well as women and concludes that both are deplorable and neither is necessary. The social institutions that oppress women as women also oppress people as people and can be altered to make a more human existence for all. So much of our society is hung upon the framework of sex-role stereotypes and their reciprocal functions that the dismantling of this structure will provide the opportunity for making a more viable life for everyone.

It is important to stress that these two ethics must work in tandem. If the first is emphasized over the second, then we have a women's rights movement, not one of women's liberation. To seek for equality alone, given the current male bias of the social values, is to assume that women want to be like men or that men are worth emulating. It is to demand that women be allowed to participate in society as we know it, to get their piece of the pie, without questioning whether that society is worth participating in. Most feminists today find this view inadequate. Those women who are personally more comfortable in what is considered the male role must realize that that role is made possible only by the existence of the female sex role; in other words, only by the subjection of women. Therefore women cannot become equal to men without the destruction of those two interdependent, mutually parasitic roles. To fail to recognize that the integration of the sex roles and the equality of the sexes will inevitably lead to basic structural change is to fail to seize the opportunity to decide the direction of those changes.

It is just as dangerous to fall into the trap of seeking liberation without due concern for equality. This is the mistake made by many left radicals. They find the general human condition to be so wretched that they feel everyone should devote her/his energies to the millennial Revolution in the belief that the liberation of women will follow naturally the liberation of people.

However, women have yet to be defined as people, even among the radicals, and it is erroneous to assume their interests are identical to those of men. For women to subsume their concerns once again is to ensure that the promise of liberation will be a spurious one. There has yet to be created or conceived by any political or social theorist a revolutionary society in which women were equal to men and their needs duly considered. The sex-role structure has never been comprehensively challenged by male philosophers, and the systems they have proposed have all presumed the existence of a sex-role structure.

Such undue emphasis on the Liberation Ethic can also lead to a sort of Radical Paradox. This is a situation in which the New Left women frequently found themselves during the early days of the movement. They found repugnant the possibility of pursuing "reformist" issues that might be achieved without altering the basic nature of the system, and thus would, they felt, only strengthen the system. However, their search for a sufficiently radical action or issue came to naught and they found themselves unable to do anything out of fear that it might be counter-revolutionary. Inactive revolutionaries are much more innocuous than active reformists.

But even among those who are not rendered impotent, the unilateral pursuit of Liberation can take its toll. Some radical women have been so appalled at the condition of most men, and the possibility of becoming even partially what they are, that they have clung to the security of the role they know while waiting for the Revolution to liberate everyone. Some men, fearing that role-reversal is a goal of the women's liberation movement, have taken a similar position. Both have failed to realize that the abolition of sex roles must be a part of any radical restructuring of society and thus have failed to explore the possible consequences of such role integration. The goal they advocate may be one of liberation, but it does not involve women's liberation.

Separated from each other, the Egalitarian Ethic and the Liberation Ethic can be crippling, but together they can be a very powerful force. Separately they speak to limited interests; together they speak to all humanity. Separately, they afford but superficial solutions; together they recognize that sexism not only oppresses women but limits the potentiality of men. Separately, neither will be achieved because both are too narrow in scope; together, they provide a vision worthy of our devotion. Separately, these two ethics liberate neither women nor men; together, they can liberate both.

# Pauline Terrelonge Stone

# Feminist Consciousness and Black Women

Like the Populist movement at the turn of the century, and the Prohibition and Anti-war movements of subsequent decades, the contemporary feminist movement is having an enormous impact on Black America. It is not so much that black people have embraced the feminist movement, nor that they have even begun to identify with it. Rather its effect is seen in the controversy it has engendered within the race concerning the exact status of black males and females, and what the ideal role of each should be. A common (and some would argue, the dominant) view within the black community at the present time is that blacks have withstood the long line of abuses perpetrated against them ever since their arrival in this country mainly because of the black woman's fortitude, inner wisdom, and sheer ability to survive. As a corollary to this emphasis on the moral, spiritual, and emotional strength of the black woman in offsetting the potential annihilation of the race, proponents of this view stress the critical role that she plays in keeping the black family together and in supporting black males. Indeed, many blacks regard the role of uniting all blacks to be the primary duty of the black woman, one that should supersede all other roles that she might want to perform, and certainly one that is essentially incompatible with her own individual liberation.[1] Pursuit of the latter is generally judged to be a selfish goal detrimental to the overall welfare of the race. In short, sexism is viewed by many blacks, both male and female, to be a factor of minimal importance in the overall oppression of the black woman. The brunt of culpability for her unequal condition is accorded to racism.[2]

The object of this essay is to challenge this point of view. It is this writer's belief that the foregoing view of black female subordination expresses a narrow perspective on the nature of social oppression in American society, and because of this, the solutions that are commonly proposed—e.g., correcting the imbalance in the black sex ratio, or building stronger black families—are doomed to serve as only partial palliatives to the problems facing black women.

The first fact that must be grasped is that the black female condition in America has developed in a society where the dominant economic form is the market economy and the sole purpose of economic activity is the making of a profit on the part of large corporations. Because profit maximization is the superordinate goal to which all other social goals are merely subsidiary, labor is a premium. Labor must not only be made as highly productive as possible, it must also be obtained at the cheapest possible cost. The manipulation of the labor market is essential to attain these dual goals and provide for the effective functioning of the American economic order.

A major strategy for manipulating labor has been the maintenance of a sexual division of labor; i.e., a situation where certain roles are designated as male, others as female. The allocation of societal functions according to gender has been based on certain biological factors that objectively differentiate the sexes and the way those factors are interpreted through the ideology of sexism. The fact that women bear children has been used to justify their relegation to the domestic sphere. Their ability to reproduce has been made a duty, to which have been added the responsibilities of nurturing the offspring, serving the spouse, and performing or supervising all domestic-related chores.

It is easy to see how the pattern of female responsibility for the domestic sphere is useful to the economic system; it has allowed certain critical societal functions to be performed without the need of providing monetary remuneration.[3]

It is generally recognized that the ideology of racism has functioned to maintain blacks in a subordinate economic state.[4] Less readily recognized, however, are the similarities of the process of racial subordination to that of female subordination. In both cases the rationale for subordination resides in characteristics ascribed by the large capitalist interests, which are almost totally white male. Moreover, both forces—sexism and racism—create an occupationally segregated labor market, thereby giving rise to a situation where there are male jobs and female jobs, white jobs and black jobs.

From a cursory view, the white female has appeared historically to enjoy a privileged status; after all, as a result of sharing the bedrooms of white males, to her fall many of the material privileges and benefits of the society. But it is essential to recognize that rarely has she achieved these amenities on her own merit; nearly always it has been through the efforts and good graces of her spouse. The apparent freedoms and material well-being enjoyed by many white women depend not on their earning them, but on their fulfilling a nurturant and supportive role and, of course, maintaining a distinctive sexual identity through a socially defined image of female attractiveness. Thus, beauty and sexual attractiveness are essential to woman's economic survival, and maintaining these assets has become a major concern second only to fulfillment of her domestic functions.

The cult of the home, like so many other aspects of white America, has unfortunately permeated the culture of Afroamerica. While the cult in black society has been subjected to indigenous permutations,[5] in essence it bears close similarities to the white pattern, as would be expected in view of the fact that the economic forces affecting the larger society also impinge on the black subculture. Thus, within Afroamerican culture (and I emphasize within) maleness creates privileges—that is, certain freedoms and rights are attached to being male. Certain sexually specific behaviors are part of the black socialization process. The result is that marriage among blacks is just as much a union of unequals as it is in the larger society; child-rearing, domestic chores, and custody of children are largely female concerns. Hence, it is erroneous to argue that the domestic patterns of white society are not replicated in the black community. The housewife model may not fit completely but it is closely approximated in the sense that black women must bear the brunt of the domestic-related chores, even when they work.

What has historically differentiated black women from most white women is the peculiar way in which the racial and sexual caste systems have interfaced. Throughout their history in America, black women have had to face a condition of double dependency—one, on their spouses or mates, two, on their employers. Although these dependencies have also been the lot of many employed white women, proportionately fewer of the latter faced both of them. Double dependency has practically always been the onus of black women. Moreover, because of the racial caste system, a significant proportion of black married women, both historically and contemporaneously, have not had the economic support of their husbands—because their husbands are either absent or underemployed and unable to find employment. What is significant about the fact that so many black women have had to contribute to their families' financial support is that society's reaction to their plight has been sexist. Because they are more economically independent of a male breadwinner than is the societal norm, many black women have been made to feel that they usurped the male role, as if they—and not society—were ultimately responsible for the black man's inability to be the main breadwinner.

It is sometimes argued that the black woman's lack of choice over whether she should or should not work renders her condition totally dissimilar to that of a white woman. While it is true that black men have had a more difficult time providing for their families than white men, and that this has forced more black women to be in the labor force than white women, it must be recognized that the roles of both groups of women were ultimately conditioned by larger economic forces: white women were conditioned not to work in the productive sector, black women were conditioned to work. Those white women who were forced by economic circumstances to work outside the home were made to feel that their behavior was somehow deviant, and in most cases they abandoned their occupational participation when it was no longer absolutely necessary to their families' financial well being. Thus, neither group of women, white or black, had an option. Consequently, the behavior of both groups of women was a direct consequence of economic forces over which they exercised little or no control.

The foregoing picture of the different though mutually consistent roles played by black and white women has not remained static over the years. In the last 25 years, dramatic changes have taken place in the composition of the female labor force. Increasing numbers of married white women have sought paid employment and black women have made major gains in earnings. In short, the labor force profiles of both groups of women have become more and more similar, especially for young women.[6]

The movement of white females into the labor sphere has been partially caused by inflation, which has made it increasingly difficult for white males to maintain a middle-class standard of living solely from their earnings. This situation bears stark similarity to that which has traditionally prevailed in black society where familial economic survival—both in the working and middle classes—generally depends on both spouses' income.

As is the case with black women, the labor force participation of white females has not relieved them of the necessity of performing the traditional female domestic chores. For both groups of women, this has had a significant impact on the nature of their occupational participation, as it is generally interpreted by employers as a sign of the inherent unreliability of female labor—i.e., as a source of potential absenteeism and turnover—and used as an added rationale for relegating women to the least prestigious, least financially remunerative and most menial tasks. Even working women who are not wives or mothers find their occupational destinies affected by employer expectations that they do or will perform dual roles.

The entrance of more women into the productive sphere of the society has not brought about the demise of occupational segregation based on sex; indeed, economists reveal that occupational segregation based on sex has become entrenched.[7] Thus, women continue to predominate in those jobs that are least secure, least subject to unionization, least lucrative in terms of working conditions and fringe benefits, and least conducive to career advancement.[8] So the recent influx of women into the labor market has not appreciably reduced the chances of males to find employment in a labor market that continues to be occupationally segregated. Women are able to be absorbed by the economy as a result of the fact that in the past 30 years there has been a phenomenal increase in some traditional female jobs, primarily in the clerical and service sectors of the economy.

Women are judged by employers to be particularly suited for clerical and service jobs for three basic reasons. One, because of their socialization, they are assumed to prefer these jobs despite the low wages.[9] Two, female socialization trains them to display the attitudes of docility and compliance essential to the functioning of bureaucracies.[10] Three, because they are assumed to be ultimately supported by men, employers feel they will not resist being shunted in or out of the economy according to its boom and bust cycle. The latter is particularly detrimental to black women since a considerable proportion of them are the sole or major suppliers of familial incomes.

What is interesting about most of these female jobs is that they increasingly demand two credentials that are more difficult for black women than white to attain. One is a relatively high level of education, at least a high school diploma. The other is the facility to read, write, and verbally communicate in mainstream English. Although it is not readily acknowledged, jobs as telephone operators, typists, secretaries, etc., commonly require an ability to use the language of white middle-class society. Because of their subcultural status and the low quality of education they receive, black women historically have been at a distinct disadvantage in manipulating the cultural symbols of the larger society. Thus, the deprecatory societal evaluation of black linguistic patterns coupled with the institutional racism of the nation's educational system has worked to black women's disadvantage in the competition between black and white female workers for clerical jobs. In 1977, the proportion of black and white working women in clerical jobs was 35.9 percent and 26.0 percent respectively.[11] Nonetheless, the rapid infiltration of black women into the clerical sphere in recent years seems to indicate that the discrimination against black women holding clerical jobs is declining. Whether they are actually achieving total equality with white women in this sphere, or whether white women hold relatively more prestigious jobs is a question that needs further investigation. What is clear is that the wage levels of black and white women workers have now almost completely converged.

While black men are also victims of white ethnocentrism and poor education, their chances of earning higher pay than black women are enhanced as racial barriers fall because many high-paying male occupations—e.g., in craft unions, municipal services, and the military—do not place such demand on the communication skills that are the sine qua non for job advancement in clerical jobs. Indeed, the military offers many black men the chance of making up the deficiencies they incurred in the nation's educational system, as well as the opportunity to gain significant social benefits that are, for many, the route to upward occupational mobility. The continued sexual stereotyping of positions in those areas that have belatedly opened up to blacks reduces the chances of black women moving out of the traditionally female, clerical jobs. Thus, the erosion of racial barriers in employment is working more to the advantage of black men than black women.[12]

It is important to recognize this point because it contradicts the commonly held view that the black woman fares infinitely better in American society than the black man. Those who advance this claim generally rest their arguments on two facts. First, a greater proportion of black women than men hold jobs that are designated as professional in the Bureau of the Census classification schema, and second, historically, black women were more likely to have graduated from high school and college than black men.

Yet it must be recognized that black women have never held high-status professional jobs in any great numbers. This is because even in the professional occupational category, rigid sexual occupational segregation persists. Black women are able to find relatively easy access to such female occupations as nursing and teaching, but have a hard time, particularly in comparison to black men, gaining access to higher status occupations such as law, medicine, and dentistry.[13] The latter are just as much male fields among blacks as among whites.

Black women's greater educational attainment is similarly misleading. First of all, in the society at large women are more likely to have graduated from high school than men, so that this being the case among blacks is not an aberration. Moreover, while the number of black female college graduates has historically exceeded that of black male graduates,[14] this was not the case in all parts of the nation,[15] and it is no longer generally true. Since the advent of a whole gamut of minority programs designed to boost black college enrollment in the seventies, black males have made strides in attaining a college education and are now equally represented among black students attending college.[16] Nor does attending college necessarily have the same impact on women as on men. A study of historically black colleges in the 1960s, containing half of all black college students, showed that the

women significantly lowered their aspirations for professional achievement by the time they were seniors, while the men maintained or
increased theirs.

> These black college-educated women appeared to be significantly
> limited by sexual constraints in their career aspirations. They
> consistently chose traditionally feminine occupations and very few
> planned to venture into occupations dominated by men. Even more
> significantly, perhaps, the women saw the "feminine" jobs they
> selected as having lower status and demanding less ability than the
> "masculine" occupations—a telling comment on how they viewed
> what they had to offer in the job world.[17]

The association of femaleness with a distinctive economic function
transcends racial lines. This fact is often obscured by certain racial
differences in female labor force participation, such as the higher
unemployment rate of black women than of white women, as well as the
tendency of black women to begin their careers in jobs lower in status,
their greater expectations of working, and their tendency to value
higher wages above job satisfaction.[18] While these differences should not
be underestimated, it is myopic to focus on them exclusively in assessing
the black female condition. Gump's and Rivers' observation based on
an extensive review of the literature on black-white differences in labor
force participation is particularly poignant here. They state:

> Much data has been presented portraying the black woman as more
> likely to enter the labor force, more interested in doing so, more
> likely to work full time and continuously, and more necessary to
> the financial welfare of her family. . . While such facts suggest a
> woman much less constricted by the traditional role than her white
> counterpart, it is equally true that black women choose occupations
> traditional for women, are motivated perhaps more by a sense of
> responsibility than by achievement need, are much more traditional
> in their sex-role attitudes than are young white women, and to
> some extent seem burdened by the responsibility they carry.
>
> Thus it appears that black women have *not* escaped many of the
> constraints imposed upon white women, though they are free of
> some of them. . . There are those who would assert too quickly the
> freedom of black women, and they must be reminded of her
> bondage.[19]

If there is much in the objective condition of black women that
warrants the development of a black feminist consciousness, why have

so many black women failed to recognize the patterns of sexism that directly impinge on their everyday lives? Why have they failed to address a social force that unremittingly thwarts their ability to compete on an equal basis in the society?

Five factors have contributed to this situation. The most formidable is that many black intellectuals and spokespeople have ignored the issue of sexism, largely because it has been viewed as a racially divisive issue. That is, a feminist consciousness has been regarded as a force that could generate internal conflict between black males and black females. It is this writer's firm conviction that far from being a source of internecine conflict, a feminist consciousness would contribute to the welfare of the race in a variety of ways.

1  It would enable black men and women to attain a more accurate and deeper level of understanding of many of the social problems that are currently undermining the viability of the race. Such problems as the black male unemployment rate, the absence of the black male in the family, the large representation of black women on welfare, and the high black "illegitimacy" rate are just a few of the many social problems afflicting blacks that are, in part at least, attributable to the operation of sexism in our society.

2  Elimination of sexism on the interpersonal level within black culture would result in each sex developing their individual talents and capacities unhindered by societal definitions of appropriate sexual behavior, thus increasing the general pool of black abilities.

3  A feminist consciousness, in ridding black males and females of their socially conditioned anxieties concerning masculinity and feminity, would foster greater psychological well-being and thereby strengthen the interpersonal bonds that are constantly being eroded and loosened by the impact of interpersonal sexism.

A second factor that helps to explain the absence of feminist consciousness among black women is the ideology of racism. Racism is so ingrained in American culture, and so entrenched among many white women, that black females have been reluctant to admit that anything affecting the white female could also affect them. Indeed, many black women have tended to see all whites regardless of sex, as sharing the same objective interest, and clearly the behavior of many white women vis-à-vis blacks has helped to validate this reaction.

A third factor is the message that emerged in the black social movement of the sixties. In one sense, this movement worked to the detriment of black women because they were told in many different ways that the liberation of the black man was more important than their own liberation. In fact, they were often given to believe that any attempt on their part to take an equal place with the black man in the movement would contribute to his emasculation.[20]

The idea of black matriarchy, another ideological ploy commonly introduced by academicians and policy makers, is a fourth factor that has suppressed the development of a feminist consciousness among black women. In a nutshell, this view holds that in their conjugal and parental relationships black women are more dominant than black men and so black and white women relate to their mates in altogether different ways.[21] It is easy to see how this view of black women could be used by some to negate the fact of black female oppression: if the black woman were indeed found to be more dominant than the black man this could be construed as meaning that she is not dependent on him, and thus not in need of liberation. In fact, scholarly exploration of the issue has revealed the idea of black matriarchy to be mythical and has shown that the relationship of black and white women to their mates is fundamentally similar. And even if a black matriarchy did exist, it would be fallacious to infer from this that the black woman is not sexually oppressed, for her subordination is a derivative of both her family-related role and her position in the productive sphere of the economy. Thus the single and married black woman are both placed in positions of subservience whenever they seek employment. Both are subjected to the manipulative tactics that are used to keep all female laborers—white and black, married and unmarried—in an unequal economic state.

What the participants in the debate on black matriarchy fail to recognize is the white bias of their viewpoints. Implicit in their arguments is the idea that any matriarchy is unnatural and deviant. To attach such a pejorative label to matriarchy, and to view the patriarchal form as a positive good or an index of normality, is to accept the normative standard of the larger white society. Given the role that the family plays in supporting and perpetuating existing unequal economic arrangements, it may be fitting for us to question whether it would not be in the best interests of blacks to work out familial relationships that deviate from the conventional patriarchal norm and approximate a more egalitarian pattern, thereby challenging the racial and sexual status quo.

A final factor that has inhibited the development of a feminist consciousness among women in American society in general, and black females in particular, has been the church. Biblical support for sexual inequality is as strong today as it ever was, and the Christian church has played a preeminent role in validating the patriarchal nature of western culture.[22] This is as true in black churches as it is in white ones, although the role of black religion in enchaining black women has been little subject to discussion.[23] The persistence of patriarchal views in black churches is undoubtedly due in some measure to the fact that most of our noted black theologians are men. But more importantly, it persists because of the deep religiosity of black people today and the fact that most black religions are basically Christian despite some deviations and modifications. For whatever reason, it is significant that the church is the most important social institution in the black community and the one in which black women (in contrast to black men) spend most of their time and energy. This dedication undoubtedly has contributed in no small part to the black female's passive acceptance of her subservient societal role. Even so-called black "nationalist" religions, which proffer a different view of the world and a substitute for the teachings of Christianity, have failed to come to terms with the subordination of black women in our society. Indeed, some have even adopted theological preachments designed to stultify the development of female talents and to push them yet further into the traditional servile role of mother and wife.[24]

In sum, black women in America have been placed in a dependent position vis-à-vis men. The source of their dependency is dual: It originates in the role they have been socialized to play in the family, and the discrimination they face when they seek remunerative employment outside the home. Because sexual dependency works to the detriment of the entire race—both male and female—all blacks, regardless of sex, need to recognize the way in which their behavior, be it familial, marital, occupational, or otherwise, is subject to social control. From this realization they need to develop alternative behavioral norms for themselves and socialization patterns for their offspring that will challenge the distribution of power in America.

The view that racism is the sole cause of black female subordination in America today exhibits a very simplistic view of the black female condition. The economic processes of the society subordinate different groups of workers in different ways, but always for the same end. Because white supremacy and male chauvinism are merely symptoms of the same economic imperatives, it is facile to argue that white pigmentation is the sine qua non for the attainment of power in America, and thus that white women share the same objective interests as white men, and have nothing in common with black women. While whiteness may be a contributory condition for the attainment of social privilege, sex and socioeconomic status are contingent conditions. Because color, gender, and wealth are at the present time collective determinants of power and privilege in America, it is almost impossible to disentangle their individual effects. Thus, those who would assert that the elimination of one type of social discrimination should have priority over all others display a naive conceptualization of the nature of power in American society and the multi-faceted character of social oppression.

## NOTES

1   Examples of literature supporting this perspective are Mae King, "Oppression and Power: The Unique Status of the Black Woman in the American Political System," *Social Science Quarterly,* 56 (1975), 116–28; Linda La Rue, "The Black Movement and Women's Liberation," *Black Scholar,* 1 (May 1970), 36–42; and Julia Mayo, "The New Black Feminism: A Minority Report," in *Contemporary Sexual Behavior: Critical Issues in the 1970's,* Joseph Zubin and John Money, eds. (Baltimore: The Johns Hopkins Press, 1973), pp. 175–86.

2   Notable exceptions are Barbara Sizemore, "Sexism and the Black Male," *Black Scholar,* 4 (March–April 1973), 2–11; Aileen Hernandez, "Small Change for Black Women," *Ms.,* 3 (August 1974), 16–18; Elizabeth Almquist, "Untangling the Effects of Race and Sex: The Disadvantaged Status of Black Women," *Social Science Quarterly,* 56 (1975), 129–42; Charmeyne D. Nelson, "Myths About Black Women Workers in Modern America," *Black Scholar,* 6 (March 1975), 11–15; and William A. Blakey, "Everybody Makes The Revolution: Some Thoughts on Racism and Sexism," *Civil Rights Digest,* 6 (Spring 1974), 11–19.

3   Margaret Bentsen, "The Political Economy of Women's Liberation," *Monthly Review,* 21 (September 1970); Juliet Mitchell, *Women's Estate* (New York: Random House, 1971), pp. 99–158; Paul Baran and Paul Sweezy, *Monopoly Capital* (New York: Monthly Review Press, 1966); Gayle Rubin, "The Traffic in Women: Notes on the 'Political Economy' of Sex," in *Toward an Anthropology of Women,* R. Reiter, ed. (New York: Monthly Review Press, 1975); Jean Gardiner, "Women's Domestic Labor," *New Left Review* (January–February 1975), 47–59; and Sheila Rowbotham, *Woman's Consciousness, Man's World* (Baltimore: Penguin Books, 1974).

4   See among others Harold Baron, "The Demand for Black Labor: Historical Notes on the Political Economy of Racism," *Radical America*, 5 (March–April 1971), 1–46.

5   For further discussion of black sex-role socialization see among others Diane K. Lewis, "The Black Family: Socialization and Sex Roles," *Phylon*, 34 (Fall 1975), 221–37; Carlfred Broderick, "Social Heterosexual Development Among Urban Negroes and Whites," *Journal of Marriage and the Family*, 27 (May 1965), 200–03; Alice R. Gold and M. Carol St. Ange, "Development of Sex-Role Stereotypes in Black and White Elementary Girls," *Developmental Psychology*, 10 (May 1974), 461; and Boone E. Hammond and Joyce Ladner, "Socialization into Sexual Behavior in a Negro Slum Ghetto," in *The Individual, Sex, and Society*, Carlfred B. Broderick and Jesse Bernard, eds. (Baltimore: Johns Hopkins, 1969), pp. 41–52.

6   See Elizabeth Almquist's article in this volume for more data on this point.

7   Barbara Reagan and Martha Blaxall, "Occupational Segregation in International Women's Year," in *Women and the Workplace*, Martha Blaxall and Barbara Reagan, eds. (Chicago: University of Chicago Press, 1976). Entire volume of the work is devoted to occupational segregation based on sex. See also Elizabeth Koontz, "Women as Minority Group," in *Voices of the New Feminism*, Mary Lou Thompson, ed. (Boston: Beacon Press, 1970), pp. 77–86.

8   Victor R. Fuchs, "Differences in Hourly Earnings Between Men and Women," *Monthly Labor Review*, 94 (May 1971), 9–15; and Elizabeth Waldman and Beverly J. McEaddy, "Where Women Work—An Analysis by Industry and Occupation," *Monthly Labor Review*, 97 (May 1974), 3–13.

9   Edward A. Nicholson and Roger D. Roderick, *Correlates of Job Attitudes Among Young Women* (Columbus: The Ohio State University Research Foundation, 1973), p. 10.

10  See Lenore Weitzman's article in this volume.

11  *Employment and Earnings* (Washington, D.C.: U.S. Government Printing Office, January 1978), p. 152.

12  Stuart H. Garfinkle, "Occupation of Women and Black Workers, 1962–74," *Monthly Labor Review*, 98 (November 1975), 25–35.

13  Elizabeth Almquist, "Untangling the Effects of Race and Sex"; and Marion Kilson, "Black Women in the Professions, 1890–1970," *Monthly Labor Review*, 100 (May 1977), 38–41.

14  Part of the reason for this is that until recently blacks were basically a rural people and it is generally the case for farmer families to withdraw males from schools to work the farm but not females since farming is a male occupation. For further discussion of how this has contributed to present-day disparities in black male and female occupational status see E. Wilbur Bock, "Farmer's Daughter Effect: The Case of the Negro Female Professionals," *Phylon* (Spring 1969), 17–26.

15  Andrew Billingsley, *Black Families in White America* (Englewood Cliffs, N.J.: Prentice-Hall, 1968), pp. 79–82.

16  According to unpublished data from the Bureau of Labor Statistics, the October 1977 Current Population Survey showed that of all black high school students who graduated in 1977, 51 percent of the men and 50 percent of the women went on to college that fall.

17   Patricia Gurin and Carolyn Gaylord, "Educational and Occupational Goals of Men and Women at Black Colleges," *Monthly Labor Review*, 99 (June 1976), pp. 13–14.

18   Patricia Cayo Sexton, R. & D. Monograph 46, *Women and Work*, Employment and Training Administration (Washington, D.C.: Department of Labor, 1977), p. 15; and Joyce O. Beckett, "Working Wives: A Racial Comparison," *Social Work*, 21 (November 1976), 463–71.

19   Janice Porter Gump and L. Wendell Rivers, *The Consideration of Race In Efforts to End Sex Bias*, National Institute of Education (Washington, D.C.: U.S. Department of Health, Education and Welfare, 1973), pp. 24–25.

20   Joyce A. Ladner, *Tomorrow's Tomorrow: The Black Woman* (Garden City, N.Y.: Doubleday & Co., 1971), p. 284; Robert Staples, *The Black Woman in America* (Chicago: Nelson Hall, 1975), pp. 174–76; Janice Gump, "Comparative Analysis of Black Women's and White Women's Sex Role Attitudes," *Journal of Consulting and Clinical Psychology*, 43 (1975), 862–63; and Cellestine Ware, *Woman Power: The Movement for Women's Liberation* (New York: Tower Publications, 1970), pp. 75–99.

21   S. Parker and R. J. Kleiner, "Social and Psychological Dimensions of Family Role Performance of the Negro Male," *Journal of Marriage and the Family*, 31 (1969), 500–06; John H. Scanzoni, *The Black Family in Modern Society* (Boston: Allyn and Bacon, 1971), Katheryn Thomas Dietrich, "A Re-examination of the Myth of Black Matriarchy," *Journal of Marriage and the Family*, 37 (May 1975), 367–74; H. H. Hyman and J. S. Reed, "Black Matriarchy Reconsidered: Evidence from Secondary Analysis of Sample Surveys," *Public Opinion Quarterly*, 33 (1969), 346–54; Robert Staples, "The Myth of the Black Matriarchy," in *The Black Family*, Robert Staples, ed. (Belmont, Calif.: Wadsworth Publishing Company, 1971), pp. 149–59; and Alan Berger and William Simon, "Black Families and the Moynihan Report: A Research Evaluation," *Social Problems*, 33 (December 1974), 145–61.

22   Simone de Beauvoir, *The Second Sex* (New York: Vintage Books, 1974); Susan Bell, *Women, From the Greeks to the French Revolution* (Belmont, Calif.: Wadsworth Publishing Co., 1973); and Alan Cuming, "Women in Greek and Pauline Thought," *Journal of the History of Ideas*, 34 (December 1973), 517–28.

23   A notable exception is Rosemary Reuther, "Crisis in Sex and Race: Black vs. Feminist Theology," *Christianity and Crisis*, 34 (April 15, 1974), 67–73; and "Continuing the Discussion: A Further Look at Feminist Theology," *Christianity and Crisis*, 34 (June 24, 1974), 139–43.

24   Barbara Sizemore, "Sexism and the Black Male" *Black Scholar*, 4 (March–April 1973), 2–11; and Harry Edwards, "Black Muslim and Negro Christian Family Relationships," *Journal of Marriage and the Family*, 30 (November 1968), 604–11.

# Barbara Bovee Polk

# Male Power and the Women's Movement*

The relationship between females and males in this and virtually every society has been a power relationship—of males over females. The current women's movement, a revitalization of earlier feminist movements, seeks to end or reverse this power relationship. As such, feminists are concerned with analyzing the nature of male power and the condition of women and developing organizations and vehicles for change that are consistent with feminist principles.

In this paper I shall consider four conceptualizations of women's oppression, their assessment of the various modes of male power, and their pre-

*Reprinted by special permission from *The Journal of Applied Behavioral Science*. "Male Power and the Women's Movement," by Barbara Bovee Polk, Vol. 10, No. 3, pp. 415–431. Copyright 1974 NTL Institute for Applied Behavioral Science.

ferred strategies for changing the status of women in contemporary society. Throughout this paper, it is important to remember that the women's movement is not an organization with officers and a unified theory and set of activities. Instead, it consists of the ideas and activities of women responding to the conditions of their oppression whether as individuals, informal small groups, or large structured organizations. Although I see women who do not consider themselves to be "women's libbers" as part of the movement to the extent that they attempt to restructure their lives in nontraditional ways, here I am concerned with the theory and activities of those women who identify with the movement.

## THE CONTEMPORARY CONDITION OF WOMEN

Many individuals have attempted to account for the historical origins of the near universal oppression of women, grounding their theories in biological differences, evolutionary genetics, economic relationships, and so on. Although these are of interest to most feminists, we are aware that whatever its origins, oppression of women exists in the present and must be combated now. For that reason most contemporary analyses do not deal in depth, if at all, with why and when questions, but rather attempt to understand the current relationship between the sexes as a basis for action.

### Modal analyses

I see four major approaches to understanding the contemporary condition of women: analyses in terms of sex roles, differences between feminine and masculine culture, male-female power relationships, and economic relationships.* Because the purpose of this paper is not to discuss the conflict and factions within the movement, I present a "modal" analysis of each viewpoint rather than ideal types. Extreme

---

*A basic tenet of the women's movement is that no one woman can speak for it. This paper expresses my own perspective on the movement, and it is limited by my own experiences, understanding, and biases. It must be read as such. The dozen women who reviewed an earlier draft suggested that I confront that problem directly. Perhaps it is useful to say, then, that by training and because I believe it is most politically effective at this time, I prefer the sex-role approach, heavily modified by acceptance of much of the cultural and power analyses. Although I believe that sexism is deeply embedded in capitalism and that its eradication will require a fundamental change in economic structure, I disagree with the socialist view outlined in this paper.

positions within each viewpoint are largely omitted and perspectives overlap to some degree, for in practice, most feminists subscribe to some combination of two or more perspectives. Although I refer to groups or writings that seem to me to fit a particular approach, it should be kept in mind that in no case is it possible to provide a "pure" example.

**Sex-role socialization**  Drawing on social-psychological analysis, this approach views the contemporary oppression of women as the result of the inculcation of socially defined sex roles. This approach is the basic one adopted by most academic social scientists, as well as well-known feminists such as Gloria Steinem, Betty Friedan, Carolyn Bird, and Germaine Greer. It is also the basic orientation of such national groups as the National Organization for Women, Women's Equity Action League, and the National Women's Political Caucus.

The main components of this analysis are:

1 Each society *arbitrarily* views a wide variety of personality characteristics, interests, and behaviors as the virtually exclusive domain of one sex or the other. The fact that societies vary in their definition of feminine and masculine roles is proof that sex roles are based on social rather than on biological factors.

2 The parceling up of human characteristics into "feminine" and "masculine" deprives all of full humanness.

3 Sex roles are systematically inculcated in individuals, beginning at birth, by parents, the educational system, peers, the media, and religious institutions, and are supported by the social sciences and the economic, political, and legal structures of society. Individuals learn appropriate roles through role models and differential reinforcement.

4 Sex roles form the core of an individual's identity. Because self-evaluation is closely linked to sex ("That's a good girl/boy") and to adequacy of sex-role performance, the propriety of the role to which one was socialized becomes difficult to dislodge in adulthood, even when it is seen as dysfunctional. In addition, individuals often link concepts of their adequacy in sex *roles* to their adequacy in *sexual* interactions and vice versa. Thus, a threat to one's role definition is perceived as a threat to one's sexual identity. Such threats are a major mechanism for psychologically locking people into traditional roles.

5 Sex roles are basic roles and thus modify expectations in virtually all other roles. Differential expectations by sex in other roles leads to differential perception of the same behavior in a woman and a man (a businessman is strong-willed; a business woman, rigid). Differential expectations and selective perception limit the extent to which individuals can step outside their sex roles and are major mechanisms for the maintenance of these roles.

6 Female and male roles form a role system in which the expectations for and behaviors of each sex have implications for the definitions of and behaviors of the other sex. (A man can't be a "gentleman" if a woman will not let him hold the door for her.)

7 The male role has higher status. This status is directly rewarding and provides access to other highly valued statuses and rewards; however, male status also places heavy pressures on men to maintain that status.

8 Males have power over females because of role definitions. "Being powerful" is itself a part of the masculine role definition. In addition, the "rationality" assigned to the male role gives men access to positions of expertise as well as credibility even when they are not experts.

**Conflicting cultures approach**    This approach focuses on value differences rather than role differences between the sexes. It points out that women who talk only in terms of role differences may seek a solution to their oppression by emulating male roles. The cultural approach is therefore a more overtly feminist analysis, focusing on the positive aspects of feminine culture. Examples of this approach include Firestone, Burris, and Solanas,[1] although the latter is quite different from the view presented here. The main ideas behind this approach follow.

1 Just as roles are dichotomized by sex, so are values. "Masculine" values include competitiveness, aggressiveness, independence, and rationality; "feminine" values include their counterparts: cooperativeness, passivity, dependence, and emotionality. These values are not inherent as male or female (according to most versions of this analysis) but are socially assigned and derived from sex-role definitions. *All* are important qualities of humanness.

2 Masculine values have higher status and constitute the dominant and visible culture of the society. They form the structure of

personal, political, and economic relationships and provide the standard for adulthood and normality.

3   Women are oppressed and devalued because they embody an alternative culture. (In one version of this analysis,[2] men are seen as colonizing women's bodies in order to subordinate an alien value system, much as men colonized the land and peoples of other civilizations.)

4   Men are socialized almost exclusively to the masculine value system, but women receive dual socialization because of the dominance of male institutions and because they must comprehend masculine values in order to survive (the slave syndrome). Dual socialization tempts women to try assimilation into the masculine culture, but it also gives women insight into the artificiality of the value dichotomization.

5   Masculine values are largely responsible for the crisis in our society. Competitiveness pits human against human and results in racism, sexism, and colonialism, as well as the rape of the natural environment in the pursuit of economic power: Aggressiveness leads to war. Exaggerated independence inhibits society's ability to solve common problems by failing to recognize the fundamental interdependence among humans and between humans and the physical environment. Excessive rationality is linked to the building of a run-away technological and scientific system incapable of recognizing and granting legitimacy to human needs and feelings.

**Power analysis**   This perspective does not deny the importance of sex roles and cultural differences in bringing about and maintaining the oppression of women, but it views them as symptomatic of the primary problem, which is the domination of females by males. Thus, it is more concerned with focusing on the mechanisms of male power than on its origins; e.g., Millett[4] and Chesler.[5] Its major tenets may be summarized as follows:

1   Men have power and privilege by virtue of their sex. They may and do oppress women in personal relationships, in groups, and on the job.

2   It is in men's interest to maintain that power and privilege. There is status in the ability to oppress someone else, regardless of the oppression one suffers oneself. In addition, power over women in

personal relationships gives men what they want, whether that be sex, smiles, chores, admiration, increased leisure, or control itself.

3 Men occupy and actively exclude women from positions of economic and political power in society. Those positions give men a heavily disproportionate share of the rewards of society, especially economic rewards.

4 Marriage is an institution of personal and sexual slavery for women, who are duped into marrying by the love ethic or economic necessity.

5 Although most males are also oppressed by the system under which we live, they are not oppressed, as females are, because of their sex.

6 Feminine roles and cultural values are the product of oppression. Idealization of them is dysfunctional to change.

7 Males have greater behavioral and economic options, including the option of oppressing women. Where individuals have wider options, they are responsible for their choices. In this way, men are responsible, individually and collectively, for their oppression of women.

8 Men oppress women through the use of brute force, by restricting options and selectively reinforcing women within these options, through control of resources and major institutions, and through expertise and access to the media.

**Socialist perspective**   This approach holds that the oppression of women is only one aspect of the destructiveness of a generally oppressive economic system and therefore contends that socialism is a prerequisite to feminism. As the basis for outlining this viewpoint, I am using the general orientation of The Socialist Worker's Party and the International Socialists, as discussed with me in conversation, and the writings of Reed.[6] Although I have chosen to use the viewpoint of socialist organizations heavily dominated by males (thus they are not feminist organizations), women in these groups often form formal or informal caucuses on feminist issues. Closely related are the analyses of the unaffiliated, all-female socialist groups, although these groups generally disagree with the following analysis by affirming the need for an independent women's movement. Their approach is represented by

Mitchell.[7] Simone de Beauvoir's work, *The Second Sex*, fits primarily into this category, although the work is so broad that it incorporates the main ideas from all analyses presented here. That de Beauvoir identifies with the socialist perspective on the women's movement as presented here is clear in her autobiography, *Force of Circumstances*.[8]

1 The oppression of women originated in the concept of private property. Women were defined as property largely because of their ability to reproduce, thereby providing new workers as well as heirs for the elite. Because private property is the institution on which capitalism is founded, the oppression of women is fundamentally linked to capitalist structures and is necessary to their continuation.

2 Sexism is functional to capitalism because it enables capitalists to buy two workers for the price of one. A man is paid a wage; his wife, who is unpaid, provides the necessary services for him to perform his job (even if she, too, has a job).

3 Women provide a cheap reserve labor force for capitalists, thereby holding down wages and increasing profits.

4 Although the rebellion of women against their roles is contrary to the interests of capitalism, an independent women's movement is not, for it separates one oppressed group from others and forestalls a coalition that could overthrow the system.

5 Equality for women is impossible until capitalism is replaced by socialism.

### Male power

These four perspectives on the contemporary condition of women differentially weigh and interpret the current sources of male power but are in general agreement as to what they are. For purposes of this discussion, I shall draw primarily on the language of the power analysts because they have given the most systematic attention to this issue.

**Normative power**    By virtue of their sex and their control of traditional sex-role definitions, men are able to manipulate women's behavior by ignoring, misrepresenting, devaluing, and discrediting women or their accomplishments, especially when women deviate from traditional roles. Some examples are the omission of women's contributions from history texts and the attribution of women's scientific discoveries and artistic achievements to men. In the extreme, the institutionalization of traditional sex-role definitions in the theories of the mental health professions allows males on a day-to-day basis to label female role deviants as "crazy" or to punish their deviations through incarceration.[9]

**Institutional power**    Not only do males have differential amounts of and access to money, education, and positions of influence, they use this control to limit life options for women and extend life options for men. For example, male control of the media, religion, and the educational system is used to influence public opinion and practice. Combined with normative power, males use these public socialization institutions to inculcate traditional role and value systems in both females and males, thereby reducing the probability that females will aspire to or succeed in moving beyond traditional roles.

When women do attempt to change or broaden their roles, they are blocked by male control of the economic institutions. Women lack skills and access to skills through formal education as well as through recognized apprenticeship and trainee programs. Denied access to well-paid jobs, women lack money, or access to money through loans that would enable them to change their condition. Thus, dominance of economic institutions by males locks women into traditional roles.

Male dominance of law and politics supports their control through other institutional means. Thus laws are made, interpreted, and enforced with male self-interest in mind. For example, the Supreme Court, with one exception, has refused to apply the Fourteenth and Fifth Amendment guarantees of "equal protection under law" to women, making necessary a *special* constitutional amendment even to establish the legal basis for female equality in society.

The two areas women are said to control, domestic life and education of the young, are delegated to them by men, who retain final authority and monitor the way in which women carry out these roles.

**Control of options through reward power**    Men use their institutional and normative power to control women's life choices not only through restricting their options but also through reinforcing choices within them. This is a subtle form of control, as Skinner makes clear; since women do receive some rewards for "appropriate" behavior, those who rebel risk losing real rewards. The recent slight broadening of options is primarily a matter of reinforcing new forms of behavior and does not change the basic control of females by males, i.e., does not change who metes out reinforcement.

**The power of expertise**    In all areas—from international affairs, space technology, and group dynamics to education, child rearing, and female sexuality—the experts are male. This is largely because male dominance of the educational institutions and the media allows males to select which individuals will become experts and which experts will receive public exposure. For a woman, this means that when she wants information or advice in any field, she must rely for the most part on males whose expertise may serve the interests of male supremacy or male values rather than her own interests.

**Psychological power**    Males, having suppressed feminine culture, have access to institutional power partly because they "fit" the value structures of the institutions better than do women (for example, see Epstein's discussion of status-set typing, and Chafetz' illustration of the interaction between sex roles and professional roles.[10]) The confidence of being "right," of fitting, gives even incompetent men an important source of psychological power over women, who have not been so wholly socialized into the masculine value structure.

**Brute force**    Not only are most men stronger than most women but they are trained to have or show confidence in their physical strength. Men physically dominate women by beating wives and girl friends or by rape and threat of rape. Rape is a form of social control that serves to restrict women's autonomy and mobility. The threat of rape is reinforced by whistling and other street hassles which, to women, implicitly carry the possibility of physical attack.

## APPROACHES TO CHANGE—A NEW SOCIETY

Surrounded by male power, from sources that overlap and reinforce one another, women find that they must totally transform society to achieve their goal of freedom from oppression. As a result, strategies for change are many and diverse, giving the women's movement the appearance of a lack of direction. However, no one tactic is intended to accomplish the entire task. Groups choose targets and activities partly on the basis of their analyses of women's oppression, partly on the basis of available opportunities for action, and partly according to the personal dispositions of any particular group or collective of women. There is, then, no easy one-to-one match between the perspectives of the participants and the activities of the movement, which I briefly review in the following section.

### De- or resocialization of oneself

Self-change is important for all perspectives, though in the socialist approach, it is seen as effected through social action. To the extent that sex-role definitions, value systems, and the power based on them are socialized characteristics, each of us to some extent participates in those definitions. The most prevalent activity in the women's movement, therefore, has been the small consciousness-raising or rap group in which women piece together an understanding of their oppression and challenge their assumptions about themselves, other women, and men. Within these groups, women find that their experiences, private fears, and self-doubts are not unique but common to many other women and related to their social conditioning. Personal experience thus becomes a basis for political analysis and action.

Most groups focus on building solidarity and support among members, replacing the distrust and dislike of other women with which many enter these groups. In addition, most groups raise questions about appropriate routes to liberation, challenge the notion that liberation means imitating male roles and values, and debate the extent to which individual freedom is possible in the absence of general structural change in the society. In this way, women begin to redefine and change themselves and build a basis for initiating larger changes.

### Changing personal interactions and micro-role systems

New definitions are useless if not put into action. All perspectives encourage actions to redefine personal relationships and micro-role systems, although they vary to some extent in the kinds of actions they favor. The sex-role analysis focuses heavily on individual change of personal relationships and the broadening of individual life options. The cultural perspective emphasizes decreasing dependence on emotional support from males and substituting strong alliances among women. The power perspective favors direct confrontation with males in all interactions—on the job, in the street, and in personal relationships.

Since, in a sex-role system, definitions are upheld and reinforced by both role actors, when a woman moves outside of traditional definitions, she forces a change in complementary roles. For example, the rap group is often important in providing support for married women seeking more egalitarian sharing of housework and child care, or attempting to return to school, take a job, or resume a career; and for single women attempting to deal with the restrictiveness of a father or boyfriend. Through an analysis of the costs and rewards to both parties in a relationship, the group helps its members find ways of decreasing the rewards (increasing the costs) for male resistance to such changes, while increasing their rewards for more egalitarian behavior.

The support function of women's groups is a step toward substituting women for men as a basic reference group. This process reduces women's reliance on the kinds of rewards they receive from men. Approval and emotional support is instead sought within the group. In this way, a new set of sisterly relationships is formed, which, for some groups, involves mutual economic support in living communes and sexual gratification in lesbian relationships, making women largely self-sufficient and males almost irrelevant.

Still, almost all women must relate to men in less personal interactions. The power analysts, in particular, help each other develop strategies for confronting rather than ignoring street hassles, for confronting and changing condescending comments and gestures in work and other settings, and for challenging the "servant chores" (making coffee, buying presents, dusting the office, providing a sympathetic ear to the boss) that are a part of many female occupations.

Learning karate and other forms of self-defense, as well as engaging in sports activities, is one popular feminist strategy for combating the physical power men have over women. Many women believe that if they develop their strength and learn to understand, use, and have confidence in their bodies, they will be less likely to be attacked physically and more able to defend themselves in the event of an attack. As men are made aware that women are able to fight back, the attacker-victim role relationship should become less frequent.

In the attempt to change others through personal interaction and micro-role system change, women undermine several sources of male power. Normative power is further reduced by destroying traditional male roles through withholding cooperation, making them irrelevant, or challenging them directly. To the extent that women provide a support group for one another, they reduce the power of males to define women's options and control their behavior through rewards. Self-defense techniques reduce the threat of brute force. These small-scale attempts at change gradually produce new bases for more egalitarian interaction than traditional practices.

### Resocialization of others

The second most prevalent activity of the women's movement has been use of or attacks on the media in order to extend the resocialization process beyond the boundaries of the movement. These activities have been engaged in primarily by women who use the sex-role perspective, which emphasizes socialization. The cultural approach and the power analysis both caution against dependence on media and media change as main tools of the movement, since the media are dominated by men. As a result, they warn, attempts by women to convey their ideas through the media will tend to distort the message in a way that ridicules or discredits the movement.

Those who use the media view it as a way of reaching and changing women who have not been exposed to rap groups. By publishing books, magazines, and articles, by speaking, producing radio and TV programs, by being interviewed or holding demonstrations covered by the media, women in the movement extend their insights to those outside it. In this way, countless women who do not identify with the movement begin to reevaluate and change their lives.

Women's access to the media also helps reshape men's understanding of the female condition. For those who believe that change can come about through convincing men of the disadvantages of their roles or of masculine values, the media provides a major vehicle for reaching and changing men. Communicating with men in this way provides the beginnings of social legitimation for legal changes and lays the groundwork for a new value system in society.

Much attention is also focused on the socialization of children. A number of groups are publishing feminist books for children and compiling lists of children's literature offering a positive image of women. *Ms.* magazine has even published a children's record, containing liberated songs. In addition, several women's groups throughout the country have formed feminist child care centers or cooperatives.

Some academic women are concerned with building a social science that defines females as full participants in society and creates and supports new definitions of women. This attempt, however, has little support among many active feminists, who point out that the social sciences are male-dominated in membership, substance, and style, thus forcing academic women to work under non- or antifeminist constraints. I myself believe that the most exciting social-psychological analyses in the past five years have taken place in feminist groups. To the extent that this thinking has filtered into academic meetings and writing, it has been a grossly watered down and devitalized version of feminist thought (my own work not excepted). Thus the movement puts little faith in the social sciences' provision of a basis for new images of women and society.

### Changing male dominance of institutions

So far, the approaches to change with which I have dealt focus heavily on undermining male normative and cultural power and substituting female group support for male approval. However, these approaches are limited by male control of social institutions, against which women have few resources. The main tactics we employ are legal action, direct action and moral pressure, and skill building.

Growing out of the civil rights movement, several legal changes in the past decade open new options to women. Under law, public accommodations must be available to women, and discrimination in hiring or pay on the basis of sex is illegal in any business or educational institution. These changes formally open the possibilities for women to travel freely, gain skills, and obtain economic and positional resources. However, none of these laws is adequately enforced. It has been incumbent upon women to identify discrimination and file suits or complaints with federal, state, or local agencies. This techinque is currently in wide use by university women, who are filing complaints against institutions with HEW. In addition, local movement groups give support and advice to individuals seeking redress of employment or pay discrimination cases and rent and loan discrimination.

Another attempt at law enforcement is a current project, coordinated through NOW, to challenge the renewal of TV and radio station FCC licenses on grounds of sexism (discrimination in employment and failure to provide fair and adequate service to a segment of the public).

Women seek to change as well as enforce laws. Campaigns, rallies and marches in support of legalized abortion, welfare rights, and child care attempt to influence public opinion and bring public pressure to bear on legislators. This tactic is especially favored by socialist groups. In addition, ad hoc groups of women have pressured politicians for new laws—the Equal Rights Amendment, laws on the treatment of female criminals, changes in marriage and divorce laws, laws and procedures governing rape cases, etc.

Direct action includes sit-ins, economic boycotts, moral pressure, and attempts to form women's unions. Sit-ins and boycotts are used to draw attention to illegal and unjust institutional practices as well as to affect the economic position of those against whom they are directed. Groups employing these tactics often negotiate their demands directly. In addition, these approaches sometimes speed up investigatory or legal action by providing adverse publicity and forcing a business or organization to defend itself publicly.

An example of successful moral pressure is the project of two Wayne State University women who analyzed the Detroit public school system's textbooks, using the latter's own guidelines on treatment of minority groups. As a result of their efforts, Detroit school guidelines now explicitly include females with other groups that must be protrayed fairly in school texts—an incentive for authors and publishers to produce such books.

Attempts to form women's unions in order to collectivize and institutionalize women's power to bargain for better working conditions, equitable pay, and job definitions that allow for promotion are underway in many parts of the country. They are necessary partly because unions have been notoriously insensitive to the needs of women. (In Detroit, some UAW leaders crossed picket lines for the first time in their lives when their female staff went on strike.) Some women are organizing unions that cut across occupational types or place of employment and are attempting to pull employed women and housewives into one union, with demands that include pay for housework. Women's unions are most strongly promoted by groups using a power analysis.

A final, and less direct, way of changing institutions is through skill building. Women's lack of power in institutions stems partly from a lack of knowledge, skills, and confidence. Many feminist projects are devoted to building women's personal and collective resources to enable them to challenge institutional power. Some groups, convinced that all individuals are capable of any activity, given the opportunity to learn and practice, build speaking and writing skills by seeking opportunities for all members to engage in those activities by assigning members to fill speaking engagements by lot rather than by degree of competence.

Some professional women are actively recruiting women into their ranks. At Wayne State University and elsewhere, women law students accompany recruiters to college campuses, talking to women about careers in law and providing information about the field, entrance requirements, and preparation for Law Board exams. Women from other professions speak at high schools and on college campuses to encourage young women to consider new career opportunities. Within professions, women are beginning to form support groups or caucuses or to change the focus of existing women's professional organizations to consider the roles of women and ways in which they can implement feminist values within their occupations. The entrance of women into prestigious fields such as law, medicine, business, and education not only gives females a basis for power within those institutions but also begins the process of building female expertise as a counter to male expertise, and in some cases begins the systematic introduction of feminist values into institutional structures.

### Building alternative institutions

Partly as a result of the cultural analysis, which argues that the institutions of society are corrupted by their weddedness to masculine values, and partly for reasons of sheer survival, many women are engaged in building alternative institutions that incorporate feminist values and can thereby serve as models for institutions in a new society.

The numerous women's self-help medical clinics primarily aim to break down male monopoly of basic medical information. They provide women with information about their bodies that enables them to stay healthy, know when something is wrong, know how to communicate with—and if necessary how to challenge—their doctors or seek alternative care. These clinics operate on the assumption that women lose control of their bodies partly through ignorance. They strive to reduce the distinctions between patients, aides, nurses, technicians, and doctors by teaching each other how to do breast and vaginal self-examinations and basic laboratory tests, and by sharing information on such topics as menopause and nutrition. Self-help groups also collect lists of doctors who are nonchauvinist and those whom women should avoid. Gradually these groups are beginning to negotiate with doctors, hospitals, and clinics for changes in the treatment of female patients, and more radically, in the structure of the medical professions.

In the field of law, a group of female lawyers in San Francisco is using its expertise to train women in law. If a client wishes, she may work in the office, including the preparation of her own legal brief in lieu of some or all of her legal fees. The approach incorporates feminist values into the practice of law by reducing mystification of the law and monopolization of expertise. Status relationships are also equalized as lawyers frequently answer phones and type letters while clients prepare legal briefs.

Another alternative institution is the commune. Although the communal movement is not feminist, many women have seen its potential for providing an alternative to the nuclear family, which power analysts in particular view as a primary oppressive institution. Communes offer women who are already married an opportunity to reduce the sex-role pressures of the nuclear family by sharing work and home roles among several adults; single women find mixed or all-female communes a way of meeting social and economic needs and reducing the pressure on them to marry; single mothers have found that collective living with others in the same position eases child care and economic problems. An important component of all these communal styles is that they increase support among women, who live together rather than in isolated homes, and reduce their dependence on males. Hence they are alternatives especially favored by women using a cultural or power approach.

In the process of working for a feminist revolution, the women's movement has attempted to structure itself around its values for a new society. Since women have been placed in a largely powerless role in society, they are especially sensitive to the degradations associated with powerlessness. Therefore, in seeking change, the movement has sought organizational techniques that do not subject women to oppression within or without the movement. Most groups have been reluctant to recruit actively, depending instead on women coming to the movement when they become aware of their own oppression as women. As mentioned earlier, the media provide indirect recruitment, but most women avoid pressuring or coercing individuals with their views.

### Problems with power and authority within the movement itself

Because feminist values emphasize the right of each woman to her own view and choice of activities, a major problem has been the coordination of activities without authoritarian leadership. Granting power to a leader puts other women in a position of subordination similar to the subordination of females to males. Groups have therefore avoided formally or informally institutionalized leadership in a variety of ways. Leadership tasks are often rotated. Steering committees are selected in representative ways to serve for short time periods. A typical practice is to send two women rather than one to speak before a group or explain a position or action to the press, on the assumption that differences in their perspective, experience, and style will reflect the diversity of the movement.

In many cities, feminist groups have organized as coalitions of smaller rap or action groups  Ideally, the coalition form assumes that differences do and will exist and leaves individuals free to support or not support the activities proposed by component groups. It provides a forum for debating ideological differences and coordinating action among those of different persuasions. There are serious criticisms within the movement of each of these organizational forms—but there is also widespread commitment to finding feminist solutions.

In this paper I have attempted to summarize the general perspectives and strategies of the women's movement. In doing so, I have omitted its many controversies—proponents of each approach often differ sharply and sometimes destructively. Each strategy has its detractors, who view it as ineffective, utopian, unnecessarily hostile, retreatist, or trivial. To males—who tend to evaluate a movement by the tightness of its organization, agreement on perspectives, goals, and tactics, and allegiance to a leader or leadership group—the women's movement looks directionless, unorganized, and ineffective. To feminists struggling with new selves and new forms of organization, the means are as important as the goals, and the struggle to coordinate efforts to obtain power for women is itself a small-scale model of a new society, one that accepts and works creatively with and for differences in viewpoint and life experience.

## NOTES

1   Shulamith Firestone, *The Dialectic of Sex* (New York: William Morrow, 1970); Barbara Burris, *The Fourth World Manifesto: An Angry Response to An Imperialist Venture Against the Women's Liberation Movement* (New Haven, Conn.: Advocate Press, 1971); and Valerie Solanas, *The SCUM Manifesto* (New York: Olympia, 1968).

2 Simone DeBeauvoir, *The Second Sex*, H. M. Parshey, trans. (New York: Alfred A. Knopf, 1953), first published in 1949.

3 Burris, *The Fourth World Manifesto.*

4 Kate Millett, *Sexual Politics* (Garden City, N.Y.: Doubleday and Co., 1970).

5 Phyllis Chesler, *Women and Madness* (New York: Doubleday and Co., 1972).

6 Evelyn Reed, *Problems of Women's Liberation: A Marxist Approach* (New York: Merit Publishers, 1969).

7 Juliet Mitchell, *Woman's Estate* (New York: Random House, 1971).

8 Simone DeBeauvoir, *Force of Circumstance* (London: Andre Deutsch, 1965).

9 See Chesler, *Women and Madness.*

10 Cynthia Fuchs Epstein, *Woman's Place: Options and Limits in Professional Careers* (Berkeley: University of California Press, 1971), ch. 3; and Janet Saltzman Chafetz, *Masculine/Feminine or Human?* (Itasca, Ill.: F. E. Peacock, 1974), pp. 60–62.

# Index